Travel and Ethnology in the Renaissance

This book offers a wide-ranging and ambitious analysis of how European travellers in India developed their perceptions of ethnic, political and religious diversity over three hundred years. It discusses the growth of novel historical and philosophical concerns, from the early and rare examples of medieval travellers such as Marco Polo, through to the more sophisticated narratives of seventeenth-century observers – religious writers such as Jesuit missionaries, or independent antiquarians such as Pietro della Valle.

The book's approach combines the detailed contextual analysis of individual narratives with an original long-term interpretation of the role of cross-cultural encounters in the European Renaissance. The author thus proposes a method of analysis which involves both the European background to travel literature and the specific Asian contexts of cultural encounter. An extremely wide range of European sources is discussed, including the often neglected but extremely important Iberian and Italian accounts of India. However, the book also discusses a number of non-European sources, Muslim and Hindu, thereby challenging simplistic interpretations of western 'orientalism'. In sum the book offers the extended and systematic treatment which the growing field of 'cultural encounters' has so far been missing.

JOAN-PAU RUBIÉS is Lecturer in International History, London School of Economics and Political Science. He has written extensively on the history of travel writing, and the political culture of early modern Spain.

Past and Present Publications

General Editor: JOANNA INNES, *Somerville College, Oxford*

Past and Present Publications comprise books similar in character to the articles in the journal *Past and Present*. Whether the volumes in the series are collections of essays – some previously published, others new studies – or monographs, they encompass a wide variety of scholarly and original works primarily concerned with social, economic and cultural changes, and their causes and consequences. They will appeal to both specialists and non-specialists and will endeavour to communicate the results of historical and allied research in the most readable and lively form.

For a list of titles in Past and Present Publications, see end of book.

Travel and Ethnology in the Renaissance

South India through European Eyes, 1250–1625

JOAN-PAU RUBIÉS

CAMBRIDGE
UNIVERSITY PRESS

PUBLISHED BY THE PRESS SYNDICATE OF THE UNIVERSITY OF CAMBRIDGE
The Pitt Building, Trumpington Street, Cambridge, United Kingdom

CAMBRIDGE UNIVERSITY PRESS
The Edinburgh Building, Cambridge, CB2 2RU, UK   http://www.cup.cam.ac.uk
40 West 20th Street, New York, NY 10011–4211, USA   http://www.cup.org
10 Stamford Road, Oakleigh, Melbourne 3166, Australia
Ruiz de Alarcón 13, 28014 Madrid, Spain

First published 2000

Printed in the United Kingdom at the University Press, Cambridge

Typeface Times 10/12 pt   3B2 *system*   [CE]

A catalogue record for this book is available from the British Library

ISBN 0 521 77055 6 hardback

This book is dedicated to the memory of my brother Joaquim Rubiés i Mirabet (1968–1992), his courage and his youth.

vous verrez à vos pieds, non plus la fameuse cité de Vijayanagar, célébrée dans la tradition et la légende, la capitale de souverains dont l'autorité s'étendait sur la moitié de l'Hindoustan, et dont l'amitié était recherchée par les plus puissants princes de l'Asie, mais mutilée par le sabre musulman et défigurée par la main du temps, l'ombre et le tombeau de sa gloire passée.

Edouard de Warren, *L'Inde anglaise* (1845)

Contents

Illustrations

PLATES

MAPS

Preface

Southern India, especially the Malabar coast and the kingdom of Vijayanagara, received many European visitors during the transition from the Middle Ages to modern times. Their travel narratives and chronicles provide a unique insight into the encounter between Europeans and a non-Christian, non-Muslim civilization, which they neither wished to ignore nor were able to dominate. In effect, this is less a book about southern India and its visitors than a book about the European Renaissance from a new perspective, emphasizing the growth of an analytical discourse about human diversity. The choice of Vijayanagara as a case-study is designed to help develop a carefully contextualized argument about the evolution of European travel literature and its intellectual content, which not only seeks to identify changes, but also aims to explain their logic. This book contends that the logic of this cultural change was driven by interactions (and often misunderstandings) with other cultures, rather than by a mere projection of European aims and ideologies. In other words, contacts with non-Europeans were intrinsically important, rather than just rhetorically important, for the development of European culture. The powerful cultural transformation of the Latin Christian world from the thirteenth to the seventeenth centuries was therefore not simply the origin of a new western way of looking and dominating: it was also a genuine, if often twisted, response to the challenge of cultural differences experienced abroad and re-evaluated in Europe.

This book therefore combines an empirical case-study, based on a systematic analysis of original sources, with an argument about the implications of this case-study for a general interpretation of the Renaissance, here broadly understood as a long-term process marked by the development of historical and naturalistic ways of thinking. The writing of this study has been constantly guided by a concern with understanding perception as a historical problem, raising questions about how realities are perceived, how 'ways of seeing' change, and which mechanisms make translation and understanding across different cultural traditions possible.

Although it is widely recognized that the cultural changes of the Renaissance must have contributed to the rise of the empirical sciences in the following centuries, there are important aspects of this contribution (especially those relating to moral and political concerns) that remain unclear. In part this is because significant genres, such as travel literature, have not been discussed in the context of an intellectual history which has been too often exclusively concerned with the more elitist genres of the humanist and scholastic traditions. Thus some of the roots of early modern 'natural and human history' have been taken for granted. Travel literature not only created an empirical ground which, by its sheer massive presence, imposed itself in the thinking of seventeenth-century theologians and philosophers: it also prompted debates about methods of exposition, induction and comparison.[1] It was an impact which cannot be understood simply by focusing on a single dramatic moment like the (actually rather muted) immediate aftermath of the discoveries of Vasco da Gama and Columbus, because the standing of travellers' accounts within the authoritative discourses of the Renaissance, and in fact their very contents, evolved in response to European intellectual concerns.[2] It is equally important to correct the still current assumption that the full intellectual impact of the discoveries only took place within the Enlightenment or its immediate antecedents, which completely neglects the Renaissance.[3]

This study has been written as an exploration of the ways in which the

---

[1] I have sketched this argument in two connected articles: J. P. Rubiés, 'New worlds and Renaissance ethnology', *History and Anthropology*, 6 (1993): 157–97, and 'Instructions for travellers: teaching the eye to see', in J. Stagl and C. Pinney (eds.) *From Travel literature to ethnography*. Special issue of *History and Anthropology*, 9 (1996): 139–90.

[2] The classic formulation of the problem of impact, with reference to America, is J. H. Elliott, *The old world and the new, 1492–1650* (Cambridge, 1970). A more nuanced view is developed in a number of articles in Kupperman (ed.) *America in European consciousness 1493–1750* (Chapel Hill and London, 1995), including the further remarks of John Elliott (pp. 391–408). D. F. Lach, *Asia in the making of Europe*, 3 vols. (Chicago, 1965–93) offers a very detailed view of the impact of Asia, although he is more concerned with the reconstruction of actual images of Asia and a judgement of their empirical validity than with analysing intellectual processes.

[3] Such is the case of the classic study of Paul Hazard, *La crise de la conscience européenne, 1680–1715* (first published Paris, 1935), who begins his analysis in the late seventeenth century. This problem is more acutely felt in the influential work of Edward Said, *Orientalism* (Harmondsworth, 1978), whose references to the literature before the late eighteenth century fail to constitute a proper reconstruction of a European tradition of thought about the Orient.

rigorous study of travel literature can illuminate these questions. It is therefore an essay about origins, events, contexts and consequences, concerned with long-term cultural changes, attentive both to the medieval background of the Renaissance and to the way the Renaissance created the conditions for the Enlightenment. It has been one of my aims to compare writers from different social backgrounds. I have also sought not to limit the analysis to travellers from a single country, which could perpetuate the false image of a series of self-enclosed national literary cultures especially inadequate for a genre whose development was crucially conditioned by its pan-European aspects (the fact that the intellectual impact of travel literature in the seventeenth and eighteenth centuries was logically centred on England and France should not of course obscure the fact that Italian and Iberian nations contributed decisively to the early production and growth of the new narrative forms).[4] I shall not, however, seek to include a description of all the images of India produced in the sixteenth century, nor a list of all the orientalist literature of this period – a task which was accomplished by Donald F. Lach in his monumental *Asia in the making of Europe*,[5] or, in a more limited way, by the works of Boies Penrose and Geneviève Bouchon.[6] Neither am I writing a history of early modern ethnology, the kind of work begun by Margaret Hodgen, Giuliano Gliozzi or Anthony Pagden, by focusing primarily on the European debates.[7] The focus of this study is rather the way travel literature, understood as a set of related genres of undeniable importance in a defining period of early European colonial expansion, informed ethnological, moral and political thought, contributing in ways still poorly understood to the transition from the theological emphasis of medieval culture to the historical and philosophical concerns of the seventeenth century. It will be my argument that the full dimension of Renaissance anthropology (in its primary form

---

[4] A Franco-centric bias dominates much of the best literature, from Geoffrey Atkinson's classic, *Les nouveaux horizons de la Renaissance française* (Geneva, 1936), to Friedrich Wolfzettel's recent *Le discours du voyageur* (Paris, 1996). The case of British scholarship is not entirely different: Kate Teltscher's *India inscribed: European and British writing on India 1600–1800* (New Delhi, 1995), despite its title devotes a very limited space to non-British sources and contexts.

[5] Lach, *Asia*. The admirably researched first two volumes (in five books) covering the sixteenth century have recently been followed by a third volume (in four further books) covering the seventeenth century, written together with E. J. Van Kley.

[6] See, respectively B. Penrose, *Travel and discovery in the Renaissance, 1420–1620* (Cambridge, Mass., 1952) and G. Bouchon, 'L'Inde dans l'Europe de la Renaissance', in C. Weinberger-Thomas (ed.) *L'Inde et l'imaginaire* (Paris, 1988), pp. 69–90.

[7] See, respectively, M. Hodgen, *Early anthropology in the sixteenth and seventeenth centuries* (Philadelphia, 1964), G. Gliozzi, *Adamo et il nuovo mondo. La nascita dell'antropologia come ideologia coloniale* (Florence, 1977) and A. Pagden, *The fall of natural man. The American Indian and the origins of comparative ethnology* (2nd edn, Cambridge, 1986).

of cosmographical literature) cannot be understood merely by studying the intellectual constructions of jurists and theologians concerned with defining the nature of man and of human political society. Writers increasingly appealed to the experience of the traveller as a source of authority for the truthfulness of particular observations concerning human diversity. And yet the traveller's experience was complex and his authority questionable. It is therefore very important to understand properly what was actually involved in the process of observing and describing a non-European society.

This is necessarily a story of European attitudes by a European historian, rather than a reconstruction of the historical realities of South India. However, both the changing context of European activities overseas and the specificity of India in the evolution of European representations of non-Europeans are central to my argument. As an idolatrous civilization with a recognizable ancient tradition, sixteenth-century India stood uniquely between the urban civilizations of the New World, unexpectedly found and quickly conquered by the Spanish, and the enormous intellectual challenge presented by the prosperous civilization of the Chinese, which would generate its own separate debate in Europe. The changing and multifarious views of Europeans in India are best understood not simply in isolation as a self-generated discourse, but rather in relation to native views and by comparison with alternative gazes. For this reason, throughout this work some attention is devoted to Islamic as well as European discourses on India. As far as my linguistic skills have permitted, I have sought to provide updated discussions of issues relating to Indian and Indo-Portuguese history which form a necessary background to many of the observations of the travellers.[8] Some of these issues require substantial comparative analysis, in particular the nature of the state in South India, which has emerged as crucial to any judgement on the empirical origins of the European idea of oriental despotism. Key themes such as idolatry, law or kingship, recurrent in many of the descriptions, are here discussed from a comparative perspective so as to interpret the analogies used by travellers and address the issue of cultural translation and mistranslation. Above all, the guiding principle of this study is to discuss the relationship between Europeans and Indians not as one between an observer and its

---

[8] The fact that the history of Vijayanagara is still to a great extent a puzzle, and that something as basic as establishing a chronology is still a matter of scholarly debate, presents considerable difficulty. The recent monograph by Burton Stein, *Vijayanagara* (Cambridge, 1989) skirted many of these issues rather than solving them. Without claiming any expertise in South Indian languages, I have attempted to use European documents and English-language scholarship in order to provide a context that is as detailed as possible.

passive object, but rather as one of genuine interaction, with special care not to simplify the historical context for the sake of rhetorical analysis.

It is also my hope that this work will be a contribution to the methodology of cultural history, understood as something wider than a history of ideas and more focused than a history of mentalities. The study of cultural encounters has emerged in recent years as a privileged field for re-thinking fundamental questions about problems of perception, identity and change. Throughout my analysis of travel accounts I have attempted to define clearly and to be faithful to three different dimensions of the process of knowledge: the tradition in which the authors of descriptions had been educated, including of course the rhetorical models and the information that each of them could be expected to know; the social strategies and political interests in which they participated, considering in particular the context of production of each text (beyond a mere sociological generalization, such as 'Marco Polo was a merchant', or 'Alessandro Valignano was a missionary'); and, finally, the experience of otherness in which the narrator may have been involved. Here I have tried to avoid the (now current) assumption that travellers only see those images they already carry, as a prejudice, from their own country.[9]

Two general ideas have emerged from the combination of these perspectives: that the history of culture can be treated as a history of language-games (to borrow a useful expression), and that travel literature is a possible form of cultural translation. I understand a 'language-game' as a set of rules and assumptions, often unconscious to the agents who use them, organized so as to meet the demands of a social context of communication. A 'language-game', therefore, encompasses any cultural activity based on the interaction of subjective agents who create and exchange mental representations in order to meet various purposes. Needless to say, there are many different kinds of conventional signs

---

[9] Edward Said's influential book, *Orientalism*, has contributed to increased awareness of the political implications of much of what has been produced in the West as 'empirical science on the Orient'. However, Said clearly overemphasizes his case when he rules out one of the fundamental dimensions of the process of 'knowing the other'; in his own words: 'the value, efficacy, strength, apparent veracity, of a written statement about the Orient therefore relies very little, and cannot instrumentally depend, on the Orient as such. On the contrary, the written statement is a presence to the reader by virtue of having excluded, displaced, made supererogatory any such *real thing* as "the Orient"' (Said, *Orientalism*, p. 21). If this were true, I do not think that most of the literature which I have studied would have even been possible. A conclusion similar to mine was reached by Karen Kupperman, *Settling with the Indians. The meeting of English and Indian cultures in America, 1580–1640* (Totowa, N.J., 1980), concerning early English descriptions of the Algonquian Indians of Virginia and New England.

which can be used in a language-game, not necessarily of a verbal kind, but also images and gestures. Language-games are not static, because through use they are constantly adapted to new situations and transformed. The tradition of a language-game produced by a community over time constitutes a discourse.[10]

A history of language-games thus implies a history of ideas, but is also broader. What makes sense of an agent's subjective experience is not just engagement with an intellectual doctrine, but also a set of purposes. Such a thing as a belief, important as it is in defining a subject's assumptions, should not therefore be taken for granted – human agents have the capacity to entertain beliefs superficially and to revise their beliefs in a context which creates new demands.[11] Most cultural activities are developed through the unconscious use of common language. While sophisticated ideas and models are crucial in a cultural tradition, they rest on a wider ability to use a variety of language-games, and thus to share in a cultural life.

One could of course argue that the formalized discourse of the elite is often more creative than the popular use of a vernacular language, and hence that Aquinas' concept of natural law is more far-reaching than Marco Polo's description of the world. It is, however, the interaction between these two kinds of discourse that I wish to address as the main subject of a cultural history of early ethnology. In fact, the non-reflective use of everyday language can be creative because of the novelty of the context in which linguistic agency takes place. This is how the languages of Christianity and civilization – that is, not just specific theological or political concepts, but rather the whole range of meanings and implications associated with different uses of these concepts – were appropriated by soldiers, merchants and missionaries in their descriptions of non-European peoples, up to the point where major intellectual assump-

---

[10] I borrow the expression, rather than the theory, from Ludwig Wittgenstein, whose approach was obviously more philosophical. It could be summarized as follows: 'language use is a form of human rule-governed activity, integrated into human transactions and social behaviour, context-dependent and purpose-relative' (*The Oxford Companion to Philosophy*, ed. by T. Honderich (Oxford, 1996), p. 461). My understanding of culture as language-games is inspired by this formulation, but is used here more historically and anthropologically. It also extends the concept of language-games to non-verbal cultural activities which carry symbolic meaning and thus require linguistic interpretation.

[11] The concept of language-game does not, however, exclude the concept of belief – beliefs are indeed the key to the 'truth value' attached by a subject to his or her mental representations, and thus crucial in defining what a subject's assumptions are. This is one reason for using 'language-game' rather than language. The point about beliefs is forcefully made by Jay M. Smith in 'No more language games: words, beliefs and the political culture of early modern France', *American Historical Review*, 102 (1997): 1413–40. I do, however, define language-game more broadly than Smith.

tions concerning the understanding of human societies could be (and needed to be) challenged.

A cultural history written as a history of language-games also implies a precision which is lacking in the concept of mentalities, too often used to generalize collective 'ways of thinking' and to analyse beliefs and behaviour without distinction.[12] In the course of this book, for instance, to speak simply of 'medieval' and 'modern' mentalities would have been inappropriate. Equally wrong is the idea that there is an 'oriental' way of thinking radically opposed to a 'western' way. In fact, even the idea that there exist some 'irrational' beliefs (such as the so-called confusion of fact and fiction some historians have identified in medieval literature on the East) cannot be accepted without criticism: what is rational is what makes sense within the context of a language-game. Rationality may in fact be defined as the human ability to learn and use different language-games, an ability related to the existence of a universal language instinct which allows all children to learn varieties of languages with common linguistic structures.[13]

This understanding of cultural history affects three alternative assumptions about human subjectivity that need to be questioned. The first one

[12] This unease with the way the 'history of mentalities' has often been practised, an unease which has guided my research, is the subject of a book by G. E. R. Lloyd, *Demystifying mentalities* (Cambridge, 1990). From a practitioner's perspective, see also the lucid article by R. Chartier, 'Intellectual history or sociocultural history? The French trajectories', in D. LaCapra and S. L. Kaplan (eds.) *Modern European intellectual history* (Ithaca, 1982). Peter Burke, *Varieties of cultural history* (Cambridge, 1997), chap. 11, has effectively defined the main problems of the history of mentalities under four propositions: the tendency to overestimate intellectual consensus in a past society, the difficulty of explaining change when so much effort is devoted to establishing shared assumptions within a reified cultural system, the tendency to treat belief systems as autonomous (although this criticism is not always applicable) and the tendency to exaggerate binary oppositions between traditional and modern, or even between logical and pre-logical. He also suggests three positive responses – the focus on interests, on categories or schemata, and on metaphors. In fact an understanding of culture as language-games does integrate the analysis of interests with the analysis of language and rhetoric, ranging from the conceptual categories used in everyday situations, with their hidden assumptions, to the different genres of cultural life. It therefore allows the historian to compare different cultures and to analyse long-term changes by defining the mechanisms of translation and transformation within a cultural system.

[13] The emphasis on this universal, biologically inherited learning ability (commonly defined as 'mentalese'), has grown in recent years. For a general exposition see S. Pinker, *The language instinct* (Harmondsworth, 1994). I will, however, stress that the existence of 'mentalese' as a fundamental hypothesis, without which so little in cognitive anthropology makes sense, does not involve accepting the existence of a 'universal people's culture'. All cultures are historical elaborations, so that the same basic linguistic skills can produce enormous differences in practice. A history of perceptions and representations needs to both include the hypothesis of 'mentalese' as part of the logic of cultural change, and the detailed analysis of its various forms and applications – which will actually help determine what mentalese *is not*.

is a form of crude materialism, according to which people's subjective life – a traveller's capacity to 'see' – was somehow determined by a kind of pre-defined power strategy, or, more simply, the ideology of a social class to which an individual is supposed to have belonged. The variety of interpretations found in travel accounts makes this kind of approach obviously simplistic.

The second assumption is a form of narrow rationalism, according to which travellers simply saw 'what was there to be seen' – unless they were clouded by the prejudices which more empirical or rational observers might easily have avoided. In fact, different interpretations of the same 'reality' can all make sense to different travellers. There is indeed no privileged position from which an interpretation of 'what was there' may be considered unchallengeable, not even the modern historian's.

Finally (and here is where the possibility of cultural translation becomes crucial), I question the idea that, because different interpretations of the same 'realities' were possible, there is no way of talking about rationality. Each interpretation was incommensurable. In particular, travellers would not be able to interpret what an indigenous culture was about, because a traveller's perspective was relative to his own culture. A traveller from the late sixteenth century would equally misjudge a medieval account. Even the modern historian cannot expect to understand properly what a Renaissance traveller saw. Yet an analysis centred on language-games helps understand why this 'radical relativism' is probably incorrect. Of course, different travellers saw different things and, of course, they relied on their own initial assumptions; but what is striking is how the *process of learning languages* (understood, in a broad sense, as language-games) allowed travellers to get involved with foreign cultures or to interpret texts produced in a different context. This ability to learn languages, however universal, was of course affected by the travellers' will to understand better, by the empirical means at their disposal and by their diverse critical skills. The existence of different languages is obvious, but insofar as translation seems to have been a possibility, the problem of relativism is in fact only a problem of degree.[14] Thus the question can be more usefully phrased as *under what*

---

[14] The case for radical incommensurability seems to be ultimately flawed, despite the spirited defence of Paul Feyerabend, *Farewell to reason* (London, 1987), pp. 265–72, who argues that it is possible to understand foreign concepts without translating them by learning a culture from scratch, as a child does. He also insists that a successful translation changes the translating language, and therefore the possibility of translation is not an argument against incommensurability. However, learning a culture from scratch does not imply that a *foreign* culture is being understood, unless it is somehow related to (i.e. translated into) an *original* culture – a point relevant to any interpretation of travel accounts as evidence for cultural encounters. To learn a different culture 'from

conditions did travel literature actually become a form of translation? This is one of the key questions which this study seeks to address.

The different chapters of the book explore a number of themes through a chronological progression, following the major narratives of Europeans in South India from the thirteenth to the early seventeenth centuries. The first chapter introduces the case-study and its sources and defines the importance of southern India, and especially Vijayanagara, in the European experience overseas. The second analyses the theme of India in the medieval Latin tradition, with a detailed analysis of Marco Polo's account and its original significance. Carrying the analysis to the fifteenth century, the third chapter studies the impact of Florentine humanism in travel literature, focusing on Poggio Bracciolini's intervention in the narrative of Nicolò Conti.

The fourth chapter then charts the emergence of the traveller as a figure of authority in European culture, using the example of the Italian adventurer Ludovico de Varthema as a model for a first-person narrative, whilst the fifth chapter, focusing on the establishment of the Portuguese in India, discusses their ambiguous attitudes towards Hindus as potential allies in a Christian imperialist project.

Chapters 6 and 7 analyse the Portuguese development of an empirical ethnology in the early decades of their colonial trade through an interpretation of the detailed works of Duarte Barbosa and Domingos Paes describing, respectively, the social world of the Malabar coast and the city of Vijayanagara. This analysis seeks to address the problem of the limits of empirical objectivity by distinguishing between descriptions of social customs and the interpretation of non-Christian religion, thus

---

scratch', then, if ever related to another (original) culture, implies a kind of translation. The very idea that a successful translation changes the translating language suggests that languages are not closed systems of meaning, which makes the argument of incommensurability irrelevant – the interesting problem is understanding when and why people engage in cultural dialogues. Feyerabend explains that the kind of incommensurability he understands is not merely to do with difference of meanings, but occurs only when the conditions of meaningfulness for the descriptive terms of one language (theory, point of view) do not permit the use of the descriptive terms of another language (theory, point of view), as can be seen in a number of historical examples (such as Aristotelian versus Newtonian science). This is also the kind of argument used by Jacques Gernet in *China and the Christian impact* (Cambridge, 1985) to argue that the Jesuits in China made a bad translation of Confucianism into Christianity. The problem here is, of course, whether there was any possible (more abstract) language from which the sharers of different cultures could understand the relative validity of their mutually exclusive original languages. Historical analysis clearly shows that an ability to transcend particular language-games is not only possible but, in fact, is one of the key elements of historical change. This is what translation actually consists of (rather than just equating one list of concepts with another).

revealing a deep chasm between the secular and religious spheres of discourse in the reports written by European merchants, but also suggesting the possibility of trans-cultural understanding through ritual, rather than doctrinal, analogies. Chapter 8 then discusses the emergence of a historical discourse in sixteenth-century India, which mediated between the indigenous historical memory and European moral and political concerns. The first part focuses on the chronicle of the history of Vijayanagara by Fernão Nunes, analysed in the context of the historiography of expansion in the Hispanic Renaissance and compared with Indian Muslim sources. The second part of the chapter then seeks to clarify the question of orientalism by distinguishing between the historical discourse generated in India and the appropriation and elaboration of this material in Europe, and in particular the emergence of the concept of oriental despotism in the political thought of Giovanni Botero in the late sixteenth century.

Finally, the last two chapters of the book, 9 and 10, explain the reasons behind the simultaneous emergence at the turn of the seventeenth century of an innovative missionary discourse on the gentile religion of India (Hinduism), and of an independent secular analysis, potentially sceptical, of Indian culture. This opposition between Jesuit apologists and lay critics leads towards a conclusion which considers the contribution of travel literature to the origins of the Enlightenment. The development of methodological distinctions between the authority of multiple empirical observations and the writing of an authoritative world history, the often self-defeating need to relate the evidence of religious diversity in an antiquarian perspective based on classical and biblical sources, and the search for a human identity across cultures beyond the growing barriers of orientalist archetypes, are all defined as consequences of the way Renaissance travel literature came to affect, and be affected by, European intellectual concerns.

Acknowledgements

The core of this book is a doctoral dissertation written at the University of Cambridge between 1987 and 1991. I am grateful to King's College for its crucial financial support and to Anthony Pagden for his insightful and open-minded supervision. The manuscript has been substantially expanded and re-written over the course of many years, and I have incurred a great many debts of advice, support and friendship. I received essential financial help from Queens' College, Cambridge, the European Institute at Florence and the Department of History at the University of Reading. It was mainly due to Brendan Bradshaw that two years as a Junior Research Fellow at Queens' College, Cambridge, were as pleasant as they were profitable. Peter Burke and Chris Pinney have been helpful over many years and their generous interest in this project has far surpassed the circumstances of a doctoral examination. The late Burton Stein was especially kind to discuss my project in the light of his then forthcoming book on Vijayanagara. I am also grateful to Wahid Behmardi who offered to check the reliability of translations from Persian. At different times I received valuable readings and suggestions from Chris Bayly, Kirti Chaudhuri, Harvey Hames, Geoffrey Hawthorn, John Headley, Tim Hochstrasser, Javed Majeed, Francesc Relaño and Sanjay Subrahmanyam. I am grateful in a very special way to David Armitage, Jaś Elsner and Peter Miller for reading the whole of the manuscript in one of its various incarnations. Melissa Calaresu has done the same and much more. My family has supported me in this project with enormous faith over many years. Two South Indian friends, Padma and Bull, offered me a delightful weekend at Draksharama by the Godavari river which has proved a source of inspiration over distance and time.

Needless to say, this book would not have been possible without the contributions of many scholars. It is in fact the case that the study of travel literature as a world-wide cultural phenomenon has emerged in the last decade as a subject in its own right, and that the subject has been (to use an expression) growing under my feet. The vast range of the material that I have considered here and perfectly sensible editorial demands have made it impossible to keep the scholarly apparatus as detailed as I had intended. None the less, I would like to acknowledge that it has only been with the help of many writers who now remain anonymous that I have been able to write this book.

A note on spelling and vocabulary

For the sake of making this book generally accessible, and given that it is not primarily destined for a specialized orientalist audience, I have accepted the editorial suggestion of simplifying the spellings for the transliteration of Arabic, Persian, Sanskrit and other Indian languages, so that Shāh becomes Shah, etc. At the cost of a small inconsistency I have allowed myself to retain oriental macrons for the names of three important writers: Ibn Battūta and Ibn Khaldūn, widely known in the West, and 'Abd al-Razzāq, whose travel narrative is especially important for the argument of this book. On the other hand, I have used traditional western forms for Avicenna and Averroes (but not Tamerlane, which I have spelt as Timur).

Throughout this book I have used a few early modern concepts which were important to the ethnological vocabulary of the period, but which either are not used in modern English, or have different meanings. Thus, 'relation' is used to mean a descriptive narrative account; 'civility' (preceding the concept of 'civilization') refers to the traits of rational and orderly behaviour found primarily in sophisticated urban societies; and 'gentilism' is the noun relative to the 'gentiles', peoples whose religious life lay outside the biblical tradition ('paganism' would be a close approximation).

1. *In search of India: the empire of Vijayanagara through European eyes*

THE PROBLEM OF INDIAN CIVILIZATION IN RENAISSANCE EUROPE: A RETROSPECTIVE VIEW

The India made famous by seventeenth-century European travellers and which occupied an increasingly prominent space in the exotic imagination of the Enlightenment was essentially the India of the Muslim-dominated Mughal empire, with its syncretic court splendour and treacherous imperial politics set against the background of a brahmin-dominated society of naked ascetics, idolatrous temples and inflexible caste rules.[1] Although Akbar's empire was first described in detail by Jesuit missionaries in the 1580s, the Mughal theme effectively belongs to a number of well-educated travellers of the seventeenth century. Some worked for the English or Dutch East India companies, although the majority were largely independent observers, mostly French. Their accounts can be conventionally classified as belonging to the post-Renaissance, a period when these travellers could work from a sophisticated understanding of the difference between the analysis of religious diversity and the analysis of diversity in forms of civilization. This is perhaps the key distinction which characterized early modern ethnology. Our question here will not be what these independent and curious travellers saw and wrote, but rather how they came to be able to describe non-European societies as they did in the light of the ethnological practices of the preceding centuries.

---

[1] For a general discussion of the eighteenth-century view of Asia see S. Murr, 'Les conditions d'émergence du discours sur l'Inde au siècle des Lumières', in *Inde et littératures* (Paris, 1983), pp. 233–84. Specifically dealing with British perceptions of Asia, see the detailed study by P. Marshall and G. Williams, *The great map of mankind. British perceptions of the world in the age of Enlightenment* (London, 1982), especially chaps. 4 and 5.

The most sophisticated European writers in the East in the sixteenth century were often Jesuit missionaries, and it is precisely when read against the images which they created that the post-Renaissance lay discourse becomes most meaningful. The importance of the Jesuits in the early history of orientalism is therefore enormous. However, they must be analysed as participating in a specialized clerical discourse, one which to some extent they shared with other religious orders. The Portuguese Fróis in Japan, the Catalan Monserrate in Mughal India, and the Italian Ricci in China – to mention three outstanding early writers – were the privileged observers of new areas of Jesuit activity, but their very condition as missionaries also limited their attitudes towards foreign cultures, however much they knew about Strabo or Aristotle and despite the fact that they learned languages which gave them access to indigenous literary traditions. It is in fact necessary to retrieve the attitudes which preceded this Counter-Reformation discourse, and this requires discussing an earlier phase in the production of travel descriptions – those written by laymen with a limited access to the authoritative languages of law and theology which only a university education could secure.

The importance of the travel literature which grew during the first half of the sixteenth century is not simply that it gave Europe many informed descriptions of non-European lands and peoples, but also that it structured the genre on the basis of the practical interests of merchants, soldiers and crown officials. These interests were reflected in the character of the two most comprehensive early Portuguese accounts of the East, the *Suma Oriental* by Tomé Pires (*c.* 1512) and the *Livro* of Duarte Barbosa (*c.* 1516). They took the form of geographical treatises that followed trade routes along the coasts of the Indian Ocean, displaying both economic and ethnological information. Remarkably full and systematic, they superseded an earlier genre, the many letters and 'relations' that had been composed following the first voyages to India and the New World, and which had been read not only in Lisbon and Seville, but also in distant commercial centres such as Florence, Venice and Nuremberg (often the letters were written by foreign merchants who in fact played an important role in these early expeditions). A few of these early accounts were published, the most important collection of this kind being the *Paesi novamenti retrovati* which first appeared in Vicenza in 1507, apparently edited by the humanist scholar Francanzano da Montalboddo. It is interesting, however, that the much more detailed descriptions by Barbosa and Pires only circulated in manuscript form and were difficult to consult until they were assembled by the Venetian civil servant Giovanni Battista Ramusio (1485–1557) in the three volumes of his ambitious collection *Delle navigationi et viaggi* (1550–9).[2]

Ramusio's edition was important both for the quantity and the quality of the material which it contained, and is the logical starting point for any analysis of early sixteenth-century interpretations of Indian civilization. This raises the question of why a collection of similar characteristics was not produced in Portugal in the first place. First of all, it must be borne in mind that the practice of collecting accounts about the new discoveries had been continuous throughout the first half of the century, so that through the hands of Germans and Italians based in Lisbon or Seville much material had made its way into the manuscript collections of the Florentine Piero Vaglienti, the Venetian Alessandro Zorzi or the Augsburg humanist Conrad Peutinger.[3] The fact that much unpublished material circulated makes the publication of the earlier major travel collections in Italy and Germany unsurprising. In this context, some historians have explained the limited initial circulation of accounts such as those by Barbosa and Pires as a result of the attempt by the Portuguese crown to prevent rival powers from having access to navigational and geographical information. The success of this policy – to the extent that it existed – was only relative, since as early as 1524 the book of Duarte Barbosa was available for translation into Castilian for Charles V (in his struggle against King John III of Portugal to claim the Spice Islands for his Spanish subjects).[4] While it seems likely that these

---

[2] G. B. Ramusio, *Navigazioni e viaggi*, ed. by M. Milanesi, 6 vols. (Turin, 1978–88), vol. II, pp. 541–780. Milanesi publishes the complete collection as it appeared in 1606. However, the three original volumes of Ramusio's collection were published in 1550 (vol. I), 1556 (vol. III) and 1559 (vol. II). There had been a second edition of the first volume in 1554, with additions by Ramusio, who died in 1557 (the 'second' volume, although finished in 1553, was published posthumously). The editions of 1563, 1574 and 1606 contained further additions, some of which (like Cesare Federici's narrative, only written in 1587) Ramusio could not have planned. In his edition of 1551, Ramusio only published a fragment of Pires' work, missing some of the more original parts. He did not even know its authorship.

[3] Piero Vaglienti's collection is now in the Biblioteca Riccardiana in Florence (ms. 1,910). The Venetian Alessandro Zorzi's more important manuscripts are in the Biblioteca Nazionale Centrale di Firenze (B.R. 233). Peutinger's Augsburg collection was dependent on the materials sent to him by Valentim Fernandes, a Moravian publisher settled in Lisbon and deeply involved in the early circulation of information concerning the Portuguese discoveries. See especially B. Greiff, *Tagebuch des Lucas Rem aus den Jahren 1494–1541* (Augsburg, 1861), and Valentim Fernandes, *O Manuscrito 'Valentim Fernandes'* ed. by A. Bião (Lisbon, 1940). A number of early letters by Florentine merchants in India have been recently collected by Marco Spallanzani, *Mercanti fiorentini nell'Asia portoghese* (Florence, 1997).

[4] For Barbosa's manuscript circulation and translation see D. F. Lach, *Asia in the making of Europe*, vol. I, p. 186, which must be complemented by G. Schurhammer, *Gesammelte Studien*, 4 vols. (Lisbon and Rome, 1965), vol. II, pp. 23–5. The Spanish translation was completed in Vitoria by the Genoese ambassador Martín Centurión with the help of

books were indeed not meant for a general public, probably the lack of a sufficient publishing infrastructure and book market in Portugal was as important as any attempt to prevent valuable information from leaking into foreign hands.[5] In any case it was difficult to prevent the Venetians, those most affected by the diversion of the spice trade through the new Atlantic route, from sending agents to collect information in Lisbon, or even interviewing in their own city independent travellers like the Italian adventurer Ludovico de Varthema or the Castilian Jew Francisco de Albuquerque.[6]

Ramusio's collection represents the application of humanist methods of faithful documentary edition and humanist ideals of systematic geographical reconstruction to the interests of Venetian commercial imperialism. Different principles, albeit no less imperialistic, dominated the public production of images of the East in Portugal. It was not until the second half of the sixteenth century that major narratives about India

Diogo Ribeiro, the Portuguese cosmographer now in the service of Charles V, to prepare for the Badajoz-Elvas junta of 1524 (the main manuscript is in Barcelona, but there are others in Madrid and Munich). It was also used for Ribeiro's important world maps of 1527 and 1529, which insisted on giving the Moluccas to Spain. It is likely that Charles secured the copy through Diogo Ribeiro himself or through any other of the various Portuguese sailors and cosmographers who abandoned King Manuel during these years seeking better prospects in Castile.

[5] In his analysis, Lach repeatedly puts forward the traditional argument for a Portuguese 'control of information'. See Lach, *Asia*, vol. I, pp. 151–4. The view has received much criticism. It seems difficult to prove that there was a systematic attempt to prevent *any* information about the new lands to 'leak' into the hands of foreign competitors, but there is little doubt that, at least in the sixteenth-century Iberian Peninsula, governments organized their own sources of information relating to colonies as a matter of state. A selective process concerning what kind of information was made available was part of the business of running an overseas empire, and the fierce competition between Portugal and Castile over the Spice Islands, for instance, certainly advised some control in the early decades of the sixteenth century. It is also true that Portuguese writers found it difficult to publish in their own country (such was the case of Mendes Pinto), and that many important chronicles, for instance the *Lendas da Índia* by Gaspar Correa and parts of Diogo do Couto's *Decadas*, were not published. Sometimes influential noblemen who did not wish the revelation of details which diminished their prestige conspired against certain chroniclers and forced revisions or even interrupted projects.

[6] For Albuquerque, see R. Cessi (ed.) 'L'itinerario indiano di Francesco dal Bocchier', *Atti della Accademia nazionale dei Lincei. Rendiconti della classe di scienze morali, storiche e filologiche*, ser. VIII, 6 (1951): 232–49, and J. Aubin, 'Francisco de Albuquerque, un juif castillan au service de l'Inde Portugaise (1510–15)', *Arquivos do Centro Cultural Português*, 7 (1973): 175–88. Cessi wrongly assumed that the author of the report was a Venetian merchant. The correct identification is given by Jean Aubin, who offers an interesting biographical sketch. Albuquerque was apparently a Jewish merchant from the kingdom of Castile who travelled to India from Cairo but was then enslaved by the Portuguese (1510) and became one of Governor Affonso d'Albuquerque's informants and interpreters. His new name was the result of conversion to Christianity in 1511, but apparently on his return to Cairo he recovered his original faith. See Braz de Albuquerque, *Comentários de Affonso d'Albuquerque*, ed. by A. Bião, 2 vols. (Coimbra, 1922–3), vol. II, p. 454, and (more precisely) Aubin, 'Francisco de Albuquerque', 182–4.

came to light, namely the chronicles of the Portuguese expansion written by Fernão Lopes de Castanheda (1551–61), João de Barros (1552–1615) and Braz de Albuquerque (1557).[7] These chroniclers, in their efforts to summarize their information, tried to synthesize ethnographical observations in short descriptive chapters, in this way making available evaluative generalizations about the oriental Indians to the European public. Although some chroniclers like Castanheda could claim a direct and long personal experience of the East, generally speaking these narratives could only give a limited role to first-hand ethnographical descriptions, because they were ruled by the aims and conventions of the epic genre.[8] There was certainly room for a degree of antiquarian curiosity within the well-written and remarkably informed narrative by the humanist court historian and bureaucrat Barros, but his *Asia* was nevertheless dominated by a very medieval-looking synthesis between patriotic aims and chivalric ideals.

The material collected by Ramusio and the Portuguese chronicles thus offered distinct images of India for European readers, but rarely attempted to define Indian civilization – a reflection of the problems of developing a lay discourse on cultural diversity outside limited practical concerns. In fact the first attempt to define Indian civilization from a comparative perspective and on the basis of personal experience was the result of the development of Christian missions in the East. Alessandro Valignano (Chieti 1539 – Macao 1606), the Jesuit Visitor to the province of India between 1574 and 1606, wrote extensively about Asian lands and peoples in the different *Summaria* which he sent to the General of the Society in Rome. His three reports became the basis for a more ambitious historical narrative written in Castilian, the *Historia del principio y progreso de la Compañia de Jesús en las Indias Orientales*, the first part of which was sent to Europe in 1584. This work influenced Jesuit historians like Giovan Pietro Maffei, who provided Europe with authoritative descriptions of the East in the late sixteenth century. Besides its focus on

---

[7] These chroniclers were followed by the historians of the reign of Manuel I, Damião de Góis and Jerónimo Osório, whose accounts of Asia were largely derivative, although not without merit. It should be noted that the work of Braz de Albuquerque has a distinctive structure. It is not a general chronicle, but it focuses on the deeds of his natural father, the famous governor Affonso de Albuquerque – hence the classical form of *commentaries* (although not written by Affonso himself, the narrative was mainly based on his papers). Braz, whose mother was a morisco slave, shared the peculiar destiny of Hernando Colón (1488–1539) of having to promote his personal cause by becoming the historian of a distinguished but ill-starred natural father.

[8] On the Portuguese chroniclers see J. B. Harrison, 'Five Portuguese historians', in C. H. Phillips (ed.) *Historians of India, Pakistan and Ceylon* (London, 1961); C. R. Boxer, *João de Barros, Portuguese humanist and historian of Asia* (New Delhi, 1981); Lach, *Asia*, vol. I, pp. 187–92.

the sanctification of Francis Xavier and in all Jesuit activities, the main interest of the *Historia* lay in the chapters describing the 'qualities' and 'customs' of the oriental Indians, the Japanese and the inhabitants of the kingdom of China.[9] Although Valignano is better known for his importance in re-shaping the Jesuit missions than for his intellectual legacy, his writings can be seen as an important landmark in the sixteenth-century European discourse on the Orient. They provided a sophisticated framework for the comparison of different peoples under the concept of rational behaviour, enshrining an idea of civility (not yet 'civilization') which was nevertheless combined with racial and religious forms of classification.

In this sense his reports, informed by a privileged education in law and theology, can be seen to express an original development that went beyond the impressive collection of travel narratives published by Ramusio a few decades earlier. While Ramusio's work had consolidated a powerful model of a world-wide empirical geography based on eye-witness accounts which benefited from humanist philological methods and thus superseded Ptolemy, Valignano and his fellow Jesuits carried European views of non-Europeans to a new natural and historical order which was in fact a meeting point between practical and theological concerns. These writings therefore represent the achievements and, at the same time, contradictions of Renaissance ethnology, and can be usefully taken as a point from which to obtain a perspective on both previous and later developments.

Perhaps the most important question is the place of India in this cultural process. It is significant that as late as 1574 European observers, having had a long history of contact with the Indian subcontinent and its peoples, acknowledged the difficulty of providing a unified image of India that made sense of its diversity. Valignano, aware of this problem, preferred to limit his observations to the western coast 'running from the city of Diu to Cape Comorin'.[10] This was, of course, the area where the Portuguese were able to exercise some direct political and religious influence by means of a regular military pressure – a long strip of land,

---

[9] See Alessandro Valignano, *Historia del principio y progreso de la Compañia de Jesús en las Indias Orientales 1542–64*, ed. by J. Wicki (Rome, 1944), chaps. 4 (pp. 22–40), 17 (pp. 126–63) and 26–27 (pp. 214–56). For a general view, see Lach, *Asia*, vol. I, pp. 257ff. A more detailed study of Valignano's policies in Japan, his key area of activity, is to be found in the introduction by J. L. Álvarez-Taladriz to Alessandro Valignano, *Sumario de las cosas del Japón*, ed. by J. L. Álvarez-Taladriz (Tokyo, 1954); J. F. Schütte, *Valignano's mission principles for Japan*, 2 vols. (Institute for Jesuit Sources, St Louis, 1980–5), and J. F. Moran, *The Japanese and the Jesuits: Alessandro Valignano in sixteenth-century Japan* (London, 1993).

[10] Valignano, *Historia*, p. 22. This corresponds to the coastline of the modern states of Gujarat, Maharastra, Karnataka, Goa and Kerala.

separated from the interior by a chain of mountains, where the Europeans had set up their earliest commercial factories and forts and a few important settlements, including the capital Goa. And yet within this limited area the difficulty of drawing a distinct image of India and its peoples was solved by recourse to a contemptuous generalization. Valignano ruthlessly described the Indian gentiles 'of many nations and languages' as inferior to Europeans: 'These people, who are almost black and go half naked, are universally contemptible and held to be base by the Portuguese and other Europeans; and the truth is that compared to them they are of little substance and lack refinement. They are, as Aristotle says, of a servile nature, because they are commonly poor, miserable and mean, and for any gain they will do the lowest things'.[11] He went on to explain that avaricious kings and lords exploited the lower castes without conscience and only kept peace and justice in order better to exploit them, that their elevated concept of *honra* and politeness did not prevent a vicious licentiousness towards women, and that the caste system was in fact an expression of tyranny and superstition. As for their religion, he noted that it contained a core of theological truth to which they added 'many chimeras and monstrosities'.[12] In conclusion, in Valignano's hierarchy of civilizations the dark-skinned Indians occupied a position slightly superior to the black Africans, since they were not entirely without reason, but were of a lower nature than the Europeans and other white peoples.[13]

The negative bias that pervades this description cannot be analysed simply as a personal opinion, even though Valignano's condition as the son of a Neapolitan aristocrat certainly contributed to the formation of his attitudes, while his education at the university of Padua helped him develop a theoretical explanation based on Aristotle. The important contrast is that in the same period a more limited contact with the Chinese or the Japanese offered to the educated missionaries led by the same Valignano not only an apparently homogeneous image of a different people with particular customs, qualities and institutions (what we would now call a different 'culture' or 'civilization'), but also higher hopes for evangelization and even a feeling of genuine admiration for their civil achievements. The non-European could actually be perceived

---

[11] Ibid. pp. 24–5.

[12] Ibid. pp. 25–32.

[13] Valignano never explains the exact relationship between his Aristotelian concept of nature, his racial classification and his cultural classification. It seems, however, apparent that he thought that cultural differences responded to natural, not simply accidental, differences, so that the Indians were not likely to become as capable Christians as the Japanese. Furthermore, colour was also an expression of these natural differences: the more vile Indians were, the more logical it appeared to him that they were also black.

as superior in the pursuit of an ideal of a well-organized society, a superiority measured by justice, education and prosperity.[14]

Valignano's views were expressed with particular clarity and forcefulness, but they do not contradict the opinions found in contemporary writers, especially among missionaries. Why were the Indians made to play such a negative role in the first clearly formulated Renaissance interpretations of Asian peoples? The answer lies partly in the very frustration of the European Catholics in their attempts to evangelize the Hindus (Muslims were from the beginning effectively regarded as a hopeless enemy). The evangelization of the gentiles, in contrast to war against the 'Moors', was more than an initial strategy to justify taking away the valuable Asiatic trade from the hands of existing merchant communities: it was an ideological imperative that went deep into Hispanic traditions of conquest and crusade. Its meaning in terms of practical needs (such as the search for indigenous allies) cannot be dissociated with the idealism that allowed the Portuguese crown to keep the empire together despite centrifugal forces and to justify it in Europe. A success so limited that in many ways amounted to failure was an important problem for European identity, especially for the missionaries themselves. For example, their greatest success in India was among the low-caste Paravas of the Fishery coast – the kind of ignorant and miserable people which Valignano despised.[15] It was largely the Jesuits' concern with the quality of their converts in India that prompted them to place hopes in other lands.

This process can already be observed in the letters of Francis Xavier (1506–52), which were read by all his followers and inspired their first ideas on the Asians. He would preach to the poor Indians of the Fishery

---

[14] The Chinese were the main focus of this idealization – the Japanese played a far more ambiguous role. For sixteenth-century European views of China see C. R. Boxer (ed.) *South China in the sixteenth century*, Hakluyt Society, 2nd series (London, 1953) and R. d'Intino (ed.) *Enformação das cousas da China. Textos do século XVI* (Lisbon, 1989). See also the recent work by Rui Loureiro, *A China na cultura Portuguesa do século XVI* (forthcoming).

[15] The Paravas were baptized by Franciscans. Their conversion in 1535–6 was apparently their own communal initiative: they sought the protection of the Portuguese fleets against rival native Muslim converts from Kayal who, with the help of Gujarati merchants, threatened their control of the pearl fisheries of the straits of Manaar (see K. McPherson, 'Paravas and Portuguese. A study of Portuguese strategy and its impact on an Indian seafaring community', *Mare Liberum*, 13 (1997): 69–82). For the Portuguese the Tirunelveli coast was of strategic navigational value, and after crushing Muslim shipping they sent the energetic Jesuits to strengthen their indirect control. In the middle of the century the Paravas flocked again to the protection of Portuguese arms against the depredations of Telugu-speaking warriors of northern origin representing the authority of the Vijayanagara captains in the area. By the time of Valignano perhaps as many as 100,000 converts were being looked after by a very small group of Jesuits.

coast, but brahmins were perfidious liars and subtle manipulators of popular ignorance, 'the most perverse people in the world'. His dreams really went towards Japan, 'the best people among the infidels', honour-loving, courteous, monogamous, without idolatry, lettered, rational and desirous to learn. Given that they had their own universities, a missionary with a good theological training would certainly be able to engage in rational disputation and convert the best among them. As it turned out, experience proved things to be more difficult, and in particular the Buddhist bonzes put up a solid intellectual resistance. Undaunted, Xavier left a few men in Japan and tried China instead, where people were generous, understanding of politics, peaceful and extremely scholarly: if they converted, the Japanese would surely follow suit.[16]

Valignano was a heir to these images, including the preference for white people as more likely to be rational, but with him a new conception of evangelization clearly emerged too, one based on the idea of adaptation, what might be described as a consciously oriented cultural exchange.[17] It was thus in the more remote China and Japan, rather than in India or south-east Asia, where this new strategy was given stronger support, almost as if Valignano's personal judgement about the inferior civilization of the brahmins directed well-trained missionaries like Matteo Ricci away from the Indian hinterland. It is not entirely coincidental that Roberto de Nobili only started his experimental work in the interior of South India in the seventeenth century, right after Valignano's death. The fact that Nobili's very different attitude towards Indian culture was *also* related to his background as a well-educated Italian aristocrat who had read Aquinas proves (if proof is needed) that the elite culture of Europe was far from rigid and homogeneous, and that social or national background did not determine a specific response to other cultures.

Xavier's and Valignano's prejudice about what they saw as the super-stitious ignorance of the Indian gentiles was not inevitable, but generally

---

[16] All the letters are collected in Francis Xavier, *Epistolae S. Francisci Xaverii*, ed. by G. Schurhammer and J. Wicki, 2 vols. (Rome, 1944–5). See in particular numbers 20, 90, 96, 97, 110 (in the above description of Xavier's view of Japanese qualities I have extracted some of the contents of letter 90, written to the Jesuits in Goa from Kagoshima on 5 November 1549; his views on brahmins can be found in a letter to the brothers in Rome from Cochin on 15 January 1544; his views on China in his letter to Ignatius of Loyola from Cochin on 29 January 1552). The saint's career in India is studied in detail in G. Schurhammer, *Francis Xavier: his life, his times*, 4 vols. (Rome, 1977), vol. II: *India 1541–45*.

[17] Background information for this 'new concept of evangelization' in Lach, *Asia*, vol. I, pp. 245–331, and J. D. Spence, *The memory palace of Matteo Ricci* (New York, 1984). See also chapter 9 below.

speaking it was shared by the Portuguese ecclesiastical bodies established in the East. It was a negative judgement of Indian civility based on apparent dissimilarities with Europe, legitimized by the immediate applicability of the concept of idolatry, and compounded by decades of missionary frustration. However, the strength of this attitude was also related to the difficulty of using a simple political image to articulate an understanding of the customs and institutions of the peoples inhabiting India. Less than in Japan, and especially unlike in China, the Europeans in India did not face a unified political system with which they could have economic, military and cultural dealings, but rather a collection of small and often volatile sultanates, principalities and semi-independent city–ports involved in oceanic trade. As Valignano recognized, it was difficult to speak about 'India' in general, because 'taking this name as it is commonly used in Europe, India contains such a great diversity of provinces and kingdoms, that it is not possible to comprehend except for those who have travelled part of them'.[18] For European observers, the fact that many of the more important states were ruled by Muslim elites was less of a problem that the fact that they were so fragmented and unstable, at a time when the ideas of political independence and stability were fundamental to the image of a successful civil life.

Akbar's Mughal empire might be seen as a clear exception, and yet this was a country in the periphery of the European vision, not really hegemonic until the latter decades of the sixteenth century and then still quite remote from Goa. Serious contacts with Akbar's court did not come until the first Jesuit mission, led by Father Rudolf Aquaviva, was sent in 1579, of which the best account is Antonio Monserrate's *Mongolicae legationis commentarius*.[19] The author belonged to a selected group of well-trained Jesuits who had been led by Valignano in 1574 to infuse a new vigour and a new orientation to the missionary path opened by Francis Xavier, despite and beyond the previous efforts of other religious orders.[20] Although the *Commentarius* did not reach Europe, Monserrate's briefer 'Relation of Akbar, king of the Mughals', written in 1582 under the illusion that Akbar might convert to Christianity, offered a powerful image of Indian (albeit not Hindu) kingship which was destined to have great impact in Europe, and which contrasts with

[18] Valignano, *Historia*, p. 22.

[19] Antonio Monserrate, 'Mongolicae legationis commentarius', ed. by H. Hosten, *Memoirs of the Asiatic Society of Bengal*, vol. III (Calcutta, 1914). There exists an English translation: *The commentary . . . on his journey to the court of Akbar*, translated by J. S. Hoyland and annotated by S. N. Banerjee (Oxford, 1922).

[20] During the first century of contacts, the Franciscan and Dominican friars in Portuguese India wrote remarkably little concerning indigenous customs and religion – in stark contrast with those sent by the Spanish to the New World.

Valignano's contemporary statement that indigenous political power was essentially tyrannical.[21]

We may conclude that there was no clear, coherent image of Indian civilization in sixteenth-century Europe – not even a simple, easily recognizable stereotype. The most complete accounts of India did not circulate extensively before 1550, and they seldom had a unitary structure. The European armchair cosmographer of the second half of the sixteenth century needed to piece together the information about India from a variety of sources, often with unhappy results. Only a few coastal areas were reasonably well known – those of Malabar, Kanará, Coromandel and Gujarat – while descriptions of more remote places such as Bengal depended on occasional expeditions.[22] The majority of these early writers concentrated their attention on either economic possibilities or on the activities of the Portuguese, although indigenous customs and basic political realities were often described as an important background. The lack of recognizable unified political structures in the Indian subcontinent (before the consolidation of the Mughals in the north) established the general context for the early experience of the Europeans in India, and determined to a great extent their difficulty in obtaining a focused image of Indian civility in a world of not one but many 'others'.

There is, however, an important exception to this, which is provided by the narratives dealing with the empire of Vijayanagara. This Hindu kingdom occupied an area about the size of Britain in the tropical southern tip of the Indian peninsula (see map 1). Narsinga and Bisnagar, the two names by which the kingdom (not without some degree of confusion) was known to Europeans, in fact became important points of reference in the late-Renaissance map of the world. Both for the quality of the sources available and for the historical importance of the 'object' of description it provides, Vijayanagara constitutes a good case-study for the central questions of this book: why did the Europeans in Asia see what they saw? – and, more specifically, how did they perceive and interpret human cultural diversity? It is for this reason that the area occupied by this kingdom will be the focus of my analysis.

---

[21] Compare 'Relaçam do Equebar, rei dos mogores' in J. Wicki (ed.) *Documenta indica*, 18 vols. (Rome, 1964–88), vol. XII, pp. 647–61, with Valignano, *Historia*, pp. 25–6. Valignano's description of Hindu kings as tyrannical should not be read in opposition to his understanding of the Muslim sultans of Gujarat and the Deccan, whose tyrannical power was an even more obvious commonplace in the ideology of the 'Estado da India'.

[22] For instance, the 1521 expedition published in *Voyage dans les deltas du Gange et de l'Irraouaddy 1521*, ed. by G. Bouchon and L. F. Thomaz (Paris, 1988), with Portuguese text and French and English translations.

Map 1 Vijayanagara (at its maximum extension, occupying the territory south of the Krishna river).

THE LAST HINDU EMPIRE

The history of the independent Hindu kingdom of Vijayanagara cannot be understood without reference to the Muslim invasions of the Indian subcontinent which gave the new military state its defensive character. From the end of the twelfth century Muslim armies composed of Turkish and Afghan soldiers invaded India from the north-west. With the military superiority of central-Asian cavalry, they succeeded in the majority of their campaigns, but unlike their predecessor of the first decades of the eleventh century, Mahmud of Ghazni, instead of limiting themselves to regular plunder they settled in Delhi. From there, they soon pushed ahead further south towards the Deccan, attacking the Hindu capitals Devagari in 1294 and Warangal in 1308 and subjecting them to tribute. This new Delhi sultanate was never a very stable political entity, but it ensured the continuous presence of a number of foreign Muslim overlords in northern India, and thus connected significant parts of the country with an expanding international Islamic world which, after the Mongol conquests, could be travelled from north Africa to China.[23]

The new Turkish rulers also invaded southern India, plundering the traditional capital of the Hoysalas Dvarasamudram in 1310, and reaching the Pandya kingdom of Madurai in the following year. But although by 1328 there was even a Turkish kingdom in Madurai, these foreign armies could never secure a hold on southern India, perhaps because local conditions did not invite a long settlement and less remote conquests still had to be defended further to the north. The land was subject to the seasonal monsoons and comprised a large plateau, separated from the commercial western coast of Kanará and Malabar by a chain of mountains. In great part it was covered by forests and hills inhabited by independent tribes, although the more urbanized areas were populated by several Hindu ethnic groups of Dravidian descent speaking a variety of related languages – Telugu, Kannada, Tamil and Malayalam. There were several wealthy cities and temples in the south, especially in

---

[23] On the Turkish invasions see the detailed work by Wolseley Haig in *The Cambridge History of India*, vol. III (Cambridge, 1928), especially chaps. 5 and 6. The South Indian perspective is summarily presented by Krishnaswami Aiyangar in ibid. pp. 467–99, and in more detail in his important work *South India and her Muhammadan invaders* (Madras, 1921). A useful overview is provided by R. Thapar in her *A history of India from the discovery to 1526* (Harmondsworth, 1966), pp. 229–40 (still valuable today). More recently, Burton Stein in his posthumous *A history of India* (Oxford, 1998), pp. 134–8, has emphasized that the Turkish horsemen did not simply defeat the native armies with surprising facility, they also defended their Indian conquests from Mongol attacks. This explains the strategic importance of Delhi for the Muslim invaders.

the fertile river deltas facing the east, but the peasant communities were strongly organized and had to be commanded locally.[24] The fragmented character of the indigenous political scene, with several thinly centralized little kingdoms ruled by groups of peasant-warriors who derived political legitimacy from Hindu brahminic consent, also helps explain why attempts to found a Muslim dynasty failed to win sufficient popular endorsement. It was therefore only through extremely violent methods that the Turkish adventurers who remained in southern India after the first plundering expeditions could maintain themselves against indigenous resistance, led in particular by the Hoysala king Vira Ballala III (1292–1342).

The exact circumstances of the foundation of the city and kingdom of Vijayanagara have long been a subject of debate, but must be seen in any case in the context of the persistence of the Hoysala power in parts of what is now modern Karnataka, against the fragility of any permanent invasion from Delhi.[25] While (as described by Ibn Battūta) Vira Ballala himself was killed in his failed campaign against the sultan of Madurai in 1342, his fortified centres in the northern frontier were the nucleus for the new kingdom of Vijayanagara, which was eventually able to defeat the isolated Turks in the south, and was also able to resist for over two centuries the Muslim armies which had settled successfully in the Deccan.

Thus, around the 1340s, two Indian brothers of the Sangama Family named Harihara and Bukka founded the new royal city by the Tungabhadra river (at the modern village of Hampi), not far from the site of the fortress of Anegondi, which until 1327 had been a focus of resistance to the Turkish armies. It seems that these Sangama brothers had in fact

---

[24] The geographical and agricultural pattern is studied in Burton Stein's fundamental *Peasant state and society in medieval South India* (New Delhi, 1980), especially pp. 30–62 and, concerning the Vijayanagara times, pp. 366–488. Against the traditional idealization of the supralocal ethnic solidarity of medieval local communities, Stein makes it clear that the peasant villages of the Tamil country were under the leadership of an elite of peasant–warrior entrepreneurs, often Telugu foreigners from the north.

[25] For a classic statement of the origins of the city, see N. Venkataramanayya, *Vijayanagara. Origin of the city and the Empire* (Madras, 1933), who insists on the idea (favoured by many scholars from Andhra) that the kingdom sprung from the attempts of an islamicized Telugu family, former servants of the Kakatiyas of Warangal, to enforce Turkish authority against the resistance of the Hoysalas – followed, however, by their apostasy and independence from Delhi. The traditional and apparently simpler view, defended by Kannada historians like B. A. Saletore in his *Social and political life in the Vijayanagara Empire*, 2 vols. (Madras, 1932), is that the Hoysalas, as agents of local resistance, were behind Vijayanagara. The most important recent contribution to the debate is by Hermann Kulke, 'Maharajas, mahants and historians. Reflections on the historiography of early Vijayanagara and Sringeri', in A. Dallapiccola and S. Zingel-Ave (eds.) *Vijayanagara: city and empire*, 2 vols. (Stuttgart, 1985), vol. I, pp. 120–43, who adopts a modified version of the Hoysala theory.

served the Kampili ruler of Anegondi, and after his defeat transferred their allegiance to the Hoysalas.[26] But the process may have been more complex than that: if we can trust a number of accounts, contemporary Arabic and Persian and sixteenth-century Sanskrit, the Sangama brothers were originally a Telugu family, former servants of the Kakatiya rulers of Warangal, who following the successive falls of Warangal (1323) and Kampili (1327) had been taken prisoners to Delhi, and after converting to Islam were sent as Turkish agents to take over the administration of the region.[27] Their apostasy and eventual emergence as a new Hindu dynasty could then be seen in the context of the vacuum created by a weakening of the Turkish military hold, and would imply rivalry with, rather than just allegiance to, the Hoysalas.

The fact is that the new kingdom expanded during the next two centuries, although not always at a steady pace, by winning over the allegiance of groups of Kannada- and Telugu-speaking warrior groups, and eventually conquering the Tamil south. The Vijayanagara rulers thus transformed the world visited by Marco Polo and Ibn Battūta into a more centralized and relatively stable kingdom, incorporating the various Hindu local cults and literary traditions, and benefiting from the new wealth created by the continuous processes of expanded land settlement and urbanization. The authority of this kingdom was vaguely held together by the threat of the Muslim invaders, who at the same time had successfully settled in the Deccan and created (against the wishes of the Delhi rulers) the independent Bahmani kingdom. Therefore, from the very beginning influential brahmin scholars and poets legitimized the kings of Vijayanagara as sustainers of a dharmic ideal of Hindu religious and social order. The successful rejection of Muslim overlords did not

---

[26] Kulke (ibid.) argues for the continuity between Vijayanagara and Hoysala powers, and for the posteriority of the brahmin Vidyaranya's role as spiritual guide of the early dynasty. The traditions presenting this Hindu sage as the main inspiration for the foundation of the city (which I shall discuss in chapter 8) would then be interpreted as sixteenth-century forgeries.

[27] Kulke (ibid.) is not convincing when he doubts the traditional account that the Sangama brothers had at some point converted to Islam. Kulke's argument that the inglorious event would have been passed in silence after their re-conversion to Hinduism begs the question of why the story that the founders of the city were sent by the king of Delhi persisted in the native accounts up to the sixteenth century, as reflected, for instance, in the story heard by Fernão Nunes in the 1530s. Sanskrit sources also dating from the sixteenth century largely agree with Nunes. The detail of religious conversion was omitted from all these accounts (indeed following Kulke's logic), but the parallels in fourteenth-century Muslim accounts such as Ibn Battūta's, who does mention conversion to Islam and whose story unambiguously concerns the sons of the king of Kampili, are striking enough and not to be ignored. Over two centuries Hindu native sources might have easily transferred the emphasis from conversion and apostasy to the more agreeable myth of the influence of the sage Vidyaranya.

however mean that Vijayanagara was isolated from Deccani influences. This is particularly clear if we consider that the remarkable success of the rulers of the new empire, who to a certain degree had become 'kings of kings', was in fact the assertion of territorial authority against both Hindu and Muslim rivals through military means.[28] While one permanent issue was consolidating the unevenly spread royal authority against a variety of centrifugal forces, the evolution of the kingdom for 200 years was to a great extent conditioned by the ability of the rulers to adapt their vast armies to changing conditions of warfare. This involved securing the importation of horses, accepting Muslim mercenaries and (as the Portuguese were to witness in the early sixteenth century) even incorporating artillery and musketeers into their campaigns.

The Sangama dynasty of Vijayanagara had a history of some 150 years marked by conflict against the Bahmani sultanate across the northern frontier, until, following a particularly difficult period of internal instability (always a recurrent problem), it gave way to a second dynasty in 1485, named after the successful general Saluva Narasimha. The rise to power of successful generals with their own territorial resources, first as regents and then as founders of new dynasties, actually became a pattern of the political history of the kingdom during the first half of the sixteenth century, underpinning a traditional weakness in the system of succession and transfer of power. Thus there was again much instability during the reign of Saluva's son Immadi Narasimha (1491–1505), which was resolved with the rise to power of the regent Narasa Nayaka, whose own son founded the Tuluva dynasty as Vira Narasimha (1505–9).[29] But it was only his brother Krishna Deva Raya (1509–29) who was able to

---

[28] Through trade, war and diplomacy Vijayanagara was culturally connected to the wider Islamic world. Secular architecture similarly reflected Muslim Deccani influences. At its most extreme, modern historical analysis suggests that the Vijayanagara kings represented a process of 'islamicization' – which would explain the adoption of titles such as 'sultan of Hindu kings' (*himduraya suratrana*) by the Sangama brothers. See P. B. Wagoner, '"Sultan among Hindu Kings": dress, titles and islamicization of Hindu culture at Vijayanagara', *Journal of Asian Studies*, 55 (1996): 851–80. In my view, this does not detract from the fact that religious conversion, or lack thereof, was a key issue, and that the dharmic ideal defined by Sanskrit brahminic culture and its South Indian vernacular variations did provide a focus of identity and legitimation for the empire of Vijayanagara. Vijayanagara was simultaneously both a Hindu bulwark against Muslim conquests (the traditional view criticized by Wagoner) and a centre of adoption of a number of international Islamic cultural values. One could even say that to some extent it was because they imitated the practices of Islamic peoples that the Vijayanagara elites were relatively efficient in resisting Islamic armies.

[29] There is still no scholarly consensus concerning the dates for all these reigns – in fact, the whole political history of the kingdom is like a jigsaw puzzle with many pieces missing. For instance, a different chronology is given by J. M. Fritz and G. Michell, *City of victory. Vijayanagara, the medieval Hindu capital of Southern India* (New York, 1991), p. 114, as follows: Saluva Narasimha, 1484–92; Immadi Narasimha, 1492–1506; Vira

consolidate this third dynasty and, through a process of centralization and conquest, led to what was then, and is still described as, the major moment of glory of Vijayanagara. This Indian king, who kept in check the powerful Muslim rulers of Bijapur as well as the Hindu kings of Orissa, became known as one of the richest in the East.[30]

However, the solidity of his achievement came into question during the reign of his brother Achyuta Deva Raya (1529–42), when factional struggle allowed the shah of Bijapur to recover the initiative. Although the Hindu empire had outlived the Bahmanis, which had disintegrated into five sultanates at the beginning of the sixteenth century, it eventually succumbed to the consequences of a spectacular military defeat against a Decanni alliance in 1565. The regent Rama Raja (1542–65), in fact an usurper from the powerful Aravidu family and whose influence went back to the times of Krishna Deva Raya, was killed in battle. More importantly, the city was shamefully abandoned by his surviving brother and destroyed, and future attempts to re-establish its authority over South India proved utterly futile.

In some ways Rama Raja had been victim of his own previous success, because he had alienated all potential allies with a ruthlessly aggressive policy. It is, however, the failure of his internal policy that, with hindsight, appears to be more conspicuous. The total defeat of 1565, which led to a new collection of Hindu regional lordships that were progressively plundered or conquered by expeditions from the Deccan, definitively uncovered the internal weakness of the Vijayanagara overlordship. A rump state of Vijayanagara under the Aravidu royal dynasty survived by moving its capital east, to Penugonda and finally Chandragiri, but (at the time when Akbar's Mughal empire was expanding in the north) it was no longer an effective political force beyond its modest regional boundaries. In fact, the new regional lords who throughout the century following the fall of the old capital competed against the Aravidu kings from their various quasi-independent cities of Madurai, Tanjore, Gingee or Mysore, were often the old nayakas, or captains, originally sent by the Vijayanagara rulers as representatives of their authority in the east and south of the peninsula.[31]

Narasimha, 1506–9; Krishna Deva Raya, 1510–29, etc. I shall discuss contentious dates only when my argument requires it.

[30] The Portuguese were told by the ruler of Gujarat, Bahadur, that in terms of wealth if the king of Cambay himself was one, the king of Narsinga was two and that of Bengal three: Barros, *Ásia*, 3 vols containing decades 1–3 (Lisbon, 1932–92), vol. I, p. 350. (Vol. III of this edition – the best available – is a facsimile of the 1563 edition.)

[31] The above summary of Vijayanagara history is of course only a brief sketch. On the political evolution of Vijayanagara the fundamental work is now Stein, *Vijayanagara*, carefully reviewed in S. Subrahmanyam, 'Agreeing to disagree: Burton Stein on

SOURCES AND GENRES: HISTORICAL AND ANTIQUARIAN PERSPECTIVES

As we have seen, the presence of political unity and centralized institutions played a crucial role in shaping the European interpretation of foreign societies in the Renaissance. The fact that Vijayanagara was a Hindu political society which was essentially defined in opposition to the religious domination of Islam (even though in reality the Vijayanagara elites may have borrowed a number of practices from their Muslim neighbours) is of great importance, especially considering the analogous European tradition of confrontation with Islam. The medieval European tendency to 'Christianize' Eastern rulers in terms of the mythical figure of the Prester John could therefore find a ready niche in non-Muslim India. It is also noteworthy that the experience of Vijayanagara made its impact before the Europeans had any full access to the more remote 'gentile' societies of Ming China or Japan. It is not comparable to the experience of the Aztec and Inca empires in America either, since these were almost immediately conquered and disorganized. The image of an idolatrous civilization presented by Vijayanagara was therefore a challenge to European narrative topoi and political ideas that had few counterparts in the sixteenth century.[32]

I shall attempt to analyse comprehensively and chronologically all European descriptions of the kingdom of Vijayanagara which involved a substantial and direct interpretation of South Indian society and culture (less important references, and accounts of a derivative character, will be

Vijayanagara', *South Asia Research*, 17 (1997): 127–39. Stein's work is to a large extent a reaction to the traditional perspective of South Indian nationalism, as summarized by K. A. Nilakanta Sastri, *A history of South India*, 3rd edn (Madras 1966), pp. 227–312. In his studies – *Peasant state* and *Vijayanagara* – Stein has emphasized instead internal economic and political processes. Other important works are R. Sewell, *A forgotten empire (Vijayanagar)* (London, 1900); S. Krishnaswami Aiyangar (ed.) *Sources of Vijayanagara history* (Madras, 1919); K. A. Nilakanta Sastri and N. Venkataramanayya, *Further sources of Vijayanagara history*, 3 vols. (Madras, 1946); J. M. Fritz, G. Michell and M. S. Nagaraja Rao, *Where kings and gods meet. The royal centre at Vijayanagara* (Tucson, 1984), and some of the articles collected in A. Dallapiccola and S. Zingel-Ave (eds.) *Vijayanagara: city and empire*. For the surviving fourth dynasty, H. Heras, *The Aravidu dynasty of Vijayanagara* (Madras, 1927), remains essential. Concerning social and economic conditions see also N. Venkataramanayya, *Studies in the history of the third dynasty of Vijayanagara* (Madras, 1935), and T. V. Mahalingam, *Administration and social life under Vijayanagara* (Madras, 1940). On the Deccan see H. K. Sherwani, *The Bahmanis of the Deccan*, 2nd edn (New Delhi, 1985).

[32] Other non-Muslim oriental societies – like Siam, Pegu and Cambodia – had a less intense effect in the European experience overseas, although they are not to be entirely neglected. For the Portuguese in Siam, see Maria da Conceição Flores, *Os portugueses e o Sião no século XVI* (Lisbon, 1995), and for Cambodia, B. Groslier, *Angkor et la Cambodge au XVIe siècle d'après les sources portugaises et espagnoles* (Paris, 1958).

treated only when they illuminate a particular point). These descriptions were all produced in the fifteenth and sixteenth centuries, until the destruction of the capital city and the disintegration of its authority in the south (1420–1570). The analysis, however, will be extended to encompass earlier and later descriptions of South India, so as to explain the process of change from the times of Marco Polo at the end of the thirteenth century to those of Pietro della Valle at the beginning of the seventeenth. The criterion that I have followed in assessing the interest of the material is the existence of a body of literature that makes an argument about the evolution of travel literature not only possible, but also enlightening. For this reason also, when descriptions of areas not directly controlled by Vijayanagara (such as the Malabar coast) throw light on the argument, they have been freely brought into the discussion. On the other hand, the survival of a fourth dynasty in Chandragiri after 1565 – in effect a rump Vijayanagara – will be analysed only to the extent that it adds significantly to the argument.

This overall exercise will necessarily involve discussing what modern historians have to say about Vijayanagara, since this is the essential tool for a critical appraisal of foreign descriptions of the empire. The group of texts formed by these descriptions provides a matrix from which to discover continuities and change throughout three centuries. It further-more serves as model and example for the main themes, genres and problems which appear in the wider cultural process of the European interpretation of oriental peoples in the Renaissance. The main purpose of this study is thus to reveal through a particular case the different registers of the process of transforming an 'experience of otherness' into a set of narratives. In interpreting each text I shall consider not only authorship, but also the expectations of audiences and, when relevant, distinct processes of transmission and re-interpretation (since quite often what was observed in India differed from what was publicized and interpreted in Europe). I will follow the principle that we need a complex interpretation for each text – something like a language-game theory – involving general rules, particular aims and diverse expectations, which I shall define in each case.

The especial value of contemporary descriptions of Vijayanagara is that they enable the historian to compare analogous material and to isolate important variables. This can be seen to operate in three ways. First, and chronologically, it is possible to compare descriptions from different periods. Second, the existence of a body of literature produced by non-European foreigners, in particular by Muslims writing in Persian and Arabic, provides an opportunity to interpret western descriptions in a wider comparative framework. Finally, the existence of many different kinds of accounts – letters, chronicles, itineraries, relations, geographical reports and cosmographies – facilitates the task of analysing the production of ethnography as related to different narrative structures. A brief discussion of the sources according to these three aspects may be useful at this point.

A chronological sequence

In order to achieve a perspective on Renaissance ethnology going back to medieval Europe and to identify the impact of fifteenth-century humanism it is possible to contrast Marco Polo's description of South India (1298) with that of another Venetian merchant who actually visited the city of Vijayanagara, Nicolò de Conti (who gave two very different reports, in 1437 and in 1441). These medieval merchant accounts can offer a perspective to assess the qualities of the two major Portuguese sources on Vijayanagara given by the horse-traders Domingos Paes (written in 1520–2) and Fernão Nunes (possibly written in 1531).[33] This second comparison can shed light on the way the new colonial conditions of Portuguese Asia affected the attitudes and descriptive skills of European observers of similar social background.

The initial ethnographic practice of those Europeans who came with the first Portuguese expeditions can be discussed more specifically with reference to letters and journals describing a novel experience of India, of which I will provide some analysis. In a few cases, these early accounts also included references to Vijayanagara, and some of them appeared in print in the *Paesi novamenti retrovati* of 1507. While some accounts of the kingdom (like the Venetian report by Francisco de Albuquerque) remained marginal, observations by the Italian Ludovico de Varthema (first published in 1510) and the Portuguese Duarte Barbosa (written *c.* 1516–18) appear in two of the most important narratives of the first half of the sixteenth century, increasing our ability to follow a continuous chronological sequence of written texts. This continuity can be taken further into the sixteenth century thanks to the existence of a final description of the city in the narrative of another Venetian merchant, Cesare Federici (published in 1587), which is based on what he saw in Vijayanagara in 1566, soon after the disastrous battle of Talikota.[34]

---

[33] The name in the manuscript, Nuniz, is commonly modernized as Nunes. I have also corrected the hypothesis of Robert Sewell in *A forgotten empire* that Nunes's account was written in 1535–7. *Circa* 1531 seems more consistent with the evidence (see chapter 8 below).

[34] I will throughout this work refer to 'the battle of Talikota' in agreement with the name by which it is commonly known. It must be stressed, however, that the battle took place some distance from that location, as discussed by Heras, *Aravidu dynasty*.

In addition to these major descriptions of the Hindu capital, second-hand references to Vijayanagara in sixteenth-century Portuguese sources can be found in the *Suma Oriental of Tomé Pires* (written between 1512 and 1515), and in the *Coloquios dos simples e drogas* which the humanist physician Garcia da Orta published in Goa (1563). Vijayanagara was also part of the background in the major chronicles dealing with Portuguese expansion: the *História do descobrimento et conquista da Índia pelos Portugueses* by Fernão Lopes de Castanheda (most of which was published between 1551 and 1554), the four decades of *Ásia* by João de Barros (published from 1552 onwards), the *Lendas da Índia* by Gaspar Correa (written during the first half of the century), and Diogo do Couto's continuation of Barros's official history (written at the turn of the century under the Spanish Habsburg dynasty).[35] Vijayanagara also appears briefly in an anonymous *Crónica do descobrimento e primeiras conquistas da India pelos Portugueses* of the first half of the century.[36]

Among those chroniclers who were actually in India, Castanheda's account of 'Narsinga' was the more substantial. It was also the more influential, because Castanheda's work was published quickly and often plagiarized and translated. Correa's observations, less systematic, are on the other hand often original, while Couto was virtually alone in discussing some of the developments of the reign of Rama Raja (there are, however, some references to this latter reign in the work of a less important writer, Leonardo Nunes, who finished his chronicle of the governorship of João de Castro in 1550).

From some of these sources, especially from the well-known chronicles by Castanheda and Barros, 'Narsinga' became a standard theme in late sixteenth-century cosmographies, notably in Giovanni Botero's *Relationi universali* (1591–6), but also in the expanded French translation of Müesnter's *Cosmographia* written by François de Belleforest (1575). By the end of the sixteenth century there was, however, a growing gap between the circulation of these reports and the changing conditions in the Indian peninsula. Some valuable accounts of a more fragmented hinterland can be usefully discussed in this context, including material by the Jesuit Valignano (written before 1584), the Franciscan Martín Ignacio de Loyola (published in 1585), the Dominican Gabriel de San Antonio (published in 1604), the Flemish merchant Jacques de Coutre

---

[35] I have maintained the name 'Correa' as it appears in the original edition of the manuscript and in English scholarship. However, modern Portuguese authors usually refer to him as 'Correia'.

[36] This manuscript was published for the first time in 1974: *Cronica do descobrimento e conquista da India pelos Portugueses* (Anonymous Codex, British Library, Egerton 20901), ed. by Luís de Albuquerque (Lisbon, 1974). It contains material similar to that used by Castanheda.

(written *c.* 1628), and, well into the seventeenth century, the Italian aristocrat Pietro della Valle (who was in Ikkeri in 1623, but whose Indian letters were only published in 1663). Furthermore, the kingdom of Vijayanagara in Chandragiri was discussed in particular detail by the Jesuits, some of whose letters were collected by Fernão Guerreiro (1603–11) and summarized by Pierre du Jarric (1608–14).[37]

The analysis of the chronological sequence is best carried taking into consideration the production of these texts, and only secondarily their circulation in Europe. For instance, and quite remarkably, the manuscripts written by Paes, Nunes, Correa and (to some extent) Couto, all of whom spent many years in Portuguese India and had a fairly detailed knowledge of the lands of Vijayanagara, remained unpublished in sixteenth-century Portugal.[38] The same happened with the later descriptions of the interior of the peninsula by Valignano and Coutre. Furthermore, as we have seen, the crucial reports by Pires and Barbosa were not printed until Ramusio produced his Italian collection in Venice, and then from imperfect copies. It is also important to examine some clear cases of direct borrowing: Barros seems to have been sent the reports by Paes and Nunes, and Castanheda drew on Barbosa, while other chroniclers often used similar sources and copied each other. Despite the interest of following the transmission and transformation of information, it is above all the evolution of the experience of describing the people, politics and religion of Vijayanagara that will provide the focus of this study.

Non-European sources

An additional advantage of this set of foreign descriptions of South India is that we have a significant number of non-European narratives, which makes it possible to develop a comparative analysis of travellers' attitudes that goes beyond sociological and national categories exclusively related to Europe. Obviously, of all non-Europeans, Muslim writers provide the sources better suited for a systematic comparison with western descriptions of South India.[39] Ibn Battūta can of course

---

[37] I exclude from this overview of the later sources the abundant accounts dealing exclusively with coastal areas, and in particular the eastern coast, although I shall refer to works of particular significance, such as those by the Venetian Gasparo Balbi (1590), the Dutch Jan Huyghen van Linschoten (1596), the Florentine Francesco Carletti (whose 'ragionamenti' were delivered in Florence in 1606) and the French François Pyrard de Laval (1611, with new editions in 1615 and 1619).

[38] Despite Couto's personal efforts, his *Decades* (written from the 1590s) were only partially published in the seventeenth century. For a summary discussion see Schurhammer, *Francis Xavier*, vol. II, pp. 612–14. The works of Correa, Paes and Nunes were not published until the second half of the nineteenth century.

[39] Another tradition of travel writing that I have considered is represented by the account

stand as a perfect contrast to Marco Polo. Amongst Indian writers educated within the parameters of a cosmopolitan Persian literary culture, possibly the most useful source for our purposes is the chronicle by Firishta, or Ferishta (d. 1623), a court historian working in the Deccani kingdoms of Ahmadnagar and Bijapur at the end of the sixteenth century. He wrote about wars with Vijayanagara (often using earlier chronicles) in a way that can be effectively compared with the Portuguese chronicles by Fernão Nunes and Diogo do Couto.[40]

An even more interesting narrative is the personal account of a journey to Vijayanagara undertaken in 1443 by the Persian ambassador ʿAbd al-Razzāq al-Samarqandī (Herat, 1413–82), who was at the service of the Timurid ruler Shah Rukh.[41] The complexity of this narrative makes a detailed comparison with European sources particularly enlightening. To what extent did differences in cultural background affect a traveller's ability to see and tell?[42] It could be argued that there was a general interpretative framework common to Persian and Western sources on Vijayanagara, centred on city, kingship and ritual, the literary elaboration of which by diverse observers was dependent neither upon a mere intertextual borrowing, nor in any simple sense on those common cultural assumptions which the Bible or the distant Hellenistic background could provide. It relied, rather, on a basic human capacity to decode and interpret an indigenous cultural system, a capacity related to the observer's training in understanding structurally similar language-games in his own culture. The logical assumptions of the natural world as an ordered one, and of history as a succession of events following an irreversible arrow of time, sustain ʿAbd al-Razzāq's empirical description

by the Russian Orthodox Christian merchant Afanasi Nikitin, who wrote about the Deccani kingdoms of South India, describing his travels there in 1469. Finally, one may also study the descriptions of Malabar found in the accounts by fifteenth-century Chinese (albeit also Muslim) navigators like Ma Huan. Whilst editorial imperatives have dictated that all these examples cannot be discussed in detail in this book, I have nevertheless drawn on them for my general formulations.

[40] A few Persian chroniclers other than Ferishta and ʿAbd al-Razzāq (discussed below) wrote about Vijayanagara, but their importance is less obvious.

[41] On ʿAbd al-Razzāq and his work see the introduction by E. M. Quatremère to his French edition, 'Notice de l'ouvrage persan qui a pour titre: Matla-assadein ou majma-albahrein', in *Notices et extraits des manuscrits de la Bibliothèque du Roi*, vol. XIV, part I (Paris, 1843), pp. 1–13; See also *Encyclopaedia of Islam*, new edn, vol. I, pp. 90–1 (article by W. Barthold and M. Shafi); E. G. Browne, *A literary history of Persia*, 4 vols (Cambridge, 1902–4), vol. III, pp. 428–30. For a recent English translation see W. M. Thackston (ed.) *A century of princes. Sources on Timurid history and art* (Cambridge, Mass., 1989), pp. 299–321.

[42] I shall not undertake a very detailed analysis of ʿAbd al-Razzāq's narrative here, but only refer to its conclusions. For a more extended treatment see my 'A western rationality? Late medieval travellers and the practice of cross-cultural encounters' (forthcoming).

no less than those of any European writer. In fact, the thematic emphases of this description of Vijayanagara – a large city in a large empire, a powerful king, a well-cultivated and fertile land, a numerous army with awesome elephants – are almost identical to those offered by Italian and Portuguese observers. Of course, while the Europeans established comparisons with Paris or Milan, 'Abd al-Razzāq referred to Herat, the Khorasani capital. He also introduced a theme which was particularly relevant to the traditions of political discourse at the Persian courts: an idealized model of monarchical rule in which a powerful king was surrounded by wise men, was able to command full authority, and brought about collective prosperity. 'Abd al-Razzāq's narrative thus went beyond the mere empirical description of human diversity in order to send a political message which had more to do with conditions at Shah Rukh's court than with those in South India. In order to do so the author had to recognize among the Indians the same political ideals he desired for his countrymen, and implicitly needed to transcend a simplistic classification of peoples based on traditional religious definitions. The fact that a single narrative combined informative and apologetic aims explains the emphasis with which the kingdom of Vijayanagara was decoded, rather than just invented, as a system of justice and power.

Perhaps the most significant result of this analysis is that, here as with many European sources, the emphatic selection of information and its literary elaboration was perfectly compatible with a fundamental reliance on the language of a common-sense description of natural and social realities. In effect 'Abd al-Razzāq's description is also a significant example of the fact that within Islam no less than within Christianity the dismissal of foreign societies on the grounds of incompatible religious ideologies was not a serious impediment to the elaboration of a descriptive discourse on human laws and customs, whenever such a need was felt – for example, as a foundation for historical writing. Indeed the Arabic ethnological tradition was not only very rich, but also prior to, and the source for, many European texts.[43] It was the product of a 'cultivated urbanity' associated with courtly high culture and basically independent of religious concerns.[44] The idea of civilization in tenth- and eleventh-century Arab ethnology involved a conventional hierarchy from the admirable Chinese to the barbarism of cannibals which was almost identical to the one used by European writers of the fifteenth century (like the traveller Nicolò Conti, a contemporary of 'Abd-al Razzāq). This does not mean, on the other hand, that some important differences

[43] A. Miquel, *La géographie humaine du monde musulman*, 4 vols. (Paris and The Hague, 1967–8); Aziz Al-Azmeh, 'Barbarians in Arab eyes', *Past and Present*, 134 (1992): 3–18.
[44] Al-Azmeh, 'Barbarians', 4 and 17.

from the European ethnological tradition cannot be detected. From an intellectual perspective, for example, within Islam there was no real language of mediation between the concepts of civility and religion, nothing like the European idea of natural law – religious themes were in this sense unassailable ('Abd al-Razzāq's implicitly idealized treatment of Vijayanagara kingship thus stood in a peculiar tension with his open condemnation of Hindu idolatry). Happy non-Muslim civilizations like China or, in a different more aberrant way, India, could not in the end be more than accidental.[45] Perhaps more significantly, the very dependence of Arab geographical writing on court culture made this kind of literature particularly vulnerable to the vicissitudes of fragile political structures. In this sense, one can reflect on the fact that the genres of travel and cosmography subsisted in late medieval Europe on a dynamic and diversified audience. This explains why Marco Polo (himself a transmitter of Arab lore) did not remain an isolated figure, as Ibn Battūta was ultimately to become.[46]

A variety of genres

European accounts of South India can be used to evaluate the development of two major analytical forms found in travel literature: the sort of itinerary with lengthy descriptions devoted to geographic, economic, ethnological and political information, on the one hand, and the historical narrative, on the other. Spatial categories organize the first, temporal ones the second. We have excellent examples of each in the accounts of Vijayanagara by Paes and Nunes, respectively. Strictly speaking, however, neither text represents a 'pure type', and the fact is that this distinction admits important degrees of variation.

The 'itinerary-type' description could closely follow a personal journey (such as in the cases of Conti, Varthema, Federici and 'Abd al-Razzāq) or rather a more systematic geographical distribution (and this was the case for Tomé Pires and Duarte Barbosa). When the personal biography is the main structuring element, as in the cases of Varthema and Coutre, a chronological sequence effectively determines the order of the narrative; the same applies to accounts of maritime expeditions, such as the journal of Vasco da Gama's first voyage. There was in fact a great degree of freedom within the narrative model of a journey to introduce systematic descriptions and reflections, particularly when the authors

---

[45] A. Miquel, 'L'Inde chez les géographes Arabes avant l'an mil', in C. Weinberger-Thomas (ed.) *L'inde et l'imaginaire* (Paris, 1988), p. 55. Climatic explanations of civilization existed which, however, did not engage with the religious sources of morality.

[46] Despite the 'vigour of Arab traders and scholars' noted by Aziz al-Azmeh, 'Barbarians', 4.

had specific interests (such as economic and political aims) or a sophisti-cated education (like Pietro della Valle in his letters). The spatial–temporal duality can thus be seen as not just a technical issue, but also a source of cultural creativity and reflection within the context of an expanding literature.

Historical narratives whose scope went beyond a direct personal experience offer a different kind of problem. The Portuguese chroniclers, despite the fact that they had sometimes been to India, usually used second-hand information in the form of archival documents, letters, indigenous chronicles and oral or written reports. Moreover, they were often more interested in portraying the deeds of the European con-querors than in the internal developments of the indigenous country. The weight of the conventions about what was to be considered a noteworthy event, together with the system of patronage that turned historians into semi-professionals of political propaganda, tended to constrain dramati-cally the pursuit of the often declared aim of truthfulness – a problem of which a number of writers were remarkably conscious.[47]

More often than not historians tended to combine chronological narratives with geographical analysis. This is clearly the case with Fernão Nunes, whose historical account of the dynasties of Vijayanagara, based on native sources, is followed by a personal description of the kingdom in his time. The humanist historian João de Barros, who never visited India, also liked to include chapters with background information as a context for his narrative of Portuguese exploits.[48] But despite these inevitable overlaps, the authors were distinctly aware that there were two main types of narrative: the historical chronicle and the description of peoples, lands and their products. They made this distinction in the knowledge of the different traditions and conventions attached to each of them. The Portuguese chronicler of India Gaspar Correa, for instance, who for many years lived in India and engaged in a wide range of activities, explained why he did not dwell on geographical matters:

> I shall write nothing about these lands, peoples and trade, because there have been others who have already done this, of which I have seen some volumes, and especially a book about all this which was written by Duarte Barbosa, *escrivão da feitoria* in Cananor. Therefore, if it pleases God, I shall only attempt to write very fully about the noble deeds of our Portuguese fighting in these parts of India.[49]

[47] See Rodrigues Lapa, *Historiadores quinhenistas* (Lisbon, 1942), pp. v–xv.
[48] For instance, Barros on Vijayanagara in his *Ásia*, vol. III, ff. 97–104. More generally, see Boxer, *João de Barros*, pp. 105–9. For all this see chapter 8 below.
[49] Correa in the preface to his *Lendas da Índia*, ed. Rodrigo José de Lima Felner, 5 vols. (Lisbon, 1858–66), vol. I, p. 3.

Barbosa, who – from his preface – also had a very clear idea of what his book was about, had previously made use of the same distinction to the opposite effect:

In this attack [on Goa being taken by Albuquerque] many noteworthy events took place which I do not relate here, in order to cut my story short, for it is not my intention to write a chronicle, but only a short summary of that which I could find out most truthfully regarding the chief places in India.[50]

Similarly, some of the more educated writers on the East, such as João de Barros and the Jesuit Monserrate, elaborated comprehensive plans in which they contemplated separate works for historical and geographical matters.[51]

It is possible to relate these two spatial and temporal emphases to the distinction between antiquarianism and history within classical and Renaissance historiography.[52] Travel would naturally suggest a picture of a society as observed at a given time, which also characterizes antiquarianism. However, in writers like the fifteenth-century humanist Flavio Biondo (who reconstructed the Roman past as distinct from his fifteenth-century Rome) this could be said to have deeper implications, because he created the picture of a distant world no longer accessible to direct observation and retrieved through physical remains, texts and inscriptions. The erudite antiquarianism of the humanists was in effect more about the pastness of the past than about the otherness of the exotic. What is, however, interesting is that the techniques of geographical and ethnographic descriptions could be shared by antiquarians and cosmographers. One could even say that it was precisely within accounts of human diversity that the Renaissance antiquarian and the Renaissance historian more fully met. Renaissance cosmography was in fact a very flexible genre with a mixed genealogy, combining ancient geography (dwelling on the diversity of places, climates and peoples), medieval

---

[50] Duarte Barbosa, *Livro em que dá relação do que viu e ouviu no Oriente*, ed. by A. Reis Machado (Lisbon 1946), p. 91.

[51] On Barros's 'universal geography' see Boxer, *João de Barros*, p. 130. On Monserrate's lost 'geography and natural history of India', see Hosten's discussion in Monserrate, 'Mongolicae legationis', 520–3. It is obvious from the few extant references to these works that, for instance, Barros's lost *Geographia universalis* was perceived to belong to the same cosmographical genre that stretched from Strabo to Botero. Similarly ambitious projects were accomplished concerning Spanish American lands, remarkably so by Gonzalo Fernández de Oviedo in his *Historia general y natural de las Indias* (1535, full edition completed in 1851–5), and Pedro Cieza de León in his *Crónica del Perú* (1553, full edition completed in 1979–86). In both these cases, the events of the conquest were set in a general geographical background which included all kinds of information, and ethnographic material here had a very prominent role.

[52] As defined by Arnaldo Momigliano, *The classical foundations of modern historiography* (Berkeley, 1990) chap. 3, especially pp. 71–3.

mirabilia (organizing strange natural phenomena in a theological world-view), and the trader's manual (with economic and navigational information). All these could be combined with personal observations within the structure of a story about travels and adventures, or even offered as illustration and test for the maxims of a political treatise.

It may be concluded that in the European Renaissance history and cosmography, equally influenced by the humanist reappropriation of classical models, were complementary genres, and together provided a wealth of empirical material which was used to illustrate and eventually change the theoretical framework for political and moral thought (as the cases of Machiavelli's *Discourses* and Botero's *Relationi universali*, at the two extremes of the sixteenth century, clearly show). The result was not only a comparative approach to human diversity, but also one which relied on the critical test of personal observations in order to establish claims to truthfulness, and which was, at the same time, able to acquire chronological depth and address fundamental problems of historical interpretation through the addition of both classical European and non-European sources.

FOREIGN DESCRIPTIONS AND NATIVE REALITIES

The role of oriental realities and even literary traditions in the creation of a European-centred world history is worth emphasizing because it runs counter to much of what the orientalist paradigm in historiography has proposed. The European interpretation of India as formulated by writers like Valignano was obviously biased against brahminic culture in accordance with specifically European values. However, this does not mean that it was a purely imaginary construction. On the contrary, any remarks about the value of the foreign descriptions of Vijayanagara depend ultimately on the existence of an 'object of description' that created the conditions for the development of this sort of literature. It was, for example, the centrality of the capital city as a recognizable physical, economic and political unity that drew all these observers in parallel directions. But here we encounter a serious problem. Because the Indian, Persian and European cultural discourses shared similar values about the importance of kingship as a central focus for political authority, or about trade as a source of wealth, it is often difficult to disentangle the subjective, culturally specific elements involved in recognizing the city of Vijayanagara as important from the possibility of appealing to a universal rational awareness of 'what there is out there to be seen'. Significant differences between cultural traditions do certainly exist, but on close analysis they often prove to be very subtle, because one needs to weigh a number of

possible analogies against the diversity of concepts and regulated practices. Thus, for instance, in order to make sense of the appreciation by
foreigners of the highly symbolic and ritual values of the annual Mahanavami festival of Vijayanagara it will not do to simply assume that the
observers understood fully what was going on just because they saw it,
nor will it suffice to do the opposite and simply state that Europeans
misrepresented everything because they lacked any understanding of the
dharmic conception of kingship: one needs to postulate instead the
existence of intersubjective elements – that is to say, a dialogue based on
contrasting and negotiating the value of different traditions.

Another difficult problem is created by the fact that current historical
interpretations of the empire of Vijayanagara rely heavily on the very
same sources we need to read critically in order to distinguish a historical
reality from a western view of it. That is to say, we can only say that a
direct observer like Domingos Paes 'shapes' what he sees according to
what he wants to see, or what his cultural background allows him to see,
because we have a different idea of what there was there to be seen. The
problem is that this latter interpretation of the modern historian – this
'what was there' – has often been constructed on the acceptance of what
a traveller like Paes wrote! We must obviously look at alternative sources
other than foreign descriptions of Vijayanagara, with the hope that they
are substantial enough to provide us with the distance we require from
the European, Arabic and Persian accounts. Therefore, an intricate
dialogue between what we can reconstruct as our interpretation of
Vijayanagara and what we think our travellers would tend to imply,
forget or exaggerate is necessary here.

The use of archaeological evidence can enormously facilitate this task.
It is remarkable that modern archaeological and art historical research
on the ruins of the city (a research largely conducted with independence
from foreign narrative sources) has produced a hypothesis which interprets the distribution of the city buildings and their religious and social
functions as having a symbolic significance according to Hindu prescrip-
tions. In the words of Fritz and Michell:

> Vijayanagara was much more than a mere 'setting' for courtly life . . .
> the layout of the city, together with its monumental architecture and
> sculpture, affirm a particular 'argument' for royal power . . . The
> Vijayanagara kings appear to have been influenced by texts (shastras)
> that provided clearly articulated models for royal behaviour that
> would result in the maintenance of moral values (dharma), and the
> increase of power and influence (artha).[53]

---

[53] Fritz, Michell and Nagaraja Rao, *Where kings and gods meet*, pp. 146–7.

And later:

> Not only is the attention of the city and empire directed towards the ruler, but the power of the king – with that of [the god–hero] Rama at its core – diffuses outward creating form and ensuring order. Vijayanagara is a cosmic city where king and god meet, not only for the affirmation of royal power, but also for the protection and welfare of the Empire.[54]

What is significant is that the results are strikingly compatible with the interpretation of a number of travellers, European or Muslim. It seems, therefore, that a system devised to impress a message of sacredness and power could be read and indeed was read as such by contemporary foreign observers. They did not need to know the Sanskrit shastras in order to appreciate the city's 'argument' somehow. We could of course wonder, in a further exercise in scepticism, whether modern archaeologists Fritz and Michell have themselves been inspired by their own knowledge of these foreign descriptions (as well as of traditional Hindu texts) when 'reading' a system of symbolic political geography into the scattered ruins of modern Hampi. However, on the whole it seems far more sensible to imagine that there indeed existed in fifteenth-century Vijayanagara a complex set of language-games, operating in the form of art, ritual, mythology and political life, which informed the life of the city and even its very layout, and that this system can be, at least in part, retrieved today by modern scholars.

In order to develop the dialogue between modern scholarly reconstruction and the critical analysis of early modern sources, the recurrence of a number of themes in different descriptions will help focus on a number of key topics. The first one is the perception of a political and economic system, that is the construction of an image of the civilization of Vijayanagara defined by its kingship, its trade, its religious organization and its social elites. A fundamental question that can help us here is whether the Portuguese interpreted the political order of Vijayanagara too much like their own Iberian 'feudal' society.

Whilst I shall argue that symbolic representations of power could be 'translated' on the basis of cross-cultural analogies, we must first recognize that we may be talking about very different kinds of state to begin with. In particular, the nature of the Vijayanagara state, and whether it can be defined as some kind of 'feudalism', is a subject of vivid debate, one which this book cannot entirely ignore. Whilst some scholars have sought parallels with European feudal monarchies, others have proposed the idea of a 'segmentary state' – one distinct from the

---

[54] Ibid. p. 151.

European medieval model. According to these writers, the main issue is precisely that Hindu kingship was ritual rather than administrative, and therefore the symbolic representation of power had a very unique role in Vijayanagara – one which (they suggest) is not comparable to European examples.[55] The emergence in the fifteenth and sixteenth centuries of a system of overlordship centred around local military chiefdoms under the authority of largely independent captains (nayakas) would, in this view, limit the development of royal administrative policies outside a core area near the capital. This position is summarized in the recent work of Burton Stein: 'The Vijayanagara era was one in which I see a new form of polity, but one with important links to earlier polities in being segmentary in character and one in which kings continued to be essentially ritual figures rather than, like contemporaries in western Europe, autocrats ruling bureaucratised, absolutist regimes'.[56]

It is not possible to do full justice here to this complex debate, which to a large extent can be seen as a slightly contrived attempt to avoid a eurocentric analysis, but two points need to be made for the sake of this book's argument: the first obvious one is that the characterization of European monarchies as either 'feudal' or 'administrative' is problematic because of the very fluidity of these concepts as applied to the European context. On the whole, over the centuries there was a tendency towards greater administrative control within a continuous tradition of state-building which might be seen to extend from the ninth to the fifteenth centuries (and even beyond). It is therefore impossible to define a

---

[55] See ibid., p. 146. While the direct anthropological model for the concept of the segmentary state is the work of A. Southall for East Africa, the current stress on the ritual and symbolic roles of the king seems to have been inspired by A. M. Hocart's interpretation of kingship in his *Kings and councillors* (Cairo, 1936; repr. Chicago, 1970). Thus Stein, in *Peasant state and society*, pp. 389–91, sees in the Mahanavami festival of Vijayanagara a confirmation of Hocart's model of ritual kingship. There are, however, reasons to suspect that Hocart has been misunderstood. His thesis can be summarized by the idea that kingship evolved from a ritual towards a political role: that ritual organization is older than government and provides the basis on which government is eventually organized. Hocart's idea is not meant to differentiate 'oriental kingship' from 'western orientalism' because, if anything, Hocart stressed the universal validity of his thesis. In that sense, his implicit message was that 'more ritual' and 'less centralized and politically organized' equals 'more primitive'.

[56] Stein, *Vijayanagara*, p. xii. See also Stein, *Peasant state and society*, pp. 8, 23–4, 265, 274, with a more detailed discussion of the idea of a segmentary state. The concept has been taken up by N. B. Dirks in his *The hollow crown. Ethnohistory of an Indian kingdom* (Cambridge, 1988), as its very title suggests – see especially pp. 28–36. This sophisticated ethnohistory is devoted to a later period of nayaka rule, after the disintegration of the Vijayanagara overlordship. The current tendency to distance South Indian kingship from 'western orientalist' models is also documented in D. Shulman, *The king and the clown in South Indian myth and poetry* (Princeton, 1985), who vaguely endorses Stein's idea of a segmentary state by tracing ambiguity in literary representations of early medieval kingship in South India.

European political system which was either purely feudal or (even less convincing) purely autocratic.[57] When it comes to establishing comparisons with an oriental state like Vijayanagara, the specific terms of an institutional comparison would require taking account of very concrete contexts, so that in effect the comparability of degrees of political centralization depends less on general categories such as 'feudal' or 'segmentary' states (which suggest too schematic an opposition between East and West) than on a specific moment in the history of each state.

The issue therefore is not the validity of the concept of feudalism as a general category, but rather finding terms that can be properly compared. It remains of crucial importance that all our travellers to southern India, Muslim and Christian, moved between worlds in which royal authority depended on a degree of aristocratic consensus and religious legitimization.[58] Certainly, in the Vijayanagara system the degree of centralization through royal state administration and prebendal distribution of lands or revenues was, for example, weaker than in Europe at the same period (but closer perhaps to Europe in the twelfth century). The strength of both the authority of local chiefs and communal rights was more prominent where the king, despite his command of huge armies and symbolic ritual, had a more limited set of legal and fiscal functions and resources. In that sense the Hindu institutional world was essentially more fragmented than the European. On the other hand, a proper understanding of the power of the nobility, the cities with their extensive privileges, and the medieval Church, invalidates the idea that in western Europe, any more than in Vijayanagara, there were (in Burton Stein's expression) 'autocrats ruling bureaucratised, absolutist regimes'. If we were to look for a fundamental difference we would need to look elsewhere. We could argue that the existence of Roman law as an independent juridical language was crucial in giving Europe political stability, not only because the idea of general public law could be opposed to feudal particularism, but more importantly because the very structure of feudal custom was transformed into a juridical system dependent on courts and parliaments. Thus from a broad comparative

---

[57] Even within the restricted period of the high Middle Ages, from the eleventh to the thirteenth centuries, the concept of a feudal state must be used flexibly and abandon the pretension of a mechanistic logic of transformation.

[58] On these grounds, some historians have insisted on the concept of 'South Indian feudalism'. See in particular K. Veluthat, *The political structure of early medieval South India* (London, 1993), who provides a critique of the traditional formulations of Indian historiography (with its emphasis on an idealized strong bureaucracy) but also of Stein's segmentary state (with its emphasis on a ritual overlordship separate from the political structure, which is seen as mainly local). See, in particular, pp. 246–67. Veluthat only discusses the centuries previous to Vijayanagara, but his assumption is that after the thirteenth century one finds variations from a defined pattern.

perspective one remarkable novelty of European feudalism (probably more significant than any particular form of fidelity and vassalage) was in fact its ability to generate a constitutional language to regulate the relationship between the king and the elites of the political community.[59] This alone, however, does not amount to a political system which we might define as 'western' in opposition to an 'oriental' model, precisely because so many other variables are important, and each political system was neither stable nor homogeneous.

Following from this, a second point that needs to be stressed is that the very idea of a ritual or ceremonial state, as opposed to an administrative one, is misleading, simply because ritual and ceremony were important in all cases and contexts. Neither was Vijayanagara kingship purely ritual (it was also held together by diplomacy, armies and treasuries), nor could European rulers from Charlemagne to Louis XIV do without their own systems of symbol and ceremony, in which ritual and propaganda assisted the use of concepts like justice and honour, fidelity and vassalage, sovereignty and tyranny, or virtue and the common good.[60] My argument will be that the existence of this symbolic dimension facilitated the efforts of foreign travellers to interpret by analogy. In some cases, the cultural distances between the mythological and conceptual traditions were vast – this would certainly be the case of European travellers in India. In other cases, as with 'Abd al-Razzāq in Vijayanagara, the increasing familiarity of the Hindu elites with a cosmopolitan Islamicite court culture, and the presence of a Khorasani community in the city, obviously facilitated the creation of common language-games. In all cases, however, what is remarkable is the way in which the essentials of a symbolic system of power, one through which a variety of political struggles for the control of resources and authority were negotiated, often seem to have been apprehended by analogy rather than through the previous knowledge of each separate literary tradition.[61]

[59] A brilliant summary of European feudalism as a dynamic force which gave flexibility to Europe is J. Strayer, 'Feudalism in Western Europe', in the comparative work by R. Coulbourn (ed.) *Feudalism in history* (Hamden, Conn., 1965), pp. 15–32. Having finally overcome static definitions of feudalism, the more recent debate amongst historians has focused on the existence, or not, of a 'feudal revolution' after the eleventh century.

[60] If one were to compare rituals of royalty across cultures – as in D. Cannadine and S. Price (eds.) *Rituals of royalty. Power and ceremonial in traditional societies* (Cambridge, 1987) – it would not be possible to isolate western monarchies as non-ritual, as opposed to Indian and African cases. There would of course be differences, and it might be said that in general the distinction between the sacred and secular dimensions of royalty is more distinct in the European tradition.

[61] The same holds true for visual representations of India: it is the homology of language-games about kingship which made it possible for an anonymous late sixteenth-century painter to make use of a tradition springing from an early woodcut of the king of

If the interpretation of the 'ritual' kingship of Vijayanagara provides an obvious thematic thread across a variety of narratives, the description of 'gentile customs' offers another. In this book, therefore, I shall repeatedly discuss those categories used by observers to identify and evaluate different customs and beliefs, especially with reference to topics of recurrent interest in ethnological literature (from peculiar religious practices to the social standing of women, to mention but two).

Thus, to conclude, although each narrative will contribute to emphasize different aspects of the process of formation of images of an Indian 'other', the analysis of the politics, customs and religion of Hindu India provides a common thread which makes it possible to explore the continuities and change from the medieval to the modern traveller.

Cochin, printed in 1508, to portray Queen Elizabeth of England ceremonially carried in a litter, as argued by D. Armitage, 'The "procession portrait" of Queen Elizabeth I. A note on a tradition', *Journal of the Warburg and Courtauld Institutes* 53 (1990): 301–7.

2. Marco Polo's India and the Latin Christian tradition

MONSTERS AND MENTALITIES

Even though ancient and medieval travel accounts are clearly less abundant than those composed and circulated after the sixteenth century, the perspective of later developments can be misleading regarding both their quantity and their significance. In particular, medieval descriptions of oriental lands and peoples form an important body of literature, which must be interpreted in terms of the basic identities valid at the time. In the West, these identities were articulated at a general level by the Church and the Carolingian idea of empire, but in practice were fragmented and conditioned by feudal structures of power which weakened public authority and only slowly gave form to states able to appeal to national feelings. This explains the importance of pilgrimage, crusade and mission as collective ideologies.[1]

---

[1] On medieval travel literature, with particular reference to images of the East, see A. P. Newton (ed.) *Travel and travellers of the Middle Ages* (London, 1926), although now rather outdated; D. F. Lach, *Asia in the making of Europe*, 3 vols. (Chicago, 1965–93), vol. I, pp. 20–48, is clear and concise, albeit dominated by empiricism as the sole analytical criterion. J. R. S. Phillips, *The medieval expansion of Europe* (Oxford, 1988) effectively summarizes a great deal of material with common sense, in particular pp. 3–17 on the early Middle Ages and pp. 187–211 for the central period. For geographical ideas see also C. R. Beazley, *The dawn of modern geography*, 3 vols. (London, 1897–1906) and G. H. T. Kimble, *Geography in the Middle Ages* (London, 1938). On medieval Christian pilgrimage the essays collected in B. N. Sargent-Baur (ed.) *Journeys towards God. Pilgrimage and crusade* (Kalamazoo, 1992) address interesting problems of interpretation. For the relationship between the first crusade and lay piety see M. Bull, *Knightly piety and the lay response to the first crusade. The Limousin and Gascony, c. 970–c. 1130* (Oxford, 1993). On ideologies of crusade and mission in general, B. Kedar, *Crusade and mission* (Princeton, 1984) provides a penetrating analysis. Western views of Islam are discussed in R. W. Southern, *Western views of Islam in the Middle Ages* (Cambridge, Mass., 1961). In the context of the crusades see also the valuable articles collected in J. Richard, *Croisés, missionaires et voyageurs: les perspectives orientales du monde latin médiéval* (London, 1983) and those in C. F. Beckingham, *Between Islam and Christendom: travellers, facts, legends in the late Middle Ages and the Renaissance* (London, 1983). With specific

Thus it was not really 'India' or 'Cathay' that constituted the societies most obviously distinct from western Europe. In fact anything outside the limits of the rather small Latin Christian world was, at the beginning of the twelfth century, a potential area for expansion – military, economic or cultural. This means that Greek Christians as well as other oriental churches, and of course Muslims and Jews, formed an initial frontier of 'otherness' no less important than those groups which could be described as gentile or barbarian. The particular ambiguities associated with the relationships with each of these groups, and which ran across a wide spectrum of possibilities concerning both religious and civil categories, indicate the complexity of the 'medieval others', to use a current expression. This complexity was indeed the basis on which a literary and pictorial tradition was formed, even though the specific products of such tradition could often be geared towards a kind of 'us–them' opposition. Therefore, rather than determining a simplistic and all-encompassing duality, crusade and mission generated novel experiences and eventually gave form to discourses which were original, in some ways even revolutionary.

It follows that we must seek to distance ourselves from the commonplace that the Orient was represented in the Middle Ages as a land of marvels populated by a collection of monstrous races, and its corollary that this 'medieval view of the other', influenced by classical authors like Pliny and Solinus and built around medieval re-workings of Greek themes such as the Alexander romance, reflects something fundamental about the medieval mentality.[2] These claims have often been supported by the analysis of the pictorial tradition that accompanied late medieval travel accounts, famously those by Marco Polo and John Mandeville.[3] And indeed this pictorial tradition, as shown by Rudolf Wittkower, emphasizes the marvellous elements in those accounts – the extremes of plenty and monstrosity linked to Edenic origins and to heathen distortions in the course of mankind's sacred history.[4] In a complementary

---

reference to the theme of India in the West, see T. Hahn, 'The Indian tradition in western medieval intellectual history', *Viator*, 9 (1978): 213–34, and for medieval ethnology in general see F. Fernández-Armesto, 'Medieval ethnography', *Journal of the Anthropological Society of London*, 13 (1982): 272–86.

[2] This view is famously expressed by Jacques Le Goff in a classic (and, in any case, evocative) essay, 'L'occident médiéval et l'océan indien: un horizon onirique', in Le Goff, *Pour un autre Moyen Age* (Paris, 1977), pp. 280–98. See also C. Weinberger-Thomas, 'Les yeux fertiles de la mémoire', in *L'Inde et l'imaginaire*, pp. 11–16.

[3] Famously the *Livre des merveilles*, codex 2810 of the Bibliothèque Nationale (Paris), and the *Livres du graunt Caam*, Ms. Bodl. 264 of the Bodleian Library (Oxford).

[4] R. Wittkower, 'Marvels of the East: a study in the history of monsters', *Journal of the Warburg and Courtauld Institutes*, 5 (1942): 159–97, and 'Marco Polo and the pictorial tradition of the marvels of the East', in *Oriente Poliano* (Rome, 1957), pp. 155–72.

way Michael Camille has given attention to the ideological aspects of the depiction of idolatry and the support this provided for the intolerant and indeed destructive activities of the crusaders,[5] while Partha Mitter has shown that travellers like Ludovico de Varthema (*c.* 1500) created an unambiguous stimulus for the bias of the illustrators when they described the gods in Indian temples as traditional European devils.[6]

Such analysis needs to be placed in context. Although several passages of the travel accounts corroborate an interest in idolatry and in the unnatural, it is in the illustrations produced in Europe that the bias becomes more obvious. In fact, as Wittkower himself concluded, these illustrations are specific products in which the artist gives coherence to a heterogeneous textual tradition. Many of the illuminated manuscripts analysed by him were destined for a late feudal aristocratic audience, while the authors of the narratives were primarily merchants and missionaries. In fact, both the Parisian *Livre des merveilles* by the 'Boucicaut master' and *Livres du graunt Caam* in Oxford by the artist Johannes belong to a rather specific period of northern French and Anglo-Norman culture which, at the turn of the fourteenth century, was dominated by a mixture of chivalric ideals, curiosity in magic and a search for the historical legitimacy of power. It would of course be a mistake to assume a homogeneous view of the other in the Middle Ages predicated on a peculiar use of sources in a specific social milieu. The problem is not merely that the relationship between texts and images has been simplified, but perhaps more seriously that the texts themselves have been simplistically read. Marco Polo does indeed describe strange animals and customs, and Mandeville certainly places some of his most significant passages in the eastward path towards earthly paradise, but these authors do many other things as well, and of greater significance. It is seriously misleading simply to assume, as both Wittkower and Camille do, that Marco Polo went to the East in search of marvels with a mind shaped by the schemes of the medieval tradition.[7] Partha Mitter, albeit carefully, also relies on this idea of schemata (inspired by the theoretical propositions of Aby Warburg and Ernst Gombrich) in order to explain why travellers would first describe their own preconceptions rather than actual observations.[8] Of course Marco Polo was influenced by an education in Venice before his departure at the age of seventeen, but that

---

[5] M. Camille, *The gothic idol. Ideology and image-making in medieval art* (Cambridge, 1989), pp. 151–64.

[6] P. Mitter, *Much maligned monsters. History of European reactions to Indian art* (Oxford, 1977), pp. 1–72.

[7] Wittkower, 'Marco Polo', p. 155, largely following Leonardo Olschki, *L'Asia di Marco Polo* (Florence, 1957); Camille, *The gothic idol*, p. 151.

[8] Mitter, *Much maligned monsters*, pp. 3–6.

cannot mean that he shared the same concerns as the Boucicaut master who illuminated his narrative for the Duke of Burgundy more than a century later. In fact, it does not even mean that he had in mind the same texts compiled at the time of his youth by encyclopaedists and educators like Vincent of Beauvais or Brunetto Latini.[9] An argument on these lines might be constructed, but it should not be taken for granted. Indeed, the actual narrative of the *Divisament dou monde* suggests an original use of specific traditions even when traditional marvels with obvious literary models are reported.[10]

For instance, the image of dog-headed men could have been borrowed from Brunetto Latini or from a popular collection of moralizing stories like the *Gesta Romanarum*, and it could also be inspired by the many thirteenth-century examples of religious iconography in which the cyno-cephali had a well-established role. In this sense the influence of early Latin encyclopaedists like Pliny, Solinus and Isidore was pervasive. But in fact the dog-headed men whom Marco Polo located in the 'island of Angaman' (Andaman) in the Bay of Bengal were more likely to be based on local hearsay.[11] These monsters had been transmitted from ancient Greek accounts to Arabic authors like the thirteenth-century cosmogra-pher Kazwini, and in fact formed part of local mythology in many parts of Asia.[12] Ibn Battūta, on his way from Bengal to 'Java' (in fact Sumatra) *c.* 1345, clearly explained that there was a Muslim community living separately in the country of the 'Barahnakar' (possibly Arakan on

---

[9] The Florentine's *Livre dou trésor* (*c.* 1265), although written in French, was of course influential in Italy as well as other parts of Europe. For its geographical ideas see book I, chaps. 115–16. Information on India derives from Solinus.

[10] Luigi Benedetto's critical edition is crucial for its thorough reconstruction of the textual tradition: Marco Polo, *Il milione*, ed. by L. F. Benedetto (Florence, 1928). A. Moule and P. Pelliot provide an English version which distinguishes and combines the evidence of the more important manuscripts: Marco Polo, *The description of the world*, ed. by A. C. Moule and P. Pelliot, 2 vols. (London, 1938). Schematically, the history of the text is as follows: we do not have the original version, which seems to have been delivered orally by Marco Polo to Rustichello, in some sections using his own notes, and written up in a medieval French with Italianisms. A good summary of this 1298–9 text is the early fourteenth-century 'F' text edited by Benedetto. This text was re-worked, with a number of cuts, in court French, possibly with Marco Polo's intervention *c.* 1307. But the original was also translated into Latin, and possibly expanded, again with Marco Polo's intervention. This 'long' Latin text is the basis for Ramusio's sixteenth-century Italian version ('R') and has been preserved in one good Latin copy ('Z'), but is entirely different from the more influential, summary translation by Friar Pipino of Bologna completed *c.* 1320. In fact the majority of the surviving manuscripts derive from the French versions (like those in Tuscan and Venetian dialects, following F), or from Pipino's Latin (who wrongly took the Venetian text as Marco Polo's original). I have used Moule's English version for references or, when making my own direct translations, from Benedetto's and Ramusio's texts.

[11] Polo, *Milione*, p. 176.

[12] On the cynocephali see Wittkower, 'Marvels of the East'.

the mainland), and that they told him stories concerning the dog-faced natives and their beautiful women, with an attitude of cultural distancing similar to that expressed by the Venetian.[13] The Dominican missionary Jordanus Catalani heard the same story, although he vaguely located it in one of the many marvellous islands between Africa and India, certain proof that the story circulated among Arab sailors.[14] It is also significant that Marco Polo seems to have heard of these people of Andaman from the neighbouring island of 'Negueram' (Nicobar), but does not say that he saw them.[15] In any case it makes sense that he also described these dog-faced people as cruel and ugly cannibals, who lived like wild beasts without any king, and who 'ate all kinds of flesh' as well as rice and milk. It is thus quite clear that an unsympathetic portrayal of the natives, possibly encouraged by the circumstances of the relationship between them and the local Muslim community who traded with them for spices, lies behind the appearance of the marvellous monster.

But Marco Polo's attitude did not simply consist of systematically interpreting strange phenomena in the light of such traditions of oriental monstrosity. In 'Basman', for instance, which was one of the eight kingdoms of 'Lesser Java' (modern Sumatra), he had discovered that the famous 'pigmies' did not exist; instead he saw stuffed monkeys.[16] He also found unicorns there which, from his detailed description, we can easily identify as rhinoceros, and he stressed that 'they are not at all like those which we say let themselves be captured by virgins'. Forest men with tails in the next kingdom, Lamori, may not be as easy to rationalize as a garbled image of orang-utans, since Marco Polo emphasizes that they have no hair. The context for all these observations is nevertheless clear and goes a long way to explain their character. By his own reckoning, the traveller spent five months in Sumatra as a member of a large expedition

---

[13] Ibn Battūta, *A través del Islam*, trans. and ed. by S. Fanjul and F. Arbós (Madrid, 1987), pp. 708–9. I have used the valuable Spanish translation by Fanjul and Arbós of the authoritative Arabic text established by C. Defrémery and B. R. Sanguinetti. The publication of the English edition by H. A. R. Gibb and C. F. Beckingham (for the Hakluyt Society), with an excellent critical apparatus, is in progress.

[14] 'There are many other diverse islands in which there are men who have the heads of dogs [*hominis caput canis habentes*], although they say that their women are beautiful': Jordanus Catalani de Sévérac, *Mirabilia descripta. Les merveilles de l'Asie*, ed. by H. Cordier (Paris, 1925), p. 120. Although Catalani's *Mirabilia descripta* was also translated into English by Henry Yule for the Hakluyt Society in 1863, the French critical edition by Henri Cordier (including a facsimile of the Latin manuscript) is better.

[15] In Nicobar, Marco Polo observed an ornamental use of fine clothes identical to the one reported by Ibn Battūta in the country of the Barahnakar. This strengthens the case for the hypothesis that the two travellers reported an almost identical story, which they both heard from the local Muslims (who probably engaged in trade between Bengal, Burma and Sumatra) despite the distance of fifty years.

[16] Polo, *Milione*, pp. 171–2.

from the Chinese Khan which took a Tartar bride to Arghun Khan in Persia. There they waited for the right weather to sail, protected from possible attacks from suspected cannibals by wooden fortifications which they had built, and trading with other natives with whom they had made a pact – probably under the fiction that they had recognized the sovereignty of the Great Khan.[17] Talking about 'Ferlec' in the same island, Marco Polo made a clear distinction between the peoples of the mountains, who 'live like beasts' and 'worship the first thing they see after getting up in the morning', and those on coastal ports who have adopted Islam through their contact with Saracen merchants.[18] It would not be surprising if the expeditionaries formed their views of a wild interior from the accounts of people from the cities. In this context, some uses of narrative language have a deeper significance than the identification of traditional monsters in an unfamiliar part of the large island. For instance, in his account of people eating their sick relatives and foreigners in the kingdom of 'Dragoian' (also on the same island) it transpires that idolatrous practices, when devilish, are ultimately equivalent to unnatural practices, because cannibalism is in fact 'a very bad and detestable custom', and thus native religious beliefs are unacceptable justifications.[19] Interestingly here idolatry is devilish *because* the custom ('usance') is bad. Indeed it is far from true that Marco Polo thought that European customs were necessarily more natural or better than those of the peoples of the East: while opposing the cannibals, he shared a great deal with the Tartars from China and Persia, and in fact his report overall constitutes a serious challenge to a simplistic definition of the natural.

An unavoidable conclusion is that we need an understanding of mental attitudes and their evolution which is more sophisticated than the concept of schemata developed by art historians; moreover, to transpose this concept into a kind of *longue durée* collective mentality can be fatal. In fact, the model of a prejudiced observer seeking to perpetuate a tradition of marvels dissolves as soon as we analyse the actual conditions of production of each text and ask what kind of travellers Marco Polo or John Mandeville were.

---

[17] Ibid. p. 172. Those five months waiting for the right weather make sense if we consider that it is difficult to sail westward between April and September due to the monsoons. In fact, we can guess with confidence that the expedition spent this period in Sumatra in the year of 1292, and that it reached Ceylon and Coromandel before the end of the same year. They were possibly in Persia by May 1293. I also note that the 'eighteen months' travelling in the Indian Ocean referred to in Rustichello's prologue are to be taken to include the whole itinerary from China to Persia, from early 1292 to mid 1293 (and not only the distance between Sumatra and Persia, which creates insurmountable chronological problems).

[18] Ibid. p. 171.   [19] Ibid. p. 174.

THE LAY TRAVELLER IN THE MEDIEVAL TRADITION

The South Indian lands and peoples which were later to be described by Europeans in the wake of Portuguese expansion were already one of the better-documented regions in the geographical literature of late medieval Europe, affording a chance to investigate the literary precedents of later accounts of Vijayanagara and the Malabar coast. The aim here will not be simply to define the basic traits of the medieval view of India which, as I argued earlier, was not an instance of a single view of the oriental other, but rather to contextualize all accounts in terms of individual authorship, the historical conditions of the locality described, and also the specific circumstances of composition and circulation. To identify the elements of a tradition going back to ancient sources is of course important, but in itself also insufficient, because any such tradition did not influence individual observers in its totality. It is, I would suggest, more revealing to study the changes and interpretations brought about by agents whose access to received images and ideas was in all cases contextual. I will therefore seek to understand the most significant late medieval representations of South India as part of the history of the genre of travel literature, with reference not only to sources and influences, but also the crusading and missionary ideologies which defined Latin Christendom against alternative societies.

Descriptions of peoples with ethnographic value – that is, descriptions predicated on the idea of an empirical difference – became a distinct (if exceptional) genre which accompanied the expansion of Europe from the twelfth century, in the north and west of Europe as well as in the Mediterranean from Spain to Jerusalem. There is of course a link in writings such as those by Gerald of Wales between the intellectual renaissance prompted by interest in classical authors and the ability to respond with literary sophistication to new situations in frontier societies such as Wales or Ireland.[20] The contrast with, for example, eleventh-century Spain, in which substantial and continuous contacts with Islamic societies did not produce any significant ethnographic practice, or with the attitudes of early crusaders (in effect armed pilgrims) in foreign settings as diverse as those between Greece and Egypt, clearly confirms that a discourse on human geography was far from being an automatic

---

[20] On Gerald of Wales see R. Bartlett, *Gerald of Wales 1146–1223* (Oxford, 1982). Also the introduction by L. Thorpe to Gerald of Wales, *The journey through Wales/The description of Wales* (Harmondsworth, 1978), pp. 9–62. Concerning the 'twelfth-century Renaissance' see R. Bolgar, *The classical heritage and its beneficiaries* (Cambridge, 1954), pp. 174–201.

consequence of the experience of cultural interaction. The Latin world had found in feudalism a basis for military strength, and in the Papacy and the crusades a religious leadership and direction which helped consolidate internal peace. However, it was the possibility of expanding the cultural horizons of the elite with reference to classical literature and science that made an empirical discourse on human diversity a substantial part of the transformation of a precarious clerical culture into a complex set of Latin and vernacular discourses. The dissemination of stereotyped images of Jews and Muslims in epic narratives such as the *Chanson de Roland* and the *Poema del mio Cid*, or in apocryphal fabrications such as the influential *Letter of Prester John*, should therefore be measured with reference to the works of contemporary well-educated clerics such as Gerald, who expressed awareness of ambiguous cultural identities outside the core of feudal Latin Christendom, or Abelard, who explored the possibilities of rational dialogue with Greek philosophy and Judaism.[21]

Gerald of Wales (1145–1223) is an interesting case in the history of the genre because besides his obvious skill as an ethnographer he also developed the figure of a traveller whose identity, unlike, let us say, the Irish Saint Brendan of the tenth-century monastic *Navigatio S. Brendani*, was not entirely conditioned by the idea of a religious quest.[22] He was of course a man of his own times. Self-awareness and an interest in human experience for which earlier centuries provide few examples have been

---

[21] In his *Dialogus inter Philosophum, Iudaeum et Christianum* (c. 1141). However, the use of rational dialogue did not necessarily lead towards tolerance of non-Christians. As Anna Abulafia has argued in chapter 6 of *Christians and Jews in the twelfth-century Renaissance* (London, 1995), since Abelard's appeal to rationality assumed that reason no less than revelation would lead to the Christian God – in fact Christ himself, as *logos*, was divine reason – it followed eventually that whilst gentile philosophers became quasi-Christians, real non-Christians, such as Jews, were irrational in not accepting Christianity. Thus attempts to rationalize Christianity easily implied a Christianization of reason which, in the existing historical conditions (and despite the open-mindedness of individuals like Abelard), would not easily tolerate the anti-Christian arguments which it provoked.

[22] The earliest surviving manuscript of the *Navigatio* is a tenth-century Carolingian copy of a text possibly dating from the late ninth century. Although it purports to describe the voyage of a sixth-century monk, it clearly belongs to a later cult. It must be noted here that, while there was an early medieval theme of travel in the literature of pre-feudal peoples – we may think here of the Anglo-Saxon poems 'The Wanderer' and 'The Seafarer' – the theme was in fact thoroughly Christianized and did not yield any kind of ethnological concern. Early medieval ethnology was entirely in the hands of encyclopaedists like Isidor, working from late antique sources and within the theological framework of Augustine. This does not, however, mean that the practice of ethnography was a cultural impossibility, only that in a very fragile tradition overwhelmed by its past and kept together by religion there was little room for its development. As exceptions we may mention here the narratives of Baltic voyages by Norse merchants Wulfstan and Ohthere appended by King Alfred in his ninth-century Anglo-Saxon translation of Orosius' *Historiae adversum paganos*.

traced in a variety of twelfth-century sources, theological and other-wise.[23] What is rather exceptional is the power with which Gerald of Wales expresses a feeling of self-importance through a kind of first-person identity – and it is not coincidental that he also composed a brief history of his own life.[24] His contribution to medieval ethnography has been properly defined by Robert Bartlett as an impressive achievement 'given the limitations of twelfth-century thought and knowledge'.[25] Of course he was an upper-class and well-educated cleric who wrote in Latin and could make use of classical models – not only the New Testament and the Latin Fathers, but also Caesar, Seneca, Cicero, Virgil, Ovid and Lucan. None the less there is no obvious model for his ethnographic works, the *Topographia Hiberniae*, the *Itinerarium Kambriae* and the *Descriptio Kambriae*. To be more precise, although Caesar's *Bellum Gallicum* may have provided initial inspiration, Gerald progressively evolved his own genre (his use of the first person is again a sign of this). Obviously the immediate stimulus to these works was the writer's role as part of an Anglo-Norman aristocracy intent on the domination of other societies, so that Gerald went to Ireland as a Norman conqueror and travelled his native Wales as a preacher. But, as we have seen, this by itself meant little if there had not also been a willingness to use literature creatively in order to clarify an ambiguous personal heritage.

Gerald seems to have started with the idea that the wonders of the West deserved as much attention as the traditional marvels of the East, and he constructed much of his account of Ireland by opposing one to the other: 'Just as the oriental countries are remarkable and distinguished for their own native prodigies, so the boundaries of the West are also made remarkable by natural wonders peculiar to them.'[26] This East of silk, precious metals and spices was associated with the crusading Levant, which indicates again how it was the process of military expansion which gave European feudal culture the stimulus to see itself as a balanced whole surrounded by extremes of outlandishness in which nature 'as if tired of its true and serious business, drew aside and went away, indulging in secret and remote freaks'.[27] Thus the Latin West

---

[23] See C. Morris, *The discovery of the individual 1050–1200* (repr. Toronto, 1987).

[24] Although within Latin Christianity there was an obvious model for autobiography in Augustine's *Confessions*, Gerald of Wales clearly departed from the Augustinian emphasis on self-denial by explicitly 'following his own desire' and seeking immortal fame as a writer: *Journey through Wales*, p. 67.

[25] Bartlett, *Gerald of Wales*, especially pp. 178–210.

[26] See the second preface of the *Topographia Hiberniae* in Gerald of Wales, *Giraldi Cambrensis opera*, vols. V and VI edited by J. F. Dimock (London, 1867–8), vol. V, p. 20.

[27] Ibid. p. 21.

stood between the Irish, naturally free and healthy but in all other respects isolated and uncivilized, and the orientals, clever and refined but also weak and poisonous. It was only in his later work concerning Wales, based on a certain capacity to identify with two sides, that the climatic oppositions broke down in order to accommodate a more subtle interplay of cultural alternatives: freedom and ingenuity on the one hand, unity and internal peace on the other.

Gerald expected literature to bring him the pleasure and the fame that the world of Church politics, with all its human misery, denied him. He was critical and ironic, and his ethnography appealed to a vast array of explanatory theories, social and economic as well as climatic. His was, however, an unsystematic analysis. A crucial fact is that Gerald's attitudes were not part of a secularized approach to the world – as Robert Bartlett has emphasized, he used moral polarities of vice and virtue in order to describe customs.[28] This moral dimension affects the traveller's literary role as direct observer of diversity. Thus, although in the first-person narrative of his *Journey through Wales* (1191) curiosity is motivated by an ideal of faithfulness to personal experience and respect for local historical truth, through various digressions it always leads from the natural and the political to the miraculous and the moralistic. The author's self finds expression in the telling of stories and opinions rather than as the protagonist of a historical experience, and although far from the Augustinian subservience to God, it does not seek to establish a meaning outside the sacred. In this sense Gerald does not really depart from the twelfth-century paradigm of religious travel, one in which crusade was a form of pilgrimage, and both chivalry and courtly love emerged as moral quests.

It may well be said that the individualistic aspects of the twelfth-century Renaissance were subsequently drowned out by the contemporary and antagonistic tendencies towards 'law, authority, system and logic', which clearly dominated the thirteenth-century clerical appropriation of chivalric and scientific themes.[29] For example, we can observe that while in the Mongol missions of the Franciscan friars John of Piano Carpini (1245–8) and William of Rubruck (1253–5) the literary model of a self-centred and critical observer persisted, in fact this essentially secular, mainly political ethnography (we are here talking about friars who acted as spies and ambassadors for the Latin West) still belonged to

---

[28] Bartlett, *Gerald of Wales*, p. 186.
[29] Morris, *The discovery of the individual*, p. 166. For the clerical appropriation of chivalric romances, especially in the case of the Grail legend, see R. S. Loomis (ed.) *Arthurian literature in the Middle Ages* (Oxford, 1959), and especially J. Frappier, *Chrétien de Troyes et le mythe du Graal* (Paris, 1972).

a restricted medium of Latin discourse, and was performed from an identity socially defined as religious. Rubruck, for instance, wrote for the crusader–king Louis IX of France, and where he succeeded in observing he failed in converting. However coherent these impressive examples of personal analysis were, they did not express open curiosity as much as the clerical control of international politics and specialized knowledge.[30]

Altogether the body of ethnographic writings produced by missionary friars between 1250 and 1350 was much more comprehensive and influential than any twelfth-century precedent. In the first place the remarkably coherent narratives by Carpini and Rubruck were prompted by the threat of the Mongol expansion from China to Hungary, which had also affected the balance of power in the Near East (it was the Mongols who effectively destroyed the Muslim Caliphate in Baghdad, only a few decades after the Latins had devastated Christian Constantinople). However, by the end of the thirteenth century, and in the context of a relatively safe passage overland, missionaries also gave first-hand descriptions of India and China.[31] Thus the writings by Franciscan and Dominican friars like John of Montecorvino, Jordanus Catalani, Odoric of Pordenone and John of Marignolli, all of which must be placed in the context of the missions undertaken between *c.* 1290 and *c.* 1350, followed upon the earlier practice of Carpini and Rubruck, and adopted the more obvious hagiographic tone of a well-established missionary purpose.

Descriptions of South India and other parts written by missionary friars thus follow from a renewed clerical tradition of western ethnography, distinct from the mere compilation of oriental marvels which ultimately derived from a few ancient Greek accounts. This new clerical tradition, which accompanied the feudal expansion of the twelfth and thirteenth centuries, can be usefully compared with another important model also created at the end of the thirteenth century, Marco Polo's *Divisament dou monde* (Description of the world). The *Divisament* is important not only because it tells us a great deal about the Orient as seen by a westerner but also because it gives expression to a new genre,

---

[30] Concerning the medieval Mongol missions the fundamental edition is Athanasius van den Wyngaert OFM (ed.) *Sinica Franciscana. Itinera et relationes fratrum minorum saeculi XIII et XIV*, vol. I (Karachi and Florence, 1929). Phillips, *The medieval expansion of Europe*, pp. 59–82, gives a useful summary. See also H. Yule, *Cathay and the way thither, being a collection of medieval notices of China*, revised by H. Cordier, Hakluyt Society, 2nd series, 4 vols. (London, 1913–16), and P. Jackson's introduction to William of Rubruck, *The mission of friar William of Rubruck*, trans. and ed. by P. Jackson, Hakluyt Society, 2nd series (London, 1990).

[31] The overland route from the Black Sea through Persia was an important focus of missionary activity, and there were references to those lands in various accounts, for instance in Pordenone's. They did not, however, generate the same quasi-eschatological interest as India and China.

and this calls for an explanation (especially since neither Herodotus nor Tacitus were in Marco Polo's mind). Thus, rather than a single composite image of oriental marvels based on Marco Polo and missionaries like Pordenone, we can in fact analyse, in the context of an expansive Latin feudal society which was creating new discourses, the abrupt appearance of an unprecedented type of narrative – the lay observer's personal observations – which challenged with its enormous popularity a fairly recent tradition of missionary discourse. This duality, in turn, may help explain the appearance of Mandeville's encyclopaedic synthesis in the middle of the fourteenth century, which under the guise of a fictional first-person traveller effectively summarized the writings of missionaries and pilgrims as well as some more traditional sources. This, paradoxically, was done with recourse to the figure of the lay observer, which helps explain why in the end the anonymous compilation proved even more popular than Marco Polo's truly lay account.[32]

Obviously the works of Marco Polo and John Mandeville deserve a systematic comparison based on the fact that they were not only the two most comprehensive and influential narratives that shaped European views of India prior to the Portuguese discoveries, but also that they represent two fundamental and, to a certain extent, alternative departures within the history of the genre. In this sense the difference goes much deeper than the mere opposition of an authentic Marco Polo at the end of the thirteenth century to a fictional Mandeville fifty years later.[33]

---

[32] I have offered an interpretation of Mandeville's work in the introduction to J. Elsner and J. P. Rubiés (eds.) *Voyages and visions. Towards a cultural history of travel* (London, 1999), pp. 37–9, and in greater detail in 'Travel writing as a genre: facts, fictions and the invention of a scientific discourse in early modern Europe', *Journeys*, 1 (2000): 5–33. For other readings see Mary Campbell, *The witness and the other world: exotic European travel writing 400–1600* (Ithaca and London, 1988), pp. 122–61; S. Greenblatt, *Marvellous possessions* (Oxford, 1991), pp. 26–51; more recently I. M. Higgins, *Writing East. The 'Travels' of Sir John Mandeville* (Philadelphia, 1997).

[33] Needless to say, Francis Wood's recent argument that Marco Polo probably did not travel very far into Asia, and simply reported a few stories that he had heard or even copied from oriental sources, is utterly unconvincing: see F. Wood, *Did Marco Polo go to China?* (London, 1995). There is an immense amount of material in the *Divisament dou monde* that is inexplicable unless we accept that he was travelling more or less where he says he went. What Marco Polo would have produced on the basis of written sources (oriental sources, if necessary) would have been at its most skilful something like Mandeville's book. Alas, we can trace Mandeville's sources almost word by word, while in order to produce Marco Polo's sources we would need to invent another Marco Polo. As for the argument that he does not mention obvious things like the Great Wall of China, we should observe that we do not necessarily have the whole of Marco Polo's narrative – in fact it seems that all the manuscripts are partial one way or the other. Furthermore, Marco Polo prepared the notes for important sections of his account of China for Kubilai Khan in the first place. The particulars of distant frontier areas and newly conquered areas – 'novelties and curiosities' – would have interested Kubilai Khan, but not what everybody knew about China. When Marco Polo dictated to

The two were originally composed in medieval French and soon translated into various other vernacular languages such as English, German and Italian, as well as Latin (the fact that the real Marco Polo was Venetian and the imaginary John Mandeville English is in this case secondary to the importance of medieval French as the central vehicle of romance literature). This of course made them much more influential than the Latin writings of either Gerald of Wales or of any of the early missionaries, excepting perhaps Odoric of Pordenone, whose account was often translated and became the main source for Mandeville's excursion to India and China.[34] Almost 145 Marco Polo manuscripts and nearly 250 for Mandeville have now been classified. This not only testifies to a long and complex tradition of translations and transformations, but also, and above all, to the appearance of a genre that transcended the limits of a restricted clerical culture and easily overtook any single instance of either chivalric romance or Bocaccioesque novella in its power to generate a European-wide culture through the medium of vernacular prose.[35]

This influence – still important in the printed literature of the sixteenth century long after Columbus and Vasco da Gama – was also reflected in the pictorial tradition of illuminated manuscripts, and in some maps with cosmographical implications (the most notable cases were the late fourteenth-century Catalan atlases produced by Majorcan Jewish artists under the patronage of the kings of Aragon).[36] Here again it is important to distinguish these products of specialized artists, which were destined

Rustichello he adopted a geographical order, following the steps of an imaginary merchant-traveller and in some cases using his notes. Often, when realizing that he had forgotten something, he would interrupt his narrative and add it. The unevenness of Marco Polo's treatment of different subjects suggests that his transition from one audience to another was not methodically planned.

[34] Van den Wyngaert, *Sinica Franciscana*, counted ninety-three manuscripts of Pordenone's relation, most of them (and often the best) in Latin. The work circulated in Italian, French and German, and apparently also in Catalan. For an analysis of Mandeville's dependence on this and other sources see C. Deluz, *Le livre de Jehan de Mandeville. Une 'géographie' au XIVe siècle* (Louvain-la-Neuve, 1988), pp. 428–91.

[35] Following J. K. Hyde, 'Real and imaginary journeys in the later Middle Ages', *Journal of the John Rylands Library*, 65 (1982): 130, we can guess that 'the vernacular versions of Marco's book . . . were favoured by laymen interested in the crusade and *mirabilia*; the Latin translation was directed towards the clergy, who were interested in missions and *mirabilia*'. As Hyde goes on to say, the book's contents challenged rather than fulfilled illusions about crusade and mission. It might, however, be added that they also challenged a traditional conception of *mirabilia*.

[36] The *Catalan Atlas* prepared *c.* 1375 by Cresques Abraham for Peter IV of Aragon, and then sent as a present to Charles V of France, included a great deal of ethnological information which was often taken from Marco Polo's account. Although using sailors' portulan charts to draw accurately the Mediterranean and Atlantic coastlines, it was the work of a specialized artist and destined for an elite audience with a political programme. Accordingly, the new empirical information was organized around a traditional T-O

for princes and lords, from other uses and audiences – there were, for instance, charts and maps which did not include pictures and legends, and whose purpose was much more practical than that of the famous atlases. While denying a simplified medieval view of the Orient based on the correspondence between marvellous tales and monstrous representations, we can nevertheless conclude that the books of Mandeville and Marco Polo influenced aristocratic culture as well as the culture of merchants and urban patricians, and in short represented the oriental world for the lay culture of late medieval Europe.

The important differences between these two texts can be analysed at the level of the authorial intention. Marco Polo was an exceptional figure placed by fortune in a position to report and describe the East for his contemporaries – a merchant who owed to his service to the Mongol prince Kubilai Khan the stimulus for a lay discourse on the diversity of human customs, and to Rustichello di Pisa the narrative framework to make his observations suitable for the wide public which enjoyed Arthurian romances.[37] These considerations are very important because there were many other merchants – above all Genoese and Venetians – who travelled abroad but never wrote about their experiences in the Orient, and it is only after the fifteenth century that, in a rather different context but clearly with the Polian model well established, these merchant accounts began to proliferate as an established genre.[38]

Rustichello openly presented Marco Polo's account as the exceptionally accurate and wide-ranging record of a world defined by the diversity of its lands and its peoples: it was a book for 'all people who wish to learn about the various races of men and the peculiarities of the various regions of the world'.[39] Natural phenomena, social customs and historical events were presented with little further interpretation: they were worth recording because they were marvellous, and they were marvellous because they were extraordinary. By contrast the anonymous author of

structure, with Jerusalem at the centre of the world. For a modern edition see *Atlas Català de Cresques Abraham*, ed. by J. Matas (Barcelona, 1975).

[37] The bibliography on Marco Polo is extremely vast. For the text see note 10 above. The notes compiled by P. Pelliot, *Notes on Marco Polo* (Paris, 1959) supersede any previous commentary, although he still owes a great deal to the nineteenth-century edition by Henry Yule. Among interpretative essays I have profited most from Olschki, *L'Asia di Marco Polo*. More recently, see J. Heers, *Marco Polo* (Paris, 1983) and J. Critchley, *Marco Polo's book* (London, 1993).

[38] In all cases it must be understood that medieval authors did not necessarily 'write' anything, as they often dictated their works. Similarly, until the end of the fourteenth century, Arthurian romances (as well as the book of Marco Polo) were listened to more often than read. There were of course differences according to genres, regions and social groups. The practice of reading alone seems to have started earlier in Italy, and spread among clerics before it reached merchants or aristocrats.

[39] From the prologue: Polo, *Milione*, p. 3.

the *Book of John Mandeville* was possibly a cleric – perhaps the Benedictine monk of Saint Omer Jean le Long, compiler and translator of many travel accounts *c.* 1351 – and his aim seems to have been to tie together Christian pilgrimage with a geographical encyclopaedia which included some of the latest reports.[40] By the way he blended all available sources, new and old (but not, significantly, Marco Polo's account), it is obvious that this writer was driven by the desire to create a comprehensive geographical vision, one which combined the pilgrims' Holy Land as centre of a universal sacred history with the variety of customs and beliefs of the most distant parts of the world. His re-working of his materials clearly suggests that he was inspired by a concern with religious reform. In effect, the extended pilgrimage to India, Cathay and the land of Prester John was a complex literary construction geared towards moral self-reflection: whilst distant lands were opposite mirrors to a Christian sacred geography, the diversity of customs eventually pointed towards a universal natural reason which the sinful Latin Christians often fell short of. The fact that Mandeville's travels could be used as a geographical source by lay readers in the centuries after its composition does not imply that it was written in order to express a lay view of the world, but rather that the intelligent writer who composed it was successful in his novel use of the figure of knight-errant in order make his theological reconstruction both inspiring and compelling.

While it is necessary to distinguish the books of Marco Polo and Mandeville as the two most important instances in the development of the genre of travel literature in the Latin West it is nevertheless unacceptable to compare Mandeville *as an observer* (which he never was) with the Venetian merchant. In order to understand medieval ethnographical practices we must therefore compare Marco Polo with those Franciscan and Dominican missionaries whose accounts did actually reflect an experience in South India and China. Of particular significance for their temporal proximity are the letters by the Franciscan John of Montecorvino, who described India on his way to China (where he was

---

[40] I have used the edition by Malcolm Letts of the oldest (*c.* 1370) and fullest manuscript of the French 'continental' text: John Mandeville, *Mandeville's travels: texts and translations*, ed. by M. Letts, Hakluyt Society, 2nd series, 2 vols. (London, 1953). It is important to acknowledge the variety of manuscript traditions and the historical importance of a number of variants, especially those produced in Liège and in England. The hypothesis that Jean le Long was the author is based on the fact that many of the key texts used in the writing of the Book of John Mandeville – such as those by William of Boldensele, Odoric of Pordenone and Hayton of Armenia – appear in his contemporary compilation, translated into French. Le Long's collection was copied several times and various manuscripts have survived, notably Bibliothèque Nationale, codex 1380. It also served as basis for some of the texts in the beautifully illuminated *Livre des merveilles* for Duke John of Burgundy (codex 2810, Biblothèque Nationale).

to work alone for many years and become the first Catholic bishop of Cambaluc until his death *c.* 1328).

The earliest of Montecorvino's letters is dated December 1292.[41] Marco Polo's book was probably dictated around 1298–9, but his observations in South India must have been made several years before, possibly on two different occasions between 1289 and 1293.[42] Therefore the experiences of the two Italians in Coromandel can be analysed as strictly contemporaneous.[43] Marco Polo travelled nevertheless in the opposite direction, from China to Europe following a sea route through Sumatra and Ceylon. It is in any case remarkable that the areas he described in coastal India formed part of an itinerary not very different from the one undertaken by John of Montecorvino and other missionaries in the following years. Descriptions of Ceylon, Coromandel, the Malabar coast and Gujarat corresponded quite logically to the main trading routes, which were also used by ambassadors and missionaries. These routes were to a great extent common to peoples from different origins and religions, including oriental Christians, but from the names of places shared by Marco Polo and the missionaries we can say with some confidence that it was the Arab–Persian culture which mediated

[41] Or perhaps 1293, according to Yule, who translated the manuscript. Wyngaert, whose edition I have followed (*Sinica Franciscana*, pp. 340–5) has 1210, but he notes that this date is an *error manifestus*. December 1292 makes more sense because according to another letter by Montecorvino written from Cambaluc in January 1305 it was 'twelve years' since the Franciscan had heard news from the West. It is very likely that the last occasion referred to was when he handed the first letter, possibly to an Italian merchant, in Saint Thomas of Mylapore, where his companion the Dominican Nicholas of Pistoia had just died. (Another Italian merchant named Peter of Lucalongo accompanied Montecorvino to China.) Menentillus of Spoleto, who from Italy then sent an Italian version of the letter to the Dominican writer Bartolomeo de Santo Concordio, also declares that he had spoken with 'him in whose arms Friar Nicholas died' – surely the bringer of the letter, if not Montecorvino himself. It is possible that Marco Polo also visited Saint Thomas's tomb at the end of 1292, but he might have done so on his earlier visit (he described in detail miracles that 'happened' in 1288, possibly from hearsay).

[42] In Ramusio's version of Marco Polo's travels (R in Benedetto's classification), which is currently considered to contain original material not found in the major French version (F), there is an explicit statement at the beginning of the 'book of India' regarding the fact that Marco Polo learnt about its many marvels from direct observation, from hearsay or even from sailors' charts. He was there first as an agent of Kubilai Khan, and later again on his way back home with the Tartar bride for Arghun Khan (*c.* 1292–3). It also appears from the prologue that in fact when he set out for his return voyage he followed the same sea route that he had just returned from – so that Marco Polo was in India at least twice, immediately before and after 1291, and thus only a few years before he dictated his memoires. His account of miracles at the tomb of Saint Thomas throughout 1288 could indicate that he visited that place soon after. Marco Polo was likely to have written notes, since he had to report to the Khan at least on his return from his first known journey.

[43] Marco Polo (*c.* 1254–*c.* 1324) was then about thirty-eight years old and John of Montecorvino (*c.* 1247–*c.* 1328) about forty-five.

between the local and the Latin spheres in this area.[44] This can of course be explained with reference to the integration which Islamic communities imposed on the trading routes. Thus it should not come as a surprise that Ibn Battūta in the middle of the fourteenth century followed similar routes and described similar places and practices to the Christian authors.

For late thirteenth-century Latin Christians, Islam was not only easily recognizable, but was also simple to deal with in practical terms. Muslims were enemies with whom both war and a working relationship were possible. The pattern in the crusading Levant, where the Franks (as all Latin Christians were known) sometimes found the culture of their declared enemies more congenial than that of Eastern Christian groups, all too often ambiguous allies, was enhanced along the land and sea routes further east by the need to dress and speak like common travellers. Genoese and Venetian merchants who traded in Egypt even while they were supposed to defend Outremer from imminent conquest, surely had no difficulties in letting their beards grow and perhaps taking a Turkish-speaking concubine in order to reach Cathay from the Black Sea, as Pegolotti advised in his *Pratica della Mercatura*.[45]

Marco Polo, whose whole career had depended on the religious tolerance of the 'Tartars' who dominated central Asia, surely spoke and read Mongol, Turkish and Persian; it is less clear whether he understood Chinese. The prevalent model in which he participated was common in many oriental courts: the king guaranteed the safety of travellers and trading communities of different confessions, although there were important variations between those rulers who gave especial privileges to one group while putting pressure on others, and those who instead established a principle of royal eclecticism under which peaceful religious disputations were often encouraged. As (according to Marco Polo) Kubilai Khan explained:

there are four prophets who are worshipped and revered all over the

---

[44] There are remarkable coincidences between Marco Polo's account and the standard views of Arab geographers concerning India and China, which showed a remarkable continuity through the centuries, as analysed by Miquel in *La géographie humaine du monde musulman*.

[45] 'Things needful for merchants who desire to make the journey to Cathay above described: In the first place you must let your beard grow long and not shave. And at Tana you should furnish yourself with a dragoman, and you must not try to save money in the matter of dragomen . . . besides the dragoman it will be well to take at least two good men servants who are acquainted with the Cumanian tongue. And if the merchant likes to take a woman with him from Tana, he can do so; if he does not like to take one there is no obligation, only if he does take one he will be kept much more comfortably . . . it will be well that she be acquainted with the Cumanian tongue as well as the men.' As translated in Yule (ed.) *Cathay and the way thither*, vol. III, pp. 151–2.

world. The Christians say that their God was Jesus Christ, the Saracens Muhammad, the Jews Moses, and the idolaters Sogomombar Can [Sakyamuni Burkhan], who was the first god of the idolaters. But I do honour and reverence to the four, that is to Him who is greatest in heaven, and truest, and to him I pray for aid.[46]

In fact, throughout the thirteenth century many Mongol Khans were more sympathetic to Nestorian Christians and Buddhists than to Muslims.[47] Along the sea routes, where the relative peace imposed by the Mongols did not reach, both Christians and Muslims were often under the protection of 'gentile idolaters' (as they would agree to call practitioners of any non-biblical religion). But in any case the conventions for economic security and ethnic coexistence were quite strong in all the important trading centres between Alexandria and South China. One could say that ports along this route followed a logic of their own – political and economic – which conditioned where travellers went, and also the cultural mediation through which local indigenous realities were analysed.[48] In this context, the distinction between direct observation and hearsay, which is a distinction which appears very clearly in Marco Polo's account, was very important.

Christian missionaries, because they sought to preach, were more likely to depend on the degree of tolerance shown by particular rulers and thus could not expect great help from Muslim princes. They obviously sought princes who either showed sympathy towards Christianity or were not actively opposed to it. On the other hand, Latin missionaries often found their oriental Christian hosts a source of complications; for William of Rubruck in Karakorum, John of Montecorvino in Peking and Jordanus Catalani in Quilon, it was the Armenians

---

[46] G. B. Ramusio, *Navigazione e viaggi*, ed. by M. Milanesi, vol. III, p. 156. The passage only occurs in Ramusio's version, so that the possibility of an interpolation cannot be excluded. However, what is known of Kubilai Khan's religious policy makes the passage entirely credible.

[47] Nestorianism, named after Nestorius of Constantinople, was condemned as heretical at the council of Ephesus (AD 431). Nestorians held that Christ's divine and human natures had to be clearly distinguished. The orthodox formula, common to both Greek and Latin churches, was eventually to define Christ as one person with two natures, some way between the Nestorian position (which emphasized the full humanity of Christ) and the monophysite alternative (which insisted on the unity of Christ's divine nature). While the monophysites grew important in Syria and Egypt, where in the seventh century they practically welcomed the Arab Muslims in order to escape orthodox oppression from Constantinople, many Nestorians had fled to Persia and survived as a minority in many parts of Asia. All these Christian communities were active when the Latin Franks turned up six centuries later.

[48] On the world of port towns in the Indian Ocean there is a considerable bibliography. See for instance K. N. Chaudhuri, *Trade and civilization in the Indian Ocean* (Cambridge, 1985).

and above all the Nestorians who were seen in the end as their most intractable enemies. This does not mean that relations with Muslims were peaceful: rather the contrary. However, when in 1321 some Franciscans travelling with the Dominican Jordanus Catalani were killed in Thana (Gujarat), they were not the victims of any inevitable ideological clash or even political complication, but simply had insisted on declaring the falsity of Muhammad in front of the Qadi and suffered the obvious consequences.[49] The model of mission created by Francis of Assisi and his biographers was confrontational and expected martyrdom as much as providential success. Preaching the enemy faith in public was in fact, when not encouraged by rulers like Kubilai Khan, a serious act of provocation, which ultimately derived from the uncompromising pursuit of Christian eschatological ideals. Otherwise a common cultural ground with Islam could be assumed by European travellers. While in Spain and Palestine exceptional men like Ramon Llull and William of Tripoli suggested more sophisticated and rationalistic approaches to mission among Muslims,[50] in the East the more challenging intellectual problems were in fact gentile idolatry and Christian heresy – the former because it was only understood superficially but in practice was influential in the form of complex traditions such as Buddhism, the latter because it challenged Latin claims to Roman universalism.

[49] There are various reports of this event which circulated in the fourteenth century, for instance as part of the travels of Odoric of Pordenone. The source for these reports was the Latin letter written by Jordanus Catalani from Gujarat in 1321, but this did not yet involve the miraculous elements. He may have written a fuller report, since in that letter he mentioned that he would be going back to the missionary centres in Persia 'on account of the canonization of the holy brethren'. It is then likely that a fuller version was constructed and that the rumours spread quickly from the oriental centres of missionary activity, with the participation of Latin merchants, and maybe also Nestorian Christians. By 1326 the Bishop of Zayton Andrew of Perugia had already heard all about it. Needless to say, all these accounts must be treated with the greatest scepticism – they belong to a hagiographic genre. Thus I have little doubt that the narrative of the martyrdom and of the subsequent transportation of the friars' relics by Pordenone is an apocryphal invention which hardly fits in tone or style with the rest of the account: the fact that there are so many different versions of Pordenone's travels, some without the miraculous passages, strengthens the case for an outright interpolation. Catalani's own judgement must be questioned, not just because, as it appears from his surviving letters, he was obsessed with winning martyrdom himself, but also because he was not in Thana when it all happened. He obviously constructed his account with the intention of creating models of missionary martyrdom, much needed if the oriental missions were to receive further support from the Latin West.

[50] William of Tripoli, the author of *De statu saracenorum* (a future source for Mandeville), was quite possibly the same Dominican friar based in Acre who according to Rustichello was sent by Gregory X to the Great Khan, but did not dare to accompany the Polo merchants all the way to Cathay. Ramon Llull, on the other hand, travelled to preach in North Africa on different occasions and was reputed to have found martyrdom in Tunis by getting himself stoned.

Throughout his account Marco Polo's cultural classifications involve references to language, dress and habits, but they also consistently refer to religious categories, that is Christians, Saracens, Jews and idolaters.[51] Within such categories there is scope for further distinctions, that is to say that there are different kinds of Christians and different kinds of idolaters (Marco Polo also describes the Assassins, the Isma'ilite sect, as a Muslim heresy). But although Marco Polo's use of religious categories expresses an awareness of the range of possibilities associated with the concepts of Christianity and idolatry, his approach is not polemical.[52] His contribution is precisely the opposite: he places religious beliefs as part of a general ethnographic language based on the observation of behaviour and always defined in terms of human diversity. Furthermore, Christianity, his own religion, needs to compete on an equal basis with other religions: in the eyes of the Great Khan whom the Venetian serves there is no reason why Christians should be persecuted, but there is no reason either why he should be baptized and deny other religions – that is, unless the Pope sends missionaries who can work such miracles that all doubts are dissolved. As the Khan explains:

How do you want me to become a Christian? You see that the Christians of these parts are so ignorant that they do not know anything and are powerless. And you see that these idolaters do what they want, and when I sit at the table the cups from the middle of the hall come to me, full of wine or drink and of other things, without anyone touching them, and I drink from them. They make the bad

---

[51] The emphasis on the religious dimension of Marco Polo's experience makes the contribution by Leonardo Olschki, *L'Asia di Marco Polo*, particularly insightful. His analysis, however, makes little reference to South India, while Nilakanta Sastri's article 'Marco Polo on India' in *Oriente Poliano* (Rome, 1957) does not really fill this gap.

[52] It is interesting that some of the passages with religious implications, such as those concerning the Great Khan's relativistic attitude towards Christianity or those describing how idolatry could bring about good social customs, were not present in the main French manuscripts and could only be read in a more obscure Latin version. One such Latin manuscript was used by Ramusio, while the discovery of another related to it, known as Z, is the most important single addition to the Marco Polo corpus made this century, through the critical editions prepared by Benedetto in 1928 and by Moule and Pelliot in 1938. Moreover, many seemingly genuine passages of a religious and sexual character are only available through Jacopo d'Acqui's fourteenth-century *Imago mundi seu chronica* (Polo, *Milione*, pp. cxciii–cxcvii). It is likely that the Latin versions, mainly destined for clerics, were composed after the first Franco-Italian version by Rustichello known as ms. F. Thus both F and Z could be genuinely Polian – from his position as a respectable Venetian merchant, Marco Polo would have been able to have interviews with the author of the new Latin version and add further details to the earlier account. Meanwhile, the French versions (mss. FA and FB) suffered a major transformation through their adaptation into court French. For this reason it is difficult and also misleading to retrieve an original Marco Polo independent of the books' various audiences.

weather go wherever they want, and they do many marvellous things
. . . and these idolaters say that they do all this through the sanctity
and virtue of their idols . . . but if you go to your pope and ask on my
behalf that he sends me a hundred men wise in your law, who in front
of these idolaters will rebuke what they do . . . and compel them so
that they no longer have the power to do the same things in front of
them, then, when I see this, I will reject them and their law and I will
be baptized.[53]

The power of providence, indistinguishable from the power of magic, is
in fact Marco Polo's criterion whenever there is an open competition
between religions.[54] Although this is not made explicit, in practice all
religions which can be seen to 'channel' magical power are accepted as
legitimate. This does not imply an idea of radical tolerance based on an
intellectual dialogue (the exploration of a rational dialogue between
religions by European writers from Abelard to Ramon Llull only took
place within a clerical genre and was of course entirely biased towards
the truth of Christianity), but rather a relative acceptance of diversity in
which confrontation, without disappearing, is nevertheless mediated by
shared cultural assumptions. Thus the whole idea of serving a pagan lord
is not justified by a complete separation between politics and religion,
but rather by the assumption that, where there is power and law, there
must also be faith.

It is from this complex experience that Marco Polo's description of
India makes a distinctive contribution to the medieval corpus. The
traditional image of oriental marvels and monsters was based on clerical
appropriations of late classical material, like the third-century *Collec-
tanea rerum memorabilium* by Solinus or the Greek Alexander romance
of pseudo-Callisthenes. These texts indeed exercised a strong influence
throughout the centuries. The Alexander romance, for example, important both in the East and in the West, shaped Latin views of India by

---

[53] Polo in Ramusio, *Navigazioni e viaggi*, vol. III, p. 157. As in note 42 above, this passage
occurs only in Ramusio's version.

[54] Such as the miracle of the shoemaker of Baghdad (found only in manuscript Z),
probably taken from the mythology of local Nestorian and Jacobite Christians living in a
hostile environment; or the stories about the tomb of Saint Thomas in South India, of
which there is little doubt that they were also local. It is also with curiosity that Marco
Polo relates his discovery of Nestorian Christians in China (again a fragment, only found
in manuscript Z). As I shall insist, the narrative makes clear that it was through its ability
to give ('providentially' or 'supernaturally') power to its followers that a religion was
usually played against the others as 'superior', in the context determined by the tolerance
which, partly for political reasons, rulers could impose. As a divided minority with
limited resources, the Christians could hardly expect to convert the Great Khan, but
local miracles, and especially the ability to be useful to the ruler, helped them to keep
their communities alive.

means of two seventh-century works, the *Marvels of the East* and the *Letter of Alexander*, even before a new Latin translation of the full romance was produced in the tenth century by Leo of Naples.[55] But the apparent continuity of themes does not contradict changes in emphasis and meaning. The Latin Alexander, it has been noted, was a more ambiguous moral figure than the Christianized Greek Alexander of Byzantine sources, or the wise Alexander of the Arabic tradition. His dialogue with the Indian brahmins about the respective virtues of the active and contemplative lives (in the *Collatio Alexandri et Dindimi* already known by Alcuin), and his journey to paradise, also identified with the island of the brahmins, acquired a particular resonance in the West because these themes raised relevant issues for Latin Christians caught in the separation between secular and religious ideals.[56] After the twelfth century both the chivalric ideals of the feudal nobility and the religious utopia of the regular clergy could find expression in further elaborations of these few sources inherited from antiquity and the East (such was indeed the significance of the use of the themes of Alexander or the Prester John in the Latin West). While those who wrote about Christian conquest in Spain or who travelled to Jerusalem as pilgrims needed to take account of some historical evidence, the sources for distant oriental realities, already stereotyped when they reached Isidor of Seville in the seventh century, never had to respond to the practical requirements of a real interaction.

Therefore, Marco Polo and his missionary contemporaries did not merely add a mass of information to those fragmentary images which, in order to suit the needs of the precarious clerical culture of the Latin world before the crusades, had been taken and adapted from Greek originals: they in fact created new genres in which the weight of authority shifted from written tradition to original observation, and new interpretative models in which the practical implications of a proper understanding of human diversity could be more important than the expression of an ethos of honour or a desire for religious satisfaction. Neither the biblical themes nor the chivalric scenes entirely disappeared from the new genres, but in Marco Polo the Prester John was given a role as a Nestorian lord subordinate to the gentile Tartar, and thus could no longer be the messianic priest–king of the twelfth-century forgery. At the

---

[55] The Latin texts are given in *Le meraviglie dell'India*, ed. by G. Tardiola (Rome, 1991), pp. 139–62. On the medieval Alexander see G. Cary, *The medieval Alexander* (Cambridge, Mass., 1956). A useful anthology of early medieval Greek and Latin texts concerning Alexander is given in English in R. Stoneman (ed.) *Legends of Alexander the Great* (London, 1994).

[56] Stoneman (ed.) *Legends*, pp. xxxiii–vi. The debate about the moral qualities of Alexander, as a king confronted with philosophers, in effect went back to his own times.

same time, the speeches of the Arthurian heroes were transferred by Rustichello to the mouths of the Il-Khans of Persia as they prepared to fight each other in historical time.

Not even the most authoritative scholastic encyclopaedias were immune to this empirical assault. For example the mid-thirteenth-century *Opus maius* by Vincent of Beauvais, which included Carpini's recent account of the Mongols together with a wide variety of classical sources, only managed to perpetuate a theological hierarchy at the cost of separating natural and historical science from metaphysics.[57] The revolutionary character of a descriptive narrative such as Marco Polo's is best appreciated when seen as an alternative to the allegorical interpretations through which thirteenth-century religious writers had domesticated the classical inheritance as well as the growing body of Arthurian literature. Here not only the narrative voice matters, but also its reception. While it was perfectly possible for pious or provincial readers of Marco Polo's travels, like the 1392 *podestà* of Ciereto, Amelio Buonaguisi, to seek mere entertainment in the book and to express utter disbelief as to its contents, and for fifteenth-century illuminators to produce stereotyped interpretations of the Great Khan or the monstrous races of India, the manuscript tradition as a whole provided Europe with the beginnings of a distinct empirical genre. Such a genre could support either the late medieval urban encyclopaedia of men like Domenico Bandino d'Arezzo or the universal chronicle of the Dominican Jacopo d'Acqui, and even encourage Aristotelian philosophers like Pietro d'Abano to challenge the geographical conceptions of Christian theologians.[58] All these uses, however, depended on external structures of meaning. Above all the *Divisament dou monde* stood, even in versions translated and summarized, as a potential model for further accounts in which marvels were no longer traditional marvels, but rather new observations of natural and human diversity.

SOUTH INDIA IN MARCO POLO'S DESCRIPTION OF THE WORLD

Marco Polo's itinerary from Ceylon to Cambay seems a little erratic, but this can be explained because he probably combined memories from two separate voyages. The account can in fact be interpreted as being remarkably coherent. It is quite clear that Marco Polo proceeded first to Coromandel, where his lengthy description of 'Maabar' (Ma'bar) sug-

---

[57] As expressed with terse lucidity by Bolgar, *The classical heritage*, p. 234.

[58] Details about the reception of Marco Polo are discussed by John Larner in a forthcoming study.

gests a long stay. He also uses this area as a starting point for further descriptions of two other kingdoms: 'Mutifili' further north (i.e. Motu-palli, by the river Godavari) and, after returning to the tomb of Saint Thomas apostle (in Mylapore), also 'Lar' somewhere in the interior (possibly Belour).[59] After some extra recollections from Ceylon which he seems to have been reminded of as he talked to Rustichello – and this includes his fullest account of Buddha, only cursorily introduced while describing Cathay – Marco Polo proceeds along the coast of the peninsula to 'Cail' (Kayal), 'Coilum' (Quilon), 'Comori' (Comorin, but here the order does not make geographical sense), 'Eli' and 'Melibar' (Malabar). From there he goes on northwards towards the ports of Gujarat, Thana and Cambay.

The description of Maabar, Motupalli and Lar can be taken without excessive anachronism to reflect a rather substantial view of the future kingdom of Vijayanagara as it stood *c.* 1290, especially detailed for the eastern coast. Interestingly for us, this period marks in fact the beginning of the Turkish incursions from Delhi that were to devastate the Deccan and South India and which have often been seen as the rationale behind the growth of the frontier kingdom of Vijayanagara after 1340. More than just fifty years and an obviously different cultural background, what separates Marco Polo's observations from those of Ibn Battūta (who was in Madurai *c.* 1344) is this historical process, and it is bearing this in mind that specific contents of his description can be analysed and compared to those of missionaries.

A systematic division of the main themes of Marco Polo's account of Maabar (see table 1) gives some clues towards the traveller's main thematic categories. But we must bear in mind that Marco Polo selected the information which he reported from a wider experience, and that one cannot take his failure to mention something as lack of observation. In fact the relative disorder of the narrative fits with the manner in which the account was delivered. It is clear from expressions like 'here he tells about the great province of Maabar', 'to turn now to other matters', or

---

[59] The identification of Lar raises the greatest problems and Pelliot (*Notes*, p. 762), following Henry Yule, interpreted it as Gujarat, since the Sanskrit *Lata* is an ancient denomination for Gujarat, and Marco Polo might have confused 'banyans' with 'brahmans'. I prefer to assume the geographical coherence of Marco Polo, who locates this kingdom in the interior towards the west from the tomb of Saint Thomas, and propose therefore to read Lar as a Hoysala centre, perhaps Belour (near the capital Dvarasamudram). The presence of brahmin or Jain merchants from the Hoysala cities trading in Coromandel is not in any case an absurdity. On the contrary, in the thirteenth century the Hoysalas expanded towards the eastern coast along the Kaveri river and founded a second capital in Kannanur. From that city they threatened the Pandya kings on the coast – those with whom Marco Polo spent some time. See Krishnaswami Aiyangar in *Cambridge History of India*, vol. III (1928), p. 481.

Table 1. *South India (Coromandel) in Marco Polo (Maabar, Greater India) and John of Montecorvino (Mebar, Upper India)*

Marco Polo (*c.* 1292–3)	Montecorvino (*c.* 1292–3)
The province of Maabar is rich and noble. Its rulers are five brothers. (1)	The land and the people. Population is abundant, there are great cities. (4)
	The Saracens control coastal ports, but not the interior. (18)
	There are few Christians and Jews. Christians are persecuted.(19)
Hot climate and nakedness. (3) Seasonal rains. (23)	Detailed account of climate in India (1), day and night (2), astronomical observations. (3) Rainy seasons. (13) Monsoons and navigation. (28) Geographical context. (27)
Hanging cane-beds. (28)	Houses made of mud and leaves. (5)
	Natural landscape, hills and rivers. (6) Water and water-tanks. (7)
	Natural products: trees and fruits all year round. (9)
	Spices are abundant and cheap: pepper, ginger, *bersi* (the Brazil tree), Indian nuts, cinnamon. (10)
Strange animals and birds. (26)	Monstrous men and animals, and terrestrial paradise, not to be found. (11)
	The variety of India and the general character of Indians. (21) Their physical aspect (colour, beauty), dress. (22)
Detailed account of pearl fisheries in the sea. The help the merchants as powerful charmers. The king gets his dues. (2)	Fish products and pearl fisheries. (26)
The king also goes naked but is honourably ornamented and rich. (4) He controls supply of pearls and precious stones. (6)	
The precious stones serve idolatrous prayers. (5)	
The king has many women, he takes any he wants. (7) He took his brother's: a family conflict. (8)	
The king has a retinue of faithful lords who serve him during life and also after death (they burn with their dead master). (9)	
The royal treasury is not spent, but each new king must increase it: it is therefore enormous. (10)	

(continued)

Table 1. (*cont.*)

Marco Polo (*c*. 1292–3)	Montecorvino (*c*. 1292–3)
The revenue is spent buying horses, which do not breed in India and must be continuously imported. They do not know how to keep them, and the merchants exploit the situation. (11) Horses breed poorly. (18) They eat flesh and rice. (27)	Horses are scarce, reserved for the king and lords. (8)
Religious self-sacrifice accepted as form of capital justice. (12)	
Strict justice. (21) Security is good, the king protects merchant-travellers. (29)	Security is good, there are few bandits, but artisans taxed and unrewarded. (24)
Polygamy and *sati*. (13)	Marriages and sexuality (no sin of flesh). (17) Death rituals (but *sati* is not mentioned). (20)
Idolatrous practices: oxen sacred (14). The *gavi*, a low race [caste] who eat ox flesh. (15) A miracle of Saint Thomas, whom the *gavi* killed. (16)	Oxen are sacred animals. Their economic uses. (12)
Food: rice, no wheat. (17) They do not drink wine (22)	Food and eating habits. (23)
Soldiers fight quite naked, poorly armed and are cowardly. (19)	Warfare. Notes Saracen mercenaries. (25)
Religious significance of hygiene (regular washing) and rules for eating (idea of pollution). (20)	
Magical arts in detail: Physiognomy, omens, tarantulas, astrology, with reference to writings. (24)	System of writing. (15)
Education of the young merchants so that they become cunning. (25)	
Temple worship (monasteries of idols) and dancing girls (28). Detailed account of ritual union of God and goddess. (29)	Idolatry. (14) Temples, worship and rituals. (16)

This table has been arranged so that the contents of the two descriptions can be easily analysed and compared. I have used the texts edited by Moule and Pelliot in Polo, *Description of the world*, vol. I, pp. 381–414, and Wyngaert, *Sinica Franciscana*, pp. 340–5. Closely related observations are always grouped together, within each description and against the other. When the two accounts differ most substantially, I have roughly followed the narrative order of the fullest account. I have given numbers between brackets to indicate the original order of the narrative for each text. It is very important to bear in mind that Marco Polo's narrative is substantially longer than Montecorvino's. Because the latter is more succinct, it manages to cover a broad number of themes. Thus the table does not intend to reflect accurately the wealth of detail of each theme, although I have sought to give some indication of this.

'now we have told you of the customs of these Braaman idolaters, let us leave them and turn to a delightful story that I forgot to tell when we were dealing with Ceylon', that either Marco Polo was speaking from memory, or Rustichello was composing the narrative with a set of notes that he needed to organize. Possibly both are true. Rustichello's intervention in the organization of the book is very likely if we consider its dual structure: the prologue contains an account of the travels of Marco Polo, and serves as justification for the validity of the main descriptive material which is, then, organized thematically following a geographical rather than a biographical order. In this way the chapter on India is not meant to be read as 'Marco Polo's experiences in Greater India', but rather as 'what Marco Polo saw and heard concerning Greater India'.

In any case it is clear that certain themes seem to engage Marco Polo's attention more than others, and this provides us with an initial contrast with John of Montecorvino's account. Even though the friar's letter and the *Divisament* constitute, strictly speaking, different genres, since Marco Polo has no mission to justify, their descriptive practices are based on the same set of assumptions. Both are valuable witnesses because they have been there, and the geographical setting is the most comprehensive mechanism through which natural and human diversity is analysed. There is indeed a kind of descriptive logic which leads the two travellers to coincide in many of their observations, and this makes the differences all the more significant.

Particularly important in Marco Polo is the recurrence of interest in religious and magical practices, which are almost never directly condemned (not at least in those manuscripts which we may consider to have been less contaminated by copyists and translators). There is also a general interest in the practice and attributes of kingly power. These two themes are treated in much less detail by John of Montecorvino. Here we can see that these differences have quite a lot to·do with the social conditions of the two observers, which affected their formal education and their ideological constraints. However, they also relate to Marco Polo's particular experience in Asia, which sets him apart from common travellers (and here I mean his overall *previous* experience as the servant of an oriental king, because Montecorvino, who had been in Armenia and Persia for many years, apparently spent thirteen months in India, and there is little to indicate that Marco Polo was there for a longer period).

Indeed, Marco Polo's seventeen years with the Great Khan could easily have inspired him with interest in royal authority, while his emphasis on magical practices has quite a lot to do with his own participation in a widespread set of magical beliefs. In this sense it is often as a man trained as a merchant who deals with other merchant communities that he approaches these themes in India. Royal justice is thus understood as the protection of the merchant-traveller, who, due to the heat, often sleeps in the streets, confident that the safety of his goods is guaranteed; omens indicate to Indian merchants when to make deals or not; Marco Polo's interest in the education of young boys is clearly focused on the sons of merchants, and he also gives a detailed account of the importation of horses and why they do not adapt to Indian soil, as opposed to Montecorvino's mere indication that horses are few and are a kind of aristocratic privilege.

The difference is in fact more significant than the mere range of themes discussed, and affects the moral interests of the travellers. The Franciscan Montecorvino was able to express in very few pages a remarkable amount of information, and he was particularly precise concerning climate, navigation, natural products and other physical conditions. In fact, his technical language indicates some scientific interests which may have been developed at the thirteenth-century universities where Marco Polo certainly never went.[60] His account of the Indians is, however, detached: although he seems to have baptized nearly one hundred people in the area around the tomb of Saint Thomas, he dismisses their beliefs and literature by declaring that they have no moral law or conception of sin. Curiously, he also declares that they have no books but then immediately adds that they write, although on palm-leafs, and only their 'accounts and prayers, that is to say charms for their idols'.[61] He also finds the apparent lack of a recognizable order in ritual worship an obvious fault, and their way of eating (with the hand, not a spoon) is 'more like pigs than men'.[62] So, while he is able to capture in a single sentence the diversity of kingdoms, languages and peoples of India, he describes the common inhabitants as shy yokels.[63] This attitude must of

[60] According to John of Marignolli who wrote c. 1350, Montecorvino had been a soldier, judge and doctor before becoming a Franciscan known for his learning and wisdom. Since it can be inferred that he was born c. 1247, it is chronologically impossible that he served Emperor Frederic, as Marignolli also declares, which casts some doubt on his report in general (although he might just have served Manfred of Hohenstaufen). According to Yule (*Cathay and the way thither*, vol. III, p. 4), Montecorvino had acted in 1272 as the envoy of Emperor Michael VIII Paleologus of Constantinople to Pope Gregory X (the same crusader pope who sent a letter to Kubilai Khan through the Polo brothers). The information is contested by Wyngaert (*Sinica Franciscana*, p. 336, n.5) who believes that here two friars have been confused. In any case, all of Montecorvino's letters express clarity of mind and a good education (he even taught Greek to the children in China), as well as a measured piety.

[61] Wyngaert, *Sinica Franciscana*, pp. 342–3: 'scriveno suoi ragioni e orasioni overo coniurasioni d'idoli'.

[62] Ibid., p. 343: 'mangiano balordamente sichome porci'.

[63] Ibid: 'sonvi li omini assai dimestichi e familiari e di poghe parole e quasi chome omini di ville'.

course be related to Montecorvino's missionary purpose. Overall he was trying to explain his limitations in his attempt to convert 'idolaters' in direct rivalry with expanding Muslims, and while no concessions were made to facile images of monstrosity, it must have been tempting to perceive a system of civil qualities which was not quite satisfactory (significantly, after many years in China the reasoning changes: the people are civilized enough, and it is only Montecorvino's isolation and the rivalry of the Nestorians that spoils the mission).[64] That it is a moral and not a racial failure is clear from his description of physical differences: the Indians are 'of an olive colour', and they are also 'very well formed'.[65]

John of Montecorvino was one of the earliest missionaries in India and in this sense his approach was only the beginning of a tradition. It is remarkable that his religious interests do not imply a less realistic narrative approach than, let us say, Marco Polo's. He explicitly looks for monsters and does not find them, in a more definite way than the Venetian, who dismisses unicorns here only to find them there. But most important is that Marco Polo is culturally less isolated: he is willing to exchange stories and participate in local traditions, and his accounts of extraordinary events – of the life of Buddha or of magical practices – corroborate this fact. While for Marco Polo the marvels of the East are defined in a world of shared understanding based on a diversity of traditions, which leads him to develop a limited form of relativism, Montecorvino sees India from outside because, as a missionary representing the Latin Church, his only legitimate marvels are Christian and orthodox. He pays less attention to the brahmins and their religion, and he of course omits to describe in detail the temple girls who sing and dance naked and whose flesh and breasts, according to Marco Polo, are so firm.

More astonishing, Montecorvino does not even record the legends concerning Saint Thomas, an obvious theme for such a pious man. The preaching of the apostle Thomas in India was an old Christian tradition (dating from at least the third century) concerning the early spread of the gospel among all the nations of the world, and which had taken a definite shape in South India with the establishment of Christian communities in Malabar by the sixth century. These communities kept in touch with the churches of Persia and Mesopotamia and used Syriac as a language for liturgy. The tradition of Saint Thomas was also known in the West

---

[64] From Montecorvino's second and third letters of 1305 and 1396: Yule, *Cathay and the way thither*, vol. III, pp. 45–58.

[65] Wyngaert, *Sinica Franciscana*, p. 343: 'sono apostutto neri, uvero iulivigni, e mouto bene formati, chosì le femine chome li omini'.

throughout the Middle Ages, but gained special prominence during the twelfth century, since the crusades put the Latins in direct touch with many Syrian Christians (in fact an alleged Indian patriarch visited Calixtus II in 1123, and some Latin pilgrims attempted to travel to the shrine later that century). Montecorvino thus had the chance to send a first-hand description of a Christian marvel to his western companions, and the subject proved less elusive than the Prester John: the traveller clearly visited the church of Mylapore, where he even buried his companion the Dominican Nicholas of Pistoia. There must, therefore, be a reason for his lack of any reference to the miracles which, according to Marco Polo, had occurred only four years earlier, in 1288. Although it is possible that the friar had written another letter, now lost, with those details, perhaps his omission is better accounted for as an expression of his limited access to the local oral traditions. Marco Polo had access to the story because he was willing to hear that the Saracens considered that the tomb belonged to a Muslim holy man and made their pilgrimage there, while the Christians – Syrian and Nestorian, not Latin and Roman – attributed the miracles to Saint Thomas instead. It is not clear how willingly Montecorvino would have listened to them.

Thus it is apparent that sharing traditions had implications which all travel writers needed to confront. Montecorvino's omission was only a response to the issue of how a missionary could relate to a sacred mythology outside its control. A later and less insightful Franciscan, Odoric of Pordenone, around 1323 found the church of Saint Thomas 'filled with idols' and in fact his popular and detailed account omits any mention of Christian miracles and becomes instead a description of idolatrous practices with some smatterings of Nestorian heresy, none of which he wants to commend.[66] Meanwhile the Dominican Jordanus Catalani, who should have heard many of these stories because he had been a few years in Quilon building a Latin church, simply states in his general account of the marvels of India written in Avignon *c.* 1329 that the Syro-Malabar community is dispersed, extremely ignorant and confuses Saint Thomas with Jesus Christ.[67] The Pope had just appointed him Bishop of Columbum (Quilon) and sent letters to the indigenous Christians (*Christianis Nastarinis de Columbo*) asking them to accept their new bishop and renounce their schism.[68] The only western friar who enthusiastically sought the benefit of the sacred powers of Saint Thomas and reported indigenous legends concerning his miracles was the rather

---

[66] Yule, *Cathay and the way thither*, vol. II, pp. 141–6. Yule publishes the Latin and Italian texts of Pordenone's travelogue, and offers an English rendering.

[67] Catalani, *Mirabilia descripta*, p. 114.

[68] Ibid., p. 39.

idiosyncratic John of Marignolli, a Florentine Franciscan who visited the grave *c.* 1348. It is no coincidence that he also found paradise near Adam's Peak in Ceylon, and described the Buddhist monks as a kind of post-Adamitic holy men. He was thus willing to conflate the accounts of Muslims and Buddhists into a Christian interpretation which was more mystical than historical and geographical.

There is no hint that Marco Polo's earlier and rather unique accept-ance of diverse traditions was at all mystical. His almost eclectic attitudes are related to both moral and magical beliefs. On the one hand, a manuscript (and not the most unreliable) mentions that he used to heal people in Venice with the earth he took from the tomb of Saint Thomas at Mylapore.[69] On the other hand it is also clear that he accepted the help of a Chinese idol when he thought he could recover some stolen goods.[70] This and other examples indicate that his regular condemnation of diabolical arts must be seen as part of an ambiguous system in which magical power, and indeed idolatry, could have both positive and negative aspects – when it was not a prudent concession to the expecta-tions of the audience.[71] Particularly remarkable is his opinion about 'Sergamoni Borghan' (Sakyamuni Burkhan, i.e. Buddha): 'had he been Christian he would surely have been a great saint with our lord Jesus Christ'.[72] This positive judgement is important because Marco Polo attributes to this saint the origin of Indian idolatry. Furthermore, although he recognizes that the Muslims think that the sacred relics of Ceylon belong to Adam, he prefers to believe that, according to the scriptures of the Christian Church, Adam was elsewhere. Thus, contrary to Marignolli's religious strategy, Marco Polo implies that it may be better to accept the validity of different religions than to collapse all sacred landscapes into a single Christian one.

It is, however, important to define with precision the possible coher-ence and the limitations of Marco Polo's relativism. His account often

---

[69] From manuscript Z; see Polo, *Description of the world*, vol. I, p. 398.

[70] Marco Polo recovered a stolen ring in Cathay through the help of an idol, although (he immediately adds) 'not by making any offering to the idol or paying homage to it' (Polo, *Milione*, p. 132). This is, again, part of a long passage describing Chinese customs which only occurs in Z.

[71] The condemnation of diabolical arts, associated with the sense of an ideological barrier peculiar to the western audience, reaches its highest point with the Tibetan magicians (in fact Buddhist Lamas), whose diabolical arts 'it is better not to relate in our book because people might marvel too much' (Polo, *Milione*, p. 112). Marco Polo, however, had already made it clear that these were the best astrologers and enchanters in those parts, so that neither Muslims nor Christians nor even Cathayan idolaters could compete with them at the Khan's court (an analysis that reflects quite precisely the relative influence of these different groups at the time).

[72] Ibid., p. 194.

implies that there is a logic in the fact that people from different lands may follow different customs, so that the king of Maabar goes almost naked in a hot country, he wears bracelets of gold with pearls in a kingdom where these are easily found, and he will pray to his idols with the prayers that his faith and the customs of his people command, indeed continuing what his ancestors used to do and told him to do.[73] This interpretation follows, as we have seen, from his own circumstances, since Marco Polo saw most of the East in the company of non-Christians, and together with food, language and dress he shared a space of religious practices without the power or the inclination to impose his own doctrine. While he wished his own sect to do well, and thus participated in the rivalry between the Christians, Moslems, Buddhists and Jews who struggled for influence at the court of the great Khan, he also accepted that the arbiter he obeyed, and who set the rules, was a pagan king.

The most important effect that this has in the narrative is that miracles were reported along with strange customs and other remarkable curiosities. A discourse on religion was not in that sense separate from a discourse on human behaviour, and although idolatry might easily be condemned, what was inescapable was the massive evidence for diversity.[74] Different beliefs justified different behaviours and altogether could no longer be reduced to monstrosity and deviance. There was a lot that one could admire as congenial to Christian ideals in the story of the life of Sakyamuni, or in the honesty and asceticism of the merchant-brahmins of Lar. Other customs, such as widows willingly jumping on to the burning pyre of their deceased husbands, or men cutting themselves into pieces in honour of their idols, were easily expected to meet with rejection, although this is not usually rationalized. Others, finally, like the account of the temple girls dancing so that the god will unite with the goddess, or the sacred oxen whose dung is also sacred, could be seen with a more detached curiosity as merely strange or ridiculous. They might

---

[73] Polo, *Description of the world*, vol. I, pp. 383–4.

[74] It is important to notice here that the occasional accusations of devilry that accompany the description of 'idolatrous' customs were not necessarily from Marco Polo, and seem to have been added by later copyists. In particular, the manuscript tradition in court French identified and edited by Pauthier in 1865 and then used by Yule (represented in Moule's 1938 edition as 'FB') seems to be particularly sensitive to the need to rationalize passages with religious implications. Some of the manuscripts of this tradition claim that Marco Polo himself was responsible for giving a version to Thibaud of Chepoy in Venice in 1308, but this does not (and can hardly) mean that Marco Polo wrote it directly in literary French. The manuscript, in any case, went through the hands of a certain Grégoire, possibly a 'second Rustichello'. Interestingly, this textual tradition, probably destined for French aristocrats, served as the basis for the spectacular illuminated manuscripts now in Paris and Oxford.

also prompt challenging comparisons, such as when the yogis of Lar declare that they go naked without any shame because they are other-worldly, and they demonstrate it by resisting the charms of young maidens without getting excited. A statement such as that wantonness is no sin in India may have made a merchant from Genoa or Barcelona wonder, since many of them, ignoring the clerical discourse, kept slaves as concubines. While Montecorvino reported the same lack of shame towards the sin of the flesh, in his letter the negative implication was clear. In the end what matters most is that Marco Polo's strange customs could be rationalized as a valid moral system: when criticized for sitting on the floor, the Indians answered that 'to sit on the earth is an honourable thing enough because we are sprung from the earth'. Any reader of the Bible would have to accept a point there, even if the Indians themselves did not read the Bible. In any case, the anecdote made the concept of honorability relative.

On the whole Marco Polo gives few value judgements and leaves a lot for his audience to decide – there is no theory of toleration nor an explicit principle of relativism. The closest we get to a statement of this kind is the observation that, because Indians in Coromandel consider black people more beautiful than white ones, they try to make children blacker, make their idols black, and also say 'that God and all the saints are black', and that 'the devils are white'.[75] However, this aesthetic principle – in reality a reverse form of colour discrimination – was also observed by the Dominican Jordanus Catalani thirty years later,[76] with no hint that it had any challenging implications. In fact he was entirely convinced by his Indian experience that 'there is no better land, or fairer, no people so honest, no victuals so good and savoury, dress so handsome, nor customs so noble, as here in our own Christendom'.[77] By contrast, what is clear and far-reaching in Marco Polo's ethnographic language (which is much more comprehensive than Catalani's) is that idolatry cannot be easily defined as something distinct from climate and customs, nor can differences be condemned wholesale. Perhaps more originally, these differences cannot be ignored either, because they are what the world is made of.[78]

A problem that must be discussed is the extent to which Marco Polo's observations should be deemed to be superficial. Is it misleading to talk

---

[75] Polo, *Description of the world*, vol. I, p. 400.

[76] 'In truth, the darker men and women are, the more beautiful they are': Catalani, *Mirabilia*, p. 115.

[77] Ibid., p. 123.

[78] On the use of climate to explain human diversity in the medieval West, see I. Metzler, 'Perceptions of hot climate in medieval cosmography and travel literature', *Reading Medieval Studies*, 23 (1997): 69–105.

about 'regular orders of monks' called yogis who serve their idols in their temples? Is it silly to add that these monks live longer than other people because of their fasts, perhaps even 200 years? We may also notice that he fails to discuss caste as a social system, even though he distinguishes groups with their own rules, such as 'a special race of men called *gavi*' who, unlike others, can eat the flesh of the ox.[79] He also discusses in detail some of the rules of purity which separate Indians from 'people who are not of their religion nor of their customs'.[80] Rather than just an inability to make subtle distinctions, all this suggests that such distinctions need not be systematic when one could assume a rather widespread analogy between different societies – in this case, we might think of the coexistence of separate cultures with a limited amount of contact in many cities of Asia. That being understood (the model was familiar in the Mediterranean), the traveller fulfilled the needs of his audience by making a few special remarks.

Indeed what becomes obvious is that Marco Polo worked from analogies, which served as a point of departure for comparisons and the establishment of differences. These analogies were nevertheless not only based on a western experience, but a much wider one, and in fact this experience could be expressed in a popular vulgar language, which made up for his lack of formal education (there is no hint of any classical culture in his book). Finally, it is also quite clear, as I have suggested, that it is not simply as a man with prejudices concerning magical powers and miracles, but rather as a man able to share local mythologies and report hearsay, that Marco Polo got most of his marvellous stuff. His description is informative partly because he was not too critical. This again makes it unique, and the fact that it was written and circulated so extensively was a very important development.

The problem of the quality of Marco Polo's observations can be discussed further by analysing the extent to which he was able to make sense of a local situation in a way that went beyond a general scheme. I shall focus on the theme of kingship, which provides a continuity with later accounts of South India throughout the Renaissance. Ma'bar was the thirteenth-century Arabic name for Coromandel, and the kings described by Marco Polo were probably the Pandyas. The political context was, however, rather fragmented, determined by the waning power of the Chola kings and the rise of regional chiefs. The dynasties of the Kakatiyas and the Hoysalas can in this context be taken to be represented by the kingdoms of 'Mutifili' in Telangana and 'Lar' in southern Karnataka. Focusing on 'Maabar', Marco Polo speaks about

---

[79] Polo, *Description of the world*, vol. I, p. 388.   [80] Ibid., p. 389.

four or five brothers dividing the province among themselves, of which the elder was 'Senderbandi Devar' (probably Sundara Pandya Dewar). He also speaks about the queen of Mutifili (possibly Rudramma Devi of Warangal) as a successful ruler. Although exact correspondences are difficult to establish, it does seem to be the case that Marco Polo is describing particular kingdoms. His account can therefore be taken to express a perception of South Indian kingship just before the devastating arrival of the Turkish conquerors.

Marco Polo's observations are best contextualized with the help of contemporary Muslim historians who wrote in Persian and witnessed the Turkish advances in the early years of the thirteenth century. In particular, the works of Wassaf and Rashid al-Din, which reflected the cosmopolitan views of the Persian Ilkhanids, were discussed by Henry Yule as corroboration of the historicity of Marco Polo's observations.[81] It is even possible to develop a working hypothesis concerning late Pandya rule in Coromandel by comparing these different sources. During the reign of Jatavarman Sundara Pandya (1251–c. 1268) this ancient ruling family had extended its dominions from the southern tip of Tamil country by advancing northwards against the Chola power and by keeping the Hoysalas in the western interior in check. Maravarman Kulasekhara (Wassaf's 'Kales Dewar') is believed to have ruled successfully afterwards for a period of forty years (1268–1310), until he was killed by one of his sons, Sundara Pandya.[82] This Sundara Pandya (the third ruler of this name according to Krishnaswami Aiyangar) in fact facilitated the Turkish raid of 1311 by fleeing to Delhi when persecuted by his rival half-brother Vira Pandya, their father's favourite.[83]

It is quite clear that, if we are to keep a minimum chronological

---

[81] Yule, *Cathay and the way thither*, vol. III, pp. 68–9. For Wassaf see H. M. Elliot and J. Dowson (eds.) *The History of India as told by its own historians*, 7 vols. (London, 1867–77), vol. III, pp. 24–54, which includes the relevant extracts on India. Wassaf, 'the panegyrist' (in fact 'Abdallah b. Fazlallah), was the author of an important history of the Mongol rulers of his own times, from Kubilai Khan to Abu Saʿid (the *Tajziat al-amsar* . . . was initially composed *c.* 1300, but a further part extended up to 1328). Rashid al-Din (*c.* 1250–1318), one of Wassafs' patrons, was possibly of Jewish origin, and a doctor. After 1298 he became extremely powerful as *wazir* (minister) in the dangerous Persian courts of Ghazan Khan and his successors Oljeitu and Abu Saʿid, until the latter was convinced that he had to get rid of him. He served the Islamicized successors of the Ilkhans whom Marco Polo had also served, and in fact he might even have met Marco Polo when the latter returned to Europe with the Tartar princess who was eventually offered to Ghazan (*c.* 1293–4). His universal history, *Jamiʿ al-tavarikh*, or 'collection of histories', was very influential.

[82] Krishnaswami Aiyangar, *South India and her Muhammadan invaders* (Madras, 1921), pp. 54–8 and in *Cambridge History of India*, vol. III, pp. 483–6. See also Wassaf's account in Elliot and Dowson, *History of India*, vol. III, pp. 49, 50 and 52–4.

[83] Krishnaswami Aiyangar, *South India*, pp. 58–9.

coherence, the four kings described by Marco Polo in 1292–3 must have been Kulasekhara and his brothers, one of whom must have been known as Sundara Pandya Dewar, a name used by various succeeding members of the royal family and which for this reason gained a quasi-mythical significance.[84] Kulasekhara might have been the eldest, Marco Polo's 'Asciar' who was lord of the prosperous port of Kayal. Another of these brothers governed the area where Saint Thomas's tomb is located, near Mylapore further north. Rashid al-Din and Wassaf both define 'Dewar' as a native title of kingship meaning 'lord of wealth' or 'lord of empire', and like Marco Polo emphasize the existence of three or four brothers ruling successfully at this time. They also shed light on another important aspect of the political system: Muslim merchants and revenue-farmers acted as ministers and, since they dominated the importation of horses from the Persian Gulf, they could have almost total control in the Indian ports. Apparently Jamaluddin Ibrahim et-Thaibi, a powerful revenue-farmer of the Persian Gulf based at Kish, supplied horses to his brother Taki-uddin et-Thaibi, who was governor at various ports like Malifattan and possibly Kayal on behalf of the Pandyas. Wassaf, who seems to have based his account of India on the testimony of this Jamaluddin, insists that thousands of horses were annually paid for with the revenues from Indian temples and their attached prostitutes, and explains, with details strikingly similar to those given by Marco Polo, that the Indians do not know how to treat their horses and many die soon afterwards.

Marco Polo's emphasis on the importation of horses thus fits the picture perfectly well. The Pandyas may have derived a military advantage over their neighbours by means of their horses, but the crucial point is that through this trade they were also connected to a wider Islamicite commercial and cultural world. It is extremely likely that it was this Arab and Persian mediation which conditioned Marco Polo's understanding of local realities, because he would have been able to communicate with these merchants. On the other hand, he was hardly in a position to learn, or even wish to learn, any native Tamil.

Historical circumstance supports this hypothesis of a Muslim mediation. According to Wassaf, in 1292 the 'Dewar' died (obviously one of the Pandya brothers, and possibly one Jatavarman Sundara Pandya II who ruled 1276–92), and his brother and successor became even more

---

[84] Nilakanta Sastri nevertheless believed that the five Pandya brothers mentioned by Marco Polo should not be identified with any contemporaries, but instead an earlier generation which the traveller knew through legendary material. See K. A. Nilakanta Sastri, 'Marco Polo on India', *Oriente Poliano* (Rome, 1957), p. 114. What makes the matter difficult to elucidate is that Sundara, who represented a human incarnation of Shiva, was a common name in the dynasty. Some evidence suggests that in fact 'Sundara Pandya Dewar' was to remain for centuries a kind of mythical king in Tamil culture.

dependent on the Muslim minister Taki-uddin, who exercised power internationally and kept the lucrative monopoly of trade for Jamaluddin. This happened around the time that Marco Polo arrived from Sumatra with his depleted party of Tartars and Chinese. This was then not an entirely new encounter: there is evidence that the Pandya rulers were already known at the court of Kubilai Khan and even considered senders of tribute. There can be little doubt that it was through these Muslim entrepreneurs that the connection had been established, and it is not surprising that Marco Polo shared with them not only the experience, but to a large extent also the interpretation, of Southern India. The world of Asia that he travelled and described had been effectively encircled, inland by the Mongol conquerors from Persia to China, and in the seas by the Muslim merchants who, inevitably, cooperated with those Mongol rulers from Persia to China too. In this context Marco Polo was not a lonely westerner in a fragmented and exotic cultural world, but rather the participant in connected oriental mythologies concerning Asian diversity. This made South Indian kingship and culture, neither Muslim, nor Christian, nor Chinese, no less enigmatic, but it certainly marked paths through which it could be approached.

By contrasting different images of kingship in Marco Polo's book, we can seek to elucidate whether his account of the southern Indian rulers amounts to a significant interpretation. The Great Khan whom he served provides a perfect counterpoint. He is portrayed as a powerful and just ruler in ways that appeal to an idealized image of universal empire. Different from the Prester John, whose special quality consists of being a mighty Christian ruler in the East, Kubilai Khan is nevertheless an admirable lord to whom the Venetian (with no hints of city-state republicanism) faithfully serves. What makes him admirable is his capacity not only to conquer, but also to be civilized. One example illustrates this kind of 'enlightened despotism':

> The present Great Khan prohibited all gambling and cheating, which used to be more prevalent among the Cathayans than anywhere else in the world. To cure them from these habits he would say: 'I have acquired you by force of arms and all that you own is mine. So, if you gamble, you are gambling with my property'. He did not, however, use this as a pretext to take anything from them.[85]

Whilst the combination of power and justice could easily be an ideal shared transculturally, Marco Polo's interest lies in the fact that this ideal was not necessarily linked to a particular religious code which separated Christians, Muslims and 'idolaters'. Thus an aristocratic code of honour

---

[85] Polo in Ramusio, *Navigazioni e viaggi*, vol. III, p. 193.

such as that prevailing in Europe at the time informs the Khan's relationship with his 'Tartar barons', and it is precisely in these passages where Rustichello's use of Arthurian literary models is most obvious. But Marco Polo's idea of justice goes beyond this code of chivalry. Fragmented and undefined as his concept might be, it encompasses many particular instances which altogether configure a wide spectrum of attributes. As a just ruler the Khan gives alms to the poor, keeps food in store to meet crises of subsistence, waives taxes to provinces struck with calamity, protects traders from robbers, facilitates travel and communication, guarantees the authenticity of paper money, tolerates different religions, and is assisted by 'right' and 'reason' as well as historical fortune.[86]

In this context, South Indian rulers are also presented as just, and Marco Polo makes a point of expressing this with various examples which often relate to the protection of foreign merchants. These kings also have a concept of honour which is displayed in various ways, often different from those elsewhere. A king is a proper king because he wears jewels, even though he goes almost naked. King Asciar has 300 women, because 'he holds himself in greatest honour who keeps more women'.[87] But however just, honourable and rich these Indian rulers might be, their political system is by contrast to the Great Khan's fragmented and volatile, so that the Pandya brothers are always at each other's throats. Marco Polo had no direct access to Tamil ideological traditions, which can be interpreted as expressing a very fluid view of Hindu kingship. On the contrary, his analysis was based on the assumption (which I mentioned earlier) that just and effective power could be exercised independently from a particular religion. Thus, although the traveller's ability to penetrate into a particular political ethos was limited to a few historical observations, it is interesting that he stresses the moral authority of the mother of the Indian kings as crucial to the maintenance of peace between them: 'But yet I tell you that it cannot fail that when their mother shall be dead they make great quarrel together and that they destroy one the other.'[88] The queen of Mutifili is also presented as exercising a great moral authority, 'a very wise lady' who has ruled for forty years on behalf of her dead husband because

God never wishes her to take another lord since he whom she loved more than herself is dead . . . Moreover I tell you quite truly that this queen has well maintained her realm with very great justice and with

---

[86] Polo, *Milione*, pp. 66–100.
[87] Polo, *Description of the world*, vol. I, p. 412.
[88] Ibid., p. 413. The original significance of the story may be related to the fact that the Pandyas practised matrilineal succession.

great right . . . she is more loved and respected by her people than ever was lady or lord of that race.[89]

This portrayal of Rudramma Devi of Warangal may be contested, but it is typically expressive of Marco Polo's way of constructing a moral understanding of alien societies.[90] This understanding is based on a kind of syncretic assumption (Indian deities here simply appear as 'God') which, while excluding a deep knowledge of indigenous literature and thought, nevertheless expresses a subjective judgement that must have originated amongst Indians themselves. In so far as they are mythical, Marco Polo's Indian rulers are more local than European.

To conclude, Marco Polo portrayed South Indian kingship superficially but not entirely inaccurately. He was particulary successful in suggesting where the weaknesses were. Those wealthy kings whose wealth consisted of pearls, jewels and a royal treasury, who were however always fighting each other, and whose expensive cavalry needed to be shipped from abroad, in effect were soon to be prey to Turkish raids. As in the case of his treatment of religion, here Marco Polo was able to offer a considerable amount of information, occasionally in remarkable detail, by simply using a very direct popular language. His ethnological discourse was independent from any allegorical interpretation, far more complex than the inherited themes of traditional marvels, and in many ways free from any major ideological constraints. It was, in fact, not only open to capturing experience, but also able to express an open-ended cultural system: his narrative practice makes the idea of an absolute opposition between eastern and western cultures nonsensical.[91]

---

[89] Ibid., p. 395.

[90] Rudramma Devi was either the widow or the daughter of Ganapati, a raja of the Kakatiya dynasty (not even the *Cambridge History of India* agrees: compare vol. III, p. 115, by Wolseley Haig and p. 484 by Krishnaswami Aiyangar, following, respectively, Muslim and local records). She fortified Warangal following the plans of her husband/ father, but in 1294 (around two years after Marco Polo's return journey), when 'Ala-ud-din attacked and plundered Devagiri in the Deccan, she abdicated in favour of her grandson, knowing that the Turks were likely to attack soon after.

[91] I must here disagree with John Critchley's recent assertion that 'In general, Polo's account of India is what any of his medieval readers would have expected to read, and indeed what Polo himself would have expected to see. Since Roman times India had been known as a land of marvels' (Critchley, *Marco Polo's book*, p. 88). Critchley is actually very careful to raise relevant questions about authorship, audience and literary context. He rightly emphasizes the agreement of Marco Polo with a number of oriental stories which he could have picked up from Muslim merchants, but he does not correctly weight these 'literary borrowings' with an analysis of the local contexts in which they operated. Thus, his views of the Saint Thomas Christians and brahmins are made to depend on ancient rhetoric, rather than the more likely analogous local native rhetoric. Excessive emphasis on literary preconception equally mars Critchley's analysis of Polo's view of oriental kingship (ibid., p. 95). The magnificence of the oriental king was not simply a

LATE MEDIEVAL IDEOLOGIES OF TRAVEL AND THE SECULARIZATION OF PILGRIMAGE

Marco Polo was unique, but his report was not the only literary genre created during that moment of transition between the thirteenth and the fourteenth centuries, when the Latins who had just begun to travel regularly in Asia suddenly had to acknowledge that Islamicized Turks and Mongols made their progress more difficult. It has often been noticed that this retreat from the East of both merchants and missionaries coincided with the effects of what may be defined as the first European 'Counter-Reformation', led by those preaching orders whose task was to keep the new lay culture of the cities under the control of Christian morality no less than to fulfil missionary ideals of conversion and martyrdom. Travel other than pilgrimage had become a cultural possibility (travel as a mere physical activity had of course always existed in many forms). However, this possibility now belonged to a society torn by inner conflict. Ideologies of travel could not be innocent. In this context, Marco Polo's narrative can be profitably compared with those of two early fourteenth-century missionaries who also visited South India, Jordanus Catalani and Odoric of Pordenone.[92]

Jordanus Catalani, a Dominican (probably from Sévérac in southern France), emphasized the marvellous character of India in a very traditional mould: 'All is wonderful in this India, because it is indeed another world.'[93] His narrative was surprisingly non-analytical and only vaguely geographical. The *Marvels described* (*c.* 1329) were composed in Avignon between missions, and future prospects were probably more important than past experiences. Therefore, although the Latin treatise contains

European idea, static through the ages, but rather an image in the making, with shades and distinctions.

[92] Reasons of space preclude me from discussing here the interesting testimony of the Franciscan John of Marignolli, who in 1338 was sent as papal legate to the Great Khan to oversee the missions of Cathay (that is, the Catholic community successfully created by Montecorvino). On his return journey Marignolli visited Ceylon and spent a whole year (1348–9) in Quilon on the Malabar coast. His recollections of this journey informed in fascinating ways the biblical historical background to a chronicle of Bohemia which he wrote *c.* 1355 for Emperor Charles IV, whom he served as chaplain after returning to Europe. See Yule, *Cathay and the way thither*, vol. III, pp. 177–201 (for his career) and pp. 209–69 (for his recollections). Unlike Jordanus, Marignolli was at pains to dismiss the existence of monstrous races and other traditional marvels. He did discuss many empirical 'marvels', like the greatness of China. He visited the tomb of Saint Thomas in Mylapore and recognized Ceylon (with Adam's foot) as being physically close to paradise, but only on the basis of the possible agreement between local legend (Christian or not) and biblical authority. Marignolli was vain and could be fooled, but he had a remarkably enquiring mind.

[93] Catalani, *Mirabilia descripta*, p. 118: 'Mirabilia sunt omnia in ista Yndia; est enim, vere, unus alter mundus.'

many elements of empirical observation, these are overwhelmed by a peculiar religious vision in which the enumeration of strange fruits and animals easily leads to a statement such as that the devil talks to people at night.[94] In the friar's 'other world' there is precious little which can be constructed as an alternative civilization.

The early ethnographic systematicity of missionaries like Carpini and Rubruck was clearly not prominent amongst Marco Polo's immediate followers. In 1330 the Franciscan Odoric of Pordenone, however, produced an orderly narrative of his travels whose logical structure is at least descriptive.[95] This friar was, in fact, a rather peculiar case. A man of obscure origin (possibly the son of a Bohemian soldier) from Pordenone in Friuli, on his return to his convent at Padua after fourteen years in the East he was asked by his superior to dictate his account to another Franciscan, William of Solagna (1330), who wrote it down in Latin. Pordenone died a few months later. His fame as a saintly missionary spread almost immediately, and his narrative was often copied and read, but there is very little in his actual travels that clearly portrays the nature of his mission or even demonstrates his supposed success as preacher, aside from the fact that few chances are missed to stress the miraculous powers of Christian symbols and prayers.[96]

There can be no doubt that his account of South India, which he visited *c.* 1322, stands out when compared to those by travellers of the same period like Marco Polo (*c.* 1293) or Ibn Battūta (*c.* 1342) as rather misleading when offering specific information.[97] Whilst Pordenone does recognize the importance of the commercial traffic in cities like Quilon on the Malabar coast and describes the manner in which pepper is grown, he is very vague about the location of cities and their political contexts. He notes the presence of native Christians (which, exaggerating,

---

[94] Ibid.

[95] On Pordenone and his book see Yule, *Cathay and the way thither*, vol. II, including the original Latin and Italian versions; Wyngaert offers a better edition of the main Latin text in his *Sinica Franciscana.*

[96] The fact that miracles concerning Friar Odoric circulated as soon as he died makes it more than likely that the manuscript tradition was tampered with at a very early stage, in order to sustain a quick road to beatification.

[97] This does not mean that the Moroccan Ibn Battūta is always reliable – he sometimes altered the facts in order to justify his behaviour, for example in his account of his trip to 'Kawlam' (Quilon), in which he had to explain his failure to deliver a valuable present from the sultan of Delhi to the Chinese Khan (Ibn Battūta, *A través del Islam*, pp. 655–9). Ibn Battūta's aims were not merely descriptive: whilst Marco Polo disappeared behind his geographical descriptions in order to reveal a network of human and natural diversities, Ibn Battūta's travels incorporated geographical observations into the general structure of an extended pilgrimage within Islam, a pilgrimage of knowledge (*talab al-'ilim*) within a community of religious learning of which he was an adventurous protagonist. But he was still much more precise than Pordenone.

he pits in a continuous struggle against the local Jews) but says nothing about the more prominent Muslims, despite the fact that many of his placenames reveal an Arabic mediation. He is certainly much more condemnatory in his treatment of idolatry than Marco Polo, and reveals none of his naturalistic relativism. While in his description of 'Coilum' (Quilon) the latter defined the differences in natural products between the Malabar coast and Europe as something positive ('they have all things different from ours and they are more beautiful and better') and offered a climatic explanation ('this comes to pass through the great heat which is the rule there'),[98] the emphasis of Pordenone's description of the same city is clearly negative: he equates marvellous customs with beastly and abominable practices (a judgement which in fact Marco Polo reserved for the savage peoples of Sumatra) and imagines non-existing human sacrifices:

Here all the people go naked, except for a cloth which they wear just to cover their nakedness, tied behind. All the people of this country worship the ox for their God and do not eat his flesh for they say that he is, as it were, a sacred creature. Six years they make him work for them and the seventh they give him rest in the common. And they observe the following abominable rite. Every morning they take two basins of gold or silver and when the ox is brought from the stall they put these under him and catch his urine in one, and his dung in the other. With the urine they wash their faces, and the dung they put over themselves . . . and they consider themselves to be sanctified for the day. This the common people do, but also the king and queen. Similarly, they worship another idol which is half man and half ox, and this idol answers questions out of his mouth, and often demands the blood of forty virgins to be given to it, for men ands women there vow their sons and daughters to that idol, just as here they vow to place them in some religious order. And many die in this way.[99] And many other things are done by that people which it would be an abomination even to write or to hear of.[100]

---

[98] Polo, *Description of the world*, vol. I, p. 415.

[99] Many Hindu worshippers offered young girls for temple service which included a form of 'religious' prostitution, and their virginity may have been taken in a public ritual, but the idea that their lives were sacrificed is mistaken.

[100] After this Pordenone goes on to describe *sati*. Yule, *Cathay and the way thither*, vol. II, pp. 295–6 (Latin) and pp. 342–3 (Italian Palatino). I have combined both versions, since they can all be considered authentic. The Italian manuscripts are in fact briefer than the main Latin recension and seem to represent a popularized account for a lay public. They have been lately published: Odorico da Pordenone, *Memoriale toscano. Viaggio in India e Cina (1318–30) di Odorico da Pordenone*, ed. by L. Monaco (Alessandria, 1990). Yule, *Cathay and the way thither*, vol. II, pp. 27–30, argued that these manuscripts were genuine and represented an early version of the narrative,

Pordenone was obviously fascinated by the idolatrous religion of the local people, reflecting the conventional interest for devilish monstrosities in non-Christian lands which we have already encountered with Jordanus Catalani. In this way he seems to have addressed the expectations of his contemporaries with little of his own to challenge them.

After the comparison Marco Polo stands out even more clearly as an exceptional author. Each travel account can be seen as a bridge between an experience of cultural difference and the demands of distinct audiences, but Marco Polo was unique in addressing the most complex audience from the widest experience. He must be seen not as a European in Asia who later reports to his own people, but rather as a man whose unique contribution – a merchant's account of human diversity – was based on a considerable experience of sharing stories as well as circumstances with a wide range of oriental peoples. Furthermore, the very separation of lay and clerical discourses in the Latin West was an essential part of its cultural history. By offering a narrative that stood next to the tradition of missionary writers, a narrative that circulated in vernacular languages as well as in Latin, Marco Polo made a very important contribution to this duality. The voice of a traveller that was neither the voice of pilgrimage or mission nor even crusade and chivalry was now part of the educational horizon of the aristocracy of the Latin West.

The implications of this new educational horizon are not easy to measure, but the task is not impossible either. The production of travel accounts between 1250 and 1350 seems to have been followed by a relative stagnation of the genre during the following century, which certainly affected the role of this kind of literature within the late medieval cultural system. It would, however, be misleading to simply analyse this process as a period of retreat, to be followed by new attitudes in the Renaissance. The growth of vernacular discourses did not stop after the Black Death, and it was in the context of the moral crisis of this period that some of the implications of the new medieval genres and institutions became more evident as, for instance, the case of John Mandeville testifies. It is curious that this fictitious account can also be seen as the most influential synthesis of the renewed clerical tradition of travel writing of the previous century, albeit now written in the vernacular and as a lay discourse. It was produced precisely when direct contacts with the East virtually stopped. This new text also corresponds with a profound change in the reading habits of Europeans, in particular

delivered by Pordenone on his way to Padua (where he then dictated a fuller account to William of Solagna, who wrote it in Latin, obviously for a clerical readership interested in the missions).

with the shift from dictating and listening to reading and writing.[101] The contrast is clear between Marco Polo's book, composed orally with Rustichello in order to be read aloud to lords and citizens, and Mandeville's creation, written in a library in order to be read privately.[102] This change was not without consequences, because the traditional means for sustaining a cultural consensus could now be circumvented, and it helps us understand why Marco Polo's tolerance of cultural diversity was in fact born out of the acceptance of collective practices, while Mandeville's – based on an idea of rational virtue – was more abstract, ideological and reformist.

Any long-term interpretation of medieval travel literature needs to address the substitution of the traditional Christian paradigm of religious pilgrimage for a new ideology of travel in which secular wisdom and practical learning took its place. The complexity of the process is quite apparent in the late Middle Ages, when competing ideologies of travel articulated the changing relationship between lay and clerical identities in the Latin West.[103] In effect attitudes to travel were intensely affected by the crisis of the dominant religious paradigm of pilgrimage, including the 'armed pilgrimage' of the crusades. The tension between the ethos of the secular aristocracy and the normative definitions of the Church was endemic in European culture, and even the chivalric romance had been subjected to a religious appropriation throughout the thirteenth century, with the quest for the Holy Grail often standing as a powerful allegory for salvation. But the religious paradigm was by no means always successful in its adaptation to new circumstances. The very emergence of Mandeville's narrative as a self-questioning, composite pilgrimage recast so as to reach the doors of paradise can be seen as a response to the failure of successive crusades throughout the previous century.

Some of the most original writers of the generation which received Marco Polo at the turn of the fourteenth century – men like Dante and the Majorcan Ramon Llull – explored the possibilities of religious allegory in the face of a fundamental system of dualities separating not only Christian and classical themes and figures, but also traditional and new genres, Latin and vernacular languages, clerical and lay discourses. They often had recourse to allegorical travel in their quest (poetic, philosophical and even mystical) for a coherent religious vision. Dante's

---

[101] See P. Saenger, 'Manières de lire médiévales', in H.-J. Martin and R. Chartier (eds.) *Histoire de l'édition française* (Paris, 1983–7), vol. I: *Le livre conquerant, du Moyen Age au milieu du XVIIe siècle*, pp. 131–41.

[102] Of course, late medieval manuscripts of Marco Polo were also read in private, and were for this reason also illuminated, but this was not the book's original form of circulation.

[103] I develop this argument in some further detail in the collaborative introduction to Elsner and Rubiés (eds.) *Voyages and visions*, pp. 29–46.

account of the death of Ulysses in the *Comedy* is a significant example. Ulysses sails to the most distant parts beyond the pillars of Hercules, reaching eventually Mount Purgatory.[104] At its sight the hero sinks with his crew, as God commands. What I find most interesting about this vision is the ambiguity that surrounds it. Whilst there is no doubt about what Ulysses stands for – an insatiable inward hunger for knowledge and new experiences, which leads him to impiously abandon his family and country of origin and to break the boundaries of fixed divine order – there is certainly a paradox in the eternal condemnation of a character who explicitly incarnates man's desire to stand above the brute beasts through the pursuit of knowledge and virtue.

While Dante condemned the worldly traveller, the Christian apologist and mystic Ramon Llull (1232–1316) recreated the image of the religious seeker in his various novels and treatises, beyond the obvious limits of traditional pilgrimage. For example, the protagonist of his encyclopaedic novel *Book of marvels* (Paris, 1285) was defined by his vocation to travel, in order to find out about the marvels of the world and recount them 'in the courts of princes and prelates, in towns, castles, cities, deserts, monasteries and all other inhabited places'.[105] The traveller's aim was to know God, and to make others know Him. Whilst internally the hero's journey was a moral and spiritual quest, externally it sought to encompass a vision of natural reality. It also found a practical expression in the missionary ideal.

However, in this secret dialogue of cultural models it was ultimately the lay figures who offered a lasting alternative. The worldly traveller sent to hell in 1300 survived in the guise of a secularized chivalric hero, and would return triumphant two centuries later as a model for imitation through the mediation of humanist educational concerns. Thus Giovanni Pontano in his treatise *The Prince*, dedicated to Alfonso duke of Calabria and published in Naples in 1490, recalled Homer's famous presentation of Ulysses as a man *qui mores hominum moltorum vidit et urbes* in support of his belief that kings needed a wide experience of the world.[106] This emphasis on travel could of course be inspired by classical ideas about

---

[104] Dante, *The Divine Comedy. Inferno*, trans. and ed. by J. D. Sinclair (New York, 1939), pp. 324–6. Dante knew Ulysses through Latin sources rather than Homer directly.

[105] Ramon Llull, *Llibre de meravelles*, ed. by M. Gustà and J. Molas (Barcelona, 1980), p. 352. At the end of the novel (pp. 353–4), Felix the seeker of marvels (who is now also a friar) becomes in fact an institution: the individual might die, but not his mission. The passage is meant to be autobiographical. Possibly the best general introduction to Llull's life and thought in English is A. Bonner (ed.) *Selected works of Ramon Llull*, 2 vols. (Princeton, 1985).

[106] In E. Garin (ed.) *Prosatori latini del quattrocento*, in *La letteratura Italiana. Storia e testi*, vol. XIII (Milan and Naples, 1952), pp. 1052–4.

knowledge (for instance Polybius had insisted that the good historian not only looks in archives, but must also learn about peoples and places through his own experience and activity) but in the following centuries, so full of sensational news, this topos reached an unprecedented importance.[107] By 1561 the Venetian popularizer Francesco Sansovino could write in the introduction to a collection of geographical relations that 'Homer, wanting to represent a most excellent and astute man in the things of the world, introduced Ulysses, not a philosopher because of his studies, but rather a practical man for having seen many peoples and many customs, from which activity it is certain that men learn more in less time than from reading a lot.'[108] Not only was the growth and consolidation of the Renaissance genre of empirical geography a vindication of Marco Polo, but in fact the very rhetoric of scientific knowledge which followed from it was based on the primacy of travel over the textual tradition.

The growing importance of such lay models indicates clearly enough why late medieval travel literature did not fall into an ideological vacuum, but does not settle the question of why the world of exceptional men like Polo, Llull and Dante eventually became the more crowded one of sixteenth-century merchant-travellers, missionaries and humanists. Again, the issue is not why various kinds of people travelled, which of course responded to a complex set of economic and political conditions that can be generally summed up with the image of an expanding Europe. Rather, one must ask why writing about foreign lands increasingly became also a practice, without assuming that a particular kind of literature naturally follows a particular kind of experience. The discourses of travel literature needed to rely, like all others, on a context of cultural traditions and practices.

Overall, the humanist genres were crucial by widening the range of legitimate moral and educational concerns and by giving shape to a discourse of civility and *humanitas* that looked beyond Christian models. However, in intellectual terms the crucial process was already well laid out after the thirteenth century with the recognition that the natural world had an autonomous rationality – not one opposed to the Christian revelation, but one which was accessible outside it, in a way that the

[107] Polybius discusses this theme in the twelfth book of his *Histories*, in his polemic against his fellow historian Timaeus, whom he accused of being a bookworm. Inevitably, he quotes the same verses from Homer. Of course Polybius himself took pride in his activities as soldier and diplomat, between the worlds of Greece and Rome. The *Histories* were recovered, translated and published by the Italian humanists in the fifteenth century, although the circulation of this particular book is less certain.

[108] Francesco Sansovino, *Del governo de i regni et delle republiche così antiche come moderne* (Venice, 1561), 'A lettori'.

modern 'gentile' nations of 'India' could comprehend no less than the pre-Christian gentile philosophers of the classical tradition. The development of a new sphere of universal discourse about human systems of laws and customs beyond the narrow possibilities offered by the Christian tradition of revealed books indeed required a new principle of legitimation and understanding. This was the role fulfilled by the ideas of human history and human nature, and, more specifically, by new interpretations of Aristotle's natural law. When, at the beginning of the sixteenth century, there was an enormous inflow of original travel descriptions, the intellectual response of European scholars and philosophers essentially followed this late medieval strategy. This explains for instance the continuity between Thomas Aquinas, Francisco de Vitoria and Hugo Grotius.

The result was that a whole area of discourse grew between providentialism and moral particularism, and enabled travel literature to have a long-term impact. Marco Polo, representative of the new urban society of the thirteenth century and its trading activities, had broken away from a purely sacred contemplation of the marvels of the world. He was still, essentially, a practical man, a merchant who had had the unusual opportunity of travelling far into the East and of entering the service of a foreign prince.[109] Ignoring any religious framework other than the superficial fact that his father and uncle had carried embassies between Kubilai Khan and the Pope, which served them as both justification and safe conduct, Marco Polo offered information potentially of interest to more people than just merchants and crusaders. Obviously the book could be read as an entertaining story, and Rustichello helped create the kind of geographical report that would fulfil the expectations of an aristocratic audience (this attempt to reach a wider audience, not Marco Polo's identity as anything other than a well-travelled merchant with lots of stories to tell, is what makes his report so different from Pegolotti's

---

[109] Leonardo Olschki, eager to provide a coherent interpretation of Marco Polo which emphasizes his qualities as an observer of men and institutions, perhaps overestimated the extent to which he had become something other than a merchant: 'né mercante né missionario, e meno di tutto un avventuriero . . . Marco ebbe un po' dell'uno e un po' dell'altro, adattandosi a essere empiricamente esperto in ogni altra attività, senza particolare vocazione, senza istruzione professionale e senza specifici còmpiti' (Olschki, *l'Asia di Marco Polo*, p. 119). The point is also made by Jacques Heers (*Marco Polo*, pp. 165–85). I find it difficult to see how Marco Polo could have failed to adopt an identity as a Latin merchant abroad by following the steps of his father and uncle, who certainly gave him a thorough education on the field. Carrying a letter from the Pope promising missionary friars does not, of course, make any medieval merchant himself a missionary. Although while in China Marco Polo certainly acted as a special agent, which broadened his experience and trained him as an observer, back in Europe he resumed a conventional identity as merchant, with modest success (see again Heers, *Marco Polo*, pp. 24–39).

Pratica della mercatura, by shifting the contents from routes, prices and products to human geography). It is not coincidental that the introductory passage written by Rustichello to the merchant's book was actually lifted from his own compilation of Arthurian romances.[110] In this introduction, a desire to know was the accepted motivation of the various listeners and readers of the travels, lords and bourgeois patricians alike, and no obvious explanation was given for why people should want to know.[111] As we have seen, miracles were reported among customs and other remarkable observations, but they did not create a separate ethnographic focus which could serve a religious purpose. In fact, it was conceivable to collect information not just because it was useful, something that the Church in the end always had to accept as legitimate, but simply because it satisfied curiosity.

There was now a danger that the completion of the picture of the human world by the incorporation of new details about peoples belonging to a non-biblical tradition would mean that the old schemes of classification had to be substantially changed. And yet the mere problem of classification was easy to solve because the Christian tradition had some vaguely defined areas of secular discourse (especially in the vernacular languages) into which the new information could be incorporated without touching the rest. In the same way that Aristotle could be made compatible with Christian theology, ancient India and contemporary Cathay could be given a place in the geographic and ethnographic map of the known world. The idea is captured by Aquinas' famous expression: *Gratia non tollit naturam sed perficit*.[112] The rational understanding of the natural world could expand and even change and still

---

[110] The relationship between the *Divisament dou monde* and a late thirteenth-century chivalric compilation attributed to Rustichello of Pisa (ms. fr. 1463 at the Bibliothèque Nationale, Paris) was discussed by Benedetto: Polo, *Milione*, pp. xiii–xxviii. Benedetto argues that in fact Rustichello simply copied a chaotic collection of manuscripts from his patron, Prince Edward of England, possibly translating the texts into the same Franco-Italian language which he later employed when writing Marco Polo's book. It seems that he had access to the Arthurian compilation in the context of Prince Edward's crusade of 1271, possibly in Sicily or Outremer (see, however, Critchley, *Marco Polo's book*, pp. 4–9). By comparing the manuscripts, Benedetto concludes that Rustichello's intervention in the creation of Marco Polo's narrative was mainly rhetorical and did not substantially affect its contents.

[111] See Critchley, *Marco Polo's book*, p. 3. Compare the expression 'Seignors enperaor et rois, dux et marquois, cueus, chevaliers et borgiois, *et toutes gens que voles savoir les deverses jenerasions des homes et les deversetés des deverses regions dou monde*, si prenés cestui livre et le faites lire' with the introduction to the Arthurian compilation: 'Seigneur emperaor et rois et princes et dux et quenz et baronz, civalier et vauvassor et borgiois et tous les peudome de ce monde *que avés talenz de delitier voz en romainz*, ci prenés ceste, et le faites lire de chief en chef' (as given by Benedetto, but italics mine).

[112] Thomas Aquinas, *Selected political writings*, ed. by A. P. d'Entreves (Oxford, 1959), p. xiii.

culminate in faith in God. The serious challenge came, however, from the secularized view of the world. Increasing trust in the expanded areas of discourse could lead to a more critical and carefree stand *vis-à-vis* the traditional definition of a revealed centre which was both theological and historical–geographical. Although Marco Polo did not compel his audience to see a natural world of unpredictable diversity *instead of* a divine creation both structured and understood in the detail, he provided (as did contemporary historians, doctors and astronomers who reported new observations) the material that could be used by those who were making that step. The traveller's 'marvels' of the world were still diversities, objects of contemplation, but the question was whether they expressed a meaning and an order, and, more specifically, whether they were evidence of a Christian moral and eschatological order. This intellectual tension found expression in the need to make faith more abstract, more privately self-disciplined.

This is what explains the necessity of a book such as Mandeville's travels, which dominated the scene from its appearance in the second half of the fourteenth century all the way to the sixteenth century. Mandeville's compilation, while creative in its literary techniques and reformist in its moral concerns, also represented a traditional appropriation of the new genre. This was an attempt to bring back theological coherence to the image of a world that was empirically diverse and could be traversed from end to end, and to restore a dimension of pilgrimage to the possibility of secular travel.

It was only the Venetian Ramusio, a travel editor with humanist concerns, who in the preface to his edition of Marco Polo most definitely enthroned the medieval account as a model of novel and accurate observation – indeed the key to improving the science of geography. His enthusiasm for Marco Polo was not entirely devoid of Venetian patriotism, but it also responded to a typically humanist concern for establishing a continuity between old and new observations. Marco Polo's descriptions, for so long taken as mere fables, could now be vindicated as a contribution to science in an age of obscurity.[113] Even when he sounded fabulous, the medieval merchant (for Ramusio, a 'gentiluomo') stood in a line that stretched from Herodotus, Pliny and Strabo to Columbus and Cortés. It is not coincidental that at the same time, with

---

[113] He writes: 'veramente è cosa meravegliosa a considerare la grandezza del viaggio . . . e oltra de questo, come il predetto gentiluomo sapesse così ordinadamente scrivere ciò che vide, essendo pochi uomini di quella sua età intelligenti de cotal dottrina, ed egli allevato tanto tempo appresso quella rozza nazione de'Tartari, senza alcuna accommodata maniera di scrivere'. Ramusio, *Navigazione e viaggi*, vol. III, p. 22 (preface to 'I viaggi di Marco Polo').

his extremely important collection, Ramusio consolidated the genre of travel writing within the high culture of the Renaissance.

Early in the Middle Ages Augustine had defined the condition of the Christian in the world as that of a pilgrim travelling towards the city of God. Many later medieval thinkers, eager to rationalize this faith, sought to define a form of natural theology that derived the idea of obedience to God from the understanding of the order of the universe. In Aquinas the rational and the natural had become the medium through which human law, both the general 'ius gentium' and the particular 'ius civile', could partake with divine law despite their being beyond the explicit contents of the Revelation. The moral challenge was that of the rationality of diversity. The cultural challenge, more insidious, was the theological justification of the new spheres of discourse, created above all through the new Aristotelian and humanist models. In the transition from the Latin Middle Ages to the Renaissance, travel accounts with ethnographic material suddenly emerged as a well-established genre and provided a ground on which these challenges would have to be met.

3. *Establishing lay science: the merchant and the humanist*

THE TRAVELLER IN ITALY: A FLORENTINE ENCOUNTER

The concern for establishing the centre of the world in a Christian perspective had strongly influenced the geographical literature of the European Middle Ages. This was, to a great extent, the result of the clerical control over culture. The starting point for a medieval traveller was the figure of the pilgrim, and it still remained so with the narrative of John Mandeville. However, the new genres of the expansion of Europe in the Renaissance tended to develop more like Marco Polo's book of marvels than Mandeville's natural-Christian synthesis. After the fifteenth century, the pilgrim lost ground steadily to more secularized travellers – to the practical reporter with specific aims, and eventually to a first-person curious observer free from any obvious external sources of authority. This transition did not come as a direct result of the discourse created by merchants living in the East like Marco Polo and Nicolò Conti, but rather through the legitimizing power of a new kind of attitude among the elite.

The fifteenth-century report given by the Venetian merchant Nicolò Conti (*c.* 1385–1469) was an important contribution to this process, and exemplifies the mechanism through which a non-clerical erudite culture and travel literature became connected. It is significant that Conti did not write an account of his travels in Asia on his own initiative, but was instead requested to describe his journey to Pope Eugene IV's secretary, the humanist Poggio Bracciolini (1380–1459). In responding to an external prompt and relying on the skills of a more professional writer, Conti was not actually departing from a medieval pattern, since in the previous two centuries it had been usual for travellers, like Marco Polo, Prince Hayton from Armenia, Friar Odoric of Pordenone, or the Moroccan Ibn Battūta, to dictate their notes and recollections to writers

85

with a specialized knowledge of literary conventions. However, Poggio Bracciolini was also, as a prominent humanist, a leading participant in a profound cultural transformation. It is thus the unique quality of his mediator, and the unique cultural context that he represented, which separates Conti from Marco Polo. Whilst Conti's travel narrative touches on themes common among late medieval authors, and to a great extent reproduces a standard set of attitudes, its subjection to the critical scrutiny of a humanist effectively points towards a new pattern that was to dominate the sixteenth century: namely, the dialogue between an unprecedented 'experience of otherness' in a context of discovery and colonization, and the concerns of European intellectuals educated in a thoroughly expanded and revised classical inheritance.

From the end of the thirteenth century, the presence of a number of Genoese and Venetian merchants attempting risky but highly profitable business in the East is attested in various documentary references. It was nevertheless exceptional for these travellers to write and circulate a full account, as in the case of Marco Polo. Their presence was not the result of a trading network with political backing, as was often the case in the Eastern Mediterranean, but rather of the isolated efforts of a few families who knew that good business consisted in gaining a direct access to special markets that would not be easily attainable to other competitors. Information was valuable and often not publicized.

Conti's family had been long established in the East, and he began his career as a young agent in Egypt and Syria. Moved by economic interest he travelled in Asia for more than thirty-five years, in the course of which he married and had children. On his way back to Europe, and while in Mecca, Conti was forced to convert in order to save his life and that of his family. It was the current practice of adventurous European merchants to adapt to the local rules of dress and language in order to avoid conflicts with political authorities, but only in the extreme cases of intolerance, or when they decided to settle abroad, did they change religion and private customs as well. Relationships with Muslims were nevertheless always potentially violent, because a pervasive tradition of religious opposition could easily fuel territorial and economic rivalries. Thus, although on his return Conti had patiently secured a safe conduct from the sultan of Egypt, he was nevertheless forced to become a renegade (back in Europe he claimed that in fact there had been an attempt to rob him, and that he accepted conversion in order to protect his family). Afterwards Conti seems to have profited from his new condition for a few years, since he was made 'trujaman' (interpreter) in Cairo. However, when four years later, in 1441, he came back to Italy in the company of oriental representatives to the council of Florence, he went straight to the Pope, hoping to be absolved and recover his place in Venetian life. Successful in his demand, Conti was to settle down as procurator of the Church of San Francesco and as a magistrate and ambassador for his native city.[1]

Nicolò Conti in fact returned at a delicate moment in the history of Latin Christendom, marked by last-minute efforts to re-unite the Latin and Eastern Churches in the face of the Turkish advance against the Greek empire, and also by a cultural revolution which affected the sources of Western identity, both religious and political. The council of Florence (1439) marked one of the clearest moments of interaction between new philological and antiquarian concerns, on the one hand, and the efforts of the Papacy to re-establish itself as the leading institution (after a long schism) for a more coherent and universal Christendom.[2] The peculiarity of the Florentine context, a republic dominated by merchant-bankers and, in particular in this period, by Cosimo Medici, can hardly be overestimated in the European perspective, because the lay culture of the humanists and their direct encounter with eastern philosophy and religion grew outside the traditional frame of royal or even aristocratic politics. In this sense the interdependence between the new Roman curia and the Florentine merchant-bankers is only an apparent paradox, and in fact goes a long way towards explaining the long-term influence of the new secular discourses, artistic, moral or scientific. Although successive popes would try to extend religious control over the new cultural forms, they would not retract from the often scandalous secularization of their Roman political structures. And while the Medici would become more aristocratic with time, this would help extend their cultural model all over Italy and beyond, rather than simply destroy it in Florence.

---

[1] For Conti's life, see Lach, *Asia in the making of Europe*, vol. I, pp. 59–60; E. Cochrane, *Historians and historiography in the Italian Renaissance* (Chicago, 1981), p. 324; J. Vives Gatell, 'Andanças e viajes de un hidalgo Español', article written originally in 1938 and reprinted in Pero Tafur, *Andanças e viajes de Pero Tafur*, ed. by F. López Estrada (Barcelona, 1982), especially pp. 62–6. Poggio and the Spanish traveller Pero Tafur offer different accounts of Conti's life. I have complemented Poggio with Tafur, considering the latter's account reliable on this point (as also argued by Vives Gatell – see note 7 below).

[2] The council was mainly devoted to convincing the Greek representatives to accept papal authority and Latin doctrine, and its short-term success depended on the willingness of the Emperor John VIII Paleologus to cast his lot with the West, combined with the admiration that Greek scholars began to feel for western humanism. Although this re-union was achieved in 1439, afterwards it did not meet with the acceptance of the majority of the Greeks. Meanwhile Eugene IV also reached agreements with representatives from the Armenian (1439), Coptic (1443) and Nestorian (1444) churches. Conti arrived during this second phase.

The humanist skills that the Papacy increasingly enlisted in its crusading plans are illustrated by the fact that Eugene IV, still occupied with the council of Florence, absolved Conti from his forced conversion to Islam, but also asked him to recount his travels to his own secretary. From Poggio's account, which he composed in Latin as part of his miscellaneous work *De varietate fortunae*, we can reconstruct the dialogue that took place between an experienced merchant of patrician origin trying to justify his apparent religious lapse and a learned and inquiring humanist able to direct his questions towards new areas of knowledge within a rapidly changing Latin cultural tradition.[3]

This interview with Poggio was not, however, the only medium through which Conti's travels were received into Europe. The Andalusian hidalgo Pero Tafur, also a traveller, claimed in his *Andanças e viajes* to have met Conti at the monastery of Mount Sinai in 1437.[4] While his account of Conti's experience has been described as being 'as brazen a piece of leg-pulling as can be imagined',[5] Poggio's has been hailed as 'the most lucid account of Indian manners and customs to be prepared by a European since Megasthenes'.[6] The denigration of Pero Tafur as unreliable is too simplistic – even at the factual level his report contains information (for instance, on the biography of Conti) which can be considered more complete than Poggio's. It was written in different conditions, and it belongs to a different genre.[7] There is still, of course, a problem of truth and representation, which we shall tackle later. Leaving

---

[3] The autograph of Poggio's *De varietate fortunae*, with his own corrections, is kept in the Biblioteca Riccardiana in Florence, ms. 871. For the early editions of this work see O. Merisalo, 'Le prime edizioni stampate del De Varietate Fortunae di Poggio Bracciolini', *Arctos. Acta Philologica Fennica*, 19 (1985): 81–102; and 20 (1986): 101–29.

[4] Tafur, *Andanças*, p. 95.

[5] Penrose, *Travel and discovery in the Renaissance*, p. 23.

[6] Lach, *Asia*, vol. I, p. 61.

[7] This problem is discussed by Vives Gatell in 'Andanças e viajes', 57–74. When the two sources contradict each other it is necessary to use discretion in interpreting them, rather than automatically giving the primacy to one or the other. Whilst Poggio states that Conti travelled in India for twenty-five years, Pero Tafur suggests a date of departure before the time of the death of Timur (1405), implying that the travels lasted at least thirty-five years (they met at Mount Sinai in 1437, and Conti would not reach Italy until 1441). In Tafur's account Conti even states that 'quarenta años a que bivo en la India con grant deseo de bolver a mi tierra' (Tafur, *Andanças*, pp. 96–7). Tafur's account is coherent in the sense that Conti's outward passage is said to have been facilitated by the stability brought by Timur's power in central Asia. It is therefore plausible to regard Poggio's isolated figure of twenty-five years as either a mistake or, more likely, as a statement referring to a particular period of Conti's travels spent in the eastern parts of 'India'. The important fact here is not that Poggio is, generally speaking, a more critical (and thus more reliable) writer than Tafur, but rather that they could both be accurate or not according to specific interests. It is easy to see that Poggio has little interest in Conti's life, and devotes most attention to obtaining a clear image of Indian society.

aside momentarily the question of whether Pero Tafur was lying or being lied to, it is in any case revealing that the secretary of the Pope provides the most secularized discourse. The two different versions of Conti's travels thus give us a unique chance to measure the actual weight of humanist skills and interests in the reception and transmission of a merchant's observations. This is the more so because Poggio's composition became one of the most widely read first-hand accounts of the East since Marco Polo.

The character of Poggio's *De varietate fortunae*, composed between 1431 and 1448, illustrates the intellectual concerns which made him one of the leading humanists of his time. The work started with an antiquarian reconstruction of the ruins of Rome that served as testimony to the destruction brought about by time. Two more sections went on to discuss events surrounding the recent pontificate of Martin V, which illustrated the changing face of Fortune; finally, Poggio added Nicolò Conti's account of distant India. There is no original philosophical principle holding together these different pieces other than a rather vague idea about the diversity and changes of Fortune through time and place.[8] This idea, on the other hand, is given a concrete form through antiquarian, historical and geographical enquiries. What is significant is that the work leads to research into historical particulars rather than towards religious consolation or traditional moral advice. Poggio's activities searching and publishing Greek and Latin manuscripts expressed a similar attitude, positivist rather than philosophical. In his violent debates of 1452 against Lorenzo Valla, Poggio took up the pious defence of classical authority against the dangers of philological criticism, but in reality the main emphasis of his works was on the actual evidence of human behaviour and its moral implications. This secular and often relativistic morality did not point towards the reform of traditional religion, but rather sought to flourish in a parallel space. (Not surprisingly, Poggio's licentious and anti-clerical writings made him popular, while Valla's more authoritative challenge to the ignorance of many in the Church got him into trouble – he was trespassing.)[9] Thus Poggio's

---

[8] See, however, the interpretation of Ouiti Merisalo in his critical edition of Poggio Bracciolini, *De varietate fortunae*, ed. by O. Merisalo (Helsinki, 1993), who argues that the different books articulate an opposition between the cruelty of contemporary Christian princes, as illustrated in the history of the recent popes, and the virtues displayed by distant worlds in time and space. I remain unconvinced, because the idea that popes can be hit by Fortune too, on account of their incompetence (in humanist idiom, their lack of proper virtue), does not really depend on a coherent idealization of pagan kings which, in reality, we would be pushed hard to find.

[9] The dispute between Poggio and Valla indicates the boundaries of Poggio's humanism. There was of course an important element of personal animosity in Poggio's successive invectives and in Valla's corresponding answers, which went back to the moment when

effort of cultural recovery led to a lay morality based on an awareness of change and variation. Both history and geography played a crucial role in defining these new humanist perspectives.[10]

Poggio's interest in Conti finds its natural cultural context in the circulation of Ptolemy's *Geography* among the Florentine humanists of his time – that is, the Byzantine geography derived from Ptolemy, brought from Greece by Manuel Chrisoloras after 1397, and translated into Latin a few years later.[11] It was also through the 1440s, while Poggio finished his *De varietate fortunae*, that Ciriaco d'Ancona, self-appointed traveller and antiquarian in Greece and Egypt, was having the *Geography* of Strabo copied in Constantinople.[12] This crucial work would also soon be translated into Latin by Guarino de Verona, immediately after the fall of Constantinople in 1453. Although many of the skills that went into this effort of recovery and translation had developed within Florentine humanist circles, it was the Papacy which, having restored its own position in Rome during the contested pontificates of Martin V (1417–31) and Eugene IV (1431–47), could give a coherent ideological direction to a new Renaissance cosmography. This is most apparent in the trajectory of Aeneas Sylvius Piccolomini, who as Pius II (1458–64) became the obvious model of a humanist pope.[13] His own *Historia rerum*

Poggio, as early as 1430, had blocked Valla's entrance into the Roman curia, apparently out of jealousy for a young arrogant competitor with superior philological skills. But beyond personal resentment one can also distinguish a difference between Valla's desire to extend philological criticism to the Bible, with all its theological consequences, and Poggio's more traditional piety. While for Valla this religious dimension, a clear precedent to Erasmian humanism, was a deeply held conviction, Poggio's activities and attitudes were notoriously secular. On Valla and the polemic see G. di Napoli, *Lorenzo Valla. Filosofia e religione nell'umanesimo Italiano* (Rome, 1971), especially pp. 30–41.

[10] On Poggio Bracciolini there is a distinct lack of monographic studies, especially considering that he is commonly referred to as one of the leading fifteenth-century humanists. See, however, R. Fubini, 'Il "teatro del mondo" nelle prospettive morali e storico-politiche di Poggio Bracciolini', in *Poggio Bracciolini 1380–1980* (Florence, 1982), pp. 1–135; F. Krantz, 'Between Bruni and Machiavelli: history, law and historicism in Poggio Bracciolini', in P. Mack and M. Jacob (eds.) *Politics and Culture in early modern Europe* (Cambridge, 1987), pp. 119–51. See also the introduction by M. Ciccuto to Poggio Bracciolini, *Facezie*, ed. by M. Ciccuto (Milan, 1994). The complete works, all in Latin, are collected in Poggio, *Opera omnia*, 4 vols. (Turin, 1964–9).

[11] On the geographical interests of the fifteenth-century humanists, and in particular those in Florence, there now exists the catalogue prepared by S. Gentile, *Firenze e la scoperta dell'America. Umanesimo e geografia nel '400 Fiorentino* (Florence, 1992), which constitutes a superb guide.

[12] Ibid., pp. 183–5. On the travels of the rather peculiar Ciriaco d'Ancona and his antiquarian interests see also R. Weiss, 'Ciriaco d'Ancona in Oriente', in A. Pertusi (ed.) *Venezia e l'Oriente fra tardo medioevo e rinascimento* (Venice, 1966), pp. 323–37.

[13] On Aeneas Sylvius there is ample literature. See, for instance, D. Maffei (ed.) *Enea Silvio Piccolomini. Atti del Convengo per il quinto centenario della morte* (Siena, 1968). Most illuminating is of course his autobiographical *Commentaria rerum memorabilium* of c. 1463. See also E. Garin, 'Ritratto di Enea Silvio Piccolomini', in his *La cultura filosofica*

ubique gestarum was an ambitious historical–geographical work motivated by the desire to prepare the crusade against the Turks on a more
empirical basis. For Pius II geography was a necessary setting for a more
precise universal history, rather than an independent focus of interest,
and his declared priority was to understand contemporary events.[14]
Although only the parts devoted to Near Asia and Europe were finished,
it is obvious that among various sources he borrowed massively from
Strabo, and that he also used Poggio's book on India (which in fact, due
to its own popularity, soon acquired an independent circulation).[15]

The unification of Christendom against internal dissent or Turkish
attack, the defence of the leading role of the Papacy after years of crisis
and scandal, or the organization of crusading enterprises, would all have
been (with little variations) recognizable motivations at the time of
Marco Polo. But by the middle of the fifteenth century the 'new men' of
the cultural arena, humanists like Poggio and Aeneas Sylvius, were
prepared to question the validity of medieval geographical accounts on
the basis of the authority and systematicity of Ptolemy or Strabo.
Furthermore, they were prepared to correct the ancients on the strength
of modern testimonies which they could control, such as that provided
by Nicolò Conti. The bias towards the recovery of classical sources and
the scarcity of recent reports meant that it was the medieval inheritance
that was more often rejected as fabulous, sometimes unfairly. In effect
Poggio's text ignores all the sources produced in the thirteenth and
fourteenth centuries, marvels and empirical first-hand observations

del Rinascimento italiano (Florence, 1961), pp. 38–59, and L. Firpo, 'Enea Silvio,
pontefice e poeta', an introductory essay to A. Sylvius [E. S. Piccolomini], *Storia di due
amanti*, ed. M. L. Doglio (Milan, 1990), pp. 5–32.

[14] Furthermore, the fact that he did not complete his project has also made his work look
more geographical than historical. Pius II explains his aims and methods in his preface:
E. S. Piccolomini, *Descripción de Asia*, ed. by F. Socas, *Biblioteca de Colón*, vol. III
(Madrid, 1992), pp. 3–5. He reveals his motivation (that is, to explain 'the losses of the
Christian republic' in the East) after discussing the Turks (ibid., pp. 257–8). The next
theme he announced was India, but he did not live to write it.

[15] On the circulation of Conti's manuscripts see M. Longhena, 'I manoscritti del IV libro
del *De Varietate Fortunae* di Poggio Bracciolini', *Bollettino della Società Geografica
Italiana* (1925): 191–215, who described thirty-one manuscripts, the vast majority in
Italian and in Latin. Pius II used the Venetian's account of 'Macinus' (in fact, Burma) in
order to describe the ancient Seres (in fact, the Chinese), which he places between India
and Cathay (Marco Polo's Cathayans not having yet been identified with Ptolemy's
Seres). See Piccolomini, *Descripción*, pp. 19–20. On the strength of ancient authority and
fame, Pius II is sceptical that the river 'Dua' (Irrawaddy) could be larger than the
Ganges, and that such an obscure king could have 10,000 elephants. This does not
detract from Conti's overall credit, but shows that the Pope felt more confident about
abundant ancient authorities than about isolated travellers' observations. In the case of
the Ganges, in particular, its primacy had a religious significance as one of the four rivers
whose source was paradise.

alike.[16] He actually thought that most of what was known in his time about India was more fabulous than true.[17] Conti's testimony was, however, seen as valuable, because his accounts 'seemed truthful, not fabrications' and Poggio could claim to have questioned the traveller closely.[18] Thus the development of cosmographical genres also gained a new legitimacy within which the merchant-traveller had an important role.

There was continuity within the tradition of cosmographical works produced around the Roman curia, from Poggio's *De varietate fortunae* (1440s) to the *Historia rerum* of Pius II (*c.* 1460) and later the *Commentariourum urbanorum octa et triginta libri* of Raffaello Volterrano (*c.* 1500).[19] Furthermore, these writings were influential beyond immediate Roman concerns, and often in unexpected ways. Thus Marco Polo and Nicolò Conti were sources of evidence for Paolo Toscanelli's advice to sail westwards to reach India in his famous 1474 letter to Ferdinando Martins.[20] Nicolò Conti's observations had already been incorporated into a *mappa mundi* produced in 1457 (known as 'Genoese' and characterized by its elliptical shape: see plates 1 and 2), which effectively started a solid tradition of mapmaking based on combining Ptolemy's maps and the observations of modern travellers in Africa and Asia – with some peculiar results, such as the separation of Ceylon and Trapobana.[21] What separated these maps from the Catalan atlas of 1375, which, as we saw, already relied on Marco Polo, was not just the presence of the Ptolemaic model, but also the illustration of an open sea through which the East could be reached, either by sailing westwards or by circumnavigating Africa. This is particularly clear in the maps produced by Enrico Martello and Francesco Rosselli at the time of Columbus' first expedition.[22] The cosmography of Pius II, printed as early as 1477, was also one of the selected geographical works read and annotated by Columbus – albeit after his first journeys of discovery, in his attempt to convince

---

[16] Well-known medieval encyclopaedism came to be despised by the learned men of letters who were opening their minds to a rediscovery of antiquity, especially after decades of virtual stagnation in the production of new geographical accounts. To a man like Poggio, for whom the great novelties had been the Greek Ptolemy or the original Pliny, Vincent of Beauvais probably did not look very exciting, although his *Speculum historiale* actually included Friar John of Carpini's rich account of the Mongols.

[17] 'Multa tum a veteribus scriptoribus, tum communi fama de Indis feruntur, quorum certa cognitio ad nos perlata arguit quaedam ex eis, fabulis quam vero esse similiora'. Poggio, *Opera omnia*, vol. II, p. 628.

[18] Ibid.

[19] Cochrane, *Historians*, pp. 44–50.

[20] This letter is only preserved through Columbus' own Latin copy.

[21] Gentile, *Firenze e la scoperta*, pp. 173–5.

[22] Ibid. pp. 239–40 and 243–7.

himself that it was, indeed, India that he had reached.[23] Among the pages of that book, in fact, he also copied Toscanelli's letter to Martins miscalculating the westerly distance between Europe and Cathay, and referring to the testimony of Nicolò Conti whom he had met in Florence.[24] Ptolemy's *Geography* had also been printed in 1477, Strabo's in 1480, and Poggio's *India recognita* (Conti's narrative) in 1492. And it was also by printing Marco Polo and Nicolò Conti that Valentim Fernandes published in Lisbon the first promotional travel collection in 1502 – that is, after the Portuguese opened the Cape route. Curiously, it was from this Portuguese version and not from the Latin original, nor from the manuscript versions already existing in Italian, that Ramusio re-translated Conti's account for his *Navigazioni e viaggi*.[25]

Therefore, besides having a direct influence on some specific projects of discovery and exploration, these Renaissance cosmographies set the tone for a genre in which merchants and soldiers were asked to answer to the critical standards of humanists. In this sense, they are the predecessors of cosmographers and travel collectors of the sixteenth century, such as Barros in Portugal, Velasco and Román in Spain, Ramusio, Sansovino, Anania, and Botero in Italy, or Postel, Thévet, Belleforest and Chappuys in France.[26]

The connection between humanism and travel literature cannot be seen as the mere anecdote of a merchant meeting the Pope's secretary in Florence. A 'cosmographer' like Toscanelli, Poggio's friend, was in fact a

---

[23] Columbus also annotated the book of Marco Polo, Pierre d'Ailly's *Imago mundi* and the elder Pliny's *Natural history*.

[24] Piccolomini, *Descripción*, a Castilian translation of Columbus' annotated copy of the *Historia rerum* with all his marginal notes, including Toscanelli's letter on p. 261. It is not impossible that Toscanelli witnessed some conversations between Poggio and Conti, which we perhaps should imagine as a humanist social event. The tradition that made Columbus the direct recipient of Toscanelli's correspondence, prominent in the life of Columbus written by his son Ferdinand, is on the other hand apocryphal. See J. Gil and C. Varela (eds.) *Cartas de particulares a Colón y Relaciones coetáneas* (Madrid, 1984), pp. 129–34.

[25] There were at least two separate Italian translations of the fourth book of Poggio's *De varietate fortunae*, known from two Florentine manuscripts. Despite the Latin edition of 1492, in the first half of the sixteenth century the circulation of Conti's original account seems to have been based on the Portuguese version of 1502 and on at least three editions of a Castilian translation by Rodrigo de Santaella (1503, 1518 and 1529), who, thinking the Venetian dialect to have been the original, translated from a manuscript in that language.

[26] These various sixteenth-century cosmographers were all educated in a culture influenced by humanist genres, and yet differed widely in the personal synthesis they developed. For example, clerics like the Augustinian Román or the Neapolitan Anania tended to offer more conservative interpretations than politicians and administrators like Juan López de Velasco or Gabriel Chappuys, independently from the fact that they also had access to excellent empirical sources. See J. P. Rubiés, 'New worlds and Renaissance ethnology', *History and Anthropology*, 6 (1993): 157–97.

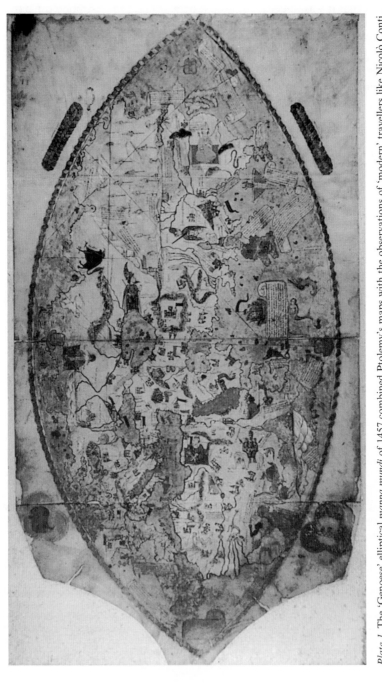

Plate 1 The 'Genoese' elliptical *mappa mundi* of 1457 combined Ptolemy's maps with the observations of 'modern' travellers like Nicolò Conti. One peculiar result was the separation of Ceylon and Trapobana.

Plate 2 Detail of India from the 'Genoese' *mappa mundi*, with the huge city of 'Bizengalia' over a mountain. The central mounted figure above the city, 'Indorum rex', is probably the king of Vijayanagara.

saintly man interested in a wide range of subjects, in particular astronomy and mathematics,[27] while Poggio himself was most famous for hunting for manuscripts in northern Europe and for his *Facetiae*, a collection of short popular stories of a sexual and anti-clerical character written in elegant Latin. However, the distance that separated Poggio from Rustichello di Pisa or from Francesco Pipino was substantially greater than that which separated Nicolò Conti from Marco Polo, and it is this distance that mattered in the long term. It was not just an issue about the credibility of a particular judgement or observation concerning, let us say, the practice of widow-burning. Poggio's exchange with Conti and its appropriation by cosmographers like Pius II or Volterrano was in fact the seed for a new model of organization of cultural spaces, in which encyclopaedic accumulation in a theological framework gave way to a critical discrimination of sources of knowledge. Information of a geographical or historical kind was no longer simply perceived as further illustration of God's marvellous creation, nor merely accepted as traditional moral example. Eventually, by the end of the sixteenth century, the idea of a *method* would come to regulate new disciplines in which empirical accounts tested generalities, and therefore could improve the human enterprise of defining the natural and the rational (in terms of logic, history, law and morality, but also the natural sciences). The scientific enterprise of the seventeenth century followed at least partly from this.

NICOLÒ CONTI'S INDIA: IDOLATRY, BARBARISM AND CIVILIZATION

The very structure of Conti's account, in two parts, betrays the pattern of mediation imposed by Poggio's interview. The first half consists of an account of his journey which is particularly valuable for the precision of its geography. There is reason to suppose that some of the itineraries described have been somehow simplified, considering that Conti did not follow a single route, but instead engaged in various journeys throughout many years. The overall structure is nevertheless both clear and coherent: Conti first travelled from Damascus towards Persia, which he reached after visiting Arabia and Baghdad. After reaching the Persian Gulf he approached India through Cambay. He then followed the western coast

---

[27] See S. Gentile, 'Toscanelli, Traversari, Niccoli e la geografia', *Rivista Geografica Italiana*, 100 (1993): 113–31. Gentile demolishes the idea that Toscanelli was a specialized geographer – no more than, let us say, his friend the theologian Nicholas of Cusa, who shared many of his scientific interests. Needless to insist that one of the key conditions for the humanist renewal was this ability of the intellectual elite to share a wide range in interests within a remarkably inter-connected social network.

but, at a certain point, turned inwards and crossed the empire of Vijayanagara, visiting the capital and various cities. He thus reached Coromandel, and from there Ceylon. He then crossed the sea to Sumatra. Afterwards he sailed north towards the port of Tenasserim and all the way to Bengal in the west. Travelling upwards along the Ganges he reached various cities, and even visited the mountains of northern India. Then he returned to the sea of Bengal and travelled to Arakan, sailing again upwards along the river. Crossing the mountains of the interior he reached the river Irrawaddy and the city of Ava in Burma. Although he discusses Cathay, it is very unlikely that he actually went there. Instead, he seems to have sailed down to Pegu, and then towards the islands of Indonesia ('greater and lesser Java'). Later he returned to the Malabar coast in South India. From Cambay he sailed towards the Red Sea and Ethiopia, and via Mount Sinai he finally reached Egypt.

In a few pages, therefore, Conti was able to give an image of Asia along trading routes similar to those used by Marco Polo on his return trip to Venice, and also by many later travellers of the sixteenth century. Having spent long periods of time in many of these places, he was able to offer precise information concerning the peculiarities of each place. Without dwelling on his personal feelings and activities, he used the idea of travel as a narrative structure for a geographic, economic and ethnological description.

Conti had travelled through much of India in the company of Persian merchants, 'adopting the dress of the country', in his own words. He also spoke Arabic. Not surprisingly, his insights are very similar to those offered by Marco Polo, and some of his descriptions and stories show remarkable coincidences which inevitably raise the question of explaining the continuity after 150 years. The humanist Poggio's intervention is made nevertheless clear by the conciseness of the account and by an air of detached objectivity, quite different from Marco Polo's ability to transmit a feeling of shared understanding between him and the customs and beliefs he describes. Poggio is in all likelihood also responsible for a few classical references which betray the presence of Pliny and Ptolemy in his mind – for instance, the mistaken identification of ancient Trapobana with Sumatra rather than Ceylon (a mistake which would have consequences for the best maps for the next 100 years).[28] But

---

[28] From his statement that nobody had been to Trapobana after a commander of Alexander's fleet (that is, Onesicritus) and a Roman citizen at the time of Emperor Claudius, it seems that Poggio, when writing this piece, was aware of Pliny's *Natural history* (Book VI, chap. 24), but did not think of Marco Polo. See N. Conti, 'The Travels of Nicolò Conti in the East', with independent pagination in R. H. Major (ed.) *India in the fifteenth century*, Hakluyt Society, 1st series (London, 1857), p. 4. I have generally used Major's translation, corrected in the light of Poggio's Latin.

nowhere is Poggio's presence clearer than in the second part of the narrative, when Conti adds a more analytical description of the 'manner and customs of the Indians' according to the humanist's direct questions. While in the first part Conti introduced his own observations about peculiar natural phenomena and customs as they came to mind (like widow-burning in Cambay, snakes in Malabar, or the curious enhancements inserted into male sexual organs in Pegu), the second part represents Poggio's clear attempt to expand that kind of knowledge according to more systematic categories and interests of his own. For instance, although Conti describes Bizengalia and South India in the first part, it is in the context of the detailed discussion of Indian customs that many more details concerning Hindu religious rituals come out. It could thus be argued that the perception, memory and language of the merchant-traveller was being pushed to new areas by the action of the educated secretary.

In order to analyse this dialogue three themes deserve particular attention: the role of cities as centres of geographical analysis, religion as a cultural marker, and the clarification of the idea of a hierarchy of civilization. In all cases, Vijayanagara plays a substantial role. At different points in the discussion it is necessary to separate the different contributions of Conti, Poggio and their possible sources. This is not always easy, but there is enough evidence to suggest an argument concerning the recurrence of certain themes.

There is a continuity between the geographical categories used by ancient Greek descriptions of India and those used by Nicolò Conti. In all these cases, big rivers provide the basic principle of regional division, while cities are often the focus of ethnographic discussions. The boundaries of different countries are much less defined. It is not, however, a direct continuity that we must consider. Although Poggio Bracciolini was to translate Diodorus Siculus' *The library of history* into Latin (which included a summary version of Megasthenes' description of India), and Strabo's detailed version was also then made available in Italy, one can assume a certain chronological precedence for Conti's interview.[29] The

---

[29] The account by Megasthenes was not the only description of India resulting from Alexander's expedition and its aftermath, but it certainly had the best reputation in the ancient world – and with good reason, since only Megasthenes seems to have ventured beyond the area near the Indus and reached Pataliputra (Patna) on the Ganges. Besides the few traces of this account that could still be read in the Latin writings of Pliny, Solinus and Pomponius Mela, Megasthenes reached the Renaissance in the West through the much closer Greek works of Diodorus, Strabo and Arrian. Even more than philosophers and poets, these historians (with Herodotus, Thucydides, Xenophon, Polybius, Plutarch, Diogenes Laertius, etc.) were the priority of Poggio and his friends when translating the flood of Greek literature brought from Constantinople, as noted by Bolgar, *The classical heritage*, pp. 434–5.

coincidence within the same humanist circles between the arrival of the best classical accounts of India and a new fresh description of the East does not therefore mean the existence of an immediate and direct collation, as much as the prevalence of an interest for the subject and a method based on the rejection of the traditional Latin image as too vague and too fabulous.

Thus, the division of India into three parts which introduces the second part of the account ('one, extending from Persia to the Indus; the second, comprising the district from the Indus to the Ganges; and the third, all that is beyond')[30] seems to satisfy the sense of order of the humanist in his effort to organize the information provided by the traveller. However, early in the sixteenth century, the Portuguese Duarte Barbosa also reported this to be a common division among the *mouros*, 'who have known it for longer than us'.[31] On the other hand, when it comes to the geography of India the alternative report of Pero Tafur is particularly vague and legendary. It therefore seems that Conti merely transmitted a division current among Muslims, and that it was Poggio who extracted it from the merchant in order to improve on the *Geography* of Ptolemy.

The fact that the voyage is structured as a succession of cities is important because it creates the analytical basis for a discourse on civilization independent of Christian theology. Furthermore, it is a category that easily lends itself to cross-cultural comparisons. The city is fundamentally a social environment and a market. In addition, local peculiarities concerning social practices and institutional arrangements may also be worthy of note. In a context of generalized wilderness in which going from one city to the other may require crossing seas and deserts or sailing huge rivers, the city stands out as a settled human community, and is evaluated according to its size and its products. This interest seems natural enough in a merchant, but points towards a more general implicit principle: that the capacity to produce a complex urban life, with all its economic and political implications, is the main measure of social and cultural achievement. In this respect, it is interesting that of all cities mentioned by Conti, Bizengalia, the capital of Vijayanagara, deserves the fullest description:

The great city of Bizengalia is situated near very steep mountains. The circumference of the city is sixty miles: its walls are carried up to the mountains and enclose the valleys at their foot, so that its extent is thereby increased. In this city there are estimated to be ninety thousand

---

[30] Conti, 'Travels', p. 21.
[31] Barbosa, *Livro em que dá relação do que viu e ouviu no Oriente*, p. 188.

men fit to bear arms. The inhabitants of this region marry as many wives as they please, who are burnt with their dead husbands. Their king is more powerful than all other kings of India. He takes to himself twelve thousand wives, of whom four thousand follow him on foot wherever he may go, and are employed solely in the service of the kitchen. A like number, more handsomely equipped, ride on horse-back. The remainder are carried by men in litters, of whom two thousand or three thousand are selected as his wives on condition that at his death they should voluntarily burn themselves with him, which is considered a great honour for them.[32]

Through this description, and others of Cambay, Calicut and a few more cities, Conti introduced in Europe the image of what Poggio's account calls 'central India' (which roughly corresponds to modern India) as an urban civilization – marked, yes, by peculiar customs, but above all by a network of cities of varying importance located on a well-defined geographical space. The kingdom of Vijayanagara itself is defined by various cities: besides the capital, Pelagonda (Penugonda) is also big and noble, Odeschiria (Udayagiri) and Cenderghiria (Chandra-giri) are both very beautiful, while on the coast he also mentions Peudifetania (Pulicat) and Malepur (Mylapore).

It is true that this kind of discourse was already prominent in earlier travel literature. For instance, the connection between Marco Polo's Venice and his long description of the Chinese city of Kinsai (Hang-Chau) has long been noticed. Here the eulogistic language of the traveller does not so much refer to the marvellous *other* as to what he interpreted as a universal quality of human civilization.[33] But unlike Conti more than a century later, Marco Polo did not find in South India any comparable city, and therefore, despite a few references to coastal city–ports like Quilon, his important description of Maabar and Lar is organized according to vaguely defined provinces and kingdoms. No city was seen as the centre, and this made the peoples of India participants of an alternative religious and cultural system which easily acquired a mythical character, rather than representatives of an alternative civiliza-tion. Within the broad identity of peculiar Indian customs and natural phenomena described by both travellers, there is a distinct change of emphasis from that which causes surprise towards that which can be understood in a comparable civic or physical context. And it is not coincidental that while in Marco Polo rulers like the Great Khan stand clearly as protagonists who define political realities, in Nicolò Conti

[32] Conti, 'Travels', p. 6.
[33] Polo, *The description of the world*, vol. I, chap. 152, pp. 326–41.

kings are only part of a wider human system and remain very much in the background.

One little example reveals with special clarity the role of Poggio in creating this sphere of comparability in terms of nature and history. Conti recounts that in the island of Ceylon there is a river with plenty of fish, which cause sickness to any one who holds them. 'The cause of this phenomenon is referred by the natives to a certain legend, which Nicolò related to me', added Poggio, 'but it appears to me that the cause is natural'.[34] And he goes on to discuss the effects of the torpedo fish known in Europe.

Human societies were no less comparable than natural phenomena. There were important foundations for this attitude in the tradition of classical and late medieval political thought, and the practical rationality of the merchant-traveller also required particular attention to cities. But the question arises whether the language of Indian civilization developed by Poggio, and which can be accepted as being sharper than Marco Polo's, was in any way different from the Greek and Roman models he knew. We can briefly consider in this context the accounts of Strabo, Diodorus and Pliny.[35]

Strabo describes Palibothra (Patna), the capital city of king Sandrocottus (Chandragupta) 'to whom Megasthenes was sent on an embassy'.[36] It is not, however, a very full description, simply telling us about the size and location of the city, and its wooden fortifications. The emphasis falls on the superiority of the tribe for which Palibothra is the capital, and on the fact that its kings must take up the name of the city as their own surname. The rest of Strabo's account of India follows similar principles: what matters are the tribes and the territory they occupy, and cities (understanding this concept generously, as any fortified town) are the natural centres of population and military struggle and have their own laws and councils – like Taxila, which, unlike King Porus, welcomed Alexander. The general climatic conditions of the country and its rivers are in any case given priority in the discussion, which seeks to establish a parallel with Egypt and Ethiopia (especially with the Nile) and emphasizes the idea of extraordinary fertility. The overall impression is that of a strong bias towards the Greek concept of the *polis* and its dependence on

---

[34] Conti, 'Travels', p. 33.

[35] It must be remembered that almost three centuries separated Diodorus and Strabo, writing at the time of Caesar and Augustus, from their main source Megasthenes, who was writing *c.* 300 BC. Arrian's works, which also contributed to the transmission of Megasthenes' account to fifteenth-century Italy, were of course composed even later, some time in the middle of the second century.

[36] Strabo, *The geography of Strabo*, trans. by H. L. Jones, 8 vols. (Cambridge, Mass. and London, 1917–32), vol. VII, p. 63 (15.1.36).

tribal identity, good climate and clear laws. Even the discussions of castes and of brahmins do little more than project the Greek ideal of a well-ordered society and its wise philosophers.[37]

This Greek ethnocentrism is confirmed by Diodorus, who also relied above all on the work of Megasthenes.[38] He again described a well-watered fertile land where famine was unknown, which must have been a contrast to the relative fragility of the Mediterranean economy. This idealization also affected the customs of the Indians: even when at war they respected farmers and their lands, knowing that it was to every-body's profit. Alexander could not conquer the people of the Ganges because of their many elephants (Diodorus did not realize that Alexander never reached so far). In fact, he insists, the Indians have never been conquered, and all their tribes are autochthonous – a misrepresentation that reflects Diodorus' nostalgia for the Greek ideal of independence and autarchy when already under the dominion of Rome. In contrast to Poggio, who creates an image of a civilized network of trading centres, Diodorus does not describe particular cities, not even Palibothra. Instead, he describes a civilizing process from hunter-gatherers clad in skins through scattered village clans and finally cities with arts, laws and religion. This account is based on local myths, he says, but it is identical to the way the Greeks became civilized, since it follows the logic of a universal human nature – one defined by reason, hands and speech. That Greek self-understanding is crucial to this idea of the civilizing process is made most clear by the fact that local myths can in fact be translated into Greek ones: Dionysus came with an army and acted as civilizing hero for the Indians. Alternatively, Heracles cleared the wilderness from beasts, had many sons and founded Palibothra. In both cases the Greek heroes founded a universal monarchy from which today's democratic fragmentation has derived. As in Strabo, the Indian caste system described by Diodorus is as rational as Plato might have imagined it, and it rests on the idea that nobody should be a slave – a wise ancient law, it is suggested, that surpasses Western models, 'since it is silly to make laws on the basis of equality, and yet to establish inequalities in social intercourse'.[39]

---

[37] For the whole account see the first part of book 15 in ibid. pp. 2–129.

[38] Diodorus Siculus, *The library of history*, trans. by C. H. Oldfather et al, 12 vols. (Cambridge, Mass. and London, 1933–67), vol. II, pp. 2–25 (book 2, chaps. 35–9).

[39] Ibid., p. 19. Diodorus' argument is obviously inconsistent. If the rejection of slavery is meant to produce a context of social equality, then it is difficult to see what the good can be of a caste system in which one cannot marry outside one's group nor change it. Diodorus, a Greek Sicilian under Roman power, would seem to have been carried away by his disgust towards the prevalence of brutal slavery in his own world, and yet still be influenced by the spell of Platonic idealism. It is also curious that in the pages describing

The account which Poggio certainly considered insufficient was that of Pliny.[40] His geographical description of India is of course mainly based on Greek sources, and does not substantially depart from them. If anything, Pliny emphasizes even more the division of India according to tribes (that is 'peoples', *gentes*), of which he identifies a vast number. These tribes are often separated by geographical barriers and occupy specific territories, and can sometimes be characterized by having a king and armies of varying size. Only a few groups deserve a description of their manners and customs, especially those which appear more extraordinary, like the Pandae, who are alone ruled by queens. But no tribe is defined by the personality of a city, and the Pandae, for instance, rule over 300 of them. Certainly Palibothros is the capital of the more powerful people of India, the Prasi, and Pliny describes it as a large and wealthy city ruled by a king with a very large army. However, the defining elements of a peculiar Indian civilization are entirely absent from the *Natural history*. Thus oriental monstrosities and weird customs appear in a separate section as illustration of the extremes of nature, not as part of an explanation of India as an alternative cultural space.[41] This is coherent with Pliny's plan to divide his matter thematically in order to record diversity. Thus, when it comes to defining a criterion for evaluating civility, Pliny remains locked in the typically Roman imperial duality of either considering that 'of all the people in the whole world the most excellent in virtue is undoubtedly the Roman', or, without bothering to justify the statement, quickly shifting to the more philosophical theme of the power of Fortune over a universally weak mankind.[42]

In Conti's time, political culture in Italy was based on such a different system of identities (Christian-providential, patriotic-republican, but also aristocratic and monarchic) that neither the Venetian merchant's possible ideology nor the Florentine humanist's curiosity could have connected entirely with the logic of the Greek *polis* as transmitted through the writings of the Roman imperial period. It is also difficult to see how they could have been satisfied with the rather threatening Roman imperial twist. Although, as we have seen, Poggio translated Diodorus into

India he writes in the present tense and does not mention Megasthenes, as if these observations could be put under the authority of his own autopsy – a traveller's principle of verification which, no less than Strabo, he claims for his universal historical compilation.

[40] See in particular Pliny, *Natural history*, trans. by H. Rackham, 10 vols. (Cambridge Mass. and London, 1938–62), vol. II, pp. 378–407 (book VI, chaps. 20–4).

[41] Ibid., pp. 518–27.

[42] 'Gentium in toto orbe praestantissima una omnium virtute haud dubie Romana extitit . . . si verum facere iudicium volumus ac repudiata omni fortunae ambitione decernere, nemo mortalium est felix' (ibid., p. 592).

Latin,[43] his political attitudes typically alternated between defending Florentine liberty in Tacitist terms against the threat from the tyrannical Duke of Milan, to presenting Alfonso of Aragon, now king of Naples, with a free rendering of Xenophon's *Cyropaedia* – a rhetorical transformation of a Persian despot into an ideal ruler. In the midst of all this, he worked for the Pope and his Roman state. The idea of civility that emerged from this complex setting was neither simply monarchical nor simply republican, but somewhere within a complex field of possibilities created by this duality, as expressed by the different genres of Renaissance political thought. It was very far from the universalization of Athenian democratic tribalism, and (at least in the case of Poggio) reluctant to grant Platonic utopias. Christianity obviously introduced a further discontinuity in the translation of local mythologies into Greek or Roman ones. Christian mythology had obliterated all others, Greek, Egyptian or Indian (it was their awareness of this problem, and of its impossibility, that made the next generation of humanists, like Ficino and Pico, embrace the syncretic philosophy of Neoplatonism).

Although the Greek principle of climatic determinism would prove congenial to the humanists' attempts to rationalize geographical diversity, the single process of civilization described by Diodorus was in this context too naive. Through the efforts of humanists like Poggio, or his colleague at the Roman curia the antiquarian Flavio Biondo, the arts of civilization had become a past that needed to be recovered. The barbarians who had marked the end of Roman civilization had introduced a fundamental discontinuity into European history (and what was recoverable of the Greek empire was then being imported too, just before the Turks conquered it, with an attitude which showed marked contrast with that of the Frankish crusaders of the century of Marco Polo). How this humanist recovery would be made compatible with the single mythology which had actually triumphed throughout the Middle Ages was less clear. But meanwhile India was approached as a transparent civilization with an opaque mythology, as a network of cities that could be placed with some precision on a map, and thus defined more by the actual diversity of economic exchanges and social customs than by a single model of the civilizing process pointing towards a kind of Platonic utopia.

We can conclude that the tension which allowed different interpretations of a civil society to take place has to be sought in the particular connotations of the concept of the city as it was used by different actors in different historical circumstances. The Greek *polis* that inspired Plato

---

[43] Or, as Valla claimed, he appropriated the translation prepared by George of Trebizond, a Byzantine scholar who had moved to Italy after the council of Florence.

and Aristotle, the European late medieval Mediterranean city – such as Conti's Venice – or the South Indian capital that he eventually described to Poggio, all had distinctive features that only the contextual use of a continuous and yet changing conceptual tradition could express.

Conti's treatment of Vijayanagara not only re-enacts a traditional assumption, it also seems to respond to a 'type' of city description which often appears in travel narratives. This type, especially influential in the formalized 'genre' of late medieval and Renaissance civic eulogies, has for instance been proposed as a systematic pattern in the travels of Pero Tafur, relating both to northern Europe and the Mediterranean.[44] In the description of Vijayanagara by Nicolò Conti given above, the situation, size, and population function as a basic framework, while a few particulars on the king and on marriage and burial customs identify the place further.

The presence of these 'types' raises the question of whether formal rhetorical training predominates over the spontaneous use of everyday language. There can be little doubt that Conti's few sentences give a clear sense of the historical particularity of Vijayanagara. What needs to be explained is the recurrence of certain themes in the Portuguese descriptions of the city written more than sixty years later. Duarte Barbosa and Domingos Paes do not seem to have relied on Conti's narrative when they came to write their own (even though they might possibly have read it). In fact cases of textual borrowing were not uncommon in the travel writing of the period, even among authors of first-hand accounts. For example, in the second half of the sixteenth century the Venetian merchant Gasparo Balbi, who travelled along the coasts of South India and all the way to Pegu, copied quite a lot from his predecessor Cesare Federici, even though he need not have done so. The fundamental reason was that copying information increased the value of accounts whose main aim was to provide information rather than being original.[45] However, the prevalence of partial plagiarism must be set against the evidence for a great deal of original reporting.

In the light of this observation it makes sense to argue that common themes were often the result of the interaction of similar cultural assumptions with similar experiences. In the case of Vijayanagara the direct experience of the physical and social reality of the city obviously plays a role of its own. As we have seen, Conti stresses the huge physical

---

[44] Vives Gatell, 'Andanças e viajes de un hidalgo español', p. 15.

[45] The concept that suffered tension was the authenticity of the personal testimony as guarantee of truthfulness. It is not the case that this guarantee was merely rhetorical: rather, trusting another person as much as oneself seems to have been an easy vice, a kind of cheap self-fashioning.

space enclosed by the walls, the remarkable quantity of people available for the army, the power of the king, his (also extraordinarily numerous) female household, and a few other key features concerning the role of women. In particular, he mentions the limitless polygamy and the practice of widow-burning, which obviously raise some implicit moral questions. In short, Conti's Vijayanagara is characterized by continuous and quantifiable greatness. We may also assume that any tendency to exaggerate, common in medieval popular narratives (including Marco Polo's *Divisament dou monde*), must have been restrained by Poggio's authoritative incredulity.

Greatness characterizes the city, but also idolatry. In the second part of the narrative, when describing religious festivals, Conti introduces some information specifically related to Vijayanagara. This information has to be understood in the context of Conti's (and Poggio's) account of Eastern religion, which follows his discussion of marriage and burial customs, and of priests and philosophers. Curiously, Conti distinguishes these two groups, the 'Bachali' and the 'Brahmins'. The Bachali, found in Cambay, in fact correspond to Indian brahmins, who 'abstain from all animal food, in particular the ox' and 'have only one wife, who is burnt with her dead husband'.[46] Conti's brahmins, instead, are portrayed as philosophers of great wisdom and virtue who are found throughout all India, particularly in Ceylon, and practise astrology and other magical arts. It is likely that the formula given to this classification, albeit based on Conti's observations, responds to Poggio's attempt to separate the wise brahmin-philosophers of the Greek tradition from the priests who preside over idolatry, and in particular over *sati*. Later, with the arrival of the Portuguese and the Church, this dichotomy would not be sustained.

In the Christian tradition, the analysis of a non-biblical religion must inevitably take idolatry as its key concept. Conti nevertheless identifies this idolatrous religion as diverse, and provides an analytical structure which makes it comparable to Christianity. He therefore refers explicitly to different gods represented by idols of different size and material, 'some of stone, some of gold, some of silver, and others of ivory'. These idols are then placed in richly painted temples 'similar to our own', and different kinds of prayers and sacrifices are offered to them. In fact they present their gods with feasts 'after the manner of the ancient heathens'.[47] With all the details pointing towards a diversity of forms but within a

---

[46] Conti, 'Travels', p. 25.
[47] Ibid., p. 27. This sentence is probably Poggio's.

recognizable structure of practices and institutions, the weight of the interpretation inevitably falls back on the biblical concept of idolatry.

Idols, in Christian discourse, are images of false gods, nothing more than a piece of material that has been given a form and worshipped. This may actually express a deviation from true worship, a deviation directly inspired by the devil. Conti's treatment, nevertheless, is not condemnatory. Like many other lay travellers without a philosophical education, he does not feel the need to dwell on the definition and implications of idolatry. He knows which are the words most appropriate to publicize what he saw in India and uses them. It is very difficult to go beyond this evidence and discuss his subjective beliefs (he was, after all, asking for the Pope's absolution for having 'provisionally' become a renegade). Conti's case is similar to that of Marco Polo. Although he travelled for many years using Arabian or Persian dress and language as a means of socialization, and married an oriental woman who gave him several children, there is no reason to doubt that he would have kept faithful to his original identity and beliefs as a Christian. In this sense he was not entirely isolated. The presence of heretical Nestorians scattered all over India 'as are the Jews among us', and the tomb of Saint Thomas at Mylapore at which they worshipped, could have given him a certain reassurance (although it is surprising that he describes the church of Saint Thomas as 'very large and beautiful', a rather inaccurate description; Duarte Barbosa would write, early in the sixteenth century, that the body was buried 'in a very small church by the sea').[48]

The denial of idols was fundamental in medieval Christian art and ideology, but the process was also ambiguous, because sacred images were essential to popular worship. Needless to say, this ambiguity was negotiated through the use of Church authority. However, the Renaissance introduced a serious challenge to this system, because pagan gods were re-introduced as new symbols of lay power and identity.[49] The encounter between Poggio and Conti in Florence indeed coincided with these cultural crossroads.[50] And yet the very actuality of oriental religion, as opposed to the possibility of appropriating ancient art and philosophy

[48] Ibid., p. 7 and Barbosa, *Livro*, p. 185.
[49] On this theme see Camille, *The gothic idol*, especially pp. 338–49. Camille gives due prominence to Walter Benjamin's analysis of the significance of the Renaissance in this respect.
[50] During his stay Conti could not have failed to notice a few striking changes, some as obvious as Brunelleschi's new cupola to the cathedral, which in size far surpassed the majority of central temple structures he had seen in any country, eastern or western. Since he was often entertained by Poggio and his friends, Conti may have even been shown Donatello's sensuous *David*, the first free-standing bronze nude since antiquity, and surely not a conventional representation of a biblical figure.

with impunity, precluded a similar attitude towards its representations. Despite the reference to ancient gentilism, which we can guess was introduced by Poggio, Conti does not present oriental art as anything but religious, and thus idolatrous.

When describing oriental religions Conti therefore follows what can be described as a regular pattern in travel accounts of this period, and which was also valid for Marco Polo. The emphasis falls on social practices involving temples and idols, such as prayer and sacrifice. Popular festivals and death and marriage rituals are also often included, and form an important aspect of Conti's description. This could be called the exoteric description. In some cases, but less often, beliefs which are associated with those practices are mentioned, especially in the form of scattered references related to the description of behaviour ('they do this because they believe . . .'). In the travel literature of this period a detailed description of native cosmology and mythology is rare indeed, at least until the end of the sixteenth century.[51] However, some of the most extraordinary practices led some of these writers to occasional reflections on the psychological aspects of religious experience. In these cases the implicit evaluation ranged from respect for the ascetic virtue and wisdom of holy men, with ambivalent attitudes towards the miraculous/magic use of power, to the condemnation of the cruelty and foolishness of the most bloody sacrifices.

It is in fact through these alternatives that the final evaluation of idolatry rests. While the so-called 'brahmins' in Ceylon are wise and admirable, the priests of India are presented as preachers manipulating popular religious feelings, for example in the case of *sati*. This leads Conti to what surely is the most crucial, tangible proof of the alien nature of Indian religion, the powerful motif of self-immolation. From his description it appears that Indian religious sacrifices involve an element of 'asking for favours', but that the practice can transcend that worldly aim and become self-destructive: the priests, who encourage the people to perform their religious duties, insist on 'how acceptable it is to the gods that they should quit this life for their sake'. Within this economy of sacred pain, the more painful and public, the better is the sacrifice. Those men who yield their lives 'as a sacrifice to their idols' are 'regarded as saints'.[52] The introduction of the word 'idols' here, instead of 'God', signals the implicit criticism of this particular religious practice. However, this criticism may by analogy be extended to any sort of religious act with negative consequences for human life: the strength of

[51] See chapter 9 below.
[52] Conti, 'Travels', p. 28.

Christianity rests, implicitly, in the absorption of all sacrifices within the eucharist. Festivals, churches and priests have on the other hand been placed in the frame of a much wider religious anthropology.

In this context, Conti introduces his description of a Vijayanagara festival:

> In Bizengalia also, at a certain time of the year, their idol is carried through the city, placed between two chariots, in which are young women richly adorned, who sing hymns to the god, and accompanied by a great concourse of people. Many, carried away by the fervour of their faith, cast themselves on the ground before the wheels, in order that they may be crushed to death, a mode of death which they say is very acceptable to their god. Others, making an incision on their side, and inserting a rope thus through their body, hang themselves to the chariot by way of ornament, and thus suspended and half dead accompany their idol. This kind of sacrifice they consider the best and most acceptable of all.[53]

Without discussing the matter fully, the Venetian asserts some important theoretical principles simply by using descriptive language. 'They say' and 'they consider' work effectively as rhetorical devices to indicate the distance which separates Christian and European beliefs from Indian ones. The acceptance of diverse beliefs in diverse social contexts raises (at least potentially) the possibility of relativism. On the other hand, the acceptance of a form of free will in different people from different cultures also shapes a typically western anthropological discourse – there is an implicit idea of a universal human dignity through choice. So, *satis* in India are expected to jump *voluntarily* into the fire with their deceased husbands, and this assumption is important despite the fact that, as the merchant explains, if they show too much timidity, priests, relatives and bystanders encourage them and, eventually, 'push' them to fulfil their duty. By assuming diversity of beliefs and free will Conti does not suggest that Indian religious practices are as good as the Latin Christian ones, but like Marco Polo he does acknowledge the existence of different possible ways of believing and acting within a common structure of human agency. As in the case of idolatry, he leaves up to the Church authorities the theological defence of the superiority of the European Christian tradition, which he can merely assume. But while Conti here does not substantially depart from Marco Polo, the lay authority of Poggio makes the implications of his discourse more obvious.

Thus the narrative context, rather than the actual description, is what carried the more important implications. In fact Conti's description of

---

[53] Ibid., pp. 28–9.

Hindu religious sacrifices followed the pattern of previous European texts, for instance the description of 'Mobar' in South India given by friar Odoric of Pordenone in 1331. Thus:

> annually on the recurrence of the day when that idol was made, the folk of the country come and take it down, and put it on a fine chariot; and then the king and the queen and all the pilgrims, and the whole body of the people, join together and draw it forth from the Church [ecclesia] with loud singing of songs and all kinds of music; and many maidens [virgines] go before by two and two, chanting in a marvellous manner. And many pilgrims who have come to this feast cast themselves under the chariot, so that its wheels may go over them, saying that they desire to die for their God. And the car passes over them, and crushes and cuts them in sunder, and so they perish on the spot . . . and their bodies they burn, declaring that they are holy, having thus devoted themselves to death for their God.[54]

This continuity also extends to Conti's attitude towards magic, understood as a practical way of exercising power over nature by using links with 'divine' realities which can be apprehended symbolically. Not unlike Marco Polo, Conti is prepared to take the claims of oriental sages to special powers seriously. He thus explains that the saintly and wise brahmins study astronomy and predict the future, that he saw one of them who was 300 years old, and that on one occasion the sailors of his ship negotiated with a demon so that he would send them a good wind. In this last event the Venetian presents himself as witness, and describes a ritual involving various actions (such as drinking blood from the neck of a cock) with obscure symbolic significance, and above all the scene of an Arab sailor being possessed by the so-called god or demon.[55] Of course Conti's attitude towards supernatural magic was common in fifteenth-century Europe, and operated within a logic of the supernatural which was largely consistent with the Christian belief in providential intervention.[56] The lack of rupture between science and magic is exemplified by the fact that Conti's account of miraculous practices comes together with a description of the navigation technology in the Indian Ocean.[57]

---

[54] Pordenone as translated by Yule, *Cathay and the way thither*, vol. II, p. 144. The Latin version is given on pp. 298–9. As in Marco Polo's account, 'Mobar' stands for the Arab Maʿabar and represents the Coromandel coast.

[55] Conti, 'Travels', p. 26.

[56] For the medieval background to the widespread belief in magic in late medieval Europe see R. Kieckhefer, *Magic in the Middle Ages* (Cambridge, 1989). The attitudes of the humanists are explored in A. Grafton, 'Humanism, magic and science', in A. Goodman and A. Mackay (eds.) *The Impact of humanism on western Europe* (London and New York, 1990), pp. 99–117.

[57] If we use modern distinctions to analyse Conti's vocabulary (ibid.) we can see that it

However, through his narrative voice, Poggio distances himself from these stories (nor was he interested in the syncretic Hermeticism of humanists of the following generation like Pico della Mirandola).

It is unnecessary to discuss all of Conti's observations of Indian religions in detail. Despite Poggio's remarkable effort to provide geographical precision, it is impossible to determine in all cases what region each observation corresponds to. But while it would be incorrect to ascribe the whole of Conti's description of Indian manners and customs to Vijayanagara, it can be said that 'central India' dominates his account, and that within central India, Bizengalia (rather than Cambay, Quilon or the Ganges) is the kingdom that presents the sharpest image of an idolatrous civilization.

The relationship between this image of an idolatrous civilization and European self-understanding is crucial to the theme of a hierarchy of civilizations. It was at this moment that the works of humanists like Flavio Biondo began to emphasize the discontinuity between standards of civilization within the classical–medieval tradition.[58] Ancient gentilism could therefore appear as a key concept in framing the understanding of contemporary gentilism, not only because it was non-Christian, but also because it could be either civilized or barbarian. Biondo's model was of course paradoxical (the Roman empire civilized Europe and extended the use of Latin, while the spread of Christianity could not prevent the triumph of barbarism; only in the fifteenth century, in a peculiar context, were the arts and letters happily revived). Poggio did not immediately seek to draw an overall parallel between India and the ancient world, despite the occasional comparison (oriental sandals 'as we see in ancient statues'),[59] but there can be little doubt that Conti's detailed account, placed next to an antiquarian reconstruction of Rome, suggested such a parallel, and in the following centuries travellers and historians outside Europe would constantly fall back on this model.

In fact, Poggio and Conti develop a hierarchy of civilizations *within* India (understood as the whole of Asia) which eventually emerges as the starting point for the comparison of Europe and India. The key contribution of the narrative is therefore the clarity with which the audience is presented with two different models for the oriental world, one positive and the other negative. In Conti's division of India into three parts, the third, that is everything beyond the Ganges, 'excels the others in riches, politeness, and magnificence, and is equal to our own

jumps ambiguously from religion ('god') to magic ('demon'), and from magic to anthropological science ('human insanity').
[58] Cochrane, *Historians and historiography*, pp. 34–40.
[59] Conti, 'Travels', p. 22.

country in the style of life and in civilization' (*vita et civili consuetudine nobis aequalis* is the expression written by Poggio).[60] From the description that follows it is apparent that the Venetian traveller uses a dualistic criterion to evaluate a culture in general terms, one which applies to style of life and forms of social organization. What is rich, humane, civilized, refined and similar to Europe is opposed to what is poor, cruel, barbarous, coarse and different from Europe. Eating on the table belongs to the civilized group, eating on a carpet is more barbarous, and so on.

From another passage it is evident that when Conti refers to a highly idealized land beyond the Ganges he is thinking about Cathay:

> Beyond this province of Macinus [Burma] is one which is superior to all others in the world, and is named Cathay. The lord of this country is called the Great Khan, which in the language of the inhabitants means Emperor. The principal city is Cambaleschia . . . [here follows a military description of the city] . . . the houses and palaces and other ornaments are *similar to those in Italy*: the men, gentle and discreet, wise, and more wealthy than any that have been before mentioned.[61]

At this point most medieval authors demonstrate an attitude surprisingly similar to the one developed by the Portuguese and the Jesuits when they encountered China (even before they concluded that China had to be identified with Marco Polo's Cathay): civil order is seen as an obvious achievement and therefore China represents an ideal model of civilization. Interestingly, however, Conti probably never went there. His account is based on hearsay. Furthermore, it is an anachronistic account, since the Great Khans had long given way to Ming China. Conti's Cathay was in part mythical.

It would be tempting to see this Cathay ruled by the Great Khan from Khan-balik as a direct borrowing from Marco Polo. Other passages in Conti's narrative, such as the account of the ingenious manner of how diamonds are taken in a mountain 'fifteen days journey beyond Bizengalia' (that is, Golkonda) are also very similar to Marco Polo's account of the same technique in the kingdom of 'Motupalli'.[62] And yet the very reference to the city of Bizengalia indicates that here we are dealing with a different account altogether, a conclusion confirmed by many other details of the same passage which Conti could not have borrowed from Marco Polo. In fact neither Conti nor Poggio seem to have depended, at least at the time of the interview, on Marco Polo's narrative.[63] Conti's

---

[60] Ibid., p. 21; Poggio, *Opera omnia*, vol. II, p. 641.
[61] Conti, 'Travels', pp. 14–15 (my emphasis).
[62] Compare Conti, 'Travels', pp. 29–30, with Polo, *Description*, vol. I, pp. 395–6.
[63] Marco Polo's account did nevertheless circulate a few years later in Florence among

Cathay is also the Cathay of his oriental companions, often Arab and Persian merchants, occasionally oriental Christians of Turkish origin. The persistence of this folkloric theme within Asia followed its own rationality – it can be imagined, for instance, that those groups whose commercial and political systems had benefited most from the 'Mongol peace' had a special attachment to the mythical Khan of Cathay. This was, for instance, the case of the Nestorian envoy who reached Rome 'from upper India' some time after Nicolò Conti, and was also interviewed by Poggio through an Armenian interpreter (he presented himself as envoy of a magnificent Christian kingdom 'twenty days journey from Cathay', which also shows that attachment to the Great Khan and to the Prester John were not separate mythical phenomena).[64]

Other examples prove that the continuity between the stories heard by Nicolò Conti and those others reported by Marco Polo was remarkable indeed – as again with the cannibals from 'Andamania', who in Poggio's account have nevertheless lost their dog-heads and limit themselves to devouring those unfortunate travellers driven there by bad weather.[65] This makes it possible to define Poggio's contribution as the clarification, through a language of civility which carried new connotations, of a cultural hierarchy which was nevertheless already part of the oriental cultural world. This cultural hierarchy was also implicit in Marco Polo, but his descriptions of peculiar customs, commercial prosperity and royal justice did not coalesce into a full model of civility.

The same is valid for the opposite model, barbarism. As opposed to the 'Cathayan' image of civilization that compares favourably with Italy, Conti's description of the cruelty and unlawful customs of the people from 'Taprobana' (Sumatra) and Java insists on the theme of inhumanity.[66] It is again in the tradition of early fourteenth-century travellers such as Marco Polo, Jordanus Catalani or Odoric of Pordenone that people in Sumatra are cruel and warlike, trade in human heads, and eat human flesh. Their customs are described as brutal (*moribus asperi*), which recalls, in the intellectual tradition to which Poggio and Conti belong, the association of what is morally repugnant with what is naturally animal. Civilization is thus understood as the social control of animal passions through 'cultural' means, such as laws

---

Poggio's fellow humanists. As I have suggested, Toscanelli used it for his letter of 1474 to Martins. The argument by W. Sensburg, 'Poggio Bracciolini und Nicolo Conti in ihrer Bedeutung für die Geografie des Renaissancezeitalters', *Mitteilungen der K. K. Geographischen Gesellschaft in Wien*, 49 (1906): 1–109, defending Poggio's use of Marco Polo's narrative on the basis of a few similarities (pp. 26–7) is unconvincing.

[64] Conti, 'Travels', pp. 31–2.

[65] Ibid., p. 8.

[66] Ibid., pp. 15–16.

and education in good customs; or, in other words, civilization (the quality of the *civili consuetudine* and the *mores*) is a process of refinement, and moral virtues are the inclinations to act in ways which contribute to the preservation of a peaceful and harmonious social order. As a consequence, certain ways of acting are 'less human': in Java *homines inhumanissimi omnium, crudelissimique inhabitant.*[67] There are many particular instances that give origin to this judgement: killing men is very easy, the law encourages debtors to become assassins as a good way of escaping slavery, desires can be satisfied without social control (i.e. a man can take as many wives as he wishes), cock-fighting and betting on such a cruel spectacle are popular amusements, and 'unclean' animals – mice, dogs, cats – are commonly eaten. Either these peoples have no laws, or they have the 'wrong' ones, since they do not prevent cruelty and other disgusting perversions (here again Conti does not mention the idea of natural law, he simply relies on the educated instincts of his audience).

It is in relation to the 'civilized' model that the more serious connection between oriental and European cultures is made, because 'Indians' not only have their own subjective approach to the world, their own ideas and beliefs, but also an opinion about the Latin Christians. Thus Conti reported that the natives of India 'call us Franks, and say that, while they call other nations blind, they themselves have two eyes and we have but one, because they consider that they excel all others in prudence'.[68]

This statement should not be read as an invention of the humanist, but rather as yet another example, a spectacular one in fact, of the importance of oriental mediation for European views of Asia, even at the level of establishing comparisons. The fact is that a very similar saying was reported by Prince Hayton (Hetoum) of Armenia in the description of Cathay included in his *Flor des estoires de la terre d'Orient*, which he dictated to Pope Clement V in 1307.[69] Hayton's sources were probably first-hand Mongol or Nestorian views. However, his account is not likely to have been used by Poggio. This is not all: Ruy González de Clavijo, Castilian ambassador to the court of Timur in 1404, offers an almost

---

[67] Poggio, *Opera omnia*, vol. II, p. 637.

[68] 'Hi nos Francos apellant, aïuntque, cum caeteras gentes coecas vocent, se duobus oculis, nos unico esse, superiores existimantes se esse prudentia' (ibid. p. 648). The geographical context for many of Conti's observations in this part of his narrative is unclear, because he was responding to Poggio's questions concerning his entire journey. Rather than reflecting the opinion of the inhabitants of 'central India' (as it might seem superficially) the statement probably refers to Cathay or 'further India', which according to Conti was the most civilized part.

[69] Hayton of Armenia, 'La flor des estoires de la terre d'Orient' in *Recueil des histoires des croisades. Documents Arméniens* (Paris, 1906), vol. II, p. 121 (for the original French version) and p. 262 (for the contemporary Latin version).

identical proverb which he heard in Samarkand from a traveller (possibly an Armenian or Genoese trader) recently arrived from the Chinese capital.[70] Similarly, the saying was reported again by the Venetian Iosafa Barbaro in relating his embassy to Uzun Hasan *c.* 1471. As the Turkish ruler of Persia and would-be ally of the Venetians explained to Barbaro, in order to praise his prudence and commercial sagacity, 'the world has three eyes, the Cathayans have two and the Franks one'. In fact Barbaro had already heard the comparison in Tana from the ambassador of the Tartar emperor (the Khan of the Golden Horde) on his return from Cathay in 1436, in a way that clearly implied that the Tartars themselves lagged behind – they had none of the eyes of the world.[71]

Although in some cases textual borrowings are not impossible (for example, the author of the book of John Mandeville obviously copied this same story from Hayton), the repeated appearance of this particular saying, with a remarkable consistency of meaning and route of transmission, is better explained by its origin in Mongol-dominated China and by its subsequent prevalence in the Mongol and Turkish-conquered lands of central Asia and Persia.[72] Even after the consolidation of the Ming dynasty in China the routes with Persia remained open to trade and political contacts for a number of decades. In effect, for much of the fourteenth and fifteenth centuries it was quite possible to connect and compare the land of the 'Cathayans' and the land of the 'Franks' from a central Asian Islamicite civilization which had itself suffered the destruction brought about by the Mongol and Turkish invasions of the late Middle Ages.[73] From this perspective one should not rush to conclude that Islamic Persian writers of this period automatically classified Latin Christian Europe as a remote and barbarous backwater: the idea of a world with two stable centres of civility at its two extremes (a civility measured by commercial prosperity, artistic skill and scientific knowledge) gained some currency among Muslim writers in the fourteenth

---

[70] Ruy González de Clavijo, *Embajada a Tamerlán*, ed. by R. Alba (Madrid, 1984), pp. 220–1.

[71] Iosafa Barbaro, 'Viaggi del Magnifico messer Josephat Barbaro', in *Viaggi fatti da Vinetia alla Tana, in Persia, in India, et in Costantinopoli*, ed. by A. Manuzio (Venice, 1545), p. 34.

[72] I am unable to offer here a detailed analysis of all the relevant passages, but see my forthcoming article 'A western rationality?' which includes a considered argument of why Poggio was very unlikely to have copied Hayton's or Clavijo's opinions.

[73] The importance of China as an economic and cultural influence over the central Asian and Persian world after the thirteenth century has been recognized more often than the emergence of the 'Franks' as a model of civilization, albeit marginal, in the same period. On this topic see the evocative argument by Marshall Hodgson, *The venture of Islam*, 3 vols. (Chicago, 1974), vol. II, pp. 329–68. Marshall Hodgson perhaps tends to exaggerate the intellectual influences of Islam in Europe, which were clearly secondary to the reception of the classical tradition.

century, so that whilst Ibn Battūta declared that 'the Chinese (it is well known) are of all peoples the most skilful and talented in the arts', in his remarkable world history of c. 1377, when discussing the spread of the sciences, the Tunisian Ibn Khaldūn reported as a new development that 'the philosophical sciences, we now hear, are greatly cultivated in the land of Rome and along the adjacent northern shore of the country of the European Christians'.[74]

The example helps establish the principle that continuities between different travellers should not always be analysed as cases of unacknowledged textual borrowing. Rather, the existence of a common oral background, fully justified by the strength of Muslim trading communities and military courts, not only helps to understand coincidences between European travellers from Marco Polo to Nicolò Conti, but also, of course, with Muslim authors like Ibn Battūta. There existed, in other words, a 'logic of spontaneous ethnographies'. A travel writer may have been stimulated to describe something by the reading of the same story in a previous author, but it is also likely that certain historical realities (what else can we call them?) would have been considered interesting by different observers and that as a consequence similar phenomena would be repeatedly described.[75] The fact that *sati* sacrifices, or the spectacle of people throwing themselves at the wheels of a chariot for the sake of a god, were so often reported in descriptions of southern India, reveals immediately the measure of a common framework of assumptions that was being challenged.

The 'marvellous' was in principle the strange, the different, what was recognized as worthy of being reported: something that did not leave the traveller indifferent. However, although a ready-made image of legendary other-worldliness was easily available, a long experience abroad blurred the distinction between the commonsensical and the strange, and allowed the travelling subject, now in command of an expanded linguistic world, to challenge the terms of precedence of an initial us–other opposition. Thus, Conti's acquaintances in India made him realize that the *Franks* had a perhaps unjustified sense of superiority and his passage on 'the three eyes of the world' is surrounded by the description of indigenous cultural achievements: calendar, coinage, military technology,

---

[74] Ibn Battūta, *A travès del Islam*, p. 723. Ibn Khaldūn, *The Muqaddimah*, trans. by F. Rosenthal, ed. by N. J. Dawood (London, 1967), p. 375.

[75] One other remarkable example of an ethnological curiosity which was reported very often in the fifteenth and sixteenth centuries, with clear cases of independent observation, is provided by the description of strange sexual customs in south-east Asia, especially in Pegu and Java. The situation is summarized in Lach, *Asia*, vol. I, p. 533 n.298. The same can be said concerning some themes of the literature on American Indians, such as cannibalism in the Caribbean or Brazil.

paper and writing, languages, slavery (!) and justice. It is also followed by the sensational statement that among the Indians pestilence is unknown, 'neither are they exposed to those diseases which carry off the population in our own countries', with the consequence that 'the number of these people and nations exceeds belief'.[76] Here, as in other instances, Conti exaggerates, but he was obviously referring to something that he had experienced (he seems to have been particularly impressed by the enormous armies of Vijayanagara). Freedom from disease, an idea already present in the Greek account of Megasthenes, must have had an important meaning in the plague-stricken Europe of the late Middle Ages.

Despite Poggio's intervention, none of these comparative aspects are developed in Conti's account as they are in the systematic reflections one finds in sixteenth-century authors, such as the historian João de Barros and a number of Jesuits. Barros, for example, also reported the proverb of the three eyes of the world, but he clearly equated this concept of civility with that of the ancients: 'in the same way that the Greeks thought that in respect of themselves all other nations were barbarians, similarly the Chinese say that they have two eyes of understanding concerning all things, that we Europeans – since they have now communicated with us – have one eye, and that all other nations are blind. And truly . . . these gentiles have all those things for which Greeks and Latins are praised'.[77] Significantly, Barros also transforms the 'Franks' and 'Latin Christians' of the late medieval sources into this 'we Europeans' of the Renaissance. However, although Poggio did not bring in the Greeks and the Romans with the full force of Barros, he had clearly framed the hierarchy of oriental civilizations within a comparative language of civility. The mythical Cathayans represented the high point of civility, next to fifteenth-century Florence and Rome; the inhabitants of the islands of southern Asia remained at the other end, verging on inhumanity. In the middle ground stood the ambiguous image of central India, more civilized than marvellous and yet, despite the magnificence of Vijayanagara, perhaps more idolatrous than civilized.

THE MERCHANT AND THE 'HIDALGO': THE PERSISTENCE OF MARVELS

As we have seen, what separated the humanist historian Barros from medieval travellers like Marco Polo or Nicolò Conti was not so much an

---

[76] Conti, 'Travels', p. 32.
[77] Barros, *Ásia*, 3 vols. (Decades I–III) (Lisbon, 1932–92), vol. III (facsimile of the 1563 edition), p. 46r.

increased appreciation of different cultures as the elaboration of an independent language of civilization to describe them. The originality of late Renaissance critical travellers was above all a matter of *degree of elaboration* of cultural references and theoretical concerns – a development associated with institutional efforts of organization of information and even ideological control, rather than the automatic effect of a new epoch-making modern 'mentality' or way of thinking. In travel literature these changes took the form of an alteration within a traditional genre. Even though in many particular instances Conti's responses are very similar to those of Marco Polo, by talking to Poggio he also revealed that he could become a more critical and keen observer than he would have remained had he been left to talk only to Pero Tafur, or to write on his own.

This fundamental point can be illustrated by looking in detail at the alternative report of Conti's narrative offered by the Andalusian knight Pero Tafur, who travelled in the eastern Mediterranean between 1436 and 1439 (although his narrative was written in Cordoba about fifteen years later). What was striking to early commentators was the great difference between this account and that of Poggio.[78] This disparity led to questioning the truthfulness of one of the witnesses, with the humanist usually being assumed to be the more reliable. I agree with Vives Gatell, who undertook a systematic comparison, that such great differences can be explained by considering the different conditions of the two writers and the circumstances of composition for each text.[79] There are sufficient details shared by the two accounts to make it difficult to believe that Tafur's encounter with Conti was a complete fabrication.[80] It is, on the other hand, unlikely that he copied from Poggio's account, because Tafur includes some original material on Conti's life which he could hardly have learnt other than by talking to him. Even if by some extraordinary chance Tafur had had access to an early manuscript of *De varietate fortunae*, he would not have used it so erratically. These precisions are important so as to establish that we have a genuine case of two independent versions of the same travel experience, one reported in

[78] These views are critically discussed by Vives Gatell, 'Andanças'.

[79] Ibid., pp. 62–74.

[80] This encounter between two travellers, the crusader-pilgrim to the East and the merchant with tales from the Prester John, is in fact far from unique. Bertrandon de la Broquière, author of a contemporary travel narrative, had a remarkably similar experience with Peter of Naples, whom he met in Pera in 1432–3: B. de la Broquière, *Le voyage d'Outremer*, ed. by C. Schefer (Paris, 1892), pp. 145–6. This not only happened at almost the same time that Tafur met Conti, but in fact the kind of text, the kind of traveller and the kind of excursus are extraordinarily analogous (although de la Broquière was more of a spy than Tafur). I believe, however, that any direct relationship can be ruled out.

1437, the other in 1441, and both included in written texts composed (also independently) a few years later. The interests and assumptions of Pero Tafur, a petty nobleman who fashioned his own role as traveller as that of a knight-errant, represent a more traditional kind of mediation than those of the humanist bureaucrat Poggio.[81]

The contextual differences can be analysed as four pairs of oppositions:

I. Pero Tafur met Conti by chance, and the information was transmitted to him orally and in a disorganized way. This he remembered and summarized a few years later. In his text, the personal encounter is as important as the description of India, and certainly more vivid. In sharp contrast Poggio interviewed Conti several times, with the intention of obtaining accurate information which he noted down immediately. He had little interest in the man himself.

II. Tafur probably did not know Italian (which must have been the language for both interviews) as well as Poggio.

III. Tafur displayed vague geographical ideas based on current medieval conceptions. His exchange with Conti does not seem to have altered them significantly. Poggio made a conscious effort to establish a true geographical image on the basis of the works attributed to Ptolemy, which he knew and corrected.

IV. Conti adapted his account to the audience he was addressing. He felt free to give advice, and probably also to exaggerate, when speaking with a foreign adventurous knight like Tafur with whom he had made friends on the road. He must have felt more intimidated by the secretary of the Pope, one of the most cultivated men he had ever met and, at the time, in the service of the spiritual head of the Roman Church.

There is a structural analogy between the two texts. Both Tafur and Poggio divided the report into two parts, a narrative of Conti's travels and a description of India. It is, however, a superficial analogy, especially when it concerns the more cosmographical part. It is not only that Poggio and Tafur selected different observations, and expressed them in different ways: the two contexts of communication were radically different, and probably Conti's words and emphases changed accordingly. Thus Tafur, albeit full of personal details on Conti's life, fails to

---

[81] In his dedication to Fernando de Guzmán, Tafur equated 'visiting foreign lands' with the great deeds that transformed a nobleman into a virtuous knight, and explained that his journey had been prompted by the peace agreed by the king of Castile with the Spanish Muslims. His journey was therefore a sublimated holy war (although it also had an educational political value). See Tafur, *Andanças e viajes*, pp. 1–2.

record names of places carefully. He remembered all kinds of legends and striking wonders. He may also have remembered marvellous things heard or read elsewhere, and added them while writing fifteen years later in Andalusia. Poggio either was not told as much, or tended to reject such information. Occasionally, he noted something fabulous with a hint of scepticism. If anything, what he had in mind were classical images such as those found in Pliny. It is particularly remarkable that Pero Tafur kept confusing the Nile with the Indus and that he referred very explicitly to the Prester John of the Indies, whom he located in India (and not in Abyssinia or somewhere near Cathay, which were the better substantiated versions of the medieval myth). He forgot or discarded any distinction between kingdoms and peoples in the East, the kind of information which is one of the main contributions of Poggio's version. Instead, he appeals to the typically medieval unified image of wonders and monsters which Conti certainly did not transmit to Poggio. It is this conception, rather than any one or other detail, which is significant of Pero Tafur's uncritical attitude. Beyond this, as to the source of exaggerations and confusions, we are left to wonder whether it was Conti who adapted to Tafur's preconceptions and ignorance, whether Tafur himself adapted to his Castilian audience, or whether maybe it was only Poggio's questions that clarified Conti's own confused memories.

Tafur's text is a continuous but disorganized prose where legends and ethnological observations mix with each other. This, however, does not detract from the validity of particular observations. A more detailed look reveals that the text consists of a series of independent themes which the author has not tried to select according to one particular standard of critical awareness, nor to reconcile in a consistent geographical picture. One may distinguish twenty such independent themes, which I shall list as they appear in the text, noting also any possible parallels in Poggio's account (see table 2).

From the comparison between Poggio and Tafur it is clear that the humanist composed a far more detailed and precise account. More importantly, he provided a narrative structure which was far more coherent than that of Tafur. But Poggio also omitted things, especially anything which seemed to confirm what he considered to be fables of an ignorant age. While Pero Tafur made use of various elements to give life to Prester John, Poggio tried to bury him. Tafur was an enthusiastic believer in Christian unity against Muslims, with interests ranging from the Spanish *reconquista*, in which he participated, to the crusading dreams in the East. His own writing may have been prompted by the fall of Constantinople, a city which he described in full decadence before its

Table 2. *Pero Tafur's version of Conti's travels*[a]

Pero Tafur	Poggio (parallels)
1. The Prester John of the Indies. Conti introduces this figure at Tafur's request. He is described as a great king obeyed by other minor kings and many gentile peoples. This image vaguely epitomizes well-known medieval sources, including the narratives of Marco Polo and Mandeville.	In contrast Poggio mentions *separately* a Nestorian king near Cathay, and the Ethiopian king. These two appear as reported by eastern emissaries to the council of Florence, whom Poggio interviewed after talking to Conti. There exists an alternative report of this interview with the Ethiopian monks, which took place in the presence of a commission of cardinals, by the antiquarian Flavio Biondo. A comparison shows that Poggio edited this information and eliminated any reference to whatever he considered excessively fabulous material, including the very name of the Prester John.[b]
2. A lengthy description of a huge mythical mountain with a flourishing civilization of priest-kings (the Prester John) which actually seems to combine the characteristics of Tibet and Ceylon and is offered almost as a utopian model.	Only details about fruits and cinnamon in Ceylon have a parallel in Poggio.
3. An isolated marvel about crabs that, in contact with the air, turn into stone.	
4. The description of a 'gentile' religious ritual, a pilgrimage including suicidal sacrifices (jumping into a pool of mud) which is based on an indigenous myth.	
5. Another rite of self-sacrifice (cutting one's head with huge scissors).	There is a parallel in Poggio.
6. A note on cannibalism. Indian Christians eat raw meat, but not human flesh.	Poggio reports cannibalism in his more focused and detailed description of Sumatra.
7. A long account of an expedition sent by the servants of the Prester John in search of the origins of the Nile. This was a well-known theme, with classical undertones and a quasi-mystical interpretation, which appears for instance at the end of the *Travels* of Mandeville. Another version of the same story, very similar to that of Tafur, was told by Peter of Naples to Bertrandon de la Broquière in late 1432, although la Broquière's Prester John was much more firmly located in Abyssinia.[c] What in Tafur is no more than a suggested mystery, Mandeville and la Broquière openly declared to be the earthly paradise. Here	Poggio on the other hand mentions asking the Ethiopian emissaries about the sources of the Nile, and his report on their answer presents a few similarities with what Tafur attributes to Conti. It is possible that Tafur heard about the Abyssinian Prester John in Egypt (where monophysite Ethiopian Christians maintained their Church despite a centuries-long Muslim rule) and mixed this information with Conti's report of India. On the other hand, on his way home Conti had stopped at a port ('Barbora') in Ethiopia. More generally, any Christian traveller in the East would have easily been familiar with accounts of the Prester John,

Table 2. *(contd.)*

Pero Tafur	Poggio (parallels)
tradition actively encouraged the geographical confusion echoed by Tafur, since both the Nile and the Ganges (as well as the Tigris and Euphrates) were meant to have their source in the middle of this land, the highest on earth, and surrounded by an impenetrable wall. Thus Tafur, or perhaps Conti at his request, repeated the mythical geography of tradition.[d]	which had been a fundamental myth in the crusading Latin kingdoms since the thirteenth century.[e]
8. A report on Indian marriage customs, especially dowries and the *sati* (including two variants).	The *sati* described by Poggio is different in the precise details, but very similar in essence.
9. A report on valuable goods from India, with emphasis on medicinal herbs and precious stones.	
10. A discussion on the best European markets for oriental products. Tafur shows a striking preference for Spain (i.e. the kingdom of Castile), his own country.	
11. Asked about Indian humanoid monsters (the kind found in Isidore of Seville and medieval encyclopaedias) Conti denies their existence, but insists on strange animals and gives some examples.	Poggio's account agrees even with some specific cases.
12. A comment on the piety of the Christians of Prester John, despite the fact that they ignore Rome, again a theme close to the Mandeville tradition.	In his own report of the Christians of Ethiopia Poggio omitted detailed information about religious practices.
13. Emphasis on the authority of the king (the Prester John) among his subjects.	
14. A report on magical practices, with a story about prediction of weather in the Red Sea through demonic intercession.	There is a very similar parallel in Poggio, despite clear differences in detail.
15. A description of big ships.	Parallel in Poggio.
16. A description of Mecca.	
17. Emphasis on the size and importance of the Nile, which is made to run from India to Ethiopia (a common medieval idea, but a surprising mistake in someone who spoke to Conti).	
18. A note on the interest of the Prester John in western Christianity and in the conquest of Jerusalem, perfectly coherent with the usual crusading meaning of the medieval myth (the Prester John was a promise of	

restoration of the original Christian paradise through the success of spiritual reform and war against the infidel).

19. A statement about the church and tomb of Saint Thomas in India, including a legend about miraculous interventions (the legendary material has parallels in Marco Polo and other medieval reports, as well as in early sixteenth-century Portuguese descriptions of the tomb of Saint Thomas in Mylapore, north of the Coromandel coast, which suggests the existence of a common indigenous source).

Poggio only mentions the church with the remains of the apostle.

20. A comment on skin colour, with the Indians darker than the Europeans, but not as dark as the Ethiopians (Africans). Tafur seems to imply a geographical continuum, in the same way as Pliny, who commented on the same point.[f]

[a] Tafur, *Andanças e viajes*, pp. 99–110.
[b] Vives Gatell, 'Andanças', pp. 71–3.
[c] Broquière, *Voyage d'Outremer*, pp. 145–6.
[d] It is very doubtful however that Conti or Tafur followed Mandeville directly, since the actual stories are completely different. The story ultimately derived from Genesis. This is why a few pages later Tafur mentions quite explicitly that the source of the Nile is the earthly paradise, as a piece of well-established mythical geography. It is, however, a river Nile that reaches as far as the tomb of Saint Thomas (in 'South India'!).
[e] The story about the failed attempt to find the source of the Nile appears to have a local Egyptian origin. It is recorded as a contemporary event in the Latin pilgrimage of Ludolphus of Suchen (1336–41), a German priest and contemporary of Mandeville with cosmographical ambitions. See Ludolphus of Suchen, *De itinere terrae sanctae liber*, ed. by F. Deycks (Stuttgart, 1851), p. 59. It would seem that the thematic connection with the Prester John, Saint Thomas the apostle of the Indies and the location of earthly paradise was generalized among crusaders and pilgrims from the fourteenth century.
[f] Pliny, *Natural history*, vol. II, pp. 390– (book VI, chap. 22).

occupation by the Turks (he also claims to have been well received by the emperor, a distant 'relative' of his).

In contrast, Poggio had an intellectual dream. He wanted to restore ancient knowledge and improve it. Conti, whom he personally questioned, could be as good a source as any old text, if critically scrutinized. Poggio's attitude towards knowledge was not without reservations. That quality of his works which also makes his contribution to travel literature novel can best be defined, in the words of F. Krantz, as 'historical and analytical realism', in which original knowledge of ancient texts and scepticism about the direct utility of classical learning are combined in a wider attitude, defined by a 'reliance on the utility of contemporary experience', and, more generally, 'a tendency, even a drive, to view reality, past and present, in terms of concrete particulars'. The result is a fundamental assumption: 'the secular relatedness and comparability, indeed, the interchangeability of [human] experience'.[82]

We may therefore say that it was Poggio, rather than Conti, who created Bizengalia for the West. Conti was to be followed by many others who risked their lives in India and dealt with its particularities. But the new critical attitudes of the humanists, which transformed the education of the social elites of the whole of Europe, were soon to influence imperial administrators and ambitious missionaries. Thus the Portuguese, who went to the East in search of 'Christians and spices', in the famous expression of one of Vasco da Gama's companions, quickly abandoned the idea of finding the Prester John and left it behind, securely located in a historical Abyssinia. Christians and spices they found, and also Muslims to wage war against, but in the middle there were other kings to negotiate with. Thus they re-created the empire of Vijayanagara.

---

[82] Krantz, 'Between Bruni and Machiavelli', pp. 150 and 121–2. However, I suspect that the 'secular', 'historical' and 'relativistic' aspects of Poggio's humanism may have been overstated in Krantz's analysis. He seems to extract almost a system of modern thought out of what was merely an implicit attitude of openness towards common opinion, and curiosity for contemporary events. This led Poggio, it is true, to challenge the traditional definitions of Fortune, Law and Virtue, but his was not really a systematic philosophical project (nor was he a terribly original historian either: Cochrane, *Historians*, pp. 28–9).

4. *Ludovico de Varthema: the curious traveller at the time of Vasco da Gama and Columbus*

CURIOSITY, DISGUISE AND THE END OF PILGRIMAGE

Ludovico de Varthema of Bologna is the second European traveller to have visited and described Vijayanagara. We know little about him, apart from what he tells us in his own book, and that, alas, is not always reliable.[1] However, when he died some time before 1517, Varthema was one of the most successful and best-known travel writers since Marco Polo.[2] On his return to Italy in 1508, after seven years in the East, he personally recounted his travels to the Venetian Senate (for which he was paid).[3] The written version which he produced soon afterwards was dedicated to members of one of the leading noble families in Rome, the Colonna-Montefeltro. It was printed in Italian in 1510 with the support of the Pope and several of his humanist-trained cardinals, and then immediately translated into Latin. For decades, Varthema's *Itinerario*

---

[1] On Varthema see Lach, *Asia*, vol. I, pp. 164–6. The bibliography on this writer is remarkably thin considering its obvious interest. The logical starting points are the modern editions: see, in Italian, *Itinerario di Ludovico de Varthema*, ed. by P. Guidici, 2nd edn (Milan, 1929), and in English *The travels of Ludovico di Varthema*, trans. by J. Winter Jones and ed. by G. P. Badger, Hakluyt Society (London, 1863). The same translation was used in Varthema, *Itinerary*, ed. by Sir Richard Carnac Temple (London, 1928). The English and Italian editors have generally defended the reliability of Varthema against some doubts cast late in the nineteenth century by L. A. Tiele in the Netherlands in 1875 and by C. Schefer, the French editor, in 1882. See Carnac Temple in Varthema, *Itinerary*, pp. xix–xxvi and P. Guidici in Varthema, *Itinerario*, pp. 40–50. Jean Aubin has recently re-taken the sceptical argument, 'Deux chrétiens au Yémen Tahiride', *Journal of the Royal Asiatic Society*, 3rd series, 3 (1993): 33–75.

[2] His latest date of death can be established through a reference in the 1517 Roman edition (see Jones in Varthema, *The travels*, p. iv).

[3] According to Marino Sanuto in his *Diarii*, 'Today [5 November] after lunch there came to the College of the Signoria a Bolognese who had come from Calicut. He explained many things about those parts, and everybody remained stupefied by the rites and customs of India. And the College gave him 25 ducats for his account'. Sanuto, *I Diarii*, 58 vols. (Venice, 1879–1903), vol. VII, p. 662.

would figure as one of the key modern authorities concerning the Portuguese discoveries in the East. In fact his work is one of the most striking successes of travel literature in the early history of printing, with at least five editions in Italian, one in Latin, three in German, and two in Castilian between only 1510 and 1523. There were several more editions later in the century, including French, Dutch and English translations.[4] Having been knighted by the king of Portugal for his services in India, Varthema could also seek to add a social emblem to his authority as traveller. And yet a relative obscurity remained attached to his persona, possibly on account of his modest origins, but especially as a result of the very elusiveness with which he constructed his identity as a traveller in India. For many sixteenth-century erudite cosmographers, like the German cleric Johannes Boemus, Varthema was not the adventurous traveller who cleverly disguised his true identity in order to penetrate Mecca or to reach the faraway islands where nutmeg and cloves grew, but rather a dubious character who may have been fooling his European audience at the same time that he fooled his oriental companions.[5] The important issue about Varthema's journey to India is therefore not just a matter of defining what kind of personal description he gave, but more broadly what kind of role he adopted as traveller and as travel writer, and how this role and this rhetoric related to his intentions. In this sense, despite Varthema's efforts to describe a novel world to his contemporaries, he can be seen with hindsight to have added more to the evolution of images of the traveller than to the evolution of images of the East.

By all appearances his journey, in the very first years of the sixteenth century, followed the same pattern as Nicolò Conti's a century earlier: disguised as a Muslim, and with a knowledge of colloquial Arabic which he acquired during a long stay at Damascus, Varthema followed the main trading routes that connected the Mediterranean with the Indian Ocean. Thus from Egypt and Syria he travelled to Arabia (including

---

[4] See the preface by the nineteenth-century translator J. Winter Jones to Varthema, *The travels*, pp. i–xvi. It is noteworthy that in the 1540s Ramusio could not find a satisfactory copy of the Italian text and had recourse to the Spanish version by Cristóbal de Arcos, which he used to correct the Italian in a number of places. He did not, however, re-translate the whole thing, as is sometimes stated.

[5] See, in particular, Johannes Boemus, whose *Omnium gentium mores, leges et ritus* of 1520 (a kind of comparative ethnology based on classical and humanist sources) is discussed by Klaus Vogel as a reaction against recent travel writers like Varthema: K. A. Vogel, 'Cultural variety in a Renaissance perspective: Johannes Boemus on 'The manners, laws and customs of all peoples' (1520)', in H. Bugge and J. P. Rubiés (eds.) *Shifting cultures. Interaction and discourse in the expansion of Europe* (Münster, 1995). Boemus indeed described Varthema in his prefatory letter as a shameless liar seeking the admiration of the populace. I remain sceptical as to whether he had any solid grounds from which to launch his attack, other than the intellectual arrogance of a conservative cleric who counted himself among the humanists and despised novel books written in the vernacular.

Mecca) all the way to Aden. He then claims to have visited Persia, and eventually reached the important commercial city–port of Cambay in Gujarat. From Cambay he descended along the western coast of India, visiting its ports but also penetrating to the interior capitals of Bijapur and Vijayanagara. He certainly spent some time in Malabar, and afterwards he sailed (or so he claims) to Ceylon, the gulf of Bengal, the Malay peninsula, Sumatra and the Spice Islands.

While some parts of Varthema's account are perfectly credible, others create a number of problems and raise the question of the *Itinerario*'s authenticity. In particular, the reality of Varthema's trip to Ormuz and the interior of Persia and of the journey beyond Coromandel (to Tarnassari, Pegu, Bengal, Malacca, the Moluccas and Java) is very much open to question. The descriptions are generally vague and confusing, although they contain some elements which can be verified with other sources. Varthema might have been unable to record or remember well these parts of his journey, especially given the dangerous conditions in which he travelled: unable to hide entirely his European background, he pretended to be a Christian renegade, captured early in his youth by Muslims and turned Mamluk. In this guise, he alternated between playing the roles of merchant, artillery-smelter, physician and fool/saint. It seems, however, more likely that at some points Varthema simply reported as direct experience what was only hearsay, with the possible aim of enhancing his role as a famous traveller. His attitude as a writer acutely aware of his own persona could be seen to support the idea that he was prone to exaggerate.

The argument ultimately depends on the geographical and chrono-logical coherence of the itinerary. From this perspective, it is clear that the journey from Diu (off Gujarat) back to Persia and then back to Cambay is not particularly logical; that the trip within Persia to Shiraz *through* Herat is impossible in the time available, and therefore an invention unless one were to believe (as Carnac Temple, one of his apologists, argued) that the capital of Khorasan has been confused with a little village elsewhere.[6] In the Bay of Bengal the itinerary again loses geographical coherence, in particular the journey to the city of Tarnassari (Tenasserim), which is wrongly placed in the Indian subcontinent (in the vicinity of Orissa). Moreover, and this is most decisive, the whole trip East of Malabar is chronologically quite impossible to fit in, especially given the fact that the seasonal monsoons limited the possibilities for

---

[6] Both the authenticity of the journey to Persia and that beyond Cape Comorin were defended by Carnac Temple (Varthema, *Itinerary*, pp. xix–xxvi). He tried to prove against previous critics the chronological feasibility of the voyage, and found ways to explain away Varthema's abundant misstatements.

navigation to certain times of the year.[7] Effectively, in the most coherent reconstruction Varthema's travels east of Yemen need to be crammed in between August 1504, which is the earliest date he could have sailed towards India, and the autumn of 1505, when he met the Portuguese in Malabar.[8] How much of India he visited within this period is an open issue, but his journey to Pegu, Malacca and the Spice Islands can be effectively ruled out. From this perspective, Varthema's account of his invented travels stands out as a sustained and informed fiction.

The certainty of this falsification is confirmed by the fact that the actual descriptions of many of the locations beyond South India offer contradictory evidence. Varthema was supposedly travelling as 'Iunus', his oriental persona as a former Christian renegade but now a saintly Muslim, speaking (it would seem) some popular Arabic. He was under the close supervision of 'Cogazionor' (Khadjeh Djoneyd), a Persian merchant with whom he had managed to associate himself as friend and future brother-in-law. All this would have limited his ability to keep notes of his observations, or to extend his social contact beyond the communities of Muslim merchants in the city–ports which he visited. But this explanation would not seem sufficient to justify a number of marked inconsistencies. For instance, if Varthema was indeed in Siam and Pegu, he failed to distinguish the indigenous Buddhist priests from the foreign merchant communities of Hindus, and he repeatedly described wife-burning in the wrong geographical context. On the other hand, those descriptions which are accurate (such as those of the nutmeg and clove trees in the Spice Islands, and some stories about trade in Pegu), Varthema could have easily obtained from his Persian companion and other traders he met in Malabar.[9]

Jean Aubin, Varthema's most recent, best-informed and harshest

---

[7] While Carnac Temple managed to cram the voyage from India to the Spice Islands between February 1505 and August of the same year, the resulting itinerary is not only unlikely but also absurd from a climatic perspective. The merchants would have travelled eastwards during the north-eastern monsoon (December to April) and returned to the west during the south-western monsoon (May to August). In reality, one would want to sail to the east in April or May (but not between June and August, when it became too dangerous) and return west from October to March.

[8] Aubin, 'Deux chrétiens', p. 36. Varthema explicitly states that he left Damascus for Mecca on April 1503, but modern critics point out that his dating of the 'feast of the sacrifices' on 24 May must refer to 1504. Varthema might have changed the date in order to accommodate an extra year for his eastern travels.

[9] In general, even when his reports are basically accurate, Varthema tends to dramatize situations in a literary fashion, and invents funny dialogues in a rather intuitive Arabic (in a way not dissimilar to the use of direct speech in various *novelle* of the period). In Portuguese India, Varthema is the most obvious precursor to Fernão Mendes Pinto, whose *Peregrinaçam* (1614) is obviously a literary recreation of a personal experience written as a novel.

critic, not only doubts these obviously flawed sections of the *Itinerario*, but also his travels north of Malabar, from Gujarat through the Kanarese coast and to Vijayanagara.[10] Instead, he argues that Varthema only left Aden in the summer of 1505, having been coerced into fighting for the ruler of Yemen over the previous year, and that he sailed straight to Calicut, where soon afterwards Almeida's Portuguese fleet also arrived (it was then that Varthema abandoned his Muslim identity in order to join them). He further believes that Varthema possibly travelled to Malabar as a mercenary Mamluk specializing in artillery, and that he might have been sent by the sultan of Egypt to assist the ruler of Calicut against the 'Franks' – although he obviously had second thoughts about it.[11]

Aubin's thesis is unnecessarily sceptical. Although it does account for some of Varthema's inventions by referring them to his need to hide a supposedly 'genuine' (rather than merely episodic) Mamluk past, it does not account for the literary and social skills which he demonstrated on his return to Europe. It also requires denying any authenticity to the element of 'curiosity' which Varthema so obviously plays up. In fact, if we discount Aubin's unnecessary hypothesis that Varthema spent August 1504 to August 1505 in Yemen (after all this part of the account, describing his imprisonment and sexual adventure with the wife of the sultan, has obviously fictional elements), it is perfectly possible that he sailed towards India at the end of the summer of 1504, after a brief interlude in Aden and Rada.[12] His imprisonment there, if we take away the elements of romance, is still feasible. More importantly, this hypothesis would have allowed him to travel with his 'Persian' trader companions up until winter (which would also explain how he picked up so many stories about other regions), facilitating also his eventual introduction to the merchant communities of Malabar.[13]

Another question is whether the account of these travels in western India makes full sense. The narrative is not particularly eventful. The circuitous itinerary from Goa to Bijapur (Varthema's 'Decan'), then to the coastal ports of Kanará and Malabar, then again towards the

---

[10] Aubin, 'Deux chrétiens', p. 38.

[11] Ibid., p. 43.

[12] Aubin finds the sojourn in Yemen more credible than the eastern travels, but accepts that it does create problems too.

[13] Varthema could not of course have met 'Cogazionor' in Khorasan, as he declares. However, even Aubin believes that he is to some extent a credible character, and suggests that they could have met in Malabar instead. At some point Varthema specifies what the Persian trader carried to India: coral, saffron, velvet brocades, knives – a sensible list. What is most curious is that Khadjeh Djoneyd adopts Varthema as companion because he is himself interested in seeing the world, rather than in mere profit. This twist obviously serves Varthema's literary needs.

interior, from Cannanor to Vijayanagara and back, before finally proceeding to Calicut, involves a remarkably long detour, in the case of Vijayanagara only for a visit of a few days (which should perhaps be dated during the winter of 1504–5). However, the description of the city conforms to the image given by earlier travellers like Nicolò Conti. It is also considerably more detailed. The narrative implies the existence of brahmin informers, either met *in situ* or on the coast. The fact that Varthema (or his party of Muslim merchants) did not take the shortest route, or that the description of Bijapur is not very vivid, does not invalidate the likelihood of a visit to Vijayanagara, which was after all renowned among traders for its beauty, wealth and cosmopolitan atmosphere. On the whole the itinerary is realistic and detailed, so that many small places are mentioned. This was, of course, a region that Varthema would have a chance to explore further when he spent some two years serving the Portuguese in Malabar (from December 1505 to December 1507).[14]

From all this it can be concluded that Varthema's experience of India in general and of Vijayanagara in particular cannot be separated entirely from his interaction with Muslim merchants first, and with the Portuguese later. While the Italian traveller stands as an independent figure in his *Itinerario*, he was effectively functioning as a spy, with claims to originality (duly exaggerated) in a context in which information was quickly becoming part of an imperial project. In fact, although we cannot be certain about how much Varthema knew when he left Italy (probably some time in 1502), he could certainly have heard about the Portuguese arrival in Calicut, because the news had reached Florence and Venice – by the means of letters written by Italian merchants in Lisbon and Egypt – as early as 1499.[15] On his way to India he found evidence of the impending struggle with the Portuguese in commercial centres such as Mecca and Aden, and for this very reason, when travelling amongst Muslim merchants, he was often accused of being a spy.

---

[14] The itinerary between the cities of the Kanarese coast, from Bhatkal north to Honavur and then south to Mangalore, is not entirely logical either, but a party of foreign merchant travellers might have had reasons to depart from a straight course.

[15] Strictly speaking, Varthema could have listened to or even read some of the manuscript Italian reports of the first expeditions of Vasco da Gama and Pedro Alvares Cabral, of the kind later published in 1507 in the collection entitled *Paesi novamente retrovati*. Conti's account, which circulated in Latin and Italian manuscripts, did not necessarily reach Varthema, but we must note the existence of Latin editions in 1485 and 1492. In 1502 the Moravian editor V. Fernandes published a Portuguese translation which accompanied his edition of the book of Marco Polo – and it was from this Portuguese text that Ramusio, again unable to procure a copy of the Italian or Latin text, made his version.

While Varthema's observations must be studied as part of the early formation of images about India in the context of the first Portuguese expeditions, what emerges as the key question is what kind of traveller Varthema really was, because his peculiar role-playing lies at the heart of his approach to non-European peoples. His travel narrative was written, in Italian, for a growing market of printed books, and on the adventurer's initiative.[16] He made use of the narrative techniques of the late medieval and Renaissance *novella* in order to produce an early form of picaresque story-telling, unchecked by any mediating figure such as Poggio, Rustichello or Friar Pipino. In fact Varthema exemplifies an original development of great consequence for the future of the genre of travel writing during the following four centuries, namely the appearance of a new degree of self-consciousness of the European traveller, elaborated as a new literary persona with parallels not only in travel literature but also in new forms of autobiography in the culture of the Renaissance.[17] One could in fact say that travel literature considerably strengthened the secularizing autobiographical trend in the culture of the Renaissance, from the rather obscure accounts written by travellers like Pero Tafur or Bertrandon de la Broquière in the fifteenth century to the more famous books published for instance by Álvar Núñez Cabeza de Vaca (1555), Hans Staden (1557), Jean de Léry (1578) or Fernão Mendes Pinto (1614) concerning their travels (real or fictional) in America and Asia.[18] Departing from its medieval precedents, the new persona elaborated by Varthema suggests a secular attitude in a more radical way than (let us say) John Mandeville, because the Italian traveller is no longer a pilgrim – he does not even care to visit the Christian holy places, and skips them when he journeys from Cairo to Damascus. In fact he opposes his experience as empirical traveller to the world of armchair cosmographers rather than to the conventional world of pious travellers. Varthema's persona also states its own validity as the source for a new genre with more confidence than either Marco Polo or Nicolò Conti,

---

[16] I do not know any earlier example of a travel narrative written and printed on the traveller's own initiative with the purpose of addressing an open market.

[17] Important forms of autobiography existed in the Middle Ages both in Muslim and Christian cultures, as a religious–intellectual genre and, more rarely, as a historical one. But in the sixteenth century autobiographical forms were used for a wider range of purposes – it could be argued that as numerous literary genres were revived, combined and transformed, new identities other than those of saints, rulers and poets could find a self-conscious expression. In this sense autobiographies essentially shadowed biographical subjects.

[18] Other autobiographical accounts of course remained unpublished – for example those by the Florentine merchants Galeotto Cei in America (*c.* 1555) or Francesco Carletti around the world (1606).

because he does not need special circumstances in order to present himself: it is his very originality as traveller that justifies his discourse.

In this way Varthema belongs to, and to a certain extent creates, the tradition of the 'curious traveller': the traveller who is not primarily a merchant, an ambassador, a spy, a conqueror, a mercenary, a pilgrim or a missionary, but rather an independent character self-defined by a desire to know other lands and peoples, and to report back on them to his own community of origin. The identity of the traveller is created in the narrative structure as the centre that organizes the world, because what he does and what happens to him provides the main argument, and what he sees or hears is in substance that which the reader learns. There is nothing sacred in Varthema's itinerary either, no search for meaning or transcendence. Unlike Felix, the protagonist of Ramon Llull's *Book of marvels*, whose role as allegorical traveller was to witness a pre-defined divine and natural order in a pre-defined moral way, or unlike any historical pilgrim, whose intention was to fit an actual empirical journey to a conventional spiritual experience by means of a sacred landscape defined by symbols and texts, Varthema's identity as traveller depends entirely on the book he writes. He is the centre of the book and the book creates his persona.

This lack of external definition is reinforced by the fact that Varthema himself is a rather obscure character, of no particular origin or occupation, a subject therefore impossible to classify by his social status or that of his family (his references to family and occupation in the text are always questionable because they sustain a false identity). As a traveller he assumes different identities as it suits different circumstances, changing dress, language, profession and even religion so as to become a soldier or a physician, a rich merchant or a humble pilgrim, a devout Christian or a Muslim holy man. There is no way to pin him down to any of these roles, since he presents himself as a clever spy. He visits Mecca as a Mamluk – probably he is the first European whose claim to having been there is genuine. At one stage in his journey to the Spice Islands he makes friends with oriental Christians, but 'Iunius' cannot reveal his 'true' identity (as a Latin Christian in disguise) because his principal companions are Muslim. At any moment he may turn out to be pretending further – even when he writes (and indeed this part of the journey is fictional). Varthema's identity is therefore reduced to his authority as a writer, and the problem of truth is reduced to the question of the truthfulness of what he says. Even when he joined the Portuguese and fought bravely at the siege of Cannanor in 1507 – a well-documented fact – Varthema was acting in a new role rather than simply returning to an original persona. His knighthood was, even for his contemporaries, an expression of his success in performing that role, rather than a guarantee of his truthfulness. Varthema thus remains primarily the author of a book and, secondarily, when we can believe him, the protagonist of a journey.

Varthema expresses very clearly his motivations, and from his words in the preface it appears that he is extending a primarily intellectual concern to the activity of travel:

> There have been many men who have devoted themselves to the investigation of the things of the world . . . Then others of greater understanding, to whom the earth has not sufficed . . . have begun to traverse the highest regions of Heaven with careful observations and vigils . . . Wherefore I, feeling a very great desire for similar results [i.e. praise from others and satisfaction to myself], and leaving alone the Heavens as a burden more suitable for the shoulders of Atlas and Hercules, determined to investigate some small portion of this our terrestrial globe; and not having any inclination (knowing myself of very slender understanding) to arrive at my desire by study of conjectures, I determined, personally, and with my own eyes [*con la propria persona e con le occhi medesmi*], to endeavour to ascertain the situation of places, the qualities of peoples, the diversities of animals, the varieties of fruitful and aromatic trees of Egypt, Syria, Arabia Deserta and Felix, Persia, India, and Ethiopia, especially remembering that the testimony of one eye witness is worth more than ten heard-says.[19]

It is apparent that Varthema presents his motives with a great deal of irony. To mock pretentious theorists by appealing to the knowledge attained through practical experience was quickly becoming a central theme in the Renaissance legitimation of novel discourses. This also suggests that Varthema's dedicatory preface has some of the elements of a rhetorical piece. Indeed, it recalls Iosafa Barbaro's preface to his account of embassies to Persia and the Black Sea, written in 1487 and well known in Venice before its publication in 1543:

> According to what men versed in geometry prove with evident demonstrations, when compared to the skies the earth is as small as a point in the middle of the circumference of a circle. And because a good part of it is either covered with waters, or intemperate on account of an excess of cold or of heat (according to the opinion of some), the part which is inhabited is even smaller. And yet men are so small that it is difficult to find any who have seen more than a very small part of this inhabitable part, and (if I am not mistaken) none

---

[19] Varthema, *The travels*, pp. 1–2, corrected from *Itinerario*, p. 335.

who have seen it all. And those who have seen a good part are mostly merchants or sailors, in which two activities, from their origins until today, my Venetian forefathers and lords have excelled so much that I can say with confidence that in this they surpass all others. Therefore, since the Roman Empire ceased to rule everywhere as it used to do, and the diversity of languages, customs and religion have, in a manner of speaking, worn out and confined this inferior world, a great deal of this small part of the earth that can be inhabited would not be known had it not been opened up by the trade and navigation of the power of the Venetians. And among them, if there is anyone today who has laboured in order to see some part of it, I can say with truth that I am one of these, having spent most of my youth and a good part of my old age in distant places, with barbarous people, and among men alien in all respects from our customs and civility. Among these peoples I have found and seen many things that to many who will hear them perhaps will seem like lies, because, in a manner of speaking, they never left Venice.[20]

Barbaro went on to justify his writing of a book with a remarkable list of ancient writers like Pliny, Solinus, Pomponious Mela, Strabo, Herodotus, Diodorus Siculus and Dionysius of Halicarnassus, and modern (mostly Venetian) ones like Marco Polo, Nicolò Conti, Pietro Quirini, Alvise da Mosto, Ambrosio Contarini and 'Iovane de Vanda Villa'.[21] This awareness that travel literature was part of a neglected and potentially useful science which could be, and indeed was, being revived, was likely to have been shared by Varthema. Both writers were obviously responding to a cultural climate influenced by humanist education and concerns (Varthema also goes on to mention Ulysses in his preface). But at the same time the rhetorical ingredient in Varthema's declaration of his aims only confirms that we cannot exclude an important dimension of fortune-seeking in his travelling to the East only some four or five years after the Portuguese had reached the Indian Ocean (in 1498). He was aware that the whole Venetian system of trading spices in the Levant was being threatened. His return to the Christian fold after his trip to the East, whether purely spontaneous or opportunistic, was certainly facilitated by his ability to sell information to the Portuguese in their struggle against the Muslim merchants and the Hindu rulers of Calicut. That he was eventually knighted by the Viceroy Almeida for his services, and later confirmed in his new aristocratic status by King Manuel in

---

[20] I translate from Ramusio's edition of the 'Viaggio della Tana e nella Persia': Ramusio, *Navigazione e viaggi*, vol. III, pp. 485–6.

[21] This 'Iovane de Vanda Villa' is of course John Mandeville, whose account had been published in Italian by this time and was being continuously reprinted.

Portugal, also suggest that Varthema's 'desire to see the world' was not a simple act of curiosity.[22] And Varthema's interest in obtaining a privilege to print and profit from his book probably indicates that an economic calculation underlay his desire to sell copies.

And yet, despite these hidden motivations, the original statement in the dedicatory preface indicates a genuine attitude confirmed by the rest of the narrative: Varthema is a very clear case of an independent and curious traveller seeking to transmit to his contemporaries a fresh and unmediated image of the world. He in fact offers himself as a model of audacity, survival and self-regulation in the dangerous world of natural and cultural differences. Thus, he justifies his return on the grounds that he has had enough of the continuous change of climates and customs, and especially by the fear of those bestial, 'inhuman men' (*inumani omini*) which he had encountered – only fictionally, as it turns out – in islands like 'Java' (Sumatra).[23] If there is any moral conclusion to the *Itinerario*, it is that the knowledge of the variety of climates and customs can help men regulate their desires and learn how to deal with novel situations. While Varthema offers the result of his efforts to his contemporaries (who therefore do not need to undertake the dangerous journey to gather the fruits), he presents himself as an essential traveller when he concludes his preface by saying that, 'since I am not good at any other kind of study, I shall continue to spend the remainder of my fleeting days in this laudable exercise'.[24]

Thus Varthema's role appears remarkable when compared to medieval precedents, because neither his social origins nor his purpose were conventionally defined, and also because he directly addressed an unlimited market with his printed book. However, compared to contemporary travellers he appears more as an extreme case in an age of growing ambiguity than as a mysterious phenomenon. In some ways he was the culmination of a process as well as the inauguration of a new possibility. If we take as a starting point Mandeville's fourteenth-century fictional synthesis, in which the first-person authority assumed a central position but remained committed to a religious geography, we can follow the emergence of the lay worldly traveller which, as I suggested earlier, culminated in the chivalric and educational models of the Renaissance.

---

[22] Varthema's career with the Portuguese, recounted in his own narrative, is to some extent confirmed by Barros, who had read the Latin version of the *Itinerary* in the collection of Simon Grynaeus: Barros, *Ásia*, vol I, pp. 388–9. There exists Portuguese documentary evidence of Varthema's activities in India and Portugal.

[23] Varthema, *Itinerario*, p. 297.

[24] Ibid., p. 337. His next project was to travel to the furthest north. Curiously, but logically, under the illusion that the Far East and the West Indies somehow coincided (the Pacific Ocean yet being undiscovered), he thought that he need not go to the New World.

THE EMERGENCE OF THE WORLDLY TRAVELLER IN THE LATE MIDDLE AGES

Mandeville's narrative centre was in the first place useful for other imaginary travels, but it also became the vehicle for historical narratives, to the point that the historical bore witness to the supernatural. One early example of this shift in emphasis is the narrative by the Catalan nobleman Ramon de Perellós, who in 1397 visited the purgatory of Saint Patrick in Ireland. From a literary point of view, his aim was to make sure that the recently deceased King John I of Aragon had not ended up in hell, a fate for which Perellós and others accused of his murder could have been made responsible. Thus Perellós appended material from the *Tractatus de Purgatorio Sancti Patricii* written by Hugh of Saltrey (an imaginary narrative of the visit of the knight Owein to purgatory) to his own ethnographical observations of Ireland, whose authenticity few scholars deny today, blending the two around a particularized Christian first person.[25]

More decisively, the extraordinary traveller represented by Marco Polo or by Mandeville, whose claims, whether real or imaginary, could hardly be authenticated (and Nicolò Conti would still remain in this category), was followed in the fifteenth century by ambassadors and humanists travelling either within Europe or further abroad: men like Ruy González de Clavijo, sent in 1403 by the king of Castile to the court of Timur, the French herald Gilles le Bouvier, who in 1451 put together a modern geography of Europe based on his travels, or the Bohemian nobleman Leo of Rozmital, who completed a wide circuit of the courts of Europe between 1465 and 1467 (through Germany, Flanders, England and France as far as Spain, Portugal and then Italy). In all these cases what sustains the narrative is the interest of an aristocratic or patrician audience for a reliable description based on personal observations. If what characterized the anonymous journal of the Castilian embassy to Timur was the almost naïve objectivity of a detailed everyday description, Gilles le Bouvier, whose book of geography (*c.* 1450) is rather impersonal and superficial, is instead interesting for his own understanding of his reasons for writing it: 'Because many people of different nations and countries find enjoyment and take pleasure, as I have done in times past, in seeing the world and the different things that it contains [*veoir le monde et les diverses choses qui y sont*], and also because many others want to know them without

---

[25] See Ramon de Perellós, 'Viatge al Purgatori nomenat de Sant Patrici', in *Novel·les amoroses i morals*, ed. by A. Pacheco and A. Bover i Font (Barcelona, 1982), pp. 9 and 23–52.

travelling there.'[26] The journey of Leo of Rozmital presents a few more ambiguities. Although the travel diaries declare his to be a 'knightly journey' across Christian kingdoms with the intention of completing a pilgrimage, there are reasons to suspect that there was a diplomatic motivation behind it, namely to enlist support for the recently excommunicated Bohemian king, George Podiebrad, a Hussite married to Rozmital's sister.[27] We could add Pope Pius II to this list of fifteenth-century secular travel writers. His *Comentarii*, describing his travels as part of his third-person autobiography (1405–64), were motivated by a desire to make sense of his pontificate in historical terms, and thus bring together the European Christians against the Turks.[28]

Here it is important to introduce a distinction. Although the author of the journal of Clavijo's embassy wrote in the third person, out of social deference, and Pius II also dictated his personal recollections in a third person reminiscent of Julius Caesar (thus in a manner appropriate for an accomplished and slightly vain humanist), the underlying principle that gave meaning and authority to these texts was a secular self-centred observer.[29] The same could be said about the two diaries of the travels of Leo of Rozmital, kept separately in German and Czech by two members of his retinue, the Nüremberg patrician, Gabriel Tetzel, and Rozmital's squire, Schaseck. The chroniclers use a generic 'we' to relate what was seen and observed by a group of people, because what mattered was the experience of their lord, not their own. But what gave authority to the text was the direct testimony of a historical experience, which in some cases was shared by a group of travellers, but sometimes was purely personal. In this sense, it is not so much the presence of self in the first person that matters, because this 'I' could be an Augustinian, providenti-

---

[26] Gilles le Bouvier, 'Le livre de la description des pays', ed. by E. T. Hamy, in *Recueil des voyages et de documents pour servir à l'histoire de la géographie*, vol. XXII (Paris, 1908), p. 29.

[27] M. Letts (ed.) *The travels of Leo of Rozmital through Germany, Flanders, England, France, Spain and Italy 1465–67*, Hakluyt Society, 2nd series (London, 1957). Letts translated the complete German text by Gabriel Tetzel into English but unfortunately only parts of the Latin version of Schaseck's journal (the Czech text having been lost). On fifteenth-century travellers in general see the introduction by J. R. Hale to Antonio de Beatis, *The travel journal of Antonio de Beatis*, ed. by J. R. Hale, Hakluyt Society, 2nd series (London, 1979).

[28] I have used the excellent English edition, A. S. Piccolomini [Pius II], *Memoirs of a Renaissance pope*, trans. and ed. by F. A. Gragg and L. C. Gabel, *Smith College Studies in History*, 5 vols. (Northampton, Mass., 1937–57).

[29] Although Gonzalo Argote de Molina, the sixteenth-century Spanish editor (1582), attributed the narrative to the ambassador Clavijo, the author always refers to the ambassadors in the third-person. He also avoids delivering any personal opinions. Alonso Fernández Mesa, a poet who accompanied the expedition (as we learn from the testimony of Pero Tafur), is perhaps a more suitable candidate.

alist self, geared towards a religious interpretation of events.[30] For example, it is remarkable that the examples we have of thirteenth- and fourteenth-century chronicles written by a first-person witness of the deeds of kings and lords, or even by a first-person king – vivid accounts such as those by James I of Aragon, Jean de Joinville or Ramon Muntaner – obsessively insist on the idea that what happens is God's will, and that human history simply witnesses to it.[31] What we find instead in the fifteenth century is an increasing number of narratives, often travel accounts, clearly written from an individual human perspective that makes sense of experience without reference to the will and power of God.

An important example is provided by the French Bertrandon de la Broquière, who in 1432 was sent by the duke of Burgundy Philip le Bon to collect information about the Near East, and in particular about the Turks. Although he presented his account 'for the amusement and distraction of the hearts of noble men who wish to see the world', this aristocratic audience was above all offered a solid geography of the possible passage for 'the conquest of Jerusalem', and in particular an account of those areas, customs and conditions which were less well known. Thus the pilgrim had been fully transformed into a spy, who took notes of what he saw with the view to supporting the organization of another crusade.[32] The traveller was himself a lesser nobleman eager to make friends with European merchants or Christian renegades in order to obtain an insight into the local scene, willing to disguise himself like a Muslim Mamluk (after proper confession) in order to cross from Syria to the Ottoman empire by land, and ready to join impromptu more formal ambassadors so as personally to get to know kings and emperors and, in particular, to study the military system of the Grand Turk. Much of what Broquière learnt depended upon the skilful use of these external mediations which he often acknowledges, in particular Frankish mer-

---

[30] The Augustinian self, which associates human personality with sin and aspires to identify an external divine will as superior, is best portrayed in Augustine's own *Confessions*.

[31] For instance Joinville, in his account of the disastrous crusade to Egypt in 1248, manages to present a badly planned and stupidly led enterprise as yet another reflection of King Louis' saintly virtues, and this is possible precisely because the religious, providentialist code is far more important than the political one. The contemporary *Book of deeds* of James I of Aragon – a quite unique medieval royal autobiography – is an even more perfect example of unabashed chivalric providentialism.

[32] See Bertrandon de la Broquière, *Le voyage d'Outremer*, ed. by C. Schefer (Paris, 1892). I quote according to the English translation by G. R. Kline, *The voyage d'Outremer by Bertrandon de la Broquière* (New York, 1988), p. 1. The background to his mission, like that of Pero Tafur's wanderings or even the cosmographical interests of Pius II, was an attempt from the crusading tradition of the Latin West to revive and confront the bleak possibility of the imminent fall of Constantinople to the Ottoman Turks.

chants (from Venice, Genoa, Florence, France or Catalonia) and peculiar adventurers (like one Antoine Passerot, who had left his native Famagusta as a political exile and ended up living in Konya as a Muslim, or one Peter of Naples, whose account of the 'Prester John' of Ethiopia, albeit to some extent genuine, is no less confused than Pero Tafur's).[33] Without departing from any conventional audience or purpose, and initially rather better informed about the legends of past crusades than about the contents of the Koran, Broquière in fact develops a novel attitude of systematic curiosity which in many ways resembles that of Varthema. If we were to compare, for example, their respective accounts of the city of Damascus (where both spent some time) we may conclude that both writers offer a realistic impression of a city that pleased them for its beauty, wealth and artistry, for its gardens and fountains, and where they heard a number of local Christian legends too.[34] On the whole, however, Broquière was more penetrating in his political analysis, possibly because it was his clear purpose to assess whether the Turks could be defeated. He found them a brave and loyal people, but inferior to the Western Christians in military technology, and therefore only victorious because they were better disciplined and informed.

What distinguishes Broquière's ethnological analysis from Jean de Joinville's occasional description of Bedouin or Tartar customs 150 years earlier is a systematicity that derives from understanding historical–political discourses as a separate genre from religious ones. If the fifteenth century witnessed the development of this kind of discourse, it is at the beginning of the sixteenth century that this kind of secularized travel account became especially important.[35] We can quickly recall texts such as those written by the humanist doctor from Nuremberg Hieronymus Münzer, who travelled to the Low Countries, France and Spain in 1494–5 fleeing from the plague, or by the Italian ambassadors Francesco Vettori, sent to Emperor Maximilian I in 1507, and Francesco Guicciardini, who kept a journal of his mission to the king of Aragon Ferdinand II in 1511. We may add more examples in the following decade, from Antonio de Beatis' account of the journey of his master Cardinal Luigi d'Aragona from Italy to Germany, Flanders and France in 1517–18, to

---

[33] Thus one of the interesting things about Broquière's narrative is that the European presence in the East appears fully described, giving us an indication of its importance and character. For the account of Peter of Naples, who had in fact settled in the Christian Ethiopian kingdom and seems after all to be genuine, see Broquière, *The voyage*, pp. 89–94.

[34] Compare Broquière, *The voyage*, pp. 21ff. to Varthema, *Itinerario*, pp. 89ff.

[35] See J. R. Hale, *Renaissance Europe. Individual and society, 1480–1520* (London, 1971), pp. 31–54. Also his introduction to Beatis, *The travel journal*.

an anonymous Italian description of what appears to be a business trip through France, the Low Countries, England, and Spain in 1517–19, probably by a Milanese merchant.[36] What is striking in this period (as opposed to the formalization of geographical relations, cosmographies, and the narratives of the Grand Tour later in the century) are the variety of origins from which secular travel writing simultaneously grew. Münzer with his scholarly erudition, Vettori with his anecdotal stories, Guicciardini with his dry criticisms, the anonymous merchant with his graphic sketches and Antonio de Beatis with his overall clerical mediocrity in fact all produced very distinctive narratives. For example, the distance that separates the collection of personal reflections and sexual *novelle* produced by Vettori from the serious geo-political analysis practised by his friend and fellow correspondent Guicciardini is startling.[37]

In this context, the early narratives of the more exotic voyages of discovery do not appear as a free-standing genre, but rather as a collection of documents which share the conventions of a general cultural development, although obviously in a peculiar way, related to original needs. Despite the fact that in his writings Columbus comes across as a devout Christian with extravagant providentialist claims, his letters and journal were also meant to construct a secular meaning from the perspective of personal observation – namely, the exploitation of economic possibilities through the manipulation of geographical and political conditions. Mission and crusade did not detract from this meaning. On the contrary, if the providentialist emphasis distorted the description, it did so in order to justify and reinforce the validity of the economic prospects: one may well argue that Columbus made the naked Caribbean Indians more handsome and rational, and their land more marvellous, the more he needed to reassure himself and his patrons that

---

[36] The Spanish section of Münzer's travelogue is published in Castilian in J. García Mercadal (ed.) *Viajes de extrangeros por España y Portugal* (Madrid, 1952), vol. I, pp. 327–418. The French part was edited by E. Ph. Goldschmidt, 'Le voyage de Hieronimus Monetarius à travers la France', *Humanisme et Renaissance*, 6 (1939): 55–75, 198–220, 324–48, 529–39. See also F. Guicciardini, 'Diario del viaggio in Spagna', in R. Palmarocchi (ed.) *Scritti autobiografici e rari* (Bari, 1936), pp. 103–24; F. Vettori, 'Viaggio in Alamagna', *Scritti storici e politici*, ed. by E. Niccolini (Bari, 1972), pp. 13–132; L. Monga (ed.) *Un mercante di Milano in Europa. Diario di viaggio del primo cinquecento* (Milan, 1985).

[37] Guicciardini's journal of his journey to Spain provided material for a proper 'relation' of his embassy. Instead, Vettori wrote for his own pleasure and that of his friends. Travel, although real enough, was not so much the subject-matter of his writings as an 'honest pleasure' for free and wealthy people which provided an occasion for collecting arguments, observations and *novelle*, in a way not dissimilar to how many Renaissance novels were constructed from a series of separate episodes (including Cervantes' *Don Quixote* and Fernão Mendes Pinto's *Peregrinaçam*).

Marco Polo's Cathayans were not too far away.[38] A similar analysis can be applied to the anonymous journal of Vasco da Gama's first expedition to India, probably written by a soldier called Alvaro Velho. Less concerned than Columbus with justifying the validity of an enterprise that had been organized, rather than merely adopted, by the monarch, this account is clearly empirical in its method and secular in its concerns, albeit not exempt from significant prejudices – most famously, those concerning the existence of 'Moors', 'Indian Christians' and 'African Blacks'.[39]

From all these examples it is clear that Varthema's narrative appears in a moment of growth in both numbers and models of travel accounts, a growth which affected travel within Europe as well as exploration outside. What distinguishes Varthema is the radical nature of his break with tradition, in the sense that the abandonment of the medieval model of travel as pilgrimage does not involve the need for justification and therefore the definition of a new social convention. Unlike his more immediate predecessors in the fifteenth century, merchants and diplomats like Caterino Zeno, Iosafa Barbaro and Ambrosio Contarini, who had travelled to the Black Sea and Persia, Varthema was not constrained by the political and economic interests of the Venetian republic.[40] The danger of secularization detected in Marco Polo is more advanced in Varthema: his only reason to travel was a curiosity for knowledge, and all the authority of the text derives from an abstract will to travel in order to see and know. Polo and Conti were defined as merchant-patricians from Venice, Varthema is simply the man from Bologna who went to see the East. Even among idle noblemen this lack of obvious purpose was atypical. The Andalusian hidalgo Pedro Tafur, for example, combined his desire to know famous and strange places through personal experience with an ideal of chivalric virtue which he wanted to associate with his social status as a member of the nobility. This led to the idea that somehow the traveller's experience of different governments and national temperaments would be useful for 'learning that which is more profitable to the republic and its establishment, in which activity those

---

[38] See Columbus, *The four voyages of Columbus*, ed. by Cecil Jane, Hakluyt Society, 2nd series, 2 vols. (London, 1930–3); Columbus, *The journal of the first voyage*, ed. by B. W. Ife (London, 1990). Among the many studies of Columbus' writings, Ife's interpretation of the narrative strategies of his journal is particularly lucid (ibid., pp, xix–xxiii).

[39] See [Alvaro Velho], *Diário da Viagem de Vasco da Gama*, ed. by D. Peres, A. Bião and A. Magalhães Basto (Porto, 1945).

[40] The embassies of Zeno, Contarini and Barbaro are summarized in Penrose, *Travel and discovery in the Renaissance*, pp. 24–5; Cochrane, *Historians and historiography in the Italian Renaissance*, p. 326; L. Lockhart, 'European contacts with Persia, 1350–1736', in P. Jackson and L. Lockhart (eds.), *The Timurid and Safavid periods, The Cambridge History of Iran*, vol. VI (1986), pp. 377–8. They were all published by Ramusio.

who do not want to be considered enemies of nobility should labour hardest'.[41] Varthema shied away from any such claims.

Perhaps the best illustration of what is novel in Varthema's narrative identity is the comparison with another independent traveller of the same period, Arnold von Harff, a knight from Cologne who visited Egypt and other places in 1496–9. In the account which he wrote in his German Lower Rhine dialect, and which circulated in a manuscript form for the use of friends and family, von Harff gave a very detailed description of Cairo, where (in a way not unlike Broquière) he was lucky to have the guidance of two German Mamluks who could also inform him about what was going on in the rather unstable sultanate. But not content with climbing pyramids and visiting Mount Sinai, von Harff claimed to have travelled to India and to the source of the Nile in the Mountains of the Moon, and thus exaggerated his actual travels with the help of a Ptolemaic map, a great deal of hearsay and even the addition of a few illustrations. Only with the better knowledge of later accounts can the journey be revealed as utterly confused. But if in this respect he seems to follow the same path as Varthema, the ultimate structure of his narrative reveals an entirely different purpose. Von Harff visited India because he needed to reach the tomb of Saint Thomas, and he climbed the Mountains of the Moon because he needed to reach the source of the Nile and find out about the location of paradise (which, as he discovered, was not really there, but near Jerusalem). For the same reason, he 'went' to Santiago of Compostela in Spain, and to Rome to see the Pope, despite the fact that his account of Rome is essentially lifted from a previous German guidebook printed in 1489, and that he could not have gone there and simultaneously sailed from Venice to Cairo, as he must have done if his dates are correct. In other words, von Harff was a serious, if shallow, pilgrim. Not content with having actually been to the Holy Land, where his experiences were far from mystical, he wished to fulfil a complete sacred landscape, like his illustrious predecessor John Mandeville, whose book, already printed in German, he certainly used to fill in all the gaps.[42]

---

[41] As expressed in his preface: Tafur, *Andanças e viajes*, pp. 1–2. Tafur thus believed that travel could make the knight effectively virtuous, both because in foreign lands he would have to prove himself worthy of his dignity (rather than just resting on the family tradition), and because he would learn political wisdom concerning different lands and peoples, which could later benefit his country. In this sense Tafur, despite his 'medieval' credulity and crusading ideals, clearly introduces major themes of the Renaissance understanding of nobility.

[42] Harff, *The pilgrimage of Arnold von Harff*, ed. by M. Letts (London, 1946). Although Letts acknowledges that the part of the narrative dealing with India (pp. 156ff.) is probably apocryphal, he is far too credulous about many other parts of the narrative and

By contrast, it was not as a pilgrim, but as a discoverer, that Varthema lied, according to the scientific–intellectual concern proposed in his preface. Which exactly are the origins of this concern? The issue that needs to be clarified is the relationship between elite and popular discourse in the ambiguous narrative type created by Varthema. Like his contemporary Vettori, who may be described as a typically curious and hedonistic humanist traveller, Varthema felt free to invent entertaining (and often sexual) anecdotes of the kind that recall Boccaccio's *novelle* and Poggio's *Facietae*.[43] But Varthema was not an ambassador having a good time. He was not a humanist, and he was not particularly learned, despite the fact that his preface shows awareness of an intellectual climate which owed a great deal to the humanists. The humanists indeed provided some of the literary models and intellectual concerns that made travel narratives richer, and travel itself a fashionable activity. But it would be a mistake to see secular travel literature as essentially a humanist genre.

It has for instance been argued, but I believe with excessive emphasis, that one of the most famous early sixteenth century travel writers, Antonio Pigafetta of Vicenza, gave expression to the concerns of a humanist education in his account of the first circumnavigation of the world in 1519–21.[44] In 1519 Pigafetta had accompanied Francesco

---

misses its point. Von Harff did not merely follow the substance of Mandeville: above all, he followed the model.

[43] These anecdotes are probably the least authentic part of Varthema's narrative, traceable to the comic and moralistic *novelle* so popular in the literature of the late Middle Ages and the Renaissance, and equally reminiscent of the sexual tales from the *Arabian Nights* current in the culture of sailors and merchants of the Indian Ocean. They offered the prospects of guaranteed literary success. In this regard the observation made by the English translator J. Winter Jones in 1863 (Varthema, *The travels*, p. ii) is astonishing: 'the translator has endeavoured to preserve the quaint dry style of the author. This must be his excuse for retaining some expressions which are hardly suited to the refinement of the present day, and for not omitting some anecdotes which a writer in modern times would hardly venture to record. *They, however, afford an additional voucher for the truth of the narrator: it is impossible to imagine them to be inventions*, and they only make us feel the more assured that we are travelling with Varthema' (my italics).

[44] On Pigafetta's account see Lach, *Asia in the making of Europe*, vol. I, pp. 173–6; Cochrane, *Historians and historiography*, p. 338 (who insists, wrongly I believe, on the idea that Pigafetta had a humanist education and followed humanist models in his 'journal'). Old editions tended to follow an Italian version published in 1536, possibly by Ramusio who, however, unable to obtain the original, translated from a previous French edition (the French critical text was published, from various manuscripts, by J. Denucé: Antonio Pigafetta, *Relation du primer voyage autour du monde* (Anvers and Paris, 1923)). I have used a recent edition of the more complete Italian version discovered in 1800 in an Ambrosian manuscript of Milan, which is apparently an early copy, and certainly the closest we have to the original (Pigafetta, *La mia longa et pericolosa navigatione*, ed. by L. Giovannini (Milan, 1989)). Giovannini includes Pigafetta's original colour illustrations of the Philippines and Spice Islands.

Chiericati, apostolic legate to the newly elected Emperor Charles V, to Barcelona. With their permission he joined Magellan when he set sail from Seville, officially as a soldier but with the real aim of recording what he saw and heard: in his own words, 'having learnt from many books which I read and from diverse persons who had conversation with his lordship [Francesco Chiericati] of the great and amazing things concerning the Ocean Sea, I decided . . . to obtain personal experience and to go and see those things that might give me satisfaction and give me a name for posterity'.[45] Despite some differences, Pigafetta and Varthema shared very similar motivations and narrative personae. They both claimed patrician origins in small Italian cities and they were both knighted for their personal exploits.[46] On their return to Italy (after visiting their respective royal courts) each first offered his story to the Venetian Senate. Afterwards both wrote their narratives in the vernacular, with limited erudition, for a wide audience, and with the support of the Pope and other aristocrats, to whom they dedicated their works (the difference being that in 1524 Pigafetta was not satisfied by the conditions offered to him in Rome and returned to Venice looking for a more profitable privilege to print his book). Both actively participated in the widening Renaissance understanding of the human subject, by which not only kings and saints, but also soldiers, adventurers and artists could be the subject of biographical and autobiographical narratives.[47] But while Iosafa Barbaro, Amerigo Vespucci, Ludovico de Varthema and Antonio Pigafetta were all educated men with a patrician background who could write with style and ideas and display technical knowledge in subjects such as geography or navigation, the true humanists were historians like Pietro Martyr of Anghiera, who lived among princes and

---

[45] As expressed in the dedicatory letter to Philippe Villers de L'Isle Adam, Grand Master of the Knights of Rhodes (Pigafetta himself was then a knight of Rhodes): Pigafetta, *La mia longa et pericolosa navigatione*, p. 53.

[46] Pigafetta was a knight of Rhodes, but it is not clear whether he obtain the dignity before or after his journey. He certainly obtained a benefice after his return, in 1524, as he struggled to get his book published in Venice. This may have decided him to dedicate the work to the Grand Master.

[47] Autobiographical genres essentially followed biographical ones, and it is worth insisting here that these were important in the Middle Ages for saints, lords, knights and, to a more limited extent, poets. The poet as a relevant subject arose with the Provençal lives of troubadours, and crystallized around the mythical aura that surrounded Dante and Petrarch. What was good for poets and clerics in the fourteenth century would inevitably be equally valid for humanists in the fifteenth, since modesty was not their main strength. By the sixteenth century soldiers, merchants and artists no less than saints, scholars, aristocrats and kings, had become proper subjects for biography. What mattered was not simply that these authors were first-hand witnesses of interesting information, but also that they were themselves, in various ways, an interesting focus of literary attention and self-discovery.

wrote about the New World according to classical models and in elegant Latin. The importance of our educated travellers simply reflects the fact that humanist culture was not that of a self-enclosed community of scholars, but rather, through literacy and other channels, affected various levels of society, connecting the urban classes of patricians, merchants, lawyers and doctors to the court and its domesticated aristocracy.

The contribution of writers like Varthema and Pigafetta, as opposed to most travellers that stayed within the boundaries of Europe, consists in the radical degree with which they portrayed themselves as de-contextualized individuals. This was helped by the fact that they moved outside the frontiers of Christian society proper; but there was more to it. While a medieval traveller like Ibn Battūta reproduced himself as a member of a religious (Islamic) institution even in India and China, or while the Spanish and the Portuguese in America and Asia also carried with them, albeit in the difficult beginnings only symbolically, the institutional reproduction of their original society (their town, their king, their priests and crosses), Varthema moves around with his single identity as an observer. There is good reason to believe that in his account he actually tried to hide the extent to which he had stepped away from his conventional Christian identity (especially given that he requested a privilege to print his narrative from a bishop and dedicated the work to a duchess).[48] In this respect his position seems to have been similar to that of Nicolò Conti.

That Varthema was not articulating an authoritative humanist discourse is confirmed by the fact that it was from this quarter that he was criticized. It was not only an armchair ethnologist like Johannes Boemus who denied his authority. The physician Garcia da Orta, who had settled in Goa and published his learned botanical treatise *Coloquios dos simples e drogas he cousas mediçinais da India* in 1563, could find no better way of casting doubt on Varthema's accuracy (with whom he disagreed with respect to the geographical origin of *benjuy/storax*) than by recalling *what kind of traveller* he was:

> As for what you say concerning Ludovico Vartomano, I have spoken here and in Portugal with men who knew him here in India, and they told me that he went about in the dress of a moor, and that he returned to us doing penance for his sins, and that this man never went beyond Calicut and Cochin, nor did we then frequent the seas which we now navigate.[49]

---

[48] Rafael Sansoni, bishop of Portueri, was the Pope's chamberlain. The book was dedicated to Agnesina di Montefeltro Colonna, duchess of Tagliacozzo and countess of Albi.

[49] I have consulted a copy of the rare 1563 Goa edition kept in the University Library,

Independent observation, therefore, did not constitute by itself a scientific authority. It was instead an arena where social, educational and religious identities could be disputed. The claim to authority that rested on pure personal experience was essentially rhetorical, and whilst a collective control of new observations could be slowly institutionalized through years of publication, criticism and corroboration, in many cases this could only be an unfinished process. This is why a whole genre of satirical and speculative writing could grow on the basis of exploiting the new rhetoric of personal travel, as Thomas More famously exemplified when in 1516 he made his character Hythlodaeus describe Utopia by inscribing his narrative within the framework of the published voyages of Amerigo Vespucci. (Little did More and his humanist friends know that the letter of the four voyages of Vespucci, known to them from the Latin translation published in 1507 by the cosmographer Martin Waldsee-müller, was in fact a forgery, although certainly based on some genuine Vespuccian material. The reality of the voyage of 1503–4 which More used as a starting point, Vespucci's fourth according to the *Quattuor navigationes* of 1507, is still a matter for debate today.)[50]

We may summarize the preceding argument by saying that two variables were important in the definition of the role of the 'curious traveller': on the one hand, an individual point of view expressed in a first-person narrative, which could be the narrative source for an empirical description (but not necessarily); and, on the other hand, a de-contextualization in respect of those ideological institutions that determined social condition and purpose. This de-contextualization, in its more radical expression, meant that the first person of the narrative became a centre of discourse. It also effectively implied that the empirical emphasis of a description, which was originally a pragmatic possibility that coexisted with an allegiance to a traditional sacred centre, could now be justified as an entirely independent secular discourse. However, there

Cambridge: Garcia da Orta, *Coloquios dos simples e drogas da India* (Goa, 1563), ff. 29v–30r. Carnac Temple tried to defend Varthema's authenticity against Orta's statement (Varthema, *The itinerary*, p. xx). Orta was in fact concerned with denying Varthema's statement that the best *benjuy* is from Sumatra (not Malacca, as Temple wrongly states) and that 'it does not come to our Christian lands' (Varthema meant Europe, but Orta seems to have understood India). Orta went on to explain that he used to take Varthema's authority seriously until he read his book, where he found many absurdities concerning Ormuz and Malacca. But, as Temple says, it is likely that Orta read the Spanish version of 1520, itself derived from the Latin of 1511, which contained a number of unclear translations. Many of Orta's criticisms are based on misreadings.

[50] For a recent discussion of the 'Vespuccian question' see the introduction to the Spanish edition of Vespucci's letters by Luciano Formisano: Amerigo Vespucci, *Cartas de viaje*, ed. by L. Formisano (Madrid, 1986). The original Italian letters are collected in A. Vespucci, *Il Mondo nuovo di Amerigo Vespucci*, ed. by M. Pozzi (Turin, 1993).

was no simple correspondence between the presence of an independent first-person traveller and the quality of empirical descriptions in a particular text. Even when, as was often the case, the claim to personal experience supported a historically genuine account, and even if we can exclude the possibility of textual tampering (like the one raised by Vespucci's published letters), the quality of a description motivated by honest intellectual curiosity depended on a training in the process of observation and in the process of writing. Varthema's account of Vijayanagara, as we shall now see, makes this quite clear.

VARTHEMA IN SOUTH INDIA

It seems reasonable to maintain the hypothesis that Varthema spent a few days in the 'extremely fertile city of *Bisinagar* in the kingdom of *Narsinga* in India', possibly in the company of a small party of Persian merchants.[51] As with previous travellers, it is the power of the king and the magnificence of the city that are the focus of his description:

The said city of Bisinagar belongs to the king of Narsinga, and is very large and strongly walled. It is situated on the side of a mountain, and is seven miles in circumference. It has three circles of walls. It is a place of great merchandise, is extremely fertile, and is endowed with all possible kinds of delicacies [gentilezze]. It occupies the most beautiful site, and possesses the best air, that could ever be: with some very beautiful places for hunting and the same for fowling, so that it appears to me a second paradise.[52]

It appears to me a second paradise . . . here Varthema uses a metaphor identical to the one which permeates the account by 'Abd al-Razzāq. The idealized perfection of a city was a crucial theme in the urban culture of Renaissance Europe, and especially of Italy. It was often also the key theme in contemporary travellers' accounts within Europe, a serious expression of patriotic pride and a way of ranking civility between nations. Varthema follows a well-defined set of categories to analyse the value of Vijayanagara: size, walls, fertility, and in particular 'site' and 'air', the classical, Hippocratic concepts by which the best climates for human habitation were defined. The concept of 'gentilezze', imperfectly translated as 'delicacies', suggests that it is a 'courteous civility' – and not

---

[51] Early European descriptions often used the word Narsinga to refer to the kingdom, and restricted the word Bisnagar to the city. This is because at the time of their arrival the rulers of Vijayanagara had the name of Narasimha, one of the incarnations of the god Vishnu.

[52] Varthema, *Itinerario*, p. 202. For my English translations I have also consulted the reliable version by J. Winter Jones (1863).

a religious paradise – that Varthema is really talking about.[53] Certainly other cities had merited similar epithets: in India itself Canonor (Cannanor) is 'big and beautiful', Bathacala (Bhatkal) is 'very noble, beautiful and walled', Decan (Bijapur) is 'extremely beautiful and very fertile' and 'walled as is custom among Christians' (i.e. with stones, as in Europe). More impressively, Damascus in Syria was 'very wealthy and populated' and the place produced 'huge quantities of grain and meat' as well as 'the greatest quantity of fruits that I ever saw'.[54] But there could be no doubt for Varthema's readers that Vijayanagara was at a peak in a hierarchy of cities. It was well located in a fertile, healthy and beautiful place. At the same time it was large, strongly defended and rich in merchandise.

Is it then the case that Varthema simply saw in Vijayanagara the same sort of thing he would like to have seen in Venice or Bologna? Could we say that European travellers shared a common ideal of a large prosperous city and that, in their attempt to recognize a well-ordered civil community, they tried to find it abroad – for instance, in India? Or is it rather that because non-European cities could successfully be described as fulfilling in some important ways the western model of a political society, they effectively presented a value-laden image that a traveller, spontaneously, transmitted to his contemporaries?

To answer this we must first note that Varthema's civic praise was not a specific European theme based on an ideal of political liberty, but rather one linked to an image of idealized monarchy which could be shared with a number of oriental observers. As in the description by 'Abd al-Razzāq (which here again offers a valid point of comparison), the meaning of Varthema's praise of Vijayanagara was not only civil, but also political: 'The king of this city is a gentile, with all his kingdom, that is to say, idolaters. He is a very powerful king, and keeps up constantly 40,000 horsemen.'[55] The power of a gentile king, already expressed in the richness, size and walls of the city, is clearly portrayed as being based on a military capacity. Varthema goes on to emphasize the key role of

---

[53] The vernacular word 'gentilezze' suggests the refined qualities and behaviour of a civil society, but the context in which it appears – the description of fertility and merchandise – may seem to indicate that the 'rare and delicate goods' consumed in sophisticated societies are intended, and this is how J. Winter-Jones translated it. The word is not to be confused with the root 'gentile', used by Varthema and many other travellers in its technical biblical sense of 'non-Christian, non-Jew', and applied in antiquity, after the Jewish model, to non-Christian (Greek, etc.) philosophers and religions, and after the Middle Ages to religions outside 'the Book' of Revelation (that is, Muslims were 'infidels' rather than gentiles, since they recognized a biblical tradition as valid). I have not used the English rendering 'pagan', nor of course 'Hindu', when the original word in any Latin language was 'gentile'.

[54] Varthema, *Itinerario*, pp. 92, 195–6, 200.

[55] Ibid., p. 202.

horses and elephants in the armies. This, in turn, brings to his mind the importance of trade in horses and its strategic implications (especially for the sea ports of the Malabar coast, where the Europeans were beginning to be involved at the time). Varthema quickly grasped the possibility of gaining political and economic benefits from the situation:

> And you must know that a horse is worth at least 300, 400, and 500 pardaus, and some are purchased for 800 pardaus, because horses are not produced there, neither are any mares found there, because those kings who hold the seaports do not allow them to be brought.[56]

The two key features that organize the whole description are therefore the city and the king. The prosperity of the first is the counterpart of the power of the second. But if the ideal city depends on external human factors, a true government and a true religion, in our western sources on Vijayanagara (as in an oriental narrative like 'Abd al-Razzāq's) we encounter the paradox of a good king with false gods. There is no open discussion of this duality, but the description itself represents it, inviting a question which indeed had profound implications for the moral and political thought of Europe. Both the success and the falsity of the system of government are expressed in unequivocal terms:

> This king of Narsinga is the wealthiest king I have ever heard spoken of. This city is situated like Milan [i.e. in the interior], but not in a plain. Here is the king's seat, and his realms are placed as it might be the realm of Naples and also Venice, so that he has the sea on both sides. His brahmins, that is his priests, say that he possesses a daily revenue of 12,000 pardaus. He is constantly at war with several moorish and gentile kings. His faith is idolatrous, and they worship the devil, like those of Calicut (when the proper time comes we will state in what manner they worship him). They live like gentiles.[57]

Varthema goes on with a description of dress, distinguishing between men of condition (*omini da bene*), who wear a short shirt and a turban 'in the moorish fashion', and common people (*populo minuto*), who go quite naked, with the exception of a piece of cloth about their middle (women are not described here, although they appear in the chapter on Calicut). As opposed to ordinary men the king deserves a special description, as hierarchically superior. It becomes apparent not only that his more sophisticated dress expresses a higher status, but also that his horse, besides its practical purpose, has a symbolic value:

> The king wears a cap of gold brocade two spans long, and when he goes to war he wears a quilted dress of cotton, and over it he puts another garment full of golden piastres, and all around it are jewels of

[56] Ibid.   [57] Ibid., pp. 206–7.

various kinds. His horse is worth more than some of our cities, on account of the ornaments which it wears. When he rides for his pleasure he is always accompanied by three or four kings, and many other lords, and five or six thousand horses. *Therefore he may be considered a very powerful lord* (my italics).[58]

The perception of symbolic power is clearly part of Varthema's cultural training. This understanding of symbols helps explain why certain 'wonders' were considered more interesting than others – that is, in what sense was the strange meaningful. It is, for instance, remarkable that (like the Khorasani ʿAbd al Razzāq) Varthema dwells on the discretion, strength and intelligence of the elephant as something note-worthy (*cosa degna de notizia*). He does so not only because elephants were rare in Europe, and always a favourite theme for literary and artistic recreation, but also because they were (like horses) an essential element of the institution of South Indian kingship, with both practical and symbolic functions. The emphasis on elephants and horses thus agrees with the central idea in Varthema's interpretation of Vijayanagara: the concentration of power in the institution of kingship. Varthema per-ceived this power to depend on high revenues and military capacity, of which the prosperity of the city and the huge armies with elephants and horses were the main expression. The rest of his observations and references ultimately refer to these premises. Thus, Varthema describes the monetary system, of interest not only because it expresses the economic order of which the king is ruler and guarantee, but also because it relates directly to the trading activities that concern foreigners such as the Portuguese. (The basic structure of the monetary system is similar to the one described by ʿAbd al-Razzāq sixty years earlier, but the numerical correspondences seem to have changed, as one would expect.)[59] Of importance for foreign merchants is also the safety of the roads and the tolerance of different creeds. The king is able to guarantee all of these in the interest of the system (and because that system needs the foreign traders). The aim of political power is the peace that brings prosperity, and because the king of Narsinga offers that, he is a good king despite the fact that the human community he governs is idolatrous and worships the devil. 'In this kingdom you can go everywhere in

[58] Ibid.
[59] The golden 'pardao' from Vijayanagara, also described by later sixteenth-century travellers like Cesare Federici and Gasparo Balbi as 'pagodo', was one of the most prestigious coins in the trade of India at that time, and its influence extended not only to neighbouring kingdoms, but also far beyong the Indian subcontinent. It commonly had the names of rulers in Sanskrit on one side and mythological figures (such as Shiva and Parvati) on the other. See O. Pinto (ed.) *Viaggi di C. Federici e G. Balbi alle Indie Orientali* (Rome, 1962), pp. xxxiii and ff.

safety.' Furthermore, 'This king is a very great friend of the Christians, especially of the king of Portugal, because he does not know much of any other Christians. When the Portuguese arrive in his territories they do them great honour.'[60] Varthema sees the political influence of the king of Narsinga extending virtually everywhere in South India, so that he is constantly at war with the Muslim ruler of Bijapur, several cities of the Kanarese coast are subject to him, and his presence is recorded in Coromandel, Ceylon and even Tarnassari in the gulf of Bengal.[61]

Varthema perceives both the symbolic expression of a system of power and its practical effectiveness, with the consequences it carries for the Europeans. He thus describes, interprets and evaluates a whole social system in a single narrative movement. For all the lack of definition which surrounds his persona, it is quite obvious that he organizes his description from the perspective of a self-appointed spy for European merchants and conquerors. In his account, the king is not identified as a historical individual, but rather perceived as a type (this might support Aubin's suspicion that Varthema was merely reporting hearsay, except that personal observations were also often described schematically). Which 'king of Narsinga' could possibly fulfil a role of authority both real and symbolic at the time of Varthema's visit? Certainly not the young Immadi Narasimha (1491–1505), the real king but a virtual prisoner all his life. The ruler at the time of Varthema's visit was probably Vira Narasimha, who had recently inherited the role of regent from his father the general Narasa Nayaka but was about to inaugurate a new dynasty by getting rid of Immadi Narasimha – only to find his authority questioned by the other captains.[62]

The problem is deeper than the lack of attention to historical personality and circumstance – it is not even clear that Varthema is right in portraying the king as *institutionally* powerful. I have mentioned earlier

[60] Varthema, *Itinerario*, pp. 206–7.

[61] It is doubtful that Varthema knew what he was writing about when he mentioned Tarnassari in this context. Tarnassari cannot in my opinion be identified with Tenasserim (Mergui) in Siam, as the English editors of Varthema, Percy Badger (1863) and Carnac Temple (1928), repeatedly did. The idea that the king of Narsinga – not a maritime power – was at war with the ruler of Tenasserim across the sea is rather ludicrous. In fact, Varthema's later description of this city is not fully consistent with any particular place.

[62] The exact circumstances of the politics of Vijayanagara during these years are not too clear, and for the time being we must rely on the authority of the Portuguese chronicle by Fernão Nunes (further discussed in later chapters), a few inscriptions and literary references, and common sense. If we place the authority of inscriptions above that of Nunes, Varthema would probably have visited Vijayanagara at the time when Immadi Narasa Nayaka (the son of the old regent Narasa Nayaka, Nunes' 'Narsenaque') was struggling to have himself accepted as regent (1503–5), and perhaps plotting to become king as Vira Narasimha (1505–9).

that modern scholars defending the idea of a 'segmentary state' insist that the symbolism surrounding the kings of Vijayanagara expressed a coherence and centrality that was more ritual than administrative. From this perspective, Varthema's emphasis on the power of the king may reveal the superficiality of his analysis, perhaps even his misunderstanding of Indian kingship – a considerable fault given that, unlike 'Abd al-Razzāq, who constructed his whole account as a utopian projection, the Italian seemed to want to provide European audiences with a reliable assessment of conditions in India.[63] To be fair, Varthema, in contrast to 'Abd al-Razzāq, shows some awareness of the distance between the claims to sovereignty of the kings of Vijayanagara and their effective control of outlying provinces. So, although the trading cities of Kanará, Bathacala (Bhatkal) and Onor (Honavur), are 'subject' to the king of Narsinga, the cities of the Malabar coast, especially Calicut, are clearly independent. (As Portuguese writers like Duarte Barbosa or the historian Barros were later to observe, the main reason for this was that the western chain of mountains running along the coast separated Malabar from the hinterland and prevented the Vijayanagara armies from finding easy access to the oceanic trading centres.)[64] Similarly, on the eastern coast of Coromandel, nominally under the jurisdiction of Vijayanagara, the power of the king is felt to be distant.[65] This, as Varthema notes, is unfortunate for the indigenous Christians – that is the Saint Thomas Christians – because they are being driven away or killed by the Muslims (according to Varthema, it was precisely the arrival of the Portuguese and their attacks on the indigenous 'Moors' on religious grounds that had provoked this persecution of native Christians).[66] The power of the

[63] For an extended analysis of 'Abd al-Razzāq's narrative as a utopian projection, see my 'A western rationality?'

[64] See Barros, Ásia, vol. I, p. 145; Duarte Barbosa, Livro em que dá relação do que viu e ouviu no Oriente, pp. 100–1.

[65] This part is rather suspect. Varthema writes about a city of 'Cioromandel' some seven days by sea after Quilon, but Coromandel was the name for the whole land along the south-east coast above the Fishery coast (it was considered under the jurisdiction of Vijayanagara, at least nominally). What is most baffling is that it is in 'Cioromandel' rather than Pulicat, which Varthema describes separately, where the Italian hears the stories about the Christians of Saint Thomas and of the saint's tomb at a distance of some twelve miles. This makes it difficult to identify the first 'Cioromandel' with a small port like, let us say, Negapattinam.

[66] 'In this land I found some Christians who told me that the body of Saint Thomas was twelve miles away from there, looked after by some Christians. They also said that since the arrival of the king of Portugal the Christians could no longer live there, because the king has killed many Muslims of that country.' Varthema adds that the Muslims kill the Christians 'secretly, in order that it may not come to the ears of the king of Narsinga, who is a great friend of the Christians, and especially of the Portuguese' (Varthema, Itinerario, p. 249). I have not seen any reference to these persecutions anywhere else. A possible explanation is that the western coast was a more important location of the

king of Vijayanagara is therefore feared, but it can also be evaded. But whilst these observations help qualify the stereotyped image of an all-powerful king, they alone do not suffice to redeem Varthema's analysis from its obvious defect of superficiality. Nor was Varthema consistent in his assessment of the relative importance of each kingdom.[67]

The most penetrating description was in reality the one that measured the degree to which the theoretical power of the king and its effective use differed. The fact that Varthema does not compare the different instruments of political centralization in Europe and Vijayanagara in any detail is a clear limitation, but Varthema's representation (and he had been in Vijayanagara for at most a few days) was a valid starting point, insofar as the interest of the Portuguese merchants and conquerors was concerned. It would be unrealistic to expect him to have dwelt on the factional struggles which we know characterized the political life of the kingdom. In the terms of the aims that informed this particular part of Varthema's narrative, the weakness lies elsewhere. His optimistic claim about the friendship of the ruler of Vijayanagara with the Portuguese conveys the illusions and hopes of the Viceroy Almeida and his successors after 1505, rather than any coherent articulation of interests and compatible beliefs.[68]

With respect to the obvious optimism concerning kingship which

struggle between the Portuguese and the Muslim merchant communities, and that retaliations in Coromandel were secondary to the Portuguese chroniclers. Alternatively, Varthema – whose geography of this areas is in any case rather suspect – reported what he heard from local Christians in Malabar. If true, his observation would seem to suggest that the derelict state in which the Portuguese would find the Christian communities of Coromandel, and in particular the tomb of Saint Thomas, in the second decade of the century was in fact a side-effect of their own violent intrusion.

67 For example, Varthema goes on to justify the primacy he gives to the king of Calicut in his description of gentile customs and religion over kings such as those of Bhatkal, Honavur, Mangalore, Cannanor, Cochin, Quilon and Vijayanagara (Narsinga), on the grounds that 'he really is the most dignified king of all those before mentioned, and he is called Samory, which in the gentile language <Malayalam> means God on earth' (*lui si è lo più digno re de tutti quisti sopraditti, e chiamase lui Samory, che viene a dire in lingua gentile Dio in terra*: ibid., p. 209). Only from a very peculiar perspective could Calicut be seen as more important than Vijayanagara, and his king more dignified. It is possible that Varthema intentionally wanted to emphasize the role of the king of Calicut, certainly the most important ruler on the Malabar coast, because of his dramatic struggle against the Portuguese. For most Europeans who had heard about the Portuguese in India between 1499 and 1510 the king of Calicut was a more 'real' figure than the king of Narsinga. But this does not quite fit with Varthema's own account of the kingdom. Similarly, that Samory means 'God on earth' is either something he was told by a Muslim, or something that he invented for the benefit of his fellow Europeans in order to categorize the gentile religion as 'devilish'. It is commonly translated 'lord of the sea'.

68 The idea of friendship between Portugal and Narsinga against a common 'Muslim' enemy probably did not develop until 1505–7, the years when Varthema fought with the Portuguese and embassies were being exchanged. There is little evidence to suggest that the king of Vijayanagara was seriously concerned with the Portuguese at the time of Varthema's alleged visit at the end of 1504. It is difficult to assess whether the claim that

seems to have been shared by so many observers, one could argue that foreign travellers were regularly deceived by appearances. That delusion, however, should not be seen as the result of any cultural inconmensurability, since these travellers seem to have interpreted the signs of royal magnificence in a way analogous to how the indigenous population was intended to do. They clearly became aware of a pre-existing symbolic system of power. When Varthema described certain oriental kings in either a positive or a negative light, he was not merely projecting religious prejudices, but rather, not unlike Marco Polo, he was responding to the stories circulating in the locality. Thus when he counterpoises the tyrannical king of Cambay, who treated himself to a diet of poison in order to murder wise men by spitting on them (although this also killed the women he slept with), to a gentile 'king of Ioghi' who performs pilgrimages and lives like a Hindu ascetic (perhaps a Rajput lord), he was probably re-telling popular stories, often garbled, heard from the Muslim merchants of Gujarat.[69] But this sultan of Cambay was no less interested in elephants than the ruler of Vijayanagara, and Varthema's description does not omit the symbolism of their parades. Symbolic interpretations solved the distance between pure graphic descriptions and pure hearsay. European travellers may have failed to measure the extent to which the institutions of government in India were not centralized, but here the narrative conventions to which they were accustomed made them converge with the ritual emphasis of the indigenous language-game, rather than attempt to analyse the different assumptions underlying it. Lamenting the financial difficulties of the monarchy, or the quasi-independent power of great noblemen and other privileged corporations, was not a common theme of geographical literature (although this kind of concern could of course be expressed in other linguistic contexts, such as parliamentary discussions). Indeed Varthema was not departing from the tendency prevalent among medieval and Renaissance historians in Europe to place their narrative emphasis on the actions, virtues and power of princes and lords who were also their patrons, rather than on their difficulties (financial or political) in maintaining their authority and extending their administration.[70]

the king favoured the Christians of Coromandel is based on a genuine local Christian tradition or is instead a European idealization.

[69] The legendary predilection for poison of Mahmud Baigara of Gujarat is well attested in a number of contemporary sources.

[70] It is perhaps Machiavelli, who with his constitutional and military analysis (rather than with his realist re-definition of political virtue) went further towards challenging a political history centred on the mere interaction of individuals. But then, by the time this kind of analysis significantly affected historiography, it could not be separated from the concomitant use of ethnological, geographical and economic literature by late Renais-

ETHNOGRAPHY AND THE PROBLEM OF RELIGION

Rather than for its political analysis, a narrative like Varthema's stands out (as it did when it was received in Europe) for its ethnographic contents, for its capacity to portray a diversity of human customs. Varthema confines his treatment of these themes for the whole of South India to his description of Calicut, claiming that in most other places (including Vijayanagara) 'they live after the manner of those of Calicut'.[71] This narrative strategy of assuming an ethnological synthesis, shared by later observers like Duarte Barbosa, shows at the same time the degree of trans-cultural similarity that the traveller was prepared to acknowledge and the degree of local difference that he was prepared to sacrifice. Why Varthema and Barbosa chose Calicut is easy to understand: this was the city where Vasco da Gama had originally landed, and in the years during the first Portuguese expeditions it was considered the most important economic and political centre on the Malabar coast. The Portuguese, in fact, first organized their trading system in India as a war against Calicut, with the assistance of allied kings such as that of Cochin, and in rivalry with the Muslim merchants (both native and foreign) who dominated its trade. Varthema's description of Calicut is indeed a model for a full (if rather unsystematic) treatment of ethnological information, inserted into a wider narrative based on the adventurous progression of the traveller through different places.

Some of these observations merit special comment because they illuminate the relationship between European prejudice and novel experience. In particular, Varthema's description of the religion of Calicut has been singled out by historians as particularly exemplary, because, as Partha Mitter remarked, 'it affected both literature and the pictorial tradition relating to Indian Gods'.[72] The German edition of the *Itinerario* printed in 1515 included two illustrations of the idol of Calicut, a devil-like figure that appeared in one woodcut eating 'souls', and in another receiving worship. The artist from Augsburg, Jorg Breu, used Varthema's text as his main source, but then, according to Mitter, turned to a European stereotype 'that closely corresponded to the description' because 'he did not have access to an actual Indian image'.[73] Partha Mitter's interpretation suggests that it was not the artist who, lacking better resources, transformed an Indian god into a popular European

sance 'reason of state' writers – writers like Giovanni Botero for whom 'Narsinga' was already an example of oriental despotism.

[71] Varthema, *Itinerario*, p. 209.
[72] Mitter, *Much maligned monsters*, pp. 16–20.
[73] Ibid., p. 18.

woodcut of the devil: Varthema himself had already performed that operation in his description, and the artist simply took the next logical step. The key issue is that, to Varthema, 'Indian gods could not be anything but demons', so that his Indian idol 'owed a great deal more to the Western tradition than to the Indian'.[74]

Mitter notes that Varthema described a king who believed in God (*Tamerani*) but was simultaneously guilty of adoring the devil (*Deumo*). It would then seem that we are concerned with a straightforward case of European Christian prejudice and condemnation taking over the whole genre and, more concretely, of Varthema setting a precedent of travellers to India demonizing Hindu art which would mark the tone for the whole century. There can of course be no doubt that from a Christian tradition (which Varthema was certainly in no position to question on his return to Rome) 'idols' were a deviation from worship of the true God, and condemnation of idolatry as devilish was a powerful commonplace. But it is noteworthy that there also existed then in Italy a powerful philosophical, Neoplatonic tradition (represented by men like Pico della Mirandola) which, following late antique literature, sought to retrieve, through esoteric interpretations, a primitive syncretic theology behind ancient (Egyptian and Greek) religions.[75] Varthema's reliance on the popular image of the devil would then reflect not an absolute need within western culture, but rather an unsophisticated choice which was intellectually more accessible and theologically safer than what might have been the choice of some contemporary humanists. Given that, therefore, reliance on prejudice was not a simple, universal, automatic operation, we must try to determine to what extent Varthema was going against his own empirical evidence when he described the idol from Calicut as a devil, and whether his overall description of the customs of Calicut (which stand as exemplary for the whole Hindu 'gentile' religion) supports such a tendency towards demonization.

Varthema introduces the theme of religion immediately after describing the city which, despite being the 'capital of India', did not impress him as much as Bijapur or Vijayanagara, on account of the ephemerality of building materials and the lack of walls, so that houses were 'very sad'. Although Varthema acknowledged practical reasons for this, Calicut's commercial importance was not therefore matched by its urban architecture. The weakness of Calicut at this level of 'civility', matched by the

[74] Ibid., and n.44 on p. 291.
[75] On the interest in Hermeticism, Cabbala and Egypt in the Italian Renaissance see E. Garin, *Ermetismo del Rinascimento* (Rome, 1988), who insists that the movement led by Ficino and Pico at the end of the fifteenth century sought to create from Christian Platonism a space of religious unity for a universal *pax fidei*.

peculiar caste system and marriage customs of its Nayar military elite, may have encouraged a more detailed account of its religion as 'alien':

The king of Calicut is a gentile and worships the devil in the way that you will see: they acknowledge that there is a God who created heaven and earth and the whole world, and say that, if he wanted to judge you and me, and a third and a fourth, he would not be able to enjoy being a lord. For this reason he has sent a spirit of his, that is, the devil, to do justice to the world, and he does good to whomever does good and evil to whomever does evil. They call him *Deumo*, and they call God *Tamerani*.[76]

It is obvious from this that Varthema's account, however garbled, is based on discussions with Hindu brahmins (which he mentions in other passages). He knew some basic, colloquial Malayalam. Even if he had those discussions in the presence of, or through, the mediation of Muslim merchants, he could share with them a basic monotheistic attitude. The distinction between a creator God and an active spirit of justice could easily reflect a distinction between Brahma and Shiva or Vishnu. 'Tamerani' easily recalls 'Tamburan', a term widely used as a title of lordship among the Nayars (and 'my lord' could of course be God).[77] 'Deumo' may stand for 'Deva', used to denote minor gods who dwell in the upper worlds, or perhaps for 'Damodara', a possible name for Vishnu. More than any specific correspondence, what matters is that a fairly believable account of the distinction between an abstract principle of God transcendent and its manifestations in the Hindu pantheon becomes a distinction between a legitimate 'God' and an illegitimate spirit-on-earth which, clearly impossible to identify with a conventional Holy Spirit, becomes a 'devil'. The paradox is that this 'devil' is here to

---

[76] Varthema, *Itinerario*, p. 213.

[77] The term was applied to the petty nayar kings but also to the divinity. Thus 'Periya Tambiran', meaning Great Lord, could be used to refer to Shiva. Father Joseph, a Syro-Malabar Christian from Cranganor who accompanied Cabral to Portugal in 1501, in his account of India uses 'Tambran' to refer to the Trimurti, the combined representation of Brahma, Shiva and Vishnu: 'These Gentiles worship one single God, creator of all things, and they say that he is one and three, and in his likeness they have made a statue with three heads. It stands wih the hands joined and is called *Tambran*': W. B. Greenlee (ed.) *The voyage of Pedro Alvares Cabral*, Hakluyt Society, 2nd series (London, 1938), p. 100. Father Joseph was in Rome and Venice in 1502, giving information about India to eager audiences, and thus it is even conceivable that Varthema had heard of him just before he left Italy. But the use of the term of lordship for the divinity was necessarily loose. Thus Barbosa described the 'Indian trinity', with Christianizing overtones, as 'Bermabesma Maceru' (which stands for 'Brahma, Vishnu, Mahesvara'), whilst he used 'Tambarane' to refer to the *lingams* carried by the *lingayats* of Vijayanagara: Barbosa, *The book of Duarte Barbosa*, ed. by M. L. Dames, Hakluyt Society, 2nd series, 2 vols. (London, 1918–21), vol. I, p. 218; as the editor Dames notes, Barbosa probably used here a Malayali word because his knowledge of Kannada was less perfect.

administer justice in a rightful way. The way Varthema solves the problem is by insisting on the basic flaw of worshipping an idol instead of God – the original criticism of idolatry shared by all biblical religions. He does this not by evolving any theological argument, but rather by assuming it, concentrating instead on the description of everyday Hindu worship:

> The king of Calicut has this *Deumo* in a chapel in his palace, in the following way: his chapel is two paces long on each side of a square, and three paces high, with a wooden door all carved with figures of devils. In the midst of it there is a devil made of metal, sitting on a chair also of metal. The said devil wears a crown made of three crowns as in the papal kingdom. It also has four horns and four teeth, with a huge mouth, and with terrifying nose and eyes. The hands are like a flesh-hook and the feet like those of a cock, so that it is a fearsome sight. Around this chapel all the paintings are also of devils. For each painting there is a Satan sitting on a chair, placed in the middle of flames from a fire, in which there are a large number of animals half a finger and one finger of the hand in length. The said Satan has a soul in his mouth with his right hand, and with the other hand he is taking a soul from below. Every morning the Brahmins, that is the priests, go and wash the idol all over with aromatic water, and after that they put perfume on him. Having thus perfumed him, they worship him.[78]

It is obvious from the above description that the woodcuts made by Breu in Germany, so similar to traditional images of European devils, are basically faithful representations of Varthema's description, including the triple crown, the horns and fangs, and the little souls being eaten one after the other by a terrifying figure (see plates 3 and 4). The only important liberty taken by the artist has been to 'humanize' the animal-like tiny figures of Varthema, and to conflate the image of the metal idol with the paintings on the wall. Other additions tending to create a traditional 'goatish' figure of a devil seem legitimate, insofar as no more details were available to the artist. But this 'filling in' was not entirely innocuous, because it created a figure that could not be an accurate representation of a Hindu statue, while Varthema's in many ways was. That is, much of Varthema's description could be applied without excessive violence to representations of Narasimha, the lion-like incarnation of Vishnu Narasimha represented in many temples in Kerala and Vijayanagara, often with fangs and a tiara-like crown. The combination of mural paintings and sculptures (albeit often wooden) in small chapels was certainly prevalent in Kerala, and we could think of the Narasimha

[78] Varthema, *Itinerario*, pp. 213–15.

temple of Chengannur as an example of the kind of statue that inspires Varthema to identify Indian 'idols' with 'devils'.[79] The crowded atmosphere of the Malabari shrines from this period is certainly accurately described by the European. Seated painted figures, colourful demons, small-scale figures at the feet of the divinities, and aggressive door guardians would also been common.

There is no doubt that Varthema decided to suggest a traditional European image of Satan eating souls in hell, and that he added a few details which supported that tradition, but it cannot be denied that much of what he wrote was in many ways accurate. Thus even the graphic description of everyday worship which follows, involving the bloody sacrifice of a cock, can be seen as fairly realistic, of course within the realm of inevitable superficiality inhabited by an observer unacquainted with the significance of a ritual code. It certainly does not depart in its language and tone from equivalent descriptions by observers who, like Father Joseph of Cranganor, had lived in Malabar for many more years, and yet still described a ceremony with 'one nude priest with a large crown of roses on his head, with large eyes and with false horns' who inflicts wounds on himself and then, bleeding, acts as oracle for the idol.[80] The prejudices of the European traveller reporting to his own people were clearly no more striking than those of an oriental Christian speaking to the same European audience. The important fact is that

---

[79] See J. C. Harle, *The art and architecture of the Indian subcontinent* (Harmondsworth, 1986), p. 350. The sculpture of Chengannur is from the eighteenth century, but the basic iconography would have been similar at the time of Varthema. Contemporary wooden sculptures, which predominated in Malabar, are unfortuntely not very likely to have survived.

[80] Compare Varthema, *Itinerario*, p. 215 with Father Joseph's relation of 1502 in Greenlee (ed.) *The voyage*, p. 100. Joseph's relation, as printed by Francanzano of Montalboddo in 1507, seems to imply that he was a native of Cranganore. We know from a Syriac letter of 1504 that he had been sent to Mesopotamia by the Church of Malabar in 1490 in order to request from Mar Simeon, their Catholicos, that a new bishop be sent: Schurhammer, *Gesammelte Studien*, vol. II, pp. 333–49. In Mesopotamia he was ordained priest. What is, however, surprising is the implication, in the published Italian relation, that Father Joseph had a limited knowledge of the language of the gentiles of Malabar: 'there are many other kinds of sacrifices which Joseph, because he did not understand the language and because he had not had many dealings with Gentiles, has not been able to explain entirely': Greenlee (ed.) *The voyage*, p. 101. It is difficult to imagine Joseph having less than a perfect command of Malayalam, since in the Church of Malabar Syriac was only used for ritual purposes. His inability to give more details may have been exaggerated by his unwillingness to do so to a Latin Christian audience, but probably what lies behind his 'difficulty of understanding' is the lack of a religious dialogue between the Malabari Christian and Hindu communities. The Christians essentially functioned like a separate caste, with a merchant community which controlled the pepper trade and had many of the aristocratic privileges of the nayars. With respect to the meaning of Hindu ritual, the Christian Indian was no less foreigner than the European in India.

Plate 3 The idol of Calicut, with a 'papal tiara' and eating souls, according to a woodcut by Augsburg artist Jorg Breu in the first German edition of Varthema's *Itinerario* (1515).
The said devil wears a crown made of three crowns as in the papal kingdom. It also has four horns and four teeth, with a huge mouth, and with terrifying nose and eyes. The hands are like a flesh-hook and the feet like those of a cock, so that it is a fearsome sight . . . The said Satan has a soul in his mouth with his right hand, and with the other hand he is taking a soul from below (Varthema's *Itinerario*, p. 214).

while Varthema described Hindu religion essentially as he observed it, he could not have easily defined it, from a Christian standpoint, as anything other than idolatrous and devilish. It would be fairer to say that Varthema interpreted Hindu gods as devils than to say that he saw European devils where he should have seen Hindu gods, because within the logic of his tradition there was no safe alternative to the universalistic claims of Christianity. Once the category of the idol is accepted, its use in India by Varthema (or in the New World by the Spanish) is impeccable. What is more remarkable is how much Varthema dared to find out and write on a subject about which publicizing opinions could be so dangerous. The fact that a philosophical language which could mediate between different religions (however biased Neoplatonism was towards Greek philosophy) had already been invented in the West, only reminds us that any traveller, even a curious and shifty traveller, was, individually, limited to a particular context and background. There was no role

Plate 4 The brahmins worshipping their 'devilish' idol: Jorg Breu's interpretation of Varthema's description.

for the speculations of Pico or Ficino in Varthema's encounter with a gentile god.

Varthema's representation of Satan marks a clear departure from the initial expectations of the Portuguese, who had been led by the legends of the Prester John and the Saint Thomas Christians, and by a general desire to perpetuate the imperialistic strategies associated with the ideology of crusade, to underestimate the massive preponderance of what could only be classified as 'gentiles'. The story of how Vasco da Gama and his companions came to misrepresent Hindus in Calicut as Christians deserves a separate analysis as an example of what might be termed 'first encounters'. By Varthema's time, the king of Calicut was instead bitterly at war with the Portuguese, as the traveller noted. Similarly, we shall need to consider with more detail the extent to which racial categories may have been important in the process of classification and evaluation of non-Europeans. For the time being, however, it is sufficient to keep in mind that Varthema described other peoples besides Indian gentiles, particularly Jews and Muslims, and Damascus impressed him no less than Vijayanagara. His journey was a progression in which different shades of diversity were uncovered, rather than a single, dramatic encounter with a demonized 'other'. There was therefore nothing especially 'alien' about the South Indians, except that they were perceived both as very important (because they were seen to offer enormous possibilities for trade, plunder and evangelization) and not yet well known.[81] If we consider Varthema's description of Calicut as a whole, with references to eating habits, sexual customs, marriage arrangements, caste differences (distinguishing six 'sorts' of gentiles: priests, warriors, artisans, fishermen, pepper-gatherers and rice-gatherers), dress codes and eating prohibitions, burial ceremonies, the administration of justice, religious worship, festivals, methods of fighting, groups of merchants, money-lending, ships and navigation, the royal palace, medical practices, the ten wonderful uses of the coconut, agricultural practices, and a number of natural products and animals, it is apparent that the fact that the inhabitants worshipped the devil did not create any global problem of interpretation. Instead, it shifted the weight of interpretation away from religion, so that what is most remarkable about sixteenth-century texts (and in stark contrast to the fascination for the wisdom of the brahmins in ancient Greek accounts) is an almost complete lack of interest in the beliefs and faith of those peoples whose material resources, military power, dress and ritual customs attracted such attention. Only the earliest descriptions of Malabar, still under the influence of the myth of the Prester John, tended to make gentiles as Christian as possible. After that, when the concept of Indian gentilism became more distinct and substantial, no knowledge of the religious and philosophical foundations of manners and customs was thought to be essential for their practical understanding. Brahmins could be described by Varthema as social agents who performed rituals – 'as priests among us' – and whose duties included taking the virginity of the king's wife and making peace in war, rather than as the upholders of a complex literary religious tradition to which he had no access.[82]

Varthema's identity as an independent observer and adventurer was not accompanied by any sophisticated intellectual concerns on his part. As a consequence, his otherwise original narrative did not produce reflections substantially different from those of Marco Polo or Nicolò Conti. The increase in the number of travel narratives brought about by the Portuguese arrival in the East did, however, create a pressure to write informative and precise descriptions. The importance of Varthema's book was not only the clarity with which the idea of the traveller as an

---

[81] At the time of writing his book, Varthema was aware that it would be one of the first to hit the market, although he may have known of the publication near Venice of a collection of reports in 1507, the *Paesi novamente retrovati*.

[82] On the brahmins – 'bramini' – see Varthema, *Itinerario*, pp. 216–17.

independent authority on the subject of human diversity was publicized, but also the degree to which the de-contextualized individual was now subjected to the pressures of a powerful literary context – that is, the one made possible by colonial imperialism. In Portuguese India as in Spanish America, 'pen, ink and paper' were an essential element of the overseas administrative machine.[83] The complexity of the Portuguese institutional presence also demanded further definition of the religious and racial modes of classification on which systematic policies had to be organized and legitimized. Throughout the Latin crusades of the previous four centuries the Europeans had painfully learnt that the distinction between Christians and non-Christians was not sufficient for political purposes – it was after all the Franks who had first sacked Constantinople, and then failed to unite to defend it against the Turks.[84] Before embarking on the analysis of the more detailed ethnological and historical models used by sixteenth-century Europeans to describe the societies of South India, it will be useful to first discuss the implications of the overall Portuguese official approach to Vijayanagara.

[83] I borrow the expression from J. H. Elliott, 'Spain and America before 1700', in L. Bethell (ed.) *Colonial Spanish America* (Cambridge, 1987), p. 63.

[84] See S. Runciman, *A history of the crusades*, vol. III: *The kingdom af Acre* (Cambridge, 1954; repr. Harmondsworth, 1978), pp. 107–31 and 465–80.

5. The Portuguese and Vijayanagara: politics, religion and classification

FIRST ENCOUNTERS AND THE PROBLEM OF CLASSIFICATION

The kingdom of Vijayanagara was the largest political unit the Portuguese found in South India, and one of its central features was its non-Muslim character – a very significant detail from the Portuguese perspective. In common with other medieval Christian nations, the Portuguese had a long tradition of contacts with Muslims in North Africa and the Mediterranean. Moreover, the ideology of crusade, common to all western Christianity, had a very special importance in the Iberian Peninsula, as a result of the process of *reconquista*, and this influence was still felt in the fifteenth century. The whole of society could be directly implicated in a providential plan and conceive itself as having recovered a lost country from the infidel rather than having just taken it, a vision sustained by the myth of a Gothic Hispanic kingdom which preceded the Arab invasions. Obviously, it is only in a limited sense that the Portuguese expansion along the western coast of Africa in the fifteenth century can be interpreted, as it often has been, as some sort of extension of *reconquista* values and aims (and of course similar arguments can be made about the Spanish in the Canary Islands and in America).[1] Among the significant differences to consider there is the fact that in this second

---

[1] The influence of the ideas of *reconquista* and crusade on the Portuguese expansion is a polemical issue. A solid synthesis of the early Portuguese ventures is the contribution by B. Diffie to B. Diffie and G. Winius, *Foundations of the Portuguese empire 1415–1580* (Oxford, 1977). See also M. Newitt, 'Prince Henry and the origins of Portuguese expansion', in M. Newitt (ed.) *The first Portuguese colonial empire* (Exeter, 1986), and more recently the various articles by L. F. Thomaz. The medieval precedents of crusade and mission in the Iberian peninsula can be explored through Kedar, *Crusade and mission* and F. Fernández-Armesto, *Before Columbus. Exploration and colonization from the Mediterranean to the Atlantic, 1229–1492* (Basingstoke, 1987). The persistence of the Muslim kingdom of Granada in southern Spain helped keep alive the idea of *reconquista* as crusade through the fourteenth and fifteenth centuries.

phase of 'feudal' expansion, trading activities, in particular the search for gold, were much more significant than territorial conquests, although violent plundering never lost its prominent place. Another difference was that the Black African tribes which were routinely enslaved were not 'Moors', and the idea of their evangelization presented special challenges. Despite the fact that the crusade in Morocco never disappeared from the mental horizon of the Portuguese kings, early colonial expansion was not really a continuation of a single process of *reconquista*. Nevertheless, it is still true that some ideological attitudes persisted, and that the Portuguese and other Europeans who reached the Indian Ocean were used to classifying and conceptualizing Muslims with a higher degree of precision than peoples belonging to a non-biblical tradition. While Muslim merchants in the Indian Ocean could be seen and treated roughly the same way as those who lived in Granada or Egypt, and the Turkish and Persian warriors of the Deccan like those from Anatolia, the gap that separated the 'gentiles' from Tenerife or Guinea from those in Calicut or Vijayanagara was a significant one.

How this gap came to be defined presents one important illustration of the use of religious and racial categories in the first encounters between Europeans and non-Europeans, and a necessary preface to the more specific question of the relationship between the Portuguese and the kingdom of Vijayanagara. Thus, if we can judge from the evidence of the journal written by one of the participants of the first expedition of Vasco da Gama (1497–9), the initial reaction of the Portuguese in India was to identify the Hindus with Christians, whom they had been led optimistically to expect there, and to regard the Muslim communities involved in oceanic trade as natural enemies, whom they could and should legitimately fight. Meeting a couple of Tunisian Moors who spoke to the Portuguese in Castilian five minutes after landing in Calicut certainly helped to dispel the initial feeling of disorientation. Most famously, the expectation that the Indians were Christians certainly shaped the interpretation of the evidence of religious temples and rituals which the Portuguese encountered, a situation described in the journal of the first expedition (probably written by the soldier Alvaro Velho):

Then they took us to a big church, in which there was the following: first the body of the church, which is as large as a monastery, all made of hewn stone and with a tiled roof. And the main door had a pillar of bronze, high as a mast, and at the top of this pillar there is a bird which looks like a cock. Another pillar, high as a man, is very thick. In the middle of the Church there is a chapel made of hewn stone with a door as large as it is needed for a man to go through, and stairs of stone that went up to this door, which was made of bronze. Inside there was a small image that they said was Our Lady. And in front of the main door of the Church, along the wall, there were seven small bells. Our captain-major [Vasco da Gama], and us with him, prayed here. We did not go into this chapel because their custom is that only certain men who serve the chapels, called *quafes*, can go in. These *quafes* [brahmins] have some threads thrown over their left shoulder and under their right arm, in the same way that the priests who say the gospel carry the stole. They threw holy water over us, and they give some white clay which the Christians of this country commonly put on their foreheads, their breasts, around the neck, and on the forearms. They did all this ceremony to the captain, and gave him some of that clay so that he would put it on. The captain gave it to be kept and made it understood that he would put it on later. And many, many other saints were painted on the walls of the church, with diadems, and their painting was different [from ours], because the teeth were so big that they came out of the mouth a whole inch, and each saint had four or five arms.[2]

Where Varthema would describe a devil, Vasco de Gama and his companions momentarily saw saints. The same empirical evidence could sustain opposite interpretations. However, it would be wrong to conceive of these as anything but relative. In both cases it was a context of previous information and future audience that shaped the choice of interpretation. As the few Portuguese who had landed in Calicut were led towards the city, followed by a crowd of people curious to see them, some entertained doubts about those saints with long teeth and many arms (for instance, at the time of kneeling down to pray, the *escrivão* João de Sá is reported by the historian Castanheda to have said that 'if these be devils, I worship the true God'). The fact that the main body of the Portuguese expedition managed to keep the Christian hypothesis alive until the next expedition by Alvares Cabral is not an indication of irrationality, but rather evidence of the importance of expectations, desires and mediations in shaping the interpretation of experience, when direct linguistic communication was not yet possible.

In his audiences with the king of Calicut, Vasco da Gama had to rely on Arabic as an intermediate language, and that meant that the well-

---

[2] I have consulted the palaeographic edition of the manuscript: [Alvaro Velho], *Diário da viagem de Vasco da Gama*, pp. 40–1, compared with the modernized text: [A. Velho], 'Relação da primeira viagem de Vasco da Gama', ed. by Luís de Albuquerque, in *Grandes viagens marítimas* (Lisbon, 1989), pp. 30–1. For a general commentary on Velho's journal, also discussing the problem of authorship, see Franz Hümmerich, 'Estudio crítico sobre o "roteiro" da primeria viagem de Vasco da Gama', in [Velho], *Diário*, part II, pp. 173–542. I have accepted the attribution to Velho as likely, but this is not a settled matter.

established Muslim merchants, who for obvious reasons did not want the Portuguese to be well received, had an enormous advantage and could even tamper with some exchanges. It is likely that the North African Moors who could speak a smattering of Genoese and Castilian (and one of them, popularly known as Monçaide, was soon brought into service by the Portuguese) helped the Portuguese sustain the belief that non-Muslim rulers were Christians, probably because they perceived that this was what the newcomers wanted to hear – they had been told that 'we came to look for Christians and spices'.[3] But the identification of Hindu merchants as Christians had already taken place in the eastern coast of Africa. There the Portuguese communicated with Arab-speaking Moors – 'black' or 'white' Moors, depending on their ethnic background – through a sailor who was himself a former captive of the Moors.[4] In Mozambique some Moors had already led the Portuguese to believe that non-Moors were Christians, and had given reports about the Prester John of Abyssinia, which the Portuguese received with tears of happiness. The Portuguese took Muslim pilots with them who, under interrogation, constantly referred to riches and Christians ahead. By the time they reached Malindi, some Indian traders were being hailed with the cry of 'Criste', even though all that the Portuguese managed to learn about them was that they did not eat beef.[5] The king of Malindi gave the

---

[3] 'Vimos buscar cristãos e especiaria': [Velho], *Diário*, p. 36. This rather apt expression was apparently uttered by a 'degredado' called João Nunes who had been sent to make first contact. He was, apparently, a New Christian with some knowledge of Arabic and Hebrew: E. G. Ravenstein (ed.) *A journal of the first voyage of Vasco da Gama, 1497–99*, Hakluyt Society (London, 1898), pp. 178–9. 'Degredados' were convicts whom the Portuguese often employed to make initial contacts. Without this concept of 'useful punishment', which helped retain and manipulate men with unusual skills and experience, many delicate missions would not have been easily accomplished. The Tunisian Monçaide became one of the chief informers of the Portuguese in the months to follow, and by the time they left he was in fact being accused in Calicut of having travelled to the emporium by previous arrangement with the Portuguese. In this light, he may have been responsible for sustaining Portuguese preconceptions.

[4] Possibly one Fernão Martins, who is later referred to as Gama's trusted interpreter. Another interpreter, Martim Affonso, was sent to speak with African tribes because he had spent a long time in Manicongo.

[5] It is not impossible that they were actually Christians from Cranganore in southern India, as suggested by S. Subrahmanyam, *The Portuguese empire in Asia, 1500–1700* (London and New York, 1993), p. 58, although I am not entirely convinced. The merchants 'showed him [Vasco da Gama] an altarpiece ['retábulo'] with Our Lady with Jesus Christ in her arms, at the foot of the cross, and with the apostles' and 'when the Indians saw the altarpiece, they threw themselves onto the ground' (the sentence is not easy to interpret, since from the second part of the sentence it would seem that it was the Portuguese who showed the altarpiece to the Indians). Afterwards 'while we stayed there they used to come to make their prayers' and 'brought us pepper and clove'. At night they celebrated a party 'for us' ([Velho], 'Relação', p. 27). Whether all these activities had been interpreted correctly by the Portuguese is far from clear. Their physical description (few clothes, long

Portuguese a pilot whom they believed to be 'Christian', but who in fact was Gujarati.[6] These identifications seem to have combined three elements: the misinformation supplied by Arabic-speaking pilots and interpreters who, as captives, may have had their own agenda; the desire of the Portuguese to find allies against Muslim enemies who were clearly rivals and whose influence was obvious everywhere in the East that mattered; and the difference between the Indian traders and those better-known black peoples from Africa whom the Portuguese associated with simple, even bestial ways of living, and with an idolatrous lack of formal religion (the 'formal idolatry' of India was in this sense a new experience). Ultimately the expectation of Christians in India went back to the older ideas of the apostolate of Saint Thomas and the might of the Prester John, ideas not entirely without foundation, but not yet set in a proper context. Lacking that, it was easy to fall back on the most optimistic interpretation and to force it upon the Arab-speaking informers whose fortune might have depended on pleasing their masters. As in the case of Columbus, who after sailing along the coast of Cuba fruitlessly searching for the evidence of the civilization of Cathay, in desperation made his crew swear that they were on the Asian mainland, in Calicut captains like Vasco da Gama could somehow impose an unrealistic official line against the private thoughts of others – even if only for the time being.

That the Portuguese did not make friends with the king of Calicut owed a great deal more to the fact that they were not willing to abide by the existing rules of exchange than to their ideological confusion. Although they were well received, their insistence on a common moral ground as Christians only exasperated a king who saw that they were not treating him with the presents that would win his special favours, nor on the other hand trading as normal merchants. The weakness of the Portuguese is that, coming from a poor country, little of what they had brought to sell was very valuable – which meant that direct trade alone would not sustain the cost of their fleets (they could pay with silver and gold, but this would not make the enterprise profitable, especially if the spices still reached the Mediterranean through the Red Sea).[7] Thus Vasco da Gama found that the king's factors laughed at his 'goods' and

---

beards and long, braided hair) suggests South Indian merchants, perhaps *chetis* from Coromandel.

[6] The idea defended by some historians that the belief in Indian Christians had been a trick by the Gujarati pilot, whose mission was to lure the Portuguese into a trap, is quite unwarranted and not particularly coherent.

[7] According to [Velho], in their first interview the king asked 'what was it that he [Vasco da Gama] had come to discover, precious stones or men? If it was men he was after, as he claimed, why did he fail to bring any presents?'; and concluded 'let him bring his merchandize to the mainland, and sell it as well as he can' ([Velho], 'Relação', p. 35).

nobody bought them. The failure of the exchange at this logical level of commerce was a real turning point, and quickly encouraged the king to listen to those foreign Muslim merchants who had negative expectations about the 'Franks' and predicted trouble ahead (quite rightly, as it turned out). As mutual suspicion grew, the opportunities for friendly exchange broke down, and Vasco da Gama, isolated in his ships, increasingly fulfilled the role of a violent rogue foreseen by his Muslim enemies. For Velho the Indians had become 'people who had no more sense than beasts', although he also thought that the Moors were responsible for all the problems.[8] Eventually Vasco da Gama left in fear of attacks and without doing any good business – but also convinced that the next expedition should come with the means to impose favourable trade conditions.

It was in Gama's interest to portray his trip as a success, which from a navigational point of view it certainly was. From the instructions received by the leader of the following expedition, Pedro Alvares Cabral, it appears that the official line was not substantially modified: the king was a 'Christian', however imperfect, and the Portuguese (pretending to be uninterested in commerce alone) were concerned with establishing a political–religious alliance on which to build a profitable trade.[9] Similarly, when announcing his success to the Catholic kings and to the Pope, King Manuel maintained the image of a Christian alliance in India against the Moors, only hinting at the fact that some heresies would need to be corrected. But meanwhile the information processed in Lisbon after the return of the first expedition in July 1499 reflected a gradual shift

---

[8] Ibid., p. 38: 'demos graças a Nosso senhor por nos tirrar de entre tais homens em que não cabe nenhuma razão, come se fossem bestas'. The Portuguese view that the foreign Muslim merchants were responsible for the negative attitude of the king of Calicut was not a mere justification. They heard it from Muslim informers in Calicut. The belief was also shared by the Christians of Malabar and expressed, for instance, in a letter written in 1504 by four Syrian priests to Mar Elias, their patriarch in Mesopotamia: 'A king sent Western Christians, who are our brothers the Franks, to these countries of India in some powerful ships . . . But in Calicut there live many Ismaelites who, moved by their inveterate hatred of the Christians, began to calumniate them to the gentile king and lied to him'. W. B. Greenlee (ed.) *The voyage of Pedro Alvares Cabral*, Hakluyt Society, 2nd series (London, 1938), pp. 95–6, translated portions of the letter. It is given in full in French by G. Bouchon, L. F. Thomaz and J. P. Costa in 'Le miroir asiatique', in M. Chandeigne (ed.) *Lisbonne hors les murs 1415–1580. L'invention du monde par les navigateurs portugais* (Paris, 1990), pp. 254–5. This letter, whose rampant providentialism and schematic analysis certainly equals that of the Portuguese themselves, was written after a number of expeditions, when hostilities had become open.

[9] The instructions are translated into English in Greenlee, *The voyage*, pp. 169ff. The instructions maintain the fiction of a common Christian identity and that the economic exchange will easily be balanced, but nevertheless suggest a cautious approach to the actual commercial and political prospects and emphasize the need for hostages and negotiations.

away from the image of Christianity in India. Initially (on the arrival of the first ship) the Florentine Girolamo Sernigi, one of the key Italian investors in Lisbon, wrote to Florence that Calicut was peopled by Christians, although odd ones: 'In this city are churches with bells, but there are no priests, and the divine offices are not performed, nor masses celebrated, but in each church there is a pillar holding water in the manner of the fonts holding our holy water, and a second pillar with balm.' He added that 'this king of Calicut eats neither meat nor fish nor anything that has been killed, nor do his barons, courtiers or other persons of quality, for they say that Jesus Christ said in his law that he who kills shall die'.[10] However, a few weeks later Sernigi corrected his views, on the basis of the reports by a Jewish trader from Alexandria whom the Portuguese had captured when they were about to leave India, and who, after converting to Christianity, was to become (as 'Gaspar da Gama') one of their chief informers on the economy of the region:[11] 'He says that in those countries there are many gentiles, that is idolaters, and only a few Christians, that the supposed churches and belfries are in reality temples of idolaters, and that the pictures within them are those of idols and not of saints. To me this seems more probable than saying that there are Christians but no divine ministrations, no priests and no sacrificial mass. He does not believe that there are any Christians of account other than some called Jacobites and those of the Prester John, who is far from Calicut, on this side of the gulf of Arabia.'[12] The destruction of the medieval image of the Prester John, who was now clearly an isolated ruler in Abyssinia far away from the small Christian communities of India, themselves surrounded in a sea of gentilism, was not then the result of direct, naked experience. It followed from the use of informers and the ordering of information at some critical distance from the ideology of messianic success that dominated the court of King Manuel.

[10] See Ravenstein (ed.) *Journal*, pp. 123–136. Ravenstein translated this letter from the manuscript in the Vaglienti collection in Florence, which gives a fuller version than the ones printed by the *Paesi novamenti retrovati* of 1507 and by Ramusio in 1550 – see Ramusio, *Navigazione e viaggi*, ed. by M. Milanesi, vol. I, pp. 607–17. Differences between different manuscript and printed versions are discussed by C. Radulet, *Os descobrimentos Portugueses e a Itália* (Lisbon, 1991), pp. 48–51. A similar opinion to Sernigi's – that the people of Calicut are Christian, but not proper ones – was given by another merchant called Guido di Tomaso Detti on the basis of an oral report by the pilot of the first ship (Biblioteca Riccardiana, ms. 1,910, 68r).

[11] In fact this Polish Jew, who spoke Venetian, was then at the service of the Muslim sultan of Bijapur, and had approached the Portuguese in order to spy on them and lure them into an ambush. He was found out and flogged until he confessed. His future service to the Portuguese king was nevertheless remarkable.

[12] Ravenstein (ed.) *Journal*, pp. 137–8. See also Ramusio, *Navigazioni*, vol. I, pp. 615–16 (with small variations, which I have used to emend the text).

The subsequent expeditions confirmed the judgement of Gaspar da Gama and extended the economic and ethnological experience of the Portuguese from Calicut to the various ports of the Malabar coast, as well as increasing the range and precision of oral reports describing other parts of India and beyond. It was thus soon accepted that there were fewer Christians than expected, notwithstanding the communities of pepper-growers in Cranganore and Quilon, whom the Portuguese theoretically undertook to protect. Distinctions between Arabs, Turks (Rumis) and local Muslims (called Mappilas on the Malabar coast) were also strengthened, like those between different groups of gentiles. However, the main ideological pattern for the colonial enterprise – an apparently religious principle of classification – would not change substantially in the following decades: the Portuguese wanted to find Christians, knew how to deal with Jews and *mouros*, and finally grouped all the rest together as *gentios* or 'idolaters'.[13]

The predominance of this religious classification raises the question of how important other categories were. It is quite clear that the first Europeans in India do not seem to have needed racial explanations to understand and evaluate the new people they encountered. Marco Polo had noted the fact that in South India people were black as just another curiosity, and emphasized the idea that they appreciated being black, and that they portrayed their devils as white.[14] The accounts of Persian and Deccani Muslims and the one written by the Russian Nikitin in the fifteenth century were much quicker to express racial prejudice than those written by the Italians and Portuguese who visited India in the sixteenth century. But that does not mean that European racism did not exist. Varthema's sexual anecdotes, for instance, invented or not, often have a racist component, like when the queen of Rhada in Yemen, driven by desire for his white body, laments that she and all her family are black.[15] Perhaps this example is less an indication of European prejudices than of attitudes which the traveller shared with his Arab and Persian companions (in some ways Varthema's use of racial categories depends upon the assumption of his different roles). However, in the *Itinerario* there seems to be an implicit ranking between white, brown and black people. Whether this hierarchy is made explicit or not seems to depend on who the writer wants to identify with at any given moment: the 'brown' Indians of Ciaul and Dabul (*colore leonato oscuro*), encountered

---

[13] The roots of the Christian idea of *idolatry* are of course in the Bible and the Fathers of the Church. This concept defined the identity of Judaism and Christianity *vis-à-vis* other traditions in the ancient world.

[14] Polo, *Description of the world*, p. 400.

[15] Varthema, *Itinerario*, pp. 142–50.

on Varthema's way to Vijayanagara and Calicut, are idolaters but uphold justice; the traveller's own whiteness makes him suspect when he is attempting to run away from his Muslim companions in Calicut; naked black people in Mozambique are described as animals, but in a context that serves to emphasize Varthema's return home, that is to his European–Christian identity.

Another case in point is the treatment of black Africans in Portuguese sources of the same period. The Portuguese category of *negros* was extensively used – western Africa was in fact divided between 'the land of the Moors' and 'the land of the blacks' – and it could have a negative connotation because black peoples were also those who were seen as bestial in their way of living and were most often subjected to slavery. But while the negative connotations of darkness went back to medieval literature, the actual experience of exploration and slave trade did not simply reinforce it; rather, it often created contexts for the modification of the stereotype.[16] Black people were sometimes admired for their skills, their courage or their feelings, and the fact that they were also 'sons of Adam' and 'rational creatures' whom God could save was emphasized by writers like Gomes Eanes de Zurara, the remarkable fifteenth-century chronicler of the Portuguese explorations and raids in Guinea.[17] Alvaro Velho in his journal expressed curiosity for the ways of living of the various tribes encountered along the way, offering evidence of a tendency to distinguish different African groups which ran counter to the simple imposition of an overarching racial category.[18] Ultimately, the paradox was that these peoples were simultaneously fully men and yet more bestial than men, capable of salvation and yet legitimate slaves. This paradox had in the end more to do with the improper identification of Christianity with civility than with colour: similar categories were

---

[16] There is a valuable analysis of the image of the African in the Portuguese travel literature of this period in J. da Silva Horta, 'A representação do Africano na literatura de viagens, do Senegal à Serra Leoa (1453–1508)', *Mare Liberum*, 2 (1991): 209–339.

[17] For Zurara [Azurara], bestiality and 'natural slavery' were attributed to either biblical condemnation or to the Platonic–Aristotelian distinction between different types of men. Compare chaps. 16 and 35 of his 1453 *Crónica do descobrimento e conquista da Guiné*, ed. by Reis Brasil (Lisbon, 1989), pp. 79 and 117.

[18] See [Velho], 'Relação', pp. 10–17. For instance, when they found some small dark men ('homens baços') dressed in skins and wearing penis-sheaths in the bay of Santa Helena above the Cape of Good Hope (Hottentots), a certain Fernão Veloso seems to have been victim of his great desire 'to go to their houses to see how they lived, what they ate and what their life was about'. As a result of this a whole party of Portuguese was ambushed, Vasco da Gama was injured, and they learnt that small bodies did not necessarily mean 'small hearts'. After the publication of Hans Burgkmair's woodcuts in 1508 illustrating Balthasar Springer's account of the expedition of Viceroy Almeida in 1505, these Hottentots, along with the Indians of Malabar, soon became a favourite subject for European artists.

applied by Zurara to the 'white' Canary Islanders and to the 'black' peoples from Guinea.[19] While the category of *negros* mattered, it was therefore a relative one. We may indeed conclude that the use of general racial classifications was in this period superficial and unsystematic. These categories did not constitute a necessary way of thinking for the whole of the late medieval European cultural tradition, nor were they exclusive to it (in fact, they were often inherited from or shared with the Arabs).[20]

Skin colour was ultimately more significant because it suggested, by association, a particular level of civility than because it defined racial traits. Although the biblical idea of a divine punishment was sometimes referred to in order to account for a colour that had negative symbolic and aesthetic associations, darkness was more often explained on account of climate and heat. And it was not a schematic climatic determinism either. As early as 1502 Amerigo Vespucci tried to account for the fact that American Indians were not black by explaining that 'nature and custom' were more significant than just physical environment in determining the blackness of Africans, as the experience of genetic observations showed, and that different conditions could be found at the same latitude.[21] The crucial issue was the relationship between religious and civil–ethnic categories. In general, it can be said that religious definitions were taken more seriously than civil or racial ones, although in practical terms their use was relative too. Many black Africans were, for instance, often described as idolaters, but others were recognized as Moors, and it is interesting that in this case 'black Moors' could be seen in a more positive light than 'white Moors' because, only superficially Muslims, they seemed more likely to adopt the European religion and customs.[22]

---

[19] Azurara, *Crónica*, pp. 210–15 on the Canary Islanders.

[20] On the subject of racism in Islam, and in particular attitudes towards blacks, see for instance B. Lewis, *Race and slavery in the Middle East* (Oxford, 1990). Bernard Lewis notes the paradox that while Islamic religious law made all men equal, the experience of Arab expansion and in particular the growth of specialized channels of African slavery created the historical conditions through which racial prejudices gained an unprecedented importance (which he does not find in antiquity). It is, however, important to remember that very often the practice differed from the theory.

[21] In his letter to Lorenzo di Pierfrancesco de Medici, trying to justify his reports against sceptics in Florence. See Vespucci, *Il mondo nuovo di Amerigo Vespucci*, pp. 95–6: 'nonn'è necessità che tutti gli uomini che abitono drento a la torida [zona] debbino esser neri di natura e di sangue comato, come sono li Etiopi . . . perché già la natura ha convertito in abito la loro negrezza, e questo lo veggiamo in queste nostre parte, ché e neri generano neri, e si un bianco [usa] con una nera, la creatura sarà bigia . . . segnale è che la natura e'l costume adopera più le forze che la compressione dell'aere e della terra'.

[22] As observed by José da Silva Horta. 'Primeros olhares sobre o Africano do Sara Occidental à serra Leoa', in L. de Albuquerque et al., *O confronto de olhar. O encontro*

When later in the sixteenth century the understanding of non-Europeans became a theoretically more complex enterprise, a combination of religion, race and climate provided some of the grounds on which comparative theories were built. It is none the less significant that this development, which reflected the increasing methodological sophistication of late Renaissance humanist culture, was already a response to the evidence of diversity of customs, rituals and laws gathered in travel collections. It is equally interesting to note that, to a large extent, the development of fairly sophisticated racial classifications in the writings of (as we saw) leading Jesuits like Valignano in the 1580s responded to the need to go beyond pure religious categories, albeit, paradoxically, to solve a religious problem. If until then dismissive racial or religious classifications were most often found in the writings of those needing to justify a political attitude (such as mistrust or violence), or to explain a political failure (successful resistance to European expansion was thus the result of the 'treacherous' character of natives and Moors), in the case of Valignano the problem was the reasons why a mission had failed. Racial arguments were in this context no more than an attempt to link the prospects of Christianization to a belief in a hierarchy of civilization by which the 'white' Chinese and Japanese were regarded as more likely to convert than 'black' South Indians. The racial–climatic element was for this reason no more than an explanation of civility, and not strictly necessary – thus in the same years, from his experience in Spanish America, the influential missionary José de Acosta sharply distinguished different levels of barbarism within a single racial framework, because all Indians were descendants of Noah who had migrated by land to the new continent and yet the Incas who built Cuzco were worlds apart from the hunter-gatherers of Brazil. Far less coherent was the attempt by another Jesuit, Alonso de Sandoval, to establish a general category of 'blacks' in his treatise on the salvation of the 'Ethiopians' of

---

dos povos na época das navegações portuguesas (Lisbon, 1991), pp. 83–4. Azurara himself did not clearly define the 'blacks' as either idolatrous or gentiles, but the concept of lawless idolaters is central in the accounts by the Venetian Ca' da Mosto in the fifteenth century (*c.* 1465, then printed in the *Paesi novamenti retrovati* of 1507 and by Ramusio), and appears in the compilations of Portuguese observations produced at the beginning of the sixteenth century (such as those by Valentim Fernandes and Duarte Pacheco Pereira). It thus seems that the well-attested use of the concept of idolatrous gentile in the medieval accounts of Asia preceded its use in Africa, and that the Portuguese, content for a long time with the concept of 'blacks', adopted it fairly late. This also suggests that despite their connections with Florentine humanists, the Portuguese, caught by the images of crusade and of the Prester John, did not make very good use of their possible medieval sources. The Moravian Valentim Fernandes published his Portuguese versions of Polo and Conti only after the discovery of the route, and when it had already been established that non-Muslim Indian kings were gentiles.

1627. If in the cases of Valignano and Acosta the aim had been to define different missionary methods for different levels of civilization, Sandoval was concerned with the spiritual life of the black slaves whom he saw arrive in Cartagena, and who had been neglected by Acosta. However, instead of simply dealing with slavery as an institution which he was in no position to eliminate, he sought to establish the obligation of baptizing slaves and protecting them against cruel treatment by defining, through an ethnographic survey, an ambiguous category of 'Negros' (improperly identified with 'Ethiopians') which included any dark-skinned peoples, not only in Africa, but also in South India, New Guinea or the Philippines.[23]

We can conclude that while the use of racial distinctions was contextual and to a remarkable extent represented one option among others – an ideological choice rather than an ideological assumption we could say – the distance between the general religious concept of gentilism and the specific description of secular civility provided the crucial gap through which a distinct image of the Indian 'other' could grow. The formation of this type of image was shared by many travellers in the first years of the Portuguese expeditions, and has left traces in a number of reports of first-time experiences written before the main ethnic stereotypes of Asian peoples had been publicized as text and image in Europe, becoming a clear referential point in the imagination of many.

One example is the letter written by Giovanni Buonagrazia, a Florentine who was captain of a ship during the second expedition of Vasco da Gama to India in 1502–3.[24] It is apparent that Buonagrazia's main interest, when writing to his father, were the exotic people he had encountered. With a few schematic but also immediate images, he distinguished between three groups: 'naked black', 'black Moors' and

---

[23] See A. de Sandoval, *Un tratado sobre la esclavitud*, ed. by E. Vila Vilar (Madrid, 1987), pp. 57ff. Although Sandoval's concerns were prompted by the personal experience of imported black slavery in America, he relied on written sources for his ethnographic survey of blacks in Africa and Asia, and these he used rather indiscriminately. For South India, for instance, he combined João de Lucena's biography of Saint Francis Xavier (which he himself had translated from Portuguese into Castilian in 1619), which contained a detailed account of his apostolate among the Paravas of the Fishery coast, Antonio de Gouvea's account of the synod of Diamper in the mountains of Malabar (1606), some traditional references to the apostolate of Saint Thomas, combined with contemporary Jesuit reports of it, and Marco Polo's description of Maabar, which Sandoval mistranslated as Malabar! To complete the picture, he added some observations about Quilon (not realizing that he had already discussed it under a different name) and about Zanzibar (unaware, apparently, that it was in Africa). The key reason for bringing together all these passages is of course to establish the continuity and success of the apostolate among 'blacks', inspired by Saint Thomas in antiquity and by Saint Francis Xavier in modern times.

[24] Biblioteca Nazionale di Firenze, Ms. Palatino, 1125, ff. 32r–40v.

'Indian gentiles'. It was clear that the black Moors of Eastern Africa were, although Muslim, more 'civil' than those in the Western coast, and for this reason Buonagrazia believed that they were closer to Christianity. But his real fascination was with the Indian gentiles. Buonagrazia did not have the long experience of those commercial factors who (like Duarte Barbosa) would stay in India for a number of years in order to build a permanent Portuguese presence, but he benefited from the accumulated knowledge of successive expeditions and was able to dispense with the illusions of the first visitors (he reported as a distinct category that there were 'very good' Indian Christians, whom he had met in Cochin). What struck him most about gentile Indian culture was an apparent incongruity: the contrast between rampant idolatry and loose moral standards, on the one hand, and 'discretion' and 'civility', on the other. In this way Indian gentiles were displayed in their full cultural otherness as morally opposite to the European Christians, rather than as would-be converts eager for missionaries.[25]

IMPERIAL IDEOLOGIES

The foreign investors whose financial role was so crucial to the first Portuguese expeditions (the Florentines alone would account for more than 20 per cent of the capital in the first fifteen years) were in a position to develop their own discourse and interests about India.[26] Their relationship with the Portuguese was often difficult, as for instance the second expedition of Vasco da Gama bears witness. Merchants like Matteo di Bergamo complained that the admiral took arbitrary decisions in order to exclude them from many profits, and made things unnecessarily violent.[27] The Portuguese captains, on the other hand, resented the

[25] For an edition of Buonagrazia's hitherto unpublished letter, with a more detailed discussion of its contents, see J. P. Rubiés, 'Giovanni di Buonagrazia's letter to his father concerning his participation in the second expedition of Vasco da Gama', *Mare Liberum*, 16 (1998): 87–112.

[26] On the Florentines in Portugal see especially M. Spallanzani, *Mercanti fiorentini nell'Asia portoghese*.

[27] Matteo di Bergamo complained in his letter to the investors that Vasco da Gama had forbidden any trade that was not supervised by the royal factor, and indeed at the prices that he set: P. Peragallo (ed.), 'Viaggio di Matteo di Bergamo in India sulla flotta di Vasco da Gama (1502–3)', *Bollettino della Società Geografica Italiana*, 4th series, 3 (1902): 92–129. He also excluded foreigners from the profits from plunder; perhaps worse still, whilst he could have reached a peaceful agreement with a compliant king of Calicut, who simply requested that the Moors who had always traded in his kingdom should continue to do so, Gama cruelly bombarded the town; then he imposed his commercial terms onto his Indian allies, the kings of Cochin and Cannanor; he also refused to let the European private merchants reduce the price of silver and alum in order to speed up the business; finally, he intended to advise the king of Portugal to

foreigners' neat benefits within their own empire, and were concerned with the profit of the crown and their own (how to distinguish these two soon became a serious problem). Although the king of Portugal needed Italian investment to finance his ships, his trump card was the appeal to military force, which, however, followed a logic of its own, a different ethical code indeed, in which the rhetoric of honour (although not necessarily the reality) was placed above the rhetoric of economic calculation. The king certainly needed an empire if he wanted to sustain his business as profitable and simultaneously draw together the different social elements of the nation around his project. The conflict between the needs of empire and those of merchants could then easily take a national tinge, but was wider than that: it was crucial to the experience of the Portuguese themselves, because while only the empire could sustain the business at a competitive level, its costs could also destroy the business.[28] In this dilemma a nationalistic ideology of empire adapted to the realities beyond the Cape of Good Hope came to supply the force that could fill the gap between ideals and realities, with all the consequences that this entailed for European attitudes towards non-Europeans.[29]

Perhaps the best illustration of this imperial ideology is given by the humanist-educated and officially minded historian João de Barros (1469–1570) in his discussion of the decision to pursue empire taken by the king and his counsellors when they sent Vasco da Gama on his second expedition. Although this chapter of *Asia* has more of a Renaissance historian's rhetorical piece than an empirical record of actual arguments, Barros none the less expresses with intelligence the ideological dilemmas involved in this decision.[30] He begins by declaring the arguments against expansion: how profitable will it be to conquer such a distant country as India? In Guinea the gentiles were 'obedient and peaceful', and gold and spices could be cheaply obtained. In India, instead, after Cabral's expedition it had become obvious that many ships would be lost in the sea, and that it would not be possible to conquer

---

attempt to exclude foreign traders from India (ibid, p. 122). Matteo concluded that the merchants should obtain securities from the king so that the Portuguese captains could not arbitrarily command them.

[28] On this duality see Diffie and Winius, *Foundations*, pp. 406–15 and Subrahmanyam, *The Portuguese*, pp. 45ff.

[29] The nationalistic element was a crucial addition to the religious identity because since the late Middle Ages the Portuguese did not simply define themselves as Christians against Moors or, secondarily, as missionaries amongst the blacks whom they enslaved; they were also, within Christianity, Portuguese as opposed to Castilians. In fact the explorations of the fifteenth century gave expression to the idea of a separate providential history against the Castilian threat of a Spanish Christian empire that would include the whole of the Iberian Peninsula once lost to the Moors.

[30] Barros, *Ásia*, vol. I, pp. 213–21.

without a substantial recourse to arms. As for the idea of evangelization, Barros also presents the doubts of the principal men of the kingdom:

> But to communicate, converse and conduct business with the people of India, whose idolatries, abuses, vices, opinions and sects even one of the apostles sent by Jesus (as Saint Thomas was) feared, and for this reason he was wary of going there simply to offer them a doctrine of peace for the salvation of their souls: how could we expect that our doctrine, however Catholic, would make an impression on them, since we took this doctrine with armed force instead of an apostolic voice – indeed we took it with the voice of men more interested in their own profit than in the salvation of that Gentile nation? And especially in so close proximity to the Moors who, precisely on account of that evangelical doctrine, were our capital enemies.[31]

Barros went on to emphatically describe the power of the Muslims in India, 'more numerous on the coast between Goa and Cochin than in North Africa between Ceuta and Alexandria', singling out in particular those foreign Muslims who had taken over the profitable trade in spices. Obviously, with the entrance of the Portuguese into India, the Moors would join forces and muster the support of the most powerful gentile kings, like the Zamorin of Calicut, against them.

But of course Barros, distinguished imperial bureaucrat for the affairs of Guinea and India, unfortunate colonial investor in Brazil, and appointed to write his history by the elderly King Manuel before his death in 1521, presented all these negative arguments only to defend more thoroughly and brilliantly an empire that was fully established (and thus, in his own eyes, fully vindicated) by the time that he composed his work.[32] The gospel certainly had to be announced, whatever the means, as was convenient to the glory of Christ. Against the Moors and the Zamorin of Calicut one could oppose a network of local alliances, especially with the kings of Cochin, Cannanor and Quilon. Barros went on to assert with confidence and optimism that trade with the Portuguese was obviously beneficial to the gentiles, and that it would enrich Portugal as well as pay for its armies and fleets. He concluded with an unambiguous return to the messianic image of the crusader-king which had indeed been so important in shaping king Manuel's sense of dynastic

---

[31] Ibid. p. 214.

[32] This particular passage of Barros's *Ásia* seems to have been composed (from a number of references) not long before the book was first published in 1552, although the first draft of this decade must date back to the 1520s and 30s. For instance, Barros declares at some point (ibid. p. 219) that by now the Portuguese have held power in India for more than fifty years. (This, according to 'o direito de usucapiones', gives a *secondary* reason why they have a right to stay, whatever the Indians think, and exclude other Europeans. I discuss the *primary* reasons below.)

tradition and historical mission, and whose roots went back to the medieval ideology of Portuguese discovery in the Atlantic:[33]

> Finally the king determined that since Our Lord had opened to him this route, until then unknown, but in whose pursuit his ancestors had struggled so hard for more than seventy years, he would pursue it. And especially seeing that already the profits from the first expedition by Pedro Alvares outweighed both the efforts of the past and the fears for the future.[34]

With the elegance of a humanist Barros reasserted the ideological principles of a medieval crusader king, and upon it he built a systematic defence of the legitimacy of the empire which was, simultaneously, a defence of royal authority and of the title adopted by King Manuel: Lord of navigation, conquest and commerce of Ethiopia, Arabia, Persia and India. Not only was the title of conqueror of infidels a just one for a king, but it was precisely upon this kind of conquest that his glory rested. The popes had put the stamp of religious legitimacy upon the title too, and this 'donation' was justified by the expenses incurred by the kingdom in the pursuit of its mission (hence the profitable business of African gold and Indian spices was now conveniently portrayed as a sacrifice of blood and labour). And here came the interesting twist: since kings were, properly speaking, only kings of their subjects, but not of the land itself, the land belonged to whomever occupied it first. A king could rule over subjects but could only be the *lord* of their land (thus the blacks from Guinea, people without fixed territorial frontiers, could offer no resistance to the Portuguese kings when they declared themselves 'lords of Guinea'). Moreover the popes, as universal lords of all Christians, could distribute the lands of non-Christians amongst the faithful (this argument was, needless to say, far from orthodox and would not have been accepted by the theologians of Salamanca). Hence, 'Gentile idolaters and heretical Moors' are all 'unjust possessors' of their lands – they may not indeed be subjects of the king of Portugal, but their lands could legitimately be taken away at any time. And since the Portuguese kings owned the sea route and the right to conquer, the commerce belonged to them too (although, of course, natives were allowed to trade, provided that they bought their safe conducts).

But what about the principles of common law, which declare the seas

---

[33] On the Manueline imperial ideology see L. F. Thomaz, 'L'idée impériale Manueline', in J. Aubin (ed.) *La découverte, le Portugal et l'Europe* (Paris, 1990). More generally, on the importance of a solid providentialist framework in the Portuguese historiographical tradition (from the fourteenth to the sixteenth centuries) see L. de Sousa Rebelo, 'Providencialismo e profecia nas crónicas portuguesas da expansão', *Bulletin of Hispanic Studies*, 71 (1994): 67–86.

[34] Barros, *Ásia*, vol. I p. 216.

to be open to all, and property a right recognized by all? Well, this law is according to Barros only valid among Christians in Europe 'who through baptism and faith follow the rule of the Roman Church, and who are also governed by the rule of Roman law in their political life' (although, to avoid a threat to the independence of Portugal from the universal claims to authority of Roman popes and emperors, he is forced to add that these principles have been accepted *because they are rational* only, without letting it go that this contradicts his main argument). Thus Barros sustains the common law principle of primary possession as far as European Christians are concerned, effectively defending a Portuguese monopoly against other Christians, but denies the same principle to any non-Christians on account of their spiritual imperfection, 'since they deny the glory that they owe to their creator and saviour'.[35] Paradoxically, the authority of the pope is stronger for the dispossession of distant gentile nations than within the Christian kingdom of Portugal.

There could hardly be a more obviously self-serving use of the concepts of justice and religious truth, and certainly Barros did not command any consensus among the leading jurists and theologians of his time, beginning with Francisco de Vitoria and concluding with Hugo Grotius, who sought to define a truly universal natural law.[36] But while this apology for the Portuguese empire can be seen as the kind of theoretical aberration that patriotic propagandists would evolve if convenient in any European court of the time, the important question for us is the extent to which it mattered in the formulation of policies in Portuguese India. One could certainly argue that actual conquest and negotiation occurred prior to the historian's justification – thus Barros's own definition of the Portuguese lordship over commerce distinguished three modes which clearly corresponded to historical practice, namely commerce with vassals in territories under direct Portuguese dominion, commerce with allied kings according to long-lasting arrangements which amounted to a colonial monopoly of valuable products, and free commerce elsewhere. And yet Barros was not the rare apologist of a spontaneous development,

---

[35] Ibid. p. 219.

[36] In fact Barros's arguments were revived in the Hispanic empire at the beginning of the seventeenth century in response to Hugo Grotius's *Mare Liberum* of 1609. Hugo Grotius himself based parts of his argument about the civil rights of gentiles and infidels on the work of Francisco de Vitoria. I have no evidence of whether Barros was targeting Vitoria specifically, but he certainly must have been at least vaguely aware of the contents of his lectures in Salamanca. On the other hand, Vitoria himself quite naïvely thought that the Portuguese traded without conquering, as opposed to the practice of the Castilians in America, and was convinced that the intentions of the Portuguese kings were entirely honourable. See F. de Vitoria, *Political writings*, ed. by A. Pagden and J. Lawrence (Cambridge, 1991), pp. 291–2 and 334.

nor was he simply projecting back a debate of his times onto an innocent past. Although he was certainly responding to the arguments which were most controversial in his own time, perhaps even in the light of parallel debates concerning the Spanish empire in America, he was also drawing on a traditional set of beliefs and attitudes and giving them a refined, literary expression. Some of his arguments may not have been heard before in India, but the attitudes which informed them were certainly around from the very times of the establishment of the imperial network of forts and factories, lurking behind the Portuguese approach to local political realities whether they were Christian, Muslim or gentile. Essentially, the principle that a rational, common law defining basic human rights applied to European Christians but not to heretics, Jews, Moors and gentiles could justify the use of force in any imperial context, but ran counter to the practice of political negotiation and commercial dealings – that is, unless one were openly to adopt moral double standards.

THE KING OF NARSINGA: THE DISTANT ALLY

The fact that they had to deal with 'gentiles' as important political powers with whom they wanted to negotiate, changed European attitudes towards them. The practical problems involved in dealing successfully with the king of Vijayanagara or with the Ming emperors of China were of a different order to those raised by the Aztecs in Mexico or even the Zamorin of Calicut, who were far more accessible – not to mention the technologically weaker Indians of the Caribbean islands, or the inhabitants of the western coast of Africa. The 500 men who accompanied Cortés to Tenochtitlan would not have succeeded in conquering Vijayanagara, whilst the fleet of ships that bombarded Calicut in 1502 could only operate along coastal areas. One may generalize by saying that whilst each situation presented its own peculiar possibilities, Europeans knew how to measure their interests against the military strength of the different peoples they encountered, and evolved alternative strategies according to the result. Thus, the same general concept of 'gentiles' acquired different meanings and connotations depending upon the particular relationship the Europeans expected to have with the peoples concerned. As a general rule, the weaker the Europeans felt, the more they tried to understand with precision, so that in their accounts those societies perceived to be more powerful easily became the more sophisticated and, at the same time, the more respected.

This is reflected in the space devoted to each 'province' or 'kingdom' in the first systematic general accounts of the East by Tomé Pires and

Duarte Barbosa.[37] The latter, for instance, deals with each coastal city or little state in a few paragraphs, paying some more attention to key entrepots or commercial areas such as Ormuz, Gujarat and Malacca; but then his narrative expands dramatically when he talks about Vijayanagara and the Malabar coast. This attention to Calicut and the south-west coast of India makes a lot of sense, because that was the area where the Portuguese first landed, settled and evolved complicated economic, political and cultural relationships. It was also the area where Duarte Barbosa spent most of his time in India. The interest in Vijayanagara, on the other hand, has to be related to the potential importance that the kingdom appeared to have (especially through its impressive capital city), even though the Portuguese presence was and would remain limited to the few traders, soldiers and other visitors which the king wished to welcome.[38]

In fact the first references to Vijayanagara recorded by the Portuguese seem to have derived from hearsay.[39] It is clear that, before crossing the mountains towards the interior or even reaching the cities of Coromandel, the Europeans formed their first impressions through local intermediaries. For instance, the author of the journal of Vasco da Gama's first expedition appended a geographical description of the kingdoms 'south of Calicut' from the oral reports of 'a man who spoke

---

[37] Observe the space devoted to Vijayanagara by Barbosa, *Livro em que dá relação do que viu e ouviu no Oriente*, pp. 94–114 and by T. Pires, *The Suma Oriental of Tomé Pires*, ed. by A. Cortesão, Hakluyt Society, 2nd series, 2 vols. (London, 1944), vol. I, pp. 63–5 (or pp. 60–5 if we include the Kanarese coast).

[38] The history of Portuguese contacts with Vijayanagara, in particular the early phases, has been summarized by D. Lopes (ed.) *Chronica dos reis de Bisnaga* (Lisbon, 1897); Sewell, *A forgotten empire*; H. Heras, 'Early relations between Vijayanagara and Portugal' *Quarterly Journal of the Mythic Society*, 16 (1925): 63–74, (Bangalore); B. S. Shastry, 'The first decade of Portuguese-Vijayanagara relations', in *Studies in Indo-Portuguese history* (Bangalore, 1981), pp. 80–91. The main primary references are found in the chronicles of Castanheda, Barros, Correa and Couto. Of great importance are the letters written by Affonso de Albuquerque and his contemporaries, published in *Cartas de Affonso de Albuquerque*, ed. by R. A. de Bulhão Pato and H. Lopes de Mendoça, 7 vols. (Lisbon, 1884–1935) (hereafter *CA*); also the 'commentaries' written in 1557 (and with revisions in 1576) by his natural son Braz de Albuquerque, *Comentários de Affonso d'Albuquerque*, by A. d'Albuquerque [sic], ed. by A. Bião, 2 vols. (Coimbra, 1922–3); finally, an anonymous report of the Cabral expedition in 1500, published in the *Paesi novamenti retrovati* in 1507, and in English in Greenlee (ed.) *The voyage*. Shastry's *Studies* and G. Bouchon, *'Regent of the sea'. Cannanore's response to Portuguese expansion, 1507–28* (Oxford, 1988) represent an effort to re-assess the indigenous perspective.

[39] I do not pretend to undertake an exhaustive list of all minor early sixteenth-century references to Vijayanagara in this chapter, a task which has recently been accomplished by J. M. dos Santos Alves, 'A cruz, os diamantes e os cavalos; Frei Luís do Salvador, primeiro missionário e embaixador português em Vijayanagara (1500–10)', *Mare Liberum*, 5 (1993): 9–20. I shall only discuss the most significant examples.

our language and came from Alexandria to this parts some thirty years ago' (that is, probably Gaspar da Gama). He seems to describe Granganor, Quilon, Kayal and Coromandel, and then he goes on with Ceylon, Sumatra, Sarnau [Siam], Tenasserim, Bengal, Malacca, Pegu and some other places.[40] Since all Hindus are still identified as Christians (apparently at this stage Gaspar did not press the distinction) the king of 'Chomandarla' (Coromandel) is also Christian.[41] The fact that he can command 100,000 soldiers – more than any other ruler – suggests that the informer is attempting to describe the king of Vijayanagara, but the descriptions are too notional and schematic to convey a sense of historical specificity (they simply include name, religion, distance from Calicut, military power in number of men, and a few important products and prices). The real descriptions of Vijayanagara began with the expedition of Pedro Alvares Cabral which left Lisbon in 1500, and although still done through intermediaries, it is remarkable how similar they were to the later reports of the Portuguese who actually visited the capital. The author of the anonymous narrative of this expedition wrote extensively about the people of Calicut and its king, now clearly an idolater 'although others have believed that they are Christians'.[42] He then added a few ideas about another king who lived beyond the mountains:

in the mountains of this kingdom [the land of Calicut] there is a very great and powerful king who is called Naramega [Narasimha], and they are idolaters. The king has two or three hundred wives. The day he dies they burn him and all of his wives with him. And this custom prevails for nearly all the others who are married when they die . . . In this kingdom there are many horses and elephants because they wage

---

[40] [Velho], *Diário*, pp. 81–5.

[41] Speaking with Amerigo Vespucci two years later Gaspar gave a similar, but equally confused, list. Gaspar spoke to Vespucci in May 1501, when the returning ships of Cabral's expedition met the ship sent by the king of Portugal to explore the coast of Brazil off the Cape Verde Islands. In his letter to Lorenzo di Pierfrancesco di Medici (collected by Piero Vaglienti) Vespucci summarized his conversation concerning what must be Vijayanagara: 'Disse ch'era stato drento in terra de l'India in uno regno che si chiama e'regno de Parlicat [Pulicat], el quale è uno grandissimo regno e ricco d'oro e di perle e di gioie e di pietre preziose; e contò esser stato dentro in terra a Mailepur [Mylapore], e a Giapatan [Jaffna? Negapattam?], e a Melata [Malacca], e a Tanaser [Tenasserim], e a Pegu, e a Scarnai [Siam], e a Bengola [Bengal], a Otezan [Orissa] e a Marchin [Narsinga?]. E questo Marghin dice sta presso de'rio grande detto Emparlicat; e questo Emparlicat è città dove è il corpo di San Tomaso apostolo, e vi sono molti Cristiani' (Vespucci, *Mondo nuovo*, p. 80). Despite the lack of geographical clarity it seems obvious that 'Parlicat' and 'Marghin' both stand for Vijayanagara. The big river called 'Emparlicat' is a mystery (if it was near Pulicat it cannot have been so big), although there are a number of large rivers going from Coromandel towards the interior.

[42] Greenlee, *The voyage*, p. 79.

war, and they have them so taught and trained that the only thing which they lack is speech, and they understand everything like human beings.[43]

Thus the author briefly remarked on some of the themes common to all foreign descriptions of Vijayanagara: the power of the king, his idolatry, the custom of *sati*, the significance of elephants and horses. The relation by priest Joseph, the Christian from Cranganor in Malabar who returned to Europe with Cabral's fleet, insists on similar (if more obviously militaristic) points:

> Towards the mountains and about three hundred miles distant from the sea is to be found a very powerful king, who is named king Narsindo, and he has a great city with three circuits of walls. It is called Besenegal. This king, as priest Joseph told, he has seen with his own eyes. When he goes with an army against his enemies, he takes with him eight hundred elephants, four thousand horses, and innumerable foot soldiers, and he says that his camp from north to south is thirty miles long, and from west to east, of equal breadth. Consequently it may be supposed that his kingdom is very extensive . . . is three thousand miles around. Its faith is idolatrous.[44]

Joseph had already described *sati*, which explains its omission here. There is little doubt that he and the anonymous writer stressed the same idea of kingly power (they may have actually met, thus Joseph might have been the informant of Cabral's companion). Both of these descriptions found their way into the first collection of travel literature published in Venice, the *Paesi novamenti retrovati* of 1507.[45] They serve to establish an important point, namely that the Portuguese first learned about Vijayanagara and identified its prominent features from Indian mediators with whom they shared the same basic descriptive priorities. The case of priest Joseph is particularly clear: a Syro-Malabar Christian on a visit to

---

[43] Ibid. p. 82. I have cut the by now tedious description of *sati*. Ramusio published the document too (*Navigazioni*, vol. I, p. 646).

[44] Greenlee, *The voyage*, p. 113.

[45] News of Vijayanagara had previously been publicized in Europe in an Italian composite letter attributed to King Manuel but in fact made from a number of reports, including those from Cabral's expedition: see S. J. Pacifici (ed.) *Copy of a letter of the king of Portugal sent to the king of Castile concerning the voyage and success of India ('Copia di una lettera del re di Portogallo mandata al re de Castella del viaggio et successo de India', Roma 1505)* (Minneapolis, 1955). Thus, after describing the manners of the people of Calicut and India, the letter went on: 'Further inland there is another kingdom of idolaters, called Barsingua, which is abundant with horses and elephants experienced in warfare. In this kingdom women are burned with their husbands' (p.19). In 1507 there appeared a fuller notice in another letter, based on the reports of Friar Luís: *Gesta proxime per Portugalenses in India, Ethiopia et aliis orientalibus terris a Serenissimo Emanuele Portugalie rege* (Nüremberg, 1507).

Rome and thus especially acceptable to the Europeans, he was interviewed in Italy and his report then used by the editor of the collection,
Francanzano da Montalboddo.[46] As he copied Joseph's information, the
humanist editor added his own explanations from many readings,
ranging from Strabo to Marco Polo. He thus explained that 'those
are called Gentiles who in ancient times worshipped idols and various
kinds of animals' before giving Joseph's elaborate description of their
'sacrifices' involving naked priests, horned figures, human blood, burning
fire and conversations with idols – a description which, as we saw, bears
comparison to Varthema's. Here the European editor and the native
Christian (who has a claim to direct observation) share a space against
an alien religion which even Joseph, 'because he had not had many
dealings with Gentiles, has not been able to explain entirely'.[47]
The powerful Narsindo was neither a new invention nor a pure act of
realistic appropriation, but part of a newly established common cultural
patrimony.

Cabral's expedition also took some Franciscan friars to India, and one
of them, Luís do Salvador, is known to have visited Vijayanagara
(probably as a missionary) in 1504 if not earlier.[48] The members of the
next two Portuguese expeditions to India, through their dealings with the
chiefs of Baticalá (Bhatkal) and Cannanor, realized that the king of
Vijayanagara exercised a vague overlordship over some of the petty
coastal kingdoms of Malabar and Kanará, which the Portuguese were
trying to turn against the Muslim merchants to their own benefit (the
Portuguese knew by then that they would have to rely on aggressive
policies in order to secure a trade monopoly of pepper and other spices).
In particular, the rulers of the ports of Bhatkal and Honavur (on the
Kanarese coast, between Goa and Cannanor) paid tribute to the kings of
Vijayanagara, and benefited from the control of the main routes of
exchange through which precious stones and rice were exported from the

---

[46] Montalboddo defined Joseph as 'truthful', 'of the highest integrity', 'of exemplary life'
and 'of great faith' (Greenlee, *The voyage*, p. 99). From Montalboddo's way of
explaining things it seems that he did not personally interview the priest, but followed a
written report and had conversations with some of the people who met him.

[47] Ibid., pp. 100–1. See chapter 4 n. 80 above for Joseph's apparent lack of insight towards
Hindu religion.

[48] Alves suggests that Friar Luís visited Vijayanagara twice, in 1503 and then again at the
beginning of 1504 (Alves, 'A cruz, os diamantes e os cavalos', pp. 12–13). I must,
however, note that much of the information on the missionary activities of Luís do
Salvador comes from hagiographic sources written in the seventeenth and eighteenth
centuries by members of his own order, namely Paulo de Trindade and Fernando da
Soledade. Although the traditions concerning his contacts with the Indian Nestorian
communities and his attempts to preach among Hindus probably had an empirical base,
they must be read with a degree of scepticism.

interior and horses brought to the capital. In the south of the peninsula, instead, the king of Venad (who ruled the port of Quilon) was at war against the captains from Vijayanagara.[49] As a result of the growing realization of this strategic presence, in 1505 the first viceroy appointed for a long term, Francisco de Almeida, was dispatched with instructions from King Manuel to establish links with Vijayanagara. Pero Fernandes Tinoco travelled in this fleet as the future *feitor* of Vijayanagara, with the idea of trading in precious stones. As soon as Almeida arrived he was told that an embassy from Vira Narasimha, Narasa Nayaka's son and recent successor, was waiting for him in Cannanor.[50]

Vira Narasimha, who at the time had trouble establishing his authority as a king (since he was in fact an usurper), must have realized that the aggressive foreigners were able to exercise a new power in the sea. His decision to approach the Portuguese was facilitated by the presence of Friar Luís who, accompanied by his nephew Pero Leitam, effectively acted as Portuguese ambassador (Friar Luís had apparently been recalled to Vijayanagara by the previous ruler, the regent Narasa Nayaka, late in 1503, and stayed in the kingdom throughout 1504).[51] According to the chronicler Castanheda, Vira Narasimha offered friendship to the Portuguese king, including the right and facilities to build fortresses on the coast, although he excepted Bhatkal, which had already been rented out to one of his vassals.[52] It seems that the king of Vijayanagara envisaged a cooperation in which he was the land power while the newcomers

---

[49] On this war see G. Bouchon, *Albuquerque. Le lion des mers d'Asie* (Paris, 1992), p. 63. Bouchon believes that on the occasion of his first visit to Quilon at the end of 1503 Affonso de Albuquerque had already masterminded an anti-Muslim alliance and decided to dispatch Luís do Salvador to Vijayanagara, but I do not know on what evidence. The information supplied in passing by Pero Fernandes Tinoco in a letter of 1505 concerning the fact that Narasa Nayaka had called Friar Luís seems to contradict Bouchon's idea.

[50] According to the chronicle of Vijayanagara by Nunes, it would seem that the regent Narasa Nayaka ('Narsenaque') became king after the assassination of the true heir, the child Immadi Narasimha. He was then succeeded by his son Vira Narasimha (1503–09). This version has been corrected by a number of historians, on the basis of a number of inscriptions suggesting that Narasa Nayaka died, still as regent, in 1503, and that his son then became a new regent as Immadi Narasa Nayaka. See Sree Rama Sarma, *Saluva dynasty of Vijayanagar* (Hyderabad, 1979), pp. 199–223. Immadi Narasa Nayaka was then responsible for the elimination of the puppet raja two years later, in 1505, thus becoming the new king as Vira Narasimha.

[51] Thus Friar Luís must have been in Vijayanagara at the time of the visit by Varthema. In the light of my discussion of Aubin's sceptical thesis in the previous chapter, I find the view expressed by Alves ('A cruz', p. 10) that Varthema was really never there and that he picked up his bits of information in the ports of Kanará and Malabar unnecessarily uncharitable.

[52] Fernão Lopes de Castanheda, *História do descobrimento & conquista da Índia pelos portugueses*, ed. by M. Lopes de Almeida, 2 vols. (Porto, 1979), vol. I, pp. 243, 251. See also Shastry, *Studies*, pp. 86–7, and Bouchon, *'Regent of the sea'*, pp. 77–8.

controlled the sea, thus strengthening both partners against rival powers. This idea was also favoured by some factions within petty kingdoms such as Cannanor, who therefore could take the risk of an anti-Muslim stance seemingly compatible with the Portuguese strategy.[53] In his embassy Vira Narasimha did not fail to send presents, and offered his sister in marriage to a Portuguese prince.

Although Almeida received the ambassadors from Vijayanagara with pomp, he decided not to do anything for the time being, to the frustration of Tinoco, who sent letters complaining about this delay to King Manuel. Tinoco was excited by the descriptions of Friar Luís, full of 'great and miraculous things' (probably a combination of prospects of great wealth and prospects of sensational conversions). He had determined to write everything he saw and heard in Vijayanagara in a special book for the king. But his letters also reveal divisions among the Portuguese about the priorities to be followed in approaching local powers – divisions soon related to the factional distribution of personal loyalties and benefits.[54] Almeida did not want to do anything despite the embassy, perhaps because he was not sure whether or not Vira Narasimha had consolidated his own power. His argument, quoted by Tinoco, that there were no spices in Vijayanagara, need not be taken seriously, since precious stones were not an unattractive prospect. On the other hand, his other argument, that it was too far from the sea, reflected a genuine difference of opinion about the best strategy for the Portuguese. It is certainly true that the immediate aim was to secure a profitable routine of trade with Portugal, and that this required the elimination of a considerable obstacle, the enmity of Calicut. Thus, while he dispatched Luís do Salvador to King Manuel with his wonderful stories, Almeida went about the business of securing the coast against pirates and enemies. The semblance of some sort of friendship did, however, have a moderating effect – for instance, when, some days before meeting the ambassadors in Cannanor, Almeida had attacked Onor (Honavur, a port inside a river in the coast of Kanará) in order to impose the commercial dominion of the Portuguese, he nevertheless maintained the distinction between burning a rival 'corsair' fleet and sparing the city, since he had learnt that the gentile king of Gersoppa was a vassal of Vijayanagara.[55] But it was not until much later, in 1508, that

---

[53] Bouchon, '*Regent of the sea*', p. 81.
[54] For Tinoco's letters, dated 21 November 1505 and 15 January 15[06] respectively see *CA*, vol. II, pp. 341–4 and vol. III, pp. 170–7.
[55] Barros, *Asia*, I, 327–33. The rather poor excuse for this attack was to recover some Persian horses which the Portuguese had stolen from a 'Moorish' ship and then left behind. It was also here in Honavur that Almeida secured the services (at least in theory) of the local corsair, Timoja, a Hindu privateer in the service of the king of Gersoppa.

Almeida sent Tinoco and Friar Luís (on his return from Portugal) to Vijayanagara.[56] And then, rather than regular trade and the right to send missionaries, Almeida insisted on the furthering of military plans, in particular the right to make a Portuguese fortress in the trading centre of Bhatkal (the most important petty coastal kingdom whose ruler was directly related to the king of Vijayanagara). Vira Narasimha's answer was now vague and non-committal – quite logically, since he was being asked to give up his best port on the western coast for very little. This whole affair set a future pattern in the relationship between the Portuguese and Vijayanagara, which was to link an agreement on friendship with such high demands that several decades of fruitless delay and negotiations ensued without achieving a substantial agreement.

It can be argued that the European visitors quickly grasped the strategic importance of the kingdom, especially with regard to the lucrative horse trade. Varthema, if not Luís do Salvador, must soon have informed Almeida that the powerful king needed to import horses from Persia and Arabia for his army, and thus whoever controlled that trade could demand high prices and negotiate the supply. Many Portuguese

---

Barros's argument that it was in order to control Timoja and his corsair ships that Almeida had gone to Honavur to burn his fleet is rather peculiar if we consider that he goes on to explain that Timoja's job was to fight off the Muslim merchants who supplied horses to the Deccan, so that they might reach Vijayanagara from Bhatkal and Honavur. Barros is effectively caught between his desire to present the Portuguese arrival as a great help to the gentile rulers and the fact that their commercial monopolies also damaged non-Muslim native interests. Gaspar da India, who acted as interpreter on this occasion, was therefore more honest when in a letter to the king he simply declared that the Portuguese had gone to Honavur to require vassalage and tribute, and attacked it in order to fully impose their terms (CA, vol. III, pp. 201–2). He speaks openly about the inhabitants as 'gentiles', while Barros introduces the word 'Moors' when he describes the combats. The point is that for Barros the gentiles were allies against the Muslims, but only for the benefit of Portugal's wars – and the very categories of 'Moor' and 'gentile' were manipulated to reach that effect.

[56] According to Alves ('A cruz', p. 14), Almeida secretly sent his own agents (a Castilian called Guadalajara, and Gaspar da Gama's son Baltasar) to Vijayanagara in 1506, probably in order to secure for himself the profitable trade in precious stones which the king had given to Tinoco. From Tinoco's letters, it indeed seems that Almeida had neglected to take the affairs of Vijayanagara seriously, publicly denigrating the kingdom, whilst at the same time promoting his personal agents like Guadalajara. On the other hand, the evidence for Baltasar's secret mission to Vijayanagara is less clear. From a letter of Gaspar da Gama (CA, vol. III, 201–4) it seems that his son Baltasar had also joined the Portuguese as an interpreter and New Christian in February 1503, and that he had previously travelled through Vijayanagara. His reports, and those of Friar Luís, allowed Gaspar to explain to the king in early 1506 that there had been much instability in the kingdom since the death of the old king (Saluva Narasimha in 1491), and that affairs seemed to have reached a low point recently, 'no more than 20,000 horses [cavalry] are now left in the kingdom'. It is far from obvious that Baltasar had been sent on a secret mission by Almeida – he rather seemed to be reporting the situation from his previous experience.

governors and viceroys, on the other hand, soon played with the idea of finding in what they called the kingdom of Narsinga an ally against the Zamorin of Calicut (who had decisively sided with local Muslim merchants rather than with the Portuguese), and, after the conquest of Goa, against the Muslim rulers of Bijapur in Deccan. Although Almeida had reacted slowly, an inflated image of prospects of wealth, conversion and military cooperation soon crystallized around the various accounts of Vira Narasimha's embassy to King Manuel, and reached Europe with Luís do Salvador. 'The king of Narsinga is one of the greatest lords in India and has sixty kings as his great vassals. His household has more than one thousand five-hundred horses' – thus the Castilian Martín Fernández de Figueroa, who had been in India, introduced him in his account of Almeida's attack on Honavur.[57] More precise were the calculations made by the anonymous author of the *Crónica do descobrimento e conquista da India pelos Portugueses*.[58] After describing Vira Narasimha's offers of friendship and expensive presents, he compared a number of first-hand reports of the king and the city: 'He is a great and very powerful lord, in lands and in vassals: he has 100,000 cavalry and foot soldiers without number and 1,000 war elephants', adding that 'he has fifteen other kings as his vassals, and some of ours who have been in the city say that they saw nine crowned kings in his palace'. Concerning the city of Bisenegaa, 'they say that it has 120,000 inhabitants, others say 150,000 and I write at least 100,000'. As for Manuel's reaction, he was certainly prone to interpret and publicize the reports of Friar Luís as yet another sign of the providential character of the imperial mission that God had given to his dynasty and his people. While the king of Cochin, imagined in Europe as a naked man carried in a palanquin, acted as a genuine ally from his rather modest kingdom in Malabar, a powerful emperor of gentiles in the mountains ready to renounce his idolatry was the best available substitute for the mythical Prester John of India.

While the Portuguese fortresses grew and the empire consolidated, a continuous shift between idealized images and improvised tactics remained central to European attitudes towards Indians, revealing the essential flexibility of the use of categories of classification according to context and choice. This can be illustrated by the policies of Almeida's successor, Governor Affonso d'Albuquerque (1509–15), who is com-

---

[57] J. B. McKenna, *A Spaniard in the Portuguese Indies. The narrative of Martín Fernández de Figueroa* (Cambridge, Mass., 1967), p. 66. The first edition of Fernández de Figueroa's *Conquista de las Indias, de Persia et Arabia que fizo la armada del rey don Manuel de Portugal* (Salamanca, 1512) was perhaps altered by Juan Agüero de Trasmiera.

[58] *Crónica do descobrimento e conquista da India pelos Portugueses* (Anonymous Codex, British Library, Egerton 20901), ed. by Luís de Albuquerque (Lisbon, 1974), p. 132.

monly considered to be the main strategist of the Portuguese empire in the East at the time of its rapid, if somewhat precarious, military expansion.[59] His carefully balanced attitude towards indigenous powers clearly shows that there existed no absolute ethical principle derived from religious classification when it came to defending the economic and military interests of the Portuguese system in India. Thus when, in February 1510, the new governor sent the Franciscan friar as his first emissary to the city of Bisnaga he intended him to act as a spy as well as a diplomat. The instructions Albuquerque gave him clearly express how he sought to present his position (keeping in mind that he had not yet taken Goa): Luís do Salvador was required to offer the new king Krishna Deva Raya (Vira Narasimha's brother) the assistance of the armies of Portugal, and should emphasize the power of his lord, King Manuel. Then he was to declare the principle that the king of Portugal wanted to make friends and trade with all gentile rulers, and fight against their common enemies, the Moors. He suggested a combined attack against the Zamorin of Calicut (although he was a gentile too) and then he promised to help Vijayanagara by taking Goa and by selling him all the horses, whose source he expected to control in Ormuz. Finally, he asked for the right to build fortresses and *feitorias* all along the coast, including Bhatkal.[60]

Albuquerque could relate trade interests and military strategy in a single negotiation. He could at the same time find a fleeting sympathy for the 'idolaters' – insofar as the Muslims, hopeless for conversion, were their common enemies. The truth is that no important missionary effort was made in the interior of Vijayanagara until late in the sixteenth century, no matter how emphatically the literature of the Franciscan order in the seventeenth century came to portray Luís do Salvador as a martyr for the faith who impressed the king of Vijayanagara with his miracles and perseverance.[61] Although generally speaking the *gentios* had

---

[59] Bouchon's *Albuquerque* (1992) is a new biography, readable and evocative, of the governor's career.

[60] These instructions are reproduced in Braz, *Comentários*, vol. I, pp. 322–4. Soon after Albuquerque sent another ambassador, Gaspar Chanoca, who was (as usual) well received, but failed to obtain Bhatkal or a commitment for concerted action against Bijapur. After the death of Friar Luís, Gaspar Chanoca was sent again. His role is mentioned by Barros, *Ásia*, vol. I, p. 202, and by Castanheda, *História*, vol. I, pp. 519–20.

[61] The hagiography of Friar Luís, from a 1772 *Notícia do que obravão os frades de S. Francisco* is printed in A. da Silva Rego (ed.) *Documentação para a história das missões do padroado português do Orientê. India*. 12 vols. (Lisbon, 1947–58), vol. V, pp. 398–400. The main religious sources are the chronicles of Fernando da Soledade, *História Seráfica cronológica da Ordem de San Francisco na Província de Portugal* (Lisbon, 1705), III, v, 4, and Paulo de Trindade, *Conquista espiritual do Oriente*, ed. by Felix Lopes, 3 vols. (Lisbon, 1962–7), I, 284–7. These accounts are crudely idealized.

always been seen as the privileged field for evangelization, the Christian clergy were quite hard pressed to sustain the religious standards of their own Indo-Portuguese community, in which even renegades to Islam were soon quite common. While political patronage and personal circumstances were crucial in shaping the flows of conversion, it was only gradually that the Church institutions discovered that they had enough trouble keeping the mixed Christian population clean from the 'contaminating influences' of idolaters whom they were supposed to convert.[62]

Albuquerque proceeded to conquer Goa, at the suggestion, indeed, of Timoja, the Indian corsair of Honavur.[63] As it turned out, Albuquerque had to conquer Goa twice, because the first time his resources were too precarious. On that occasion the Adil Shah concluded a peace with Vijayanagara and overpowered the Portuguese during the monsoon (May 1510). However, it cannot be claimed that Vijayanagara actively supported the Adil Shah; it seems that Krishna Deva Raya simply made a tactical peace in order to attack the ruler of Bijapur when he was busy elsewhere. For the second, successful conquest (November 1510) the 'king' of Gersoppa, nominally also a vassal of the king of Vijayanagara, supplied 15,000 troops as well as Timoja's fleet. But although Goa had in the past been disputed between Vijayanagara and Bijapur, Albuquerque took it from the Muslim ruler only to create a Portuguese stronghold and settlement, sustained by a monopoly of the trade in horses which was in open competition with the 'friendly' ports of Bhatkal and Cannanor.[64]

There exist references to the missions of Friar Luís in the Portuguese chronicles of Castanheda and Correa, in the *Comentários* of Braz de Albuquerque, and in the contemporary letters of Tinoco and Albuquerque. Castanheda presented Friar Luís primarily as a missionary trying to convert the king, but it is clear that he had been sent with political instructions too (at least until Gaspar Chanoca joined him following the conquest of Goa). Friar Luís may have been accompanied by an interpreter called Lourenço Prego (*CA*, vol. II, p. 74).

62 Albuquerque's sympathy for the *gentios* over the *mouros* is stated by Braz, *Comentários*, vol. II, p. 317: 'Albuquerque's objective was to keep him waiting [the Adil Shah of Bijapur] until he found out whether the king of Narsinga had reached a decision about his proposal that the king should make a determined effort to conquer the kingdom of Deccan, because he preferred his friendship as a gentile to that of the Adil Shah, who was a moor, and with whom he could not therefore ever have a true friendship, for the sake of the Turks'. For more general attitudes towards the Hindus see A. da Silva Rego, *História das missões do padroado português do Oriente*; Lach, *Asia*, vol. I, pp. 229–45; M. N. Pearson, *The Portuguese in India* (Cambridge, 1987), pp. 116–30.

63 For the role of Timoja see Shastry, *Studies*, pp. 92–121.

64 Albuquerque argues for the advantages of holding Goa and the horse monopoly in his letters to King Manuel, especially 1 April 1512, 4 December 1513 and 1 January 1514. He is very explicit: 'Goa in your power will make both the kings of Narsinga and Deccan pay tribute . . . because the king of Narsinga, in order to secure Bhatkal, and his ports, and the supply of horses to his lands, will have to do whatever you request' (letter of 1 April 1512, *CA*, vol. I, p. 54); 'I have determined that the horses from Arabia and Persia should all be in your hand . . . first, in order to favour the port of Goa with the high

Thus, despite the declaration of such a positive attitude towards the non-Muslim would-be Christians, Albuquerque was eventually prepared to let his new friends down.

In fact the ambiguity of the relationship had become most obvious in the months following the conquest of Goa. Friar Luís reported that the king of Vijayanagara delayed giving an answer to his requests for an alliance because he did not desire to give away Bhatkal, accusing Albuquerque of simultaneously having offered his friendship to the Adil Shah. In response, Albuquerque indeed opened negotiations with Bijapur, hoping to force Krishna Deva Raya to agree to his conditions if only to keep his own supply of horses.[65] He may have felt justified because Friar Luís had warned him against trusting men like Timoja, who had apparently written to Krishna Deva Raya offering Goa to Vijayanagara before the Portuguese had consolidated their position there. In any case, it is clear that Albuquerque consciously played with the need for horses of both Vijayanagara and Bijapur, turning one against the other. No wonder that, in the meanwhile, Father Luís do Salvador was killed in mysterious circumstances, apparently by a Turk on behalf of the sultan of Bijapur. But this did not stop the negotiations. Between 1511 and 1514 Albuquerque and Krishna Deva Raya exchanged several further embassies, often at the Indian's initiative, but it was obvious that they were all keeping contacts with their 'common enemies' in order to strengthen their respective positions in negotiation. Whenever

duties paid by the horses . . . and also because the king of Narsinga and those of Deccan will desire and strive for peace with you, seeing that it is in your power to give them victory over each other, because without doubt whoever has the horses from Arabia and Persia will win . . . and finally in order to ruin the port of Bhatkal' (letter of 4 December 1513, *CA*, vol. I, p. 199). The ambassadors of Vijayanagara of course complained, and in November 1514 demanded that the horses be allowed to go to their ports, but to no avail: 'I answered that . . . if he wanted any horses, he should send for them to the port of Goa, that I would always give them to him before the Turks' (letter of 27 November 1514, *CA*, vol. I, p. 341). In such conditions of monopoly the price of horses was of course exorbitant, and not surprisingly the treaty with Narsinga against the Adil Shah again fell through.

[65] Braz de Albuquerque, *Comentários*, vol. II, pp. 31–3. This important passage reporting Friar Luís's letter to Albuquerque is ambiguous – it is not entirely clear whether Krishna Deva Raya simply accused Albuquerque of double dealing (as I have suggested, taking the simplest reading) or whether he himself had reached a momentary peace with the Adil Shah, which he did not wish to jeopardize, and was waiting to see who ended up controlling Goa. This would fit with Castanheda, *História*, vol. I, p. 520, who explains that the king of Vijayanagara was not really very pleased with the Portuguese taking Goa, because he feared losing the supply of horses that the *mouros* had never denied him. This suggests that the fluctuating opposition between Hindus and Muslims did not really interfere with trading conditions until the arrival of the Portuguese. In other words, the Portuguese attempt to establish a monopoly of imported horses favoured neither Vijayanagara nor Bijapur.

Albuquerque detected that the king of Vijayanagara was serious, he raised the stakes of his demands, and eventually met with further ambiguity and delays.[66]

The Portuguese were rivals of the *mouros* in their attempt to secure good trading conditions from the local powers, but for the same reason they were prepared to negotiate with Muslims and betray Hindus when it was in their best interest. Albuquerque had to write to the king explaining that it was not possible to defeat the *mouros* by trading with local Christians and gentiles alone, because their best cities were filled with Muslim merchants who were richer and, therefore, too powerful to be just ignored.[67] But the Portuguese were not alone in playing this sort of game, and as far as war and trade were concerned there was more cultural understanding than cultural shock between the Asians and the western newcomers. Romila Thapar has summarized the situation in fifteenth-century India: 'a Hindu ruler saw nothing unusual in allying with and obtaining aid from a Muslim ruler in order to fight another Hindu ruler, and the same held true for other Hindu dynasties'.[68] Despite the fact that the defence of Hindu identity was part of the political mythology of Vijayanagara, its rulers were actually successful insofar as, acting as one power among many, they welcomed methods and allies from the Deccani sultanates. On the other hand, they were eventually destroyed when Aliya Rama Raja, failing to maintain this flexible attitude, actually forced his Muslim neighbours to unite against a common enemy (which was by then the only important surviving Hindu kingdom in the peninsula). This led to the disastrous military defeat of 1565.[69]

---

[66] According to the information contained in Albuquerque's letters and the *Comentários*, this stalemate happened at least three times: in 1510–11, in late 1513/early 1514, and in late 1514. Eventually, even crucial allies like Timoja, who had initially been offered an important role in the administration and defence of the island of Goa, ended up seeking refuge in Vijayanagara (where he died in 1512 of an overdose of opium).

[67] See letter dated 25 October 1515, *CA*, vol. I, pp. 306–7.

[68] R. Thapar, *A history of India*, p. 281.

[69] A traditional account in K. A. Nilakanta Sastri, *A history of South India*, 3rd edn (Madras, 1966). Rama Raya's policies, which led to the defeat at Talikota, are newly assessed in Stein, *Vijayanagara*, pp. 113–21. It must, however, be noticed that it seems unfair to assume that without Rama Raja's personal ambitions and aggressive policies, the kingdom would not have been overrun. One could instead note that the tradition of independent generals taking over the regency and eliminating puppet kings was well established, that the legitimate rule of a king with personality like Krishna Deva Raya was the exception rather than the rule, and that indeed during the contested succession of Achyuta Deva Raya in 1542–3, the invitations to the ruler of Bijapur to take control in the midst of anarchy came from all quarters. In this context Aliya Rama Raja could be seen as the restorer of a Hindu central authority, in the context of a fundamentally weak system of succession, whose methods proved nevertheless counter-productive.

In this context, the Portuguese may have been original in claiming a lordship over the sea, but not in trying to use military power to improve trading opportunities. The lack of success of any long-lasting alliance against Bijapur was due to the fact that, quite often, either the Portuguese or the Hindus preferred to agree with the sultanate when circumstances dictated. The idea of a Christian alliance with Vijayanagara (not unlike the idea of a Christian–Mongol alliance against the Saracens in the thirteenth century, or a European–Persian alliance against the Ottoman Turks between the fifteenth and the seventeenth centuries) was always available, but it only occasionally became a practical reality. Embassies were exchanged on several occasions after 1505, especially when Albuquerque was in command between 1509 and 1515, and in 1521 Krishna Deva Raya offered the lands surrounding the island of Goa to the Portuguese in order to weaken the Adil Shah.[70] However, no formal agreement was reached until many years later, in 1547, perhaps because the Portuguese could not really secure a monopoly of Persian and Arabian horses in Goa, and this fundamental weakness made their political demands (such as a fort in Bhatkal, on which Almeida and Albuquerque repeatedly insisted) excessive.[71]

The lack of articulation of the alliance between the Portuguese and Vijayanagara was due to the fact that systematic opposition to the Muslim powers did not benefit either party. Although in 1548 the prime minister and virtual usurper Rama Raja and viceroy João de Castro tried to implement their formal agreement of the previous year against the king of Bijapur, this was quite exceptional. Rather, it can be said that an intermittent presence of Portuguese *feitores* specialized in horse-trading in the Hindu capital, the occasional participation of Portuguese soldiers and renegades as mercenaries in the wars of the Deccan, or the failed attempt by an unscrupulous governor like Martim Affonso de Sousa to plunder the wealthy Hindu temple complex of Tirumalai-Tirupati in 1543, constitute a more faithful reflection of the meagre results of the diplomatic exchange between the Portuguese and Vijaya-nagara than the actual terms of the circumstantial treaty signed in 1547. The idea of outright conquest was never entirely abandoned by the Portuguese, and in fact estimated as possible as late as the 1540s,

---

[70] On the gift of the lands of Bardes and Salsette in 1521 see Castanheda, *História*, vol. II, pp. 94–5, who explains that the gift was no more than a convenient side effect of the victory of Krishna Deva Raya over the Adil Shah in the interior (the fortified towns of Raichur and Belgaum). Barros's version (*Ásia*, vol. III, ff. 103r–104r) suggests, however, that the Portuguese were not invited to the Goan hinterland by Krishna Deva Raya, but opportunistically exploited a breakdown of local authority to seize the land.

[71] Lopes, *Chrónica*, published the contents of this interesting treaty of 1547.

although its economic cost was also seen to be excessive.[72] What motivated a governor like Martim Affonso de Sousa in 1543 to attempt the plunder of one of the most emblematic temples of the kingdom was the calculation (born out of desperation) that immediate wealth was more valuable to a Portuguese empire in continuous financial distress that the unclear friendship with unreliable allies who could be ultimately defined as gentiles and blacks. Even then, it was probably only the succession crisis in Vijayanagara at the death of Achyuta Deva Raya that made the undertaking plausible (and in the end it proved not to be so) – as it was the growing authority of Rama Raja four years later that made a formal alliance possible.

To a great extent the perception of this political ambivalence was distorted by the distance that separated Europe from India. While vague rumours persisted in Europe about the conversion to Christianity of the ruler of the fabulously rich kingdom of Bisinagar, this image pointed towards a mythical model of politics that emphasized unity and simplicity where real fragmentation had taken over. Thus in 1511, after the conquests of Goa and Malacca, an anonymous Florentine (possibly a cleric) wrote to a friend in Venice that 'this king Narsinga is ready to convert to Christianity', and in a flight of imagination foresaw his enormous armies of horses and elephants crushing the Moors (he was of course unaware of the fact that Friar Luís, the great Christian missionary, had been murdered in the meanwhile).[73] But simplistic interpretations could go either way, and certainly another bias had been in operation when Vincenzo Quirini, a Venetian ambassador in Portugal, wrote in 1506 that the Portuguese trade in the East had no future because the king of Calicut would easily 'move the king of Narsi, who is a great lord, and his neighbour, friend and relative . . . to prevent the pepper from going the new way [towards the Portuguese in Cochin and Cannanor] and to make it go to Calicut as it used to do' – or in other words, 'it is understood that the Portuguese route is not very solid,

---

[72] I discuss Portuguese plans to conquer the Deccan, and Martim Affonso de Sousa's unglamorous expedition to the 'pagode of Tremel', in chapter 8 below.

[73] 'Copia di un capitolo de una lettera scripta da Firenze per . . . a Vinezia a ser Zuane di Santi, a di 19 Novembre 1911': 'Ancora voglio sapiate che il re di Portogallo ha facto una grande amititia con il re di Bisinagar, che si chiama re Narsinga, dove stete Santo Tomaso a predicar in quella città di Bisinagar, la qual città è di 900,000 caxe. Et in ditto Regno è il corpo di ditto S. Tomaso. Stimase questo Re Narsinga se habia presto a ridur a farsi Cristiano, et questo per esser gentile, che più tosto si riducano che non fanno ogni altra setta. Dicto re e potentissimo et tiene a L. in LX. over LXX milia cavalli da guerra, et mile e dusento helephanti pur da guerra, in modo tale che, essendo questo, si stima che Mori andrano presto sotto et sarano ruinati', Biblioteca Nazionale de Firenze, ms. B. R. 233 (Zorzi collection), 103r–104v.

because it entirely rests upon the head of the king of Narsi'.[74] Both interpretations were more than just mistaken, they were deeply implausible too, as the pattern of actual contacts in the following decades reveals. Sporadic Portuguese visits to the capital city, trade in Coromandel and settlements like the town of São Tomé in Mylapore, piracy and counter-piracy in the coast of Kanará, or missionary success amongst the poor inhabitants of the Fishery coast – the fragmentary character of all these contacts suggests that the impressive kingdom was not held together as a national-territorial entity comparable to most European states of the time, nor were the Portuguese with their limited resources and contradictory purposes able to rule and act as a coherent imperial power in such a vast and complex world.[75]

One can therefore conclude that the political attitude of empire-builders like Albuquerque (biased as it was) not only responded to a political context which was far from simple, but in fact articulated a secular analysis which was potentially at odds with the idealistic emphasis of traditional ideologies. This attitude is best illustrated by referring to the letters sent by the governor to King Manuel. In December 1510, soon after taking Goa for the second time, he insisted upon the desirability of winning the king of Narsinga as an ally against the *mouros*. His plans were to ask for a site on which to build a fortress and to organize combined military operations against the Muslims of the Deccan and the Malabar coast. In exchange, he offered Krishna Deva Raya exclusive access to the Arabian and Persian horses imported by sea. Thus:

> I am sending a messenger to Narsinga, and also some horses to the king of Narsinga to represent him the deed of Goa . . . and to see whether with this deed of Goa we can take away from him the credit they give to the Turks and the fear they have for them, and make him see that we are as good fighting in the land as we are in the sea, and thus I shall see whether I can make him move his armies against the Turks of Daquem [meaning the Muslim rulers of the Deccani king-

---

[74] 'Relazione delle Indie Orientale di Vincenzo Quirini nel 1506', in *Relazioni degli ambasciatori veneti al senato*, ed. by E. Albèri, 15 vols. (Florence, 1839–63), vol. XV pp. 5–19.

[75] On piracy on the western coast of India see G. Bouchon, 'L'évolution de la piraterie sur la côte malabare au cours du XVIe siècle', in G. Bouchon, *L'Asie du sud à l'époque des grandes découvertes*, collected studies (London, 1987), XII. On the Coromandel trade and the Portuguese settlements, see S. Subrahmanyam, *Improvising empire. Portuguese trade and settlement in the Bay of Bengal 1500–1700* (Oxford, 1990), chaps. 3 and 4. Concerning missionaries on the Fishery coast see Lach, *Asia*, vol. I, pp. 235ff. and McPherson, 'Paravas and Portuguese'.

doms, in particular the Adil Khans of Bijapur] *and wish for our true friendship* (my italics).[76]

The value of such a true friendship is better understood by looking at a subsequent passage in the same letter, where Albuquerque explains the strategic value of Goa:

> In a very short time your men could enter into the kingdom of Daquem *and of Narsinga*, because the strength of the Turks is not by itself very big, were it not that the Gentiles are their subjects and go to war with them; and the Gentiles are people full of novelties, and if they found a Portuguese captain who gave them free scale and pay, there would then be one-hundred thousand footmen with him, and they take the rent from the land for pay; and the Turks are divided among themselves, and all their strength consists of Gentile foot soldiers (my italics).[77]

The observation that the 'gentiles' love novelties is a derogatory one because it implies political (and moral) weakness, and was commonly used in this sense by Renaissance historians such as the Florentine Guicciardini.[78]

Albuquerque realized that the Muslim military aristocracy depended on the cooperation of the Hindu population to remain in power, and hoped to devise a scheme by which the Portuguese, if they could win a few battles against divided enemies, would be able to substitute them as rulers of the country. The prospect proved to be beyond their powers (the main point of Albuquerque's letters was in fact to justify a militaristic approach in the Orient, even against the resistance of many at the court or already settled in Malabar, and to ask for more armed men from Portugal). Even the more limited idea of controlling the oceanic trade and establishing a monopoly of the spice market would eventually fail. Nevertheless, it is obvious that there was a manipulative attitude towards oriental peoples that went beyond the self-professed belief in abstract, moral, religiously based principles. Without any need to read the contemporary writings of Machiavelli, Albuquerque in South India, like Hernán Cortés in Mexico, was able to make honesty relative to the useful.[79]

---

[76] Letter of 22 December 1510, *CA*, vol. I, p. 28.

[77] Ibid. pp. 28–9.

[78] For instance, in his *History of Italy* (on the Neapolitans): 'such is the nature of the people, who are inclined to hope more than they ought to, and tolerate less than is necessary, and to be always dissatisfied with the present state of affairs': Guicciardini, *Storia d'Italia*, 3 vols. (Milan, 1988), vol. I, pp. 178–9.

[79] Albuquerque did not of course work this out theoretically, nor did he engage with the subtleties of Machiavellian thought. For his cultural models he drew inspiration from a typically Renaissance blend of chivalric and classical models, from the Spanish hero of the reconquest, El Cid, to the Greek conqueror Alexander.

Paradoxically, this 'political' way of interpreting non-Christians and non-Europeans did not in fact degrade them, but rather assimilated them into the rest of humanity, because a classification according to religion was subjected to a manipulative anthropological conception. The very use of political analysis implied a level of agency which was above providential history. Essentially, while the historian (or the poet and playwright) could portray Christians defeating Moors for the glory of God, he simultaneously described exchangeable roles.

Albuquerque understood the convenience of making agreements with indigenous powers, but insisted that no trust should be placed in them, 'because the friendship you may establish with any Indian king or lord, my Lord, unless there are safeguards, you can be sure that as soon as you turn your back you will have them for enemies'.[80] Friendship ultimately depended on power, in particular the ability to appear militarily strong (and, to achieve this, in the long term it was necessary actually to be militarily strong). These are again the same sort of ideas we find expressed in contemporary political thinking. The king of Portugal should trust good soldiers and good fortresses rather than good words, and this conception explicitly included the ruler of Vijayanagara:

And the king of Narsinga, does not he have friendship and peace with you? and he secretly helps the Sabaio [the Adil Khan, sultan of Bijapur] against us; and inside Besnigar, did not a *rumi* kill friar Luís? and he did not do anything about it; and the first time that we took Goa from the Moors, we killed one of his captains, and he felt very bad about the taking of Goa, and has much fear of your majesty.[81]

Fear backed by an occasional display of violence was to achieve the political aims which friendship alone could not: 'What pulled down the arrogance of the kingdom of Daquem, and made Narsinga be so much afraid of us, but the fact that we took Goa, which is placed right between them?'[82] This political conception was not exclusive to a single governor such as Albuquerque. In a world in which so much actually depended on exploiting the skills of criminal exiles, renegades and converts, Portuguese of more humble origins, for instance the anonymous interpreter and ambassador who wrote the illuminating *Lembrança d'algumas cousas*

---

[80] Letter of 1 April 1512, *CA*, vol. I, p. 39.
[81] Ibid. *Sabaio* was originally the description for Yusuf Adil Khan (1490–1510), a Turkish slave of the Bahmani king who when the Bahmani sultanate disintegrated took over the south-western territory of the kingdom, with its capital at Bijapur, thus founding the dynasty of the Adil Shahs. His succesor Ismail (1510–34) was at the beginning also referred to as *Sabaio*, but eventually the Portuguese sources agree in naming him (and his successors) as *Idalcão*, a rendering for Adil Khan.
[82] Ibid. p. 56.

que se passaram quando António de Brito e Diogo Pereira foram a Bengala (1521), often display a similar political rationality in which the non-European *other* is integrated. The point is not merely that the religious classification was replaced by a more general political conception of a manipulative character, but, more precisely, that the complicated relationships of interest and power which were established with diverse peoples were articulated at the cultural level by a sophisticated game of shifting identities. The more obvious ideological divisions were therefore no more than the starting point for a continuous exercise of conceptual subversion and recreation.

What strikes the reader of documents such as the *Lembrança* is not the clever apology for Portuguese piracy, nor the obvious self-advancement of the author, but more interestingly the creative elaboration of new language-games in accordance with situations of conflict and dialogue with local powers. This implies that a basis was being defined for the mutual understanding of peoples with different cultural backgrounds and, moreover, that such a basis was not stable, nor did it depend on the attitude of a single subject. In fact, individual identities, European or otherwise, were ultimately absorbed by the language-games they tried to learn, shape and control. In this sense the disquieting individual who changed dress and religion, like one Cristovão Jusarte in Bengal, was not doing anything substantially different from the members of the rival embassy who preferred to present themselves as faithful servants voicing the truthful friendship offered to the sultan by their lord the Christian king of Portugal.[83]

To what extent was the recognition of the non-Muslim character of the empire of Vijayanagara influential in shaping European attitudes towards it? Why did European observers attach such importance to the perception of political unity in foreign societies? I have attempted to clarify these questions by looking at the approach of the leaders of the Portuguese expansion towards Vijayanagara. On the basis of the letters of Governor Albuquerque it has been made clear that the religious principle of classification of foreign societies was dependent on a political rationality which was shared by indigenous and invading powers alike. This political rationality operated on the basis of measuring one's power against the enemy's in an attempt to further profitable activities, either trade (regulated by local customs and laws, and exceptionally by international treaties) or tribute and plunder, linked to the claims of political dominion. A further question remains: how did this 'practical rationality' in which men, because of their nature, can be made friends

---

[83] *Voyage dans les deltas du Gange et de l'Irraouaddy*, pp. 329–34.

but not trusted, relate to the image of Asia transmitted to the West in descriptive narratives? This I shall try to answer next by examining the ethnographic practice developed by men such as the *escrivão de feitor* of Cannanor Duarte Barbosa in South India, in what we might define as the unprecedented creation of an empirical imperial ethnology.

6. The practice of ethnography: Indian customs and castes

THE BIRTH OF A COLONIAL ETHNOGRAPHY

The Portuguese presence in Asia after 1499 entailed an important leap both in the amount of information regarding oriental societies which was available, and in the variety of generic forms it took. By virtue of the works written in the early decades of European activity in India, and notwithstanding the fact that the majority were only published years later or remained in manuscript form, South India, and in particular the Malabar coast, was to become one of the better mapped areas of the Renaissance world.[1] This is why, despite its increasingly limited political importance, 'Calicut' still figured prominently in late Renaissance cosmographies such as Giovanni Botero's *Relationi universali*, alongside China, Persia, Turkey or the 'Great Mogor' of India. Perhaps more importantly, the early descriptions of South India set standards of accuracy and comprehensiveness which remained valid for much of the ethnography of the early modern period. Much more clearly than in the relatively hazy reports of Marco Polo, it is in the narratives of Varthema, Barbosa, Pires, Paes and Nunes that one finds the obvious precedents of such 'modern' ethnographical treatises as Abbé Dubois' classic *Character, manners and customs of the people of India and of their institutions religious and civil* of 1806.

Dubois' treatise, although originally written in French from Jesuit materials, accompanied the consolidation of the British empire in India, and its impact can best be understood as part of a colonial context.[2] As

---

[1] The accounts of Vijayanagara by Domingos Paes and Fernão Nunes remained unpublished, the works by Duarte Barbosa and Tomé Pires only appeared (incomplete) in Ramusio's edition some forty years after they had been written.

[2] Dubois had apparently gone to India fleeing the French Revolution, seeking material and spiritual refuge in exotic missions (his political views can be described as reactionary). The first edition of the *Character, manners and customs* was published in English in 1817. A substantially different version was published in French in 1825. Various editions

Mark Wilks, the acting president of Mysore, wrote in 1807, the manuscript could be used as a manual for the servants of the English
Company: 'Every Englishman residing in India is interested in the
knowledge of those peculiarities in the Indian castes which may enable
him to conduct with the natives the ordinary intercourse of civility and
business without offending their prejudices.'[3]

The fact that the Portuguese Pires, Barbosa, Paes and Nunes would
have agreed wholeheartedly with this claim sets them apart from their
ancient and medieval predecessors as an altogether new category of
'colonial ethnographers'. In fact, they introduced an understanding of
India as a caste society into Europe. The point here is not to claim any
direct influence across the centuries: between these early Portuguese
writers, published by Ramusio in his travel collection, and the late
French Jesuits of the Coromandel coast whose work, via Dubois, was so
valuable to the British, there stood a formidable tradition of seventeenth-
century missionary writers on South Indian religion: Italian Jesuits like
Roberto de Nobili or Dutch Protestants like Abraham Rogerius. Rather,
my aim is to understand the early emergence of an ethnographical
attitude, one whose logic extends beyond the obvious observation that it
was part of a colonial system, simply because not all colonial systems
work in the same way. This chapter shall therefore try to uncover the
cultural basis on which the ethnographical practice of the early Portuguese writers rested. This involves, before anything else, identifying their
social and political background.

While Marco Polo and Varthema may have been motivated by the
desire to 'sell' information, to the Great Khan or to Venetian and
Portuguese merchants, they were also engaged in selling a romance:
Marco Polo sold marvels, and Varthema the idea of himself as traveller
and adventurer. We have scant data about men like Pires, Paes, Nunes
and Barbosa, authors of outstandingly empirical descriptions, but
perhaps enough to identify them as members of a fairly homogenous
social group of settled merchants and crown officials in Portuguese
India. They may perhaps best be described as an urban patriciate
transposed to India, men who often had to struggle hard to obtain
official positions and whose obvious destination was the community of

continued to appear throughout the century in India and in England, with a new English
translation in 1897. Jean-Antoine Dubois was essentially a plagiarist, as has recently been
explained by Sylvia Murr, who has studied the thought of the Jesuit missionary G. L.
Coeurdoux (1691–1779), whose manuscripts Dubois followed. On this, and on his
anglophilia, see Sylvia Murr, *L'Inde philosophique entre Bossuet et Voltaire*, 2 vols. (Paris,
1987), vol. II, chap. 1.

[3] Abbé J. A. Dubois, *Character, manners and customs of the people of India* (1806), 3rd edn
by Rev. G. U. Pope (Madras, 1879), p. viii.

casados (married settlers) of the Portuguese enclaves. Their social horizon might have been ultimately aristocratic, but rather than a 'middle nobility' they were still essentially a merchant class with vertical connections at the court.[4]

We know enough about Tomé Pires (*c.* 1470–1524) to support this image. He was an apothecary in the service of the crown as factor of drugs, and he reached India in 1511 in order to obtain information and specimens.[5] Between 1512 and 1515 he supervised the spice trade in the *feitoria* of Malacca, collecting much of the material for his *Suma Oriental*.[6] He visited Java and eventually returned to Cochin (1515–16) to finally become head of the first Portuguese embassy sent to China in 1517, in which capacity he was imprisoned until he died seven years later.[7] Unfortunately, our knowledge of Domingos Paes and Fernão Nunes is far less certain, outside their involvement with trading expedi-

---

[4] Recent historians, focusing on the opposition to Governor Albuquerque from Cochin and Cannanor have identified these crown officials and settled private merchants (including Duarte Barbosa) as a kind of 'middle nobility' with connections at the court. See, for instance, the excellent article by I. Guerreiro and V. L. G. Rodrigues, 'O grupo de Cochim e a oposição a Afonso de Albuquerque', *Studia*, 51 (1992): 119–44, where they mention the categories of 'cavaleiros-fidalgos' and 'moradores de casa d'el-rei' (p. 130). More generally, see the biographical sketches by Bouchon and Thomaz in *Voyage dans les deltas du Gange et de l'Irraouaddy*, and by various authors in a special number of *Mare Liberum*, 5 (1993). In view of the evidence, I remain, however, sceptical about how appropriate the category of 'middle nobility' really is – could all these people actually claim the privileges of noblemen in legal and political matters? Or should we at least distinguish various social levels behind each aristocratic faction? Most of the men who had to struggle to become interpreters, clerks and traders were certainly not *fidalgos*, nor could they use the title of *dom*. Service in India was a possible route to social promotion in a strongly hierarchical society – but only for the few who made it. As A. Cortesão wrote, men like Pires, though of humble origin, were trusted by the king and his governors because they 'had more education than the great majority of Portuguese noblemen then in India': Pires, *The Suma Oriental of Tomé Pires*, vol. I p. xxviii.

[5] For biographical details, see A. Cortesão in Pires, *Suma*, vol. I, pp. xviii–lxiii.

[6] In Malacca Pires was *escrivão* and *contador de feitoria*, as well as *vedor das drogarias*. Effectively he combined two jobs in a rather troublesome factory – one reason why he soon requested a larger salary.

[7] Pires is best known as a leading member of the 1517 embassy to China which never returned. After an auspicious beginning, the high-handed Portuguese captains on the coast made a number of mistakes and the ambassadors, instead of seeing the emperor in Peking, were recalled to Canton, tortured and imprisoned. In the light of what they learnt about the fate of Malacca, bombarded into submission by Albuquerque, the Chinese indulged their own xenophobic instincts and refused to accept the Portuguese traders for decades to come, classifying them as pirates instead (but not without good reason, if we are to judge by Portuguese plans to create a fortress near Canton). It seems that Pires died in 1524, although at least two of his colleagues survived and even smuggled letters out of China – copies of which reached João de Barros together with the accounts of Vijayanagara by Nunes and Paes: see R. d'Intino (ed.) *Enformação das cousas da China. Textos do século XVI* (Lisbon, 1989), pp. 1–53. The memory of these prisoners was kept alive in Barros's chronicle and even in novels such as *Peregrinaçam* by Fernão Mendes Pinto, where a half-Chinese daughter of Pires appears as a character.

tions to Vijayanagara. Paes was a horse-trader in the company of Cristovão de Figueiredo, an important *casado* from Goa. His description of the Indian capital city *c*. 1521 seems to be the only document about his activities. Fernão Nunes, or Nuniz, another horse-trader active some ten years later, seems to have been a slightly less marginal figure, as is suggested by the fact that he was able to trade in horses on his own, while Paes was simply the obscure member of a party. He can perhaps be identified with the Fernão Nunes who in 1512 was *escrivão de feitor* of Calicut, and who in 1526 appears as *escrivão de fazenda* in Cochin.[8] In 1533 – after his return from Vijayanagara – Nunes was *provedor-mor dos defuntos* in Cochin, and in 1538 he was rich enough to be considered for a loan to the king of Portugal.[9] Three years later – in 1541 – he signed a document in Goa by which the *vedor de fazenda* and provisional governor of the city, F. Rodrigues de Castello Branco, appropriated the rents from the Hindu temples.[10] Finally, in 1547 he was a *casado* in the Portuguese capital, and purchased the position of *almoxarife* of the city.[11]

The *escrivão de feitoria* of Cannanor and occasional interpreter Duarte Barbosa, whose biography is better known, illustrates best the interests and circumstances of this group of writers.[12] Having accompanied his

---

[8] According to the chronicler Castanheda, Nunes was asked by the influential *vedor de fazenda* Afonso Mexía to read the document by which an alternative succession to the governorship of Portuguese India was opened in 1526 in Cochin, so that it fell on Lopo Vaz de Sampaio instead of Pero de Mascarenhas, the captain of Malacca. See Castanheda, *História*, vol. II, p. 392.

[9] *Gavetas do Torre do Tombo*, ed. by A. da Silva Rego, 12 vols. (Lisbon, 1960–77), vol. IV, p. 378 and X, p. 172.

[10] A. da Silva Rego (ed.) *Documentação para a história das missões do padroado português do Oriente*, vol. II, pp. 293–303.

[11] Apparently he was still alive in 1565. For these details see Schurhammer, *Francis Xavier, his life, his times*, vol. II, p. 669.

[12] Since Ramusio there has been a pervasive tendency to confuse two individuals called Duarte Barbosa. One of them was a son of Diogo Barbosa, a servant of Alvaro Bragança who participated in João de Nova's expedition to India (1501) but later followed his patron to Castile. Diogo Barbosa thus settled in Seville, welcomed Magellan at his home, and allowed him to marry his daughter. This faction of dissatisfied Portuguese used their knowledge of the East to organize the first expedition round the world for Charles I of Castile against their natural lord. Duarte Barbosa, Diogo's son, accompanied Magellan in 1519, and died in Cebu a few days after him, in 1521 (Barros, *Ásia*, vol. III, ff. 145v–147v: the most complete report of the expedition is Pigafetta's). The second Duarte Barbosa – *our* Duarte Barbosa, specialist in Malabari language and customs and author of the *Livro* – was the nephew of Gonçalo Gil Barbosa and accompanied him when he sailed with Cabral in 1500 and became the first *feitor* of Cochin (Barros, *Ásia*, vol. I, p. 198). This Duarte Barbosa could never have accompanied Magellan because in 1520 and 1527 he was signing documents in Cannanor, and is mentioned by Barros still as *escrivão* at Cannanor in 1529. There existed a third Duarte Barbosa in India, a pilot. See G. Schurhammer, 'Doppelgänger in Portugiesisch-Asien', in Schurhammer, *Gesammelte Studien*, vol. II, pp. 121–47.

uncle Gonçalo Gil Barbosa to India on Cabral's expedition, he assisted him when he took the important role of commercial factor at the time when the first permanent Portuguese *feitorias* in India were set up, first in Cochin (1500–2) and then in Cannanor (1502–5).[13] He learnt Malayalam well and became an important interpreter, exceptionally trusted (like his uncle) by the local rulers and merchants. Duarte accompanied his uncle to Portugal in 1506 but returned to India in 1511. After this date, Duarte Barbosa was mainly attached to Cannanor as chief *escrivão de feitor.* Initially he found it difficult to obtain his full position, perhaps because he was not trusted by Governor Albuquerque. At the beginning of 1513, he wrote to the king against the governor's militaristic policies, joining a chorus of opposition from those interested in preserving the trade of Cochin and Cannanor against the shift of power to Goa and the possibility of peace with Calicut.[14] In response, Albuquerque transferred him to Calicut, and in 1514 he even tried to imprison him, but Barbosa was too useful and too well connected locally to be dislodged. It seems to have been at this time that he composed his description of India, of which he probably left a copy on his return to Portugal in 1516 (which was the basis for the Spanish and Italian translations which circulated in the sixteenth century).[15] Possibly as a reward for this and other services, he was made 'Cavaleiro da Casa del rei' and granted the position of *escrivão* in Calicut. In 1517 he returned to India with his wife, and after 1518, the job in Calicut not having materialized, he again occupied his cherished position at Cannanor, where he lived as a prominent *casado* until as late as 1546.

What this career illustrates is that the unprecedented ethnographic analysis displayed in a text like Barbosa's *Book of what I saw and heard in the Orient* was the intellectual creation of a colonial elite in formation whose novel horizon was a settled, prosperous life in India. Men like Pires, Barbosa, Paes and Nunes were nominally agents for the crusading and missionary ideals of the crown, but actually tended to develop their own contacts and interests locally, to the point exemplified by Barbosa's criticism of the ambitious imperial plans developed by Albuquerque. In

---

[13] In 1502 Gonçalo Gil was transferred from Cochin to Cannanor, where he organized the *feitoria* until 1506, when he left for Portugal at the command of a ship.

[14] *CA*, vol. III, pp. 48–51.

[15] Barbosa's prologue giving the date of 1516 is only found in Ramusio's version, but does not seem to be false – there is no reason to suspect that anyone would have interpolated it. On the other hand, it is possible that Barbosa revised the manuscript in the following years, which would explain why he writes about the expedition to the Red Sea by Lopo Soares de Albergaria in 1517, and a number of other additions. The existence of different versions by the author could also help explain the proliferation of manuscripts with significant variations.

fact within this colonial middle elite there was room for a variety of political visions: if in January 1513 Barbosa openly wrote about the necessity of keeping peace with the Indian allies to King Don Manuel, in the context of a widespread opposition to Albuquerque and his authoritarian style, Pires, on the other hand, writing at about the same time from Malacca, seems to have supported a more aggressive approach, praising war against all kinds of infidels and commending the leadership of the 'hearty, most prudent and skilled in war' Albuquerque.[16] He defends the conquest of Goa by praising its benefits to the point of exaggeration, and his argument that 'as doors are the defence of houses, so are seaports the help, defence and main protection of provinces and kingdoms' could have been dictated by the governor who conquered the city.[17] The situation in the distant commercial entrepot of Malacca, recently seized against formidable opposition, was certainly more precarious than in Cannanor and stimulated this kind of thinking, but there was also a high degree of factionalism related to the distribution of lucrative jobs which may have motivated support for, or opposition to, a particular governor or viceroy.[18] Ultimately the different views of empire expressed by those who emphasized trade over conquest, or by those who defended the need for imperial action, were really two gradations within a common ideological system (Barbosa would for instance have insisted on the convenience of waging war against Calicut, and in his *Livro* he seems to approve of Albuquerque's conquests in Ormuz, Goa and Malacca, while Pires, in his prologue, openly declared how necessary and excellent trade was). It is, therefore, no coincidence that despite their different ideological stances Barbosa and Pires share an almost identical intellectual aim, to give a fresh account based on direct experience and reliable reports of the ethnological and economic realities of the Asian world encountered by the Portuguese.

[16] See Pires, *Suma*, pp. 323–4. The fact that Pires mentions Albuquerque as still alive in his prologue suggests that the *Suma Oriental* was composed between 1511, when Pires reached India, and 1515, when the governor died. Some passages in the book are clearly dated. In particular, Pires indicates that the leader of the Coromandel trading community and prominent ally of the Portuguese 'Bemdara Nina Chatuu' (that is Nina Chatu, the Bendara of Malacca) died in January 1514 *as Pires was writing his Suma*. Since this occurs at the end of the description, the book could be dated 1513–14, although Pires might have added things about India and Ceylon on his return to Cochin and before his departure for China in 1515–16.

[17] Ibid., p. 56.

[18] Thus Pires seems to have sought direct favour from Albuquerque, which may help explain his different stance. In Portugal Pires's patron seems to have been Jorge de Vasconcelos, who had an important position as *provedor* in the Casa da Mina e India. Curiously, as things turned out, it was from Albuquerque's successor and rival Lopo Soares de Albergaria that Pires obtained his best (if unfortunate) appointment as first ambassador to China.

This makes it possible to identify here the early forms of institutional support and political motivation that stimulated the creation of clear ethnographical models within the context of a geographical discourse. From a material perspective, the aim was to secure stable patterns of trade and local security in the face of a growing but fragile network of Portuguese outposts – a system which benefited best those who could combine an official position in a commercial town like Cochin, Cannanor, Goa or Malacca with the development of private business. Culturally, the ethnographic models rested on commonsense descriptions which relied on the narrative possibilities of everyday language with independence from the more rigid conventions of traditional literary models. It was the engagement with the local languages and language-games – Barbosa was a specialist in Malayalam, and Nunes probably learnt Kannada – and not with Ptolemy, whom Pires openly declared to be irrelevant to his purposes, that led to the creation of this colonial ethnography. In the medieval traditions of Europe and Asia, art, science and law were defined primarily in relationship to religion. However, Barbosa, Pires, Paes and Nunes developed an ethnographical practice in which the behaviour of the people (their *customs*) was described with more detail than their doctrines or beliefs. They followed in the steps of Marco Polo, Conti and Varthema, but more systematically because they wrote to meet the aims of a system of European institutions now implanted in foreign lands.

Thus, in their descriptions of lands and peoples, human culture came to be judged, effectively, as *civilized behaviour*, and ranked hierarchically according to political and economic success. Law was not presented as a system of rules which must follow certain universal principles, but rather as a political guarantee to safety, peace and fair dealing. Because of its single-minded empiricism, this approach both skipped over and went beyond the classical Greek distinction between nature ('physis') and custom ('nomos'). As 'geographers' these merchants were interested in particular conditions, and therefore they provided quantitative information. The curious traveller like Varthema felt free to exaggerate to an extent that contrasts with the moderation of Tomé Pires, for instance. Pires may never have been in Vijayanagara, but his description is perhaps the least outlandish version of the rhetorical common-place about the greatness of the city:

> The kingdom of Narsimgua is large and very important . . . [follows a description of its limits]. In older times the kingdom of Narsimgua was much greater than it is now and embraced almost the whole of the Deccan . . . the king is a Gentile of Kanarese nation, and on the other hand he is a Kling [*quelim*]; in his court the language is mixed, but his

natural speech is Kanarese.[19] The king is a warrior and he often goes to field with more than forty thousand mounted men and a large number on foot. He must have five hundred elephants, two hundred of which are for war.[20] He is always at war, sometimes with the Deccan, sometimes with Orissa, and sometimes inside his own country. He has great captains and many mercenaries. When he rests it is in Biznagar, a city of twenty thousand inhabitants,[21] which lies between two mountain ranges. The houses there are not usually very much ornamented. The king's houses or palaces are large and well built, and the king has a good following of noblemen and horsemen. He has great lords with him and he is held in great respect. There are a thousand girl entertainers in his court, and four or five thousand men of the same profession. These are Klings and not Kanarese, because the people of this province of Talimgo [Telingana] are more graceful.[22]

One important aspect of these Portuguese descriptions is that they can refer with relative familiarity to local concepts of ethnic and social classification. Thus Pires here distinguished the Kanarese from the Klings – the Kannada from the Tamils and Telugu. Barbosa also explains that in Malabar they all speak *maliama*, Malayalam, and that the language of the *chatis* (merchants) from Coromandel – Tamil – differs from Malayalam 'as it is with the Castilians and Portuguese'.[23] In

[19] This means that ethnically the king represents both Kannada (Kanarese) and Tamil or Telugu (Kling) peoples, albeit he mainly speaks Kannada. It is a little surprising that Pires seems to include both Telugu peoples (whose speech was very similar to Kannada) and Tamil peoples (closer to Malayalam) under the same concept. In Malacca Pires must have become familiar with the Klings from Coromandel because they formed a very important community of foreign merchants who were actually allies of the Portuguese – in fact the word comes from the Malay *keling* to refer to Indians from the Coromandel coast. These Klings could therefore be Tamil or Telugu, and indeed further down Pires identifies the Klings with the inhabitants of Telingana. On the other hand, a few decades later the Portuguese in Coromandel came to distinguish the Telugu from the Tamils as Badagas (from the Tamil 'northerners').

[20] This according to the Paris ms., with which Ramusio here agrees. As observed by A. Cortesão (Pires, *Suma*, p. 64), the Lisbon ms. here has 300,000 mounted men and 800 elephants – much more enthusiastic. For quotations I have followed A. Cortesão's edition, which includes both the best Portuguese version (based on a Paris manuscript) and an English translation which notes the variants (such as those in Ramusio's partial version). I have also considered the text recently and meticulously edited by Rui Loureiro, *O manuscrito de Lisboa da 'Suma Oriental' de Tomé Pires* (Macao, 1996). Loureiro discusses the manuscript tradition in detail (ibid., pp. 32–43). All the copies of Pires's account now available are imperfect, but the Lisbon ms. is clearly worse.

[21] The Lisbon manuscript here says 50,000. On the other hand, 20,000 *vizinhos* may be best translated as 20,000 households (like Ramusio, who translated 20,000 *fuochi*).

[22] Pires, *Suma*, pp. 64–5 and 351.

[23] Barbosa, *Livro em que dá relação do que viu e ouviu no Oriente* (1946 edn), pp. 120 and 158. The book of Duarte Barbosa requires a special textual note because no satisfactory text is yet available. The first Portuguese edition of 1821, prepared by S. F. de Mendo Trigoso, amalgamated a Portuguese manuscript from the Cadaval Library – a late copy

their description of castes in Malabar, both Pires and Barbosa clearly distinguish the brahmins and the nayars, the dominant religious and military groups. Barbosa's description of the nayars is particularly full and goes over many pages (historians like Castanheda, Barros and Correa discussed this aristocratic group in some detail too).[24] Although the classification and treatment of other groups becomes less even, the attempt to be precise cannot be doubted – not least when Barbosa distinguishes as many as eighteen castes, 'eighteen laws of native Gentiles'.[25]

The word most used by Barbosa to distinguish these social groups is 'law' (*lei*). The implicit meaning of this concept, as used in Barbosa's report, is the formal recognition of a social regulation which defines a

of irregular quality written in two hands – with Ramusio's Italian text, which was based on a Spanish translation of 1524 of which we have various copies (the best manuscript, in Barcelona, has been translated into English). I have consulted this 'amalgamated Portuguese edition', including Ramusio's material, in the version published by Reis Machado in 1946 (Barbosa, *Livro* (1946)). The English translation, *The book of Duarte Barbosa*. ed. by M. L. Dames, is in some ways better, since it distinguishes the passages from different sources and gives a critical commentary. Three further sixteenth-century Portuguese manuscripts, two in the National Library of Lisbon and one in the archive of Torre do Tombo, have been identified – see Schurhammer, *Gesammelte Studien*, vol. IV, pp. 23–5. There has recently appeared an edition of one of these manuscripts (National Library of Lisbon, ms. 9163), available in the modernized transcription of M. A. da Veiga e Sousa: Barbosa, *Livro do que viu e ouviu no Oriente* (Lisbon, 1989). Unfortunately, this is not yet a critical edition, which is now in course of publication by the same person. It is noteworthy that the sixteenth-century manuscript used by Sousa appears truncated, or perhaps unexpanded, in a number of places, in particular the beginning and the section on Vijayanagara. In the meanwhile, another version of Barbosa's book from a manuscript in the Fronteira Library was published by L. Ribeiro (ed.) 'Uma geografia quinhentista', *Studia*, 7 (1961): 151–318, albeit strangely attributed to Barros. This latter version, in many places disorderly and truncated, often coincides with the Castilian and Ramusio texts where these differ from the Cadaval manuscript. The wording has been substantially altered from the other Portuguese manuscripts, but it does not seem to be a re-translation from the Castilian. It is not impossible that the Castilian translation of 1524 should be considered as a better version than many of the Portuguese manuscripts, because it has suffered fewer cuts and alterations. The translation was made by the Genoese ambassador Martín Centurión assisted by Diogo Ribeiro, a Portuguese in the service of Charles V (I of Castile) as his royal cosmographer, and owner of the original copy. It was probably meant to be used in the *junta* of Badajoz-Elvas, in which the emperor Charles I of Castile and the king of Portugal tried to settle their dispute concerning the discovery and possession of the Moluccas, and Ribeiro used it later for his maps. In this study I have compared all these versions, using the editions by Dames and Reis Machado as my main English and Portuguese texts, correcting them in the light of Sousa's published text, and taking account of the Fronteira and Barcelona versions too.

[24] Castanheda, *História*, vol. I, pp. 37–41; Barros, *Ásia*, vol. I, pp. 351–8; Correa, *Lendas da Índia*, vol. I, pp. 353–7.

[25] Barbosa, *Livro* (1946), p. 120: 'dezoito leis de gentios naturales'. The reliability of Barbosa's analysis of caste is defended by Dames (ed.) in *The book*, vol. II, pp. 70–1, on the basis of modern identifications.

limited group, rather than the looser idea of accepted and characteristic behaviour, for which he uses 'custom' (*costume*) or 'use' (*uso*). At the other extreme, his 'law' does not necessarily imply the written constitution of a kingdom nor even the particular commands and regulations issued by a temporal sovereign power.[26] Barbosa's use of the concept of 'law' was in fact analogous to the distinction between different religious communities in the biblical tradition: Jews, Christians and Muslims. The novel point is that the *gentios* can be said to have 'different laws within a common law' – different moral identities within the same religious system. For instance, in Narsinga 'there are three *leis* [classes] of Gentiles, each of them has a distinct law of their own, and similarly their customs are very different one from the other'.[27] These moral codes are more than just social or professional differences: they are exclusive and transmit from generation to generation – in particular the eighteen 'laws' of Malabar: 'each one is separate, and they cannot touch others nor mix through marriage; and besides these eighteen classes of Gentiles who are natives of Malabar, which I have described, there are others of foreign peoples, traders and merchants in the land'.[28]

The same is observed by Pires: 'In Malabar a son cannot be more important than his father . . . and a Nayar is always a Nayar, and in all crafts, and among jesters, singers and sorcerers, the son has to follow his father's profession'.[29]

Pires and Barbosa thus define each group by distinguishing rules of untouchability and hierarchy, possibilities for marriage, professional activities, and special prohibitions such as those concerning food. Barbosa also notes that some groups have their special idols and superstitious beliefs. What is striking about this clear definition of caste, and more generally about the way this group of sources develops an ethnographic analysis, is the extent to which there are parallels between

[26] The use of the word 'caste' in early sources, and its derivation from a generic to a technical use, is documented in *Hobson-Jobson. The Anglo-Indian Dictionary*, ed. by H. Yule and A. C. Burnell, 2nd edn (London, 1903), pp. 170–1. It thus appears that although the word was already in use in the fifteenth century in the writings of the Venetian Ca' da Mosto to refer to a particualr ethnic-racial group, it really took its modern sense (to describe a sectarian-professional endogamous group) in Portuguese India during the second half of the sixteenth century. Occasionally Barbosa uses the word *sorte*, but not caste. See Barbosa, *Livro* (1946), p. 63 ('há neste reino outra sorte de Gentios che chaman Baneanes'). Ibid., p. 140 has 'As mulheres naires . . . não dormem com homem mais baixo que sua casta', but the transcription by Sousa, based on a variant sixteenth-century manuscript, corrects: 'estas mulheres não dormem com outra gente mais baixa' (Barbosa, *Livro* (1989), p. 93). Pires, on the other hand, has no specific concept for 'caste' – or even *lei* – and sometimes uses 'people' or 'nation'.

[27] Barbosa, *Livro* (1946), p. 107.

[28] Ibid., p. 157.

[29] Pires, *Suma*, p. 72.

descriptions. This can of course be explained on account of the social homogeneity amongst these different authors, as I have argued. However, it is also necessary to take account of the fact that these writers were engaged in an original process of decoding indigenous rules. They had the advantage of a long and direct experience, but clearly they also benefited from a serious attempt to 'map' difference in order to guide the behaviour of the Portuguese.

This owed much to the peculiar context of the Portuguese empire in Asia. With the exception of the main towns such as Goa and the missions, the Portuguese could not really try to change the indigenous ways of living, but sought instead to reach a series of agreements with local powers that would give them the dominant role. It was only on the sea that the Portuguese could consider themselves in full command. The image we have of early sixteenth-century Cannanor, for instance, drawn by the chronicler Gaspar Correa, is that of an indigenous town by the beach, under the palm trees, onto which a foreign fortress has been superimposed, with its little port, walls, tower, hospital, churches, *feitoria* and Christian town.[30] Correa's pictorial perspective emphasized these Portuguese constructions, as his voluminous *Lendas da India* emphasized the deeds and misdeeds of his fellow countrymen. But the background of a different cultural reality is something which imposed a presence even if only by extending its boundaries outside the picture. It could not be simply written out of the imagination, and therefore had to be mapped.

It is from this perspective – living in the 'Portuguese quarter' of a petty indigenous kingdom shared by various socio-cultural communities – that Barbosa, for many years *escrivão de feitor* at Cannanor, approached his subject matter. The statement of his aims and method in his preface (which only appears in Ramusio's Italian edition), may be valid for the whole group of sources:

> I Duarte Barbosa, a gentleman of the right noble city of Lisbon, having sailed for a great part of my youth over the seas of India . . . and having travelled by land as well through many and diverse regions lying in the neighbourhood thereof, and having seen and heard at that time many things which I esteemed marvellous and astonishing inasmuch as they had never been seen or heard by our forefathers, have resolved to write them down for the profit of all men, even as I saw them or understood them day by day, endeavouring to set forth in this my book the towns and the boundaries of all those kingdoms where I have either been myself or as to which I have learnt from

[30] Correa's pictures are reproduced in the nineteenth-century edition of the *Lendas da Índia* by R. J. de Lima Felner. For Cannanor see vol. III, p. 11. On Cannanor in the early sixteenth century see G. Bouchon, *'Regent of the sea'.*

trustworthy persons, stating which are the kingdoms of the Moors and which of the Gentiles, and the customs thereof. Nor have I omitted the trade of those countries and the kinds of merchandise found therein, and the places where they are produced, and whither they are carried.[31]

This statement is revealing because it sketches all the key elements necessary for an understanding of the genre: its derivation from a personal experience of travel, the fact that it deals with what is different (*varie e diverse cose . . . maravigliose e stupende*) as defined by opposition to a tradition (*li nostri antichi*). It also provides, albeit schematically, the main categories which define the subject matter, that is, towns and kingdoms, the religion and customs of the inhabitants, and the traffic of merchandise. It even defines the identity of the author – a citizen of Lisbon – and its audience – universal. Furthermore, it goes on to express a concern for empirical reliability, based on a clear distinction between what has been seen by the author and hearsay:

Inasmuch as, besides those things which I have myself seen, I have always taken pleasure in enquiring from Moors, Christians and Gentiles regarding the manners and customs of those countries of which they had knowledge, and their statements I have none the less painfully compared one with another to the end that I might have a more certain knowledge of the truth thereof, which has ever been my chief desire as it should be of all who write on such matters.[32]

THE PERCEPTION OF CULTURAL DIFFERENCE

Of course different authors pursued this same programme with different emphases. So, while Pires seemed to restrain his admiration for the greatness of Vijayanagara by noting that the houses are not very ornamented, and by giving numerical assessments of the size of population and armies which are not wildly above the average, Barbosa seems to have insisted on the fact that the inhabitants are, in most respects, 'almost like us' – rich, tawny, prosperous and well organized, rather than naked, black and poor. For instance, 'the natives of the land are Gentiles . . . they are of a brown colour, almost white . . . they are men of good stature, and their physiognomies are nearly like ours'.[33] Later, 'The king and the people from this land marry in a way

---

[31] Barbosa, *The book*, vol. I, p. 1, translation corrected from Ramusio, *Navigazioni e viaggi*, vol. II, p. 543. Although missing in all surviving manuscripts, there is no good reason to suspect that Ramusio would have interpolated this preface, dated 1516.

[32] Barbosa, *The book*, vol. I, p. 2, corrected from Ramusio, *Navigazioni*, vol. II, p. 543.

[33] See Barbosa, *Livro* (1946), pp. 103–4.

similar to ours, and they have a marriage-law' – an observation which is meant to contrast with what Barbosa says about the people of Calicut, who have no 'marriage-law' ('não têm lei de casamento').[34] (This favourable comparison was made more explicit by the historian Castanheda in his version of Barbosa's account: 'the king of Vijayanagara is more refined in his habits of eating and dress than the kings of Malabar'.)[35] Although Barbosa also described many substantial differences between 'us' and 'them', and in particular a number of rather horrific idolatrous sacrifices, these were not used to create a dramatic distance between Portugal and Vijayanagara. In fact the most obvious condemnations of vain and cruel customs appear to be additions by Ramusio.[36]

Thus, for Barbosa, Vijayanagara represented a society which could equal or surpass his own, with the remarkable exception of gruesome ceremonies like *sati*, hook-swinging and deflowering with stone idols (whether honourable prostitution and aristocratic polygamy really bothered him is less easy to ascertain). More generally, his underlying message was that Vijayanagara was a uniquely wealthy and extremely cosmopolitan centre of trade – indeed, for its traffic, safety and fair dealing, a great place for business. Thus: 'this is a great king and the richest found in this world. He has great cities wherein live many merchants, Moors and Gentiles of great wealth who deal with rich merchandise, chiefly in precious stones, which are held in great esteem in that kingdom'.[37]

---

[34] Ibid., p. 108. On the other hand, Barbosa carefully describes *rules*, however bewildering to a European, which tell who can sleep with whom, who cares for children, and who inherits and succeeds in Calicut. In that sense there is a 'law'.

[35] Castanheda, *História*, vol. I, p. 247.

[36] This is particularly clear in the comment that follows the description of a hook-swinging ceremony, 'a miserable and pitiful thing', which is one of the very few passages not found in any version other than Ramusio's. See Barbosa, *The book*, vol. I, pp. 219–20, including Dames' note 1 on p. 219. For Barbosa's description of Vijayanagara there is a serious discrepancy between the long text given in the Cadaval manuscript, the additions found in the Spanish rendering (ibid., pp. 198–228) whose validity is confirmed in the Fronteira text (Ribeiro (ed.) 'Una geografia quinhenista', pp. 244–53), and the shorter version published by Sousa (Barbosa, *Livro* (1989), pp. 64–9). I have treated the sections given in the Spanish (and Ramusian) version as authentic. This includes virtually all the second half of the account: the description of armies, the relationship between warriors ansd prostitutes, the three classes of lords, brahmins, and *lingayats*, and a number of bloody religious sacrifices.

[37] Barbosa, *Livro* (1946), p. 114: '[el-rei] é mui grande e mais rico de mercadoria que se acha no mundo, e tem mui grandes cidades, onde vivem muitos mercadores mouros e gentios de muito dinhero e grosso trato, principalmente de pedraria, que neste reino é mui estimada'. Ribeiro (ed.) 'Una geografia', has instead: 'ho reino de narsymgua he muito riquo e muy grande e o mais ryqo de mercadorias que ateguora se no mundo sabe. Neste reyno haa muitas e muy grandes çidades'. Dames' translation seems incorrect here.

It is not clear whether Barbosa actually visited the kingdom. He probably learnt a great deal from 'informed and critical' hearsay, although his detailed descriptions of male and female dress, the streets and houses of the capital city, and ceremonies like *sati*, suggest that he witnessed much of it too. Thus in his account of the ritual deflowering of girls, Barbosa takes us to the temple at night with music and the whole family, adding that he does not know the details of what exactly happens behind the curtains (precisely because the curtains hide it). His description of a young maiden on the way to her marriage, half naked, bleeding from two sharp iron hooks in her loins which are set in a tall water-lift 'like those used in Castile for drawing water from wells', and contentedly throwing lemons to her husband, is also extremely visual.[38] In any case the interpretation of Vijayanagara as a place of trade was not simply his own. In the new colonial context more fundamental than the personal rhetorical emphasis by individual writers is the general agreement between descriptions, and the question is really to what extent the parallels found between these various descriptions of Malabar and Vijayanagara are based on the systematic use of a common stock of general categories of classification, or rather on particular observations which happen to coincide.

Although Ptolemy and Strabo were well known in early sixteenth-century Europe, there is no evidence that writers like Barbosa and Pires drew from them any formalized models of geographical and ethnographical description – at least nothing comparable to the reliance on classical and medieval models of historical writing exploited by Barros, Castanheda and Correa. It was only late in the sixteenth century that humanist methods for travellers teaching 'what to describe' began to proliferate in Europe.[39] It seems, therefore, that

---

[38] There are many similar examples. In this light, the suggestion put forward by Alves, 'A cruz, os diamantes e os cavalos', p. 18, n.28, that Duarte Barbosa could have learnt his information concerning Vijayanagara from Luís do Salvador because they met in the years 1500–6, or the one by S. Subrahmanyam, *Improvising empire*, p. 49, that he probably learnt about Pulicat from the Italians Corsali and Strozzi who were there in 1515–16, are equally unnecessary if we consider that by the time Barbosa wrote his book he had spent many years in India and in different places. Not only is he likely to have made occasional trips to the interior and to the eastern coast of the peninsula, but he could have also collected reports from indigenous sources – as he himself declares when he explains that he learnt many things from the Moors, or that he learnt stories about the miracles of Saint Thomas from the Christians of Quilon. He also remarks that both Gentiles and Moors worship at the tomb of Saint Thomas, saying that it is 'coisa sua', and that in fact the small and derelict church in Mylapore is looked after by 'a poor Moor'.

[39] See J. P. Rubiés, 'Instructions for travellers: teaching the eye to see', in J. Stagl and C. Pinney (eds.) *From travel literature to ethnography. History and Anthropology*, 9 (1996): 139–90.

Pires and Barbosa wrote on the basis of a very broad and vague consensus about the proper subject of geography. As we saw in Barbosa's preface, he wanted to talk about the boundaries and inhabited centres of each kingdom, to distinguish the religion and customs of the inhabitants, and to discuss in detail the merchandise for each place. There is little doubt that this is precisely what he does.

However, by compiling a comparative table of the various descriptions of Malabar written by Varthema, Pires and Barbosa, we can be more precise (see table 3). It would seem that the interplay of these broadly shared aims with the particular realities of historical Malabar led to further parallels, affecting sub-categories such as the kinds of customs described or, more generally, the kinds of emphasis and simplification employed. These parallels spring from the use of a shared everyday language, with its full range of European connotations, in its attempt to 'decode Malabar' according to certain aims. In other words, the parallels between descriptions spring from analogies within a complex process, rather than just from an immediate set of 'prejudices' or an immediate 'empirical observation'.

Table 3. *Customs of Malabar and Calicut: analytical categories*[a]

	Pires (1512–15)	Barbosa (1512–18)	Varthema (1504–10)
I Physical setting	Size and limits of Malabar (1), climate (2), landscape (14).	Size and limits of Malabar (1).	[only Calicut – Malabar not treated as a unity] Climate (13).
II Natural products	Detailed analysis of trade and local products, considering each kingdom (18) and then in general, imports of rice (17), production of palm trees, betel, arecas, pepper, ginger, coconuts, coir, etc. (22). Shipping (16). Pirates (20).	[Information on animals, fruits and spices appears scattered among the description of other Malabar kingdoms further south]	Spices (15), fruits (16) and rice (17). Very detailed. Animals and birds (20).
III Trade	[As above.]	See professional castes (21) and foreign or Moorish merchants (22). Ships and itineraries (23).	Traders and navigation (13). Bankers and money-lenders (19).
IV Cities	Various kingdoms described separately (18). Emphasis on ports (16).	[There is a separate narrative, describing Calicut with other kingdoms of Malabar.]	Picturesque. description of Calicut (1), starting point of narrative.

V Rulers and government	Distinguishes various kingdoms (18). Kings and lords also discussed in section describing brahmins (6). The kings of Malabar listed aside (15).	Very thorough account of Calicut kingship. Legendary origins (2), death and succession ceremonies (8), oaths and obligations, and prime minister (9), role of 'prince' (10), writing officials (11), women servants (12), special attentions (14), betel and food (15), travel (16). Emphasis on ceremonial customs.	The king (2), his religion (2) and eating habits (3). Death and succession ceremonies (7) (23). The royal palace (14) (22).
VI War and enemies	Portuguese fortresses (4). Observations relating to nayars (5) (19). All kingdoms at war with each other (18).	Observations in section relating to nayars (20).	Way of fighting (12), with emphasis on nayars and ceremonial procedures.
VII Law and religious classification	Native Christians (13), Moors and Gentiles (23). Condemns idolatry (11). Confuses Hindu 'trinity' with Christianity (3). Consciously superficial.	Justice kept by a governor in Calicut, with punishments according to caste and religion (17). Minor offences (18). Mentions belief of brahmins in gentile 'trinity' (19) and *mouros* (22). See XII.	Justice, with emphasis on punishments (10).
VIII Ethnic identity	Generalizes about people and their language emphasizing nayar customs (5). See XII.	Language and caste system (3). Physical description and dress (4), ceremonial customs of kings (5).	Religion of the king and idolatrous practices (2).
IX Religious customs	Extended discussion of brahmins (6). Offences (8). Prohibitions (6) (10).	Idol worship and kingship ceremonies (13). See separate castes in XII, with full description of brahmins, and of nayar superstition.	Eating ceremonies of kingship (3). Bathing and perfuming (11). Annual feast and sacrifice (24).
X Marriage and sexual customs	Discusses rules of succession and sexuality among brahmins (6) and nayars (10).	Kings (6) and nayars (20) marriage and matrilineal succession. Detailed account, with emphasis on the sexual freedom of women. Maidenhood ceremonies (7) (20).	Merchants exchange women, and among 'the others' (nayars) women sleep with whom they please (8).

XI Other customs	Emphasis on health issues (7). Nayar loyalty and sacrifice (5). *Sati* described outside Malabar, in Kanará.	Many details on food, dress and marriage appear in the particular description of each caste (19–22). Note nayar death ceremonies (20).	Dress and food (6) (9). Medicine and doctors (18). How poor women feed and raise their children (19).
XII Social divisions	Brahmins (6), nayars (5, 10) and more than ten other groups (11). Detailed description, but simpler than Barbosa. Discusses power and inequality (9) (21).	Brahmins (19), nayars (20) and 15 further castes (21). Also foreign Hindu merchants (*chatis, baneanes*), and local and foreign *mouros* (22). Explained hierarchically and in extreme detail.	Brahmins (4). Nayars and four other sorts of people (distinguishes six castes in total) (5)
XIII Wonders	Charmed snakes (12).	Snakes (21).	

[a] In this table, numbers between brackets indicate the place that each item of description occupies in the sequence of each narrative. It must be observed that while both Pires and Barbosa claim to describe the land of Malabar in general, Barbosa in fact focuses on the kingdom of Calicut, but leaves the description of the city as a separate section. Varthema's description of customs in Calicut is meant to be applicable to other kingdoms in South India. Both Barbosa and Varthema have therefore further sections dealing with other cities and kingdoms of Malabar. It must also be borne in mind that some of the descriptions are lengthier than others, and in that sense parallel descriptions are not equivalent. Barbosa's description is fuller than either of the other two, and Pires's account is the shortest (it is more detailed when dealing with Indonesia, the Moluccas and China).

Table 3 again reveals the emphasis of each author. Varthema is the more superficial but nevertheless remarkably in line with writers committed to preparing reliable geographical guides. Pires is more precise on the economic and political situation, and Barbosa particularly informative about socio-cultural aspects. Barbosa's account of Vijayanagara follows the same general pattern of description that he had used for Calicut (see table 4), although with a far less detailed account of the lower castes, and perhaps more emphasis on how the city's setting and size, the power and justice of its kings, and the prosperity of its trade in horses and precious stones all relate to each other.

While Barbosa does not neglect to give a precise view of the provinces of the kingdom, of its economic life, and of the way the army functions, it is remarkable how detailed his descriptions of dress, personal ornament and women's customs is. This attention in fact gives a special flair to his interpretation of the society of Vijayanagara. He fully describes prostitution, rivalries in the royal palace, women as *sati*, live burials, and a number of maidenhood ceremonies as distinct from those customs peculiar to Malabar, clearly keeping this account of women in Vijayana-

Table 4. *Geography and customs of Vijayanagara: Barbosa on Narsinga (1512–18)*[a]

I Physical setting	The kingdom and its provinces (1). Geographical and geological landscape (2). The city's environment (7).
II Natural products	Landscape: wild and strange animals (3). The kingdom's natural products, cattle and crops (5). Hunting (36b).
III Trade	Many merchants in the city (11). Goods: precious stones etc. (13). Coins (14). Elephants and horses (20). Conclusion: the city is a rich trading centre and the king is very rich (35).
IV Cities	Density of urbanized population (4). The capital, political, economic and cultural centre: its size, population, walls, etc. (8). Streets and buildings (10).
V Rulers and government	Provincial lords and governors (6) (15). The king: his name, title and religion (9). Luxurious lifestyle of rulers (15). The distribution of horses is a symbol of power relationships (21).
VI War and enemies	Strategic importance of the physical setting (2). Armies: size (22), role of women (23)(34) and recruitment policy (24). Vijayanagara's enemies (32). The style of warfare (33) (36a).
VII Law and religious classification	Safety and justice stimulate trade (12–13). The king controls his lords exercising justice (20). Soldiers have different 'laws' (24). See VIII.
VIII Ethnic identity	Different languages (1). Religious groups and physical types (16). Male and female dress and luxury (17).
IX Religious customs	Brahmins (27) and *lingayats* (28). Detailed discussion of idolatrous customs: *sati* (26), live burials (29), hook-swinging (30), maidenhood sacrifice (31).
X Marriage and sexual customs	Detailed account. Women are pretty, elegant and good dancers (18). Marriage is related to politics and economic position (19). Different practices for different social groups (26–29).
XI Other customs	Describes special food and dress characteristic of the main social groups (25–28).
XII Social divisions	Distinguishes three leading castes: lords (25), brahmins (27) and *lingayats* (28).
XIII Wonders	Animals (3).

[a] This table follows the longest Portuguese version from the Cadaval Library (Barbosa (1946), *Livro*), incorporating those sections found in the Spanish translation and in Ramusio which can be corroborated with the text edited by L. Ribeiro ('Una geografia'). I have distinguished the two different endings with the letters a (Cadaval ms.) and b (Ramusio and Ribeiro texts). The shorter manuscript published by Sousa covers numbers 1–21.

gara separate from his analysis of the matrilineal patterns of Calicut. The clarity with which these distinctive patterns of behaviour are identified matches, therefore, the clarity with which they are narrated, not simply as being different from Europe, but also as having a cultural consistency of their own. This is particularly clear in the description of the nayar women of Malabar:

> The Nayre women are very independent, and dispose of themselves as they please with Bramanes and Nayres, but they do not sleep with men of lower caste [of lower condition] under pain of death . . . the more lovers she has the greater is her honour. Each one of them passes a day with her from midday on one day till midday on the next day, and so they continue living quietly without any disturbance nor quarrels among them. If any of them wishes to leave her, he leaves her, and takes another, and she also if she is weary of a man, she tells him to go, and he does so, or makes terms with her. Any children they may have stay with the mother who has to bring them up, for they hold them not to be the children of any man [they do not know whose children they are] . . . their heirs are their nephews, sons of their sisters . . . This rule the kings made for the Nayres in order that there should be nothing to hold them back from their service . . . These [Nayar] women do not work except to prepare their own food, and to earn their living with their bodies, for in addition to the three or four lovers, whom every woman has, they never refuse themselves to any *Bramene* or *Nayre* who gives them money. These women are very clean [and well attired], and look after themselves very much, and they consider it a matter of great honour and gallantry and pride themselves greatly to be able to give pleasure to men, and believe that every woman who dies a virgin is damned [she does not go to paradise].[40]

What is important about this description is that a social system which breaks almost every important European convention about family life is not portrayed as 'savage' and 'bestial', nor monstrous, nor legendary, nor utopian, but simply as empirical, traditional and civil. What Barbosa has portrayed is not an image of 'otherness', but rather a complex set of social rules which happen to be different. In fact, whenever he finds analogies with his European background he exploits them, so that brahmins and nayars are openly shown to be analogous to European priests and noblemen, the religious and military dominant classes of a three-ordered society. This analogy, on the other hand, does not prevent him from describing as distinctive of India the strength of the division

---

[40] Barbosa, *Livro* (1946), pp. 140, 141, 147, and noting in square brackets the most significant variants from Barbosa, *Livro* (1989), pp. 93 and 99.

that separates the lower castes, not only from the two above them, but also between themselves.

To the extent that chroniclers like Fernão Lopes de Castanheda also included chapter-length ethnographic descriptions in their historical works, they followed a similar rhetoric. Castanheda, in particular, seems to have used Barbosa's work for his description of the society and customs of Vijayanagara – as he also did when he wrote about Gujarat.[41] He did not copy him slavishly and, writing some thirty years later, had a few things to add from other sources (he mentions the reports of Vijayanagara which he heard from Moorish merchants, and his valuable account of Pegu far surpasses Barbosa's because Castanheda had probably been there).[42] Thus Castanheda gives a detailed account of the gallant duels for the sake for their lovers which occupied so much of the attention of the nobility of Vijayanagara, describes their arms and armour, and explains how the brahmins exploited the superstitious beliefs of kings ('because they believe very much in charms and oracles') to obtain huge alms from them. He also introduces his own judgements, for instance that the kings of Vijayanagara, 'while thoroughly upholding justice to foreigners, especially to merchants, with their vassals they keep none and are great tyrants'.[43] These were in essence additions to an existing model of human geography which already had its own clear rhetoric and analytic conventions – and it was as an expression of that model that Castanheda's description of Vijayanagara was copied, adapted and translated in Europe, first by Portuguese historians like Damião de Góis and Jerónimo Osório, then by others abroad like Alonso de Ulloa in Italy or Simon Goulard in France, until it reached readers like Michel de Montaigne.[44]

[41] For Gujarat compare Barbosa, *Livro* (1946), pp. 62–7 with Castanheda, *História*, vol. I, pp. 805–8 (book III, chap. 130). For Vijayanagara, ibid., pp. 244–50 (book II, chap. 16). It is noteworthy that Castanheda agrees with Barbosa's account of Vijayanagara especially in those latter parts not included in the manuscript edited by Sousa in 1989. It seems, therefore, possible that two different versions circulated separately and were later combined.

[42] It seems that Castanheda wrote his ten books after his return from Asia in 1538 after roughly ten years over there. Their publication began in 1551 but was interrupted because of opposition at the court, perhaps instigated by his rival, Barros. Barros published his work almost simultaneously, but he seems to have been working on his drafts from an earlier stage.

[43] Castanheda, *História*, vol. I, p. 248.

[44] Montaigne read a description of Vijayanagara (*c.* 1588) from Simon Goulard's *Histoire de Portugal* (Geneva, 1581), a French translation from the elegant Latin history of the reign of Manuel I written by the Portuguese bishop Jerónimo Osório (*De rebus Emmanuelis gestis*, 1571). Osório had to a great extent copied the Portuguese history of King Manuel written by the humanist courtier Damião de Góis (*Chronica do felicissimo rei dom Emanuel*, 1566), whose main source for Vijayanagara was obviously Castanheda's second book (1552). Thus Montaigne annotated his essays on cultural relativism –

While there was soon a clear model of how to describe customs, analysis of religion was more of a problem. It was not a lack of interest, but rather a cultural insecurity, which explains why Castanheda would begin his account of the people of Vijayanagara with a confused mixture of God and devils, superstitions and true beliefs, priests and prostitutes:

They have many and diverse idolatries, and believe a lot in charms and omens. They believe principally in one single God, whom they confess to be the lord of all things, and afterwards in the devils. They believe that these devils can harm them, and for this reason they honour them greatly. Thus they dedicate houses to them, called pagodes, and they have many in the kingdom which are very sumptuous and have great income. In these temples they have religious men of their sect, called brahmins, and in others unmarried women who earn with their bodies for the temple, and many young girls brought up to do the same when they reach the right age.[45]

What makes this otherwise plausible account rather strange is the attempt to find European parallels without actually engaging in any serious comparison. Barbosa similarly seeks for analogies, and, with Tomé Pires, identifies the Trinity as the object of worship of the brahmins: 'three persons in a single God which they confess exists from the beginnings of the world' – thus translating the major triad of Brahma, Shiva and Vishnu (which was often represented in three-headed sculptures) into a Christian idiom.[46] Despite his accurate and detached description of behaviour, which for instance means that he admires the beauty of idolatrous festivals and excludes any mention of the devil from the ritual worship of the brahmins, Barbosa is ill prepared to retrieve any system of meaning from indigenous literature of whose existence he was nevertheless well aware: 'these brahmins are learned in their idolatries

for instance that 'the taste of good and evil things depends on our opinion' – on the basis of a French translation of Osório's Latin version of Góis' summary of Castanheda's re-working of Barbosa's description – all in the space of some seventy years. Compare Goulard, *Histoire*, pp. 159–60 and Damião de Góis, *Chronica do felicissimo rei dom Emanuel*, ed. by D. Lopes, 4 vols. (Coimbra, 1949–55), vol. II, chap. 6.

45 Castanheda, *História*, vol. I, p. 244.

46 He calls this Trinity *Berma, Besma, Maiceru* (for Brahma, Vishnu, Mahesvara). See Barbosa, *Livro* (1989), p. 91. A similar, even more emphatic passage appears in the description of Gujarat, where the brahmins even enter the Christian churches 'worshipping our images and always asking for Saint Mary, as men who know something about this. Concerning our way of honouring the Church, they say that there is very little difference between us and them' (ibid., p. 37). This passage was similarly adopted by Castanheda. The idea that the Indian gentiles worshipped the Trinity went back to the early Portuguese confusion about Hindu religion, and kept appearing throughout the sixteenth century. For instance Nunes, when discussing the brahmins of Bysnaga, mentions the Hindu Trinity, *Tricembeca*. See Lopes (ed.) *Chronica dos reis de Bisnaga*, p. 75.

[*letrados em suas idolatrias*], and they have many books about them, and the kings esteem them highly'.[47] Unable to find any recognition of 'our Lord Jesus Christ', he concludes in disappointment that 'they believe and respect many vanities, which they do not declare according to the Truth'.[48]

Similarly, he finds devotion among the Christians of Malabar, but also much ignorance ('the majority lack both doctrine and baptism, and only have the name of Christians, because in his time Saint Thomas baptized anyone who wanted to be Christian') and does not entirely trust the 'Armenian' priests who follow the Chaldean (Syriac) rite. They are certainly very pious, but they also baptize for money and it is not clear if they 'recite the whole office, as do our friars'.[49] His enthusiasm for the miracles of Saint Thomas did not preclude the vague realization that Indian Christianity could not be entirely assimilated to the European religion.

To conclude, the *escrivão de feitoria* of Cannanor was obviously better prepared to observe customs systematically than to enter into a systematic dialogue about beliefs. He did not of course have a humanist education but, more importantly, he did not have a proper cultural space in which to discuss religion, since that discourse properly belonged to the authorities of the Church. It is with this crucial omission that the Portuguese ethnographers transformed the isolated observations of Marco Polo and Nicolò Conti into a systematic, even quantitative 'map' of kingdoms, customs and castes. Known in Europe through Ramusio's collection and the historical works of Castanheda and Barros, they set standards for a Renaissance ethnology based on naturalistic and historical assumptions, within the framework of a secularized, rather than a metaphysical, idea of order.

---

[47] Barbosa, *Livro* (1946), p. 138 (passage not found in Sousa's text). It is interesting that in his version of Barbosa's account of the religion of the brahmins from Gujarat, Castanheda, less sympathetic, did introduce devils. It has often been remarked that Castanheda's history tends towards a simplistic and monotonous opposition of the Portuguese fighting against the Moors and winning with God's providential help (Harrison, 'Five Portuguese historians', pp. 165–6). However, it would also be fair to stress that Castanheda's chronicle is often more faithful to the basic pattern of events, and more likely to describe gentile customs as they were recorded in primary documents by men like Barbosa and Pires, than the more elegant or vivid compositions respectively written by Barros and Correa.

[48] Barbosa, *Livro* (1989) p. 91: 'crêem e honram muitas vaidades que não dizem com a verdade'. This 'vaidades' from Sousa's text agrees with the Spanish-Ramusian text and is therefore preferable to the paradoxical 'verdades' in Reis Machado's 1946 edition of Barbosa, *Livro*, p. 138.

[49] Barbosa, *Livro* (1946), pp. 172–3.

7. *The social and political order: Vijayanagara decoded*

A JOURNEY ACROSS THE MOUNTAINS

Some time after 1531 an anonymous Portuguese in Goa collected two descriptions of Vijayanagara and sent them to Europe, probably to the official chronicler of the Portuguese Indies, the humanist-educated João de Barros:

> it seemed necessary to do what your honour desired of me, namely, to search for men who had formerly been in Bisnaga; for I know that no one goes there without bringing away his quire of paper written about its affairs. Thus I obtained this summary from one Domingos Paes, who is around, and who went to Bisnaga in the time of Crisnarao [Krishna Deva Raya] when Cristóvão de Figueiredo was there. And because a man can not say everything, I obtained another from Fernão Nuniz, who was there for three years trading in horses (which did not prove remunerative). Since one relates things which another does not, I send both the summaries which they wrote over there, one, as I said, at the time of Crisnarao, the other sent from there six months ago. I have done this so that your honour can gather what is useful to you from both.[1]

The sender was not wrong in thinking that the two long and detailed reports, by Domingos Paes and Fernão Nunes, complemented each other. The narrative of Paes, the earlier document, was presented as the

---

[1] Sewell, *A forgotten empire (Vijayanagar)*, p. 235. I have checked all translations with the original text as first published by Lopes (ed.) *Chronica dos reis de Bisnaga*. I have also consulted the unique manuscript in the Bibliothèque Nationale of Paris (ms. Portugais 65, 1r–106v), which attests to the accuracy of Lopes's edition. The manuscript, a late sixteenth-century copy, is carefully written and in an excellent state of conservation. Pages 88–9 are left blank, perhaps to include pictures of the Mahanavami festival. It is possible that the copyist is responsible for placing Nunes's chronicle *before* the introductory letter and Paes's report. The material on Vijayanagara is followed by copies (in a different hand) of some letters from the same period written by Portuguese captives in China (104r–135v), now published elsewhere.

account of a personal experience rather than as a systematic geographical description of the kind attempted by Duarte Barbosa. Paes in fact approached Vijayanagara with the eye of an external observer who does not think any detail is irrelevant, and therefore uses a very 'physical' narrative thread. Leaving 'India' (i.e. Portuguese India) from the coastal city of Bhatkal, the expedition followed the route of the packoxen loaded with merchandise, and crossed the mountains towards an alien country-side that combined urban settlement and wilderness. Paes's general frame of description is clearly geopolitical and economic, with a sophisticated understanding of the interactions between physical conditions and human activity. The plateau behind the mountains has a different climate from that of the coast, without 'winters' of continuous rain (the monsoons), and water must be collected in artificial tanks which, because of the continuous wind, are often muddy. But irrigation secures sub-stantial crops of rice and other grain, which means that this is a very fertile and populous kingdom, with many towns surrounded by tree groves (of mangoes, jack-fruits, tamarinds), a great variety of cattle and fowl, and cotton in abundance. There are few wild woods, and some trees are so huge that they serve as resting-places for whole caravans of travelling merchants.[2] Thus Paes takes us along the road towards the king and his city, stopping only to describe an extraordinary temple. With original precision, almost everything he thinks noteworthy is either quantified or compared to the world known to the Portuguese, and thus translated into measurable standards.

The Portuguese expedition first went to meet the king in the new city of Nagalapur (near modern Hospett),[3] built in honour of Krishna Deva Raya's beloved wife. Here Paes describes the brahmins, the king, his daily

---

[2] Lopes (ed.) *Chronica*, pp. 80–2. Although the analysis of perceptions of the economic geography of India is not my main concern here, it must be understood that it plays an important role in most travel accounts of the period. With respect to Vijayanagara, Paes certainly is quite outstanding, but lucid observations are also found in Barbosa (who discusses, for instance, the difficulty of crossing the 'serra' above Kanará and Malabar, speculates from the evidence of fossils that the whole coastline used to be covered by the sea, and lists the main products and crops from Vijayanagara). Similarly, the chronicler Gaspar Correa devotes an interesting passage to the analysis of the policy of water management which allowed the water collected during the rainy season to support rice crops all the year round – crucial for the subsistence of the poor. He effectively uncovers the economic interdependence between the rice from 'Bisnega' sold in Malabar, which travelled down the rivers to the ports of Kanará or was imported from Coromandel; the pepper from the 'serra' of Malabar, which was acquired from the Christian producers at a low price in exchange for rice and cotton clothes; and thus the structure of the bulk trade in entrepots like Cochin, dominated by local Muslim merchants until the arrival of the Portuguese. See Correa, *Lendas da Índia*, vol. I, pp. 428–9.

[3] This is the identification suggested by Sewell, *Forgotten empire*, but it presents some problems, since Paes said that the new city was 'one league' (*hũa legoa*) from Vijayanagara, and 13 km, the distance from Hospett to Hampi, is perhaps excessive. See

routine, his favourite minister, and also his household of eunuchs and wives. It is only after a brief embassy that Paes and his party finally proceed towards the capital city. We are led through several circles of walls, 'and from here to the king's palace is all streets and rows of houses, very beautiful, and houses of captains and other rich and honourable men; you will see rows of houses with many figures and decorations pleasant to look at'.[4] We thus walk with the Portuguese traveller through the streets of an extraordinary city – not a fabulous city taken from a book of chivalry, which is what the Castilian soldier Bernal Díaz saw in Tenochtitlan during the conquest of Mexico, scarcely a year earlier, but something much closer to a European city of his own time.[5] Paes's eye is caught by many details, his prose is prolix and often repetitious. We are shown the landscape and buildings surrounding the city, and its economic life. We visit the city itself, with its water-tanks, temples, streets and market. We witness an important religious festival and an impressive military parade. Finally, thanks to a special permission secured by the Portuguese leader Figueiredo directly from the king, we enter into Krishna Deva Raya's private palace. Paes does not fail to climb a hill and contemplate the city below him. He compares it with Rome: 'I could not see it all, because it is placed among hills, but what I saw from there seemed to me as large as Rome, and very beautiful to look at'.[6]

With Paes a modern traveller can also follow the ruins of the site of Hampi, temple by temple and road by road, up to the very same hill where the strange landscape unfolds in all directions (see plates 5 and 6).[7]

Lopes (ed.) *Chronica*, p. 93. From his other various estimates, it seems that Paes uses the Portuguese league of about 6 km.

[4] Sewell, *Forgotten empire*, p. 254.

[5] Consider the famous passage by Bernal Díaz del Castillo, *Historia verdadera de la conquista de la Nueva España*, ed. by Miguel-León Portilla, 2 vols. (Madrid, 1984), vol. I, pp. 310–11: 'y desde que vimos tantas ciudades y villas pobladas en el agua, y en tierra firme otras grandes poblaciones, y aquella calzada tan derecha por nivel como iba a México, nos quedamos admirados, y decíamos que parecía a las cosas y encantamiento que cuentan en el libro de Amadís . . . y no es de maravillar que yo aquí lo escriba desta manera, porque hay que ponderar mucho en ello, que no sé cómo lo cuente, ver cosas nunca vistas y aún soñadas, como vimos'. For Paes, instead, a huge *lingam* is not as tall as 'the needle of St Peter's at Rome' (Sewell, *Forgotten empire*, p. 241), the wall of the palace of the king encloses 'a greater space than all the castle of Lisbon' (p. 254), and the temples in the streets belong to groups of merchants and artisans 'like the confraternities you know of in our parts' (p. 256).

[6] Lopes (ed.) *Chronica*, p. 96. Probably this hill was the one known as Matanga Parvatam, placed above the agricultural area between the large temple complexes along the river in the north and the urban centre in the south. The stone steps are still in good condition today and it offers a spectacular view of the ruins of the city.

[7] Today's archaeologists base many of their interpretations on the authority of Domingos Paes – see, for instance, A. H. Longhurst, *Hampi ruins described and illustrated* (Calcutta, 1917), and Fritz, Michell and Nagaraja Rao, *Where kings and Gods meet*.

Plate 5 Sasivikallu Ganesa statue from Hampi, Vijayanagara.

In this temple of Darcha [a city on the road from Bhatkal] is an idol in the figure of a man as to his body, and the face is that of an elephant with trunk and tusks, and with three arms on each side and six hands, of which arms they say that already four are gone, and when all fall then the world will be destroyed; they have this as article of faith according to their prophecies. They feed the idol every day, for they say that he eats; and while he eats, women who belong to that pagoda dance in front of him' (Sewell, *A Forgotten Empire*, p. 241, corrected from Lopes, *Chronica dos reis de Bisnaga*, pp. 84–5).

Plate 6 Pampapati (Virupaksha, i.e. Shiva) temple at Hampi, as seen from the south, with the Tungabhadra river behind.

Outside the walls of the city, on the northern side, there are three very beautiful pagodas . . . another is called Aōperadianar, and this is the one which they hold in most veneration and to which they make great pilgrimages . . . They make a pilgrimage to this first gate [*gopura*]; this gate has a very high tower all covered with rows of men and women and hunting scenes and many other stories, and as the tower goes narrowing towards the top so the images diminish in size. Passing this first gate you come at once into a large courtyard with another gate of the same sort as the first, except that it is all rather smaller; and passing this second gate there is a large court with verandas on stone pillars [*mandapas*] all around it and in the middle of this court is the house of the idol (Sewell, *A Forgotten Empire*, pp. 260–1, corrected from Lopes, *Chronica*, pp. 98–9).

Paes does not, however, go very deep inside – both literally and metaphorically. He saw the palace, but not the women's quarters, which represented the private dimension of Vijayanagara royalty. He also remained on the surface of the indigenous religion. An anecdote can serve to exemplify this: after crossing the various towered gates and inner courtyards of the popular Virupaksha (Shiva) temple by the river, Paes gave something to a brahmin so as to be allowed into the main shrine, but all he could see was a series of idols, the principal among which 'is a round stone without any decoration (*sem nenhũa fegura*); they have great devotion for it'.[8] And he steps out again, having made no attempt to interpret the shape and meaning of a *lingam*.

While in Paes's relation the king plays a central role, he appears almost like the logical extension of the landscape, as the perfect ruler of an integrated system that stretched from the wild forests and cultivated areas of the empire to the public spectacle of the city. The description of Krishna Deva Raya was particularly realistic, a rather fat and cheerful man who 'has on his face signs of small-pox'.[9] This 'humanized' perspective was unconventional, but the implicit message less so: we are still being presented with a king who effectively acted as the symbolic centre of an indigenous system of power. In that sense, the question which remains is whether Paes was able to 'decode' to any significant extent the language of the indigenous culture – and more precisely, whether he could actually read a symbolic language on the basis of a minute apprehension of its physical manifestations, but without actually dominating its inner religious code.

The strength and limits of the narrative approach of Domingos Paes can be assessed by comparison with that of Fernão Nunes, who did not confine his account of Vijayanagara to his impressions as a traveller and instead was able to offer a chronicle. Of all writers about the capital he is perhaps the one who acquired a better knowledge of the local language – he spent three years in Vijayanagara, and must therefore have learnt at least Kannada.[10] At the end of his chronicle, Nunes also describes the place and the people, but he does so from the focused perspective of someone who tries to uncover a political system centred on kingship. The kings provided the thread of his historical narrative, and it was only as a digression that he also brought in a discussion of religion and customs, on account of the prominent political role of lords and brahmins. Nunes in fact appears to have been familiar with some Indian literature, probably the *Ramayana* epic, which was of particular importance to the ideology of the Vijayanagara elites in this period: 'they say that in former times all this land was inhabited by monkeys, and that in those days they

---

[8] Lopes, *Chronica*, p. 100. Sewell (*Forgotten empire*, p. 261) translates 'fegura' as 'shape', but perhaps a figurative decoration is intended. It is not clear why Paes calls the Virupaksha temple Aôperiadanar, but the word is clearly written in the manuscript (f. 81v). It might be an attempt to render Ardhanarishvara, the image of the union of Shiva and Parvati (Virupaksha and Pampa) in the temple.

[9] Sewell, *Forgotten empire*, pp. 246–7.

[10] Kannada, known by the Portuguese as 'Kanarese', was spoken in the area between the coast (south of Goa) and the capital city. Telugu, a closely related language spoken in Andhra, was also important at the court, especially because some of the most powerful Indian chiefs and captains (including the Saluva and Aravidu royal dynasties) came from Telugu-speaking areas and had their power base on the north-east of the kingdom. In fact the Vijayanagara heartland combined these two key linguistic groups.

could speak. They have books full of their own stories of great deeds of chivalry.' He, however, dismissed this as a ridiculous fantasy, 'foolish tales about their idols such as it is not rational for men to believe'.[11]

Notwithstanding his contempt for Indian beliefs, Nunes wrote history and, from indigenous sources, interpreted a political system remarkably similar to that of European feudalism. Paes, on the other hand, probably never heard as much about Hindu traditions and mythology. His description of his visit to the main Virupaksha temple, mentioned above, suggested almost complete oblivion to the sacred landscape that surrounded him.[12] However, by describing the streets and the festivals in full detail he effectively transmitted a vision of justice, abundance, pleasure and piety. It was not the heavenly paradise evoked by the Persian ambassador 'Abd al-Razzāq, in his narrative of a journey to Vijayanagara, but perhaps an intuition of the 'four ends of man' of traditional Hindu literature – *dharma* (duty), *artha* (profit), *kama* (love) and *moksha* (spiritual liberation). This was a moral vision that the *Ramayana*, in its mythological language of virtuous kingship, also sought to express, and which informed to a large extent the classical Sanskrit literature of India.

THE MISSING LANGUAGE

But what could Paes, as a European, possibly have perceived? If we want to proceed with an assessment of his 'possible intuition' as a cultural bridge, we need to analyse more systematically what separated the two cultural traditions, and the extent to which analogies could have been misleading. Although Paes's narrative is too detailed for me to discuss fully here, there are a few points where his description of public royal rituals – religious and political – invites a comparison with indigenous sources and archaeological reconstruction. However, no such comparison is possible without a previous (if perhaps tentative) identification of a number of significant referents within the Vijayanagara cultural system. I have mentioned, in this respect, the importance of the epic poem *Ramayana* in this period, which inspired much of Vijayanagara art and kingship (although by no means exclusively). This is attested by the

---

[11] Lopes (ed.) *Chronica*, p. 75: 'dizem que em outro tempo esta terra toda foy de bogios, e que neste tempo fallavão elles, tem livros cheos d'estorias suas de gramdes cavallaryas . . . bestidões de suas ydolatrias, que não esta em rezão d'omenes terem taes opiniõis'.

[12] It is the view of John Fritz and George Michell that the sacred landscape of Vijayanagara was focused on two overlapping mythologies, one associated with Virupaksha (Shiva) as the consort of the river goddess Pampa – hence the name Hampi – and another based on the episodes of the *Ramayana* associated with Rama's allies. Thus the sage Matanga is at the same time the father of the river goddess Pampa and the protector of the monkeys Sugriva and Hanuman. Fritz and Michell, *City of victory*, pp. 49–56.

didactic representation of this epic in the reliefs on the walls of the Hazara Rama (Ramachandra) temple in the central enclosure of the city, Krishna Deva Raya's chapel, which was showed to Cristovão de Figueiredo and Domingos Paes in 1520 (see plate 7). If, as it seems, the temple was built and endowed c. 1513, the Portuguese must have seen it a few years after its completion. We can also note that the mythological associations of the sacred geography of the imperial city involved the *Ramayana* too. For example, it was believed that one of the key locations of Valmiki's epic, the Rishyamuka hill by the river Pampa where Rama encountered the monkey-king Sugriva and enlisted Hanuman, was near Hampi (near the Matanga Parvatam hill ascended by Paes, named precisely after the powerful sage who protected Sugriva in Valmiki's poem).[13] In this context, Nunes's awareness of 'chivalric stories' about monkeys who could talk is not merely casual, but points towards the encounter with a significant referent of the native mythology.

Obviously any attempt to analyse imaginative, religious and political analogies between the cultural tradition of Portuguese travellers like Paes and Nunes, and the Hindu world they described, raises some problems. To begin with, the reconstruction of a Vijayanagara cultural system from sources like the *Ramayana* cannot be undertaken lightly, because it is not possible to read directly, from the Hindu classical tradition, the values that *actually* informed the life of the Hindu empire. Possibly more than 2,000 years separated the first versions of the Indian epics (the *Ramayana* and also the *Mahabharata*) from the reign of Krishna Deva Raya, and throughout this period the Sanskrit brahminic tradition had been repeatedly interpreted and modified to suit local contexts. Romila Thapar has defined the *Ramayana* as 'a charter of validation for monarchy' in the regional kingdoms of India from about AD 700, and its use accompanied the process of Sanskritization of new areas.[14] The

---

[13] These associations have been discussed by Fritz and Michell, ibid. p. 50.

[14] R. Thapar, 'Epic and history: tradition, dissent and politics in India', *Past and Present*, 125 (1989): 3–26, at 15–17. It is often said that the artistic and literary history of the south follows a different rhythm from that of the north, with a *décalage* of a few centuries. This is true both for processes of Sanskritization (from c. 500), and Islamization (from c. 1300), possibly because successive invading elites (first Aryan and then Persian-Turkish) are seen to advance from the north. Thus it is well known that the languages of South India are not Indo-Aryan, but Dravidian, although they adopted many Sanskrit forms. Tamil, in particular, became a sophisticated literary medium at a very early stage, and was part of a 'classical' southern Indian artistic achievement under the Chola dynasty (especially c. 900–c. 1200). By the time of the late Pandya, Hoysala, Kakatiya and Vijayanagara dynasties (which might be conventionally described as within the 'late medieval period' of Indian history, c. 1200–c. 1600) the cultural movement was less marked by the introduction of brahminic culture to new areas than by the expansion of regional language variations, in Tamil, Kannada or Telugu, of previously Sanskrit themes.

Plate 7 Stone reliefs from the southern side of the Hazara Rama (Ramachandra) temple at Vijayanagara, believed to have been the 'state chapel' within the royal palace.

we entered a courtyard . . . very well plastered . . . we mounted four or five steps and entered some beautiful houses . . . there is a building there built on many pillars, which are of stone-work, and the work of the roof and the rest is made the same way. The pillars and all are gilded so well that they seem all of gold. After the entrance of this building in the middle nave there is a canopy standing on four pillars and covered with many images of dancing women, besides other images in the stone-work. All of this is also gilded, with some red colour on the under-sides of the leaves which stand out of the stone-work. You should know that they do not use this house, because it belongs to their idol and to the temple. At the end of this there is a small closed door where the idol is. Whenever they want to celebrate a festival for the idol they carry it on a golden throne and put it under the canopy, which is made for this purpose, and then the brahmans come to perform their ceremonies, and the dancing-girls come to dance (Sewell, *A Forgotten Empire*, pp. 286–7, corrected from Lopes, *Chronica*, pp. 119–20, from a visit to the royal palace).

literature of Vijayanagara, like the literature of medieval India in general, was essentially a re-creation of a classical tradition, in Sanskrit or in any of the vernacular languages patronized in the courts, through the medium of a number of conventional genres which gave ample scope for stylistic and thematic transformations.[15]

[15] It is not easy to piece together the literary history of Vijayanagara. I have found most useful Shulman, *The king and the clown in South Indian myth and poetry* and Wagoner *Tidings of the king*. For legal texts, P. V. Kane, *History of Dharmasastra*, 5 vols. (Poona,

In this sense the 'classical' and mythological tradition of Vijayanagara written in Sanskrit was indeed analogous to the European classical and mythological tradition written in Latin and Greek. These traditions did not determine, for example, a particular discourse on kingship. They were, rather, sources of inspiration, offering an imaginative and technical language with which the inevitable tension between inherited ideals and the requirements of particular situations could be negotiated. However, and this is the key difficulty which we need to consider, the parallel between the structuring roles of the classical literatures of India and Europe cannot be developed very far without revealing a number of very important differences which question the validity of apparent analogies. To begin with, the division, within a European classical inheritance, between 'Christian-religious' and a 'Latin-Greek secular' strands has no correspondence within the Hindu traditional sources. Furthermore, the strategies for reading and incorporating the traditional within the local and the new were very different in each case. One could argue that the way in which an old epic like the *Ramayana* was adapted to new contexts in India worked towards the elimination of a sense of historical change, emphasizing recurrent patterns of alteration and restoration (mediated by the dharmic principles of cosmic and moral order) over precisely defined events. By contrast, the Christian tradition entertained at its core – with the themes of the fall, incarnation and final judgement – a profound sense of historical discontinuity. It also defined itself far more than Hinduism by opposition to, rather than through the incorporation of, alternative cults. These features of European Christianity – the cultivation of a distinctly non-religious classical tradition, a precise sense of historical change and an emphasis on mythological exclusivism – altogether amounted to the separation of religious and secular discourses. Needless to say, this separation was only accentuated throughout the Renaissance, with the combined impact of humanism and the various reformations. Therefore we are not here faced with a difference between static ('oriental') and changing ('western') traditions – the Hindu brahminical tradition was certainly flexible – but rather with different attitudes towards tradition. Europeans, with their emphases on structured empirical discourses and wide-ranging philosophical scepticism, came to oppose experience to tradition (not without the loss of a great deal of

1930–62). For the nayaka period see also V. N. Rao, D. Shulman and S. Subrahmanyam, *Symbols of substance. Court and state in Nayaka period Tamil Nadu* (Delhi, 1992), and for Telugu love poetry A. K. Ramanujan, V. Narayana Rao and D. Shulman, *When God is a customer. Telugu courtesan songs by Ksetrayya and others* (Berkeley and Los Angeles, 1994). Venkataramanayya, *Studies in the history of the third dynasty of Vijayanagara*, provides a general historical context in which literary sources are used generously.

mythological belief). Hindu culture on the other hand, with its many variations, was geared towards the fluid recreation of coherence at every stage. The intellectual methods of the brahminical schools were in effect so abstract that no sense of historical difference or change could be recognized as a fundamental problem.[16]

Therefore, whilst Europeans shared with the gentile inhabitants of Vijayanagara their reliance on a religious mythology, what separated them was not only the distinctive character of their religion (relevant as this was), but more importantly the fact that the role of such mythology within their own cultural system was fast becoming entirely different – more confined, one might say. At the time of Paes's visit, this process of European divergence was at a mid-point in which symbolic and mythical ritualism could still be shared languages across cultures, but this kind of encounter was a fading possibility.

A key theme in Paes's description in which the two trajectories – European and Indian – can be seen to diverge is the image of kingship, and specifically the models of royal sacrality. The epic hero Rama, a God incarnate but ambiguously unaware of it, could possibly have been compared with sacred kings of the ancient Near East such as David or even Alexander, but he was (to extend the metaphor) neither as exclusive and other-worldly as Christ in his divinity, nor as definitely human as the most supreme western Christian emperor, Charlemagne. A king like Krishna Deva Raya was, by virtue of his metaphorical association with Rama, more sacred than King Manuel of Portugal could ever be as a national sovereign acting with the grace of God in a world of sin. As a sixteenth-century Telugu account of the exemplary reign of Krishna Deva Raya made clear, 'first of all you should know that the king of the lion-throne is none other than an emanation of Vishnu'.[17] One need not *add* supernatural grace to Indian kingship. Simply by becoming part of a sacred landscape, kingship *was* sacred – the ritual, not the law, made the king (which helps explain why royal successions were so contested and political authority generally so unstable). The extent to which Krishna Deva Raya combined in one person ritual or sacred attributes with secular authority therefore posed a challenge to the assumptions of a sixteenth-century European observer like Domingos Paes.[18]

If the sacredness of kingship was beyond European expectations, the importance of epic mythologies presented an equally formidable barrier.

---

[16] With perhaps the exception of Muslim domination, which by threatening ritual kingship also threatened one of the fundamental mechanisms for the reproduction of *dharma*.

[17] Wagoner, *Tidings*, p. 89.

[18] The Indian king did of course also depend upon brahminic assistance, but this is another matter.

Taking the European tradition as a term of reference, the *Ramayana* did not operate at the level of Homer's *Odyssey*, which is the usual comparison, nor of Camões' *Os Lusíadas*, which would seem appropriate in the circumstances, but in many respects should be seen as something closer to the books of the Old Testament: it presented a moral and political model, expressed in a mythological language, within a fundamental religious framework. Obviously the Indian epics were not meant to sustain the doctrinal orthodoxy of a historical revelation like the books of the Bible, but the point here is that they were a *serious* mythology, unlike the *Iliad* and the *Odyssey*, which in European Christianity no longer performed the canonical, even sacred, role they may have had in ancient Greece. Similarly, whilst Camões' epic poem (1572) may be comparable to the *Ramayana* in its tendency to idealize historical figures, to involve anthropomorphic gods and to promote a political-moral identity (that of Portugal as an imperial nation fulfilling a providential mission), as the expression of a 'poetic genre' which took special liberties and was nor meant to be 'believed', the epic of the Renaissance did not have an overarching role comparable to that of the Hindu epic in Vijayanagara. That is, Camões may have read the best chronicles to get his details, he was certainly attempting to be a good Christian when he brought in pious justifications, but in effect his poem operated within a uniquely western fictional space, delimited by secular history on the one hand and by dogmatic theology on the other. I am not here therefore describing two radical alternatives, Hindu and western, in a simple field of action concerning the definition of political authority, but rather two cultural fields of action, two traditions, in which the fundamental dilemma – how to sacralize power – was similar, but the symbolic strategies – to incorporate or to separate – were quite opposite.[19]

We need of course to consider in some more detail the political and religious culture of Vijayanagara which Europeans would have encountered, in order to establish more exactly how it adapted the brahminic tradition, and in particular what specific, contextually defined values lay behind the image of sacred kingship. Both Vijayanagara art

---

[19] In characterizing a tradition as a whole I must emphasize long-term patterns rather than specific contradictions, but it must be understood that the ultimate impossibility of the Christian–classical synthesis of the Renaissance was a subtle thing, and many sixteenth-century educated Europeans would only have been aware of their own attempts to build it. Thus Camões, following Vergil, presented Venus as an agent of divine providence in his epic poem about Gama's voyage – and his ecclesiastical censor had to explain away this embarrassing use of 'gentile gods' by recourse to poetic licence. Indeed, poetic licence alone allowed the western cultural system of the Renaissance to sort out its inner contradictions. The crucial point remains that this western system increasingly defined fictional, 'poetic' literature as a separate domain from either history or religion.

and dynastic tradition show a significant eclecticism, with Shiva and Vishnu equally honoured in special temples, and in diverse manifestations.[20] Historians tend to agree that while the Shaivite emphasis may have predominated as a royal cult in the first century of the history of the kingdom, with the new dynasties of the late fifteenth and sixteenth centuries there was a more distinct patronage of Vishnu cults, evident in the temples built in the capital city by Krishna Deva Raya and his successor Achyuta, and also in the patronage of temple complexes in the east such as that of Tirumalai-Tirupati near Chandragiri.[21] This shift was not separate from the actual evolution of personal and regional power-bases for kings and aspiring factions alike. The new imperial city of the fourteenth century had grown near the Shaiva temple of Hampi, and this growth was accompanied by the patronage of the *matha* (monastery) of Sringeri, located between the old Hoysala capitals and Vijayanagara. Sringeri became the base from which learned brahmins like Vidyaranya, a teacher of Advaita philosophy, set up a programme of intellectual reconstruction for dharmic orthodoxy under the shadow of the new kingdom – in fact claiming for Vidyaranya a crucial role in its very inception: Vijayanagara would be Vidyanagara, and the learned brahmin would be the guide of the victorious warrior.[22] Whether the legendary claims of the brahmins be true or not, in any case it can be established that their patronage was one of the key elements of the cultural policies of kings Bukka I and Harihara II at the end of the fourteenth century.[23]

[20] For a detailed discussion of religion in Vijayanagara, see Konduri Sarojini Devi, *Religion in Vijayanagara empire* (New Delhi, 1990), who summarizes a great deal of information and emphasizes the royal policy of religious tolerance.

[21] It is worth insisting that whilst sectarian cults could easily degenerate into petty squabbles, there were also efforts of synthesis, philosophical or iconographic, based on an understanding of a common religious purpose beyond this rivalry. The Shiva devotee did not necessarily exclude other gods, although he may have wished to focus on his personal devotion. Sometimes attributes of the rival god are incorporated in the other's main temple. For instance, there are a number of Shaivite figures in the Ramachandra temple built by Krishna Deva Raya. 'Harihara', the name of some of the more prominent members of the Sangama dynasty, literally meant 'Vishnu and Shiva', and the Harihara image in the Hoysala temple of the town of the same name near Sringeri is a representation of half of each god. It has also been suggested that Venkateshvara (Vishnu), god of Tirumalai-Tirupati, was originally Harihara too.

[22] Vidyaranya (*d.* 1386), also known as Madhavacarya in his earlier works, is classified as a Shaiva teacher of Advaita philosophy: Sarojini Devi, *Religion*, pp. 57–64. She, however, denies that he is to be identified with Madhavacarya (p. 13). The revival of Advaita philosophy in Sringeri implied a return to the transcendental monism of Shankara – often, it has been suggested, against the former influence of Jains. Too strict an ascription to Shaivism seems far-fetched, since Shankara's thought was essentially supra-sectarian, although it is true that in this period two enormously influential Vaishnava thinkers had emerged in the south, Ramanuja (twelfth century) and Madhva (thirteenth century), defending increasingly dualistic views.

[23] The claims of the Shaiva *matha* of Sringeri and the complex historiographical debate

On the other hand, the patronage of Tirupati, initiated by the Saluva and Tuluva dynasties as a way of consolidating their power base in the eastern part of the kingdom, could not fail to grow even further after the transfer of the imperial title to Chandragiri late in the sixteenth century.

Eclecticism (of a kind impossible in Europe) none the less remained essential to the religious–political legitimacy of the kingdom, because its strength derived from the collaboration of military elites with different regional and ethnic origins under the protective umbrella of sacred kingship. In a society divided by caste and sect, there was little else that could be called a political community. Religious patronage to some extent made up for the lack of political cohesion, providing a minimum ideological allegiance against the continuous threat of disintegration. In this light sectarian politics were no more than secondary reflections of a system based upon the principle of growth through incorporation. Tribal gods were identified with brahminic deities, and these were all represented in the political capitals in a number of manifestations which had their own followings. South Indian culture had also incorporated in a very distinctive way local cults to the 'mother goddess' of blood and power, and to various male warrior-gods, into its brahminic tradition – in particular, the goddess Durga was central to the Mahanavami festival, one of the most important political-religious rituals in Vijayanagara.[24] As old shrines like the Virupaksha temple by the Tungabhadra river (in itself an example of a river goddess, Pampa, having become the consort of a brahminic god) became popular centres of pilgrimage, ritual needs augmented, and the temples grew in concentric rectangles, gaining ever more spectacular additional enclosures, with their high towered gates (*gopuras*), elaborate pillared galleries and halls (*mandapas*), and secondary shrines. This kind of growth, which came to characterize Vijayanagara architecture, was of course possible because religious patronage was widespread among the elite. Islam and Jainism were also at least tolerated in Vijayanagara. Muslims were some of the best cavalry, and Islamicite influence was growing all over South India. Jains, on the other hand, were an established indigenous group which had exercised an

surrounding them have been discussed by Kulke, 'Maharajas, mahants and historians', pp. 130–6. Kulke is quite sceptical about the tradition that says that the *matha* was established by the philosopher Shankara *c.* 800. Instead, he believes that the legend was invented in the late fourteenth century in order to increase the prestige of the new religious establishment. He further suggests that rather than providing an initial impetus for the Sangama dynasty *c.* 1336, Vidyaranya only came to play an important role in Sringeri after *c.* 1374, building on the work of previous brahmin teachers although certainly developing a special relationship with the Vijayanagara kings.

[24] The interplay of these local goddesses and warriors and the brahminical tradition is discussed in S. Bayly, *Saints, goddesses and kings: Muslims and Christians in South Indian society 1700–1900* (Cambridge, 1989), pp. 27–44.

important cultural influence in the Hoysala royal courts (in the eleventh to the fourteenth centuries), although in the Vijayanagara period their position was receding under the pressure of the unfriendly competition of Bhakti cults. In this, as in everything else, kings could not fail to benefit from spreading their protection and patronage above sectarian distinctions (and it can be guessed that to that extent they welcomed Christian friars, like Luís do Salvador, too).

The originality of the Vijayanagara synthesis has been recently argued by Burton Stein from the analysis of political forms, in the form of a 'centralized prebendalism' superimposed upon traditional South Indian kingship as a response to the new military needs created by the competition of Muslim states in the north.[25] By contrast, Vijayanagara 'high' culture seems to have been fundamentally conservative and accumulative, geared towards the support of brahminical culture, and with emphasis on elaborate ornamentation and the eclectic patronage of traditional local deities. Although the kings developed their own devotional and political preferences through their patronage of temples, poets and philosophers, there is little evidence of any significant thematic innovation originating from the capital and imposed throughout the kingdom.[26] The style in art and architecture reflects this lack of originality: temples conservatively follow a southern 'Dravida' late-Chola model rather than the 'Vesara' synthesis of the Deccan favoured by the Hoysalas (with many buildings clustered at the site). The new Vijayanagara temples do incorporate some Deccani elements, whilst a new influence is most obvious in the many Muslim elements of the surviving secular architecture. Overall, what characterized the Vijayanagara synthesis is gigantism and a creative use and abuse of ornamentation within the structurally conservative models of the south.[27] A similar principle is apparent in its religious policies. The incorporation of new deities was usually the corollary to the incorporation of new lands – and most often what was brought to the capital was a new image of an old god.[28]

---

[25] Stein, *Vijayanagara*, pp. 140–6.

[26] Thus Thapar relativizes the idea of a 'Hindu' revival: *A history of India from the discovery to 1526*, pp. 333–5. Paradoxically, Stein prefers to see more originality in areas outside politics, which is, however, the one where some (of his own) claims can be substantiated. See Stein, *Vijayanagara*, p. xii.

[27] On Vijayanagara religious architecture in the general context of Indian art see J. C. Harle, *The art and architecture of the Indian subcontinent*, pp. 328–41. For individual temples, G. Michell, *The Penguin guide to the monuments of India*, vol. I: *Buddhist, Jain, Hindu* (Harmondsworth, 1989), pp. 397–403. Concerning the secular architecture of the capitals there is now the study by G. Michell, *The Vijayanagara courtly style* (New Delhi, 1992).

[28] When in 1513 Krisna Deva Raya successfully attacked the Gajapati ruler of Orissa, he took the image of Krishna in the Udayagiri fortress to his 'city of victory'.

Possibly the most precise answer to the question of what distinguished the Vijayanagara political–religious synthesis can be found in literary sources for which we can reconstruct a historical context. Two of our most informative Vijayanagara sources, the *Amuktamalyada* and the *Rayavacakamu*, both composed in the Telugu vernacular, deal with political success in terms which try to combine practical advice with *dharma*, on the basis of the image of the perfect king (that is to say, a manifestation of the divine Vishnu on earth). In both cases they represent a list of political maxims by incorporating sources of an independent origin, essentially conventional compendia with echoes from Kautilya's *Artha Sastra*, into the main body of the text.[29] Thus, for instance, in the *Amuktamalyada*, 'if when a king is bestowing equal attention to the *vargas, dharma* [religion], *artha* [wealth], and *kama* [love], by chance he shows more attention to *dharma*, it would be like allowing the surplus water intended to irrigate other fields [to] overflow and fertilize corn-fields. It would only conduce to enjoy [sic] of the sovereign'.[30] Or again, in the *Rayavacakamu*, the key to prosperity is dharmic conduct: 'if your majesty walks in the path of *dharma*, it is bound to rain thrice a month and the land will yield plenty'.[31] The *Amuktamalyada* was attributed to Krishna Deva Raya, while the *Rayavacakamu* is believed to have been written in the late sixteenth or early seventeenth centuries, although fictionally set back in his time. Although written at different times and in different contexts, from their contents one could argue that both works have a common root in brahminic culture, and that taken together they express a continuity in the concern for defining a Hindu royalty able to successfully maintain imperial authority. For instance the *Rayavacakamu* represented an attempt to define the qualities of divine kingship against the political crisis of South India, after the actual fragmentation of

[29] I have worked from the partial translations in A. Rangasvami Sarasvati, 'Political maxims of the emperor-poet Krishnadeva Raya', *Journal of Indian History*, 4 (1926): 61–88, and K. A. Nilakanta Sastri and N. Venkataramanayya, *Further sources of Vijayanagara History*, 3 vols. (Madras, 1946). I have subsequently been able to compare the latter to the more fluid translation of the *Rayavacakamu* by Philip Wagoner, *Tidings of the king*. Wagoner identifies the source for these maxims as the *Sabhapati Vacanamu*, a mid sixteenth-century prose work. It is, on the other hand, noteworthy that the *Amuktamalyada* seems to include advice specifically designed for the conditions of Vijayanagara.

[30] Rangasvami Sarasvati, 'Political maxims', p. 76. The translator, by rendering *dharma* as 'religion', and *artha* as 'wealth', is actually only giving an approximate equivalent, which can never do full justice to the complexity of each of these concepts, especially when one considers them in their dynamic relationships. Thus in certain contexts *dharma* should be translated as 'virtue', or 'law'. This dynamism is perfectly expressed in dramatic Sanskrit literature, such as the plays of Kalidasa, which focus on the complex relationship between love and duty.

[31] Nilakanta Sastri and Venkataramanayya, *Further sources*, vol. III, p. 141.

imperial authority, by projecting the image of Krishna Deva Raya as accomplished imperial dharmic ruler against Islamic pressure (which is portrayed as demonic). Written in the context of the virtually independent Telugu-speaking Nayaka court of Madurai, and probably by a brahmin counsellor, this work could not attempt to revive a unified Vijayanagara authority such as the one still claimed at the time by the rulers of Chandragiri, but instead sought to inform the political vision of a Nayaka lord according to the now quasi-mythical dharmic traditions of the earlier empire.[32]

The *Amuktamalyada* describes even more effectively the necessary relationship between royal power and brahminical tradition, one which reinforces their combined political dominance by connecting the local-historical to the cosmic-divine.[33] The story – about the virtuous daughter of an accomplished sage, Vishnuchitta of Srivillipittur – builds on a tradition of Vishnu worship, but at the same time brings together different South Indian 'local deities', and even claims to kingship, through the cumulative technique of telling a story within the story. The god often appears as a character, commanding the writing of the poem or even telling a story himself. The brahmin–sage is given a chance to present a sectarian Vaishnava philosophy and demolish its opponents.[34] The theme that holds together these diverse stories is ultimately based on classical Sanskrit drama and poetry: saints ('ascetic sages' and 'saintly maidens') interrelate with kings following a cosmic-godly pattern, in a

---

[32] Concerning the *Rayavacakamu* see the English translation and interesting study by Wagoner, *Tidings*, who argues that this work, written in the original form of an imaginary diplomatic report, in fact expresses a Hindu cultural answer to the pressure from Islam after the defeat of Talikota, by establishing a political doctrine in the form of an idealized historical account of the foundation of the kingdom and the successful reign of Krishna Deva Raya. Thus the courts of the nayakas from the end of the sixteenth century modelled their symbols of authority on the earlier success of Vijayanagara.

[33] My analysis of this work is necessarily very brief. For more details see Krishnaswami Aiyangar, *Sources of Vijayanagar History*, pp. 132–3, Rangasvami Sarasvati, 'Political maxims', pp. 61–4, and Sarojini Devi, *Religion*, pp. 91–5.

[34] Through the sage Vishnuchitta's disputations in the Pandya court, the author presents his sectarian views about the superiority of Vishnu and demolishes with his Visistadvaita philosophy (the qualified monism of Ramanuja, which insists on the direct relationship between an eternal human soul and God) all the alternative philosophical systems: Advaita, Sankhya and others. The emphasis on the god Venkatesvara and the obvious use of Tamil sources in a Telugu text seem to point towards a brahmin of Tirumalai-Tirupati, and a follower of Ramanuja's philosophy, as the possible author, perhaps trying to promote his sectarian views at the court. Some dynasties of musician–poets based on this temple were famous for defending similar philosophical and devotional views in this period. The establishment of Telugu nayakas in Madurai in the reign of Achyuta, in particular the adoption of Vaishnavism by Visvanatha Nayaka after obtaining control of the Pandya kingdom, may provide a meaningful context for the fabrication. However, in her analysis K. Sarojini Devi still insists on attributing the work to Krishna Deva Raya: *Religion*, pp. 91–5.

social search for a balance between *kama* (love) and *dharma* (moral order), which is also the condition for *artha* (prosperity). In the end kingship strengthens its sacred claims by establishing a pattern of renunciation which subjects the wielder of power to the master of learning.

Other examples, such as a poetic description of the coronation of Krishna's successor Achyuta in Vijayanagara in the *Achyutarayabhyudayam* of Rajanatha (*c.* 1535) point towards similar concerns and solutions.[35] In this case the ceremony of consecration according to traditional rules was by no means an empty ritual, since Achyuta's succession was seriously contested by a powerful faction. In the poet's description, the universalistic idea is expressed by the image of women from all countries attending to and performing a number of tasks. Women symbolized the various localities and therefore their service at the capital was also a symbolic strategy of incorporation. The facts may not be entirely correct (as a historical account, even if strictly contemporary, the poetic description is obviously incomplete and biased), but the extreme traditionalism with which kingship was portrayed according to dharmic ideal is what counted.[36]

The main limitation to using this kind of literary source is that we might be tempted to define the political and religious thought of the Vijayanagara period exclusively through the views of the brahmins, who always had their own axe to grind. Brahminic cultural dominance was unquestionable, but for instance the nayaka class may have held their own opinions about political affairs. The 'political maxims of Krishna Deva Raya' may actually be the political maxims *for* Krishna Deva Raya or one of his successors, perhaps even for those nayakas who used the Vijayanagara overlordship as a way of establishing their own regional power. When using these sources to compare a native political–religious ideology to the assumptions of European observers, we are effectively constrained within a brahminical discourse.

The pursuit of analogies remains tempting but elusive, because similar components – a sense of moral law inspired in the divine, a devotion based on faith, and an idea of spiritual perfection attained through asceticism – developed in Europe through a more narrowly defined cultural framework, involving a universal Church, a unique revelation and the ultimate separation of faith and reason. What emerges from the

---

[35] Krishnaswami Aiyangar, *Sources*, pp. 108–9 and 158–70. I also follow the analysis by D. Sridhara Babu, 'Kingship: state and religion in South India', inaugural dissertation (Göttingen, 1975), pp. 56ff. This Sanskrit work is considered as factually accurate by a number of Indian historians, although it is, nevertheless, essentially a court panegyric.

[36] As noted by D. Sridhara Babu in his conclusion, ibid., pp. 144–6.

analysis of the political-religious literature of Vijayanagara is that the brahminic discourse did not seek theological coherence as much as a flexible language of sacredness – unlike Christianity, which tended to reduce the scope of that language for the sake of doctrinal coherence. The key concept which we need to consider is *dharma*. At the same time supernatural, cosmic and social, it cannot be reduced to the European idea of *law*, in which the divine, the natural and the human are continuously distinguished and defined in relationship with each other. As Clifford Geertz wrote, the problem with translating dharma is that we find 'less a splintering of meaning . . . than imprecision of meaning', that is the expansion of a semantic domain 'to near infinite dimensions'.[37] Since everything has a 'law' according to its 'nature', no natural–human distinction is really possible, and no conflict of 'natural reason' against 'animal nature' is really moral. On the other hand, this 'law' does not have a universal expression, but relates to different groups as separate and in fact defines them as such. What gives unity to the dharmic cultural system is precisely the collective acceptance of the validity of the general frame of reference as a system of classification and orientation. *Dharma* is about everybody and everything having their own *dharma*, and kingship – the cornerstone of socio-political *dharma* – is about keeping the system of sacred relatedness together.

REACHING FOR THE CENTRE

It is obvious then that the difference in the definition of the fundamental domains of law actually implied different conceptions of kingship. Here again, at a superficial level we notice analogies. The Indian as well as the European believed in a centre, both political and ideal. Kingship was seen in all cases as a guarantee of order, and therefore the king was portrayed as a symbol of the prosperous social community, generally

[37] C. Geertz, *Local knowledge* (New York, 1983), pp. 197–9. On Hindu *dharma* and legal codes see J. D. M. Derrett, *Religion, law and the state in India* (London, 1968). I have also consulted the recent translation of the *Laws of Manu*, ed. by W. Doniger and B. K. Smith (Harmondsworth, 1991). Kane, *History of Dharmasastra*, vol. I, pp. 374–81, discusses the contribution of Madhavacarya, the brahmin who helped restore Hindu orthodoxy at the time of the growth of the Vijayanagara kingdom (he is, as I said, usually identified with Vidyaranya). Ibid., vol. III deals with ideas of kingship and justice. For justice in Vijayanagara there is the problem that sources tend to be idealistic and a number of historians follow suit. For instance Saletore, *Social and political life in the Vijayanagara Empire*, vol. I, chap. 7 posits the correspondence between classical prescription and Krishna Deva Raya's practice, but remains superficial for lack of historical contextualization. That is, while he attempts to criticize foreign observers like 'Abd al-Razzāq or Nunes on the basis of legal traditions, he fails to prove that these traditions were in fact an accurate guide to historical practice – could they ever be?

speaking the empire but, more emphatically, the city. This is clearly the meeting point between Nunes and his native sources: the history of Vijayanagara is a history of its kings, and the greatness of the kingdom has much to do with the virtue and success of its rulers.

However, in Vijayanagara the king was also a sacred figure who dramatized the search for a balance between virtue (*dharma*) and pleasure (*kama*). Because of his sacredness the king not only held supreme power but, through the mediation of the brahmins, whose temples he endowed, he also held supreme renunciation. In the rich sacred landscape of India there was no god or shrine that needed to be excluded, because the role of the king as a centre was merely dramatic and political. He enacted a cosmic pattern for the community, but he did not define the religious as such. There was no expectation of substantial change in a universe in which truth had existed fully from the beginning – history was in that sense cyclical.

Christianity had followed an altogether different course. Medieval pilgrims ultimately sought, in the Holy Land, the centre of the world. The story of Christ was a central historical event that defined past and future for eternity. Of course much of Christian piety and symbolism was abstract and mystical, like much of Hinduism, but Christian theological discourse occupied a radically different space. It set limits and defined boundaries where the brahminical tradition was open and fluid, it proclaimed universality where the brahminical tradition put up barriers and introduced distinctions. I argued earlier that John Mandeville had sought to include a map of the known world in his pilgrimage towards a reformed Christianity. By the time Paes and Nunes went to Vijayanagara, Prester John had become a purely historical Abyssinian ruler struggling to break out of his isolation, and the oriental Christians had been reduced to their modest size and described according to the castes and customs of the Malabar coast. The next stages in the rather sad history of the encounter of Roman Catholicism with indigenous Christianity would be the discovery of heresy, followed by various attempts to enforce papal authority, doctrine and rite in the context of mutual disappointment.[38]

Therefore, although European travellers liked Vijayanagara because

---

[38] On the Saint Thomas Christians see the summary in Lach, *Asia in the making of Europe*, vol. I, pp. 266–71, as well as L. W. Brown, *The Indian Christians of Saint Thomas* (Cambridge, 1956). Concerning the Portuguese settlement in Mylapore and its legends see also G. Schurhammer, *Francis Xavier: his life, his times*, vol. II, pp. 550–605, which includes a detailed account of the settlement at the time of the visit of Francis Xavier in 1545 (it is remarkable that his admirable scholarship does not prevent Schurhammer from maintaining a hagiographic interpretation). For the latter part of the century see S. Subrahmanyam, *Improvising empire*, chap. 3.

they found in it a centre, it was also, necessarily for them, a secular centre, outside any sacred landscape. Only a syncretic and mystical approach, inspired perhaps by Neoplatonism, could now conceive of bringing back the European language of sacrality to those areas that fell outside the orthodox path. This remained a lively but minority option for the European intellectual elite. Generally speaking, the Portuguese played a safer, more orthodox game. They indeed attempted to colonize the sacred landscape of India by appropriating, for instance, the remains, the legends and the physical space of the tomb of Saint Thomas the apostle in Mylapore. They filled their new sacred geography with missionary martyrs like Luís do Salvador or, much more famously, Francis Xavier. In this way they extended with sword, cross and pen their own thin veil of imaginary meanings while demonizing, manipulating or ignoring the thick texture of indigenous myths. Remaining nevertheless restricted to their own limited resources, and in contrast with the Spanish experience in the New World unable to conquer all, the Portuguese could hope to destroy little. The alternative to which the Jesuits committed themselves – conversion through cultural dialogue – had to rely on the acknowledgement of a centralized system of power defined in secular terms. Not surprisingly, it was also as part of a political purpose – to establish kingship over all religious traditions – that rulers such as Akbar listened to the Jesuits later in the century. Christians were welcome to sit in a room already crowded with Muslims, Hindus, Jains and Jews, and expound their doctrines, so that the king might judge them.

The predilection for centrality, the king as centre, is very obvious in Nunes, but receives a special emphasis in the narrative of Paes. This idea of the centre implicitly carries ideals of justice, wealth and power, but can also exclude the local and the contingent. The description of the king's power, even though it may be presented in secular and historical terms, creates a periphery in the discourse. To a remarkable extent, Paes succeeds in bringing this periphery into the centre by making all the details of the journey relevant to the final discovery. Although Nunes provides a more systematic interpretation of the kingdom's political system, with a special discussion of the revenues and the power of the military chiefs, it is Paes who gets closer to decoding the sacred nature of kingship. This cosmic dimension is, however, only hinted at, because his perspective is popular, that of an uninitiate. He observes a Hindu festival in much the same way as many Catholics might have participated in a procession, without really caring very much about the official theological discourses which underpinned it. But of course, Paes only observes, without full participation, because he does not want to contaminate his own identity with idolatry.

From the beginning, Paes explains that the ritual character of such festivals, and the reverence with which they are pursued, is reminiscent of Europe: 'You should know that among these gentiles there are days when they celebrate their feasts, as we do, and they have their days of fasting, when all day they eat nothing, and eat only at midnight.'[39] The most important festival, which starts on 12 September and lasts nine days, takes place at the royal palace in the capital city, and brings together all the important people of the kingdom: the king himself comes from his new city, so do all the prostitutes ('mulheres solteiras do reyno'),[40] and all the captains, kings and great lords who are not engaged in war or in the defence of remote frontiers. The festival is therefore a 'meeting at the centre'.

Paes then describes in full detail the inner courts of the palace complex, where the festival takes place. These huge courtyards are surrounded by walls and well guarded. The inner area is a space of display surrounded by low verandas, occupied by the lords and chiefs of the kingdom. The dancing girls ('mulheres solteyras') stand in two circles by the gates, adorned with many jewels. There are also eleven lofty wooden scaffoldings, specially made for the occasion, adorned with colourful cotton cloths, and three double-storeyed stone platforms, also hung with embroidered cloths. Here the king, his guests (including the Portuguese) and his household (favourites and eunuchs) may watch the spectacle. The principal platform stands on pillars 'shaped like elephants and other figures', and is called (like the city) 'house of victory', after the recent and successful war against Orissa (see plate 8).[41] A special gate connects this platform to the private palace of the king, where his 12,000 women servants live.

This is, so far, a picture of *artha* (power and abundance), and – as Nunes acknowledged in his own description of the festival – also of *kama*: 'in this way during these nine days they are obliged to search for those things which will give pleasure to the king'.[42] The arrangement soon acquires, however, a religious dimension in which the king is the connecting figure, while the 'house of victory' that separates the public and the private palaces is the connecting space.[43]

Thus, in the 'house of victory' the king has a rich throne, with a golden

[39] Lopes (ed.) *Chronica*, p. 100.
[40] Ibid., p. 104. The Mahanavami festival followed a lunar calendar (the first day of the month Asvina) and for this reason it started on a different day each year. This serves Sewell to date Paes's stay at 1520, although if Correa is not mistaken, it would seem that Figueiredo had already been sent to Vijayanagara as factor in 1517.
[41] Ibid., p. 101.   [42] Ibid., p. 67.
[43] My interpretation of Paes's account follows here the suggestions put forward in Fritz, Michell and Nagaraja Rao, *Where kings and gods meet*.

Plate 8 Mahanavami platform in the royal enclosure of Vijayanagara, seen from the south-west.
  and on the left side of the north of this open space is a great one-storeyed building . . .
  This building stands on pillars shaped like elephants and other figures, and is all open in
  the front. They climb to it by staircases made of stone. Around it, underneath, is a
  corridor paved with very good flagstones, where stand some of the people looking at the
  festival. This building is called the House of Victory, because it was made on occasion of
  the king returning from the war of Orissa (Sewell, *A Forgotten Empire*, p. 263, corrected
  from Lopes, *Chronica*, p. 101).

'idol', adorned with precious stones and flowers, and also a little shrine
made of cloth, which also belongs to the 'idol'. During the festival the
king sits on some cushions in front of this idol.[44]

  Paes was able to follow closely the rituals, and described them in great
detail. According to his observations, every morning the king performed
some ceremonies and prayers inside the shrine of the idol, and then, with
the help of several brahmins, he threw white roses and perfume to a
specified number of horses (eleven) and elephants (four), beautifully
adorned, who stood in the courtyard while the women danced. The ritual
involved several entrances and exits, in which the king, clearly acting on
behalf of the 'idol', and under the close supervision of brahmins,
alternatively became private and public, giver and receiver, actor and

[44] Lopes (ed.) *Chronica*, pp. 102–3.

spectator. At some point the curtains of the shrine were opened and the king, sitting inside, contemplated the sacrifice of twenty-four buffaloes and 150 sheep. Before retiring to his private quarters, the king received the ritual salutation and occasional gifts of his favourites, lords and chiefs.[45]

A different set of ceremonies, mainly involving wrestling and dancing, took place in the afternoons; and again a third set at night, by the light of lamps and torches, with other plays and stage battles, and also fireworks. The main emphasis of the description is on a procession of triumphal carts, horses, elephants and women. Paes is particularly interested in the ritual significance of horses, and in the extraordinary value of the precious stones and gold that the queens' maidens wear and display. At the close of each day, and before anyone eats anything, the king again performs the rituals involving the idol, similar to those of the morning, and witnesses the sacrifice of cattle, whose number is increased on the very last day.[46]

The presence of the idol unequivocally brings a dimension of sacrality (*dharma*) into the festival, but Paes is again unable to provide any identification of a distinctive mythological background – nothing that may allow us to identify the 'idol' with Durga, perhaps, with the king probably impersonating Rama.[47] On the other hand, the social and political implications of the ritual arrangements interest him a great deal – and, in that sense, *dharma* (which is also a social code) is present in the description. This reflects the area in which an analogy with a Portuguese

---

[45] Ibid., pp. 103–4.
[46] Ibid., pp. 105–10.
[47] Sarojini Devi, *Religion*, pp. 272–5, identifies this idol (Kalasa) with Durga on the basis of the *Markandeya Purana*. The nine days of the festival (hence the name Mahanavami or Navaratri) commemorate Durga's nine incarnations and victories against evil forces (the buffaloes sacrificed each day may represent the demon Mahisha, the most famous of Durga's foes). This would certainly be a fit prologue to the final parade of the armies of Vijayanagara on the tenth day (*Vijaya dasami*), which would refer to the expedition of Rama against Ravana. As Paes declares later, this same 'idol' was placed in the royal tent in front of which the military parade took place. Seen from this perspective, the ritual would associate the power of the female goddess to the military aims of the king of Vijayanagara, who during the ritual performs the role of Rama (and Vijayanagara is confirmed as Kishkindha, the country of Sugriva and Hanuman). After the ritual, which took place at the end of the monsoon, the war season was open. There is some additional evidence to suggest the identification of the king with the hero of the *Ramayana*. The temple of Rama at the edge of the royal enclosure was situated north of the large enclosure with the stone platform, in all probability the area where the festival took place. It is believed to have been built by Krishna Deva Raya *c*. 1513, and has been defined as 'the nucleus of the royal centre' (Fritz, Michell and Nagaraja Rao, *Where kings and gods meet*, p. 149), separating the private and public areas of royal activity. The walls of this temple depict episodes from the epic which involve celebrations of kingship with armies, dancing women and entertainers, i.e., similar scenes to those shown to Paes during his visit.

popular festival or a royal celebration would have been most immediate, and, from time to time, Paes does refer to the festival 'of the body of God' (Corpus Christi) in Lisbon.[48] The festival is not merely a display of wealth and art, but also of order and hierarchy, and Paes is eager to identify the special rights and pre-eminences of every group.

For instance, the prime minister Salvatinica (Saluva Timma), who made Krishna Deva Raya king, organizes everything, and his is the first triumphal car.[49] After the king has sat down, only the important kings 'of his race' who have given him their daughters in marriage can also sit, and stay near him. A special exception is made for wrestlers and dancing-women, who can eat betel and sit when they please.[50] Paes expresses his surprise that such women (whom he has earlier established are much honoured prostitutes attached to temples and living in the best streets) are allowed to become so wealthy.[51] It is only after the king is sitting in comfort, both he and the idol fanned with coloured horsetails by the brahmins who stand nearby, that the captains and principal men ('capitãees' and 'gente honrrada') are allowed to enter, in turn, and to position themselves on the verandas, followed by the captains of the king's guard, first those who carry shield and sword, and then the archers.[52] In summary, 'the officers of the household go about organising the people, and keeping all in their places. They are distributed among the doors so that nobody may come in apart from those whom they want to'.[53]

A similar sense of order is observed in the procession of women and eunuchs which comes from the private section of the palace – some of these women are hardly able to move because of the sheer quantity of gold and jewels that they wear.[54] But there can be little doubt that Paes was even more impressed by the display of power and magnificence involved in the army parade that he witnessed after the festival:

> I have no words to express what I saw there . . . in order to see all and tell about it, I went along with my head so often turned from one side to the other that I almost fell from my horse with my senses lost . . . I was truly so out of my wits that it seemed to me as if I was seeing a vision, and that I was in a dream.[55]

This dream-like experience was not so much a necessary outcome of an expedition into 'otherness', which never shook the deep conventional

---

[48] Lopes (ed.) *Chronica*, pp. 107 and 113.
[49] Ibid., pp. 105 and 107, but on p. 91 Paes called him Temersea, i.e., Timma Raya.
[50] Ibid., pp. 105–6.   [51] Ibid., pp. 106–7. Also p. 85.
[52] Ibid., p. 106.   [53] Ibid., p. 105.
[54] Ibid., pp. 108–9. See also Nunes in ibid. p. 67.
[55] Ibid., pp. 113–14.

beliefs of the Christian trader, as the result of a desperate attempt to see everything and record every detail. The shouting and shield-beating of the colourful crowd eventually overstretched his ability to hear and count.

Despite the fact that our indigenous sources for the interpretation of the festival are largely indirect, they do suggest the accuracy of Paes's description. However superficial, and perhaps thanks to the fact that it must remain superficial, his account does not fall into the trap (which so often affects the historical value of indigenous sources) of presenting ideal prescriptive rules as all there is to learn about a ritual event.[56] The reliability of Paes is confirmed by the fact that some ten or twelve years later Nunes, independently, provided a description which is remarkably similar, although differing in some details.[57] Nunes is sometimes more precise (for instance, the 'nine [not eleven] lofty wooden scaffoldings' are in fact 'castles' made by the principal captains of the kingdom), and sometimes he gives different numbers (thus, in the sacrifice, 'the first day they kill nine male buffaloes and nine sheep and nine goats, and thenceforward they kill each day more, always doubling the number').[58] But the general pattern of the ritual is clearly identical. One could argue that Nunes summarized more, but was probably in a position to distinguish and calculate better. Where the two accounts really differ is in emphasis, because, almost like a premonition of later trends, Nunes hints at a novel combination of wild ethnocentrism and secular cynicism. Thus the nine days of the festival may be celebrated 'in honour of the nine months during which Our Lady bore her Son in the womb' (*a honrra dos nove meses que nossa senhora trouxe seu filho no ventre*).[59] Despite his access to indigenous traditions, Nunes ultimately interprets all religious practices either as a corrupted Christianity or, more often, as purely political rituals: 'others say that they only do this because at this time the captains come to pay their rents to the king'.[60]

---

[56] There is, for instance, a description of the coronation of Krishna Deva Raya in the *Rayavacakamu*, as I said from a later tradition (late sixteenth or early seventeenth century). See Wagoner, *Tidings*, pp. 87–8. Here the king appears as a quasi-mythical model of wisdom and virtue, mainly in traditional brahminic terms. This account of Krishna's coronation ceremony clearly distorts the actual events by simplifying the line of royal succession towards a more 'lawful' model, and consequently presents the coronation 'as it is prescribed in the sastras'. The source is therefore valuable as an expression of the *idea* of the ritual, which involves reciting sacred texts (such as the abridged *Ramayana*), and specifies baths, gifts, music, dress and meals. The king has little initiative, and it is the lords, brahmins and court officials who invest him with sacrality. Afterwards he asks for instruction – a typical trick of Indian didactic literature, namely another occasion to explain to the king the full conventions of how he should rule according to *dharma*.

[57] Lopes (ed.) *Chronica*, pp. 66–8.

[58] Ibid., p. 66.   [59] Ibid.   [60] Ibid.

Confined within a more strictly descriptive language, Paes never offers an explanation that reduces the effect of the picture as a complex totality. The strength of his account is its very simplicity, the willingness to depict without offering explanations. It is only within this rhetoric that a symbolic bridge, however incomplete, could cross the distance between Portuguese Christian values and the Hindu rituals of Vijayanagara. We can say with some confidence that the bridge was genuine but indeed flimsy. On the other hand, an analysis of the social and political order, remarkable in its increasing precision, does emerge at this unpretentious descriptive level.

Paes gives a very brief explanation of the inner workings of a system that will allow a ruler to maintain an army of one million fighting men, including 35,000 armoured horsemen, so that 'he is the most feared king of any known in these parts'.[61] Developing patterns of thought very common in sixteenth-century Europe, he thinks that the economic prosperity brought by the many merchants prevents the kingdom from becoming empty of people, because it creates a balance between soldiers and men employed in other activities. He also observes with admiration the technical skill of the Muslim mercenaries, and then comments on the religious caste, the brahmins, who are 'like friars with us' and are seen everywhere in the kingdom. They follow special food prohibitions, are of a lighter complexion than the majority and have beautiful but modest wives. They are, as holy men, held in honour by the king. Although Paes had explained earlier that, besides these lettered men who look after the temples, other brahmins work as royal governors of towns and cities, and still others are merchants or landowners, he also remarks that 'they have little stomach for the use of arms' – and are, in this sense, not very useful to the king.[62]

The problem is, therefore, the collection of sufficient revenues to pay for the army. As Paes goes on to explain, the king's captains are in fact like noblemen, who hold towns and territories. They are obliged to maintain a substantial number of troops ready for battle, according to their revenues, and in addition they have to offer annual payments to the king. The troops are chosen and paid so as to give 'the best' possible troops. The king has also a number of troops whom he pays directly from the revenues of the capital city, and in particular many horses and elephants. His captains, and some other petty kings who are also his vassals, send him presents on his birthday, and when he has children. In fact, the annual offering of revenues is very much part of the ritual, as it takes place during the New Year festival, soon after the other festival is

[61] Ibid., p. 114.   [62] Ibid., pp. 87–8 and 114.

finished.[63] In order to preserve this wealth the kings have a well-supplied treasury into which they must ordinarily put more than they take out.[64]

The pattern of Paes's description can be recognized in any modern attempt to understand the political system of Vijayanagara, but clearly here this 'system' is portrayed at its best. The chronicle written by Nunes during the time of a weaker king, Achyuta Raya, offers a glimpse of what happened when the supreme ruler was not in full command. However, Nunes's understanding of political change still leaves us in a simplified political world in which everything depends on the personality of the ruler; that is, unless we are able to uncover the inner tensions of a system that necessarily, if only by analogy with other aristocratic, 'feudal' systems, must have suffered divisions and factions. I am talking not only about rivalry between chiefs, or between chiefs and brahmins, but also between the king and his almost independent captains, who (from Paes's description) were in a position to tax lands and raise armies before they had to submit to royal authority. Burton Stein has convincingly shown some of these tensions in operation,[65] but we do not, in fact, need to wait for modern scholarship to find them. Fernão Nunes, in his chronicle of the kings of Vijayanagara, not only portrayed the rulers with their human weakness: he also thought that the social fabric, with its greedy brahmins and overtaxed peasants, was faulty. By restoring time to a description of otherness, he went beyond the system of social customs of Barbosa and the colourful human geography of Paes, and identified the movements of political improvement and corruption in their historical particularity.

---

[63] According to Paes, it took place on the eleventh day of October the year he was there, that is to say the new moon with which the first month of the year began. On that occasion everybody wore nice dresses.

[64] Lopes (ed.) *Chronica*, pp. 115–16.

[65] This is perhaps the main theme of Stein, *Vijayanagara*.

8. The historical dimension: from native traditions to European orientalism

The Portuguese and Spanish chronicles of overseas discovery and conquest written in the sixteenth century constitute an important group among the genres of Renaissance historiography. Rather than drawing on pure classical models, they followed a vigorous indigenous tradition of medieval chronicles, books of 'deeds' of kings and lords often written by secular authors, but providentialist and moralistic none the less. This was a tradition very much marked by the mythologisation of the process of territorial expansion of the Christian kingdoms as a kind of reconquest or crusade, which by the twelfth century had fused the concepts of *patria* and Christendom.[1] In Portugal, as in other parts of the Iberian Peninsula, these chronicles thus evolved from feudal epic towards a prose narrative centred on royal dynasties and a vaguely defined nation. The new emphasis on collective achievements (notwithstanding the hierarchical character of these societies) is especially obvious in the fourteenth and fifteenth centuries. It made it possible to accommodate the fact that whilst the truly valid historical enemies were Muslim infidels, often the actual enemies were rival Christian powers. We might consider the examples of Ramon Muntaner (1256–1336), self-appointed chronicler of the providential success of the House of Barcelona and their Catalan

---

[1] On the complexities of the early phases of this process, from the ninth to the thirteenth centuries, see P. Linehan, *History and the historians of medieval Spain* (Oxford, 1993). For the fusion of the concepts of *patria* and Christendom see p. 294. R. Fletcher *The quest for El Cid* (Oxford, 1989), has insisted on the obvious point that the ideology of crusade was often superimposed on a process of conquest which obeyed more opportunistic motivations. However, there is no denying the global psychological impact of the long-standing ideas of reconquest and religious war in medieval Christian Spain (ideological idealism does not require lack of base material motives, nor even lack of contradictions, in order to be a historical force).

251

subjects against Muslim and French–Angevin enemies alike, or the Portuguese Fernão Lopes (c. 1380–c. 1460), whose account of the succession struggle of 1383–5, which saw the triumph of the House of Avis, was marked by a remarkably populist, anti-Castilian rhetoric. Similarly in Castile, increasingly the hegemonic power in the peninsula, there was a logical continuity between the twelfth-century appropriation of the theme of the restoration of the pre-Islamic Visigothic Christian kingdom to proclaim a kind of pan-Hispanic imperialism (a move which of course did not please its Christian neighbours), and the conquest of Granada by the Catholic kings at the end of the fifteenth century. This conquest was formulated as the completion of a process of re-conquest, finally made possible, in sharp contrast with decades of civil disorder, by the leading role of a strong Castilian monarchy in union with Aragon.

Within these three historiographical traditions of the Iberian Peninsula – Portuguese, Castilian and Catalan–Aragonese – rival political projects coexisted with a remarkably homogeneous rhetoric of expansion based on a religious and monarchical ideology. By extending these narratives to overseas conquests, the chroniclers of the fifteenth and sixteenth centuries could perpetuate social ideals and rhetorical techniques that belonged to the medieval chivalric ethos, colouring empirical accounts and if necessary distorting them (it was thus that in Cortés' letters to Emperor Charles, Mesoamerican temples were described as 'mosques', in an obvious appeal to the ideology of the conquest of Granada as support for that of idolatrous Mexico).[2] In their accounts of the exploration of Africa, or of the conquests of the New World and India, they wrote tales of honourable struggle and providential success in praise of particular princes and their loyal subjects.

The fact that from the fifteenth century some of these chroniclers were also aware of classical models did not alter significantly the nature of the exercise, it simply widened the range of rhetorical skills at the disposal of the writer and his critics.[3] Thus, in Portugal and Spain, Livy could serve as an elegant model for a rhetoric of overseas expansion precisely because his *History of Rome* already articulated a Roman myth of national origins and sustained imperialism. Stylish humanist historians like João de Barros in Portugal, who researched thoroughly, planned

---

[2] Especially in the first and second letters. See H. Cortés, *Cartas de relación*, ed. by A. Delgado Gómez (Madrid, 1993), pp. 142, 195, etc.

[3] As early as 1390 Pero López de Ayala, the chancellor of Castile, translated Livy into Castilian, but this does not alter the essentially medieval character of his own chronicles, however admirably informed and measured in tone (R. B. Tate, 'López de Ayala, humanist historian?', *Hispanic Review*, 25 (1957): 157–74). In reality Ayala's translation was made from the French version of Pierre Bersiure: J. Simon Díaz, *Bibliografía de las literaturas hispánicas*, 3 vols. (Madrid, 1963), vol. I, p. 207.

logically and wrote carefully, were only the more sophisticated propagators of essentially tribal myths, interpreting the activities of greedy predators as the agents of Christianity and civilization (although in some cases, like the Spanish historian Pedro Cieza de León in Peru, these writers were also able to express with remarkable depth their anguish for the contradictions between declared aims and performed cruelties).[4] The more polished Renaissance historians brought about a shift of emphasis, outlining broad geographical perspectives (like Barros for Portuguese Asia, or Gonzalo Fernández de Oviedo in the New World), inventing classical orations which dramatized the conflicts between conquerors and conquered (like Gómara in his version of the conquests of Mexico and Peru), and reaching a wider audience, perhaps even engaging in elaborate ideological justifications of their patrons' prestige and rights (like Peter Martyr of Anghiera and Jerónimo Osório with their Latin histories). Authors like Oviedo or Diogo do Couto could also reflect on the paradoxical fact that providential success was not always fully realized, and that the respective failings of Spanish and Portuguese Christians – essentially moral failings – must be responsible for not a few tragedies and misfortunes in their respective imperial ventures.

All these educated writers did not, however, lose their dependence on more popular sources: those letters and descriptive 'relations' written by men who by seeking to establish a personal record of merits also established an empirical record of historical events, and whose basic moral world, the subjection of the ruthless prosecution of personal profit to the discipline of service to God, king and *patria*, the armchair writers often echoed. In authors like Barros, classical literary models thus coexisted with a medieval heart which was dynastic, feudal-epic and nationalist, in a formula which came to define the Hispanic Renaissance.

The comparison of the writings of armchair historians with their sources is often one of the most fruitful ways of assessing subtle shifts of emphasis and interpretation. For example, José da Silva Horta's recent analysis of the way in which Barros used the chronicle by Zurara uncovers the subtle change from the fifteenth-century emphasis on divine predestination in the rhetorical formulation of Prince Henry's initiative as promoter of commercial and piratical expeditions along the coasts of Africa, to a new emphasis on the perception of the hero's personal political responsibility, from the vantage point of the historian who knows that the early forays in Guinea were actually the beginnings of a

---

[4] Among the more ambitious and sophisticated chroniclers of overseas discovery and conquest, Pedro Cieza de León was exceptional in that he was self-educated, having travelled in the Indies very young, and in that sense was not an armchair historian.

more ambitious imperial enterprise.[5] Barros's move is, indeed, a transformation shaped by a rigid ideological scheme, of a national myth in the light of new historical perspectives, that is, an elaboration rather than an abandonment of medieval principles and identities. One could argue that this same moral language and mythical horizon to a large extent still framed the consciousness of imperial crisis expressed by writers like Couto, Barros's official continuator, at the turn of the seventeenth century.

The imperial stimulus meant that the late medieval and early modern historiography in the Iberian Peninsula was one of the most vigorous in Europe for this period. The primary milieu for this historiographical genre was certainly the court, and its function was essentially propaganda. Gomes Eanes de Zurara's prologue to his 1448 chronicle of the discovery and conquest of Guinea (coastal western Africa) shows an author fully aware that he had been commissioned to fashion an exemplary image of the extraordinary deeds and virtues of Prince Henry from his maritime initiatives, effectively a myth which would serve the House of Avis both at home and abroad.[6] However, this exercise was not straightforward: as Zurara reflected, praise for some was often read as neglect for others. Another historian, Fernão Lopes, had defined the essential problem a few years earlier (c. 1443): 'The force of interest has often given to many of those charged with the writing of history a great deal of licence with truth' – an 'interest' which included patriotism as well as aristocratic family honour.[7] The writing of history actually involved a balancing act between telling and not telling, conditioned by the powerful principles of exemplarity and, increasingly too, accuracy. As a result, historians constantly struggled with an ideal of historical truth, rooted, to a great extent, in an idea of personal experience, either direct or secondary. For Fernão Lopes de Castanheda, having been in India was a guarantee that he would not be easily deceived by his sources.[8] While humanist authors like João de Barros, or López de Gómara who wrote about the Spanish conquest of America, displayed a remarkable command of style and overall plan, the more 'popular'

[5] J. da Silva Horta, 'Uma leitura de Zurara por João de Barros's, in *Amar, sentir e viver a História. Estudos de homenagem a Joaquim Veríssimo Serrão* (Lisbon, 1995), pp. 673–702.

[6] Azurara, *Crónica do descobrimento e conquista da Guiné*, pp. 25–7. Azurara (or Zurara) was the successor of Fernão Lopes in his job as keeper of the royal archives (*guarda-mor da Torre do Tombo*).

[7] F. Lopes, *Crónica de D. João I*, ed. by H. Baquero Moreno (Lisbon, 1983), p. 84. These are the opening words of his prologue to the chronicle of John I of the House of Avis. In the name of impartiality Lopes went on to develop, with superb skill, a no less patriotic and partisan interpretation of the events of 1383–5 which led to the establishment of the Avis dynasty.

[8] Castanheda, *História*, vol. I, pp. 494–5 (from the prologue to book 3).

writers like Gaspar Correa or Bernal Díaz del Castillo often displayed an extreme emphasis on observed detail and were able to present their personal experience as a corrective to the rhetorical bias of the more educated writers (a claim for authority which was, of course, another rhetorical trick).[9]

There was certainly a progression in terms of what could be deemed as acceptably accurate throughout the period, from the obvious exaggerations of Ramon Muntaner in his account of Catalan victories in Sicily to the careful conflation of documents of sixteenth-century writers like the Aragonese Jerónimo Zurita. To some extent, the very multiplication of historical narratives, often contradictory, combined with humanist critical standards, created a context which helped define strict standards of accuracy. Primary narratives of conquest and discovery, in particular, where immediate information for the sake of a global imperial enterprise was often more important than political education, show a remarkably high standard of empirical accuracy, forming habits of composition which even appear almost instinctively in otherwise polemical documents. But this was never a process that fully eliminated the personal and political bias in the production and transformation of narratives, nor was a tendency towards criticism and honesty independent of individual talents. That writers like Castanheda, in their accounts of Portuguese exploits in India, needed to respond to the pressure of the imperial doctrine prevailing at the court at any given time, did not necessarily determine their mode of writing, or even their essential truthfulness.[10]

What made the chronicles of conquest overseas original was, in the first place, the fact that the figure of the king necessarily diminished, because the ruler could only be made the direct protagonist of imperial policy in a European context. In this sense these narratives accelerated a process which had been only incipient in European historiography. Conquerors and governors, and the nation in general (Catalans, Casti-

---

[9] On Portuguese historiography see A. F. G. Bell, *Gaspar Correa* (Oxford, 1924) and *Diogo do Couto* (Oxford, 1924); Rodrigues Lapa, *Historiadores quinhenistas* (Lisbon, 1942); Harrison, 'Five Portuguese historians'; Boxer, *João de Barros*. The claim to personal experience became part of the rhetorical repertoire of Europeans writers settled overseas, who were developing a distinctive historical consciousness by the end of the sixteenth century. In Portuguese India, an example would be Diogo do Couto.

[10] Castanheda is an exceptionally valuable historian from a factual perspective, less restrained in his provision of detail (including damning detail) than his great rival João de Barros, for whom social decorum was crucial to his task as historian. Rather than brute truth, Barros sought educational truth according to an imperial ideological programme. But Castanheda was not immune to the reception of royal orthodoxy concerning the basic myths of the discovery, as has been shown by Rebelo, 'Providencialismo e profecia', 77–9.

lians, Portuguese), became protagonists.[11] It was the collective deeds of the Portuguese or their interactions that, in the end, justified and organized the historical narrative of writers like Castanheda.[12] Moreover, by placing these adventurers in specific alien contexts the chroniclers were in a position to respond to the need for a geographical and ethnographical background peopled with something more than stereotypes and symbols. Indians and Moors – and, more particularly, their kings and their captains – became historical agents next to the Castilians and the Portuguese. As such, they were able to make (at least implicitly) historical choices. They not only interacted with Europeans, but also had concerns of their own. The case of Vijayanagara offers a wide range of examples. Thus Correa described in detail the dynastic struggles at the death of King Achyuta in the fourth book of his *Lendas*, while Barros wrote about the wars of Krishna Deva Raya in his third decade, and Couto included an important summary of Vijayanagara history in the sixth decade.[13]

That Indians would emerge as dignified historical agents agreed not only with classical precedents, but also with the Spanish late medieval historiographical treatment of the Moors of Granada. This found its fullest expression in sixteenth-century literature, for instance with the

---

[11] Muntaner's fourteenth-century account of the Catalan Company in Greece stands as a precocious example of this essentially sixteenth-century model. It is worth noting that under successive dynastic unions the idea of a 'Spanish' nation progressively (but never fully) integrated different national traditions. The fact of Castilian dominance and the resistance it provoked meant that the term remained problematic. From the times of the Catholic kings in effect two different uses existed side by side: whilst Catalan and Portuguese humanist writers like Margarit, Góis and Barros referred to 'Spain' in its classical sense, encompassing the different nations of 'Hispania', chroniclers like Pedro Cieza de León described the conquerors of Peru as a single 'Spanish' nation, although in fact they were almost exclusively subjects of the crown of Castile. The incorporation of Portugal into the Spanish crown after 1580 did not clarify the concept either.

[12] This was in no way meant to diminish the glory of the kings of Portugal, to whom the chronicles were dedicated. Thus Castanheda, even when dedicating the first book of his *History of the discovery and conquest of India by the Portuguese* to John III, made it explicit that the fact that the Portuguese conquests were overseas and without the personal leadership of the king placed them above any achievement of the ancients – Greeks, Romans or 'barbarians' (Castanheda, *História*, vol. I, p. 4). The inevitable consequence was that the emphasis shifted from the glorification of the kings to the glorification of the nation.

[13] Diogo do Couto, decade VI, book 5, chap. 5, which includes his summary of Vijayanagara history, corresponds to vol. XIV, pp. 376–85 of the eighteenth-century combined edition of Barros and Couto, *Da Ásia* (Lisbon, 1777–88). The original edition of 1614 is very rare because most copies were burnt. Given the lack of modern editions of Couto's decades, I will quote by decade, book and chapter. Couto's 'sixth' decade was in reality his third, the system of numbering having been adjusted to the idea that his work was an official continuation of Barros's text (Barros produced four decades, although the fourth was not published until 1615 by João Baptista Lavanha, thus overlapping with Couto's 'fourth', published in 1602).

beautiful anonymous novella *Abencerraje* (1565), a rhetorical elaboration of a popular frontier theme around the themes of love and honour across cultures.[14] One must be wary, however, of assimilating these nice literary explorations to actual patterns of relationships with non-Christians, especially in their colonial contexts. The *moriscos* of Granada were being driven to rebellion and even expelled from Spain at the same time as the love of the Abencerraje and its implied theme of generosity towards honourable enemies became a theme in popular poetry – in a way similar to how the violent suppression of the Araucanian Indians of Chile could nevertheless inspire a conqueror like Alonso de Ercilla to sing of their courage in a magnificent, classically inspired, perhaps even subtly ambivalent epic poem *La Araucana* (1597).

Another, more remarkable, step was to write a chronicle exclusively focused on the history of an indigenous society without any reference to the providential Christian background that ultimately underpinned all European chronicles. This is what Fernão Nunes accomplished with his account of Vijayanagara, preceding the efforts of the official historians Barros and Couto to incorporate a historical vision of the Hindu kingdom in their narratives (and, in fact, in his own account of the wars of Krishna Deva Raya, Barros merely summarized a section of Nunes's work).

THE EUROPEAN HISTORIAN AND HIS NATIVE SOURCES

The rarity of Nunes's indigenous focus raises the question of whether a particular explanation is needed. Unlike some of the early historians of the American Indies who wrote about indigenous traditions (for instance Inca Garcilaso, famous for his publications on pre-Hispanic Peru in the early seventeenth century), Nunes was not of mixed ancestry, responding to a complex personal heritage. Neither was he a missionary concerned with the salvation of human souls, like those Franciscan, Dominican and Jesuit writers who wrote the history of the Aztecs in the 1570s and 80s by organizing interviews and retrieving an indigenous chronicle. He was not motivated by a royal commission either, like the humanist doctor Francisco Hernández, whose Latin history of the 'antiquities' of Mexico (one largely based on the previous work of the Franciscan missionary Bernardino of Sahagún) responded to a unique context – in 1570 he had been sent by Philip II to lead what amounts to the first systematic

---

[14] *El Abencerraje (novela y romancero)*, ed. by F. López Estrada (Madrid, 1987), including a discussion of different versions. On the general literary context, see also S. Carrasco Urgoiti, *El moro de Granada en la literatura (del siglo XV al siglo XVII)*, (Madrid, 1956).

naturalist scientific expedition to the New World. This enterprise, we might note here, finds no real parallel in Portuguese Asia.

Nunes's circumstances also set him apart from a historian like Pedro Cieza de León, whose record of Peruvian pre-Hispanic history c. 1550, although standing as an autonomous part of his magnificent chronicle, and fully based on Inca traditions through interviews with the men charged with keeping the kingdom's memory, clearly belonged to the context of a successful, if tragic, conquest. From this perspective Inca civilization, however admirable, was necessarily interpreted by Cieza in the light of the triumph of Christianity, and his judgement of the rationality of Indians was inevitably bound up with actual debates about the character of their idolatry. Accordingly, Cieza's rationalization of the Inca myths of origin was simultaneously a dogmatic guarantee of the Christian monopoly of divine power and a humanitarian attempt to set limits to the devil's hold on Indian civility.

All these preoccupations were absent from Nunes's chronicle. In contrast with sixteenth-century writers on Mexican and Peruvian 'antiquities', he wrote exclusively as an external observer, not free from value judgements but certainly free from the twin (and sometimes incompatible) responsibilities of converting and preserving the conquered, which so deeply affected Spanish writers in America. For this reason, his account of Vijayanagara in the 1530s can be better compared to the more widespread phenomenon of contemporary European interest in the history of the Ottoman Turks.[15] Vijayanagara, like the Ottoman empire, represented a civilized, essentially independent and perhaps even threatening non-Christian society, and this justified an attempt to understand it in the terms of its origins and development, that is, in terms of a secular, historical tradition. Such an exercise required the learning of languages and, ultimately, the translation of indigenous sources. Although Paes, suggesting a smattering of antiquarian erudition, occasionally compared the peoples of Vijayanagara with the ancient Romans,[16] Nunes found nothing in the Bible or in the histories of Alexander in India which he could use as a frame of reference for his account. Stretching the narrative back to the thirteenth century, and

---

[15] On the Ottoman empire the number of publications was enormous in the first half of the sixteenth century alone. For a detailed list see C. Gölner, *Turcica: die europäischen Turkendrücke des XVI Jahrhunderts*, 2 vols. (Berlin, 1961–8). Concerning fifteenth-century accounts, also very numerous, see Cochrane, *Historians and historiography*, pp. 328–37.

[16] 'There are other shoes that have nothing but soles, but on top are some straps which help to keep them on the feet. They are made like those which of old the Romans were wont to wear, as you will find on figures in some papers or antiquities which come from Italy': Sewell, *A forgotten empire*, p. 252.

carrying it forward to his own times, he wrote about what he observed, what he was told and, crucially, what he found in native writings. He did not necessarily read a Dravidian script, or of course Sanskrit. It is more likely that he understood the local language and had a Kanarese or Telugu chronicle read aloud to him by a native, possibly a brahmin who had access to a copy. Thus the chronicle – that is, the historical part of Nunes's narrative – must have been the result of a collaboration, although as he approached his own times Nunes obviously elaborated the material with his own judgements and observations. This collaborative use of native sources is not of course entirely isolated. Diogo do Couto, for example, working well after the fall of the city, also wrote about Vijayanagara 'according to their writings'.[17]

It was perfectly logical that this use of native chronicles would accommodate an emphasis on legendary origins, because interest in a mythical past with some claims to historical validity was something early European travellers could understand as being analogous to what was common in their own societies. The mythical foundation of Vijayanagara *c.* 1336 is a well-known theme in the indigenous tradition, as has been recorded by European historians from the beginning of the nineteenth century.[18] The most influential version of this tradition, expressed in a number of brief Kannada chronicles, is associated with the figure of

---

[17] That is, 'segundo suas escrituras'. See Couto, VI, 5, 5: 'Do fundamento deste Reino Canará, e origem de seus reis com todos os que até hoje reinaram: e donde nasceo chamarem a este Reino de Bisnagá, e de Narsinga'. Couto, based in Goa in the late sixteenth century, might possibly have had direct access to a Kanarese chronicle, but this is not certain – he is also known for having appropriated the work of people like Agostinho de Azevedo, who translated indigenous sources, as his own. On the other hand, the process followed by Nunes is not too different from the one which allowed Mark Wilks, resident for the East India Company at the court of Mysore, to present a version of Vijayanagara history in English in 1810 on the basis of an eighteenth-century Kannada cotton scroll written by a brahmin. The parallel is the more intriguing if we consider that almost three centuries separated these two efforts to bring the history of Vijayanagara into a European language.

[18] Nunes begins his chronicle with the year 1230. This is not really a mistake of a hundred years on the part of Nunes, as Sewell thought, because it is very likely that he was following a native year in the Salivahana-Saka era (Nunes actually writes 'na era de mil e duzentos e trinta anos'). The SS era begins in AD 78, supposedly after the Shaka (invading Scythian) kings of the first century, and follows a solar calendar (Hindus used a solar as well as a lunar calendar for religious festivals). Thus in some of the native accounts of the foundation of the city by Vidyaranya, the year given is usually SS 1258 (AD 1336) – a date accepted by modern historians. Nunes's chronology is generally consistent provided we change Christian for native years: his SS 1230 corresponds to AD 1308 – close enough to the years when the eunuch Malik Nayb, general of sultan 'Ala ad-Din, actually attacked the Kakatiya and Hoysala capitals of Warangal (1309) and Dvarasamudra (1310). This basically fits with the gist of Nunes's story. Couto, who followed a slightly different version of the native account of the origins of the city, begins with the Indian year SS 1220, but like Nunes fails to notice a discrepancy and even writes 'nos anos de mil duzentos e vinte *de nossa Redempção*'.

Vidyaranya and bears remarkable similarities to Nunes's account.[19] Couto, independently, also recorded a similar story, which proves that it was well known.[20] The comparison between these different versions offers us a rare opportunity to explore how the Europeans related their own historiographical practice to the native tradition.

The myth of origin of Vijayanagara has two central themes. The first one is that a holy man – a wise and ascetic brahmin called Vidyaranya, sometimes explicitly associated with the worship of Virupaksha by the Tungabhadra river – chose two famous brothers, Harihara and Bukka, to build a city on that spot, guaranteeing sacredness and, consequently, promising worldly success. In the *Keladinripavijayam*, for instance, the emphasis of Vidyaranya's sacred mission is the need for the establishment of a virtuous, dharmic rule under the tutelary power of Virupaksha, the local god.[21] In these sources the role of the sage is more clearly delineated than the origin of the first kings, whose exact position, between the Hoysala dynasty of southern Karnataka and the Muslim rulers of Delhi, is ambiguous.

This is also true of Couto's Portuguese version of the foundation of the city, which resembles a classical explanation of the origins of civil society by secularizing the role of the sage, so that the 'holy man' is above all a lawgiver. In this account, the first king of Vijayanagara was merely a local shepherd who brought milk to the sage, and the foundational emphasis is on the establishment of imperial overlordship over local chiefs and tribes. The successful fight against the Muslims of Delhi,

---

[19] See Nilakanta Sastri and Venkataramanayya, *Further sources of Vijayanagara history*, vol. III, pp. 6–8, summarizing the *Keladinripavijayam*. Also pp. 9–15, summarizing the *Vidyaranya Vrttanta* and the *Vidyaranya Kalajnana*, two of the manuscripts collected by the British military surveyor and antiquarian Colonel Colin Mackenzie in the early nineteenth century. N. Venkataramanayya considered these traditions essentially reliable and of considerable antiquity (tracing the *Vidyaranya Kalajnana* back to the close of the fifteenth century). He therefore used them to support his controversial interpretation of the foundation of the kingdom by Harihara and Bukka. However, more recently H. Kulke has been sceptical about the value of the material associated with Vidyaranya, arguing instead that the sage did not help found Vijayanagara, but intervened quite a few years later, establishing a 'new system of [religious and legal] orthodoxy to counteract the influence of Islamic inroads into South India': Kulke, 'Maharajas, mahants and historians', p. 135. This act of 'intentional cultural policy' would explain the legendary associations between the new royal line and the centre of religious learning at Sringeri which became Vidyaranya's base. Furthermore, the agreement of many chronicles would be no more than an effect of the success of the strategy cultivated at Sringeri over the centuries, involving (for example) the sixteenth-century forgery of temple inscriptions, dated back to the foundation of the kingdom. Kulke believes that chronicles like the *Vidyaranya Kalajnana* should be dated after 1580. I must observe, however, that Nunes's chronicle is good evidence that the legend held full sway during the reign of Krishna Deva Raya if not earlier.

[20] Couto, VI, 5, 5.

[21] Sastri and Venkataramanayya, *Further sources*, vol. III, pp. 6–8.

which is the second important theme of the indigenous tradition, and the foundation, as a memorial, of the 'city of victory' (*Visajá Nager*), are clearly portrayed by Couto as later developments.[22]

Without abandoning the emphasis on the role of the hermit–sage, Nunes followed those South Indian traditions which also insisted on the identity of Harihara and Bukka as dignified prisoners, and, subsequently, successful ministers of Delhi.[23] According to Nunes the king of Bisnaga – that is, the Hindu king of the region of Kanará (modern Karnataka) – lost his city, Nagundy, to the sultan of Delhi. He and his people, according to a ritual sense of honour, sacrificed all their families before giving themselves up.[24] However, the sultan's new governor, one Meliquy niby (Malik Nayb), proved unable to subdue the local people, and finally the Sultan proclaimed an old minister of the kingdom – one of the few who had not participated in the collective suicide – as king. This was the origin of the new dynasty.[25] The foundation of a new city

---

[22] Couto, VI, 5, 5.

[23] As in the *Vidyaranya Vrttanta* and *Vidyaranya Kalajnana*, in Sastri and Venkataramanayya, *Further sources*, vol. III, pp. 9–15.

[24] This king of Bisnaga *c.* 1310 must be the Hoysala ruler, since Vijayanagara, properly speaking, did not exist. Anegondi is an old fortified site and temple complex on the northern side of the Tungabhadra river, opposite the sacred area of Vijayanagara. It was important in the fourteenth and fifteenth centuries. Nunes's account is to that extent coherent. Stein considers Anegondi a key fortress of the kingdom of Kampili, which became a new regional power and an important centre of resistance to the Turkish invaders in the early fourteenth century, until Muhammad b. Tughluq crushed it in 1327: Stein, *Vijayanagara*, pp. 18–19. Nunes's account then appears as a version of the destruction of Kampili, and suggests a kind of continuity between Kampili and Vijayanagara, which a number of modern historians support. Nunes does not, however, mention Ibn Battūta's observation that Muhammad b. Tughluq sent Khvaja Jahan against Kampili because its ruler (Kampiladevaraya) had protected a Muslim rebel emir from Devagiri, Baha' ad-Din Gurshasp: Ibn Battūta, *A través del Islam*, pp. 571–2.

[25] Therefore, Nunes agrees with the Kannada chronicles in presenting the new dynasty as originally an agency of Delhi, although he does not mention any wars against the Hoysalas on behalf of the sultan. The *Vidyaranya Vrttanta* and the *Vidyaranya Kalajnana* make it quite clear that the Sangama brothers had originally been ministers of the king of Warangal in Telingana, were later sent by their captor, the sultan of Delhi, to fight against the Ballalas (Vira Ballala III, 1292–1342, was the last Hoysala ruler), and became the governors in the name of the sultan. The connection with Kampili/Anegundi is possibly made by the *Vidyaranya Kalajnana*, which states that after fleeing Warangal the two brothers became the treasurers of one Ramanatha, identified as the son of Kampiladevaraya by N. Venkataramanayya (Nilakanta Sastri and Venkataramanayya, *Further sources*, vol. I, p. 30). Ibn Battūta claims to have befriended in Delhi the sons of the king of Kampili, who had converted to Islam and were serving the sultan. Although for Nunes it was only the king's ministers who survived in Anegondi, given the disparate nature of these sources perhaps the coincidences are still more significant than the differences. Curiously, in the indigenous tradition it is lord Shiva who, through Vidyaranya, elects the founders to perform the peculiar role of crushing the Hindu resistance, although after their victory the idea that they are serving Delhi vanishes without trace, and the logical possibility that they had previously converted to Islam is

'that would never be captured by his enemies' at the other side of the river followed as a consequence of a prodigious hunting scene, in which the hares pursued the dogs. This event the holy 'hermit' interpreted for the king, 'Deva Raya' (Deoráo), as a divine sign that the city should be built there.[26] Thus the city received the name of the hermit, Vydiajuna, but, in Nunes's words, 'in the course of time this name has become corrupted, and it is now called Bisnaga'.[27] Nunes also explains that the temple in which all kings have to worship before they are crowned, and to which they offer many prayers and annual feasts, was then built in honour of this hermit. (This can only be the temple of Virupaksha by the river). The temple in fact provides a key to the sacred continuity of the city.

There can be little doubt of the identity of Nunes's 'Vydiajuua' with the Hindu Vidyaranya, the association of this foundational myth with the worship at the Virupaksha temple in Hampi, and the importance of a perceived link between the military success of the new dynasty and the dharmic rule legitimized by the Shaiva brahmin. The fact that the etymology of Vijayanagara provided by Couto – 'city of victory' – is more widely accepted by modern historians, and that the exact origins of the first kings – indeed, the very nature of their relationship with the Hoysalas and the Turkish sultans – are unclear, only points towards the diversity of indigenous sources consulted by the Portuguese historians.[28] Thus, although neither Nunes nor Couto match any known native source perfectly, the fundamental fact is that they both reflect very closely a native self-understanding, of a historical–legendary character, as it existed in the sixteenth century. They both include a 'dharmic' element crucial to indigenous identity, defined in opposition to political disintegration and to Muslim domination, and expressed in terms of a sacred landscape and origins.

The importance of the myth of origin in the Hindu tradition is attested not only by the existence of many versions, but also by the fact that

---

not mentioned (if anything these contradictions suggest that the legend might be genuine).

[26] Here Nunes entirely agrees with the traditional legends. One indigenous explanation of this scene, found in the *Rayavacakamu*, is that where hares are stronger than dogs, an extraordinary (divine) power protects the weak against the strong – a good location for a city that must protect its inhabitants against all attacks.

[27] Sewell, *A forgotten empire*, pp. 291–300. Nunes thus agrees with the *Keladinripavijayam* in giving the etymology of the city as Vidya-nagara after the sage. Couto, instead, clearly states that the name is the more military Vijaya-nagara.

[28] The use of the name Vidyanagara by many sixteenth-century poets is well attested, sometimes alongside Vijayanagara. This is the case, for instance, in the *Achyutarayabhyudayam* (1530s) by the court poet Rajanatha, an idealized but contemporary account of Achyuta's first years as king which includes a conventional poetic description of the city.

changes between these versions are marks of intentionality. In the *Rayavakacamu* it is possible to interpret this intentionality in the light of the tenor of the whole work. This Telugu prose composition was written well after the fall of the city, and therefore its foundation could be interpreted retrospectively, giving a fixed term for the duration of its prosperity (360 years, thus wrongly beginning SS 1127 / *c.* AD205).[29] The point of this work is to present Krishna Deva Raya as a perfect – and thus mythical – king, a model of dharmic rule set against the attacks of the Deccani sultans which could serve in the troubled circumstances of the nayaka courts *c.* 1600.[30] Interestingly, this dharmic aspect dominates the account of the foundation myth to the point that the theme of the origins of the dynasty disappears altogether. Vidyaranya controls the entire process, and accordingly the city is called Vidyanagara. The shift towards Vaishnavism is also apparent: although the writer does not deny the association of the site with Pampa and Virupaksha, the role of Lakshmi (Vishnu's wife) as bestower of prosperity, and Matanga's power as the protector of Sugriva (Vishnu's ally), are here more prominent in the definition of the city's significance and location. Although the fictional author of this work is the ambassador of a Vijayanagara nayaka (a captain of the kingdom) at the court of Krishna Deva Raya, writing a report for his master, the emphasis on ritual legitimacy underpinning what amounts to a treatise on practical politics makes it difficult to imagine an author who was not also a politically active brahmin. His particular treatment of the foundational myth confirms that the legend was a fundamental element in the identity of the kingdom even after the demise of the city that had come to define it. It also suggests that native versions of the myth could be made to be very diverse.

This also implies that the intentionality of Nunes or Couto cannot be easily distinguished from the intentionality of their sources. What Couto's use of his materials also reveals is that he did not accept the indigenous account uncritically, and felt inclined to tamper with it (rather unwisely, as it turns out). A Goa settler (*casado*) like Nunes, Couto (1542–1616) shared with the horse-trader the belief that these 'oriental gentiles' are full of silly tales, 'one thousand inventions

---

[29] Wagoner, *Tidings of the king*, pp. 12–33. Although the work was written after the fall of the city, it was fictionally set sixty years before its destruction, at the beginning of the reign of Krishna Deva Raya (not a perfect reckoning, since this reign began in 1509, not 1505).

[30] I follow Wagoner in ibid., pp. 25ff. The work was sponsored by the court of the nayakas of Madurai *c.* 1600, and therefore sought to trace a direct legitimacy from the period of Krishna Deva Raya, sidestepping the sovereign claims of the Aravidu dynasty of Chandragiri-Vellore.

[*patranhas*] so as to provide their kings with an honourable origin'.[31] What is, on the other hand, rather surprising, is how he muddled his own history of Vijayanagara: in his attempt to clarify the matter, in effect Couto amalgamated indigenous traditions with various European references. He thus invented a false coherence, perpetrating a number of serious confusions. For instance, Saluva Narasimha and Narasa Nayaka become the same individual; battles against the Bahmani kingdom are often confused with battles against the sultans of Delhi; the chronology, combining Christian and native dates, extends over three and a half centuries, and in order to fill in this inflated period, both Krishna Deva Raya and Rama Raja appear twice, in the fifteenth century and then again in the sixteenth century, as separate characters. It is obvious that this confusion goes far beyond the possible limitations of the Kanarese chronicle, and is mainly a result of Couto's attempt to match it with European sources.[32] His biggest blunders appear precisely when he wants to prove his erudition, as when he writes that the early fifteenth-century Castilian ambassador to Timur, Ruy González de Clavijo, in his references to a Christian king of India, was actually talking about the king of Vijayanagara and 'his' vassals the Christians of Saint Thomas.[33] Worse still, despite continuous reference to writers like Barros, Castanheda and Góis, Couto is even unable to offer an accurate view of the history of the kingdom during the years of the Portuguese in India in the first half of the sixteenth century. His inability to match the coherence of Barros (who in his account of the wars of Krishna Deva Raya at least followed Nunes closely) or the overall accuracy of Castanheda (who, as we saw,

---

[31] Couto, VI, 5, 5.

[32] Couto's concluding statement can only be read today as a little tragicomic: 'and in this way the origin of this kingdom and its kings has been understood and clarified, and the confusion which there was about its names has been eliminated' (ibid.); Couto was particularly proud of his etymological work, that is, the distinction between 'Bisnagá', which he identified as a corrupt rendering of 'Visaja Nager', that is 'city of victory', and 'Narsinga', the name given to the kingdom after its ruler 'Narsinga Naique' (Narasimha Nayaka) by the Italian travellers of the fifteenth century (he must have been referring to Varthema). About this he was right.

[33] See Ruy González de Clavijo, *Embajada a Tamerlán*, ed. by R. Alba (Madrid, 1984), pp. 197–8. The author of the account of Clavijo's embassy merely reported a battle between Timur and a (North Indian) king 'about twelve years ago' (he was writing at the end of 1404 or a few years later, and must refer to Timur's attack on Delhi of 1398). He described this Indian king as a Christian, probably because the central Asian Mongols (from whom the story must have come) were likely to have classified the Hindus along with the Christians as 'idolaters'. In reality Timur's opponents in Delhi were Muslim overlords. The Castilian traveller also heard stories about Parsis and the legend of Saint Thomas, all of which confirmed his belief that all Indian 'infidels' were heretical Christians 'like the Greeks'. Couto could easily have read the edition of Clavijo's embassy published by the humanist antiquarian Gonzalo Argote de Molina in Seville in 1582.

copied Barbosa in his description of Vijayanagara) is all the more remarkable if we consider that Couto was well read in classical authors, and that after 1595 he was also the keeper of records at Goa under Philip I (II of Castile). In the midst of this historiographical disaster, which may to some extent be explained by the disparity between Couto's Jesuit education and his active life as a soldier in India, his one positive contribution is the attempt to take seriously the original records of the inhabitants of Vijayanagara as a source for historical reconstruction.[34]

Working with similar principles, but with the advantage of having spent a considerable period living as a foreigner in Vijayanagara, Nunes produced a long and balanced chronicle of the kingdom – without doubt, the single most useful work for modern historians of Vijayanagara since its publication in 1897. It is none the less (and as one would expect) very partial, organized chronologically along a succession of vaguely characterized kings, whose exact names and dates may be easily contested. These problems have, of course, much to do with the quality of the sources to which Nunes had access, and the cursory description of the first reigns possibly reflects the structure of a Kannada account of the foundation of the kingdom and its first dynasty.[35] Consequently, the chronicle becomes fuller and more critical as it approaches the writer's

---

[34] Aubrey Bell, *Diogo do Couto*, presented this historian sympathetically as a Renaissance combination of classical learning, direct observation and lively style, that is, a man more educated than Gaspar Correa and less distant from his subject matter than João de Barros. Undeniably dedicated, and also able to launch into moral diatribes against the shortcomings of the Portuguese elite, it would seem, however, that Couto's critical skills did not always match his intellectual ambition. For a recent assessment see the important study of Maria Augusta Lima Cruz (ed.) *Diogo do Couto e a década 8a da Ásia*, 2 vols. (Lisbon, 1993), including a scrupulous critical edition of the eighth decade. A great deal of work remains to be done on a historian who often stands alone as an authority but many of whose manuscripts were lost or mutilated. Possibly because his royal appointment as the continuator of Barros dated from 1595, the majority of the decades written by Couto were completed and sent to Europe in his late years, between 1597 and 1601 (this included decades 4 to 7). The actual publication of all these decades was delayed until 1612–16, except his fourth decade, published in 1602. Couto was forced to rewrite decade 7 after the ship carrying it was captured at sea, and decades 8 and 9 after they were stolen from him (1615–16). Decade 10, which had been written as early as 1593 in order to attract the patronage of Philip II of Castile (it dealt with the years of his personal rule after the union of crowns in 1580), remained unpublished until the eighteenth century. Decade 11 was lost in Portugal, and decade 12 was left unfinished.

[35] Even in this earlier part Nunes maintains his own narrative voice. He will, for instance, explain the etymology of a name, or introduce his own comments about local customs, as in this passage: 'On the death of that king Bucarao there came to the throne his son called Pureoyre Deorao, which in Canará means 'powerful lord', and he coined the money of *pardaos* which even now they call *puroure deorao*; and from that time it has become custom to call coins by the names of the kings that made them, and it is because of this that there are so many names of *pardaos* in the kingdom of Bisnaga' (Sewell, *Forgotten empire*, p. 301). Some turns of phrase seem to suggest that Nunes took notes from oral reports and then, selectively, wrote his own summary.

own times. There is a substantial increase of historical detail for the period of Narasa Nayaka's regency (1491–1503) and then again during the rule of Krishna Deva Raya, his second son (1509–29). The analysis of the organization of the kingdom at the time of Achyuta Raya in the 1530s is the most personal and perceptive part of the composition.

Two fundamental qualities emerge from the progression of Nunes' narrative: first, the sense of order, in almost purely secular terms, that the writer imposes on his material; second, the internal dialectic of two fundamental models of kingship, 'good' and 'bad', which develops throughout. These two qualities are in fact interconnected, so that Nunes actually fashions his indigenous material into a form of Renaissance historiography, not so much inspired by classical models – references to the Latin or Greek traditions are remarkably absent – as in terms of practical politics. It is only in this restricted sense that Nunes may be compared to a contemporary Italian historian like Guicciardini. Formally, Nunes's work is closer to the fourteenth-century chronicles of Pero López de Ayala or Fernão Lopes, who wrote with a strong sense of political exemplariness, than to the rhetorical elaboration and psychological sophistication of the best humanist historians.

Thus what connects Vijayanagara to the European tradition is not just that history builds a political identity around a dynasty of kings but, more ambitiously, that it has an exemplary role: it is a source of advice for the practical politician. Both the political maxims of Krishna Deva Raya in the *Amuktamalyada* and the account of his success as the head of a conquest state in the *Rayavacakamu* are in the last analysis an advice book and a 'mirror for princes'. In that sense, Christian, Hindu and Muslim historical genres shared a common educational purpose. But, in the indigenous literature, this enterprise was also associated with an attempt to link the authority of the mythical and universal to the allegiances of the local. Nunes had to omit this. As a foreigner, he could not write from a local sectarian perspective, and had no duty to praise any particular king (although he was of course vulnerable to the bias of his informants). As a Latin Christian, he had access to few mechanisms that might have allowed him to take the religious dimension of the indigenous tradition seriously, even though he commented on the many things that the gentiles did to win 'paradise' from their 'God'; moreover, he was writing in a Gentile context in which Christian providentialism and morality had little opportunity to frame the discourse.

For all these reasons, what Nunes produced was a secularized system of practical politics. He had no need to oppose Aristotle and Tacitus, or Fortune and Prudence, to Christian piety and providence. He had no need to develop an amalgamation of practical advice and revealed law into a system of natural morality based on historical consensus. Without any further ideological demands, he wrote about tyranny and kingship at the minimal meeting point of all medieval traditions, the practical concerns of the human community where the different laws of Christians, Jews, Muslims and even gentiles necessarily talked to each other.[36]

From this perspective, Nunes's chronicle thoroughly questions the assumption that had governed earlier European descriptions of Vijaya-nagara: that the king of such a vast state and wealthy city was simply very powerful. More critical than Paes, he portrays a dynamic system in which qualities counter-balance defects, and the greatness of Vijayana-gara is in fact shadowed by instability. The virtuous king, Krishna Deva Raya, is succeeded by a cowardly tyrant, his brother Achyuta, who is detested by everyone. Often the king is only a puppet of a powerful lord, and the faithful minister is actually involved in political intrigue. The power of the king is, in fact, counter-balanced by the power of great chiefs, whose names are thus listed as worthy of notice, and the armies are raised to the detriment of the peasant population. Trade is not conducted with such justice that one can escape having to bribe the king and his officials.[37]

It is not that Nunes portrays a dark, negative image of Vijayanagara: on the contrary, his rhetorical sophistication allows him to write about admirable aspects and others which he detests. He recognizes, for example, that thieves are thoroughly persecuted, and that as a consequence the city is safe.[38] The brahmin priests are described as 'despicable men' (*homenes muito despreziveis*), but he later portrays another caste of 'better brahmins' who hold the administrative offices of the kingdom and are 'honest men, given to merchandise, very subtle and intelligent, very good at accounts, lean and well-formed, albeit unfit for hard work'.[39] The point here is that Nunes introduces caste distinctions in order to offer a balanced interpretation of the merits of the civilization of Vijayanagara.[40] Other passages confirm that his personal experience,

---

[36] The existence of this practical meeting point does not, however, imply a statement of religious and political equality. It reveals, instead, continuity with medieval attitudes, in which religious coexistence enshrined rather than dissolved political hierarchies. Tolerance of other religions was less an aim than a method.

[37] Lopes (ed.) *Chronica dos reis de Bisnaga*, p. 68.

[38] Ibid., pp. 68–9.

[39] Ibid., p. 75. Nunes might perhaps be referring here to Jains, a select group in Vijayanagara. He distinguishes these 'brahmins', who neither kill living beings nor eat them, from the Kanarese who worship devils, monkeys and buffaloes in their temples of idols. However, he also writes that the former believe in the 'Holy Trinity' (called *Tricebemca*) – this does not fit with Jainism if (as it seems) the Trimurti is here meant.

[40] Nunes distinguishes caste with the concept of 'criação de homenes' (lineages of men), or 'gente' (people).

no longer the glimpses of the occasional visitor who is entertained as ambassador, but now the insight and perhaps also the bitterness bred of three years trying unsuccessfully to prosper by selling horses, leads him towards an image in which the pretensions of ideal kingship, although not completely obliterated, are nevertheless reduced to human proportions.

One example may suffice to show the dramatic rather than the stereotyped character of Nunes's chronicle. Contrary to the more idealized version of the *Rayavacakamu*, which portrays a legitimate Vira Narasimha (1503–9) listening to the brahmins, who recount the exemplary story of Vidyaranya, and then voluntarily renouncing the kingdom in favour of his brother Krishna Deva Raya, Nunes gives us a dramatic version of their relationship. He explains that Busbalrao (Vira Narasimha) was one of the five sons of the regent Narsenaque (Narasa Nayaka), himself portrayed as an usurper to the throne. Krishna was a second son to Narsenaque and thus brother of this Busbalrao. The latter, however, wanted him to be blinded so as so secure the succession of his own eight-year-old son. It was only the trickery of the minister, Sallvatina (Saluva Timma), that saved Krishna from a by no means untypical fate, and brought him to power.

At this crucial point a special relationship is established between the king and his minister. Seeing the threat, Krishna's first reaction had been to renounce any claims to power, 'that his desire was to pass this world as a *jogui*'.[41] Paradoxically, this helped convince the 'wise minister' that he should be king (the renunciation which the *Rayavacakamu* made normative is here no less valid for being tactical). Afterwards, their exemplary partnership makes Krishna Deva Raya the most successful of all kings of Vijayanagara. He becomes patron of arts and builder of cities and water-tanks. Above all, he becomes conqueror of his neighbours, both Hindus (the Gajapati ruler of Orissa) and Muslims (the Deccani sultans, in particular the Adil Shah of Bijapur). Not unlike the *Rayavacakamu*, Nunes offers here a detailed account of political strategy and military campaigns, in which the king proves himself to be courageous, prudent, pious and magnanimous.[42]

At the end of Krishna's reign the pattern of renunciation recurs: Krishna, wanting to rest and secure his succession, decides to abdicate and make his six-year-old son king. Saluva Timma will lose his job as prime minister and become Krishna's counsellor. Fatally, during the festival the boy dies. Krishna suspects that he has been poisoned by the son of Saluva Timma, whom he had also made a great lord. Bringing

---

[41] Sewell, *Forgotten empire*, p. 315.   [42] Ibid., pp. 315–58.

together the old minister and his family – indeed, a powerful court faction – Krishna delivers to his hitherto faithful servant what seems to be the only direct speech of the chronicle, all the more dramatic because of its paradoxical reasoning:

I always held you as my great friend, and for forty years you have been governor in this kingdom, which you gave me; but for this I am under no obligation to you, because in doing so you acted in a way contrary to your duty. You were bound, since the king my brother commanded so, to put out my eyes; yet you did not carry out his will nor obey his words, but rather cheated him and the eyes of a goat were instead put out, wherefore, since you did not fulfil his command, you were a traitor; and so are your sons, for whom I have done so much. Now I have learnt that my son died of poison given to him by you and your sons, and for that you are all here made prisoners.[43]

Questioning the concept of duty itself, the relationship between the king and his counsellor ends in a tale of treachery, disappointment, rebellion and punishment.[44] Not long after this, Krishna Deva Raya also sickens and dies 'with pains in the groin, of which die all the kings of Bisnaga'.[45] With him dies sacred authority too. His successor, Achyuta, who since his brother's accession to power had been kept confined in the fortress of Chamdegary (Chandragiri), 'gave himself over to vice and tyranny'. He is 'a man of very little honesty ... he has never done anything except those things that are desired by his two brothers-in-law, who are men very evilly disposed and great Jews'.[46]

[43] Lopes, *Chronica*, p. 52. There are a number of examples of indirect speech in Nunes's chronicle, but this example of direct speech is unique. The question arises whether Nunes made up the short speech after the fashion of classical and European historians (direct speech is found in medieval vernacular chronicles as early as the thirteenth century), or perhaps followed his Indian informants. There is no lack of direct speech in the *Rayavacakamu*, for instance. Nunes mentions, however, that when Krishna Deva Raya moved against his minister he requested the assistance of Portuguese horse-traders, which suggests that Nunes may have had access to their views on this event, or perhaps was even there as a witness.

[44] When focusing on the relationship between king and minister, as with his emphasis on the renunciation of power, Nunes also hit the nail on the head. Both themes were important issues in the Indian concept of kingship and figure prominently, for instance, in the *Rayavacakamu*, which is (curiously enough) also built around the relationship between Krishna Deva Raya and Saluva Timma.

[45] Sewell, *Forgotten empire*, p. 362. The Portuguese text is more explicit, but of difficult interpretation: 'neste tempo adoeceo de doemça que todollos seus antecessores morrerão, com dar das verylhas e dos campanhões, de que morrem os reys de Bisnaga': Lopes (ed.), *Chronica*, p. 54. The implication seems to be that this disease is related to the sexual functions of the kings of Vijayanagara.

[46] Sewell, *Forgotten empire*, p. 367. Achyuta Deva Raya was half-brother of Krishna Deva Raya – their father was Narasa Nayaka, but they had different mothers. The two brothers-in-law who controlled Achyuta were the Salakarajus, later to claim a regency on Achyuta's death in 1542, something which actually provoked a civil war.

Here suddenly a European language of contempt creeps in, marked by a traditional anti-Jewish discourse (used metaphorically) and by the concept of tyranny (used analytically), but surely Nunes was also expressing an indigenous feeling of political opposition of which he had been made a participant: 'the captains and the people . . . lived in great discontent, and believed that if the kingdom should ever be lost, it would be during the life of this king Chitarao [Achyuta Raya], because he had destroyed the principal men of his kingdom and killed their sons and taken their goods, all on the advice of his brothers-in-law . . . he is a man that they hold to be of little force of character, and very negligent of those things which are needed for the well-being of his kingdom and state'.[47] Some details are clearly only meaningful with reference to native ritual language: thus Achyuta Raya does not even sit on the throne of gold and precious stones at the Mahanavami festival, 'for they say that whoever sits on it has to be a very truthful king, one who speaks the whole truth, and this king does not do so'.[48] That is, Nunes picks up (from his informants) that this king, because of his immorality, has lost the sacred character accorded to him in the indigenous tradition. Whether Achyuta actually had not sat in the throne is secondary; the point is that he was not believed fit to sit there. But beyond this symbolic dimension, the whole political analysis comes to depend on the negative judgement of the king's moral and political capacity, and Nunes interprets the humiliating attacks on the kingdom by Ismail Adil Shah (or Adil Khan) of Bijapur in 1531 as the direct result of the internal weakness caused by Achyuta's bad leadership (leading to the loss of Raichur, the city taken with great effort by Krishna Deva Raya).[49] This is why the captains and the people were so pessimistic about the future of the kingdom.

In this interpretation it is often difficult to determine the precise boundaries between native views and European rhetorical elaboration. Certainly, the fact that the Portuguese writer must have followed to some extent a native source does not imply that the modern historian can accept Nunes's interpretation uncritically. First, in matters of historical interpretation, native views need not be in agreement with each other, especially if they reflect a factional struggle which was still alive when the documents were composed. It is thus extremely likely that the 'captains and the people' whose dissatisfaction Nunes represents as a universal

[47] Lopes, *Chronica*, pp. 58–9.   [48] Ibid., p. 67.
[49] Ibid., pp. 57–8. The Adil Shah who attacked the capital of Vijayanagara in 1531, recovering Raichur, was Ismail Adil Shah (1510–34). Nunes blames this event on the Salakarajus, Achyuta's brothers-in-law. Nunes wrote his chronicle a few months afterwards.

voice should be associated with the faction of Aliya Rama Raja, who would eventually fight for a regency after the death of Achyuta Deva Raya. Our real problem here is the scarcity of detailed sources, which means that the basic events of the period remain unclear and can only be reconstructed, imaginatively, by giving credence to some of the biased accounts. The interpretation of the reign of Achyuta Deva Raya (1520–42) and its complicated aftermath, which was marked by a dynastic crisis, is a case in point. Although we have Muslim, Portuguese and native sources, all we can say with certainty is that they do not agree with each other, the first being confused, the second favourable to Rama Raja, the latter to Achyuta, and all, in their own ways, severely limited. In fact, no twentieth-century interpretation of this reign is fully satisfactory. Burton Stein, for instance, taking a line which is quite different from Nunes's views on Achyuta's tyranny, argues that this ruler survived the early threats of the future regent, Rama Raja, 'by his courage and impressive allies of his own'.[50] Unfortunately Achyuta still depended on the support of brahmin military commanders (an inheritance from Krishna's attempt to balance local chiefly powers) and, as Nunes observed, on the powerful Salakarajus, his brothers-in-law.[51] Thus, whilst Stein changes the emphasis from Nunes's moralistic condemnation of tyranny to a functional analysis of power politics, in which the destabilizing action is attributed to Rama Raja rather than the king's faction, he must conclude that the inability of Achyuta to contain the growth of factionalism (a structural problem of all aristocratic systems) casts a doubt on his political success.

Nunes may only have been expressing sympathy for lords who belonged to an opposing faction, and he adopted with suspicious ease a dualistic scheme of good and bad kingship incarnated in Krishna and his successor, but his negative judgement of Achyuta was not entirely without historical justification. Stein's discussion, which follows the interpretation of South Indian historians like N. Venkataramanayya, relies on native sources which are not necessarily a better authority than Correa and Nunes. In effect he follows the basic outline of a Sanskrit historical poem in honour of Achyuta, the *Achyutarayabhyudayam* by

---

[50] Stein, *Vijayanagara*, p. 68. Stein (pp. 113–17) also provides a detailed background to this dynastic struggle, focused on the beginning and the end of Achyuta's reign, which seems to go quite a long way towards correcting Nunes. However, other Portuguese sources like Gaspar Correa would also seem to disagree with Stein's interpretation. The account by the Deccani historian Firishta has not been satisfactorily fitted in either.

[51] Thus, in Stein's own words (ibid., p. 116), in 1530 Salakaraju Tirumala 'vigorously counter-attacked' Quili Qutb Shah, the sultan of Golkonda (Vijayanagara's Muslim enemy on the north-eastern frontier), forcing him to abandon his campaign against the fortress of Kondavidu.

Rajanatha.[52] However, of all sources this remains the most problematic from a historian's perspective. Although it has been considered uniquely reliable by a number of modern Indian historians, because many of the events narrated can be corroborated with the help of other literary sources and epigraphical material, there can be no doubt that the intention of the poet was to simply glorify his existing patron. For instance, the coronation of the king in Tirupati, which occupies an important part of the poem, had an obvious political significance. It legitimized the succession in the most important Vaishnava temple of the kingdom against rival claims (which the poem does not mention), and it consolidated the position of Salakaraju as minister, since Achyuta's son by his daughter, Cina Venkatadri, was declared heir apparent. But the poem is also intent on bringing out the religious significance of the coronation ritual: young women from all countries attended the king, representing the universal claims of kingship, and Achyuta is symbolically married to the earth. Throughout the rest of the poem this emphasis on the ritual relationships surrounding the figure of the king is maintained, and accompanies the account of the victories of Achyuta against his enemies. Thus, whilst leading an expedition to the south to punish the rebellious Chola (Tamil) governor Chellappa and his ally the Chera king of Travancore, Achyuta is repeatedly seen as worshipper in a number of important temples, as holding the attention of poets and scholars, and as focus of all kinds of royal pleasures, all according to ritual orthodoxy. The passivity of this role is to some extent explained by the fact that the eventual protagonist of the expedition to the south is the general Salakaraju, acting on the king's behalf.

There can therefore be little doubt that this poem is a piece of historical propaganda serving the interests of the same court faction criticized by Nunes. And from this perspective, the account of the campaign against the new ruler of Bijapur, Ibrahim Adil Shah, in 1535 is of particular significance, portraying a double victory, first in a siege of Raichur and then on the banks of the Krishna river, which stands in sharp contrast not only to the previous humiliation of the Hindu ruler in his own city, described by both Nunes and Firishta but not by the poet, but also to the details of this campaign against Raichur as explained by Barros, who devoted a significant part of his fourth decade to the

---

[52] For an outline of this poem see Krishnaswami Aiyangar, *Sources of Vijayanagar history*, pp. 108–9 and 158–69 (including extracts with English summaries). See also his edition of 1945. Unfortunately, Stein does not actually discuss his use of sources in any detail. N. Venkataramanayya's optimistic interpretation of the reign of Achuyta was elaborated in his *Studies in the history of the third dynasty of Vijayanagara*, and then summarized in Nilakanta Sastri and Venkataramanayya, *Further sources*, vol. I, 232–9.

discussion of the Deccani politics of these years.[53] The exact terms of this 'victory' can be suspected of gross exaggeration: Achyuta's aim was to recover Raichur, which he had given away to Ibrahim's father four years earlier in the first place, and he failed to do it (although a reader of the poem may miss this detail). In fact, if we follow Barros, Achyuta's real advantage was the opportunistic alliance of a fascinating and powerful figure, Asad Khan, Turkish ruler of Belgaum and one of the most influential captains of Bijapur. Asad Khan in the end betrayed the Hindu ruler, since his aim had always been to protect himself against the arbitrary power of the new Adil Shah, and to restore his own influence, which had been threatened by a succession crisis in Bijapur in 1534–5.[54] In this light, the sultan's submission as described in the Sanskrit poem was no more than an agreement by Ibrahim Adil Shah to compensate Achyuta with some of the fertile lands south and east of Raichur – not a high price for a young prince who in effect was still seeking to consolidate his contested position as ruler.[55]

[53] João de Barros [and Joao Baptista Lavanha], *Quarta decada da Asia* (Madrid, 1615), book VII. In particular, for the campaign of Raichur, chap. 7–8 (pp. 432–9). This fourth decade was left unfinished by Barros and was only completed in 1615 by João Baptista Lavanha, under the patronage of King Philip II (III of Castile). Lavanha, however, was an extremely scrupulous editor, and always indicates which information came from Barros and which he needed to add from other published chronicles. On the whole, book VII is Barros's own account. The account of the brief reign of Mallu Khan given by the court historian of Bijapur, Firishta, is in some ways quite different: M. Q. Ferishta, *History of the rise of the Mahomedan power in India till the year 1612*, ed. by J. Briggs, 4 vols. (Calcutta, 1908–10), vol. III, pp. 73–7. However, we cannot simply assume that he is more reliable than the Portuguese, as Briggs does (ibid., p. 76, note). Although one would want to believe that the Persian writer had a superior access to local primary sources, he tended simply to copy previous chronicles which were often biased and of very irregular quality. His obvious confusions of events that happened only sixty years before he wrote (*c.* 1590s) are thus notorious. For many events that can be tested with independent documents, the accuracy of Barros and Correa (who after all were contemporary writers) is generally superior.

[54] Ismail's second son Ibrahim Adil Shah (1535–58) is famous for having restored Sunnism in Bijapur during his reign despite the Shiite tradition of the dynasty, on the strength of a Deccani factional reaction opposed to the dominance of foreign Iranian officers (some of these officers, degraded in Bijapur, were employed a few years later by Rama Raja of Vijayanagara, who is said by Firishta to have had the Koran placed before him when they paid their respects). The Portuguese were in a good position to know about the succession crisis in Bijapur because they had been drawn into an agreement with Asad Khan, who promised the lands of Salsette and Bardes surrounding Goa. The influential Goa *casado* Cristovão de Figueiredo, horse-factor in Vijayanagara in 1517, leader of the expedition which had assisted Krishna Deva Raya in 1520 against Raichur and companion of Domingos Paes, was the Portuguese representative during these wars of Achyuta too, and was given the administration of the rents of the new lands of Salsette. Concerning the fascinating career of Asad Khan, decisive in the triangle formed by Bijapur, Goa and Vijayanagara, Schurhammer, *Francis Xavier*, vol. II, pp. 191–2, 234, 269–70, 391–401, contains a number of important observations.

[55] Compare *Achyutarayabhyudayam*, canto XI, with Barros, *Quarta decada*, VII, 7. Barros's

In conclusion, no account so obviously based on creating an image of sacred kingship as Rajanatha's poem could have failed to give us a very selective view of these events, even if we accept the basic historical reality of the military campaigns which are being described.[56] Only the impossibility of escaping the bias of the indigenous sources, today as in the sixteenth century, can explain the contrast between Nunes's portrayal of Achyuta and the Salakaraju brothers as responsible for the unpopular intervention of the shah of Bijapur in the affairs of the kingdom, and Stein's contrary suggestion that it was Aliya Rama Raja who unscrupulously pursued his own ambitions to the throne by allegedly allying himself with Muslim powers.[57] It would seem that the need to capture a language of collective Hindu interests, and the possibility of its factional manipulation, was already alive in sixteenth-century Vijayanagara. True, brahminic historical sources never developed the distinction between myth and history, a notion crucial to Greek and western historiography (even if it was not always respected), or the idea of a narrative genre based on a clear chronology, despite the fact that a kind of chronological sequence was apparent in the Kanarese royal chronicle used by Nunes. But an indigenous historical narrative voice certainly existed, and obviously performed an ideological function which was not lost on contemporaries.[58]

The way in which Gaspar Correa (1496–1563) dealt with the succession crisis of 1542–3 at the death of Achyuta confirms the receptiveness of Portuguese writers to this 'native voice'. The narrative, despite a few

account of these conflicts is remarkably detailed and consistent, and must have been based on the reports of Portuguese participants like Cristovão de Figueiredo, or a number of Portuguese renegades who worked for the sultan of Golkonda. The incidents related by Firishta as referring to 1535–6 (*History*, vol. III, pp. 80–92) actually correspond to 1542. This renders Sewell's interpretation confused (Sewell, *Forgotten empire*, pp. 167–77) and, combined with Firishta's unreliability in the use of Indian rulers' names, misled N. Venkataramanayya into giving a fanciful account of the central years of the reign of Achyuta (Nilakanta Sastri and Venkataramanayya, *Further sources*, vol. I, pp. 236–7), taken up by Stein too (*Vijayanagara*, p. 116).

[56] For an analysis of some passages in the poem see Sridhara Babu, 'Kingship: state and religion in South India', especially pp. 56–60 (for the coronation ceremony and its significance). Its historical validity was defended by Venkataramanayya, *Studies*, and again by Krishnaswami Aiyangar in his 1945 edition of the poem.

[57] This same bias colours Stein's interpretation of Rama Raja's role in the succession crisis of 1542–3 at the death of Achyuta, entirely against the views expressed by the Portuguese chronicler Correa.

[58] One interesting question which lies beyond the scope of this study is the impact that Persian historiography may have had among Vijayanagara writers, in the light of the intense relationship between the Deccani courts and the court of Vijayanagara, which, for instance, had a clear impact on civil architecture and military technology. This influence, to the extent that it existed, would have been more important in the sixteenth century. It does not seem to have reached the stage of direct imitations of historical chronicles of the kind written by Firishta or the Mughal courtiers.

confusions, seems to do justice to the complexity of the events described.[59] However, Correa at the same time clearly offered a moral interpretation, one which, following a factional pattern analogous to that earlier developed by Nunes, was favourable to Rama Raja and negative towards Achyuta and the Salakaraju faction. The regent Salakaraju Tirumala, in particular, is consistently portrayed as a 'tyrant' and usurper, whilst his opponent Rama Raja, equally unscrupulous in his methods, emerges on the whole as a prudent regent, 'a man of great wisdom' championing a legitimate succession. What is perhaps most interesting here is the quality of the language of political virtue and legitimacy employed by Correa: tyranny is not simply a lack of proper succession, but also a personal way of doing things, a moral mis-behaviour and systematic disregard for laws and political consensus, which endangers the interests of the state as a whole.

Therefore, whilst it is obvious that Correa's bias colours his interpret-ation of events, it would be wrong to see him as simply distorting the facts to suit his hero, because he also tells us about Rama Raja's military failures, or his cruelty towards his enemies. The question is, how reliable is he as a historian? From a number of passages in his *Legends of India* it would seem fair to say that Correa, unlike Barros who compared and organized sources, was accurate only as far as his personal experience allowed, and that whenever his sources failed him he let himself be carried by the dramatic and the exemplary. On the other hand, his knowledge of the 1540s is often superior to that of any other Portuguese writer, and as a Goa *casado* (where he had settled in 1530) Correa was actually quite close to the events of Vijayanagara (he was, for example, able to describe the temple of Tirumalai-Tirupati first-hand).[60] We can safely conclude that Correa offers a genuine historical interpretation of the events of 1542, one based on a view of the common good of the kingdom of Vijayanagara, threatened by ambitious regents, independent captains, and (most ominously) a Muslim takeover led by the Adil Shah of Bijapur. In this light Rama Raja, albeit ambitious and unscrupulous in his methods, saves the day. Correa's political vision is perhaps debatable, but is generally consistent.[61]

Could this view have been entirely his own? Everything seems to point

---

[59] Correa, *Lendas da Índia*, vol. IV, pp. 247–9 and 276–83. For reasons of space I omit a summary analysis of the narrative.

[60] Ibid., pp. 301–2. Both Schurhammer, *Francis Xavier*, vol. I, p. 365 n.57 and Heras, *The Aravidu dynasty of Vijayanagara*, pp. 2–12, emphasize the reliability of Correa's account.

[61] Correa may have underestimated Rama Raja's role in the succession crisis, and thus his duplicity. The rivalry between his family faction, who had married Krishna Deva Raya's daughters, and the Salakarajus, who had married their sister to Achyuta Deva Raya, went back many years.

towards the opposite, namely, that although his analytical language is European, he is transmitting one local, native interpretation (however factional). The point is, simply, that the concerns expressed by Correa's historical voice are those of someone involved in the conflict – and his native sources are very likely to have transmitted these concerns. Of course the Portuguese in Goa had an interest in the political stability of Vijayanagara, if only for the sake of the trade in horses and the possibility of territorial expansion on the Kanarese coast. The evidence suggests that throughout the 1540s and 50s Portuguese attitudes, following the same pattern of opportunism towards gentile powers that had crystallized under Albuquerque, remained tuned to the shifting politics of the region, marked by the ascent of Rama Raja and his increasing ability to mobilize the resources of the kingdom.[62] However, the intricacy of the account of the succession crisis in 1542 given by Correa goes far beyond such basic concerns. In fact, I should like to argue that behind the European language of tyranny and political legitimacy used by Correa, quite unlike the ritual–religious language usual in Hindu sources, there appears a remarkably perceptive, if partial, account of a political dynamic which is genuinely South Indian. The ease with which Vijayanagara slides towards a succession crisis, the mechanisms used by different factions to eliminate rivals, the tendency of the captains to oppose central authority and to become 'like kings' in their own areas of dominion, the use of royal and temple treasuries to build military factions, the pattern of relationships with the Deccani powers, involving the payment of huge sums of money to buy peace, and the basic truth that the kingdom's tendency to political fragmentation made a Muslim dynastic takeover a real possibility: all these are penetrating analyses of the nature of power in sixteenth-century Vijayanagara, and reveal the same tendencies which modern historians have laboured to define.

It is possible to re-consider Nunes' originality and importance in the light of the preceding discussion. Simple as his scheme of virtue and vice may be, Nunes's achievement as a historian needs to be measured against the standards of the historical models he had inherited. Not only did he

---

[62] One may consider here the attempted attack on the temple of Tirumalai-Tirupati by governor Martim Afonso de Sousa in 1543, described by Correa and Couto; the plans to conquer the Deccan or Vijayanagara floated at the court of João III (and abandoned only because of the impossibility of assembling all the necessary men at the same time – 10,000 soldiers, according to Dom Aleixo de Meneses); the formal treaty against Bijapur subscribed between Viceroy João de Castro and Rama Raja (as regent) in 1547, followed by the embassies of Tristão de Payva to the Hindu capital; and the attack by Rama Raja against the Portuguese town of São Tomé in Coromandel in 1559, also described by Couto (who is our main source for these latter events). This interest culminated with the destruction of the city in 1565.

undertake to write about a non-European kingdom with languages and gods very different from the known traditions, but he also developed the medieval chronicle so as to generate a dramatic tension in place of the usual dynastic or nationalistic propaganda. More surprisingly, he did so with little reference to ancient classical models.[63] Only personal engagement with the local tradition could have helped him here. Most other historians of Portuguese Asia or Spanish America were committed to writing about indigenous peoples only with reference to a European military, or spiritual, conquest (we saw that this was the case even with writers who developed a sympathetic understanding of indigenous historical traditions, authors such as the Spanish Pedro Cieza de León on Peru). The interest of Nunes's work therefore derives from the relatively neutral ground on which the history of Vijayanagara was met.

The nature of this common ground is in itself of great importance and takes us back to the issues discussed in the previous chapter: the western cultural background to which Nunes, Correa and Couto belonged was increasingly, and emphatically, historically minded, whilst in contrast Hindu Indian civilization has been often been defined (albeit with some exaggeration) as conspicuously lacking in historiography.[64] There is, of course, a great deal of factual historical material which served as basis for a number of genres within Indian literature. The *Rayavakacamu* is a case in point: though not a historical piece in the sense of Nunes's chronicle, and much more obviously fictional, it did nevertheless develop, rather exceptionally within the Hindu tradition, as a prose composition with a concrete political message which was clearly inspired by a historical memory and constructed as such. Certainly the main impetus of this composition was towards the creation of a mythical image of dharmic rule, incarnated in Krishna Deva Raya.

This 'mythical' character of Indian historical traditions was recognized by João de Barros, who, describing the palm-leaf writings of the gentiles

---

[63] Which would have been essentially Greek, because with very few exceptions, such as Tacitus' *Germania*, the Romans were clearly uninterested in the history of peoples other than themselves, especially as a world-conquering power. They assumed the Greek universalist scientific interest, but not a real curiosity for other peoples' past and mythology (especially the past of barbarian nations).

[64] A typical judgement is that of A. L. Basham: 'Having no real historical tradition, the Indian memory of earlier conquerors coming from the north-west – Greeks, Sakas, Kushanas, and Hunas – was so vague that it was quite ineffectual as a warning [of the menace of Turkish invasions from the eleventh century] to the rulers of the time'. *A cultural history of India*, ed. by A. L. Basham (Oxford, 1975), p. 52. More significant than this, or any individual historical judgement, is the fact that pre-Islamic Indian historiography occupies no space in this 'cultural history of India' (and Islamic contributions to the genre are subsumed within the general discussion of topics like miniature painting, Persian literature or Mughal contacts with the English), in sharp contrast with the parallel post-war recasting of 'The legacy of Greece' and 'The legacy of Rome'.

of Malabar, explained that 'the majority of their writings on religion, the creation of the world, its antiquity and population, the multiplication of men, and the chronicles of earlier kings, all are in the form of fables like those of the Greeks and the Latins, and almost like a metamorphosis of transmutations'.[65] The hidden reference to Ovid did not so much seek to disqualify poetic fiction (Barros had himself written a chivalric novel) as to insist on the need to separate historical and poetical genres. The Portuguese writer was not of course about to include the biblical account of origins within his definition of historical fables, as some *philosophes* were able to do from the end of the seventeenth century, and in this sense his position may be deemed profoundly ethnocentric. The important point, however, is that the classical distinction between history and myth was unequivocally a guiding principle of his task as historian. This does not contradict the essential rhetorical quality, educational and thus moral and political, of western historiography. It simply means that this rhetoric was increasingly conditioned by concerns for scientific truth, relative impartiality of the narrative voice, chronological coherence, search for causal explanations and documentary rigour. We can understand that Barros, aware of these concerns, failed to consider the myth-making qualities of his own historical mode of thinking, which he effectively shared with those Indian chronicles he had dismissed as 'fabulous'.

There was therefore a meeting point, defined by the mythical value of the historical narrative, which could be understood by Indians and westerners alike, and which provided Nunes with a ground on which to build. What he produced was necessarily something very different from his indigenous sources, but not entirely unrelated to them. There were other writers who were aware of indigenous chronicles in their descriptions of Portuguese Asia, for instance in the brief sketches by Barros and Couto of East Africa, Persia, Malabar, Gujarat, Ceylon, Siam or China.[66] Missionaries like Gaspar da Cruz and Martín de Rada offered some indigenous historical perspectives in their accounts of China in the 1560s and 70s, and after 1580 a number of Jesuit histories on the Mughals, Japan and China were similarly able to combine native writings with personal observations. However, we probably need to wait for the doctor–philosopher and *libertin* François Bernier, author of the *Histoire*

---

[65] Barros, *Ásia*, vol. I, p. 352. Barros went on to explain that he had had the chronicles of the kings of Malabar, with the history of 'Saramá Perimal' of Quilon and his conversion to Islam, translated for him, and he summarized the story.

[66] The loss of Barros's historical 'Geography', to which he constantly refers in his decades, has deprived us of a fundamental source of the humanist's use of oriental materials, often only mentioned in passing in the main epic narrative.

de la dernière révolution des états du Grand Mogol (Paris 1670), before we find a European history dealing exclusively with non-European affairs that surpasses in scope and penetration the early and almost unnoticed achievement of Nunes the horse-trader. Following Bernier in the Mughal court, another important European historian of India is the Venetian gunner and quack Nicolò Manucci, who wrote *c.* 1699. But perhaps the closest parallel to Nunes's use of a native chronicle is found in the seventeenth-century Portuguese accounts of Ceylon.[67]

MUSLIM HISTORIANS OF INDIA

In order fully to appreciate the importance of the European standards of historical coherence we can briefly consider how Muslim historians dealt with similar subjects. Particularly revealing is the Persian history of Firishta, who wrote many decades after the demise of the city of Vijayanagara, roughly at the same time as Couto and the author of the *Rayavacakamu*. Based in Bijapur (where he lived from 1589 to 1623), he could be expected to be in close touch with the historical memory of the Deccani region. He was the heir of a historiographical tradition that went back to the Bahmani kingdom of the fourteenth and fifteenth centuries, but also took advantage of the interest in Hindu literature at the Mughal court, which meant, for instance, that he could read the Persian translation of the *Mahabharata* by Akbar's historian and ideologue, Abul Fazl. I shall only discuss two aspects of Firishta here: his general attitude towards Hindu culture, and the way he treats particular episodes.[68]

---

[67] A view of Ceylon explicitly based on a Sinhalese royal chronicle, the *Rajavaliya*, appears in Couto's fifth decade (1612), but as Georg Schurhammer has demonstrated, it was an indecent plagiarism of the work of the Augustinian Agostinho de Azevedo (Schurhammer, *Francis Xavier*, vol. I, pp. 614–18). What is interesting is that Couto (that is, Azevedo) revealed the oral–poetic method of delivery of these 'writings': 'Dizem as suas Chronicas, e nós ouvimos cantar a hum principe de Ceilão em versos a seu modo, que hum interprete nos hia declarando, porque todas suas antiguidades andam postas em verso, e se camtam em suas festas.' See Couto, V, 2, 10, to compare with [Agostinho d'Azevedo] 'Estado da India' (BL ms. Add. 28,461, no. 36), in *Documentação ultramarina portuguesa*, ed. by A. de Silva Rego, 6 vols. (Lisbon, 1960), vol. I, 197–263, at p. 242. Azevedo met Sinhalese princes in Goa *c.* 1587, probably at the same time as he met the historian Couto, and was introduced to their royal chronicles. A later, more sophisticated use of Sinhalese chronicles was integrated by the Jesuit Fernão de Queyroz into his *Conquista temporal e espiritual de Ceylão* of 1687 (Colombo, 1916). For a sensible discussion of the significance of this work as a 'view of the other' in contrast with actual Sinhalese chronicles, see Chandra Richard de Silva, 'Beyond the Cape: the Portuguese encounter with the peoples of South Asia', in S. B. Schwartz (ed.) *Implicit understandings: observing, reporting and reflecting on the encounters between Europeans and other peoples in the early modern era* (Cambridge, 1994), pp. 308–21.

[68] I have used the second edition of John Briggs' translation: Ferishta, *History of the rise of*

Perhaps what is most obvious is the way the Persian writer seems to depend on his written sources. In his first chapter he used the *Mahabharata* as the basis for a summary of Hindu cosmogonic beliefs and the starting point for a history of pre-Islamic Hindustan, displaying a certain awareness of the fact that Hindus often disagreed about fundamental beliefs. Firishta's summary account in effect amounts to a secularization of Hindu myths as garbled history, including an attempt to explain the origins of the caste system. His attempt to create a continuous historical narrative involved a great deal of legendary conquests, often made to relate to Persian figures from the Shah Nama or the history of 'Iskandar' (Alexander). When necessary, Firishta emphasized the validity of the biblical account of origins against Hindu beliefs. But his hostility to Hindu religion was more than just Muslim–biblical: he also used a fundamental distinction between the 'natural' paganism of pre-Muslim Persia, based on worshipping the sun and the stars, and the corrupting worship of images, set up in India at some historical point by a king at the instigation of a brahmin (this distinction of course served to protect many pre-Islamic Persian epic heroes from the stigma of outright idolatry).

What emerges most clearly in this prologue is that whilst the writer artificially created much of the historical continuity between episodes of ancient Indian history, often misplacing events, he also captured the essential patterns of dynastic power and crisis of the Muslim historical period. Here, among the many chapters devoted to the history of the Deccani dynasties, we often find the kings of Vijayanagara playing a stereotyped role which could perhaps be defined as being regularly beaten up by Muslim armies and forced to pay huge ransoms. This humiliating role is, of course, in perfect agreement with the plan of the work, an account of Muslim conquests in India. Vijayanagara represented, as Babur the founder of the Mughal dynasty himself wrote in his memoirs, 'the greatest both in territory and army among the pagan rulers' at the time of his conquest of northern India.[69] According to Firishta, already in the fourteenth century 'the princes of the house of Bahmuny maintained their superiority by valour only; for in power, wealth and extent of country, the rajas of Beejanuggur exceeded them'.[70] The contest between Muslims and idolaters, in which the latter always

---

the Mahomedan power. Briggs, whose first edition appeared in 1829, often closely followed the 1794 translation by Jonathan Scott, chaplain of the East India Company and secretary to Warren Hastings for his Persian correspondence.

[69] Babur, *Babur-Nama (Memoirs of Babur)*, trans. and ed. by A. S. Beveridge, 2 vols. (London, 1921), p. 483.

[70] Ferishta, *History*, vol. II, p. 337.

came out worst, was enhanced by the superior wealth and numbers of the beaten enemy (of course this is a cheap rhetorical trick, not exclusive to Muslim historiography).

It seems possible that the facility with which Firishta accepted the role of Vijayanagara as a dumb enemy helps explain why he was so likely to garble his account of the affairs of the kingdom. A good example is his version of Ibrahim Adil Shah's intervention in the succession crisis at the end of Achyuta's reign, which I mentioned earlier when discussing Gaspar Correa's account of these events.[71] With the help of the Portuguese chronicle, we are able to identify a mysterious figure like Firishta's imbecile but powerful 'Bhoj Tirmul Ray' as Salakaraju Tirumala, who became regent on behalf of his nephew Venkata I, disposed of him, and then had to confront the opposition of many captains led by Rama Raja. Firishta's account of how Bhoj Tirmul Ray called for the help of Ibrahim from Bijapur, followed by his eventual and tragic suicide, is probably essentially reliable, since it involved specific Deccani interventions – it certainly fits to some extent with Correa's version. But it is only possible to make sense of the whole story by adding central figures entirely missing from Firishta's picture, like king Achyuta himself, whilst being sceptical about much that surrounds the possibly genuine details. In fact the dynastic succession described by Firishta can only have had a historical basis if we accept that different figures have been mixed up. The patterns of usurpation and betrayal by generals, uncles and nephews are all displayed, but not usually the correct storyline or the individual identifications.

Is there, however, any further logic behind this apparent confusion? Indeed. To begin with, the Persian writer is keen to identify some of the Hindu rulers as quasi-mythical figures who act as a type throughout the narrative. Thus for the fourteenth century we find a haughty 'Krishna Ray' who is repeatedly humiliated by the first Bahmanis; in the fifteenth century we have an amorphous 'Dew Ray', or Deva Raya, who is forced to marry his daughter to the Muslim sultan with all pomp, and eventually tries to imitate his military techniques, cavalry and archers, in order to reverse a string of defeats (to no avail: in the end he is forced to pay tribute); and for the sixteenth century Rama Raja occupies the centre stage. What is really significant is that all these types incarnate the

---

[71] Compare Correa, *Lendas*, vol. V, pp. 247–9 and 276–83, to Ferishta, *History*, vol. III, pp. 80–6. There is no point in reproducing Firishta's whole passage here, because it is as intricate as it is misleading. The accounts of modern historians like Sewell (1900), Heras (1927), Nilakenta Sastri (1955), and Stein (1989), need to be read with a certain amount of scepticism when they follow it, explicitly or implicitly. For example, Firishta gives the date of AH 942 / AD 1535–6 for the succession crisis in Vijayanagara; this must be a mistake for AH 949.

powerful king defeated, rather than the powerful king as such. This is perhaps the reason why Krishna Deva Raya, the most emblematic figure in the Hindu tradition, is largely absent from Firishta's account of the sixteenth century.[72]

The only real exception to this general rule of minimizing any Hindu victories is the detailed description of Rama Raja's interventions in the Deccan, almost invariably in combination with one Muslim power against the other. There can be little doubt about the historical reality of many of the alliances and counter-alliances of the 1540s and 1550s described in Firishta's account, a period when Rama Raja could count not only on the traditional rivalry between Bijapur and Golkonda, but also on the war between the Adil Shahs and the rulers of Ahmadnagar, and thus prospered by siding for a few years with one, then with the other. Whilst modern historians may understand that Rama Raja cleverly weakened the ruler of Bijapur, his main enemy, by first allying with his Muslim rivals, and then transforming him into his own pawn, Firishta instead focuses on the shortcomings of the Muslim rulers. He suggests, therefore, that the real causes for the success of Rama Raja were the tyranny of Ibrahim Adil Shah (as opposed to the fidelity and wisdom of his captain Asad Khan), and the rivalry between the Muslim sultans, which for a number of years was out of control. In any case this criticism of the sultans, which comes surprisingly forceful, is only made explicit because eventually they can be shown to have reacted against the excessive power and insolence of the idolaters, reaching a historical agreement to briefly revive the power of a united Muslim army (as had been the case during the Bahmani period) and thus destroy the hegemony of Vijayanagara. In this way, the success of the Muslim alliance in the battle of Talikota is the real justification for the previous display of Rama Raja's opportunistic advances.

In no other chapter are the victories of the Hindu armies described so cogently, nor the rivalries between Muslim sultans so objectively narrated. This is partly because the events of this period were close to the historical memory of Firishta's time of writing, some forty years later; but the contrast with the neglect of the reign of Krishna Deva Raya only

---

[72] Ferishta, *History*, vol. III, p. 80. To some extent Krishna Deva Raya may be identified with a certain 'Shew Ray', whose death signals the end of an uninterrupted succession of Vijayanagara kings of 700 years and opens the way for the chaos that followed. In fact, Firishta seems to have merged three different figures into 'Shew Ray': the last of the Sangama rulers, Saluva Narasimha and Krishna Deva Raya. Firishta does describe a failed expedition by Ismail Adil Shah against Raichur in 1519, in which his defeat at the river Krishna is attributed to his indulgence in wine. Sewell has identified this conflict with the famous battle of Raichur of 1520. But Firishta makes no mention of the name of the victorious raja of Vijayanagara.

a few further decades earlier is still too dramatic. It seems clear that Firishta was here setting the stage for a considered discussion of why the holy war against the infidel should have been undertaken, and with such success. To begin with, there was a religious offence which was obviously intolerable: 'In the first expedition, when Ali Adil Shah had invited Rama Raja to his assistance, the Hindus committed great outrages at Ahmadnagar, and omitted no mark of disrespect to the religion of the faithful, singing and performing their abominations and superstitious worship in the very Mosques.'[73] The king of Bijapur was therefore simply performing his duty when, according the Firishta, he conceived the holy war:

> [His advisers said that] the king's desire to humble the pride of the Raja of Vijayanagara [Beejanuggur] was undoubtedly meritorious and highly politic, but could never be effected unless by the union of all the Mohammedan kings of the Deccan, as the revenues of Rama Raja, collected from sixty seaports and numerous flourishing cities and districts, amounted to an immense sum.[74]

The recognition of the superior resources of the king of Vijayanagara led to the formulation of a religious theory about the historical significance of the politics of the Deccan:

> [Mustafa Khan, envoy of Ibrahim Qutb Shah of Golkonda, said that] during the times of the Bahmani princes the whole strength of the Muslim power was united under one king, which maintained the balance against the force of the raja of Vijayanagara; that now, though the Mussalman power was divided, policy required that all the princes of the faithful should unite in restraining the increasing power of their common enemy . . . in order that the people of their several dominions, who should be considered as being committed by the Almighty to their care, might repose in safety from the oppression of unbelievers.[75]

There is evidence here of some nostalgia for an earlier period when the Bahmanis ruled and their armies massacred unbelievers 'in so relentless a manner, that pregnant women and children at the breast even, did not escape the sword'.[76] The historical voice of the Muslim historian (sometimes Firishta, sometimes his sources) does not always advocate such cruelty – at some point he commends 'the general custom in the Deccan' which is 'to spare the lives of prisoners in war, and not to shed the blood of an enemy's unarmed subjects'.[77] However, bloodshed is still the corollary of a victory of such importance as that against Rama Raja. It

---

[73] Ibid., p. 132. (In the following quotations I have modernized proper names so as to avoid an excessive sense of archaism).
[74] Ibid., p. 123.   [75] Ibid., pp. 124–5.   [76] Ibid., vol. II, p. 316.
[77] Ibid., p. 319.

seems clear that Firishta saw in this event one of the high points of his narrative. In the midst of the battle, and after the Hindu infantry had been devastated by the artillery of Husain Nizam Shah of Ahmadnagar, the king was captured and immediately beheaded, and his head placed at the point of a spear:

> The Hindus, according to custom, when they saw their chief destroyed fled in the utmost disorder from the field, and were pursued by the allies with such success, that the river was dyed red with blood. It is computed, by the best authorities, that above one hundred thousand infidels were slain during the action and in the pursuit ... the advanced troops penetrated to Vijayanagara, which they plundered, razed the chief buildings to the ground, and committed every species of excess.[78]

This is of course not so different from what one can read in Livy – it is in the nature of both barbarians and idolaters to lose any discipline when confronted with defeat. Firishta's essential point is that the Hindus may sometimes win because of their wealth and numbers, or their desperate determination to protect their idols, but not on account of their virtue: rather the contrary, it is the Muslims, the true moral subjects, who only need to restrain themselves from vicious passions in order to succeed as agents of the faith.

Despite the primacy of this moral vision, Firishta's description of the battle of Talikota is in any case valuable for its many details, although his bias is also apparent – in his insistence on Rama Raja's intolerable arrogance, and in his neglect of the fact, attested by the Venetian traveller Cesare Federici, that the Hindu army had been betrayed by its Muslim cavalry.[79] We can conclude that for much of his narrative Firishta is extremely unreliable, even though his account may have a factual basis,

---

[78] Ibid., vol. III, pp. 130–1. The rhetorical expression 'razed to the ground' elicits comment. Heras, *Aravidu dynasty*, pp. 218–28 points out that the city of Vijayanagara was not sacked immediately, but only after a few days which the Muslim armies spent plundering the enemy's camp (Rama Raja's surviving brother Tirumala, the puppet king Sadashiva and many of the wealthy captains might have organized a resistance but fled instead). He also insists that the image of the total destruction of the city given by Firishta has to be qualified in the light of the survival of many buildings. Obviously the timber, brick and plaster upper levels of temples and palaces, and the more movable sculptures, were destroyed or damaged, but not the stone and mortar foundations. Important buildings often had upper floors which stood upon columns. It has also been noted that Shaiva temples survived better than Vaishnava ones: Michell, *The Vijayanagara courtly style*, p. 3. It seems clear, however, that after a few months of occupation and systematic plunder the city had suffered not only a great deal of physical destruction; it had also lost its mythical aura, which Tirumala as new regent would seek to recreate in vain.

[79] I discuss the western sources of the battle on p. 304 below. Heras, *Aravidu dynasty*, pp. 199–217 is more careful than Sewell, *Forgotten empire*, pp. 196–209.

because from his Deccani perspective (which was also that of many of his sources) Vijayanagara represented only 'the other', whose role was to fall victim to the success of Muslim sultans. In this sense Firishta was more 'orientalist' than Nunes, who had no vested interest of the kind. Whilst Nunes and Correa offered a limited view of the history of Vijayanagara, in comparable passages Firishta is both more partial and more confused. The existence of a rhetorical emphasis based on the idea of holy war was of course not exclusive to Islam – the same idea dominated, as we saw, the main Portuguese chronicles of conquest. However, the level of sophistication with which sixteenth-century Spanish and Portuguese writers made the theme of providential success compatible with empirical research, narrative coherence and educational versatility was clearly superior, and in this sense Firishta's crude presentation of interactions with the enemy can perhaps be better compared to the way thirteenth-century Iberian chronicles depicted their Muslim opponents in the peninsula.

The most important observation is that Muslim historiography of non-Muslim peoples, even when detailed and reliable, does not seem to have seriously grown out of the rhetorical model of the holy war. For example, Zinadim's magnificent sixteenth-century chronicle of the wars against 'the Franks' in Malabar is a good example of the fact that a fresh historical genre, empirical and coherent, could develop in India in response to the arrival of the Portuguese, and yet only do so around the idea of a religious–military confrontation. Zinadim (Zain-ud-din), probably a Muslim trader from Calicut, thus dedicated his Arabic *Gift of the defenders of the faith* to Ali Adil Shah of Bijapur in order to 'incite the believers to the war against the worshippers of the cross, as is their obligation, since these Christians invaded a Muslim territory, capturing, killing, and converting a great number of the believers, and then forcing Muslim women to give them Christian sons who would continue the struggle'.[80] The chronicle was not only a history of the peaceful penetration of Islam in Malabar (including an insightful description of 'pagan' customs) and of the cruel depredations of the Portuguese, but also an elaboration of the theory of holy war, defining Malabar as a Muslim territory (disregarding the fact that its rulers were Hindu) and stressing the need for action and unity among Muslim rulers. Sympathy for the

---

[80] D. Lopes (ed.) *Historia dos Portugueses no Malabar por Zinadim. Manuscripto arabe do seculo XVI* (Lisbon, 1898), p. 5. Lopes used better manuscripts than M. J. Rowlandson, who published an English version in 1833. The events described in the chronicle go as far as 1585, but the dedication must be prior to 1579, when Ali Adil Shah was murdered. This suggests, according to Lopes, that the work had a continuator, although this does not detract from its overall coherence. The year 1575 is a likely date for the first version.

ruler of Calicut and his people was logical in a work which described Hindus as future Muslim converts and which did not hide the fact that the Hindu kings of Malabar depended upon Muslim traders for their prosperity. However, the strength and validity of this friendship only became essential to a Muslim historical discourse in the face of the serious threat posed by the Franks.

Thus the question was not really the sheer weight of historical experience, but rather the way it was culturally elaborated within a set of language-games. Centuries of rule over Hindu subjects did not automatically confer upon the Muslim elites of the Deccan more analytical insight than some Europeans achieved in a few decades, and the early achievement of a talented individual like Al-Biruni remained practically unsurpassed because the scientific geographical genre which he cultivated was marginal in Indo-Muslim education. Although certainly much cultural contact went on which historians did not care to record (or perhaps even *actively avoided* to acknowledge), and despite the undeniable originality of the cultural syncretism achieved occasionally by individual patrons like the Mughal ruler Akbar, the crucial issue is that the attention of the Muslim historian was not ordinarily directed towards understanding native politics and religion, but rather towards the glorification of military dynasties according to Persian cultural models, with the denunciation of personalities and factions as the writer's possible main local theme. Firishta is a representative writer because little in his rhetoric, other than the style, is peculiar to him.[81]

If we define orientalism as a manipulative historical gaze based on a crude separation between *us* and *other*, and which denies the representation of this *other* any intrinsic voice, then there was very little in the Muslim discourse about Hindu India which was less orientalist than what contemporary Europeans perceived and wrote. Just as Goa, a mere eight days' distance from Vijayanagara, looked towards Europe rather than India for its structures of discourse, so the Muslim elites of the Deccan looked towards other Muslim courts rather than their Hindu neighbours, whom they probably resembled more in everyday practice

---

[81] This is clear if we compare Firishta's account of the fall of Vijayanagara with the rather absurd version given by a contemporary historian, the Mughal official Nizam-ud-din Ahmad Bakhshi (1551–94), who in a few lines explains that the Muslim kings were about to be defeated when a cannon ball accidentally hit Rama Raja, turning the tide of the battle: Nizamuddin, *The Tabaqat-i-Akbari*, trans. by Brajendranath De, ed. by Baini Prashad, 3 vols. (Calcutta, 1911–39), vol. III, pp. 141–4. Here again the role of the kings of Vijayanagara, mainly rhetorical, is to be outwitted by the Muslim sultans, and we cannot expect the details of the battle to be accurate. Nizamuddin's work was in fact one of the sources for Firishta (although not for the section on the Deccan), and possibly his main inspiration. Similar conclusions are reached by Peter Hardy in his *Historians of Medieval India. Studies in Indo-Muslim historical writing* (London, 1960), p. 114.

than they ever wished to acknowledge by the testimony of the written record. Perhaps the fact that they looked as far away as Persia for their cultural models (Herat, the Timurid capital, was still a key model in Babur's historical memory when he conquered Delhi) ironically made the Indo-Muslim elites less prone to idealize kingship in Vijayanagara than a fifteenth-century Khorasani like 'Abd al-Razzāq could have been. But this leaves open the field for a definition of orientalism that goes beyond the simple scheme of opposition between the gaze of a dominant elite and its objectified victim. What is most obvious about the development of historical discourses in sixteenth-century Europe is the growth in quantity and complexity of the narratives dealing with the non-Christian, non-European others. The paradox that needs to be clarified is how more information and more theoretical elaboration, rather than dissolving the fundamental problem of orientalist manipulation, simply shifted the ground. The roles of the other multiplied, historical observation led to historical comparisons, and yet the question of whose identities were at stake in the creation and use of discourse remained necessarily problematic.

RE-DEFINING ORIENTALISM

'Orientalism' has traditionally been defined as a western imperialist attitude in which the colonized subjects are perceived according to purely western ideological concerns. It has however become obvious that there were equally ideological biases in 'oriental' Muslim views of other oriental peoples (logically so, since western powers never had a monopoly of imperialist attitudes). Perhaps more significant than this unsurprising parallel is the evidence for the existence, in a common geographical space, of not one, but many discourses. At least three 'historiographical voices', Portuguese Christian, Telugu Hindu and Persian Muslim, sought to give meaning to the experience of the crisis of Vijayanagara at the end of the sixteenth century. Interestingly, although these historiographical traditions were all different, they did not develop in complete isolation from each other: rather, they acquired new traits through diverse kinds of interaction. And yet they maintained distinctive distances, which are often difficult to measure. Defining the particular quality of each historiographical tradition is therefore no less important than understanding the possibility of interaction.

The comparison between Portuguese and Muslim historians in India has allowed us to establish the relative sophistication of the European writers – even those writers from a country which was intellectually at the periphery of the Renaissance. However, this still leaves unanswered the question of the extent to which even the most informed travellers, however reliable and impartial as witnesses of events, and however willing to record native accounts, were essentially projecting their own cultural assumptions. Did Fernão Nunes impose a European 'feudal' understanding of society and politics onto his experience of Vijayanagara? Or can we claim that his analysis is fundamentally an original and, to some extent, lucid response to a peculiar reality, much as I suggested that Gaspar Correa, despite his use of European concepts like tyranny, was also writing about the nature of power in Vijayanagara?

Nunes's chronicle is as much an original combination of indigenous sources and Portuguese attitudes as his political interpretation is an attempt to 'translate' Vijayanagara patterns into more general models, analogous to European ones. One may argue that, even within the narrow framework of the court politics of the 1520s, he fails to mention some of the important historical movements emphasized recently by Burton Stein, such as the long rise to power of Aravidu Bukka and his son Rama Raja.[82] It must be borne in mind, however, that Nunes's experience of Vijayanagara was ultimately limited. It is not just that the terms of his language may have been simplistic when dealing with foreign social and cultural realities, or that he lacked our historical hindsight: his individual experience was also limited in time and space. Furthermore, the very native sources at his disposal were likely to omit many of the issues identified as significant by the modern historian. As I argued above, Barbosa, Paes, Barros and Nunes are occasionally better guides than some of these native sources. It is only when we keep all these considerations in mind that Nunes's account can be criticized fairly from the position of a modern reconstruction.

Stein has defined the fundamental problem in one sentence: 'the Vijayanagara kingdom, at the moment when its central authority was greatest, was a weakly-centralised polity'.[83] This weakness was due to the fact that the kings owed their power over local communities and temples to a caste of military overlords, the nayakas, who ultimately manipulated and contested the central institution of authority. The pattern of all crises of succession is strikingly similar: the prime ministers and generals who lead the royal armies to restore authority also go on to build up family factions, and eventually replace existing kings. The centralized prebendalism of a conquest state directed against an interior, as much as an exterior, enemy, led to the creation of powerful provincial generals in control of substantial resources and armies. (This pattern in fact would

---

[82] Stein, *Vijayanagara*, p. 113.   [83] Ibid., p. 121.

be carried over to the period of multiple nayaka courts after the destruction of the city).

There is little of this that the language used by Nunes fails to capture. He emphasizes the luxurious private life of the king (within the 'female' side of his palace), and his public display of military power,[84] but he also reveals the delicate balance of power between him and his captains. The royal ministers are few in number: a *regedor do reyno* (prime minister, probably also general of the royal army), a *tisoureyro* (treasurer) with the *escrivães de fazemda* (scribes of the exchequer), a *thisoureiro moor* (chief treasurer), a *porteiro moor* (head porter, i.e., commander of the palace guards), and two special officers in charge of key goods: jewels, and horses.[85]

We are here forced to translate Portuguese terms into indigenous realities, making suppositions such as that these *escrivãos de fazemda* were in charge of keeping a record of the revenues from the king's own lands and customs duties.[86] (It is worth recalling that Nunes may himself have had administrative experience as an official for the Portuguese king in India). Despite this linguistic distortion it is very clear that the administration thus described, with a very limited amount of paperwork and no sense of a secular constitution, is in fact in the hands of a powerful aristocracy: the king 'has no controller of the revenues nor other officers, nor officers of his house, but only the captains of his kingdom'.[87] Thus, for instance, 'Salvanayque [Chellappa Saluva Nayaka], who now is minister . . . is lord of Charamãodel [Coromandel] and of Nagapatão [Negapattinam], and Tamgor [Tanjavur], and Bomgarin, and Dapatao, and Truguel, and Caullim, and all these are cities; these territories are all very large, and they border on Ceylon'.[88] Thus, the current prime minister is actually lord of a substantial portion of the Tamil country.

In this context, the king's method of dealing with rebellious lords is not so much by the development of an independent central administration, as by the reliance on ultimate military superiority. This entails, of course, that if the king ceases to be the most powerful general, then the most powerful general will become king. In fact, the same minister (Saluva Nayaka) who had always supported Krishna Deva Raya, and guaranteed the enthronement of Achyuta in 1529, rebelled soon afterwards in 1531, leading a coalition of many other Tamil chiefs.[89]

---

[84] Lopes (ed.) *Chronica*, pp. 61–3.   [85] Ibid., p. 71.
[86] Here I follow Sewell's suggestion (*Forgotten empire*, p. 384).
[87] Ibid., p. 384.   [88] Lopes, *Chronica*, p. 72.
[89] See Stein, *Vijayanagara*, pp. 48–51. Stein insists that in 1529 Achyuta's succession was only secured against the pretender Rama Raja. However, he seems to be following the

Nunes dwells in detail, and with the precision of someone used to keeping numerical records, on the nature of this 'nobility':

These captains are like rentiers who hold all the lands of this king, and besides keeping all these people [600,000 foot-soldiers and 24,000 horsemen] at their own cost, they also pay to him every year sixty lakhs [6,000,000] of rents as royal dues. The lands, they say, yield a hundred and twenty lakhs [12,000,000] of which they pay sixty to the king, and the rest they retain for the pay of the soldiers and the expenses of the elephants which they are obliged to maintain. For this reason the common people suffer much hardship, those who hold the land being so tyrannical.[90]

Despite his claims to revenues from the whole land, and a lucrative monopoly on the importation of horses, this king has little direct political contact with his subjects, except through his lords. Peasants are portrayed as having to pay as much as nine-tenths of their produce to them.[91] The king, on the other hand, must spend more than half his revenues to keep his own soldiers, horses and elephants. He also keeps more than 4,000 women, who perform all kinds of services within the palace, and as many as 2,000 artisans paid by the day.[92] Nunes explains that he needs to keep a close watch on his lords, who therefore 'are always at court . . . obliged to be always with the king', and are not allowed to settle themselves in cities or towns, which are administered by proxy. Those lords who do not keep the appropriate number of soldiers 'are severely punished and their estates confiscated'.[93]

These captains – about 200, says Nunes – imitate on a smaller scale the lifestyle of the king: '[the captains of this kingdom] make use of litters and palanquins' and 'when a captain dies all his wives, however many he has, burn themselves'.[94] They all have secretaries who connect them permanently to the court, and who naturally act as spies: 'so that nothing happens which they do not soon learn'.[95] Nunes emphasizes that these captains, all 'gentios' (Hindus), are compelled to pay a fixed amount and to maintain a number of forces 'according to the lands and revenues that

interpretation of Venkataramanayya (*Further sources*, vol. I, pp. 234–6), who relies disproportionally on Firishta's botched passage. I also believe that Sewell was wrong in dating Nunes's chronicle as late as 1536–7. This narrative actually stops at the beginning of Achyuta's reign, when Saluva Nayaka (Chellappa) was still his minister. It should therefore be dated 1531, just before the rebellion of Saluva Nayaka for which there exists inscriptional evidence. Nunes actually reflects the climate of dissatisfaction that would have preceded it. This revised chronology, and the scepticism which must be thrown upon any account of the reign of Achyuta based on Firishta, also means that Stein's emphasis on Rama Raja's machinations as a cause for Saluva Nayaka's rebellion is probably unjustified.

[90] Lopes (ed.) *Chronica*, p. 64.   [91] Ibid., p. 68.   [92] Ibid., pp. 69–70.
[93] Ibid., p. 64.   [94] Ibid., pp. 74 and 77.   [95] Ibid., p. 65.

they have'.[96] He even provides a list of eleven important captains, which includes details of the territories they hold, and the amounts of men and *pardaos* that they supply each year.[97]

There can be little doubt that Nunes's understanding of European institutions did not prevent him in any fundamental way from conceptualizing the specific nature of political life in Vijayanagara. Rather, the analogous character of many institutions such as kingship, or even of ideological schemes such as the three-ordered division of society, actually helped him to introduce distinctions into the description of Indian peoples. Thus, *bramines* were like European friars and priests, while *nayaques* were compared to noblemen.

This homology would have been disastrous if it had been used to *hide* differences. However, it could be, and actually was, often used to provide a basis on which to build distinctive descriptions. In the analysis of political institutions, Nunes was able to show that Vijayanagara kings were remarkably successful in maintaining criminal justice, but he did not transmit any sense of a political constitution comparable to those of contemporary European principalities. The Indian king could thus nominally give and take lordships as he willed, without committing himself to any written law other than the mere record of all his deeds and sayings, which was kept scrupulously by palace officials. As a result, 'he never issues written letters for the favours he bestows or the commands he gives'.[98] When analysing society, Nunes again drew important parallels. Supporting brahmins with economic benefits, for instance, was translated as 'giving charity' in a way reminiscent of the endowment of monasteries in Europe.[99] But the long account of brahmin marriage and funeral practices at the end of the manuscript could leave the reader in no doubt that there were substantial differences between them and their Christian counterparts. It is in this careful observation of customary behaviour that travellers contributed most creatively to an ethnological discourse.

Does all this mean that there was no hint of 'orientalism'? I have mentioned earlier the considerable limitation posed by the lack of a legitimate cultural space that may have enabled secular travellers to approach religion from a comparative perspective. Nevertheless, the descriptions of the kind I have been analysing are far from being mere

---

[96] Ibid., p. 74.
[97] Ibid., pp. 72–4. According to Paes, one *pardao* had the value of 360 Portuguese *reis* (Sewell, *Forgotten empire*, pp. 282–3). This gold coin minted at Vijayanagara had prestige all over the Indian peninsula.
[98] Lopes, *Chronica*, p. 65: 'não passa cartas nem alvaras das merces que faz'.
[99] Ibid., p. 68.

'orientalist' constructions. In fact, it is possible to trace the *later* emergence of orientalism as Vijayanagara was progressively incorporated into more central areas of the European system of cultural discourses. If we take 'orientalism' to mean an attitude by which the other (and, only circumstantially, the *oriental* other) is defined more in terms of one's own system of power and identity than in terms of a genuine exchange, then it appears that, in the case of the Renaissance re-invention of the theme, 'orientalism' increased with distance, a distance which could be both physical and mental. That is to say that, rather than in the first-hand report of Nunes the merchant, it is in the summary of his account in the history of the vernacular humanist Barros, who was committed to an apology of the Portuguese empire, that orientalism took shape. And more clearly still, it was in the universal system of political cosmography of the Counter-Reformation scholar, Giovanni Botero, who summarized Barros and various travellers, that Vijayanagara became a stereotyped model of oriental tyranny. Paradoxically, all this occurred as the kingdom itself fragmented, and only a shadow remained of the mythical glory of the 'city of victory'.

João de Barros (1498–1570) published the third decade of *Ásia* in 1563, in which he devoted two chapters to explaining certain events relating to Vijayanagara.[100] It was part of his plan to offer an indigenous background to the narrative of the Portuguese expansion, but it also seems that this interest was, in the context of the decades, generally limited to the relevance such a background might have for the understanding and proper representation of Portuguese affairs. Barros thus justified including a section on the king of Narsinga because his wars with the Adil Shah of Bijapur favoured the Portuguese expansion in the 'terras firmes' (hinterland) surrounding Goa. This king was traditionally an ally of the Portuguese. But Barros emphatically chose to describe the power of such a king in terms of military ability, because it was only his power that interested him. He probably had the narratives of Paes and Nunes in front of him, and decided to disregard the kind of colourful picture supplied by the former:

> Now, if we gave notice of the way in which the king is served, and of the apparel of his household, this would be something with which to judge his wealth and power; but these are things which belong to refined and haughty princes, who with gold, silver and much political skill want to turn their houses into temples of worship, and service to their persons into a kind of idolatry, and by these means they want to

---

[100] Barros, *Ásia*, vol. III, ff.97r–104r (decade III, book 4, chaps. 4–5).

be served by their peoples. Therefore, we shall leave aside all these superstitions.[101]

Thus Barros rejected the extraordinary display of the festival, so carefully described by the Portuguese horse-traders, precisely because it succeeded in suggesting the sacredness of kingship in an idolatrous context – and certainly Barros would not like his own lords to mirror themselves in bad examples. Thus he turned to his feudal epic ideal: 'because the power and being of a prince cannot be reasonably noticed better in anything other than the order and apparel appertaining to military practice'.[102] Barros returned to Nunes, and then summarized, with elegant and measured style, his account of the prebendal system that allowed the king to concentrate revenues and raise huge armies.[103] This served as a good basis for a more detailed account of the expedition against the fortress of Raichur, in which Barros could describe not only the indigenous military campaign and diplomatic exchange, but also the decisive intervention of Cristovão de Figueiredo and his Portuguese men as the providential allies of the gentile king. Curiously, this section of Nunes's chronicle was precisely the one in which the Portuguese became protagonists (much as Xenophon's Greek mercenaries were the heroes of his account of Persian wars).

Barros's incipient orientalism was only the starting point for authors writing about Vijayanagara in Europe. The South Indian kingdom never attracted as much interest as the Ottoman state or, later in the sixteenth century, Mughal India, Japan or China, but its presence is remarkable none the less. For instance François de Belleforest, in his 1575 French translation of Münster's influential cosmography, included a description of the *Royaume de Narsinga* as part of his improvements on the original.[104] However, Belleforest lacked the geographical or historical perspective to summarize the original sources he found in Ramusio's collection without making serious mistakes and distorting the original emphasis. He thus used Barbosa's full account and Varthema's sketch in order to create an image of Vijayanagara, and yet he did not use information from these travellers to criticize the Greek sources, as Ramusio wanted, but rather tried to combine these new descriptions with some dubious identifications from Ptolemy's geography. Furthermore, he expanded the original accounts with unnecessary verbosity, while at the same time failing to realize that the oriental kingdom had been

---

[101] Ibid., f. 97v.   [102] Ibid.

[103] He attributed this account to indigenous officers of the exchequer: 'segundo o que temos sabido dos oficiais de fazemda daquele príncipe' (ibid.).

[104] François de Belleforest, *La cosmographie universelle de tout le monde* 2 vols. (Paris, 1575), vol. II, p. 1660.

destroyed ten years before he published his universal cosmography. It was not simply that Belleforest could hardly have had access to something like Cesare Federici's account of the fall of Vijayanagara, only published in 1587, but more importantly he suffered from the theological tendency to create a cosmographical encyclopaedia which would be as definite an account of God's created world as possible – and therefore, the historical dimension did not play a coherent role.

Giovanni Botero (1544–1617), a failed would-be Jesuit but successful counsellor of Cardinal Federico Borromeo, also included Vijayanagara in one of the most important cosmographies of the Renaissance.[105] In the various volumes of his *Relationi universali* (Rome, 1591–6) he brought together an immense mass of geographical and anthropological information, which he tried to organize according to broad methodical categories (like 'resources', 'government' and 'religion') so that it might serve to test his own political and economic theories, as explained in *Delle cause della grandezza e magnificenza delle città* (Rome, 1588) and *Della ragion di stato* (Rome, 1589). The second and most popular part of his *Relationi* (1592), dealing with the political organization of the most important nations of the known world, included Botero's fullest account of Narsinga.[106] It was based on the historians Barros and Osório, but also on the various accounts published in Ramusio's travel collection (which included those by Conti, Varthema, Barbosa, Pires and, in later editions, Federici). Unfortunately, the fact that Botero wrote his summary with a wider perspective than Barros did not prevent him from trying to extract some political lessons which had little to do with the conditions in which the original descriptions had been written. He looked for a comparative framework where particulars could be assembled and understood according to more general conditions. Asia was, in his opinion, a land where specific climatic conditions encouraged great empires, and also the source of all ancient sciences, of the events of sacred history, and of many valuable spices; Europe, instead, derived its superior strength from its diversity and divisions, which were explained

---

[105] See F. Chabod, 'Giovanni Botero', in *Scritti sul Rinascimento* (Turin, 1974), pp. 269–458; Lach, *Asia*, vol. II, pp. 235–49. I have discussed Botero as cosmographer in Rubiés, 'New worlds and Renaissance ethnology', pp. 178–81.

[106] There was also one section devoted to Narsinga in the first part (1591), which was more like a world geography (part I, book II). The most interesting discussion is, however, in the second part (1592). I have based my analysis on the first full Italian edition: Giovanni Botero, *Relationi universali* (Vicenza, 1595–6), compared with the latest and most complete version (Venice, 1618). I have used the English version by Robert Johnson as the basis for my quotations of the description of Narsinga: Botero, *The travellers breviat, or an historicall description of the most famous kingdomes in the world*, translated by I. R. [Robert Johnson] (London, 1601).

by a combination of natural causes (the geographical setting) and human qualities (the characters and skills of its different peoples).[107]

Botero's interpretation of Vijayanagara became the best known in seventeenth-century Europe, as the second part of the *Relationi* was translated independently as a short historical description of the most famous kingdoms of the world. In England, for instance, Robert Johnson's *The travellers breviat* (London, 1601), first printed anonymously but with Botero's material arranged in a different order, was repeatedly republished, often in revised and enlarged editions (1603, 1608, 1616, 1630).[108]

The result of several overlays of epitomes was to produce a text that responded more to the interpretative needs of European writers than to the original experiences of those who went, saw and heard. However, in reality, Botero had not made any direct effort to *change* the story, nor had he tried to depart consciously from the empirical model of knowledge sustained by the figure of the traveller. On the contrary, he even compared Conti with Varthema and complained about their inconsistencies in measuring the size of the city of Bisnagar.[109] Some of his blunders result from a misguided attempt to make things clear: 'In Narsinga are two imperial cities; Narsinga and Bisnagar: by reason whereof he is termed sometime king of Narsinga, sometime King of Bisnagar.'[110] There is also a concern with finding models useful in the context of the political thought of the West, which could feed on the interpretative emphasis of the original Portuguese descriptions. Vijayanagara is a land prodigiously abundant 'with all good things'. This soon reaches fantastic proportions, reminiscent of ancient and medieval accounts of the marvels of India. 'The waters . . . doe woonderfully coole, moisten, and inrich this land, causing the graine and cattell to prosper above imagination.'[111]

---

[107] Botero, *Relationi* (1618), part I (book 1), pp. 1–2; part I (book 2), p. 102; part II, p. 45.

[108] From his introduction, which alters somewhat Botero's own analysis of the balance between the different parts of the world which derived from his comparative perspective, it appears that Johnson was less interested in Asia as a modern reality than in developing the idea that the Europeans were morally superior, and thus – a remarkable statement with few equal precedents – fit to rule the world: 'so it seemeth that nature hath created this people [the Europeans] fit to rule and govern others, as men far surpassing all other nations in wisdome, courage and industrie' (Botero, *Travellers breviat*, pp. 2–3). He does not thus discuss like Botero the 'natural', climatically determined potential of Asia for great empires. Johnson's translation was re-edited in 1603. The versions of 1608 and 1616 were enlarged and reorganized by the same Johnson and had a new introduction. In 1630 John Haviland published a further revision of Johnson's translation. Throughout these editions the European sections were updated, but remote areas like Narsinga still closely followed Botero's 1592 text.

[109] Botero, *Relationi* (1618), part I (book 2), p. 113.

[110] Botero, *Travellers breviat*, p. 140.   [111] Ibid., p. 139.

Thus, while some details are close to the original descriptions – the diversity of provinces and languages within the kingdom, the fact that it depends on horses imported from the Indian Ocean, or the relationship established with the Portuguese on the coast – the central concern of Botero's text, namely, to understand the power of the king to raise huge armies and to present himself as a very rich and powerful lord, is rationalized in a way that completely misses the internal mechanisms by which power and revenues were distributed in the South Indian empire. The author tries to explain the military power by appealing to an image of *oriental despotism* which, in fact, enhances the power of the king at the expense of the common people. Thus, we are told that 'He is absolute lord of the bodies and goods of his subiects [*padrone de i fondi del suo stato*], which he shareth to himselfe and his captaines, leaving the people nothing but their hands and labour . . . all these barbarous princes [*prencipi orientali*] maintaine not peace and iustice, as arches whereupon to lay the groundworke of their estates, but armes, conquest and the nurserie of continuall soldierie'.[112] Botero had been clearly impressed by Barros's account of Vijayanagara military might, but before reproducing the expedition to Raciel (Raichur) he introduced some negative reflections. A quick comparison with a Christian prince, the king of France, allowed Botero to show that if this king were absolute, as 'potentates of the East' are, and therefore richer, he would be able to raise huge armies. However, since wealth is better distributed in Europe, thanks to the variety of rights and laws that limit the power of the king, 'the peazants live wel here, in comparison of the villagois of India, Polonia and Lithuania'.[113] Botero even offered a quantitative analysis of the differences between the French and Vijayanagara regimes. In France he estimated an annual rent of 15,000,000 scudi, as opposed to 12,000,000 in Vijayanagara. However, while the king of Vijayanagara could dispose of

---

[112] Ibid., p. 140. Compare with Botero, *Relationi* (1595–6), part II, p. 201r: 'essendo il re padrone de [tutti] i fondi del suo stato (non resta a i popoli altro che le braccia e la fatica) egli è cosa verisimile che, compartendo egli tutto ciò che se ne cava d'entrata, tra lui et i capitani suddetti (egli ne tira un terzo per se, e gli altre due terzi restano ai capitani) alcuni di loro tiranno summe grandissime. Dalche si vede che la più parte dei prencipi orientali, perchè non hanno per fine ne la pace nè la giustitia, ma la vittoria et la potenza, rivolgono tutte le loro facoltà all'intertenimento della militia, e di altro non si curano.' Although Johnson's translation here seems to be a little free, using the concept of 'absolute lord' for 'padroni de tutti i fondi del suo stato' and translating 'prencipi orientali' by 'barbarous princes', on the whole he faithfully captures Botero's expressions. The expressions 'governo despotico' and 'padrone assoluto de i suoi domini' (with an emphasis on the ruler's unlimited control of the persons of his subjects and their goods) also appear in Botero's analysis of comparable regimes.

[113] Botero, *Travellers breviat*, p. 141. Compare Botero, *Relationi* (1595–6), part II, p. 201r: 'i contadini vivono in quel regno [France] largamente, e in Levante, massime nell'India, sono (come anche in Polonia e Lituania) in conto di schiavi'.

all his goods for his military campaigns, the French kings only controlled 1,500,000, and the rest was in the hands of the Church (6,000,000) or private owners (7,500,000). The real financial advantage of the French kings was their ability to tax additionally for about 8,000,000. Thus the French kings were potentially more wealthy, because although their armies were actually smaller, they did not need to monopolize rents or ruin their peasants. Ultimately their wealth came from taxing the private wealth of their subjects. The king of Vijayanagara, by contrast, spent most of his rents (some 9,000,000 scudi) on his army of about 40,000 elite foot soldiers (which Botero wrongly defines as *nairs*) and 20,000 horsemen. Additionally, his 200 captains (Nunes's nayakas) also exercised similar despotic monopolies in their dominions, and raised their own small armies – they gave a third of their revenues to the king and kept the rest.[114]

Oriental despotism is therefore seen to be founded upon an excessive concentration of authority and revenues. In the third part of his *Relationi*, devoted to the religions of the world, Botero would find in his depiction of devilish idolatry of the 'Narsingani' a perfect complement to this image of political excess.[115]

Narsinga is not of course the main source, let alone the only one, for the late Renaissance image of despotism: in Botero's own *Relationi* the concept is constructed from a variety of oriental models, with examples that range from Muscovy and Turkey to China, Siam and the Mughal court. In all these cases the concept seems to acquire distinctive shades according to a variety of historical realities, although the general concept also seems to guide the way these realities are interpreted.[116] There is no simple exportation of a Greek–European idea of despotism, nor of course a transparent reading of oriental systems of government. Unprecedented access to new empirical realities, and the intellectual challenge of interpreting them from a particular set of Counter-Reformation, reason-of-state concerns, explain the way Botero both adopts and,

---

[114] All of Botero's data for Vijayanagara are taken from Barros, who took them from Nunes.

[115] Botero, *Relationi* (1595–6), part III (book 2), 54v: 'The peoples of Narsinga believe first of all in one God, Lord of the universe: and afterwards in the devils [*demonii*], authors of all evil [*autori d'ogni mali*]. For this reason they do more honour to these devils than to Him, and build for them many and magnificent temples [*pagodi*] with great rents.' The structure of this analysis of Hinduism, with the separation of a God–Creator and his devilish agents, is surprisingly similar to the one underlying Varthema's 1510 description of the religion of Calicut.

[116] On this topic see also the useful article by W. G. L. Randles, ''Peuples sauvages' et 'états despotiques': la pertinence, au XVIe siècle, de la grille aristotélicienne pour classer les nouvelles sociétés révélées par les découvertes en Brésil, en Afrique et en Asie', *Mare Liberum* 3 (1991): 299–307.

through comparisons, elaborates with originality the concept of despotism in 1592. In his analysis of Akbar's Mughal state, Botero had announced the general thesis that oriental kings could muster enormous armies because they could arm men scantily, feed them poorly, and kill them easily. The whole state was a military machine and few other social needs were catered for. Of course, all these kings were tyrants, who ruled through the fear of their subjects and the love of elite bodies of soldier-slaves, rather than the love of their subjects and the fear of their enemies.[117] The comparison between Narsinga and France gave further illustration of the idea that the overconcentration of resources in the hands of the king and the military aristocracy had a social cost, paid by peasants and citizens, and was relatively wasteful. Despotism was therefore a form of fiscal overexploitation without global efficiency, determined by a military elite unconcerned with ordinary justice. But this was not exclusive to Indian or idolatrous societies: in the same work Turkey was the key example of a Muslim universal monarchy ruled according to the principles of despotism, opposed to the Catholic monarchy of Spain, in which royal government was subjected to religion and justice. The consequence of the fact that the Sultan owned everything and his subjects were his slaves was that the people were overexploited, the country was underpopulated, commerce was in the hands of foreigners, and prominent state officials lived by stealing from their own subjects.[118]

Of course we would be right in thinking that in this ideologically

[117] Botero, *Relationi* (1595–6), part II, ff. 203–4.

[118] Ibid., f. 223. On the European theme of the Ottoman state as despotic, see also the excellent book by L. Valensi, *The birth of the despot. Venice and the Sublime Porte* (Ithaca and London, 1993), who emphasizes the distance between the description of the Ottoman state in the Venetian relations up to 1570, which are generally neutral or even admiring, and the shift of language towards the idea of despotism in the following decades, culminating in Botero's formulation. Valensi sees this delegitimizing shift as deriving from the relative weakness of the Ottoman state in this period, combined with the crisis of republican regimes all over Europe, and in particular the fear of absolute monarchies in oligarchic Venice. The invention of despotism would be a result of the anti-tyrannical rhetoric of the period. Valensi remains vague about the exact relationship between Botero and his possible Venetian models and imitators, although she insists on the commonality of an Aristotelian political language. The 'invention of despotism', it must be made clear, was not uniquely nor even primarily Venetian-Republican: it derived from a broader debate which might be best termed the crisis of mixed constitutions. Rather than a choice between monarchy and republic, what was at stake for writers like Botero (or the Englishman Giles Fletcher in Russia) was the debate about *the nature of the monarchy*, constitutional or absolute. Although Valensi is right in insisting on the central importance of Turkey as a kind of 'European mirror', she somehow neglects the wider comparative context of Botero's development of the idea of oriental despotism. Botero did not simply transfer the Turkish model elsewhere in the Orient: he developed his model through multiple empirical comparisons, using the best sources available in Europe at the time.

charged and simplistic reading of the Ottoman state Botero's judgement was conditioned by his own religious allegiance in the context of a military threat intensely felt in sixteenth-century Italy: but precisely the strength and originality of his concept of despotism is that it is constructed comparatively, so that ultimately religious variables are peripheral to the analysis. This, for instance, is illustrated by the example of Muscovy, a nominally Christian (albeit Greek orthodox and thus heretical) state which shared its absolutism with Turkey – as an Ottoman vizir himself was known to have observed – and which was also overly imperialist, with disastrous effects for the population. Here the marks of absolutism were not only unbound cruelty towards ordinary people, but also restrictions on travel and contact with the exterior, promoting a general ignorance which allowed the Tsars to set themselves up, through an elaborate court pomp, as objects of quasi-idolatrous worship.

Not only could Christian rulers be despots, but oriental rulers could also be 'good'. Thus in China we find the peculiar example of a benevolent despotism, so that whilst the king is obeyed 'almost like a God' and there is no hereditary nobility to stand in his way, on the other hand justice and prosperity flourish, because peace and the conservation of the state are the only aims of the political system. Of course Botero here had been influenced by missionary sources, especially the Castilian Augustinian Juan González de Mendoza's history of China, which idealized China (these were also the years when the Jesuit Matteo Ricci was beginning to develop his original method of accommodation).[119] Above all, what the Chinese example of a benevolent despotism reveals is that there was not a simple abstract idea of despotism mechanically applied to oriental societies, but rather that the connotations of the concept varied from one context to another. Despotism emerged as an analytical concept with a wide range of possible meanings, with a core definition of power without limitations (religious, legal, constitutional, educational, economic and geographical), and a variety of examples of both the way in which these limitations were missing, and the various aims and effects of the despotic system. Despotism became oriental because most societies with centralized political systems (however superficially) which by 1590 presented an alternative to the European experience were located in the East.[120] Many were perceived to be powerful,

---

[119] Botero did not necessarily interpret promising fields of missionary activity in a positive political light, as the example of 'tyrannical Japan' shows.

[120] Thus Botero discussed the examples of Turkey, Muscovy, Tartary, China, Siam, the Mughal empire, Vijayanagara, Calicut, Persia and Japan. In Africa, he discussed the 'Xeriffe' of Mauritania, the 'Prester John' of Abyssinia, and what little was known of Monomotapa. The Prester John provided Botero with another example of Christian despotism, with a 'tyrannical' ruler whose subjects are treated like slaves and worship

very few were seen to be stable and well ordered, and none could be described as constitutionally balanced.

The relationship between Narsinga as an empirical model and the idea of despotism is then an excellent example of the way travel literature contributed to the intellectual culture of early modern Europe. The contribution was both decisive and methodologically complex. Whilst the different travel accounts and historical works, often remarkably empirical, did not entail a common interpretation of the political and cultural realities they described, they were not a pure expression of empiricism either. They all involved multiple acts of interpretation, and simultaneously lent themselves to a selective and, generally, more ideological treatment in Europe. Botero in particular transcended the level of a simple compilation of descriptions of the typical Renaissance cosmographer and developed a comparative analysis concerning the relative strength of states from an economic and constitutional analysis, and their peculiar historical tendencies. Perhaps the more important implications, famously elaborated by Montesquieu more than a century later, were the positive effects of the existence of legal and structural limitations on royal power. Narsinga did not, in Botero's framework, generate the concept of despotism: it sustained it, offering a new and credible location, a representational model, for concerns which were obviously more European than Greek.

In this way Botero tested and developed his political philosophy, an exercise through which the people of Vijayanagara, first stripped of their gods by Nunes, and then of the beauty of their landscape, city and festivals by Barros, became mere despots, defined now in purely secular terms (they simply happened to be idolatrous despots) against a European 'us': they had become *what we do not want to be.*

FROM A MYTH OF VICTORY TO A MYTH OF DESTRUCTION

Thanks to one of the three maps prepared by the cartographer Jacopo Gastaldi to accompany the first volume of Ramusio's travel collection, by 1554 Besinagar had been firmly set in the midst of the new European 'map of the world'. Throughout one century of intensive dialogue with

him as if he were holy (Botero, *Travellers breviat*, p. 171). On the other hand, Calicut was discussed mainly for its importance as an area of contact with the Portuguese (ibid., pp. 143–6). Despite the existence of kings, the lack of a powerful centralized political system precludes the discussion of their system of government as despotic and, instead, the argument focuses on the analysis of the nayars as a military elite, of which, as in Barbosa's time, what seems most interesting is their community of women (Botero ingenuously suggests that the ruler who introduced the practice knew Plato's *Republic*).

the *Geography* of Ptolemy, travel accounts had thus provided the information that enabled Renaissance Europe to supersede the ancients (see plate 9).[121] On the strength of the references contained in Ramusio's collection or in the Portuguese historians, occasional observations about Vijayanagara appeared in the historical, cosmographical or moralistic literature of the second half of the sixteenth century. Paolo Giovio, who corresponded with Barros, in his *History of his own times* of 1550 knew of the wealth and horses of the king of Narsingam.[122] The French Louis Le Roy in his *De la vicissitude ou varieté des choses en l'univers* of 1575 thought that Narsingue supported his case about the concurrence of armed strength and excellence in learning, while the Italian Pomponio Torelli found place in his treatise *Del debito del cavalliero* of 1596 for praising the women who, in order to inspire the soldiers to chivalric deeds, accompanied the armies of Vijayanagara to the field (they were actually prostitutes).[123]

In all these cases the humanist historians of the late Renaissance merely summarized and often misunderstood their information, and very few compared sources with the originality and ambition of Botero. They were in fact at the end of a long chain of the transmission of knowledge, as can be exemplified in the case of Michel de Montaigne. In one of his late additions to his essays (after 1588) he confirmed his view that 'the taste of good and evil things depends on our opinion' (the title of the essay announces its relativist point) with a reference to the custom of Narsinga, according to which 'even today' wives, concubines and other servants burnt themselves on the pyre of their dead husbands or masters. Montaigne was responding to the impact of his readings of the history of the Spanish and Portuguese conquests, in particular Simon Goulard's 1581 French version of Jerónimo Osório's *De rebus Emmanuelis* of 1571.[124] However, Bishop Osório here had done little more than to re-

---

[121] Gastaldi's map of India seems to have been based in particular on the geographical overview of India introduced by Barros at various points in his first decade (1552), and extracted by Ramusio for the second edition of the first volume of the *Navigazioni e viaggi* (1554). This can be seen by details such as the depiction of the river Nagundii (for the Tungabhadra), which in Barros's account, and faithfully on the map, mistakenly runs north from the Western Ghats (over Cannanor) to Besinagar and then falls eastwards 'across Orixa', all the way to its two mouths in the gulf of Bengal, by the cities of Godavarii and Masulipatam on the seventeenth degree of latitude (these two mouths are of course intended for the independent rivers Krishna and Godavari). See Ramusio, *Navigazioni e viaggi*, vol. II, p. 1064.

[122] Paolo Giovio, *Historiarum sui temporis*, in Giovio, *Opera*, vols. III–IV, ed. by D. Visconti (Rome 1956–64), vol. III, p. 233.

[123] For all these examples see Lach, *Asia*, vol. II, pp. 219, 227 and 311.

[124] Compare Michel de Montaigne, *The complete essays*, ed. by M. Screech, (Harmondsworth, 1993), p. 54, C, with [Goulard] *Histoire de Portugal*, p. 160. It is obvious that for this exotic information Montaigne followed his source very closely.

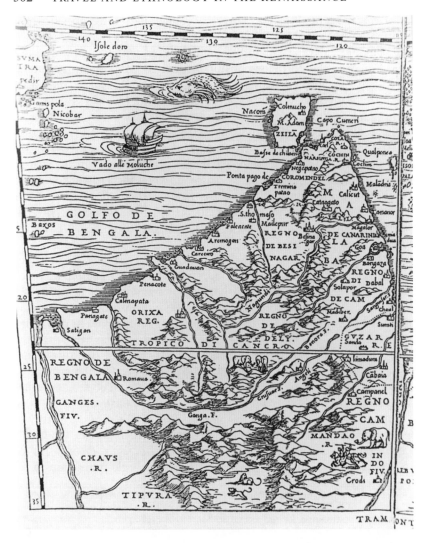

Plate 9 India, including Besinagar, from a map prepared by Jacopo Gastaldi with materials from Ramusio's *Navigazioni e viaggi* and published in the first volume of the collection (2nd edn, Venice 1554).

To all students of Geography: in these three maps the sea-coasts have been represented according to the navigational charts of the Portuguese, and the interior according to the writers contained in this first volume. Readers can therefore use the maps in order to obtain summary information of all the things that they will find in the volume, seeing in their proper locations the rivers, mountains, cities, provinces, and principal capes of Africa, Arabia, India and the Molucca islands . . . we believe that with this a part of the modern Geography will be so well illustrated that there will be little need to continue struggling with Ptolemy's maps (G. B. Ramusio).

write in elegant Latin the 1566 Portuguese chronicle by the humanist historian Damião de Góis, who had already summarized Castanheda's detailed but rough description of Vijayanagara, published in 1552. (It was his humanist rhetoric that made Osório's work attractive to the Protestant Goulard).[125] And yet Castanheda himself, as we have seen, seems to have followed Barbosa for the majority of his observations on the kingdom. Thus, just as Botero was developing a new theory of oriental despotism with Nunes's data, so Montaigne put observations which were ultimately Duarte Barbosa's to new uses.[126] Similar chains of transmission allowed episodes from the history of South India to enter the new world history written in Renaissance Europe. Thus, through Barros and Botero the battle of Raichur between Krishna Deva Raya and the Adil Shah of Bijapur became part of the historiography of the Portuguese conquest of India, and was mentioned by authoritative writers from the Renaissance to the Enlightenment – by Osório in the sixteenth century, Faria y Sousa in the seventeenth, and Lafitau in the eighteenth.[127]

However, what is most remarkable is that all these references were in a sense anachronistic: only a static image of Vijayanagara effectively reached Europe. Most maps, including Gastaldi's, showed 'Narsinga' and 'Besinagar' as separate kingdoms. More important, few of the writers of the late sixteenth century seem to have reflected on the disastrous end of the city that had sustained the myth of Vijayanagara, even though its portrayal figured prominently in the vivid narrative of the travels of a Venetian merchant, Cesare Federici, published in 1587, translated into English in 1588, and then incorporated into the collections of Hakluyt (1599–1600) and into a new edition of Ramusio (1606).[128] Nor could seventeenth-century writers profit from Couto's

---

[125] Compare H. Osorius, *De rebus Emmanuelis regis lusitaniae libri XII* (Lisbon, 1571), pp. 162–4, with Damião de Góis, *Chronica do felicissimo rei Dom Emanuel*, ed. by D. Lopes, 4 vols. (Coimbra, 1949–55), vol. II, pp. 21–4, and Castanheda, *História*, vol. I, pp. 244–50. It would seem that Góis summarized Castanheda's detailed description, and Osório summarized Góis. Castanheda's description of the customs and conditions of sixteenth-century Vijayanagara was the most detailed published in Europe until 1897.

[126] Montaigne also found the self-sacrifice of Hindu devotees on the Coromandel coast – throwing themselves under the wheels of a chariot carrying their idol, or cutting flesh from their bodies as an offering – as an argument for the re-examination of suicide from a supra-Christian perspective, in his essay 'A custom of the isle of Cea' (see Montaigne, *Complete essays*, p. 405). It is of course evident that Montaigne was not original in picking out *satis* and the *juggernaut* as sources of wonderment: what is new in Montaigne is spelling out a relativistic interpretation of this wonderment, through the literary context of the essay.

[127] Sewell, *Forgotten empire*, pp. 144–5, mentions these authors, but he is mistaken is describing Osório as a later historian than Faria y Sousa.

[128] Concerning Federici (*c.* 1535–1600), which was spelt Fedrici in contemporary

detailed account of the battle of Talikota in his eighth decade, written before 1614 but only published in 1673, except through the summary in Manuel de Faria y Sousa's posthumous *Asia portuguesa* (1666–75).[129] The circumstances of Faria y Sousa's career, a historian of unprecedented vision who, with Tacitean style and in Castilian language, wrote about the Portuguese overseas from the court at Madrid, only delayed the publication further.[130] The fact is that the gap between the observation in 1566 of an event with immediate and devastating consequences in South India (among other things, it seriously damaged the most profitable trade of Goa), and the publication of conventional travel and historical narratives in Europe decades later, helped consolidate in late sixteenth-century Europe the image of a ghost empire as it had been observed before 1535.[131]

Federici did, however, capture a new image of the city and empire. He travelled in Asia from 1563 to 1581, obviously seeking economic profit, and visited Vijayanagara during the first half of 1566, the year after the battle of Talikota, concluding that it was no longer a good place to conduct business. The version of the battle that he was able to hear during his seven-month stay in the ruined city emphasized that Rama Raja and his brothers – 'three tyrant brothers' – had been betrayed by two Muslim captains in the midst of the battle.[132] After the sack of the

documents, see the introduction to the very reliable critical edition of his account by Olga Pinto (ed.) *Viaggi di C. Federici e G. Balbi alle Indie Orientali* (Rome, 1962), pp. xxii–vi.

[129] Manuel de Faria y Sousa, *Asia portuguesa*, 3 vols. (Lisbon, 1666–75), vol. II, pp. 432–3.

[130] *Asia portuguesa* was written in the 1630s but only published after the separation of Portugal from Spain. Manuel's son Pedro felt obliged to justify in his prologue (dated 1662) the fact that the book had been dedicated to Philip IV of Castile (and written in beautiful Castilian) by retrospectively presenting his father as a prophet of the restoration. The fact of course is that before 1640 many Portuguese writers like Couto and Faria y Sousa were unable to predict the eventual independence of their nation, and worked for a Portuguese identity within the universalist system of the Catholic monarchy of Spain.

[131] The impact in Goa of the destruction of the Hindu capital was not only economic: it also gave new room to the Adil Shah of Bijapur to seek a comprehensive alliance against the Portuguese. Thus, in 1570–1 his siege of Goa, combined with simultaneous attacks from Ahmadnagar, was of unprecedented ambition. However, not all foresaw this danger in 1566–7, since the Portuguese were able to make quick and significant gains in the ports of the Kanarese coast, like Honavur or Mangalore. Afterwards, the increasing economic difficulties of the Portuguese made the idea that 1565 was a catastrophe for Goa appealing to later analysts – thus it was central to Couto's interpretation of the effects of Talikota in his eighth decade.

[132] Federici's account is very valuable for his proximity to the date and place of the battle. He was, however, bound to report the version of the citizens of Vijayanagara. Diogo do Couto, in his fairly detailed account of the battle, missed – like Firishta – this observation, emphasizing instead the chivalric imprudence of Rama Raja (Firishta called it unbearable arrogance), and the decisive technological advantage of the army of Ahmadnagar with their field artillery (Couto, VIII, 14–15; Compare with the variant

city (a sack in fact initiated by the flight of the surviving members of the ruling family) the new king Tirumala, Rama Raja's brother and former governor of the empire, was attempting to revive the capital under Federici's own eyes, but he failed to regain credit. Not recognized by many of the lords, he actually cheated the traders who brought him horses from Goa, and eventually, unable to dispel the idea that the place was doomed, in 1587 was forced to move the capital to Penukonda, a fortress-town further east. During Federici's visit the old capital was still safe (foreigners could sleep outside during the hot summer) and the royal palace was still impressive, but wilderness was gradually overcoming the city, while the roads were full of thieves and very dangerous:

I rested in Bezenger seven moneths, although in one moneth I might have discharged all my businesse, for it was necessary to rest there untill the wayes were cleere of theeves, which at that time ranged up and downe. And in the time I rested there, I saw many strange and beastly deeds [*cose strane e bestiali*] done by the Gentiles.[133]

The century and a half that separated Federici from his earlier compatriot, Nicolò Conti, is expressed through a considerable change in style. Both had travelled for many years, attempting to reverse their misfortunes through repeated expeditions to distant places like Pegu, risky but potentially very profitable. However, Federici was more aware of himself as an interesting subject than Conti would have dared to be, and the petty difficulties of the merchant-traveller – for instance his assault by thieves when he returned from Vijayanagara to Goa in the middle of the monsoon – had now become a possible literary theme (this was the inheritance left by travellers like Varthema). Moreover, even though by Renaissance standards Federici's material is not particularly well organized, there now existed a context, institutional and mental, which allowed him to be much more precise than Conti had been. This

---

manuscript version in Lima Cruz (ed.) *Diogo do Couto*, vol. I, pp. 180–9 which corresponds to Couto, VIII, 2, 10). Firishta, however, seems to imply that the Hindus also had artillery, although he agrees that the battle at some point was going badly for the allies and that the strength of the artillery of the Nizam Shah of Ahmadnagar, who was personally seeking revenge for the sack of his capital, was decisive in breaking the main body of Rama Raja's army and capturing the elderly ruler (who was reported to be ninety). Couto gives details about the role of the different brothers of Rama Raja which Firishta neglects to mention. His source were some Portuguese soldiers, probably fighting with Rama Raja. The two writers are, however, in remarkable agreement about the fundamentals.

[133] 'The Voyage and Travell of M. Caesar Fredericke, marchant of Venice, into the East India', translated by T. Hickock, in R. Hakluyt (ed.) *Principal navigations, voyages, traffiques and discoveries of the English nation*, ed. by J. Masefield, 7 vols. (London, 1907), vol. III, pp. 198–269, at pp. 213–14. I have compared Hickock's 1588 translation, generally faithful, with the Italian original: Pinto (ed.), *Viaggi*, p. 16.

framework was made possible by the Portuguese colonial system, and by the consolidation of travel writing as a European genre. Thus as a summary of trading prospects between Syria and Malacca, the account by Federici, and a similar one by his compatriot Gasparo Balbi, are much superior to Conti's observations. Federici no longer needed the promptings of a humanist like Poggio to keep a detailed diary – although he seems to have sought the assistance of a friar to prepare a summary for publication.[134] But perhaps the most striking difference that singles out Federici's description of Vijayanagara is a change of tone, now coloured by a perception of the historicity of the world. With the demise of the magnificent city, something more subtle than the mere guarantee of safe and profitable trade had died. In the dilapidated order of a decaying city gentile rulers were all tyrants, and strange customs, of which Federici seems only to notice *sati* sacrifices and similarly cruel burial practices, had become filthy and repugnant:

> Besides these, there are an infinite number of beastly qualities [*bestialità*] among them, of which I have no desire to write. I was desirous to know the cause why these women would so wilfully burne themselves <against nature and law>, and it was told mee that this law was of an ancient time, to make provision against the slaughters which women made of their husbands.[135]

After this reference to brahminic misogynism, the last glimpse caught by a European of the Hindu empire emphasized the loss of that strength and magnificence which earlier foreign visitors had admired:

> the sonne of this Temeragio [Tirumala Raja] had put to death the lawfull king [Sadashiva Raya] which he had in prison, for which cause the barons and noblemen in that kingdome would not acknowledge him to be their king, and by these means there are many kings, and

---

[134] This friar was Bartholomeo Dionigi da Fano, who appears as editor at the end of the Italian version of the voyage (Pinto, *Viaggi*, p. 68). His intervention may explain the moral tone of some of the comments on strange customs, the concluding remarks about the need to be an honest merchant, and the omission of sexually explicit observations which texts of this kind hardly ever failed to include (such as the description of the introduction of gold and silver balls into the genitals of male Peguans).

[135] Hakluyt, *Principal navigations*, vol. III, pp. 215–16. Compare with Pinto (ed.) *Viaggi*, p. 18. The misogynist interpretation of *sati* – as a measure to prevent women from poisoning their husbands – was long-standing and already reported in the ancient world by Diodorus Siculus. Whilst Federici's description of the practice did not depart from an earlier interest in the custom, his was certainly much more detailed. He did not hide his horror, perhaps because, as he explains, his dwelling in Vijayanagara was unfortunately located by the northern door of the city walls through which all processions passed in order to reach a field by the river Tungabhadra, where the burnings took place. However, the important expression 'against nature and law' was added by the English translator.

great division in that kingdome; and the city of Bezeneger is not altogether destroyed, yet the houses stand still, but empty, and there is dwelling in them nothing, as is reported, but tygers and other wilde beastes.[136]

---

[136] Hakluyt, *Principal navigations*, p. 216; Pinto (ed.) *Viaggi*, p. 19, where Federici describes Tirumala Raja as 're tirano'.

9. The missionary discovery of South Indian religion: opening the doors of idolatry

Throughout the sixteenth century Europeans in India and elsewhere overseas had elaborated an ethnological language with which they could approach human diversity in its natural setting through an immediate use of common analytical categories. They had also captured a historical vision which, in its inclusion of alien traditions, went far beyond previous European rhetorical conventions. The gap that still separated discourse generated overseas and discourse at home now offered ample room for the creation of orientalist clichés, but the power of the new historical vision was precisely its ability to do the opposite, to historicize Europe's other and thus challenge any clichés. The answer had to be an intellectual debate in which empirical issues could not be ignored.

In South India, Federici had witnessed, along with the end of the old and most splendid Vijayanagara, also the end of a phase in the history of European attitudes towards gentile civilization. Of course a rump kingdom of Vijayanagara survived for a few decades in the Indian hinterland and, perhaps more important, the idea of a mythical dharmic kingdom remained central to the political imagination of Hindu southern India. But the context had been transformed. Now European travellers confronted the problem of how to grapple with a civilization which had lost its political centre. The intellectual debate of the seventeenth century would certainly focus on China and the American Indians, Persia or the Mughal empire, rather than Hindu India, but the response given by Europeans to the problem of an obviously idolatrous urban and commercial civilization in India remained significant. One answer was to look at the religious dimension with a new kind of analysis that only the missionaries of Counter-Reformation Europe were prepared to undertake. Another possibility was to deepen the secular gaze and to ask openly the questions about human nature and cultural diversity which sceptical humanists in Europe had already begun to confront. These two answers had one thing in common: they challenged the convention of describing behaviour without analysing beliefs which had dominated travel literature and historiography since the late Middle Ages. On the other hand, the differences between these two discourses, one clerical, the other secular, to a large extent determined the shape of the Enlightenment anthropological debate. It is these two answers which the last two chapters of this historical essay will seek to discuss.

THE BIRTH OF A NEW GENRE

At the turn of the seventeenth century the Portuguese Jesuit Fernão Guerreiro (1550–1617), writing from the professed house at Lisbon, defined the Jesuit enterprise as 'opening the doors' of that immense gentile world of the oriental provinces to the reception of the gospel with (heroically) a mere 600 men.[1] He went on to describe the Jesuits' exploits in five volumes, returning to each location year after year, compiling and extracting the famous 'annual letters' sent from the missions in order to offer a systematic account of the activities of the Company in the East between 1600 and 1609.[2] However, Guerreiro's opening claim stopped short of the more radical image proposed by the Dutch Protestant writer Abraham Rogerius in the title of a book published in 1651, *De opendeure tot het Verbogen Heydendom* ('The open door to the understanding of hidden paganism'), best known in Europe through the French translation of 1670 as *La porte ouverte pour parvenir à la connoissance du paganisme caché* (see plate 10). Indeed, there was a substantial and very revealing change of emphasis from the Jesuit attempt to open the doors of idolatry to the reception of the gospel through missionary work, to Rogerius' more self-reflective metaphor of opening the door to the European understanding of the hidden meaning of idolatry with a treatise on gentile religion. But the two movements were hardly unrelated. The doors of idolatry could not have been opened by the sheer impulse of Protestant divines in India, who were few and far between. What made Rogerius' book with its claims to an esoteric account of the gentile faith possible were the Catholic precedents, and especially the fact that by the beginning of the seventeenth century there already existed a

---

[1] Fernão Guerreiro, *Relação anual das coisas que fizeram os padres da Companhia de Jesus nas suas missões . . . nos annos de 1600 a 1609*, ed. by A. Viegas, 3 vols. (Coimbra, 1930–42), vol. I.

[2] Guerreiro conceived his work as a continuation of Luis de Guzmán's *Historia de las missiones que han hecho los religiosos de la Compañía de Jesús, para predicar el sancto evangelio en la India Oriental, y en los reynos de la China y Japón* (Alcalá, 1601), a key historical synthesis of the Jesuit missions up until the turn of the century written in Castilian. The five volumes by Guerreiro were published in 1603, 1605, 1607, 1609 and 1611. Some parts were translated into Castilian and into German.

Plate 10 Title page of the French edition of Abraham Rogerius' treatise, *Le Théatre de L'idolatrie, ou la porte ouverte pour parvenir à la connoissance du paganisme caché* (Amsterdam, 1670). The same devil who has set fire to the *sati*'s funeral pyre paradoxically announces the book's open door to the discovery of the esoteric secrets of pagan religion. The title page of the Dutch edition offered instead eight engraved images (based on real-life sketches) of ascetic behaviour, including a number of bloody rituals – hook-swinging, juggernauts, *satis* – presided over by four-armed or elephant-headed idols, and accompanied by the noisy music of trumpets and timbals.

network of Catholic missions extending well beyond Portuguese dominion and, more often than not, led by the Jesuits, who, through their letters and histories, had practically monopolized the European discourse about oriental religions and, at the same time, restricted the European understanding of these religions.

To a large extent, Catholic missionaries provided the models and the contexts from which men like Rogerius could pluck with theological gloves the poisonous flower of idolatry and send it to Europe for display. And yet, opening the doors of idolatry, attempting to understand a non-Christian, not even a biblical religion, and taking idols as serious evidence for doctrine – that was precisely what Latin Christians had been reluctant to do until the seventeenth century. It had been all right to describe peculiar customs, such as the burning of 300 women when a king of Vijayanagara died, or the sexual freedom of the nayars of Malabar, all of which obviously violated natural and divine law. But should not the doors to the doctrines of brahmins remain closed if, as indeed it was generally understood, the devil stood behind those idols, those false gods whose obvious aesthetic monstrosity so logically seemed to correspond to such equally monstrous sacrifices? Why glorify the devil – for what else could the idols stand for? This is a question which, by the end of the sixteenth century, had been laid bare by the evolution of European ethnological genres, and would increasingly come to play a role in the criticism of religion. However, here we may want to consider that the intellectual discovery of Indian religion was not simply an inevitable step in the acquisition of knowledge after decades of European exploration, trade and even colonization in Asia. Rather, it seems to have been the fruit of a complex impulse which was to a large extent determined by the paradoxical position of a crucial figure in the history of Europeans overseas, the Christian missionary.

This 'opening of the door' of gentile beliefs was the result of two separate developments: first, the desire and need for missionary success within the changing logic of a Counter-Reformation theory of salvation, a logic subjected after *c.* 1580 to the increasing historicization of human political and religious diversity, and of the missionary movement itself. (This followed from the fact that the Catholic commitment to missionary activities was much more than an ideological justification: the Catholic elites, clerical but also lay, took the missionary enterprise very seriously.) The second development was the effective crisis of the European system of imperial Catholicism, based on an Iberian leadership which after 1600 could no longer be sustained, not only against Protestantism, but also within the Catholic world. The collapse of the Spanish and Portuguese colonial empires in Asia in the first half of the seventeenth century – two separate systems under one crown – meant not only that from about 1605 the Dutch were able to trade on the Coromandel coast (Rogerius' main area of contact with Hinduism), but also that an account such as *De open-deure* would not lie buried in the archives of a religious order, and be dismissed from the authoritative Catholic historical synthesis as a bunch of vain and undignified fables, which is what the Jesuit humanist historian Giovanni Maffei did when he published his Latin history of India and its missions in 1588. Rather, through the publication of Rogerius' work, an analysis of Hinduism was made available to a lay audience, and may even be seen as a stepping stone in the path towards the Enlightenment.

Despite the antiquarian and theological speculations which distinguished the anonymous preface that accompanied the various editions of Rogerius' treatise in Holland, in reality Rogerius' own approach was rather descriptive and indeed not very different from that of many of his Catholic predecessors. How he obtained his information also reveals a similarity with methods earlier used by the Jesuits. Rogerius had spent ten years (1632–42) ministering to the Christians in the now consolidated Dutch trading colony of Pulicat, near the ancient tomb of Saint Thomas of Mylapore, where after 1524 the Portuguese had established one of their cities. (They had vainly attempted to prevent the establishment of the Dutch colony early in the century.) Rogerius, as he explains, interviewed many times an Indian brahmin informer called Padmanaba. This was far from unique. In fact, most accounts of Hinduism depended on a dialogue with one or more brahmin informers who could acquire the scriptures and read them. Although it has sometimes been asserted that the collaboration of a brahmin was extremely difficult to obtain, much of the evidence seems to suggest that, given the huge diversity of Hindu sects and the lack of a rigid corporate organization, whenever a European living in India really wanted to gain access to these texts, and provided he was tactful, he could obtain some.[3]

In this respect, it is symptomatic that brahminical secrecy appears as an explanation of European ignorance of Hinduism precisely in those periods when we also hear of Jesuits in Goa stealing scriptures in order to ridicule their opponents, in a concerted campaign to eradicate idolatry from the 'Estado da India'. Curiously, the writings (apparently in Mahrati) thus confiscated in 1558 and 1559 were discussed in the more

---

[3] The reluctance of brahmins to make their writings available is discussed in Lach, *Asia in the making of Europe*, vol. I, p. 280, and also mentioned by R. Loureiro, 'O descobrimento da civilizacão Indiana nas cartas Jesuítas (século XVI)', in B. Ares Queija and S. Gruzinski (eds.) *Entre dos mundos. Fronteras culturales y agentes mediadores* (Seville, 1997), p. 320.

intelligent letters of Luis Fróis, a Jesuit who would later make his career in Japan, but were then dismissed by the historian Maffei from his official narrative.[4] In his letters Fróis explained enthusiastically how the Jesuits received a learned brahmin from Goa, baptized as Manoel d'Oliveira, who revealed to them the existence of a library of Hindu writings which a devout brahmin from the mainland had collected through eight years of patient work. This the Portuguese duly stole. This treasure-trove included the eighteen books of the *Mahabharata*. Manoel d'Oliveira translated portions into Portuguese, which were then immediately used to force the Goa brahmins into a medieval-style public disputation in which their teachings could be ridiculed. The Hindus pleaded in vain their lack of knowledge of philosophy (the learned brahmins lived, they said, in the kingdom of Vijayanagara). They were regularly forced to listen to the Christian clerics, including Manoel d'Oliveira, preaching against the absurdity of their own religious texts and the falsity of the teachings therein contained. At the same time, the translated texts were sent to the General in Rome, to be used as evidence of the ignorance which the devil had instilled in the brahmins so as to secure their service (in all the early Jesuit accounts of Hinduism the devil is an active agent, which ultimately justifies an aggressive stance towards the brahmins and their rituals). Fróis also commented on the contrast between the civility of the brahmins in matters of social honour – their subtlety in civil matters – and the obvious absurdity of their beliefs.

It does therefore seem necessary to relate the lack of availability of these texts before the period after 1580 to clerical attitudes of utter and offensive contempt. The question is when, and why, attitudes changed. Interestingly enough, they did so first of all within Catholic missionary discourse, and in a particular period between 1580 and 1620. Before this period not only was there a general consensus among clerical writers to ignore gentile mythology, but furthermore, as we have seen in the writings of Portuguese writers like Duarte Barbosa or Fernão Nunes, at a time when the Inquisition was really vigilant, there was no real room for a lay discourse on gentile religion to challenge the clerical monopoly. One might say that orientalist history and ethnology had been born soul-less.

The different orientations of the religious orders in charge of evangelization also contributed to the slowness with which a discourse on Indian gentile religion evolved. We have reason to suspect that not all the records of the activities of the Franciscan order have survived, but until

---

[4] See the account in Fróis' important letter – repeatedly printed in the sixteenth century – written from Goa on 14 November 1559, in J. Wicki (ed.) *Documenta indica*, 18 vols. (Rome 1964–88), vol. V, pp. 334–9).

the arrival of Francis Xavier in 1541 there is little doubt that they were the more numerous group in India. There were also a few Dominicans, and the Augustinians would arrive later in the sixteenth century (their presence became important after 1596, when an influential member of the order, Aleixo de Meneses, became archbishop of Goa).[5] As missionaries, the Franciscan friars were particularly successful in the lands surrounding Goa, especially in the island of Bardes. However, the Jesuit order alone would develop, throughout decades of missionary activity in Asia, a more sophisticated, ambitious and versatile approach to evangelization, combining novel organizational skills with outstanding intellectual effort. This leading role of the Jesuits in Asia is to a large extent unparalleled in Spanish America, and can be seen as a response to the need to operate under native dominion, and outside the Portuguese imperial shadow, if those nations perceived to be the more civilized were also to be converted.

This direction was in the beginning personally determined by the charismatic leadership of Francis Xavier, and to some extent can be related to the very originality of the Jesuits as a religious order. The core value of the Jesuit ethos (as defined in the spiritual exercises of Ignatius of Loyola) was the transformation of mystic devotion into an active apostolic ministry which took many forms (often improvised, rather than planned, by the first generation of Jesuits during the middle centuries of the sixteenth century). With the enthusiastic patronage of John III of Portugal, and under the leadership of one of Ignatius' ablest companions, missions to non-Christians in Asia soon grew to become one of the most emblematic of the Jesuit ministries (in contrast, their activities in the New World only began twenty years later, in the 1560s, and were conditioned by the strength of the older orders in key areas of settlement like New Spain). Unlike the mendicant orders, the organization of the Society was centralized for the sake of the practicalities of its ministry, and its members were not encumbered with the limitations of conventual life. They could effectively change dress and abode as they felt the need, working in small numbers, and they could to a larger extent than usual

---

[5] The Franciscans, with pioneering figures like Luís do Salvador, also had a primacy in Vijayanagara and among the Saint Thomas Christians, but the scarcity of men with leadership abilities meant that initial educational and missionary efforts in these areas did not find continuity. In reality the mendicant convents sank within the cultural mediocrity of the political centres of Indo-Portuguese society. The Jesuits would also pour far too many resources into Goa, but at least the College of Saint Paul and the professed house in the capital served as the basis for more ambitious activities by a minority of well-trained and talented members (often non-Portuguese) in distant missions. Early in the seventeenth century the India-born Friar Paulo de Trindade, today our main source for Franciscan activities, felt obliged to elaborate his history of the 'Spiritual conquest of India' by his order as an implicit answer to Jesuit triumphalism.

operate as an international organization, characterized not only by a fresh, secular outlook, but also by a comprehensive system of formation (including their own colleges) and information (through a wide system of correspondence).

This made it possible for the Jesuits to approach a problem which distinguished the Asian missions from those in Spanish America and the Philippines, namely, how to evangelize free nations, thus depending on the patronage, or at least the tolerance, of powerful non-Christian princes. As we saw, the assumption of Francis Xavier – often expressed in his letters – was that signs of civilization were also signs of rationality, and that this should facilitate conversions. But the fact that he set his sights upon Japan and China as idealized missionary fields does not mean that he saw the necessity for a careful study of their gentile traditions, and even less in the case of India. It is therefore within the Jesuit order that the contrast between the early neglect of Hinduism and its eventual discovery as a necessary tool to evangelization is most obvious.[6]

It is in fact remarkable how the missionary analysis of Indian gentile religion grew after 1580, and in particular, within the Jesuit order, after 1600. The works of the Augustinian Azevedo, and the Jesuits Fenicio, Rubino, Gonçalves, Nobili, Fernandes and Garcia, to which we may add the Franciscan Negrão and, in a special category, Thomas Stephens, were all produced within thirty years of each other. In 1603 Agostinho de Azevedo, using notes taken in the 1580s, prepared a report for Philip III (with the title of 'Estado da India') which includes an original summary of Hindu religion, from Shaiva Sanskrit and Tamil texts (Diogo do Couto plagiarized the chapters on Hindu religion in his fifth decade, published in 1612). The year 1603 was also when Matteo Ricci published in Chinese *The true sense of the doctrine of the Lord of Heaven* ('Tianzhy Shiyi'), an edited version of Christianity for Confucian mandarins. In 1608 Antonio Rubino, from the Jesuit mission at the court of Vijayana-gara in Chandragiri and Vellore prepared a brief account of the history and religion of Vijayanagara (*Relatione d'alchune cose principali del regno de Bisnagà*), whilst the following year in Calicut his fellow Jesuit Jacomé Fenicio, also Italian, wrote a substantial account of Hinduism in Portuguese, *Livro da seita dos Indios Orientais*, which was mainly based on material in Malayalam. At the same time, in Agra the leader of the long-standing third mission to the Mughal court Jerome Xavier (a grandnephew of Francis Xavier) completed the Persian translation of his

---

[6] Loureiro, 'O descobrimento', offers an introductory discussion of the 'discovery' of Indian civilization in sixteenth-century Jesuit letters, although without analysing changes in their method and vision.

Christian treatise 'Source of life' (*Fuente de vida*), written for the emperor Jahangir. Whilst Roberto de Nobili, in Madurai since 1606, defended himself against critics within his own order with an apology of his methods (his *Informatio*, 'On Indian Customs', was written in 1613 with the support of his ordinary superior, the Catalan Francesc Ros, Jesuit archbishop among the Saint Thomas Christians of Malabar), and whilst Trigault successfully publicized Ricci's method in China with the Latin version of the history of his mission, translated from Ricci's own account (*De Christiana expeditione apud Sinas*, Augsburg 1615), Diogo Gonçalves prepared in his 'History of Malabar' (*Historia do Malavar*) another discussion of Hindu religion in Portuguese, from Malayalam and Sanskrit sources. Further north in Portuguese India another Jesuit, the Englishman Thomas Stephens, made use of Sanskrit models to write the *Kristana Purana*, an epic poem teaching Christianity in Mahrati. And in 1616 another father, Gonçalo Fernandes Trancoso, had a number of Hindu writings translated into Portuguese, although his aim was not apologetic, but rather to refute, on the intellectual grounds chosen by his superiors, the interpretations of Hindu practices put forward by Nobili – his former companion in Madurai – in the *Informatio* of 1613. This affair was still reverberating in Goa during the conference of 1619 (where Nobili defended his method as theologically sound) when the Roman traveller Pietro della Valle met a Franciscan, Francisco Negrão, in Isfahan, who showed him his account of the gentile religions of Vijayanagara and Ceylon. And it was also during these first decades of the seventeenth century that a Portuguese Jesuit, Francisco Garcia, later to confront an anti-Latin rebellion of Saint Thomas Christians (of Syriac rite) in his capacity as archbishop in the Serra, translated into Portuguese various literary texts from Sanskrit and Mahrati, 'Gentile histories of India' such as the history of king Vicramaditu and the thirty-two perfections.

This explosion of writings based on Hindu texts reveals a number of aspects of the logic of missionary work, and raises a few important problems related to that logic. The most obvious point is that research into Hindu religion to a large extent followed from the effort to teach Christianity more effectively by using the original vernacular languages – in this sense, this early orientalist research was the culmination of the tradition of writing catechisms and grammars in various native languages which had characterized the efforts of the missionaries since the times of Francis Xavier. To use a native language was only the first step to using a native genre or to relating with a native set of social assumptions, and the ordinary lack of effective means of coercion against gentiles meant that in order to win over native intellectual elites, one could not rely on the assumption that European languages and customs would become a common ground. But more was at stake here. The experiments of Roberto de Nobili represented a watershed in the development of the tendency of accommodation favoured from the times of Valignano's visit in the 1570s, because they pushed the limits of accommodation to the point where they involved not only serious study of the Sanskrit tradition (in order to understand what form of Christianity would be acceptable to the social elite of India), but also raising the issue of which Indian social customs could be acceptable to Christianity. This provoked a crisis within the missionary discourse, because a fundamental ambiguity, the quasi-identification of civil and religious spheres which had sustained European self-confidence from the late Middle Ages to the Renaissance, was shattered by the need to re-examine which non-European customs were acceptable as compatible with Christianity.

Thus the new research into Indian religion was accompanied by an intense debate about the difference between Christianity and European civilization, one which originated within the Jesuit order but also had consequences for the standing of the order in Europe. It is not coincidental that the development of a similarly bold method of accommodation in China by Matteo Ricci and his companions took place at the turn of the century, and also met with opposition from within the order and, much more determined and more damaging, from the mendicant orders. Whilst a bull from Gregory XV in 1623, following an intense debate in Rome, accepted the validity of Nobili's methods (thus seemingly settling the issue), the Chinese rites controversy began to emerge in the 1640s, and no papal intervention would be able to settle the dispute, which continued right into the eighteenth century.

In these circumstances, the papacy's attempt to mediate between rival orders and national groups and, in the light of the decline of Portuguese power in India, to orchestrate missionary activities from Rome through the creation of the congregation of the *Propaganda fide*, were all futile. The papacy of course always depended on the powers on the ground, and the very success of the Jesuits depended on their own ability to shift their emphasis across national borders in Europe as the hegemony on the ground was transferred from Spain and Portugal to France. In fact, despite their marked international character, the Jesuits were unable fully to neutralize the existence of national rivalries within their own order, and many of their problems in Asia derived from Portuguese resentment of the influential role of Spanish and Italian members. To make things worse, any tension which could be neutralized within the order often found a second manifestation in the opposition, even hatred, of the other orders. This rift was never healed. Whilst in the 1630s the papacy maintained its support for Nobili, and even ordained Christian brahmins as bishops for Muslim-dominated areas like Bijapur and Golkonda, the Indo-Portuguese ecclesiastical establishment, in typically reactionary fashion, refused to acknowledge this native clergy in Goa. A famous example is that of Matteo de Castro Mahalo, a brahmin from Dewar ordained in Rome in 1631 but never allowed to carry out his tasks in India, so that he was forced to return to Europe. The Propaganda's attempt to work through hitherto marginal religious orders like the Theatines, the Carmelites or the Capuchins (so as to break the nationalist deadlock within the old orders) did not of course allow Rome to achieve what earlier popes had failed to do with their most successful, better trained and motivated missionary tool, the Jesuits.

By the time Rogerius was working in Coromandel, between 1632 and 1642, Jesuit missionaries had produced a very substantial body of writings analysing Hindu religion, but in fact this production was itself part of a deep crisis in their missionary methods which involved both a new, more experimental and sophisticated orientation, and a debate about the limits and implications of these experiments.

A CRISIS OF MISSIONARY METHODS

In his history of the Jesuit order in India written *c.* 1583, Alessandro Valignano found inspiration in the pioneering activities of Francis Xavier for what he saw as the needs of the mission during his own times. It is perhaps inevitable that a man whose aim was to reform and govern would project some of his views back onto a prestigious forerunner, but Valignano actually used the correspondence of Francis Xavier to support his own preference for Japan and China. In those letters he also found evidence of the opinion that the natives from southern India ('los Indios naturales destas partes') were naturally disinclined to Christianity, because of their proclivity to sinfulness. This perception explained Xavier's choice to work in coastal areas (Travancore, Pescaria and Coromandel) and his apparent neglect of the immense gentilism of the South Indian hinterland, and especially the kingdom of Vijayanagara. In fact, Valignano saw Xavier's choice as a rational one, for three reasons: because of the power of the Hindu military and religious castes, and especially the brahmins, 'whose dignity and power is based on their laws and ceremonies, so that to destroy their laws implies their own destruction'; because Francis Xavier was intelligent enough to realize that the black gentiles were naturally less rational than white peoples, and thus temperamentally unlikely to receive and keep God's commands (unless coerced by Portuguese dominion, he added); and finally, because to make

Christians among the people of Malabar was politically more important than to convert those from the interior.[7] But these views did not prevent Valignano from offering his own interpretation of the kingdom of Vijayanagara, since his historical perspective was not simply spiritual, but also political and commercial. He had himself travelled inland, from São Tomé to Goa, during his visit to the province in 1577 (the route was still used by Portuguese traders in horses and precious stones), and he was also aware that the Portuguese colony of São Tomé was within that kingdom's jurisdiction. His historical vision thus included the glorious past of Bisnaga, 'until a few years ago one of the largest, most powerful and wealthy kingdoms in all the Orient', and an idea of how a succession crisis led to wars and, eventually, to the destruction of the capital.[8] The ruins of the city were testimony to the fact that the city 'had been one of the greatest things found in this Orient', but the succeeding state of Vijayanagara, although diminished, was still of considerable wealth and military power. Valignano made a fine distinction between the *badagás* (Telugu-speaking military elites) and the other peoples of southern India, because the Vijayanagara dominant class was wealthier, more militaristic and knightly, and their cities were walled 'like our fortresses'. However, they were no less black and idolatrous, and in particular the splendour of their temples, which were very well made, was horrifying ('cosa de espanto').[9]

Valignano's pessimistic assessment about the prospects of the gospel in India was therefore rooted in a historical vision, which stands in sharp contrast with the views of contemporaries like the Spanish discalced Franciscan Martín Ignacio de Loyola, who in 1584 travelled through South India on his way from China to Rome. Martín Ignacio's opinions were, like Valignano's, conditioned by his missionary aims. In fact, his 'itinerary' described an extraordinary world tour marked by the project to penetrate China from the Spanish Philippines. Although he and his companions ended up in a prison (as foreigners without licence to visit the kingdom) and were lucky to escape alive, this did not deter the

---

[7] Valignano, *Historia del principio y progreso de la Compañía de Jesús*, pp. 69–70.

[8] Ibid., pp. 79–80: 'Esta ciudad [Saõ Tomé] está en el reyno de Bisnagá, que por otro nombre se llama Narsinga, el qual pocos años atrás era uno de los mayores, más poderosos y ricos reynos que avía en todo el oriente ... faltando succesión de la verdadera progenie de los reyes, se movieron en él diversas guerras por causa del suceder, y se levantaron muchos señores principales contra el que agora govierna. Y en una guerra fue destruida y asolada la grande ciudad de Bisnagá, que era ciudad real y cabeça de toda aquella tierra, tan populosa, rica y bastezida, que dizen avía en ella cerca de mil templos.' Interestingly, Valignano emphasized the internal rebellions of great captains, rather than the attack of foreign Muslim powers.

[9] Ibid., p. 81.

Franciscan from maintaining very optimistic views about the prospects of conversion in all the oriental kingdoms which he visited or heard about on his return journey. In his account (which was summarized by the Augustinian Juan González de Mendoza in his famous book on China of 1585) the people of Vijayanagara, no less than those of Cochinchina or Siam, 'would easily convert to the Gospel if someone went and preached to them' – a consequence of the fact that they firmly believed in the immortality of the soul, for otherwise (he noted), women and servants of deceased kings would not so happily join their funeral pyres![10]

This kind of argument, and the conventional description of the wealth and power of the king which the traveller probably picked up in São Tomé, just shows how superficial was the orientalism of many inexperienced missionaries, and how much more mature was Valignano's position. What Martín Ignacio lacked was a theory of the relationship between idolatry and civilization which defined particular gentile traditions as coherent wholes (this lack of coherence is apparent in the diverse treatment given to Bisnagà, where the people are said to be naturally peaceful, and the more negative description of idolatry in Tuticorin – the old Pandya kingdom – further south).[11] In contrast, that very decade of the 1580s saw the Jesuit elaboration of distinct classifications of gentile nations according to a systematic analysis of civilization, in America by José de Acosta and in the Orient by Valignano.

As we saw in the earlier discussion of Valignano's negative view of India, his racism was both a reflection of the historical frustration of the missionary enterprise among the Hindu elites of South India, and a personal prejudice that served to sustain a preference for more distant missions in Japan and China.[12] The influence of the brahmins seemed both more pervasive and more unassailable than that of two other cultural elites, the Chinese mandarins or the Buddhist bonzes, and it was only because Roberto de Nobili (shortly after Valignano's death) decided to re-define the brahmins as a social rather than a religious elite that a strategy of accommodation became possible in India.

We may here conclude that the personal roles of both Valignano and Nobili were crucial, first in perpetuating the intellectual neglect of the brahmins as a field for Jesuits missions (relative to other areas of missionary activity), and then in reversing that policy after 1606 (although in a rather experimental fashion). But neither Valignano nor Nobili – who shared an Italian aristocratic origin – were acting in

[10] J. González de Mendoza, *Historia del gran reino de la China*, ed. by R. Alba (Madrid, 1990), p. 391.
[11] Compare ibid., p. 391 and pp. 394–5.
[12] See chapter 1 above.

complete isolation within their order, and in the same way that the visitor in 1583 could find inspiration in Francis Xavier's opinions of forty years earlier, Nobili could consider the case of another Italian Jesuit, Alessandro Leni, who in 1599 already dressed like an Indian ascetic (a yogi) in order to gain respect as an itinerant spiritual authority. In fact, as is obvious from the preceding list of early European accounts of Hinduism, Nobili was only the most audacious and successful among a whole generation of missionary writers who, working from a historical analysis of their own mission, felt the need increasingly to understand gentilism as something more than a set of devilish aberrations.

The shift towards the analysis of religion, beyond the general descriptions of idolatry of the generation working in the 1560s and 70s, was thus an active move by an elite group that had maintained quite effectively its monopoly of discourse on religion, but had not obtained the expected results. It was, in fact, a recognition of the mistake of excluding gentile India made by the highly educated Valignano when as leader of a new generation of missionaries (many of them Spanish or Italian) he set up an innovative strategy of adaptation to engage those civilized elites which the Europeans could not otherwise coerce into belief. To some extent, as we saw, Valignano's move had been political – his job was to set priorities. But twenty years later the Jesuits could no longer contemplate their existing monopoly of missionary initiative in Asia as stable or permanent: Jesuits and friars were fighting each other in the formerly promising mission of Japan under a shared threat of expulsion, whilst the Dutch and the English were challenging Portuguese trade and control of the seas. Not even the prosperity of the old Portuguese colonies in South India was secure. In the new circumstances, and with the arrival of a new generation of educated Italian Jesuits, Nobili became Valignano's redemption for his sin of anti-Indian prejudice.[13] Seen from a long-term perspective, the missionary monopoly of analysis of religion both delayed and deepened the study of Hinduism.

---

[13] The role of Italians as innovators within the eastern missions was to a large extent a consequence of the intellectual mediocrity of the average Portuguese members, a situation which logically followed from the increasingly nationalistic tendencies within the *padroado*. Reliance on Italian members actually increased at the turn of the century, because the first object of Portuguese animosity was the Spanish members. Paradoxically, the very union of the Portuguese and Spanish crowns after 1580 had increased the difficulties for Castilian participation (natives from the crown of Aragon were seen as more acceptable), since now the threat of a complete imperial takeover supported from the Philippines was felt more strongly. But the elimination of the Spanish presence solved little, because the increasing need to rely on Italian members in positions of leadership also meant that they were resented more acutely by the Portuguese. In order to solve this problem, throughout the seventeenth century Rome increasingly sent French and northern Europeans members to the most promising missionary areas.

The Jesuit mission in Vijayanagara perfectly exemplifies this shift. The possibility of a mission to the Hindu kingdom had been contemplated as early as 1563, when some Jesuits at the city of Bijapur (invited by its Muslim ruler) met the ambassador of Vijayanagara and, after a brief religious discussion (he was a brahmin), requested to visit his city.[14] But this initiative was not exploited, and a few years later it was of course too late. Thus it was not until 1597 when, in the context of the consolidation of the kingdom of Vijayanagara in Chandragiri (which became the royal court in 1592), the Visitor of the province, Nicolas Pimenta, decided to send missionaries to the court of Venkata II and those of the largely independent nayakas of Gingee, Madurai and Tanjore.[15] Pimenta's momentous decision implied the extension to South India of the policy of working through political elites already followed in the Mughal court and in China, in contrast with the Jesuits' earlier, and quite successful, work with the low-caste Paravas of the Fishery coast (it did not however imply the espousal of a sophisticated policy of accommodation: Pimenta would later become one of Nobili's major enemies on account of his method). In parallel, Pimenta attempted to establish a mission in Calicut, which for much of the century had been out of range due to traditional wars against the Portuguese (Fenicio's treatise on Hinduism would grow from this experience). But the logical base for the new mission in Vijayanagara was the Jesuit house in São Tomé, a city which throughout the century had grown to become a prosperous and largely independent mercantile community, controlled by a Portuguese oligarchy which traded across the sea to Bengal, Pegu and Malacca.

Although the Jesuits (like other orders) found inspiration in living near the tomb of Saint Thomas, by now fully integrated as a local saint in the Indo-Portuguese Catholic pantheon, they were also conscious that they had utterly failed to convert the Telugu-speaking military elite of the land to Christianity. Thus the mission of 'Bisnaga', effectively established in 1598, became the first serious attempt by the Jesuits to approach a major Hindu royal court in the interior of the peninsula. As such, it was enthusiastically described by Guerreiro in his annual reports throughout the first decade of the seventeenth century, until the whole mission was

---

[14] Wicki (ed.) *Documenta indica*, vol. V, pp. 141–2. Letter by Gonçalo Rodriguez SI. to Antonio de Quadros SI. In fact the Jesuit accompanied a Dominican, Antonio Pegado, and both travelled as representatives from the archbishop of Goa, with whom the sultan wanted to be on good terms for political reasons. They offered the sultan of Bijapur a copy of Aquinas' *Summa contra gentiles*. The sultan entertained them with a festival and impressed the missionaries with the good manners of his court.

[15] Pimenta's visit was the basis for a long and very informative report on the state of the South Indian missions published in Latin Europe with the title *Epistola patris Nicolai Pimentae . . . ad R. P. Claudium Aquavivam* (Rome, 1601).

suddenly interrupted in 1610 (and the Jesuit historian was forced to cast a discreet veil of silence over this failure).

The story of the failure of this mission illustrates both the importance of the indigenous political context and, more significantly, the debate about accommodation that this kind of enterprise necessarily raised, but which many Catholic churchmen were reluctant to face. The first few years had been marked by optimism. The Jesuits were introduced to the king by an influential courtier, Oba Raya, a father-in-law to Venkata II, who became their protector. It is therefore likely that the fortunes of the Jesuit mission were associated from the beginning with those of an important faction within the Indian state. Oba Raya was the head of the Gobburi family, with interests in the lands east of Chandragiri near the port of Pulicat, and at the end of the sixteenth century he may be seen as the promoter of an alliance with the king of Portugal. Inviting the Jesuits to the court was a way of securing a good relationship with São Tomé, still under the nominal sovereignty of Vijayanagara (the actual administration of justice was divided, but the king's representatives held a fort and collected customs duties). This was a time when the menacing shadow of Akbar's empire was being felt in southern India, and when a Mughal ambassador arrived at Venkata's court in 1600, he was even lodged with the Jesuits. Since they had another mission group in Agra, the Jesuits could ascertain that it was indeed Akbar's intention – he was then busy conquering Ahmadnagar in the Deccan – eventually to subject the whole of southern India. Vijayanagara needed the tactical support of both Bijapur, directly threatened by Akbar, and of the Portuguese, who were an active sea power along the Coromandel coast, in order to resist the Mughals and the sultan of Golkonda – especially the latter, who posed the most immediate territorial threat to the Telugu-speaking core of the kingdom, at the north-eastern frontier. The Jesuits effectively became intermediaries in the correspondence between the courts of Chandragiri and Madrid. But Venkata II not only desired an agreement against his Muslim neighbours, he was also keen to emulate Akbar's own custom of religious patronage, which extended beyond any specific religious tradition – Muslim or Hindu – to include the Jesuits. The Christian fathers were prestigious for their western learning, and useful for the insight that they could offer into the influence of the Franks in Europe and in the world.

Thus Venkata II was willing to listen to the Jesuits, and invited them to build churches in his main cities which he himself would support with rents from villages. By 1601 three Jesuits led by Belchior Coutinho lived in Chandragiri, and throughout a whole decade this small group of two fathers and one lay brother (a group which was replenished whenever

necessary) remained near the court.[16] The king entertained them personally and guaranteed their freedom to seek converts, but this was of
course not at all the same as personally considering the possibility of
conversion – in this Venkata II was again close to Akbar. What
necessarily struck the oriental rulers as either odd or offensive is that
Christian missionaries insisted on the fact that their way of salvation was
unique, and exclusive of all others.

Thus the fundamental problem faced by the Jesuits is that, as the years
passed, the novelty of the initial contacts wore off, but no real progress
was made because nobody who mattered wanted to be baptized.
Although in 1604 and 1605 the Provincial of the new Jesuit jurisdiction
of Malabar, Alberto Laerzio, emphasizing the size of the population of
the kingdom, wrote about the expectation of great conversions, and
while the progress of the mission was followed closely by the pious king
Philip III of Castile (II of Portugal), in the next few years only a handful
of people were baptized, mainly servants of the Jesuits and the occasional
poor old man. Not only were they few, they were also socially weak
converts. Typically, educated Hindus claimed that their own religion was
as good as the Christian one for salvation, and therefore there was little
point in abandoning their ancestral customs.[17]

These poor results were eventually seen by Antonio Rubino
(1578–1643), one of the members of the mission since 1606, as a problem
of method, as he explained in a letter of September 1609 from Vellore to
the General Claudio Aquaviva (one of those letters that the Jesuits wrote
only for themselves, not for the general European public):

It is unbelievable how closed the door to the holy faith is in this
kingdom, and all this comes from the aversion and great hatred that
they feel towards us, because they know that we are the priests of the
Portuguese, who eat the flesh of cows, drink wine . . . and although we
in this kingdom abstain from those things, however, our black dress is
enough to make them run away and hate us like the plague, and as I
said it is enough for them to know that we are priests of the

---

[16] For the details of this mission (but not the interpretation) I largely follow the valuable
account in Heras, *The Aravidu dynasty of Vijayanagara*, chap. 22, which is mainly based
on the Jesuit letters, of which he prints a number. I have consulted further material from
the Archivium Romanum Societatis Iesu (ARSI), Goa 14, 15, 16, 24 and 33.

[17] Heras, *Aravidu dynasty*, p. 484, quoting a letter of November 1606 by the Portuguese
father Manoel Roiz from São Tomé, in which for the first time the opinion is clearly
expressed that hopes of conversions were slim, 'por estarem estes negros muito
obstinados naquelle diabolico fundamento . . . porque aindaque reconhecem a nossa lei
por boa, dizem que tambem a sua he boa, e que nella se poden salvar, e que nella querem
viver, pois he conforme aos seus costumes e de seus antepasados (letter reproduced in
ibid., p. 595).

Portuguese. In order to obtain results we need to dress, eat and in matters political do as they do, as far as possible.[18]

The separation of matters political from matters religious thus resulted from acknowledging the unpleasant truth that western civilization, as represented by the Portuguese in India, could not command universal admiration, and in fact while the Jesuits were individually respected for their rigorous chastity and for their learning, they were closely associated with the Portuguese. Although a missionary could not be relativist about religious truth, he might be so concerning social customs. Here Rubino clearly advocated (and surely echoed) Nobili's method of accommodation, following the same precise line of reasoning. In fact he concluded by revealing that he hoped that the Provincial Laerzio, who was sponsoring Nobili and who had visited the mission in Vijayanagara on a number of occasions, would allow him to try the new approach in a new place not already sullied by the image of the Portuguese. Rubino, Nobili and Laerzio were of course all Italian.

The coincidence between the two young missionaries was more than just regional or chronological. Sent to Vijayanagara in 1606 (the same year Nobili started his experiments in Madurai), Rubino was a well-educated member of the order, with knowledge of theology and mathematics. He had replaced the deceased Francesco Ricio in order to become the mission's specialist in gentile languages (the main one in that court was Telugu), and thus was able to dispute about the erroneous beliefs of the idolaters and the truth of Christianity.[19] The Jesuits in Chandragiri and Vellore (which, conquered by Venkata II in 1604, soon became the kingdom's capital) used European art, cosmography and science in order to attract the admiration of the gentile elites, and Rubino, for instance, introduced himself by offering a *mappa mundi* with Telugu inscriptions. His knowledge of astronomy and mathematics similarly impressed his hosts. However, this was not sufficient: a systematic theological conversation with brahmins also required increas-

---

[18] Ibid., p. 618.

[19] Francesco Ricio (born in Montesardo, Abruzzo, *c.* 1546) knew Tamil and Telugu and by default – Coutinho being slower with languages – became the intellectual figure of the mission of Chandragiri until his death in 1606. He wrote a Telugu grammar and a summary of Christian doctrine based on a Konkani model, as well as some mysteries of the life of Christ. However, according to his superior Laerzio, he found it more difficult to learn Sanskrit. The catalogue of the members of the province of India in 1594, probably by Valignano, indicated in the confidential section 'poco ingenio, juicio y prudencia, sabe poco' (*Documenta indica*, vol. XVI, p. 984). The Piedmontese Rubino, a younger man (born near Turin *c.* 1581, according to the Jesuit catalogue of 1608), had come to assist Ricio in 1606, only to see him die a few months later, and soon took great responsibilities. Laerzio's catalogue of 1608 described him as 'ingenium et uidicium bonum, cum prudentiam aliquam' (*ARSI*, Goa 24, II, ff. 426v–440r, no. 24).

ing knowledge of their beliefs, and it was in this context that we encounter evidence of serious indological research, in the form of a brief treatise on the history and religion of Vijayanagara ('Account of some of the principal things of the kingdom of Bisnaga') written by Rubino from Chandragiri in 1608 – a year before the letter quoted above. This was the first European treatise discussing the religious traditions of Vijayanagara; like Nobili's experiments and his intense study of Tamil and Sanskrit literary traditions, it logically coincided with a crisis of missionary methods in South India.

Despite the initial kindness of Venkata II towards the Jesuits, and despite Rubino's willingness to penetrate the secrets of Hinduism and adopt new methods (he became Superior of the mission at Coutinho's death in 1610), the small mission of Vijayanagara died in 1611, apparently because king Philip III ordered that it should be interrupted. There were a number of reasons for this failure. From the point of view of Vijayanagara the patronage of the Jesuits was part of an alliance with the Portuguese, and this meant that the missionaries suffered from the opportunism underlying a fragile relationship. Their position became difficult when the king moved against São Tomé in 1606 in order to protect his Hindu subjects from a Portuguese attack, the result of a brawl in which a Portuguese *casado* had been murdered on account of a young woman. This affair coincided with the arrival of the Dutch on the coast of Coromandel, and after their formal establishment in Pulicat in 1610 – a clever move that ensured that Venkata II no longer depended on one single European maritime power – the Portuguese position was fatally weakened. The fact that Venkata II was an old man and his court divided by the prospect of a succession crisis isolated the Jesuits further, and it seems that the same Gobburi faction which had welcomed the priests a decade earlier was now supporting an alternative policy of agreement with the Dutch.[20]

The years from 1606 to 1610 were therefore crucial, because Venkata II was simultaneously corresponding with Philip III, even referring to the old friendship of the times of Vira Narasimha, and considering his

[20] It appears that an anti-Portuguese court faction led by Venkata II's dominant queen and her brother Jaga Raya (both childern of the elder Oba Raya) used exaggerated reports of the Portuguese attack of 1606 in order to convince Venkata II to bring in the Dutch as an alternative to the Portuguese. See letter by Coutinho to the General Aquaviva, November 1606 (Heras, *Aravidu dynasty*, pp. 597–8). Although in the following years Venkata II prohibited the nayaka of Gingee from letting the Dutch into his ports, he seems to have been unable to impose his own preference for the Portuguese alliance upon the Gobburi faction (whose rents in the Pulicat lands would benefit from the new trade). Venkata II's preference must to some extent have been inspired by the Jesuits. But then, in 1614, the old king was not even able to impose his young nephew as successor against the ambitions of the same Gobburi faction.

options with the Dutch. As early as 1609 Rubino had noted that the king's attitude towards the missionaries was cooler than it used to be, although he attributed this to the opposition of the brahmins. When the Jesuits were asked to move out by the king of Portugal in 1610, therefore, the Indian court already had low expectations of the Portuguese alliance and had given its permission to the Dutch to settle in Pulicat. This was followed by a fully fledged military assault on São Tomé in 1611 in order to exact a considerable amount of money. On this occasion Antonio Rubino acted as peacemaker, in the end successfully, but not without first spending a couple of months in a prison until a ransom was collected. Even viceroy Jeronimo d'Azevedo, who had always seen the mission of Vijayanagara as politically useful, now concluded that the departure of the Jesuits from the court only made the king's willingness to prefer the Dutch stronger.[21]

It would seem that as important as the opportunism of the Hindu ruler was the opportunism of the Portuguese and Spanish authorities. In February 1610, the king had asked the Viceroy Ruy Lourenço de Tavora to study the possibility of conquering Vijayanagara and plundering Tirupati.[22] Only a few days later, the viceroy was also asked by the king's authority to recall the missionaries, due to their scandalous behaviour. It is quite certain that the king and his council of Portugal (which acted as a largely independent body within the Spanish monarchy) had been misled by false accusations, but it is also apparent that the very model of missionary work entertained at the court was ambivalent. In fact, the ruthlessness with which the idea of an alliance with Vijayanagara was put aside (in sharp contrast to the letters of only three years earlier) was more a product of Iberian impatience than of a full awareness of the extent to which Venkata II was already negotiating with the Dutch. The imperial system of Spain and Portugal all too often operated on the assumption that the conversion of gentiles was best combined with their conquest, and missionary experiments were only justified when conquest was impossible for the time being. The possibility that oriental converts would remain truly Catholic and under the obedience of Rome without

---

[21] In a letter of 1613 to the king, regretting the decision to abandon the mission in Chandragiri. See ibid., pp. 481–2.

[22] *Documentos remetidos da Índia, ou livros das Monções*, ed. by R. A. de Bulhão Pato (vols. I–IV) and A. da Silva Rego (vols. VI–X) (Lisbon, 1880–1982), vol. I, p. 359. Although in the king's name, the letter was however not personally written by Philip III (of Castile), but by the former viceroy, Francisco da Gama, count of Vidigueira and apparently in charge of the affairs of Portuguese India. The idea was not altogether new. As we saw (chapter 8 above) similar projects were floated following the succession crisis of Vijayanagara in 1542–3, including Governor Martim Affonso de Sousa's frustrated attack on Tirupati, and Dom Aleixo de Meneses's advice to the king concerning a hypothetical Portuguese conquest of the Deccan.

any European clerical supervision was rarely imagined, and the fact that the Spanish empire was already a confederation of largely independent Catholic nations under one royal authority only made it easier to assume that the logical outcome of massive conversion was political subjection. Native reactions to this political principle were of course logically violent, and it is no coincidence that the death of the first Christian martyrs in Japan, the Spanish Franciscans and their Japanese converts crucified in Nagasaki in 1597, had been caused by a report that the king of Spain and Portugal intended to use native converts to Christianity as a first step to conquering the islands from the Philippines.

As in Japan, the Jesuits in Vijayanagara suffered from the inextricable mixture of religious and political purposes of their patrons, both European and native, a mixture which all too often they also sought to exploit. As in Japan and as in the Mughal empire, after 1600 the Jesuits of Vijayanagara were caught under the embarrassing umbrella of an imperial power which was neither convincingly peaceful nor able to resist the naval challenge of the Dutch and the English. But they also suffered more in particular from the resentment that their growth and their methods earned them among clerics from outside the order, and which in India was further incensed by the leading intellectual role of many non-Portuguese members. Thus King Philip's decision to interrupt the mission of Vijayanagara was caused by the criticism received from the secular clergy of São Tomé, expressed in an obviously slanderous letter by the Portuguese Antonio Viles.[23]

It is worth analysing this letter. Viles claimed that the Jesuits in Vijayanagara were not making any converts, that their aim was to acquire rents for themselves (such as they had accumulated in São Thomé), and that for this purpose they mistranslated letters from Europe and misused their native language skills. He also wrote that a lay Italian brother who was also a professional painter, Fontebona, was making indecent pictures, of gentile idols and of the king playing erotic games with his naked wives in the water.[24] While some of these criticisms had a real basis (there had indeed been very few converts, the Jesuits were of course concerned with securing a financial basis for their

---

[23] This is Heras's interpretation, which seems well supported by contemporary documents. However, the Flemish merchant-traveller Jacques de Coutre believed that the reasons for the Jesuit retreat were poor results, political instability and above all the presence of Dutch traders in Vellore. He claims to have visited the mission of Madurai in 1611, where he met Fontebona, and afterwards visited King Venkata II and his two capitals: Jacques de Coutre, *Andanzas asiáticas*, ed. by E. Stols, B. Teensma and J. Werberckmoes (Madrid, 1991), pp. 239 and 245–9. Whether Coutre would have heard the whole story is debatable.

[24] Letter printed in appendix in Heras, *Aravidu dynasty*, pp. 634–7.

activities, and Fontebona, who was very successful at the court for his European naturalism, not only painted Christian images, but also secular themes when he was asked to do so by the king), the fundamental accusation that the aims of the Jesuits were not religious was of course incorrect, and it is surprising that the Superiors agreed to withdraw the mission, a temporary measure that, in the unstable political circumstances of the following decade, became permanent. Antonio Viles's letter was in fact part of a concerted campaign against the Jesuits in India orchestrated by the secular clergy whose power was limited to the areas of Portuguese settlement. It was calculated to do maximum damage, including accusations that the Jesuits were following a similar path in China and the Fishery coast, and culminated in the fantastic proposal to eliminate the autonomy of the religious orders and subject them to the power of the Portuguese clergy. In fact, Viles even suggested that the influence of the Italians in the religious orders would lead to a religious schism like those in Holland and England (thus the Franciscans, although poor and largely ignorant of indigenous languages, were safer than the Jesuits).[25]

Obviously, behind this dispute among rival ecclesiastical powers there was a genuine revulsion at the methods of partial indigenization which the less intellectual among the Portuguese perceived as a foreign heresy. These were also the issues that were at stake in the Nobili affair, which exploded during the same years, although his case was distinguished by the fact that he even had many in his own order against him. Nobili was also distinguished by his unique success in actually winning over some influential brahmins and captains, and by the solidity of his theological reasoning, all of which earned him the support of his superiors and eventually of the Papacy; but obviously any sign of weakness (such as the lack of results in Vijayanagara) was exploited by those jealous of the Jesuits. Even in Japan and China, where the Society could claim some remarkable success, the 'foreign' Spanish friars from the Philippines created much trouble by refusing to countenance a corporate monopoly of evangelization. In the less promising field of South India, the fact that Rubino failed, but Nobili succeeded, can be explained by the special circumstances of each case. Whilst Nobili struggled for half a century to create the basis of a South Indian Christian community largely independent from Portuguese India, Rubino worked on the Coromandel and Fishery coasts, often making use of his remarkable grasp of indigenous

---

[25] Although the Superior, Coutinho, was Portuguese, the mission of Vijayanagara was dominated for many years by Italians, first Ricio and then Rubino and Fontebona. The attack by Viles coincided with Coutinho's retirement and death.

affairs, but still forced to operate in his double condition of foreigner (too Portuguese for the Indians, too Italian for the Portuguese) within the contradictions of the declining Iberian power. He eventually inherited Valignano's old job as Visitor of the Far Eastern missions, and in his last years launched a couple of clandestine expeditions to Japan (after it had become a 'closed country' in 1640) that, unsurprisingly in the light of previous savage persecutions, ended up in tortures, apostasies and martyrdoms (including his own). Before that, he was fully caught up in the rites controversy fuelled by the Dominicans from Manila, and his report discussing the missionary method of accommodation in China earned him the posthumous honour of being placed on the index of forbidden books. Regardless of these personal trajectories, an important conclusion is that all these experiments raised the same kind of opposition, an opposition which was only in part political and much more fundamentally a question of cultural identity: one could not alter the social forms of Christianity without affecting the understanding that the majority of Europeans had of their own religion.

THE ANALYSIS OF INDIAN RELIGION

Rubino's 1608 *Account of the main things of the kingdom of Vijayanagara* is an important document, hitherto unpublished, describing the conditions of a Hindu state and its religion in the early seventeenth century.[26] It is probably the most detailed account of the late kingdom of Vijayanagara in Chandragiri–Vellore at the moment of its maximum influence. The literary model of the Jesuit relation describing the conditions of a new kingdom was of course well established within the order and had even been publicized for the European public, from the letters of Francis Xavier and Cosme de Torres describing Japan and its religious sects in 1551 and 1552 to the more systematic and formalized account of Akbar's empire by Antonio Monserrate in 1582. However, Rubino was the first to provide an equivalent analysis of a South Indian kingdom, and his condition of missionary allowed him to combine the ethnographic and historical interests of sixteenth-century writers like Barbosa, Paes and Nunes with a particularized discussion of gentile idolatry and its significance. Despite his superior knowledge of mathematics and

---

[26] *ARSI*, Goa 33i, ff. 320r–325v. For a transcription of the Italian original, with an English translation and a detailed commentary justifying the dating and attribution of authorship, see J. P. Rubiés, 'The Jesuit discovery of Hinduism: Antonio Rubino's account of the history and religion of Vijayanagara (1608)', forthcoming in a special volume of *Archiv für Religionsgeschichte* devoted to the birth of comparative religion in the seventeenth century.

astronomy, Rubino's views in this document are not very different from those expressed by his companions Coutinho and Fontebona in some of their letters, and he even repeats some of their observations. After only two years living in the cities of Vijayanagara, Rubino was thus to a large extent expressing a common understanding of a small group of Jesuits about the kingdom's idolatrous civilization. For all these reasons, his account can serve as a starting point for a discussion of the key ideas and methods of the new indological literature produced by Catholic missionaries in this period.

The document begins with a historical summary which adopts an indigenous mythical perspective, introducing the puranic doctrine of the four ages, or *yugas*, and locating the events of the *Ramayana* within that cosmological process of decline. Rubino is of course merely reporting the 'opinion' of the gentiles – the puranic chronology of cycles of more than four million years was incompatible with the much shorter biblical calculations (there is no doubt that Rubino was attracted to the details of this doctrine through his own discussions with brahmins about mathematics and astronomy – he was curious about their precise methods of astrological calculation, and introduced them to Galileo's recent observations of the planets with a telescope). This cosmological myth in any case served Rubino to introduce a very sketchy genealogy of the kings of South India in this current 'fourth age' of Kali.

The character of this summary suggests that Rubino's historical vision was here only an echo of the concerns of the court of the Aravidu Venkata II, quickly connecting the significant events of an immediate dynastic memory with the mythical, cosmological perspective of the brahmins. Thus, there is no transition from the legendary figures of the medieval South Indian kingdoms (Chera, Chola and Pandya) to the times of 'Narsinga Raiulu' (Saluva Narasimha Raya), identified as ruler of Vijayanagara at the time of the arrival of the Portuguese. The Muslim invasion of the early fourteenth century is not even mentioned. Effectively, the dynastic historical memory is confined to the last hundred years, and only truly comes to life with the emergence of Rama Raja (uncle of Venkata II) as usurper.[27] Interestingly, the dharmic identity of the old kingdom of Vijayanagara – including the legendary origins and sacred geography of the first capital as defined in the Kanarese sources for Nunes's chronicle – is also entirely lost. The old city is now only a wild forest without special significance.

By contrast, the battle of Talikota which saw the end of the old kingdom receives a great deal of attention. On the whole the account is

---

[27] The reigns of Krishna Deva Raya and Achyuta are mentioned very briefly.

(as one would expect) recognizably historical, with emphasis on the role of the Nizam-il-Mulk of Ahmadnagar as leader of the Muslim alliance, and the arrogance of Rama Raja as a cause for the Hindu defeat. Although Rubino's final interpretation is purely Portuguese (the defeat was a divine punishment for Rama Raja's attack on the city of São Tomé in 1559), the details which he offers of the battle reveal the perspective of the Aravidu ruling family. Thus Tirumala Raja, effective founder of the new dynasty, is seen as a prudent counsellor to his elder brother Rama Raja. During the battle both he and Venkatadri defeated their respective Muslim enemies, and it was only Rama Raja who failed to stop the sultan of Ahmadnagar. The participation of Tirumala Raja and his son Venkata – the king at Rubino's time – in the murder of Sadashiva is also passed in silence.

Rubino's attachment to the historical role and royal legitimacy of this branch of the Aravidu family is consistent with his presentation of Venkata II as an affable, learned, good-looking and prudent elderly ruler. This view is obviously conditioned by the hopes of conversion entertained by the fathers, and by their kind treatment at the court, and is only marred by the comment that Venkata II is not sufficiently severe with his vassals with respect to criminal justice and especially by his weakness for his favourite wife – surely a reflection of the conditions at the court. In fact, Rubino is quite clear about the existence of an impending succession crisis, which would in fact fatally weaken the kingdom in the following decades after the death of Venkata II in 1614.

What is most significant in Rubino's positive presentation of Venkata II and the kingdom's political and economic potential is the contrast with his very negative account of the brahmins and Hindu religion. This duality, which amounts to a limited version of the separation between civility and religion at the heart of Nobili's new method of accommodation, does not really involve a definition of civility as a relative category, as opposed to the fundamentalist attitude towards religious truth that any Catholic missionary must entertain: Rubino is not in the business of identifying brahminical customs as naturally acceptable civil arrangements. Rather, his more simple emphasis is on the personal qualities of the king as prudent ruler in terms which could be held as universally valid from a European perspective. No hint of the oriental despotism defined by Rubino's older contemporary and compatriot, Botero, is here suggested (although it is difficult to believe that Rubino was unaware of his *Relationi*). Although Botero's real concerns were no less with the world-wide spread of Catholicism as the true religion than with politics and economics, the critical depth of the secular portion of his analysis did not serve the missionaries in their strategy of accommodation.[28] The political strength of western civility could not be a pre-requisite for Christianity. On the contrary, what distinguishes Rubino's interpretation is the sharp contrast between the acceptance of the Indian political system as represented by the almost perfect rule of a virtuous king (a rule whose splendour is expressed by the Mahanavami festival, in a ritual here described as purely royal), and his willingness to confront and analyse idolatry in its many particulars as a religious system devised by the devil.

Rubino's analysis of gentile religion is therefore really a deeply felt attack against the brahmins as ministers of the devil ('ministri infernali'), an attack obviously coloured by the Jesuits' direct struggle against them for the souls of the king and his people. This condemnation begins with the spiritual leader of Venkata II, the Vaishnava Tatacharya whom Rubino perceived as a lusty, vicious man. This kind of criticism, based on the anti-sexual morality and aesthetics of Christianity, then extends to different categories of yogis and brahmins. Like Nobili in Madurai, the Jesuits adopted the identity of *sannayasi* (a conventional ascetic religious figure) offered to them by Venkata II on account of their chastity in order to identify sexual indulgence as the most obvious sign of the devilish character of both the Hindu religious caste and of a number of their festivals. Rubino, of course, was not prepared to consider that within the gentile religious system there could be a plurality of forms of holiness, some involving chastity, others the contrary. But the point is not the obvious one that he was necessarily biased: what is interesting about his account is that he was able to identify particular forms of worship and religious organization, quite realistically described, as logical expressions of this devilish character. The indecency of the *lingam*, the violent sectarian disputes between Vaishnavas and Shaivas, the dancing girls and temple prostitutes, the bloody sacrifices, the collective deflowering of virgins by priests as a religious celebration, the monstrosity of four-armed figures, the food offerings to gods, all these did not need to be discovered and analysed, they presented themselves as simple evidence. Religious sculptures were so obviously dishonest that 'from here the fathers take evident arguments in order to demonstrate that Peremal [Vishnu] cannot be God'. The *avatars* of Vishnu were of course a perverse imitation of Christ's incarnation, as was Krishna's very name, and nothing could be more automatic than to identify gentile gods and goddesses as the idols against whom the biblical God needed to be recognized as true creator.

---

[28] One wonders whether Botero's ideas might have evolved differently had he been allowed to become a Jesuit missionary in the East, an option which he was refused.

There was a bitterness in Rubino's analysis that had been born of experience. The example of Gabriel de San Antonio, a Castilian Dominican who after a complicated attempt to establish a mission in Cambodia travelled through Vijayanagara in 1600, shows – like the similar example of Martín Ignacio de Loyola discussed earlier – that the first vision of gentile religion was not the most negative. In his *Breve y verdadera relación de los sucesos del reino de Camboxa* (Valladolid, 1604), Gabriel de San Antonio offered a positive if perhaps naive image of the brahmins of Madurai: they are 'natural philosophers' in the guise of Socrates and Plato, and their philosophical academies (i.e., *mathas*) are, like the University of Salamanca, full of men able to understand Latin and eager to become Christian. He personally attended one of these academies for over a week. Although gentile temples and festivals, with their prostitutes and sacrifices, are all obviously idolatrous, this idolatry is none the less depicted as naturalistic, and is focused on the sun, the moon and the stars; the yogis are admirable for their ascetical piety too.[29]

There is little in Rubino's more mature and condemnatory analysis of Indian idolatry that would not have been recognizable to a missionary in the New World describing the religions of Mexico or Peru. What was new was the task of describing and giving names in unconquered territory. Rubino transformed the prevailing, rather vague image of idolatrous excess, which would have been familiar in most European accounts of India, not by developing a new theology, but simply by, unproblematically, offering names of gods, temples and festivals, by counting carts, torches and singers, and by distinguishing different types of brahmins and even the different marks in their foreheads. He made no effort to hide the reverence with which these brahmins were held in their society and their enormous wealth, nor the attachment of the nobility to the devil Peremal as a providential power – but he gave no hint either that there was a need to explain these beliefs historically, or to insinuate that a kernel of natural philosophy could be hidden behind all these abominations. For Rubino, the nature of Hinduism as devilish idolatry did not represent a problem of interpretation, it was the nature of the missionary method alone that needed elucidation.

In this light, the originality of Nobili emerges most clearly. Nobili shared with Rubino the basic distinction between a valid Indian civil tradition and a completely misguided religion. Unlike influential Jesuit writers on the New World, such as José de Acosta, these two Italians in India did not assume that European civilization needed to be defined as superior to that of any gentiles, and therefore a pre-requisite for effective

---

[29] See R. Ferrando (ed.) *Relaciones de la Camboya y el Japón* (Madrid, 1988), pp. 105–11.

evangelization. Rubino, for instance, described Hindu marriages, salutations or the peculiar custom of washing bodies with regularity without any need to condemn them, in contrast with the superstitious beliefs in omens, or cruel customs like *sati*, which (having witnessed a young girl trying to hide among the crowd but being pushed into the fire) were obviously of devilish inspiration. Christianity alone seems to have been his criterion of judgement, and even the caste system was described as negative mainly because it was a way of sustaining the power of the brahmins – otherwise, its sectarian effects could simply be compared to the wars between Guelfs and Ghibellines. But unlike Rubino, Nobili analysed the nature of Hinduism as a cultural and literary tradition as well as a religious one. The frontiers between civil arrangements and religious ones, he concluded, needed to be defined more carefully than Rubino's analysis would have allowed for, because the brahmins as a social caste could not be converted unless their tradition was, to some extent, accepted as valid. Nobili's revolutionary move was to reject the distinction between an acceptable military caste and a devilish brahminical caste in order to distinguish between an acceptable caste of learned men and their idolatrous beliefs. This required reading their literary tradition as more than just religious and devilish: it also had to be defined as moral and philosophical according to the universal principles of natural law.

The distance between Rubino and Nobili was the distance between learning about an idolatrous tradition as a system in order to prove it wrong to its practitioners, and introducing Christian philosophical distinctions into it as part of that same process, to the point when gentile idolatry dissolved into three separate realms: social practice, natural belief and devilish superstition. Much of the indological literature written by missionaries during the first two decades of the seventeenth century – the treatises by Azevedo, Fenicio, Gonçalves and Fernandes – moves between these two extremes.[30] The earlier writers Azevedo and Fenicio, writing before 1610, assumed a logical continuity between erroneous doctrine and peculiar rituals. However, the debate generated by Nobili's experiments with accommodation, which exploded in the following years, meant that the distinction between legitimate civil diversity and illegitimate religious diversity came to affect, and even dominate, the indological literature of the Jesuits. Two illuminating examples are the treatises written by the Portuguese Jesuits Diogo Gonçalves and Gonçalo Fernades.

Diogo Gonçalves, who composed his 'History of Malabar' (1615) from the Jesuits mission at Quilon, differs from Fenicio (who had also recently

---

[30] For a detailed discussion of some of these writers see Rubiés, 'Jesuit discovery'.

worked in Malabar) not in his method, combining exposition and criticism as distinct parts of the discourse on gentile religion, but in his clear and systematic use of separate categories of religion and civilization.[31] Thus his whole treatise is divided in two parts, dealing with 'political customs' and 'sects and superstitions'. Although the bulk of his criticisms is directed against erroneous religious beliefs, there is also an important section discussing unjust and abusive political customs (often caste-specific), including divorce, matrilineal rules of consanguinity, polygamous marriages, *sati* (although not practised in Malabar), private vengeances, the arbitrary use of power, and the extreme exclusions of the caste system. Gonçalves actually praises the caste system as a means of defining social distinctions, since social equality is not (in his view) natural, and even the idea that the nobility and the plebs should not ordinarily touch each other appears, in principle, tolerable to him. He, however, criticizes those strict rules of heredity that deny the individual the chance to follow a personal (and natural) inclination towards a new profession, or the cruelty of the rule of untouchability as it is actually applied, denying the ultimate common bond of humanity between noblemen and commoners. He therefore interprets the caste system as a natural system of social distinctions which the Malabaris have exaggerated to the point of becoming inhuman, impractical, and thus irrational.[32]

Many of these injustices are not interpreted simply as isolated errors, but rather as the consequence of having the wrong principle in civil society: because in Malabari society individuals are exclusively moved by private interests, there is a lack of true friendship and public trust.[33] But Gonçalves' aim is not to condemn the Indians on all accounts, secular and religious. Ultimately, secular vices are the result of lack of true religion. What is interesting is that the distinction between valid civil customs and those which violate natural law allows Gonçalves to support Nobili in his understanding of the brahminical thread as an acceptable sign of social dignity.[34] The paradox is that, whilst Nobili

---

[31] Gonçalves also discussed the interior of the kingdom of Travancore. The unique manuscript of his history was edited in 1955 by Josef Wicki SJ, who provides details about the life of Gonçalves: see Diogo Gonçalves, *Historia do Malavar*, ed. by J. Wicki (Münster, 1955). Gonçalves displays a clear understanding of the different languages, Sanskrit and Malayalam vernacular, used by the brahmins. His informant he describes as a 'topaz brane', a half-Portuguese Christian brahmin called Manuel de Souza.

[32] Ibid., pp. 102–3.

[33] Ibid., pp. 106–7.

[34] Ibid., p. 21. The king of Travancore tried to use the brahminical thread, and the king of Cochin, who had that exclusive privilege because of his peculiar descent, refused to talk to him, 'from which one can understand that the use of the thread is not a religious ceremony, but a sign of political dignity'. Gonçalves' distinction between 'barbaric' and

preferred to reconstruct Indian civility as originally atheistic (he used the evidence for Buddhism in ancient India as a way of doing this) in order to be able to argue historically for the non-religious character of brahminic marks of social distinction, Gonçalves fell back on analogical readings, which allowed him to suggest that the brahminic thread could stand for the Trinity, rather than Shiva, Brahma and Vishnu. He probably did not realize that by seeking an analogy between Vishnu as the Father, Shiva as the Spirit, and Brahma as the Son, he was actually contradicting himself, and undermining the core distinction of Nobili's method.[35]

In stark opposition to Gonçalves, Gonçalo Fernandes adopted the distinction between civil customs and religious ones only in order to deny the validity of Nobili's arguments. He was the most unlikely of all early indologists. A retired soldier, who entered the Jesuit order in India and who had started the mission of Madurai, he was appalled by Nobili's attempt to shed the image of the *prangui* (Frank) in order to make his message more acceptable to the caste-conscious brahminic elite of the city. For Nobili's project implied rejecting not only Fernandes' method of ministration to the low-caste Paravas, but also what Fernandes personally stood for: the common Portuguese as a model of a Christian man. Thus, in 1610, Fernandes became Nobili's first denunciator. His research into Hindu beliefs was not conducted out of missionary needs, but only in order to respond to Nobili at the intellectual level on which the argument about his method was conducted within the Jesuit order – from this perspective Fernandes was a precursor of those friars who would attack the Jesuits in China throughout the second half of the seventeenth century.[36] Thus the 'Summary of the ceremonies and way of

'sinful' customs (ibid., p. 95) defines a sphere of cultural diversity which is not explicitly against revealed or rational divine laws, however unpalatable some strange customs may be to European taste. Thus Gonçalves actually distinguishes three categories of alien customs: those which are barbaric but may be acceptable (and he discusses some in his account of the political customs of Malabar); those which are not acceptable according to natural reason (and which he discusses in a special section criticizing erroneous civil customs); and those which are unacceptable on a purely religious basis (and which figure in a section refuting idolatrous beliefs and rituals, and defending the truth of the revelation).

[35] Ibid., Gonçalves goes on: 'O trazerem tres dobras ou tres linhas hé em significação de treus deuses que adorão, Brama, Viznu, Maguechurem; o que se pode fazer à honra da Sanctissima Trindade'. This of course fully contradicts the previous statement that this is not really a religious ceremony, but instead a political dignity. What Gonçalves unwittingly conveys is that the exclusive social use of the religious ceremony is politically determined.

[36] Interestingly, the origins of the Chinese rites controversy also lie within the Jesuit order. When the Spanish mendicant friars from Manila were allowed to undertake missionary work in China by the Pope in 1633, they sought the books written by the Jesuits themselves criticizing Ricci's method, and in particular they derived much of their

proceeding of the brahmins of this part of India, according to their own laws and the doctrines of their doctors' (1616) was an extensive treatise, prepared from a translation of the Sanskrit shastras into Tamil, and then into Portuguese by Fernandes himself, with the assistance of some native interpreters.[37]

The need to destroy Nobili's position prompted Fernandes to pursue his analysis of the ceremonies of the brahmins with remarkable systematicity and subtlety. He had a clear grasp of the differences between the four Vedas (Rig Veda, Yagur Veda, Sama Veda and Atharva Veda) and of the way they applied to the different castes. A particular concern was to establish the religious significance of the figure of the *sannayasi*, the chaste, ascetic, contemplative brahmin to which Nobili aspired to equate himself. From Fernandes' account of what the Sanskrit books actually said, and especially the *Laws of Manu*, it appeared self-evident that civil and religious elements could not be separated in the tradition of the brahmins, and that the *sannayasi* was no more than a brahmin in his most developed spiritual stage. Nobili had won a great deal of support by quoting Sanskrit authorities against the superficial views of European observers unacquainted with the intellectual sources of the native tradition. Now Fernandes felt able to quote the same scriptures against him, and prove that his distinctions between civil and religious aspects were false. Nobili had compromised with outright idolatry.

Nobili himself would of course have countered those claims, with the confidence of someone who personally read Sanskrit and who had obtained from his teacher – a Telugu brahmin called Shivadharma – direct access to the Vedas.[38] In the *Informatio* concerning a number of

inspiration from Longobardi's treatise of *c.* 1623. This is ironic and perhaps sad, since Longobardi was Ricci's direct successor as head of the Chinese mission, and certainly cannot be accused of having reacted against accommodation on a purely nationalistic basis. Thus the early chronology of the Indian and Chinese debates overlaps interestingly: Ricci died in 1610, the same year that Fernandes launched the attack against Nobili, and through Trigault's Latin rendition of his history of the Chinese mission his work soon became known and admired in Europe; but Nobili's triumph in Rome of 1623, which buried the conflict about Indian rites for a few decades, coincided with the growth of dissensions in China and with the crystallization of Longobardi's public opposition to Ricci's method.

[37] See J. Wicki's modern edition of this treatise: *Tratado do P. Gonçalo Fernandes Trancoso sobre o Hinduísmo*, ed. by J. Wicki (Lisbon, 1973). The clash between Fernandes and Nobili has been analysed by V. Cronin, *A pearl to India. The life of Roberto de Nobili* (London, 1959) and, more recently, in an excellent article by Ines Zupanov, 'Aristocratic analogies and demotic descriptions in the seventeenth century Madurai Mission', *Representations*, 41 (1993): 123–48.

[38] Nobili defined the four traditional Vedas as 'little more than a disorderly congeries of various opinions bearing partly on divine, partly on human subjects, a jumble where religious and civil precepts are miscellaneously put together': Roberto de Nobili, *On Indian customs*, ed. by S. Rajamanickam (Palayamkottai, 1972), p. 42.

Indian customs, which he dictated to his companion Antonio Vico in 1613 – three years after his initial apology against Fernandes' accusations – he could present the brahmins as primarily a caste of learned men presiding over a plurality of religions or sects, but not necessarily attached to any of them.[39] Nobili could for instance contend, by reference to India's Buddhist past, that Buddhism was a kind of rational atheism with a surprisingly Cartesian ring, which proved that not all brahmins had to be Hindu believers in order to remain brahmins, and that the Vedas were just a collection of legal opinions, not a strictly religious text.[40] Idolatry in its various forms (and here Nobili distinguished the Advaita, Vaishnava, Madhva, and Shaiva schools of medieval South India) represented a deist reaction against the primordial atheism of the Buddhists, culminating with Shankara; but also its subsequent fragmentation and degeneration.[41] Nobili could thus simultaneously engage the brahmins as the restorer of a 'lost spiritual Veda' by appealing to their monotheistic philosophy above the heads of all idols, and deny against European critics that the brahmins were, as a social group, necessarily identified with idolatry – in fact some remained Buddhist or Jain. In all this, Nobili was of course very much shaping his discoveries according to a personal vision, but he was skilful enough to reduce his views to a number of uncontentious propositions, and no less than 108 learned brahmins from Madurai, Vijayanagara and Tanjore were prepared to testify to their truth.

The opposition between Nobili and Fernandes has been analysed by Ines Zupanov as representing a fissure within European culture, one dividing the idealism of an aristocratic identity educated in the universal values of humanist theology, and the realism of a more popular gaze

[39] For a valuable English translation of this important treatise by S. Rajamanickam see ibid. The other two key Latin treatises by Nobili are his *Apologia* of 1610, his first reaction to criticism; and his more mature *Narratio fundamentorum quibus missio Madurensis stabilitur*, written for the Goa conference of 1619. Apparently, for tactical reasons this was then presented as the work of Nobili's supporter the Catalan Francesc Ros, archbishop of the Saint Thomas Christians.

[40] Thus these Buddhists 'far from approving any of these laws [currently associated with the brahmins] go to the length of rejecting or questioning the very possibility of any law. Talk to them of a religious law; they are sceptical about it, since they reject all faith or all knowledge by faith; for them all knowledge worth the name is restricted to knowledge by inference or by intuition; many of them indeed admit of no other means of knowing than that produced by clear perception and clear evidence' (Nobili, *On Indian customes*, p. 41).

[41] As Nobili explained in his own Tamil treatises, idolatry was therefore the imperfect response of the gentile whose sinful ancestors had denied God's law, and even his very existence, but who, still unsatisfied, instinctively sought Him. Idolatry was established through human means (the vanity of the powerful, the sorrow of those coping with death, the wonder of the ignorant, and the love of those who were grateful to great men). The role of the devil was therefore quite secondary. Needless to say, the path of truth and virtue was now accessible through Christian revelation alone.

based on the direct experience of radical otherness through sensory perceptions.[42] This formulation is perhaps exaggerated – the very existence of Fernandes' treatise is evidence of the fact that ultimately Nobili had no monopoly of intellectual arguments which used native discourse, whilst the example of the aristocratic, university-educated Valignano and his views of India should prevent us from describing the belief in radical otherness, based on the experience of observed behaviour, as only typical of men like Fernandes. At heart, the dispute was more theological than social or national. Certainly the impulse to penetrate idolatrous religion as an intellectual tradition, and to re-write it according to the demands of a theory of salvation for the whole of mankind, was an initiative that only a socially and intellectually confident missionary like Nobili could undertake; but once the move had been made, opponents had to respond in the same manner. The history of idolatrous religions became part of the history of gentile nations, and it became urgent not to ignore either of them. What the controversy does represent is a rift between the abstract universalist ideals of Christianity and the narrow sense of identity attached to a particular historical form of religion. Nobili and Fernandes shared the conviction that only within the Church was there salvation for a sinful mankind, but whilst Nobili, with a historical vision of the Church, was able to see many social and cultural forms as irrelevant to salvation, Fernandes universalized his own social and cultural identity.[43]

The debate about Indian religion was then really a debate about Christianity. If one could be a Christian brahmin, wearing a loincloth and praying in Tamil, one need not speak Portuguese or dress like a European in order to be a Christian. Fernandes could devote his life to the Parava fishermen of the coast because, as a European priest, all religious authority remained in his hands: the Indian convert who remained culturally not European was a devout Christian, but not a Christian with power and authority. Nobili's approach was not only a

---

[42] Zupanov, 'Aristocratic analogies', pp. 123–5. For a more extensive and very intelligent treatment of Nobili from a non-theological perspective, see also I. G. Zupanov, 'Writing and acting culture: the Jesuit experiments in 17th century South India' (Ph.D. thesis, University of California at Berkeley, 1991; on microfilm, 1994).

[43] Thus to present Fernandes as 'a painter who objectified without participating', as Zupanov does ('Aristocratic analogies', p. 141), is excessive. He was no modern anthropologist seeking to portray diversity as gloriously incommensurable, because his description of brahminism as radically other carried an implicit and profound condemnation: the idolatry of the brahmins was essentially devilish, and this devil, like the God whose denial he symbolized, was the same in Europe as in India. Whilst Nobili insisted that only some specifically religious elements in Hinduism were devilish (this was the point of his interpretation), Fernandes' non-participatory gaze condemned the whole lot.

matter of dressing as a Hindu holy man in order to facilitate conversions, but also of understanding a gentile civil tradition as valid in its own terms, insofar as it could be made compatible with Christian and natural law – in this sense Hindu civilization was not different from classical Greece and Rome.[44] It was Nobili who, for the first time, translated Hindu *dharma*, with its various meanings, into European ideas of virtue and social custom, including the *ius gentium* and *recta ratio*.[45] But these distinctions were an intrusion into the native religion: he told his audience of brahmins what their thread meant – so as to render it innocuous from a Christian perspective. In 1623, Pope Gregory XV actually issued a bull explaining what idolatry and what civil custom were, in the religion of the brahmins, according to a particular western reading of Sanskrit writings, and with the necessary support of a historical interpretation of ancient brahminism. The fact that some Indians would give a religious meaning to their own customs only expressed their ignorance of their own tradition.[46]

It is doubtful that the brahminical religion could stand such a dissection, based on alien philosophical concepts, without changing in nature, but it is doubtful that Christians themselves could have applied the same distinctions with rigour to their own tradition without changing its nature too. The very experience of the Reformation proved this. Fernandes was not only stating the obvious when he insisted that the rituals of the brahmins were the rituals of an idolatrous caste: he was also denying Nobili the space to look back at ancient Christianity (as he actually did in order to defend the sanctity of his method in the light of apostolic examples) and thus acquire the power to question the intrinsic spiritual value of many popular devotional practices. Nobili had brought together the separate discourses of Aquinas the theologian and Barbosa

[44] A particularly brilliant passage in Nobili, *On Indian customs*, p. 45: 'For should you condemn those laws as a complex whole on the score that they are regarded, albeit falsely, as received on a superstitiously divine authority, by the same token you must condemn well nigh all the laws derived from non-Christian states and in large measure still in force even in our day; you must condemn all the Papirian laws which to a great extent were either confirmed or written by Numa, as well as ten out of the twelve tables of Rome and those transcribed from the tables of Draco, of Solon and Cyvengy. The same holds true for the assembly of the Areopagus, for the kings and ephors of Sparta, for the senators of ancient Rome, for whom the legal profession meant that they were dedicated men and priests.'

[45] S. Arokiasamy, *Dharma, Hindu and Christian according to Roberto de Nobili* (Rome, 1986), especially pp. 21–2, 115–16, 294.

[46] The bull was based on the report prepared in 1622 by the Irish Bishop Peter Lombard at the request of the Pope in order to settle the dispute about Nobili's method. Lombard, obviously, took the side of Nobili and his immediate superiors in India, Alberto Laerzio and Francesc Ros. See Cronin, *Pearl to India*, pp. 221–30, who translates the document (p. 228).

the ethnographer, and had accepted a gentile religious tradition as an autonomous and effective rival with which a deep philosophical dialogue had to be established. All of this could one day be turned against the unspoken assumptions that gave Christianity in Europe its authoritative role.

Ines Zupanov has insisted how unfair it is to assume that the intellectual flexibility of Nobili and his openness to adaptation were necessarily 'nicer' than Fernandes' reactionary conservatism: they also entailed an identification of the Roman aristocrat with the Tamil brahmin, against both the low-caste Hindu and the lower-class Portuguese (although, in his attempt to explain his need to disentangle himself from the common image of the Portuguese *prangui*, Nobili went further: what he was rejecting were the low moral standards of the half-Portuguese *topaz* and the Jew).[47] At a more substantial level, Fernandes had a point when he rejected the separation of the religious and civil ritual identities of the brahmin as an artificial imposition, although his answer was more instinctive than theological. However, the intellectual brilliance of Nobili as an orientalist, and the depth of his understanding of Hinduism, are equally undeniable, and assisted both his own apology of his method of local adaptation and his actual dialogue with brahmins over the fact that Christianity was the only path to salvation. It is important to stress that no concessions were made at this point: Nobili's theology was extremely orthodox within the rigid parameters of the council of Trent, and he never allowed himself the pseudo-rationalistic claims of Ramon Llull, or the unempirical lucubrations of Athanasius

---

[47] In his first apology of 1610, Nobili obviously played on social and racial prejudices in order to justify his rejection of the image of the *prangui*. In order to refute that all Christians were called *prangui*, and that the word *prangui* could stand for all white European men, he insisted that the people of Madurai had not been exposed to Portuguese noblemen, but only *topazes* (natives dressing like the Portuguese and speaking a few words of their language, but not really European by blood) and Jews (referring to independent Portuguese horse-traders, men like Paes and Nunes, some of whom were New Christians). On both accounts Nobili was exaggerating, in order to carve for himself a legitimate space for the new image of the Christian aristocratic learned man, one acceptable to the European elites as well as to the brahmins. For this, he needed to say that 'when I speak of the *pranguis*, one should not believe that I refer to the true Portuguese'. See the French edition of the *Apologia* by P. Dahmen (ed.) *Un Jésuite Brahme. Robert de Nobili S. I. 1577–1656* (Louvain, 1924), pp. 158–60. Nobili seemed to be forgetting that Henrique Henriques (1529–1600), the Jesuit who had sustained the mission among the Paravas on the Fishery coast with impressive exemplariness for over fifty years, author of a Tamil grammar as well as two Tamil catechisms and a Tamil *Flos Sanctorum* (these were printed in Tamil characters in India in 1576, 1577 and 1586), and in fact Gonçalo Fernandes' mentor, was himself of Jewish origin. The Franciscans had expelled him, but in its early days the Jesuits, under Ignatius, prided themselves on accepting New Christians.

Kircher.[48] Similarly, his key supporter in India, Francesc Ros, had been chosen as the first Latin archbishop of the Saint Thomas Christians, because he accepted with conviction the native use of local dress or the traditional Syriac liturgy, but would never compromise with any hint of Nestorian heresy.

Through his orientalism, Nobili thus accomplished three things: to argue from within Hinduism with Hindus, to argue against his Catholic critics with reference to an Indian cultural authority, and finally to create a Christian literature in Indian languages, adapted to peculiar social customs and literary expectations. Zupanov has insisted that his personal aim was to become a saint, by opening the door of paganism in order to let the light of reason in.[49] But when a door is opened, something can come out too. Historically, his role was to force a debate about the difference between religious and civil customs which was already implicit in the duality which we have observed, within the literature of expansion, between the careful historical analysis of behaviour and the shallow analysis of religious belief, and which the Enlightenment would turn against Christianity by simply asking back all the same questions: what is the cause of superstition, other than ignorance? what is a ritual, a spiritual action or a national custom? what are these religious texts which our ancestors gave us, other than a historical product which needs to be analysed and de-mythologized in order to eliminate absurd opinions? Which is, after all, the core of rational philosophical truth hidden behind the fables? Ironically, it was the destiny of missionaries like Nobili to contribute to this questioning through their intelligence and their zeal.[50]

TOWARDS A EUROPEAN DEBATE

There was thus an argument for keeping the door to an understanding of idolatry firmly shut. But it was never the Jesuits' intention to publicize their findings. For instance, Fernão Guerreiro in his *Relação anual*

---

[48] Llull's *Art*, the mystic vision of the structural reality of God which would (the missionary hoped) allow him to rationally explain the Christian mysteries to unbelievers, amounted to creating a new rhetoric to facilitate the Christian dialogue with Jews and Muslims – a rhetoric in part inspired by Jewish Kabbala and oriental exemplary genres, but ultimately dependent on a new revelation for winning logical arguments. Nobili avoids all this: he depends on the discipline of an established theological language, and in particular the distinctions of Aquinas, in order to analyse both gentility and Christianity, while his dialogue with non-Christians is an empirical one.

[49] Zupanov, 'Writing and acting', p. xxxi.

[50] G. Colas, 'Vie légumineuse et pensée travestie. A propos de l'adaptation des Jésuites en Inde aux XVIIe et XVIIIe siècles', *Purusartha*, 19 (1996): 199–220, offers a very stimulating discussion of the evolution of Jesuit adaptation after Nobili, from the perspective of the late seventeenth-century French Jesuit mission in South India.

presented the mission at Vijayanagara in a hopeful light, especially the idea that King Venkata might be converted, but the emphasis was on the friendliness of the gentiles towards the missionaries and the Portuguese, and occasionally on stories that suggested the miraculous workings of Christian providence.[51] Over the years it became necessary to find explanations for the lack of conversions – such as the strength of idolatry in that kingdom, or even the reluctance of the gentiles to become low caste by accepting the religion of the Portuguese – but no suggestion was ever given that the truth of Christianity was anything but obvious. Although the need to learn native language and customs was presented as a reason for the delay in conversions, Guerreiro did not even imply that the Jesuits were undertaking research into Indian religion in order to confuse the worshippers of the devil.

Only the order's enthusiasm for Nobili's mission made it possible for European readers to be offered some evidence of the Jesuits' concern for method. In the fifth and last volume of Guerreiro's series (originally published in 1611) Nobili's experiments received a great deal of attention, and in particular his willingness to conform to the dress and rule of the brahmins in order to overcome their 'superstition' concerning caste pollution. This unprecedented image of a Christian *sannayasi* transmitted by Guerreiro was taken directly from Nobili's own letters, and included an acknowledgement that he was learning Brahmin letters – Tamil and Sanskrit – and thus was able to present his Christian message as a restoration of the spiritual Veda, of which the religions of 'Vesmú, Bramá e Rutrú' (Vishnu, Brahma and Shiva) only had adulterated traces.[52] It was the confidence of Nobili in his method, and Guerreiro's desire to publicize this apparent success as an inspirational model, which suddenly offered the reader in Europe an exceptional glimpse of actual missionary research into Hinduism. However, it was still apology and propaganda rather than curiosity.[53]

Similarly, Pierre du Jarric's important three-volume history of the Jesuit missions, *Histoire des choses plus memorables advenues tant ez Indes Orientales que autres païs de la decouverte des Portugais* (Bordeaux 1608, 1610, 1614) was essentially a tool of propaganda (du Jarric being himself a Jesuit), and although the French writer synthesized the letters sent from Vijayanagara with more penetration and literary

---

[51] Guerreiro, *Relação anual*, vol. I, pp. 40–3 (for the year 1601); pp. 315–21 (for the years 1602–3); vol. II, pp. 141–6 (for the years 1604–5); pp. 321–3 (for the years 1606–7); vol. III, pp. 76–7 (for the year 1608).

[52] Ibid., vol. III, pp. 89–113, with reference to the years 1608 and 1609.

[53] Another important window into the methods of Nobili in South India was given in the Italian *Ragvagli d'alcune missioni fatte dalli padri della Compagnia di Giesù nell'Indie orientali* (Rome, 1615), pp. 107–59.

accomplishment than his model Guerreiro, he did not really seek to offer an exposition of the gentile system of beliefs; rather, if he focused on the intellectual reaction of King Venkata to the propositions of the missionaries it was in order to make the hope of conversion logically plausible.[54]

In fact, the impact of the indological efforts of the Catholic missionaries in Europe was mainly derivative. Thus, as we saw, Diogo do Couto managed to incorporate Azevedo's account into his fifth decade, finally published in 1612, whilst in 1619 Fenicio's treatise was sent to Europe by Father Manuel Barradas, who made a compressed version of it for the Portuguese scholar (and canon of Evora) Manuel Severim de Faria, and thus could inform the historian Manuel de Faria y Sousa for his *Asia portuguesa*.[55] More mysteriously, Fenicio's treatise was also used by the Dutch cleric Philippus Baldaeus, an appropriation which was of course entirely unintended by the Jesuits as well as entirely unacknowledged by the Protestant writer, but which also proved the more influential, since Baldaeus's 1672 *Naauwkeurige beschryving van Malabar en Choromandel* ('A true and exact description of Malabar and Coromandel') had many readers in the late seventeenth century and, with Rogerius, informed the enlightened view of brahmanism.[56]

The only interpretative account of Hinduism publicized by the Jesuits themselves in the seventeenth century was Athanasius Kircher's view of the religion of the brahmins in his famous *China illustrata* (Amsterdam, 1667), but it is immediately apparent that, however influential among lovers of Neoplatonic universalist syncretism, this was an extravagant interpretation rather than a mainstream Jesuit discourse.[57] It certainly had very little to do with Nobili's own views, which Kircher entirely ignored despite his possible access to some of the materials received in Rome. Kircher's views of India were, however, part of an attempt to

---

[54] Pierre du Jarric, *Histoire des choses plus memorables* . . . 3 parts (Bordeaux, 1608–14), part I, pp. 566–602.

[55] See Faria y Sousa, *Asia portuguesa*, vol. II, pp. 655–706. Sousa had actually completed this work by 1640, but the secession of Portugal from the Spanish monarchy prevented its immediate publication until 1666–75. The book also reached an English readership through the rendition of John Stevens (1694–5).

[56] Baldaeus' account of Hinduism relied on Rogerius as well as Fenicio's manuscript, which he might have pillaged from the Jesuit seminary of Jaffnapatam in Ceylon when the Dutch conquered it. Baldaeus (1632–72) was a missionary in Ceylon between 1656 and 1665, and witnessed the definitive establishment of the Dutch in the former Portuguese South Indian enclaves. The three parts of his book discussed the coasts of southern India, Ceylon and Hinduism.

[57] For a modern English rendering see A. Kircher, *China illustrata*, trans. by Charles Van Tuyl (Bloomington, Ind., 1987), especially part III, chaps. 3–7 (pp. 137–58). The fullest account of the theological meaning of Kircher's orientalism is D. Pastine, *La nascita dell'idolatria. L'Oriente religioso di Athanasius Kircher* (Florence, 1978). On pp. 266–87 Pastine develops a comparison with Nobili.

present a full historical vision of idolatry in a world perspective. They were a recognition that the history of the missions could no longer be the history of Catholic triumphs, but also needed to be grounded on an antiquarian basis which made sense of the new evidence with reference to both classical and biblical sources. The strategy had been advanced by the Protestant antiquarian who edited Rogerius' treatise in 1652, with a preface suggesting that many of the elements of Indian idolatry, explained historically through a diffusionist model, could be rationalized sympathetically as the gropings of natural reason in the darkness of ignorance.[58] Similarly, in Kircher's idealized reconstruction, brahminism was part of a universal idolatry that had its roots in the ancient world, especially in Egypt, and then spread to the whole of the Orient, including both China and India.[59] The idea was not new to the period – already influential Greek sources like Philostratus' *Life of Apollonius of Tyana* presented the Indian brahmin (located at the edge of a geography more symbolic than real) as a spiritual equivalent of the Egyptian seeker of wisdom, and teacher of the Greek philosopher; the analogies between the Platonic doctrine of the transmigration of the souls usually attributed to Pythagoras, and the very similar doctrines reported in India from the sixteenth century, made the case compelling to any classical scholar.

What is, however, paradoxical is the deep conservatism of Kircher's intellectual solution in the light of the research conducted by members of his own order on the ground. Kircher made no distinction between religion and civilization, which as we have seen was the cornerstone of Nobili's method. Instead, Kircher saw all civilizations as essentially religious (the hypothesis of atheism, encountered by Nobili in India's Buddhist past, was excluded from this vision). His missionary hope was based on the idea that all idolatry had a common source, which had a naturalistic root and a monotheistic spiritual direction. Thus there was a universal religious ground that could be used as basis for a universal conversion to Christianity, as the logical historical culmination of the

[58] In other words, the recognition that hidden behind its cloak of fables there was a philosophical core to paganism – a 'true foundation' which was construed as essentially deistic and Platonic – which could be used as a tool for conversions. See A. Rogerius, *Le théatre de l'idolatrie, ou la porte ouverte à la connoissance du paganisme caché* (Amsterdam, 1670), 'Au lecteur'. The important preface to the readers is signed by A. W. JCtus (Leyden, 26 December 1650). W. Caland, modern editor of Rogerius' Dutch treatise, identifies him with Andreas Wissowatius: A. Rogerius, *De open-deure tot het verborgen heydendom*, ed. by W. Caland (The Hague, 1915), p. xxvii. The French edition of 1670 included further annotations of an antiquarian nature, probably by the same writer.

[59] It seems obvious that the primacy corresponds to the Leyden professor writing in 1650, since Kircher only wrote his *China illustrata* with the material brought to Rome from China and Tibet in the 1650s and 60s.

single process of sacred history. As Dino Pastine has insisted, Kircher's originality lies in the application of analogical methods of interpretation to a biblical view of universal history which is essentially Augustinian: a story of fall and redemption.[60]

The point is not that Kircher's antiquarian universalism and Nobili's Thomistic methods were contradictory, but rather that the Jesuits were not prepared to incorporate the fine distinctions of their method into a European self-understanding. The Catholic structure of religious discourse, based as it was on a strict respect for tradition and authority, did not seek to spread knowledge of gentilism for its own sake. However, they were forced to do so, first by the existence of a Protestant antiquarian scholarship and of a growing number of lay travellers who dared to discuss non-Christian religions, and later (and more embarrassingly) by the explosion of the rites controversy over China in the second half of the seventeenth century. This allowed the lay *philosophes* to play the Dominican against the Jesuit, whilst entering the debate about religion and despotism in China with renewed sources of information. In fact Kircher's work was a mid-seventeenth century response to this trend: the *China illustrata* (1667), read alongside the *Oedipus Aegyptiacus* (1652–4), the *Arca Noe* (1675) and the *Turris Babel* (1679), used the antiquarian perspective to counter new interpretations of the Pentateuch which, like the polygenistic doctrine of 'men before Adam' of Isaac la Peyrère, could be used by sceptical libertines against traditional Christianity.

By then it was already too late, because the clerical monopoly on religious discourse had been shattered and even a system as comprehensive as Kircher's could be criticized as being full of holes. In Europe lay writers – whether Catholic or Protestant – were now in a position to combine the systematic distinction between religious beliefs and civil behaviour pursued by the accommodationist Jesuits with the historical perspective of Kircher and other antiquarians, and thus propose another history of religion – one which was in the end no more than a philosophical and critical history of civilization.

Religious dissension in Europe and the inheritance of classical humanism were of course crucial conditions for the emergence of this sceptical analysis of religion, a tradition represented for instance by Montaigne and Bayle.[61] This relativist tradition created a pressure on conservative definitions of religion without which the theories of Jesuits

---

[60] Pastine, *La nascita*, p. 28.
[61] Of course, scepticism was not the same as atheism (both Montaigne and Bayle can be construed as fideists). It did however imply a separation, or tension, between what was understood as faith and reason.

like Lafitau would have been unnecessary, and the eighteenth-century Enlightenment impossible.[62] But mediating between the humanist education which made the questions possible, and the empirical reality of human diversity which had now become essential to any answers, there was always the figure of the lay traveller informing the European essay writer. This lay traveller, as an independent figure writing for a European public, was in the seventeenth century a very powerful voice, one able to go beyond the practical concerns of the Portuguese factor and horse-trader, and, more importantly, one able to write history and discuss religion in a way that challenged the authoritative voices of the official chronicler and the missionary. Jan Huygen van Linschoten, François Pyrard de Laval, Francesco Carletti, Jacques de Coutre, William Methwold, Pietro della Valle, François Le Gouz de la Boullaye, Jean Baptiste Tavernier, François Bernier, Manuel Godinho, Jean de Thévenot, John Fryer, Niccolao Manucci, and Giovanni-Francesco Gemelli Careri (to mention only the more influential or original travellers writing on India) constituted altogether a new phenomenon, one increasingly obvious in the European book market of the second half of the century. Although some of them were still associated with particular colonial ventures and religious perspectives, on the whole they offered personal views, and certainly views better informed than those of Varthema a century earlier. Not all of them shared relativist opinions – in fact relativist writers like Bernier were in a minority – but their evidence could be used in Europe nevertheless. Unlike their ancestor Marco Polo, who could hardly be believed, and their predecessor Varthema, who was a shifty character, the independent traveller of the seventeenth century had finally emerged as the new authority for a new science of mankind.

---

[62] The declared purpose of Lafitau was to refute a purely rationalist and historical understanding of human laws, beliefs and customs: Pagden, *The fall of natural man*, p. 200. Similarly, in the seventeenth century Catholic fathers such as Gassendi and Mersenne had tried to reconcile religion and science with a compromise between Christian fideism and a historical and naturalistic understanding of the world. See R. H. Popkin, *The history of scepticism from Erasmus to Spinoza* (Berkeley, 1979), pp. 129–50.

10. *From humanism to scepticism: the independent traveller in the seventeenth century*

SAMUEL PURCHAS AND THE COSMOGRAPHICAL PILGRIMAGE

The English parson Samuel Purchas (1577–1626) is best known as the successor of Richard Hakluyt for the massive twenty books of his *Pilgrimes* (London, 1625), in which he collected the travel accounts of all times 'not by one professing methodically to deliver the historie of nature according to rules of art, nor philosophically to discuss and dispute; but as in a way of discourse, by each traveller relating what in that kind he hath seene'.[1] The distinction between methodical exposition according to general analytical headings, and the original narratives of the travellers using their own words 'in a way of discourse', was one crucial to the culture of the late Renaissance, especially in England, and supported the new ideas of scientific method developed by contemporaries of Purchas like Francis Bacon.[2] Purchas himself explained this when he defined his travel collection as a kind of natural history: 'As David prepared materials for Solomon's temple; or (if that be too arrogant) as Alexander furnished Aristotle with huntsmen and observers of creatures to acquaint him with their diversified natures; or (if that also seeme too ambitious) as sense, by induction of particulars, yeeldeth the premisses to reasons syllogisticall arguing . . . so here Purchas and his pilgrimes minister individuall and sensible materials (as it were stones, bricks and mortar) to those universal speculators to their theoreticall structures'.[3] The point was not simply to distinguish the empirical observations of the traveller and the general theories of the scholar, but rather to bring critical skills

---

[1] Samuel Purchas, *Hakluytus posthumus; or, Purchas his pilgrimes* (London, 1625), 'To the reader'.
[2] I have discussed this in 'Instructions for travellers: teaching the eye to see', pp. 139–90.
[3] Purchas, *Hakluytus*, 'To the reader'.

to the distance that separated them, under the guise of methodical awareness.

Unlike Bacon, Purchas was personally less interested in methodical awareness than in the shape of the temple he wished to build. Critics have often emphasized how imperfect were many of the summaries and translations of travel accounts which he laboriously prepared, especially in contrast with those of his predecessor Richard Hakluyt, who (possibly inspired by Ramusio's high standards of editorial fidelity) was careful to reproduce his documents word by word. Whilst Purchas has often been defended on the grounds that he made available much new material in print, what perhaps needs to be emphasized is that his project was more theoretical than empirical.[4] Before being a collector of 'pilgrimes', he was a pilgrim himself – not one who physically travelled around the world, but rather a Cambridge-educated theologian who travelled by reading books from his study, with the aim of reaching that particular location expressed by his motto 'unus deus, una veritas'. Purchas's collection of 'sensible materials' was not therefore the primary focus of his work: of greater importance was the theological–geographical temple of the whole world which he had built in his mind. This found expression in his massive *Pilgrimage, or relations of the world and the religions observed in all ages and places discovered from the creation unto this present*. This earlier work (not to be confused with the *Pilgrimes*) was first published in 1613 and dedicated to the archbishop of Canterbury, George Abbot, a circumstance which secured for Purchas a chaplaincy to the archbishop, and shortly afterward a rectory in London.[5]

Purchas can be seen as a true successor to the author of the book by Sir John Mandeville – which helps explains why, suspending his critical faculties, he insisted on Mandeville's status as a great traveller. He was also the Protestant counterpart to Giovanni Botero (though probably not his emulator, since only the political sections of the *Relationi universali* were available in English when Purchas conceived his project). Purchas' *Pilgrimage* was essentially a universal cosmography based on all the travel literature he could lay his hands on, guided by the desire to define the place of newly discovered religious diversity in a Christian

---

[4] The bibliography concerning Purchas is scarce. See, however, E. G. R. Taylor, *Late Tudor and early Stuart geography, 1583–1650* (London, 1934), pp. 53–66. The recent publication of *The Purchas Handbook*, edited by L. E. Pennington, Hakluyt Society, 2nd series, 2 vols. (London, 1997), provides essential reference material and will help rectify a traditional historiographical neglect.

[5] Published again with additions in 1614 and 1617. The fourth edition of the *Pilgrimage, or relations of the world* appeared in 1626 appended to the *Hakluytus posthumus*. It benefited from the papers collected by Hakluyt, which after his death Purchas managed to acquire despite Hakluyt's antipathy towards him.

framework, and supported by a world-historical perspective which inevitably rested on biblical and classical foundations. 'Religion is my more proper aime', he declared, and his theme was that whilst all men agreed 'that there should bee a Religion', they disagreed in their practice of it. He distinguished of course between the many heathen superstitions of Asia, Africa and America, and the 'true' religion of Christians alone – by which he meant the Protestants and especially those from Great Britain, who thus stood as a new Israel among pagans. Catholics Purchas rhetorically equated with gentile idolaters, and found standard arguments for this equation in the similarity he detected between popish rites and those of the ancient Chaldeans and Egyptians. Not only were Catholics drinking from the original fountains of paganism, they were also surpassed by the gentiles in their devotions (and here Purchas could quote the very Jesuits as witnesses to the asceticism of the devilish Indian yogis, thus taking the wind out of their own claims to sanctity).

Both Purchas's ideological stance and his method had important implications that are revealing of the tension between humanism and scepticism which characterized the seventeenth century. In this light Purchas in fact appears as a man of medieval aims and modern perspectives. The ideological implications are particularly obvious: in order to maintain his claims in favour of Christianity, Purchas needed both to cleanse it from any superstition which might be seen as idolatrous – as Protestants insisted when they criticized Catholics – and to justify his claims historically with a critical scrutiny of revelation. This could, however, only lead to the infinite search for an impossible point of ecclesiastical purity, a process which effectively condemned seventeenth-century Protestantism to further fragmentation, and to the ultimate disintegration of the authority of the Bible from an antiquarian critical perspective (which implied a historicization of the Jewish sources of Christian revelation). What made this process uncontrollable was not only the implicit challenge of authority which followed from any open act of reformation, but also the fact that the defence of the truth of Christianity necessitated the monogenistic assumption of the unity of mankind, expressed in Purchas's thesis that the religious instinct was universal. He needed to exclude atheism as an effective possibility. The empirical evidence of gentile idolatry was therefore an argument against scepticism, and justified the reader's journey through the ugly face of its multiplicity – but it could be challenged if Europeans declared themselves atheists, or if they successfully proved that gentiles in China were so. Arguments about natural religion and atheism, like the related arguments about the age of the world or about the origins of the American Indians, came to dominate the seventeenth century because of their theological implications. There was nothing that men like Purchas could do to bury a debate that their own antiquarian perspective made inevitable, and which effectively led to the Socinian and vaguely deist beliefs of the Enlightenment.

In this ideological context, the importance of Purchas's work really lay in the method which he had proclaimed of giving the voice of truth to the individual travellers, and then trying to arrange their observations into a coherent whole. The often noted imperfections of Purchas's own laborious execution are really secondary. In the *Pilgrimage* the material was methodically organized in a massive synthesis so as to cover all places and then, within each place, to offer a full historical sequence organized according to the chronology of travellers' reports. Unfortunately, the staggering multiplicity of the sources, combined with Purchas's personal limitations, meant that in reality this universal history of religion was repetitious and often failed to maintain a steady chronological progression. The example of 'the kingdome of Narsinga and Bisnagar' is again perfectly illustrative.[6] No writer before Purchas had assembled so much from so many writers about this kingdom – in this sense his account stands as the true culmination of the process started by Conti and Poggio 200 years earlier, when they joined together the authorities of empirical traveller and secular humanist to place 'Bizengalia' on the European map of the world. Purchas thus combined modern authors like Barros, Osório, Federici, Botero, Linschoten, Floris and Balbi, even Jesuit authorities like du Jarric, with older writers like Pordenone, Mandeville, Conti and Varthema. His account ranged from the earliest European reports of South Indian rites and customs to the latest Jesuit descriptions of the court of Venkata II or the nayakas of Gingee and Madurai. However, although he described the location of Bisnagar and the power of its kings, his aim was not to offer a proper history of the kingdom, but simply to describe its religion as idolatrous and cruel, to emphasize the power of brahmins as sectarian and ridicule their beliefs about the creation of the world, and to locate the Christian legend of Saint Thomas in this heathen landscape. He was essentially following the Jesuits here, and he even described Nobili's discoveries and disputations, not really aware of the controversial implications of his method.

Whilst Purchas failed in his attempt to synthesize his material effectively, he in fact returned the authority of discourse to the individual authors whose accounts he used, first within the structure of the *Pilgrimage*, and then, more clearly, in his continuation of Hakluyt's task with the *Pilgrimes*. That massive body of evidence, like the sixteenth-

[6] Purchas, *Pilgrimage*, book V, chap. 11.

century collections which inspired him, and like those others which were published later in the seventeenth century (notably the *Relations de divers voyages curieux* by Melchisédech Thévenot in France), emerged now as a key instrument for the philosopher in Europe. In this way the historical perspective created by the antiquarian scholarship of humanist cosmographers and theologians fell increasingly into the hands of the rationalist philosopher, with his own secular approach to the questions of mankind's role in creation, of the very character of creation, and even of the anthropological nature of religious beliefs.

What is perhaps most important is that the humanist philosopher was not simply competing against the clerical authorities for the interpretation of merchant accounts and missionary letters, with their peculiar limitations of perspective: he was also often travelling to the East, as a merchant-humanist, as a gentleman-humanist or even as an educated adventurer. The legacy of the travel literature of the Renaissance to the seventeenth-century transformation of the European discourse on human diversity therefore needs to be analysed at two levels: as a change in the quality of the secular gaze of the authoritative observer, and as a change in the assumptions that governed the ethnological debate, from an essentially theological language towards a fully secular understanding of nature and history. In the following pages I shall seek to illustrate these two themes through the remarkable example of the Italian traveller Pietro della Valle (1586–1652). In his concrete ideological context, della Valle stands as a lay example of that Roman Catholic synthesis of the baroque age which, as we saw when discussing Nobili, unwittingly mediated between the chivalric piety of the Counter-Reformation and the corrosive distinctions of an increasingly analytical historical discourse. But as representative of a type, his significance is larger: he is also a counter-figure to the armchair cosmographer, Protestant or Catholic. By revealing the open-ended character of the antiquarian project by means of his own reflective gaze, the educated traveller eroded the authority of writers like Botero and Purchas, and especially their theological bias, in ways that would eventually elude the controls of any particular system of ideological censorship.

PIETRO DELLA VALLE AND THE PILGRIMAGE OF HUMANIST WISDOM

I carried with me from Persia a great desire to go to Cambay because of what I had heard about it, having been told that in that city, which is one of the most ancient of India, the gentile people are very numerous and beyond measure observant of their rites, so that there more than anywhere else I would be able to see many fine curiosities [*belle curiosità*] of these idolaters.[7]

With this unambiguous declaration of intellectual curiosity, the Roman aristocrat Pietro della Valle introduced in a letter of 1623 his expedition from the Dutch factory at Surat (where despite being Catholic he was kindly hosted as a gentleman-traveller) towards the mysterious customs, rites and temples of gentile India. Pietro della Valle was particularly aware of the diversity of oriental nations and religions, and of the distinction between Muslims and non-Muslims, since he had already spent more than eight years travelling in the dominions of the Ottoman Turks and at the court of the Persian Shah Abbas.[8] He learnt

---

[7] *Viaggi di Pietro della Valle il pellegrino descritti da liu medesimo in lettere familiari all'erudito suo amico Mario Schipano. Parte terza, cioè l'India, co'l ritorno alla patria* (Rome, 1663), p. 36 (hereafter *India*). This is part of the first complete and more reliable edition of the *Viaggi*, published in Rome by Biagio Deversin between 1658 and 1663, including: part II concerning *Persia*, in two volumes (1658); a second edition of part I concerning *Turkey* (1662); finally part III concerning *India* (1663). The printers were Vitale Mascardi and (for the second printing) Iacomo Dragondelli. The first part, the letters from Turkey, had been previously published in 1650 by della Valle himself before his death. However, only the 1662 reprint also includes the life of della Valle by Giovan Pietro Bellori, and an engraving of the author (drawn during his lifetime). There is no modern critical edition of the Italian text, except for the first volume of the second part, concerning Persia, which was published as *I viaggi di Pietro della Valle. Lettere dalla Persia*, vol. I, ed. by F. Gaeta and L. Lockhart (Rome, 1972) (hereafter *Lettere dalla Persia*). I have used this superior text for quotations from this section. One of the contributions of this excellent edition is the restoration of passages suppressed by ecclesiastical censorship because they dealt with Christian theology or missionary policy, from the clean copy of the letters prepared for the publishers by della Valle, and now kept in the Società Geografica Italiana (as already noted in I. Ciampi, *Della vita e delle opera di Pietro della Valle il Pellegrino* (Rome, 1880); however della Valle died before he could supervise the edition of the Indian letters). Even more valuable, however, is the original journal of della Valle covering the years 1616–26, from which he then wrote the letters which he sent to Mario Schipano in Naples, with small alterations. I have consulted this journal (Biblioteca Apostolica Vaticana (BAV), Ms. Ottob. 3,382) for the sections on India, and have been able to ascertain that on the whole della Valle simply copied a chunk of his journal each time he wrote to Schipano, adding, however, an introductory paragraph, and including the marginalia. The journal includes words and inscriptions in oriental languages not found in the printed edition, but on the whole the published letters (excepting censored passages) represented the journal as he wrote it. In English there exists the generally reliable early translation by George Havers (1664), edited and annotated for the Hakluyt Society as *The travels of Pietro della Valle in India from the old English translation of 1664 by G. Havers*, ed. by E. Grey, 2 vols. (London, 1892). The modern version by George Bull (ed) *The pilgrim. The travels of Pietro della Valle* (London, 1990), improves Grey's translation but unfortunately is only an abridgement. I have benefited from these translations for my own and, as indicated, I have occasionally followed George Bull's.

[8] Della Valle began his travels in 1614 as a pilgrim in order to forget a frustrated love. After visiting Constantinople and Egypt, he crossed Palestine towards Syria, fulfilling his pilgrimage to the Holy Land. However, instead of going back home he turned towards Baghdad in 1616, where he married. He went on to Isfahan, and spent the next six years in Persia (January 1617 to January 1623). He finally went on to Surat and then to Goa in

some Arabic and spoke Turkish and Persian fluently, copied ancient inscriptions, collected oriental manuscripts, dug up Egyptian mummies, researched Arabic science, translated or even composed Persian literature, and dressed according to the custom of each place. In Baghdad he had also fallen in love with and married Sitti Maani Joerida, a Syrian Christian woman (Arabic-speaking and Nestorian) from a well-established family. After her tragic death in Persia, he carried with him her embalmed body, in order to bury it later with due aristocratic pomp in his native Rome.[9]

There could be no doubt for the European reader of della Valle's fifty-four long and detailed letters, which were originally published in Italian in the middle of the seventeenth century, that he was an uncommon traveller.[10] Self-styled 'the pilgrim', his pilgrimage was decisively a pilgrimage of curiosity. However, unlike the adventurer Varthema who had preceded him by over more than a century, he was not an obscure figure with unclear aims who had picked up his rhetoric of self-fashioning from echoes of humanist intellectual culture: rather, della Valle was a truly well-educated gentleman, with connections with the Roman court,

India, which he used as a base to visit the gentile petty courts of Ikkeri and Olala. In 1624 he began his return journey, reaching Rome in 1626 through the Middle East and southern Italy.

9 Della Valle met his 'Babylonian' bride in the autumn of 1616, when she was eighteen, and (although she was technically a Nestorian Christian) they married within a few weeks. In order to defeat his religious scruples della Valle noted that for Maani and her family Nestorianism was an ethnic identity rather than a doctrinal position, so that 'the biggest error found among them today may well be ignorance'. Her family followed della Valle and Maani to Persia, but the attempt to settle a Syrian-Catholic Christian community near Isfahan, under Rome's ecclesiastical authority, eventually failed. Having decided to leave Persia, in 1621, and on the way to Hormuz, Maani fell ill and died after a miscarriage. In order to transport her embalmed body, della Valle had to hide it from the crew of the English ship which took him to Surat. On his return to Rome he published an account of her magnificent Christian burial (*Nel funerale de Sitti Maani Gioerida sua consorte*, Rome, 1627). Soon afterwards he married (not without scandal in the Roman court) Mariuccia, an orphan girl adopted in Persia by his former wife, and who accompanied Pietro to India and Europe.

10 Della Valle's letters, divided into three parts, were published in Rome long after his return in 1626. In 1650 the eighteen letters from 'Turkey', including all the Ottoman dominions appeared, in 1658 the eighteen letters from Persia, in two volumes because they were longer, and in 1663, eighteen further letters from India, including the return home. Thus the Persian and Indian letters were all published after della Valle's death in 1652 by his sons. They suffered some cuts by the ecclesiastical censors. Originally della Valle had arranged to send the letters regularly to his Neapolitan friend Mario Schipano, who was supposed to edit them for publication (although he failed to do so). It is likely that it was in order to avoid the rigid ecclesiastical censorship of baroque Rome that della Valle, despite his social standing, delayed their publication on his return. The manuscript della Valle prepared for the publisher was generally a faithful reproduction of his letters, which themselves followed faithfully his journal with the mere addition of some introductory material.

and a man fully aware that he was creating his own myth as traveller from the social and religious values of the chivalric Renaissance and the Catholic Counter-Reformation. He did not hide behind his writing. His letters were in fact his carefully kept and extremely detailed journal, periodically dispatched to a friend in Europe in large chunks. With their publication, Europe was no longer being offered just another contribution to the growing number of books of travels written by merchants, missionaries and adventurers, which scholars like Botero and Purchas could then collect and summarize: della Valle gave the European reader an authoritative lay voice which not only observed, but also discoursed, about all the subjects of scientific curiosity of the age.[11] Politics, religion, manners, morality, music, food and dress, landscape, antiquities and natural history were all open to the traveller's scrutiny, whose insights into oriental matters were personal and, at the same time, informed by previous reading (della Valle did not hesitate to correct written authorities in the light of his experience for the benefit of the empirical record). Della Valle was both the recorder and the interpreter of the East: his ethnological language was no longer the spontaneous description of customs and rituals, nor was his religious discourse simply one of observation and condemnation. Instead, della Valle compared and researched, asked questions and listened to answers. Although he was not really a thinker, although he never hinted at any identity other than that of a Catholic Christian with a great deal of aristocratic self-importance, and although his linguistic skills and observations were often still limited (which led him to a number of superficial judgements), this self-styled pilgrim and citizen of the world opened his mind to both Europeans and non-Europeans, Christians and non-Christians, Catholics and non-Catholics.[12]

[11] Possibly the closest model were the Latin letters of the Flemish humanist Ogier of Busbecq, ambassador of Emperor Ferdinand to the Ottoman court in 1555–62, which were published through the 1580s as addressed to his friend Nicholas Michault (albeit in a fictionalized, rhetorically elaborated form). A full version appeared in Leyden in 1633. For the more recent scholarship see Z. R. W. M. von Martels, 'Augerius Gislenius Busbequius: leven en werk van de keizerlijke gezant aan het hof van Süleyman de Grote. Een biografische, literaire en historische studie met editie van onuigegeven teksten' (Ph.D. thesis, University of Groningen, 1989). Della Valle, whose style is more spontaneous but less ironic, in effect belongs to a very different generation.

[12] I must therefore disagree with the judgement of J. D. Gurney, who in his otherwise excellent article 'Pietro della Valle and the limits of perception', *Bulletin of the School of Oriental and African Studies*, 49 (1986): 193–216, argues for della Valle's subservience to conventional Renaissance stereotypes. Focusing on della Valle's crucial six-year Persian experience, Gurney emphasizes the traveller's aristocratic self-fashioning as a reason for his profound ethnocentrism, despite all his efforts to learn languages, so that only his casual discovery of the heterodox and eclectic intellectual life of Lar in 1622 stands in opposition to a lack of cultural relativism in many of his previous observations. Gurney

Guided by his own religious belief in the universality of the human spirit, which he formulated in the Neoplatonic and Neostoic language of the late Renaissance, della Valle in effect tested the limits of humanity. His own marriage to an oriental Christian, a romantic rather than a purely practical action, stands as proof and metaphor for this attitude, but the example of a *sati* from Ikkeri in Karnataka is perhaps even more revealing: for della Valle a woman who was planning to throw herself into her husband's funeral pyre deserved more than just the stereotyped horror and compassion of the traditional European accounts. Thus breaking with a literary tradition which went back to the fourteenth century, he individualised her experience, recorded her words, and then composed for her a few sonnets.

In fact della Valle's conversation with Giaccamà, the Telugu *sati* of Ikkeri, was the culmination of a desire to penetrate gentile India as a peculiar cultural reality. This desire had formed in Persia, inspired by hearsay and occasional contact with Indian merchants, especially Gujarati Banians.[13] It had been disciplined by the reading of ancient writers like Strabo and Herodotus, so that when della Valle initiated his intensive tour of the temples of Cambay from his base at Surat he was ready to develop a theory of Hinduism based on the allegorical analogy between Graeco-Egyptian and brahminical doctrines. A visit to a 'hospital of birds' was therefore not only an act of curiosity, but also illustrated the

is certainly right in stating that della Valle's idealized politics were still those of a crusader-missionary, and that his taste was fastidiously aristocratic according to Italian conventions (the fact that he could easily pay for his own travels over so many years is of course significant). However, it is inappropriate to stress 'thorough ethnocentrism' in someone who went as far as della Valle did in his attempt to understand sympathetically and with penetration people fom different religious backgrounds, with very few real precedents in his own culture (Montaigne himself would have insisted that the evidence of cultural relativism was an argument for modestly keeping to one's own tradition, however flawed, rather than imagining that one could find better customs elsewhere). Obviously it was not a matter for della Valle to gratuitously drop his Catholic militancy altogether, nor to look at other cultures from assumptions other than his own – in this sense his ethnocentrism was inevitable, and any question about 'limits of perception', rather than 'logic of perception', is bound to produce this result. What della Valle did that was original was to often actually change his initial impressions through continuous contact and curious conversation, something remarkable because, whilst all cultures are self-centred, not all of them are open to learning from the other. Della Valle's 'classical and Christian' lenses through which he viewed oriental societies (to use Gurney's apt metaphor) did not blind him to the appreciation of diversity, because those lenses had a universalizing component as well as a parochial one. He sought for true nobility and true love among foreigners – and, by implication, for the universal contents of civilization and knowledge. It was not a matter of putting his European lenses aside, but rather of using them with an open mind, something which, from a comparative perspective, della Valle cannot really be accused of having failed to accomplish.

13 The Gujarati Banians (*Vanias*) were a very prominent elite group of Hindu and Jain merchants.

gentiles' rigorous observation of superstitions according to a universal system of idolatry: 'for as the Indian gentiles, along with Pythagoras and the ancient Egyptians (the first authors of this opinion, according to Herodotus), believe in the transmigration of souls, not only from man to man but also from man to brute beast, they account it no less a work of charity to do good to animals than to men'.[14]

As it turned out, della Valle's experience in Gujarat was only a prologue to his Indian experience. His analysis of Hinduism did not depend on a single methodical exposition, but instead grew through the spontaneous observations of his journal, which he continued in southern India. By following this progression we can ascertain that the traveller allowed new experiences to alter his views. Thus in Goa della Valle was confronted with the reality of an Indo-Portuguese society whose political decline, as he had begun to suspect in Persia, did not tally with the image created by historians like Barros. Instead, he described a society with few real Portuguese and many wretched naked slaves, a society whose ostentatious, xenophobic and prudish attitudes (whether originally Portuguese, or perhaps specifically Indo-Portuguese, this he could not fully judge) the Italian sometimes found more alien and distasteful than those of many oriental peoples.[15] In contrast, his readiness to praise the Dutch for their kindness and humanity suggests that a European identity based on polite civility could be more powerful than one based on religious confession.[16]

Paradoxically, this alienation from the Catholic Europeans in India stimulated della Valle to attempt a more intimate, subtler understanding of the oriental gentile. Goa in effect was an opportunity for a more ambitious undertaking: to visit Indian gentiles in lands where their religion could be observed in a pure state. It is striking the extent to which della Valle formulated this as his particular desire, in his own words 'to see some land of the gentiles where they themselves have dominion and observe their rites without being subjected to Christians or

---

[14] Bull (ed.) *The pilgrim*, p. 222.

[15] Della Valle was upset in particular by the suspicion that fell over him for travelling with his Georgian foster-daughter Mariuccia, a girl of about thirteen years old in 1623. They were forced to live separately in Goa. He attributed this suspicion to the incestuous habits of the Portuguese (della Valle, *India*, p. 119). Della Valle would, however, later marry this same Mariuccia on his return to Rome, a decision which caused much suspicion and disapproval amongst his aristocratic peers. She added fourteen children to his already existing illegitimate issue.

[16] For his praise of the Dutch see ibid., p. 24. Despite his contempt for the Portuguese, della Valle made many friends in Goa, a number of them priests, and also acted as informer on Persian affairs to the viceroy, Don Francisco da Gama, who treated him courteously. But he found as much fault with the unwise policies of the Portuguese in India as with their unrefined manners.

Muslims'.[17] A Portuguese embassy to the ruler of Ikkeri, Venkatapa Nayaka, one of those military chiefs who had succeeded in establishing his power on the ruins of the fragmented authority of Vijayanagara, proved the perfect opportunity for an expedition upcountry from Honavur across the mountains of northern Karnataka.[18] This trip, and the return through Mangalore in order to visit the queen of Olala (see map 2), allowed della Valle to have a number of dialogues with the petty kings and queens of southern India, pitching his now well-developed identity as a curious gentleman-traveller from Rome (in India he returned to wearing European garb) against the humanity of gentile idolaters.

I shall discuss three of these dialogues which are especially revealing of the distance that separated della Valle from the practical aims of sixteenth-century travellers. The first one is the encounter with Venkatapa. Although his growing influence above the Kanarese coast created problems for the Portuguese, the modesty of his court could hardly represent a model of gentile kingship for an aristocrat whose immediate European referents were the Papacy on the one hand and the Spanish monarchy on the other, and whose oriental experiences had allowed him closely to observe Ottoman and Persian grandeur in Constantinople and Isfahan. Della Valle's trip to Ikkeri thus constituted a confrontation with the new dimensions of South Indian kingship. In his letter written from Goa in October 1623, before departing, he introduced this Indian ruler as the local inheritor of Vijayanagara authority:

> This prince Venkatapà Naieka used to be a vassal and minister of the great king of Vidià-Nagar [Vijayanagara], which the Portuguese improperly call Bisnagà. But after the fall of the king of Vidià-Nagar, who a few years ago, with his death, lost a great part of his state and was almost extinguished (which was caused by wars raised against him by his neighbours), Venkatapà Naieka, like many other nayakas who used to be his vassals and ministers, became absolute prince of that part of the state which he had under his care; which, because he is a good soldier, he has increased a great deal, occupying the lands of

---

[17] Ibid., p. 135.
[18] The embassy of 1623 was motivated by the recent expansion of Ikkeri to the Kanarese coast, where the Portuguese obtained much of their pepper in this period. Since 1569, exploiting the retreat of native power after the battle of Talikota, the Portuguese controlled the ports of Honavur, Barcelore and Mangalore. However, in 1618 their local allies (and some of their own troops) were defeated by the forces of Ikkeri. This forced the Portuguese to send an ambassador, a former horse-trader called João Fernandes Leitão, to seek an agreement with Venkatapa, who naturally wanted to sell the pepper at a higher price and exploit a monopoly in his lands. Della Valle had befriended Leitão and was therefore able to accompany him.

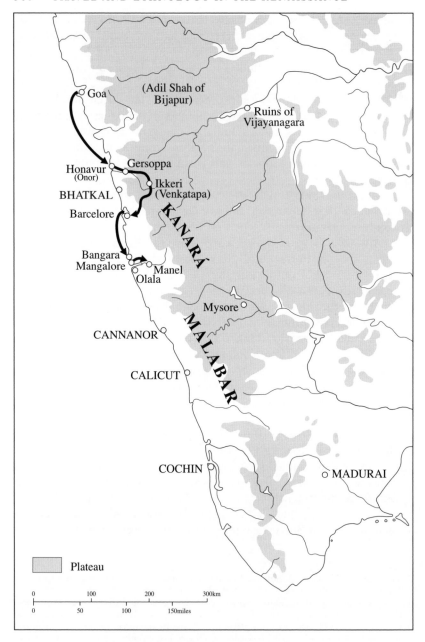

Map 2 Pietro della Valle's journey to Ikkeri and Olala

many other nayakas and petty princes who were his neighbours. With all this, his reputation has grown so much that, after also going to war against the Portuguese and giving them a good beating, now they not only treat him as friend, and try to keep his friendship, but in order to consolidate it they even send this embassy in the name of the king of Portugal.[19]

What is striking about della Valle's account of this embassy is that his contempt for the increasing weakness of the Portuguese (and their inflated chivalric rhetoric) was matched by his scepticism about Venkatapa's claims to kingship.[20] The native ruler possessed no monumental armies, cities or palaces, but only modest towns and small forts. In fact, the traveller's attention was increasingly diverted to the observation of the landscape, which impressed him for its pastoral beauty.[21] Della Valle also explored with keen interest the temples and religious customs of the Virasaiva sect which predominated in those lands (the nayaka was himself a *lingayat*). Whilst the natural and social setting of southern India came to life in the pages of his journal, della Valle's judgement of the royal court became harsher:

> I call him king because the Portuguese themselves and the Indians in imitation do so, but in truth Venkatapà Naieka does not deserve to be called king – not only because his predecessors were a few years ago vassals and simple Nayakas (that is feudatory princes, or rather provincial governors under the king of Vijayanagara), so that today he reigns as absolute ruler by usurpation, and in effect he is no more than a rebel . . . but also much more by reason of the small size of his territory, however great it may be in comparison with that held by other Indian gentile princes . . . In short, Venkatapà Naieka, although now absolute, should in my opinion be called a petty king rather than a king.[22]

---

[19] Della Valle, *India*, p. 138. At the time of della Valle's visit the eastern kingdom of Vijayanagara, caught in a war of succession, no longer exercised authority in Kanará.

[20] Despite the Portuguese tendency to portray their Asian opponents as kings and emperors, a tendency clearly reminiscent of chivalric romances, Venkatapa Nayaka had 'neither state, court nor appearance befitting a true king' (ibid., p. 154).

[21] The pastoral beauty of the landscape during the passage towards Gersoppa is admired as 'one of the most delightful journeys that I ever made in my life' (ibid., p. 158). Climbing the Ghat, della Valle compares it favourably with the Italian Apennines, except for the fact that the latter are more urbanized and sumptuous, 'the Indian Ghat having no other beauty besides what nature, liberal yet unpolished, gives it' (p.160). Whilst the combination of 'city, lakes, fields and woods mingled together' made Ikkeri a very pleasant town, with its dark and smallish houses it was not a model of urban civilization.

[22] Ibid., p. 177–8. It is certainly the case that the dynasty of Keladi chiefs from which Venkatapa descended did appropriate the claims to kingship of the Vijayanagara tradition throughout the seventeenth century, as exemplified in the Sanskrit poem *Sivatattvaratnakara*, written *c.* 1709 by a member of the family, the Shaiva chief Keladi

The arrival at the capital, and the first ceremonial audience, would only confirm della Valle's ironic distance with respect to both the native ruler and the embassy's aims. The travellers were taken through successive gates to meet the king and his courtiers, towards a restricted space which was therefore symbolically defined as qualitatively superior. However, this message did not impress della Valle: 'all in all there were few people, a small show and little wealth, signs which demonstrated the smallness of this court and prince'.[23] His detailed description clearly 'decoded' the ceremonial exchange that followed as a symbolic interaction, involving the creation of a shared language of honour through which power was both used and acquired. The real negotiations, which took place behind the scenes, only confirmed what had been obvious through this ritual exchange: the Portuguese were being humiliated by an impudent Indian chief. Della Valle believed that it was in fact their own fault: they lacked true knowledge of politics, and royal ministers like the ambassador and former horse-trader Fernandes Leitão commonly looked at their own interest rather than the interest of their state. The portrait of native pettiness was in effect also a portrait of Portuguese decline.

But the fact that both partners of the exchange were undistinguished did not disentangle della Valle from his own obligation personally to behave according to a sophisticated sense of decorum. He carefully chose black silk for his garments, to mark discretely his personal mourning for his wife. If he willingly occupied the last place in the room (secretly laughing within) it was only because he wanted to indulge the vanity of the Portuguese. However, he made sure that his position as curious Roman traveller, who had been in the greatest courts of the East, was made known. In fact the attention of the journal shifts from the embassy itself to the fact that della Valle, with his superior intellectual standpoint, was observing native customs. He was able to determine the latitude of Ikkeri and place it in the scientific map of the world. He was also repeatedly invited to admire the dexterity of temple dancing girls (which he did, although deploring their movements as either extravagant or lascivious), and the court was even disappointed when he failed to attend a wrestling match. By the end of his stay of a few weeks in November

---

Basava (Krishnaswami Aiyangar, *Sources of Vijayanagara history*, pp. 194–202 and 337–64). Among other things, the poem described the construction of Ikkeri as a beautiful and magnificent capital, and Venkatapa as a great warrior and religious, even literary patron – in fact the perfect dharmic ruler. Modern historians accept that Venkatapa's rule (1602–29) was crucial for the consolidation of the royal claims of the new dynasty.

[23] Della Valle, *India*, pp. 183–4.

1623, the traveller had effectively transformed his marginality as neutral observer into a position of cultural authority, emerging as victor in a symbolic contest which transcended its local context. The kings of both India and Spain, despite all their ritual trappings, had been de-mystified by his gaze.

Similar analyses may be applied to della Valle's encounters with the queen of Olala and the king of Calicut. Any idea that the king was the centre of a religious and political system – the idea which had sustained both native and foreign descriptions of Vijayanagara from the Middle Ages – was abandoned, and the figures in the landscape instead became humanized. The meeting with the queen of Olala is of particular importance because of the significance that della Valle attached to female figures as inspiration for his romantic vision across cultures. Della Valle was especially interested in codes of honour.[24] Although he understood that kingship in India was often through matrilineal succession, he did not believe this to be in itself dishonourable (in fact he acknowledged that the reason the natives gave, that matrilineal succession was more secure, was surely correct). However, the strict observation of specific caste rules he found less acceptable: in Calicut nayar women had as many men as they pleased, in Ikkeri the king was expected to have various wives, and everywhere temple dancing girls were also public prostitutes.[25]

The queen of Olala represented another chance to meet an interesting figure, one about whom he had already read in Portuguese chronicles when he was in Persia, and made special because she was both a female sovereign, 'something extraordinary in other countries', and gentile in religion (see plate 11). Her main exploits consisted of having divorced her husband and neighbour, the king of Banguel, and then resisted him and his allies the Portuguese with a decisive victory in 1618, with the help of Venkatapa Nayaka (although the price she had to pay was increasing submission to her new protector). Della Valle went especially to a remote village where the queen was staying and accosted her in the street, immediately establishing his prerogative as traveller-observer:

> we saw from afar the queen of Olala coming towards us, on foot, alone without any other woman, only accompanied by four or six foot soldiers before her, all naked after their manner except a cloth over

---

[24] In this trip he also reported stories about the 'base' behaviour of the queen of Gersoppa, who accepted a low-caste man as her champion, and the 'dignified' example of Venkatapa's wife, who refused to have intercourse with him after he had slept with a Moorish woman.

[25] For della Valle's brief observations about matrilineal succession and the nayar women see, *India*, pp. 274 and 285–6.

Plate 11 Pietro della Valle meets the queen of Olala, as depicted (imaginatively) in the German edition of his letters, *Reiss-Beschreibung in unterschiedliche theile der welt* (Geneva, 1674). The Swiss-German editor actually used the engravings from the Dutch edition. *Der voortreffelkyke reizen van Pietro della Valle* (Amsterdam, 1664–5), with slight variations (especially in the facial expressions). It is remarkable how rapidly the Dutch, French, English and German translations followed the complete original Italian.

their shame, and another like a sheet worn across the shoulders as a cape. Each had a sword in his hand, or at most a sword and buckler. There were also as many behind her of the same sort, one of them carrying a rather ordinary umbrella made of palm-leaves over her. She was as black as a natural Ethiopian [African], fat and broad-waisted, but not heavy, for she walked rather nimbly. Her age, it seemed to me, was about forty, although the Portuguese had described her to me as being much older. She was clothed, or rather covered from the waist down, with a plain piece of coarse white cotton, and her feet were bare as is usual among gentile Indian women, whichever their social condition . . . Above the waist the queen was naked, but with a similar cloth tied round her head and falling over her breasts and shoulders. In brief, her aspect and habit were, to tell the truth, more those of a kitchen wench or laundress than a delicate and noble queen.[26]

Della Valle was not, however, attempting to deride the idea of feminine majesty. The queen, Abag-Devì, showed her royal quality 'in her speech rather than her presence', with her graceful voice and judicious words. Even though her corpulence (della Valle noted) was a bit too obvious below her waist, as a result of the Indian custom of wearing the cotton garb quite tight, she must have been beautiful when she was young. Della Valle – this is what matters – considered a conversation with her no less curious and interesting than one with Shah Abbas. He was quick to distance himself from the discredited image of the Portuguese by stating his Roman identity, before explaining that, after travelling the world for ten years he had been moved by the fame of the queen's qualities to come and offer his service to her. It is difficult to believe that the queen was much impressed by this pompous introduction (on a later occasion she refused to receive della Valle again), and there was perhaps some sarcasm in her asking what the traveller wished to see in those woods of hers if, as he claimed, he had already seen the courts of the Great Turk, the Persian, the Mughal, and her immediate overlord Venkatapa Nayaka.

In fact, the queen (who was busy supervising some irrigation system) had been forewarned of the visit of the extravagant gentleman. She asked him about his health whilst travelling in so many countries, and whether he had left home for some love or similar tragic cause. She had actually hit upon the original cause of della Valle's pilgrimage, his desire to recover from a woman's disfavour, and yet (as he writes) 'I concealed my first misfortunes and told the queen that I had not left my country for any such reason, but only out of a desire to see divers countries and

[26] Ibid., p. 227.

customs, and to learn many things which are learnt by travelling the world.'[27] The significance of della Valle's lie was not any sense of superiority, but rather the need to support the Ulysses-like persona which he had acquired throughout his travels. This persona required that others identified him for what he had become in order to establish an aristocracy of polite curiosity across cultural barriers. However humble the Indian gentiles, however mistaken their worship, a simple detail could sustain the universality of both female and royal dignities. He thus considered that he honoured the wench-looking queen by keeping his head uncovered whilst talking to her.

Perhaps the encounter which best exemplifies della Valle's quest for a positive and universal human quality behind cultural and religious differences is the dialogue with the *sati* Giaccamà, with whom he conversed during his stay at Ikkeri. When he first saw her performing a ritual procession of despair, he immediately drew a distinction between the cruel and barbarous custom of the country, and the generosity and virtue of its victim. He then conceived the idea of 'honouring her funeral' with his compassionate affection.[28] Four days later della Valle sought the woman at home, and found her surrounded by drummers (her husband himself used to be a drummer) 'in very good humour, talking and laughing in conversation as a bride would have done in our countries'.[29] They then had a long conversation concerning his curiosity and her sacrifice. It became apparent that two older, less generous wives did not want to die and preferred to look after their children, but that Giaccamà (then scarcely thirty years old) was willing to leave her children in the care of others in order to die. She insisted that she was acting unconstrained and of her own free will, for the sake of the glory of herself and her family (although her relatives also explained that this principle was not always observed among the wealthy). Finally, and this was Giaccamà's gift to the traveller, and a justification of his visit, 'she regarded herself very fortunate that I had gone to see her, and very honoured by my visit and presence, as well as by the fame I would carry of her to my country'. Della Valle, seeing that it was impossible to dissuade her, instead promised 'that in the world her name would remain immortal'.[30]

Della Valle's three sonnets to Giaccamà, which have survived in a manuscript now at the Vatican Library, do not constitute a literary masterpiece, but they convey what is perhaps most novel in this most

---

[27] Ibid., p. 229: 'solo per desiderio di veder terre e costumi diversi, e per apprender molte cose che peregrinando'l mondo si apprendono'.
[28] Ibid., p. 194.   [29] Ibid., p. 201.   [30] Ibid., p. 203.

moving passage of the pilgrim's *Viaggi*: della Valle celebrated human virtue within a non-Christian system of beliefs and behaviour with more emphasis than he condemned the cruel customs of a gentile nation. The three sonnets explore three aspects of the event: the deserving virtue of the widow, the contrast between her faithfulness and the falsity of her religion, and della Valle's own parallel sadness for the loss of his wife, although met, properly, with Christian and Stoic resignation.[31] Since della Valle's original pilgrimage was in itself a denial of the temptation of suicide caused by a woman's rejection of his love, Giaccamà's choice re-enacted his own dilemma, creating a sympathy of feeling made even more dramatic by the contrast of religious doctrines. This of course entailed a lamentation for the barbarity of the gentile custom, but only to make female virtue the more outstanding. In a passage of his original diary (which the ecclesiastical censors later suppressed) the traveller even added that 'this made me laugh of our women, who take it as a great thing to go and enclose themselves forever in a monastery, which is so much less of a sacrifice than dying'.[32] However unfair the comment – it was in fact more a criticism of religious hypocrisy than an endorsement of female oppression – it did imply a self-reflective gaze. As is apparent from della Valle's previous discussion of *sati*, based on hearsay, in the letter written from Surat nine months earlier, the traveller's curiosity for this custom was in fact more concerned with the psychology of the freedom and will of the widow than with any religious or sociological explanation. Della Valle wondered whether the will of the widow was really free or conditioned by social pressure, much as the will of women who married in Europe was often sadly conditioned by their relatives

---

[31] I have transcribed these sonnets, hitherto unpublished, in an appendix. Kate Teltscher, who has recently emphasized how della Valle's literary recreation of the *sati* as a tragic figure exemplifies the ambivalent attitude of European travellers towards Indian women, is thus incorrect in assuming the sonnet's non-existence: K. Teltscher, *India inscribed. European and British writing on India 1600–1800* (New Delhi, 1997), pp. 56–9. Strangely, Teltscher concludes her discussion of the literary treatment of *sati* in the travel literature of this period with a return to the very Saidian position which much of her valuable analysis of diversity and ambivalence seemed previously to undermine: 'the Indian woman becomes the focus of male European desires and fears: a body to be veiled, revealed or consumed in flames. An ambivalent compound of chastity, sexual appetite, and the death wish, she is a fantasy woman in an imaginary land' (ibid., p. 68). In most cases, and certainly in the case of della Valle, the projection of the fears and desires of the European male traveller is compatible with an empiricism which equals or even surpasses the recording of ordinary observation (male or female) in Europe.

[32] BAV, Ottob. 3,382, f. 217r: 'me licentiai da lei, assai più mesto[?] della sua morte ch'ella stesso, maledicendo il costume dell'India, che con le donne è tanto spietato, *e burlandomi delle donne nostre, che hanno per grande actione l'andarsi a rinchiado per sempre in un monasterio, che del morire e tanto manco'.*

when they chose a husband, so that 'though apparently not forced', in effect they were 'compelled into the decision by the pressure of circumstances'.[33] Della Valle sought spiritual equality in a world of cultural differences, rather than an explanation of reasons for cultural differences which might serve to either justify the European Christians as superior, or to question their superiority. This (a mark of liberal Catholicism) in fact set him apart from the sceptical analysis of *sati* as mainly evidence of religious superstition and clerical abuse which characterized a number of seventeenth-century independent travellers, like the French doctor and disciple of Gassendi, François Bernier (see plate 12).[34]

Encounters with women allowed della Valle to elaborate the powerful western idea of love, Platonic and chivalric, as basis for a trans-cultural synthesis. Marrying an oriental Christian opened the door to the project of a restored unity between East and West under Catholic patronage; feeling compassion for an Indian *sati* allowed the traveller to rescue virtue from the trappings of devilish idolatry. This was a romantic as well as an aristocratic solution to the problem of cultural diversity, one inspired by Renaissance Platonism, which made it possible to associate the hypothesis of a primitive philosophical truth behind the universal system of idolatry uncovered by antiquarian research with the direct evidence of virtuous behaviour among gentiles. But this solution stood among others in seventeenth-century Europe, in the same way that della Valle stood as one among many travellers. The most far-reaching seventeenth century response to the problem of cultural diversity in general, and the virtue of the gentiles in particular, was sceptical in the tradition of Montaigne and the *libertins*, in opposition to a confessional Christian position, whether Protestant or Catholic.[35] It is therefore of particular importance briefly to analyse the way della Valle dealt with gentile religion from his apparently never questioned Catholic identity.

---

[33] Della Valle, *India*, p. 65.

[34] For Bernier's account of *sati* see F. Bernier, *Voyage dans les etats du Grand Mogol*, ed. F. B. Hattacharya (Fayard, 1981), pp. 232–40. Telstcher, *India*, p. 67, notes that Bernier, unlike della Valle, succeeded in dissuading a *sati* from her sacrifice by invoking her children's destitution (in fact he threatened her with making sure that the Muslim Agah, who was his, as well as her former husband's, employer, would not provide a pension for her orphans if she burnt herself). This intervention, Teltscher concludes, only enhances the traveller's sense of western superiority: 'Bernier steals the widow's glory to become the hero himself'.

[35] For this topic, E. G. O'Flaherty, 'Relativism and criticism in seventeenth-century French thought' (Ph.D. thesis, University of Cambridge, 1987), is of particular value. See also S. Zoli, *L'Europa libertina tra controriforma e illuminismo. L'Oriente dei libertini e le origini dell'illuminismo* (Bologna, 1989).

Plate 12 An Indian *sati*, with François Bernier (dressed in French costume) watching from the right side (*Voyages de François Bernier . . . contenant la description des Etats du Grand Mogol*, 2 vols. Amsterdam, 1709). In reality, Bernier was not a passive observer – he engaged with the widow and put enormous pressure on her so that she would desist from her undertaking. Bernier would also have been dressed in oriental garb.

CATHOLIC IDEALISM AND THE SCEPTICAL CHALLENGE

It may seem surprising that neither della Valle nor the ecclesiastical censors (who carefully removed from the published letters any opinion bearing upon Catholic theology or politics) acknowledged an intellectual threat in the antiquarian analysis of Hinduism. This intellectual optimism was in reality a gamble rather than a consistent tradition, and responded to the climate in Rome during the first decades of the seventeenth century under popes Paul V, Gregory XV and Urban VIII. This climate was conditioned by the need to meet the secular thinking of the late Renaissance (scientific, political and historical) on its own grounds, and supported by the comprehensive edifice built by Counter-Reformation writers in the previous decades. It was not really a free-thinking environment because the Inquisition was a very real presence, but at the same time learned academies such as the Umoristi, to which della Valle belonged, were popular amongst the social elite, and both human history and natural science were believed to be necessarily supportive of Catholicism within a broad universalist encyclopaedia.[36]

Della Valle confronted the problem of gentile religions early on in Persia. While the ancient local religion of the Gauris (Parsis) was difficult to research, his conversations with Gujarati merchants in Isfahan allowed him to write a long dissertation about Indian idolatry, which could supersede modern authorities like Botero in the light of his new philological enquiries.[37] This initial research allowed him to obtain some basic notions about caste divisions and about popular mythologies, in particular the Indian epic of the *Ramayana*. Above all, it allowed him to formulate a preliminary hypothesis about the meaning of idolatry, which he understood as the divinization of human kings and heroes 'as it also happened in our countries with Jupiter, Mars and others'.[38] Della Valle never ceased to revise his views in the light of new discoveries. Thus a few years later, still in Combrù on the Persian coast, he exploited new opportunities to extend his enquiries, observing a religious festival, learning from an ascetic brahmin about the existence of the Sanskrit language, and asking about the meaning of the *lingam* (which quite surprisingly, although repeatedly described and even drawn in his journal, he never identified as a phallic representation).[39] By the time della Valle left Persia he had even started a collection of Sanskrit and other Indian manuscripts which he could not then read, but which he planned to have translated in Europe as the occasion arose. (In Ikkeri he also requested and obtained a small book in Kannada, the local language, from the ambassador of Venkatapa.)

It is quite clear that his method was antiquarian and philological,

---

[36] The complexity of the subject makes it difficult to refer to an acceptable synthesis of the intellectual life in Italy in the crucial period between 1580 and 1640, and in particular the role of history and science, despite the existence of a great deal of excellent monographic material on outstanding figures like Sarpi and Galileo. Certainly della Valle participated, through personal connections and dilettante interest, in the Italian system of learning, patronage and debate, which between 1600 and 1620 had in Rome perhaps its main centre. For example, after his ceremony of departure celebrated in Naples in 1614, della Valle was accompanied by his friend Mario Schipano, a humanist doctor, and Marcello Giustiniani and his wife Caterina Boccalini, daughter of the recently deceased Traiano Boccalini. Della Valle took Boccalini's *Ragguagli di Parnaso* (1612) on his travels, along with a small library on Turkey and the Near East.

[37] Della Valle, *Lettere dalla Persia*, ed. by Gaeta and Lockhart, pp. 68–77 (letter from Isfahan, December 1617).

[38] Ibid., p. 69.

[39] Della Valle, *Persia*, vol. II, pp. 505–11 (November 1622).

backed by conversations with brahmins and direct observation: he would ask for the meaning of particular names, draw plans of temples, learn to identify the different gods and their attributes, and copy Sanskrit spellings. He would also carefully observe popular festivals. However, the frame of reference was always comparison with ancient idolatry as described in classical texts, and he relied especially on writers of history and geography like Diodorus Siculus or Strabo. It is probably from these readings that he developed his view that specific, rather than structural, similarities between different kinds of idolatry had to be explained by assuming an Egyptian genealogical primacy, 'since the Egyptians, who were descended from Cham, son of Noah, were extremely ancient peoples', and 'it is known that there always was navigation and commerce between Egypt and India by the Southern sea'.[40] Della Valle was not alone in formulating this diffusionist hypothesis concerning the ancient history of idolatry in these dates, but it would be rash to conclude that he simply borrowed it from his contemporaries like Lorenzo Pignoria: rather, we seem to be finding here a typical instance of the parallel development of a theory by two contemporaries who are looking at new evidence from similar assumptions. The antiquarian culture of the early seventeenth century, based on ancient Greek sources, pursued through philological methods, and constrained by biblical authority, made the idea of Egyptian origins a logical possibility.[41]

---

[40] Della Valle, *India*, p. 57. The diffusionist model was explicitly suggested by Diodorus Siculus, who identified the Greek Dionysus with the Egyptian Osiris: Della Valle, *Lettere dalla Persia*, p. 76. In Arrian and Strabo, Dionysus was also said to have travelled to India.

[41] Lorenzo Pignoria's *Le vere e nove imagini de gli dei delli antichi . . . et un discorso intorno le deità dell'Indie orientali et occidentali* (Padua, 1615) was an illustrated and updated edition of Vincenzo Cartari's standard iconographical classical pantheon (Venice, 1556). Annotated with antiquarian observations, Pignoria's edition included an additional discourse, 'Imagini degli dei Indiani', concerning the analogies and relationship between Egyptian, Mexican and Indian idols, observing, for instance, that the figure with an elephant head described by the Jesuit Luís Fróis in 1560, 'Ganissone' (Ganesha), obviously followed the Egyptian tendency to combine human and animal features (p. XXVII). However, this treatise was published after della Valle left Europe in 1614. The traveller certainly kept in close correspondence with Europeans and it is not impossible that he learnt about the book's novel hypothesis in Constantinople or Persia. He actually refers to Vincenzo Cartari's *Imagini degle dei* in a letter from Isfahan of May 1619 (della Valle, *Lettere dalla Persia*, p. 345), although he may have been using an earlier edition. Della Valle could also have known some of the arguments discussed by Pignoria in his previous Egyptological work, the *Vestustissimae tabulae Aeneae explicatio* (Venice, 1605). However, della Valle does not mention any of Pignoria's works – for instance when he casually suggests for the first time the similarity between the Indian worship of the cow as sacred and the Egyptian cult of Apis, in his early letter from Isfahan of December 1617 (della Valle, *Lettere dalla Persia*, p. 73). His analysis is generaly fuller than Pignoria's. Above all, what is crucial is that ancient Egypt was the logical starting point for any antiquarian analysis of idolatry, because ancient Greek

Interestingly, della Valle's theory was challenged by a brahmin from Gujarat, who claimed that some of his books had been written by the Greek philosopher Pythagoras, 'something which agrees with what Philostratus says that Iarcha [the brahmin] told Apollonius [the Greek traveller], namely, that concerning the soul the Indians believed that which Pythagoras had taught them, and which they then had taught the Egyptians'.[42] In effect, for reasons of his own, Philostratus had completely reversed the traditional order within the diffusionist model.[43] Della Valle, however, was able to maintain his original theory by appealing to the authority of another Greek author, Diogenes Laertius, whose biography of Pythagoras did not include any journey to India. When, therefore, the brahmin went on to insist that Brahma was himself Pythagoras, della Valle was ready to dismiss the whole idea:

This would be interesting news indeed, and perhaps unheard in Europe, that Pythagoras is worshipped stupidly as God in India; but without wanting to offend Becà Azarg [the brahmin], I do not believe it. Either he did not say this and I misunderstood him for lack of a better interpreter, or if he said that, he was here wrong, because he heard some other European talk about Pythagoras as the author of the foolish opinion [*stolta opinione*] of the transmigration of the souls.[44]

writers pointed to Egypt as the ultimate source of Greek culture. In Italy, as early as the end of the fifteenth century, there had been a great deal of interest in circles of Platonist humanists and artists in discovering mystical or Hermetic interpretations of Egyptian religion, positing a 'prisca theologia' whose core was both retrievable (through the Hermetic–Pythagorean corpus) and partially valid (since it had served as basis for Mosaic law). Although antiquarians like the Calvinist Isaac Casaubon demolished the Hermetic core of the Egyptian paradigm by proving the late Greek origin of the corpus (as part of his 1614 attack on Baronius's Catholic history of the early Church), thirty and forty years later Athanasius Kircher still maintained his laborious Hermetic Egyptological research with the help of della Valle's Coptic manuscripts and a great deal of absurd etymologies. On this topic in general see E. Iversen, *The myth of Egypt and its hieroglyphs in European tradition* (Copenhagen, 1961).

42 Della Valle, *India*, p. 58.

43 Della Valle read Philostratus' *Life of Apollonius* without realizing that it was essentially a fictional text. Although it reversed the diffusionist tendency by giving primacy to India, Philostratus' story supported the idea of an ancient common core of rational pagan wisdom behind the multiplicity of idolatrous cults.

44 Della Valle, *India*, p. 58. The idea that a brahmin's idea of the origins of Hinduism could have been prompted by interaction with a western traveller is not absurd, however strange it may seem if we simply assume that brahmins were the authoritative repositories of their own tradition and identity. The English chaplain at Surat, Henry Lord, in his polemic against the brahmins, and in order to weaken their high moral ground in favour of the Christian revelation, insisted that their abstinence from flesh and wine was borrowed from Pythagoras. His important *Display of two forraigne sects in the East Indies* (i.e. Banians and Parsis), the first printed account of Hinduism to appear in Europe, was published in London in 1630, but Lord was in Gujarat in the latter half of the 1620s, closely following della Valle's visit. We may be wise to conclude that traditions are often reactive to articulate foreign observers.

In effect, and this was conclusive, both Egyptian and brahminical doctrines appeared, from Greek references, to be more ancient than Pythagoras.

This passage shows quite clearly both the depth and flexibility of della Valle's antiquarian opinions, and his use of a classical framework in order to criticize and evaluate native authorities. His position was essentially open: he could contemplate both the possibility of a diversity of idols emerging from separate human models, or the transformation of the same hero-king according to diffusion and linguistic diversity. He was also able to distinguish the 'atheistic' philosophy of the Japanese Buddhists (which he learnt from a Christian Japanese who was on his way to Rome) from the basically deistic idolatry of India. However, on the other hand, della Valle's use of the chronological tables of the Jesuit theologian Roberto Bellarmino (and not, significantly, the more far-reaching work of Joseph Scaliger) allowed him to pursue this reconstruction of ancient idolatry without departing from the biblical framework which he was bound to accept.[45] Della Valle belonged to a generation which, having received the new authorities of the Italian Counter-Reformation like the same Bellarmino, Cesare Baronius or Antonio Possevino, could trust history to clarify, rather than challenge, Catholic orthodoxy.[46] Whilst della Valle was not *a priori* trying to question Indian authorities (rather the contrary), all his curiosity was never used to question the fundamental assumption that idolatry was both devilish and irrational. In this sense, there is a delicate balance between the relativism of his analysis of customs and his scrupulous observance of religious orthodoxy, one which mirrors the tension between his sympathy for the *sati*'s personal virtue

---

[45] Della Valle's mention of Bellarmino's work must refer to his *Brevi chronologia ab orbe condito usque ad annum 1612* which accompanied his *De scriptoribus ecclesiasticis liber unus* (1612). The Calvinist Scaliger's *Opus novus de emendatione temporum* had been published in 1583, and immediately transformed the Renaissance science of chronology (inevitably based on the Bible) into a systematic antiquarian discipline, through a better understanding of classical and oriental sources, and with the crucial aid of mathematical astronomy. If not earlier, della Valle would have become acquainted with the figure of Scaliger – and of his interest in Samaritan traditions – during his antiquarian correspondence with Peiresc in the late 1620s, after his return to Rome (see P. Miller, 'A philologist, a traveller and an antiquary rediscover the Samaritans in seventeenth-century Paris, Rome and Aix', in H. Zedelmaier and M. Mulsow (eds.), *Gelehrsamkeit als Praxis: Arbeitsweisen, Funktionen, Grenzbereiche* (forthcoming)). Della Valle, like Peiresc, believed that in matters of civility and scholarship Europeans should cooperate with each other, even if they did not share religious convictions. Through civil conversation, in fact, Catholics could attract intelligent Protestants to their faith.

[46] Bellarmino insisted in his own chronological work that anachronism was often a sign of heresy. The key historical and antiquarian works of the Counter-Reformation were published in Italy in the 1580s and 90s, including Baronius' *Annales ecclesiastiae* (1588–) and Possevino's critical catalogue, the *Apparatus ad omnium gentium historiarum* (1597).

and his criticism of the cruel customs which she upheld. The contemptuous words which disqualified the worship of any gods other than the true God, or the doctrine of transmigration of the souls, were only a ritual reminder that the issue here was history, not religion.

In a number of passages della Valle makes this fundamental understanding of the devilish contents of idolatry clear. Certainly, behind the extravagant cults which evolved due to the vanity of kings and heroes there existed a theistic belief, but the use of oracles was not simply a question of human vanity and ignorance, revealing instead a serious intercourse with the devil. Thus della Valle did not question the veracity of his Gujarati informer Natù when he asserted that the oracles did indeed predict the future, because, as was the case with many of his own European witch-hunting contemporaries, a humanist education did not exclude a firm belief in the reality of the devil. It was logically simple to transform Christian exclusiveness into charitable contempt: 'The baniani know the devil to be a very evil thing, but the poor wretches do not imagine the extent to which they are under his influence.'[47] This belief emerged even more forcefully when he was given a chance to study closely the naked yogis of Cambay, and in this case (perhaps because they refused to befriend him) without any charitable undertones: their unworldliness was studied arrogance, their chastity probably hypocritical, 'since it is known that in secret many of them do vile acts when they have an opportunity', and above all their books and exercises, whether spiritual or erudite, 'consist in nothing but the arts of divination, the secrets of herbs and other things of nature, and magic and spells'. The conclusion was clear: 'by way of such exercises, prayers, fastings and such similar superstitions, they arrive (it seems to them) at revelations, which in effect are nothing other than commerce with the devil'.[48]

The intense South Indian journey, and in particular the opportunity to study closely Shaiva worship in Kanara, with its explicitly sexual themes, only offered further arguments to sustain this interpretation: 'indeed, the greatest part of their worship of their gods consists in nothing but music, songs and dances, not only pleasant but in effect lascivious, and in serving their idols as if they were living persons'. This idolatrous sensualism stood directly in contrast with an intellectual religion based on learning, which is the aspect that della Valle valued most.

I once asked an old priest who was held more knowing than others, grey and clad all in white, carrying a staff like a shepherd's crook in his

[47] Della Valle, *Lettere dalla Persia*, p. 75.
[48] Della Valle, *India*, pp. 80–1. These yogis were seen by della Valle on 3 March 1623 at a Vaishnava temple outside Cambay, in the village of Causary.

hand, what books he had read and what had he studied? adding that I myself delighted in reading, and that if he would speak to me about anything I would answer him. He told me that all books were made only that men might with them known God; but if God were known, what was the purpose of books? as if he knew God very well. I replied that all thought they knew God, but few knew him properly, and therefore he should beware that himself was not one of those.[49]

This remarkable passage shows not only della Valle's desire for religious dialogue and the Indian's capacity to reply with intelligence, but also the fact that the independent traveller of the seventeenth century, by seeking to analyse diversity from an intellectual viewpoint, was actually undermining European popular religion. Would della Valle have expected Italian peasants and *lazzaroni* to read books in order to learn true religion? Or was religious truth only for the few? In fact, his position was contradictory, because the Counter-Reformation elites not only expected Catholic ritual to sustain popular belief, they in fact often participated with enthusiasm. Della Valle's happiness at the news of the canonization of Philip Neri and Teresa of Avila, Ignatius of Loyola and Francis Xavier, was unrestrained, as his diary of the events of 1623 attests, and he willingly joined the festivities in Goa in honour of Saint Teresa (a favourite of his), participating in the baroque masquerade with his Arabian dress, and even creating a multi-lingual emblem in honour of her twelve virtues.[50] Della Valle's religious confidence, it may even be argued, was the foundation of his remarkably relaxed dialogue with the Christian heretic, with the Muslim and with the gentile.

Ultimately, this dialogue with non-Christians rested upon the same dualistic level of belief in the devil which we encountered in earlier travellers like Marco Polo and Ludovico de Varthema. The traveller was simply a committed agent and witness of a struggle between God and his rival. When, on occasion, della Valle spat upon a statue in a private chapel of the queen of Olala, not a common idol from the established brahminic pantheon, but rather a 'devil' (as his interpreter explained) which the people feared for its power, his action was spontaneous and certainly not just there for the benefit of the European readers.[51] In fact,

---

[49] Ibid., p. 204.

[50] Ibid., p. 127. Della Valle later re-used the idea of this emblem (with epitaphs in twelve languages describing twelve virtues) for the sepulchre which he commissioned for the solemn funeral of Sitti Maani in Rome. She was buried in the family chapel of Saint Paul of Aracoeli.

[51] Ibid., pp. 253–4. However, the statue (della Valle noted) did not look like the devil in European representations: rather he was a handsome young man with four hands and wearing a diadem, with a knife in his hand and riding upon another man. It was not therefore the image itself which prompted della Valle to a ritual act of defiance, but

della Valle was for all his curiosity and politeness profoundly imbued with a crusading ideology, which had taken him to participate in anti-corsair skirmishes in North Africa in 1611, and which through his travels found expression in his hatred for the Ottoman Turks, seen as relentless oppressors of Christians (in sharp contrast with the more cynical Shah Abbas of Persia, whom della Valle believed could be turned into an ally, so much so that soon after reaching Persia he offered to fight in his army against the Turks).[52] Della Valle liked to think of himself as a gentleman-warrior no less than poet, musician and lover, following the Renaissance model of a courtier who was equally able to use the sword and the pen.

However, despite all these marks of traditionalism, what really distinguished the new traveller's persona was his intellectualism: not only his desire to discuss customs and beliefs with the local people, and especially the better educated amongst them, but above all his decision, unprecedented from a lay perspective, to explore gentile religion from a historical and antiquarian perspective. This went beyond the mere elevation of the Renaissance courtier into a genuinely cosmopolitan setting. His curiosity was methodical, even though his analysis evolved spontaneously and appears rather dispersed throughout his letters. This curiosity was also intellectually courageous. It is thus significant that he planned to have translated into Italian 'for the sake of the curious' a book of Indian divination, obtained from those very yogis whose practice he had just defined as outright commerce with the devil.[53] This was more far-reaching than just writing a Turkish grammar or collecting a couple of mummies. The wide range of della Valle's orientalist research was sustained by a supreme confidence, reminiscent of Ramon Llull's more primitive version of Christian rationalism, that linguistic and antiquarian expertise could only help sustain the traditional system of mission and crusade.

---

rather the fearful belief of the local inhabitants (as he interpreted it). Concerning the origins and importance of these local warrior gods, worshipped (like the queen of Olala's) in small shrines around trees, see Bayly, *Saints, goddesses and kings*, pp. 28–32.

[52] Della Valle explains this decision to stay in Persia to fight the Turks in detail in his letter of December 1617 (della Valle, *Lettere dalla Persia*, pp. 91–6). At his most aggressive he wrote that 'even at night, while sleeping, I dream about the greatest harm that I may cause to the Turks, our common enemies'. His pet crusading project consisted of forging an anti-Ottoman alliance between Persia and the Cossacks from the kingdom of Poland. But his plan had also a constructive aspect: to create a 'New Rome' in Persia, a self-governing city of oriental and Latin Christians (specifically including his relatives from Baghdad) under Shah Abbas and Roman Catholic sponsorship. Both plans – crusade and mission – failed.

[53] Della Valle, *India*, p. 82: 'procurerò anco che possa vedersi un giorno da'curiosi in nostra lingua'. He had obtained a Persian version of the book for that purpose.

What della Valle was able to do which was new in European ethnology was to interpret a variety of forms of social behaviour in the light of a variety of religious and scientific beliefs, and to discuss some of these beliefs, without collapsing one dimension into the other. In this sense della Valle shared the Thomist distinction developed by the Jesuits between valid civil customs which were relative to place and time, and a universal religious truth which could only be Christian. He showed awareness of the contemporary debate within the Jesuit order caused by Nobili's experiments, but although he discussed some of the criticisms and counter-arguments in a letter from Surat, he prudently declined to suggest a conclusion, or to add anything in his letters from Goa, where the issue was burning in the expectation of a papal decision.[54] But della Valle was quite decisive in his use of the distinction when discussing Hindu customs from personal observation. The use of cow dung to varnish the pavements of houses, for instance, 'I took for a superstitious rite of religion, but since I better understand that it is used only for elegance and ornament [*per pulitezza e per ornamento*]'.[55] In fact, not only did the Portuguese use the custom in Goa, but della Valle would also try it in Italy, since it was said that these pavements were good against the plague. This was a practical solution to the lack of better pavements, unlike the caste prohibitions of the gentile elite, which used the same cow dung to purify a room before eating there 'out of superstition'.

These distinctions marked both the quality and the limitation of della Valle's relativism. The essential mark of his cultural analysis was the confidence in the rational value of his own religion. He could distance himself from the beliefs of the prince of Olala by pointing out that 'the purity of my religion does not depend on eating things or touching others, but on doing good or bad works' – but he never applied a sceptical analysis of religion that might be turned against Catholic doctrine.[56] In this sense della Valle stands very far from the scepticism of later travellers like François Bernier, whose pitiless assault on Hinduism in his *Lettre a Monsieur Chapelain* of 1667, because it was a secular analysis, was dangerously capable of simply being turned back against Christianity.[57]

---

[54] Della Valle discusses in particular the debate about the status of the brahminical thread in his letter from Surat: ibid., pp. 67–9. Although in Persia della Valle was close to the Portuguese Augustinians, rivals of the Jesuits, in Goa he befriended the latter.

[55] Ibid., p. 166.

[56] Ibid., p. 239. This prince was the queen's adolescent son, who entertained della Valle with a meal and asked him many questions about Europe.

[57] For Bernier's discussion of Hinduism see Bernier, *Voyage*, pp. 227–65. For a discussion of his attitudes towards India, see S. Murr, 'La politique 'au Mogol' selon Bernier:

The profoundly different nature of this French traveller's attitude merits some illustration. The scepticism of Bernier's analysis of Hinduism resided in the irony with which his anti-religious and anti-clerical diatribe was reserved for gentile beliefs and the role of the brahmins, but not for Christians. The fact that his discussion of religion as superstition excluded the agency of the devil and focused instead on social indoctrination implied a secularizing reversal of the missionary condemnation of the idolaters as manipulators of a natural religious instinct. This, of course, opened the way for more disturbing possibilities of self-reflection, made explicit by the refusal to accept any explanations of extraordinary events other than natural ones. In this sense the first paragraph of the letter on Hinduism gives an important key to an understanding of what follows, by stressing the fundamental comparability of European and non-European belief systems: Bernier compares the childish terror of the common people of France in reaction to an eclipse in 1654 to the superstitious beliefs of the Indian gentiles in reaction to another eclipse in 1666. Both are dismissed as ridiculous in front of the scientific truth of naturalistic astronomer-philosophers. Similarly, Bernier's attack on the Indian idea of reincarnation also involved a direct attack on western Platonism, referring for instance to Gassendi's atomist criticism of the alchemical and animist science of Robert Fludd.[58]

As with Nobili, the paradox of della Valle's position lies in the way he contributed to the emergence of this sceptical outlook he never endorsed. If he is far from Bernier, he stands even further from the irreverent attitude towards biblical authority developed by Pierre Bayle in his *Dictionnaire historique et critique* (1696), both rejecting the validity of allegorical readings, and deploring the moral coherence of literal ones. This attitude (whose tenor was revolutionary whatever we choose to believe about Bayle's private beliefs) was to a large extent sustained by the antiquarian scholarship and travel literature of the seventeenth century, to which della Valle's oriental manuscripts and letters had contributed so much.[59]

---

appareil conceptuel, rhétorique stratégique, philosophie morale', in J. Pouchepadass and H. Stern, *De la royauté à l'état. Anthropologie et histoire du politique dans le monde indien* (Paris, 1991), pp. 239–311, and P. Burke, 'The philosopher as traveller: Bernier's Orient', in J. Elsner and J. P. Rubiés (eds.) *Voyages and visions. Towards a cultural history of travel* (London, 1999), pp. 124–37.

[58] Bernier, *Voyage*, pp. 227 and 263.

[59] Through the mediation of Nicholas-Claude Fabri de Peiresc, della Valle's Samaritan manuscripts contributed to the research behind the 1645 Parisian polyglot Bible by the Oratorian priest Jean Morin. On this issue see P. Miller, 'An antiquary between philology and history. Peiresc and the Samaritans', in D. Kelley (ed.) *History and the disciplines. The reclassification of knowledge in early modern Europe* (Rochester and London, 1997), as well as Miller, 'A philologist, a traveller and an antiquary'. For evidence of the impact

In his persona as independent observer as well as in his antiquarian research, the Italian traveller was pointing towards a future of cultural self-criticism in which he would have refused to participate, one perhaps best represented by Giovanni Paolo Marana's Turkish spy, whose apocryphal letters were published in French and English at the end of the century, inaugurating the genre that would lead to Montesquieu's *Persian letters*.[60] Mahmut the Turk, piously Muslim but anti-dogmatic in the face of European culture, was no more than a reversal of della Valle the rationalist Catholic observer. In order fully to criticize European civil and religious assumptions the figure of an outsider – an oriental traveller, or a savage from Canada – provided a rhetorical voice which made relativism obvious and criticism ambiguous (this ambiguity was of course necessary under Louis XIV's censorship: the real voice of Mahmut was in reality Cartesian rather than strictly Muslim). But this figure needed a convincing form and gaze – and both the form and the gaze of this intelligent traveller were in the first place the creation of Europeans like della Valle.

It is the force and depth with which della Valle transformed empirical observation into antiquarian research and speculation which also sets him apart from late sixteenth-century travellers in southern India, foreign witnesses of the decline of Portuguese Goa like the Dutch Jan Huyghen van Linschoten,[61] the Florentine Francesco Carletti,[62] the

of this correspondence in the later seventeenth century see also the *Antiquitates ecclesiae orientalis* (London 1682) edited by the English biblical scholar Richard Simon. Not insignificantly, Simon was the key figure behind Pierre Bayle's biblical scepticism. In his 1683 *Pensées sur la comète*, Bayle repeatedly based thoughts on the observations of recent travellers, including della Valle (in this he was no different from Montaigne, except that Montaigne relied on Léry, Osório and Gómara, rather than Bernier, Tavernier or Rycaut). On the other hand, della Valle's Coptic manuscripts were used by Athanasius Kircher in his epoch-making *Lingua Aegyptiaca restituta* (Rome, 1644). On della Valle's oriental manuscripts and poetry see E. Rossi, 'Versi Turchi e altri scritti inediti di Pietro della Valle', *Rivista degli Studi Orientali*, 22 (1947): 92–8, and 'Poesie inedite in Persiano di Pietro della Valle', *Revista degli Studi Orientali*, 28 (1953): 108–17. More generally on his contribution to orientalism, see P. G. Bietenholz, *Pietro della Valle (1586–1652). Studien zur Geschichte der Orientkenntnis und des Orientbildes im Abendlande* (Stuttgart, 1962).

60 First published in French in 1684, an expanded version of the letters (with seven more volumes) appeared in English as *Letters writ by a Turkish spy* between 1691 and 1694. This expansion is of uncertain authorship, but carried the same spirit as the original.

61 Linschoten's *Itinerario. Voyage ofte schipvaert van J. H. V. L. naar Oost ofte Portugals Indien* was first published in Dutch in 1595–6, and was soon translated into English (1598) and Latin (1599). I have used the modern edition of the old English version: Jan Huyghen van Linschoten, *The voyage to the East Indies, from the English translation of 1598*, ed. by A. C. Burnell and P. A. Tiele, 2 vols. (London, 1885), with critical annotation.

62 Carletti visited Goa on his westward return trip to Europe from an improvised tour of the world from 1594 to 1602. He delivered his six 'ragionamenti' (oral discourses) to the

Frenchman François Pyrard de Laval,[63] or the Flemish Jacques de Coutre.[64] The more systematic and influential of these writers was Linschoten, who had worked within the Iberian system throughout the 1580s but then, on returning home in 1592, immediately joined the Dutch rebels as the supreme spy.[65] He thus produced an encyclopaedic regional account of Portuguese India – one which distinguished different ethnic groups and castes, and which was especially detailed and accurate when describing the society of Goa and its trade.[66] The importance of Linschoten's *Itinerario* was clearly related to the information which it offered the Dutch, an emphasis which was far from the personal, erudite and speculative qualities of della Valle's *Viaggi*. Similarly, whilst Jacques de Coutre – another Netherlander in Portuguese India, but one whose family remained faithful to the Spanish monarchy and to Catholicism – was the exceptional witness of the conditions in the interior of the southern peninsula, and in particular the fragmentation of political authority in the second decade of the seventeenth century, his excursions into history, and many of his judgements on politics or religion, were often remarkably superficial.[67] For example, Coutre's version of the

---

Grand Duke of Tuscany in 1606, although they were not published until 1701, and only in a summarized version. For a better manuscript, the basis for all critical editions, see F. Carletti, *Ragionamento del mio viaggio intorno al mondo*, ed. by G. Silvestro (Turin, 1958).

[63] There is a recent edition of the *Voyage de François Pyrard de Laval aux Indes orientales (1601–11)*, ed. by Xavier de Castro, 2 vols. (Paris, 1998). The first three editions were published in 1611, 1615 and 1619.

[64] Coutre's account of his life and adventures in southern India and other parts of the Portuguese and Spanish empires between 1592 and 1623 was never published. It was written or perhaps dictated in Portuguese by Jacques and translated into Castilian by his Goa-born son Estevan in 1640, shortly after Jacques' death. For further particulars see the recent edition (which is also the first), Jacques de Coutre, *Andanzas asiáticas*, ed. by E. Stols, B. Teensma and J. Werberckmoes (Madrid, 1991).

[65] Linschoten's family connections in Seville allowed him to enter the service of the new archbishop of Goa Vicente de Fonseca, who obviously did not expect him to eventually turn Protestant and decisively break the Portuguese and Italian control of primary information on the East.

[66] Linschoten, *The voyage*, vol. I, pp. 175–222. The Portuguese emerged here, as in della Valle's account twenty years later, or as in Francesco Carletti's 'ragionamento' of his stay in the city in 1600–1 during his journey around the world, as an 'other', with their predominant *mestiço* population, their pompous and punctilious codes of honour, and their inflated stories of sexual jealousies, infidelities and poisonings. Although Carletti's account of India – the fourth 'ragionamento' – is very entertaining, information about actual conditions in India is unreliable except for Malabar, Goa and its environs.

[67] Like many Flemish traders and skilled workers, Coutre's family saw the Iberian Peninsula as an area of economic opportunity. Thus their fortune was made through the exploitation of the declining Hispanic colonial system from inside rather than by challenging it from outside (Jacques and his brother even married Indo-Portuguese women in Goa). Coutre's account of his life was written after his expulsion from India in 1623, where all foreigners increasingly became suspected of performing Linschoten's

history of Vijayanagara (which confuses the circumstances of the fall of the capital city with the much older history of the Bahmani dynasty of the Deccan) is a typical example of badly understood, or badly remembered, popular hearsay, despite the fact that as a privileged foreign merchant dealing with luxury commodities, Coutre had actually met many nayaka lords and even the king of Vijayanagara in Vellore.[68] He was certainly able to offer his European readers dramatic images of exotic customs and tell lively stories drawn from local life, describing, for example, the harsh conditions of work in the diamond mines of the southern Deccan.[69] However, in his judgements he did not go beyond deploring the 'barbarism' of idolatrous sacrifices like hook-swinging, *sati* and *lingayat* burials.

What is crucial is that none of these travellers, who were essentially independent merchants with a taste for adventure, emerges as an antiquarian.[70] They all wrote in order to sell information and, secondarily, entertainment, but they rarely confronted intellectual issues. We may only find a genuine precedent to della Valle's erudite attitudes in the letters of the Florentine Filippo Sassetti, also a merchant who, whilst trying to recover his family's fortunes as agent of the Rovellasca commercial interests in the spice monopoly, still participated in a circle of humanist correspondents, including the Grand Duke of Tuscany and the Academia degli Alterati in Florence.[71] He thus used his wide readings

spying role, and was conventionally addressed to Philip III as a justification and promise of service to the crown.

[68] See Coutre, *Andanzas*, pp. 245–8. On this trip to the interior Coutre often resided with the Jesuits, including Gonzalo Fernandes and Roberto de Nobili in Madurai, but he makes many little mistakes. Thus he wrongly names Fernandes and Nobili 'Pero' and 'Andrés', and Venkata II of Vijayanagara, 'Rama'. He wrongly suggests that the Jesuit bishop of the Saint Thomas Christians was Italian (Francesc Ros was Catalan). He is correct when he declares that the mission of Vijayanagara was temporarily deserted in 1611 for lack of results and because the Dutch were now trading with the king, although he was naturally unaware that Philip III had also ordered the interruption of the mission due to the scandal of Fontebona's supposedly erotic paintings (Coutre met Fontebona in Madurai). All this, and many other details, suggest that Coutre did not invent this and subsequent expeditions, but rather that he wrote, or dictated, from memory and without notes, many years after the events.

[69] Coutre's first expedition to the diamond mines of southern India (ibid., pp. 237–57) took him from Cochin, across the Ghats inhabited by the Christians of Saint Thomas, to Madurai and then Vellore and Chandragiri in Vijayanagara. From there he visited Tirupati and reached the mines in Nandial.

[70] François Pyrard de Laval's account of Goa, Malabar and the Maldives is a special case, since the successive editions of the text were edited and extensively augmented by Pierre Bergeron, an erudite canon working with Pyrard. But this could not transform the merchant's simple observations – it rather meant that much was taken from Linschoten in order to give the account a more encyclopaedic character.

[71] For the more recent and reliable edition of these letters see F. Sassetti, *Lettere di vari paesi*, ed. by V. Bramanti (Milan, 1970). Garcia da Orta's humanist dialogues, the

of classical and modern authors to scrutinize India, exploring natural and human history in the light of his personal experience in the coasts of Malabar and Kanará between 1583 and 1588. He noted the decline in power of the gentiles and the progressive triumph of Muslim rulers, analysed the caste system, identified the Indian brahmins with Pliny's ancient *Bracmenes*, speculated about the natural causes for differences in colour among humans (dismissing a crude climatic determinism), learnt about Sanskrit language and literature, and compared the Indians' admirable knowledge of mathematics (which, he was ready to suggest, ante-dated that of the Arabs) with what he understood as their confused use of Aristotelian philosophical concepts.[72] In fact Sassetti preceded della Valle and other seventeenth-century travellers in many specific ways, speculating about the Egyptian and ancient Mediterranean origins of Indian idolatry, and showing contempt for the vanity of gentile superstition on the basis of western rationalistic values.[73] With remarkable insight and originality, he defined the unity of India through its common religious tradition (of course idolatrous) despite political, ethnic or even caste divisions, and interpreted the instability of southern Indian monarchies as being a result of the feudal system which prevailed in Vijayanagara and the Deccan.[74]

Obviously in this case the merchant fully participated in the erudite, humanist culture of the aristocracy. Albeit lacking the immediacy of della Valle's style as a writer, and visited by death before he could return to Italy to see the publication of his letters, Sassetti was nevertheless able to establish a relationship with the modern authority of the travel collectors Ramusio and Thévet which foreshadowed della Valle's position with respect to his contemporaries Botero and Purchas: his lay voice

---

Coloquios dos simples e drogas exceptionally published in Goa in 1563, might be seen as another example of erudite travel writing in the second half of the sixteenth century, but Orta's medical interests meant that he mainly discussed medical botany, precluding a wider discusssion of ethnological themes.

[72] The key letters discussing Indian religion and culture are those sent from Cochin to Franceso Valori (December 1583), Pier Vettori (January 1585), Lorenzo Canigiano (January 1585) and Ferdinand of Medici (February 1585). Sassetti, *Lettere*, nos. 95, 103, 106 and 107.

[73] See especially ibid., pp. 422–3, from the letter to Pier Vettori.

[74] 'Fu questo Zamalucco [Nizam Shah of Ahmadnagar], di casta moro, uno de'quatro capitani che si ribellarono al re del Canarà . . . le quali mutazioni seguono e seguiranno sempre in questi parti, per dare questi principi carichi di capitani dieci, dodici, undici e ventimila cavalli, non pure a vita d'un uomo, ma traspassa el grado nella successione, in maniera che quella gente non riconosce più il suo signore vero, se non come un suddito de'feudatari riconoscono il primo signore del feudo, o meno' (ibid., p. 522). Here Sassetti was speaking generally and somewhat inaccurately of the Deccan and southern India as a political unity, conflating the Bahmani kingdom and Vijayanagara. Unlike Coutre, he had to rely on informants from Goa and Cochin.

could be used to question the empirical and ideological validity of a cosmographical synthesis, not only because his authority as observer was enhanced by social position and education, but also through his direct participation in erudite debates.

The actual impact of della Valle's orientalist research in seventeenth-century European antiquarianism was greater and on the whole notable, especially through his correspondence with men like Peiresc and Kircher, previous to the publication of his *Viaggi*. It is clear that his desire to interpret his findings and to make his discoveries public preceded his international contacts, but it was the intense flowering of orientalist projects in Rome, Paris and Vienna in the decades following his return to Rome which effectively ensured that his Samaritan and Coptic manuscripts were published and their significance (ultimately theological) discussed by Catholic and Protestant scholars alike.[75] However, the ecumenism of this antiquarian effort did not in the short term dissolve the theological and political differences that separated confessional camps. Della Valle did not therefore abandon his conventional perspectives on an anti-Ottoman alliance with Persia, or his pet project of a Catholic mission to Georgia. In the latter project he was particularly successful, first by offering the Barberini Pope Urban VIII (who for this reason made him chamberlain of honour) an optimistic account of the prospects in Georgia based on his observations from Persia, and afterwards, under the umbrella of the Propaganda Fide, by providing regular diplomatic advice for the rather incompetent Theatine missionaries who had been sent. (The Theatines, pious, conservative and inexperienced, were an odd choice for the job, but understandable as the Propaganda's attempt to avoid the controversial and overly influential Jesuits; della Valle's more sensible recommendation had been to send Jesuits from Europe, or the discalced Carmelites already in Persia.)[76]

There is, however, evidence in della Valle's journal and letters of these Roman years that after a long period of cosmopolitan independence the Roman atmosphere proved stifling, even under the leadership of a

---

[75] See note 59 above.

[76] *Informatione della Georgia* (1626) was only published, in France, by Melchisédech Thévenot in 1663. I have consulted the original seventeenth-century Italian manuscript in BAV, Barberini Lat. 5,181; della Valle's correspondence with the Theatine fathers led by Father Avitabile has been published by F. Andreu, 'Carteggio inedito di Pietro della Valle col P. Avitabile e i missionari Teatini della Georgia', *Regnum Dei*, 23–4 (1950): 57–99; 25 (1951): 19–50; 26–7 (1951): 118–38. Della Valle was aware that the Georgians followed the Greek rite, but he was naively optimistic about their willingness to follow the Roman rite, because they were not 'people of letters'. Rather, they were seen as a freedom-loving martial nation, able to create quite a lot of trouble for both Persians and Turks.

liberal-minded Pope who was also surrounded by some of della Valle's erudite friends. One instance of this disappointment was the poor reception of his encomiastic portrait of Shah Abbas, published in 1628 and dedicated in fact to the Pope's nephew, Cardinal Francesco Barberini. The Roman censorship refused to allow the distribution of the book because the portrayal of an infidel ruler as a heroic and prudent king, and the justification of his policies towards Christians as no worse than Christian policies towards Jews and infidels, was ideologically disturbing in the context of the current debate about reason of state. The official Catholic position was that true religion was a requisite for truly great politics, and that no real parallel existed between Christians and non-Christians. For della Valle, the demystification of petty South Indian kings did not involve a general condemnation of oriental despotism: it resulted from the stark contrast presented by Shah Abbas, who stood as a prudent, rather than tyrannical, king, fulfilling reason-of-state ideals above religious definitions.[77] Effectively, with his separation of true religion from political rationality, della Valle entered the world of men like Galileo, who similarly sought to constrain clerical authority to strictly religious matters in order to give free rein to rational enquiry. They both suffered (although della Valle certainly suffered less) under the superficially liberal regime of the baroque Papacy, on account of their imaginative understanding of what was possible for a lay gaze within the Counter-Reformation.

This is why the real challenge – the real flowering of sceptical seeds towards the Enlightenment – would have to come from the Netherlands, England and France. Due to censorship, the orientalist projects in which della Valle's manuscripts played such an important role – especially the polyglot Bible – actually developed in France rather than in Rome. Although the literature in Italian concerning oriental courts (such as Constantinople) remained important, the critical mass of independent travellers whose accounts after 1650 contributed so much to the crystallization of notions of oriental despotism, natural religion, and the relativity of human customs, was mainly French and, to a lesser extent,

---

[77] Della Valle wanted to publish the book in Rome but, unable to do so, tried in Venice, pretending, however, that the initiative was the publisher Francesco Baba's. Despite the prohibition the work actually circulated among European erudites through personal gifts. I have consulted a copy of *Delle conditioni di Abbas, Re di Persia* (Venice, 1628) in the Biblioteca Apostolica Vaticana (R. I. iv. 84) which has valuable marginalia by a contemporary critic, who seems to have known della Valle as well as the circumstances of the book's prohibition. This reader (perhaps the recipient of the book, Cardinal Barberini) associated oriental tyranny with the incommensurability between Christianity and other religions, whilst della Valle implied that moral and political systems were essentially comparable from a rational perspective, whatever the quality of the religion.

English. Writing within a few years of each other, and often feeding into a public debate, Bernier and Tavernier, Thévenot and Chardin, Rycaut and Galland, had a larger impact than any isolated traveller like della Valle could have achieved (in effect the long-term impact of the *Viaggi* was related to their incorporation into this northern European cultural horizon). In effect della Valle stood in the same position with regards to François Bernier as his contemporary Nobili in relation to the author of the philosophical preface to Rogerius' *Open door*: they were both outstandingly sophisticated products of a Roman world which was suddenly retreating from the confident Catholic assertion of the turn of the seventeenth century (however tinged by compromise with reason of state, cultural adaptation and antiquarian perspectives), to increasing dependence on the emerging French-dominated culture of *libertins* and deists which would set the tone in Europe after 1650.[78] One was a world that sanctified Ignatius of Loyola but could not take Copernicanism; the other was scandalized by, but also welcomed, the new philosophy of Gassendi and Descartes.

Thus, even at his most radical, della Valle's philosophy was Platonic and Neostoic rather than *libertin*. This is evident in the humanist oration concerning his travels which he delivered to the Academy of the Umoristi on his return, which after reviewing the diversity of the world and its changeability concluded that 'virtue alone is worth our esteem'.[79] This opposition between universal vanity and universal virtue was of course previous to any experience as traveller: the world simply served to illustrate a philosophical truth which belonged to della Valle's education in the humanism of the late Renaissance. A similar judgement could be made about the issues raised in the fuller description of della Valle's philosophical wisdom offered by his first biographer, Bellori, in the 1662 edition of the *Viaggi*:

> He used to say, concerning human customs, that vices and virtues can be found in all places, and that the good and the bad are disseminated all over; he had not found anything better, or worse, than mankind;

---

[78] For a classic assessment of the shape and significance of this cultural climate, and of its reliance on travel literature, see Hazard, *La crise de la conscience européene*, still important today, although confining the phenomenon rather arbitrarily to the period 1680–1715.

[79] 'La virtù sola conchiudo esser degna di stima', from 'Oratione del sig. Pietro della Valle recitata in Roma nella Accademia degli Humoristi, nella quale restrigne tutte o le maggiori parti delle cose più degne da lui osservate ne suoi viaggi' (BAV, Barberini Lat. 5,206). This (quite different from the oration that he had drafted in Persia) remains unpublished. I am planning to edit it. We know from Bellori's biography that della Valle's oration was offered as a response to a previous oration on the utility of voyages by Angelo Filatrello – a subject conventional in this period.

opinion and custom are extremely powerful; all profess to know, but ignorance is common; misfortunes are many, and successful outcomes few; those are always ready, these rarely happen to us; nature in all lands is a common mother: it distributes her gifts to all, and where some are missing others compensate; however, only few among the mortals know how to use these gifts, and the majority abuse them to their own harm. Finally, he used to say that among all the things he had seen, one alone he had vainly searched for and not found, through all his travels, for many years, in many places, in the midst of humble, high and royal fortunes. This was that he had never encountered a man who was entirely happy; rather the contrary, he had found many, without number, who were extremely unhappy.[80]

Here again the traveller's experience could tinge his moral philosophy with a certain scepticism, and even a naturalistic relativism, congenial to Lipsius and Montaigne, without openly addressing any theological issues. This remained in seventeenth-century Rome the key formal limitation to a self-proclaimed citizenship of the world.

Della Valle therefore exemplifies a particular version of the integration of the empirical traveller and the humanist-educated philosopher and antiquarian. Analysed alongside other well-known seventeenth-century independent travellers in the Orient like Bernier, La Boullaye, Tavernier, Chardin, Thévenot and Rycaut, creators of what was perhaps the key component of the ethnological reading-list of the early Enlightenment, what is most distinguishable is della Valle's fashioning of a persona of pious learned curiosity whose romance of tragic love and triumph of human wisdom were staged in a universal theatre, for posterity no less than for his own times. If we can judge from the circulation of his work in Italian, French, Dutch, English and German in quick succession over less than fifteen years, his own correspondence with the international network of antiquarians of the seventeenth century, his participation in the life of learned academies like the 'Umoristi' of Rome, and finally, the existence of no less than two biographies of his life (like Bellori's) which soon prefaced the Italian edition of his letters, it is clear that della Valle's self-fashioning as a curious and cosmopolitan pilgrim was socially re-fashioned, and found a niche in the intellectual gallery of baroque Europe.

Della Valle's unpremeditated style, unconventional, fresh and direct, dominated by the idea of making accessible the naked truth in unadorned language, can be seen as a literary equivalent of Caravaggio's contemporary radical naturalism, equally pious but also sharing a considerable

---

[80] Della Valle, *Turquia* (1662), 'Vita di Pietro della Valle il pellegrino'.

potential for overt sensuality and thus moral scandal.[81] What della Valle accomplished was to institutionalize a new model of historical prose which inherited Renaissance ideals of truthfulness, participated in an erudite, humanistic antiquarianism, and (through the accident of Mario Schipano's failure to perform his commission) went beyond restrictive conventions of rhetorical order and propriety. Thus della Valle's legacy pointed towards the Enlightenment in two fundamental ways: by participating in a sophisticated manner in the creation of the persona of the gentleman-traveller of the Grand Tour, and by proposing a philosophical discourse concerning human diversity which encompassed both civil and religious themes – a discourse effectively sustained by a practice of naturalistic observation and enquiry which might have been best defined as scientific, had della Valle's personal experience not been so whimsical. But much as he was a predecessor, della Valle was also an inheritor, and for this reason can serve us as epilogue for our analysis of the evolution of the travel literature of the Renaissance.

[81] It would of course be exaggerating, and also unnecessary, to suggest that della Valle's style was directly inspired by Caravaggio's naturalism. On the other hand, he was certainly aware of the dispute about Caravaggio's style, since it dominated the academies of Rome during the years of della Valle's formation, before disappointment in love and war drove him to assume the pilgrim's garb in 1614. Eventually Caravaggio and della Valle would share the same biographer, Giovan Pietro Bellori. Della Valle's interest in painting is well attested, and when he left for Turkey, Egypt and the Holy Land he took along, in his pay, a young Flemish painter called John (who had previously been working in Naples). John accompanied him to Persia too. Unfortunately his paintings appear to have been lost. Although the editor of the *Viaggi* Biagio Deversin had planned a full fourth part with illustrations, he could only find a few schematic drawings of temples and palaces in India.

Conclusion: Before orientalism

Della Valle's naturalistic and antiquarian gaze owed a great deal to his immediate intellectual environment, but is impossible to understand without the three centuries and a half of travel writing which separated him from Marco Polo. It is in particular necessary to assess the impact of the multiplication of travel narratives throughout the sixteenth century. These were important, I would argue, not for their sheer quantity, but for the position which they occupied in a structure of discourse. They offered images of distant, other worlds, among which India was only one peculiar location. These worlds became far less distant because European presence was continuous, in the form of a colonial activity whose most important effect was not so much the establishment of western dominance (only relative in Asia in the sixteenth century) as the consolidation of structural interaction. The crucial issue is not therefore simply which images were transmitted (although they mattered), but also which was the authority given to travel literature within a multi-faceted cosmographical discourse.

Within the cosmographical genres of the Renaissance, no theme had implications as profound as the analysis of human diversity, and especially cultural and religious diversity. The fundamental breakthrough, I have sought to argue, was not simply to record, but also to interpret difference. This, however, did not take place within a single ethnological practice. Throughout this period European ethnology was, one might say, scattered among geographical, historical, philosophical and literary genres, and travel literature reflected with its sheer diversity of form and reception this plurality. However, one distinction seems more profound and important than any other – the division between two analytical languages, one religious and another historical (sociological, economic and political) which, throughout this study, I have termed the languages of Christianity and civilization. The birth of modern ethnology essentially consisted in the coming together of these two languages,

388

through mutual interaction, into a single anthropological debate. Della Valle's antiquarian interests exemplify well this coming together, and its implications. In his letters the skills of the merchant as empirical observer of the diversity of human behaviour, and Christian concern with problems of religious definition, prompted mainly (as we have seen) by the dilemmas of the missionary project, finally met in a new level of independent secular discourse able to relativize beliefs in the light of analysed behaviour. In effect this coming together represented a triumph for secular history, because it widened its range and depth with natural-istic and antiquarian perspectives beyond the conventions of Renaissance historiography.

The nature of travel as knowledge is therefore a major issue in the understanding of this process. This debate, among modern historians, has been dominated by the issue of orientalism. The authority of foreign observers of India, for instance, and the validity of their empiricism has been questioned, as an expression of European desire for dominance, or as example of the inability of Europeans to transcend their own prejudices and assumptions in order to really understand other cultures. This questioning attitude, however, stands in sharp contrast to the assumption of many modern historians of South India, who have emphasized the crucial role of foreign descriptions for our understanding of its history. Logically the issue has generated a full historiographical debate. Thus, whilst the publication in English in 1900 of the two key European sixteenth-century sources for the history of Vijayanagara, the chronicles of Paes and Nunes, was welcomed by their editor Robert Sewell – a prime representative of British colonial antiquarianism – as 'documents of peculiar and unique value', many Indian historians of the succeeding generation rather looked for alternative indigenous sources (imperfect though they were), because reliance on foreign interpretations also implied a reliance on the preconceptions of intrusive powers which were seen to have brought eventual imperial domination. This explains why Burton Stein, in what is probably the most recent and innovative synthesis of the history of Vijayanagara, was ready to fend off the ghost of orientalism:

> These Portuguese merchant adventurers [Paes and Nuniz] knew no Indian languages well enough to correct their visual impressions through understandings obtained from verbal or written views of Indians. Vijayanagara kings of the sixteenth century were presented as oriental despots whose authority consisted partly of sacred power founded upon, or regenerated by, royal sacrifices and partly on feudal relations between them and great territorial lords ('captains'). Finally, to these was added the orientalist notion of the fabulous riches of Asia

which was supported by the splendours of the city itself, its vastness, its monumentality, and the wealth of its citizens.[1]

This view is certainly unfair. As we have seen, Paes and Nunes did not insist at all on the ideas of 'oriental despotism', 'fabulous riches' or 'feudal relationships' in their descriptions of Vijayanagara. These concepts are later European cultural elaborations, all too often assumed as obvious by modern scholars without further explanation. Although it may be possible to construct an orientalist interpretation of Vijayanagara using the descriptions of Paes and Nunes, as in fact Giovanni Botero did, there is no underlying assumption of an essentially different Orient in these writers which would necessarily lead to such an interpretation. Paes and Nunes do not seem particularly ill informed when it comes to Indian views either. The whole of Nunes's chronicle was most probably based on local oral or written traditions which can be traced back to Kannada and Telugu texts. In fact, what is surprising is the extent to which it is precisely in the quality of their personal observations, rather than in their transmission of local traditions, that the accounts of Paes and Nunes have been consistently confirmed by recent revisionist archaeological findings and anti-orientalist research into the political history of the kingdom.

A similar conclusion has been recently reached by Meera Nanda in a study of European travel accounts of the Mughal empire under Shah Jahan and Aurangzeb, focusing mainly on the second half of the seventeenth century. These accounts were limited by cultural preconceptions, but they also stand in stark contrast to the Persian chronicles of the period – the key indigenous sources for the empire as a whole – for their information on trade and the economy, on political forms of organization, and on social life and religious practices. They are geographically accurate and historically useful, the more so because they do not speak with a single voice. Instead, they engage in a debate among themselves concerning the validity of their observations.[2]

The frontiers between empirical observation and conditioned interpretation will of course remain difficult to establish, but what is perhaps more interesting is that today the roles of one century ago can be reversed, so that whilst Indian historians like Meera Nanda can appropriate to a large extent the secular western gaze as their own, many western critics insist on questioning it. An interesting example of the persistence of an anti-orientalist attitude, very much influenced by the work of literary critic Edward Said, is the recent book by Kate Teltscher,

---

[1] Stein, *Vijayanagara*, p. 3.

[2] M. Nanda, *European travel accounts during the reigns of Shahjahan and Aurangzeb* (Kurukshetra, 1994), especially the conclusions on pp. 157–62.

India inscribed, which, with Purchas, della Valle and Bernier, takes up where I leave off in order to study European and British writing on India from 1600 to 1800.[3] The comparison between the travel literature of the two periods is in part illustrative of the impact of two different colonial contexts, the earlier one (mainly marked by Portuguese enterprise) limited and conditioned, and the latter (culminating in the British power in India) fully fledged. The comparison is also revealing of what the modern problem of colonial representation owes to its pre-1600 past, in particular to what I have sought to describe as a long European 'Renaissance'. But perhaps the more important contrast is a difference of approach: whilst Kate Teltscher seeks to qualify the simplifications of Said's anti-orientalism by emphasizing rhetorical plurality and historical contextualization for diverse texts, she still contends that a strictly historical element is irrelevant to the analysis of the contents of travel accounts. This is where the approach adopted in this study differs. Travel literature was not simply, or primarily, a technique for colonial justi-fication. Although such ideological justifications did exist, the main impetus for this literature was scientific and instrumental. It was not, however, objective and disinterested. The real alternative is not between objective science and ideological distortion, but rather between different kinds of techniques of knowledge adapted to different kinds of aims and challenges.

One conclusion of this study is that the critical analysis of travel accounts, as texts conditioned by concrete assumptions and intentions, not only helps us relativize their empirical value (which is in itself useful considering how intrinsically important these sources often are); it also helps us reconstruct the actual experiences which conditioned the growth of early modern ethnology by reference to a number of key scenarios, techniques and problems.

To begin with, it is important to recognize the specificity of each colonial context. India's historical significance as an area of cultural encounter differed from others, in Asia or outside. Because of the existence of literary sources that went back to antiquity, and the persistence of contacts throughout the Middle Ages, India had a deeper resonance in Renaissance Europe as an epitome of difference than either China or Japan.[4] On the other hand, the challenge posed by the idea of a gentile civilization – which was in the long term the key intellectual

---

[3] Teltscher, *India inscribed*.

[4] Europe's main 'other' from the Middle Ages was of course Islam, in this period mainly represented by the Ottoman empire and, secondarily, Persia and the Mughal empire. Unfortunately the analysis of the peculiarities of the Middle Eastern scene – the original focus of Said's analysis of orientalism – has to be left out of this study.

problem – would prove more powerful in the Far East than in India, to a large extent because Hindu India was receding politically before Muslim overlords, and also because conventional European ideas of rationality and civilization were easier to fit with what was found in Japan and, especially, in China. The idolatry of India always seemed particularly obvious and irrational, and the fact that for many decades the Jesuit missionary discourse virtually monopolized the European encounter with Japan and China, and that the threat of a European conquest, even a partial one, was on the whole kept at bay, only helped to enhance the image of an alternative civilization. The missionary hopes of a conversion based on rational dialogue in fact conditioned much of the European analysis of China in the sixteenth century, and the crisis of this hope brought about by the rites controversy accompanied the reversal of the idealized image of China in the Enlightenment.

The New World provides another key scenario whose impact was peculiar to this period. In America, and especially in Mexico and Peru, the rapid conquest of large numbers of Indian communities, some of which were remarkably urbanized and sophisticated, accelerated the debate about the morality of conquest, the nature of barbarian societies, the place of the new discoveries in world history, and the persistence of idolatry despite apparent conversions. It also shifted the debate from the analysis of alternative civilizations to the justification of the political and religious subjugation of non-Europeans, or to the success and failure of assimilation. Although under the power of Spanish conquerors the western Indies became a subject of debate more openly and immediately than oriental India, in the long term the challenge of oriental civilizations was perhaps more pervasive. The themes of the novelty and the transformation of the New World, rather than its capacity permanently to challenge European assumptions, came to define American otherness.[5]

---

[5] This is not the place to discuss in detail the impact of the New World in European consciousness and the debates it generated, a topic which, unlike India, has received a great deal of attention. See especially B. Keen, *The Aztec image in Western thought* (New Brunswick, 1971); Elliott, *The old world and the new*; A. Gerbi, *The dispute of the New World. The history of a polemic 1750–1900* (Pittsburgh, 1973); L. Hanke, *All mankind is one. A study of the disputation between Bartolomé de Las Casas and Juan Ginés de Sepúlveda on the religious and intellectual capacity of the American Indians* (DeKalb, Ill., 1974); G. Baudot, *Utopie et histoire au Mexique* (Toulouse, 1977); Gliozzi, *Adamo e il nuovo mondo*; Pagden, *The fall of natural man*; A. Pagden, *European encounters with the New World, from Renaissance to Romanticism* (New Haven and London, 1993); S. MacCormack, *Religion in the Andes. Vision and imagination in early colonial Peru* (Princeton, 1991); B. Pastor, *The armature of conquest. Spanish accounts of the discovery of America, 1492–1589* (Stanford, 1992). S. Greenblatt (ed.) *New world encounters* (Berkeley, 1994); Kupperman (ed.) *America in European consciousness*; P. Seed, *Ceremonies of possession in Europe's conquest of the New World, 1492–1640* (Cambridge, 1995).

The denial of a simple orientalist prejudice as a way of interpreting Renaissance travel literature goes beyond the definition of the specificity of southern India in the European debate about gentile civilizations, and encompasses also an understanding of the way in which observers, in India or elsewhere, were able to perceive, or failed to perceive, indigenous realities. Although each text (as we have sought to show) possesses its own particular qualities and needs to be understood according to the specific circumstances of its composition, primary accounts also reveal a possibility of cultural understanding that cannot be reduced to the mere imposition upon an alien world of a set of European prejudices. It is not just that travellers had to take account of empirical sensations which came to them from 'outside', and which they were then able to interpret in various ways. More importantly, I have sought to argue that they could decode a cultural system, or more precisely a number of indigenous language-games, despite obvious and varying limitations in their levels of understanding. There was, in other words, a kind of inter-cultural dialogue going on, without which many of the accounts are unthinkable.

This dialogue was based on initial cultural homologies, but in the context of some travellers' personal involvement with the realities of southern India it went further than that, becoming a positive act of translation. The limits of such a dialogue are obvious: the constraints of space and time, the depth and complexity of initial assumptions, and ultimately, perhaps decisively, the need born out of political expediency not to change one's assumptions beyond a certain point. But these limits do not detract from the fact that people from different cultures were to a large extent able to meet and learn about each other.[6]

Learning about other peoples was, however, always a risk, because it challenged the organization of cultural spaces which made identity and

---

[6] For a more wide-ranging discussion of translation in cultural encounters see my 'Introduction' to H. Bugge and J. P. Rubiés (eds.) *Shifting cultures. Interaction and discourse in the expansion of Europe* (Münster, 1995). Important material can also be found in some of the articles collected in S. B. Schwartz (ed.) *Implicit understandings: observing, reporting and reflecting on the encounters between Europeans and other peoples in the early modern era* (Cambridge, 1994). With my emphasis on translatability across cultures, I differ from Patricia Seed, who in her interesting *Ceremonies of possession* emphasizes instead the creation of separate national-linguistic domains, with mutually unintelligible assumptions, in the European encounter with the New World. Certainly, different national and religious cultures can be distinguished in the cosmographical literature of this period. However, from a more general perspective here I would insist on how close the different European vernacular languages were to each other (because of their common Latin erudite tradition, but also due to the fact that their diverse literary developments continually interacted throughout the whole period). Furthermore, I would also insist in the gradual erosion of linguistic barriers in the case of encounters with hitherto isolated cultural communities across the world, something which can be exemplified by the role of Castilian and Portuguese as colonial languages.

morality possible. In particular, for Christians and Muslims alike, these spaces relied on a religious centre, a revealed tradition which the practice of inter-cultural understanding (even the use of everyday language for practical purposes) often questioned in subtle ways. Sophisticated narrative strategies were developed to deal with this threat, and often the very practice of colonial power implied the exportation of European mythologies to new settings – as the Portuguese re-creation of the myth of Saint Thomas in India exemplifies. However, these adaptations were seldom cost-free: Saint Thomas in India or the virgin of Guadalupe in Mexico all involved a compromise with native traditions and were the product of creole, rather than just European, identities. On the whole, learning from others often implied that an original centre became less of a centre. The history of cultural translations is therefore also the history of identities, of their creation and dissolution in a continuous process of reproduction and change. European and Persian travellers to Vijayanagara were able to decode indigenous language-games because they had a few initial homologies to work with, but also because, through their experience of otherness, they were able to move in the periphery of their own tradition and to change it. We may generalize by saying that any original practice, a practice which responds to a particular historical context, is in some degree creative and thus changes tradition, even when it takes the form of attempting to 'repeat' tradition.

One important feature of Renaissance travel literature was that it was a peripheral discourse within the European system of knowledge, justified by practical aims rather than theoretical concerns, but with an immense potential for suggesting new problems. The movement from the merchant-traveller to the philosophical traveller was also a movement from the popular to the elite discourses. Many of the Italian and Portuguese travellers of the sixteenth century who preceded della Valle – traders, soldiers and fortune-seekers – could not, for instance, openly discuss the beliefs of Indian idolators, partly because they were not trained in theology, law or the humanities, and more importantly because they regularly avoided trespassing upon the territory of clerics. It was left to missionaries like Nobili to explore, let us say, the possible parallels and differences between natural law and Hindu *dharma*. Common travellers also lacked the erudition to compare and contrast different sources within a scholarly discipline, so that it was left to collectors and cosmographers like Ramusio and Botero to revise Ptolemy in the light of new reports. Similarly, it was left to erudite writers like the Jesuit historian Sebastiam Gonçalves to identify Bisnagá with Marco Polo's kingdom of Var (i.e., Lar) in South India, thus casting a net of cosmographical self-referentiality within the body of travel literature.[7] But popular travellers were on the other hand able to identify, for instance, the city of Vijayanagara as the centre of a complex non-Christian civil society, and to re-create through their analysis of the institution of kingship many of the political, economic and ritual language-games which regulated that society. They could place the city on a local map and contribute to a reconstruction of native history from native sources, oral or written. Thus travellers elaborated, on the basis of their experience of South India and its social and religious system, a detailed empirical description based on ethnographic and historical models which were to a large extent independent of religious dogmas. By defining or assuming similarities in a variety of language-games, foreign travellers came to terms with differences which belonged to a world of 'otherness'.

The two assumptions central to this practice were the ideas of *nature* and *history*, and their practical use was a legacy that seventeenth-century educated travellers like della Valle could endorse with greater authority. Effectively, the use of conceptual categories of classification – as we have seen in the analysis of ethnographic descriptions from Marco Polo to Duarte Barbosa – followed a logic which institutionalized naturalism: the assumption that the world is ordered, that it follows laws (with or without lawgivers) and regularities, and that these regularities also affect human behaviour. The development of historiographic genres, from Barros and Nunes to Couto and Valignano, consolidated in a similar fashion the discipline of a historical order, based on the idea that contingent events follow one another in an irreversible sequence. Stories about the very arrival of the Portuguese, their military and spiritual conquests, or the sudden destruction of a Hindu metropolis, all implied a science of change which overlay the geographic and ethnographic science of continuities.[8] What is most important to establish here is that the naturalistic and historical assumptions were implicit in the use of everyday language for the simplest of empirical descriptions – those many narratives guided by the key principle of the faithfulness to personal experience which in this period established the traveller's authority in Europe. The conviction that empirical observation and even participation were possible was the fundamental rhetorical component of the genre of travel literature, defining it despite its multiplicity of purpose

[7] Sebastiam Gonçalves, *Primeira parte da História dos religiosos da Companhia de Jesus*, ed. by J. Wicki, 3 vols. (Coimbra 1957–62), vol. I, p. 135. This work was written in 1604–14.

[8] I am not here discussing possible conceptions of time and history. The idea of cyclical history, like the idea that time is only one more human illusion, could be entertained in Europe in the fifteenth and sixteenth centuries. However, these were not the organizing assumptions of the narratives which I analyze – assumptions whose logical consequences were increasingly allowed to shape discourse.

and form. Travel accounts were not simply bricks with which the Renaissance cosmographer, as architect of knowledge, could build a world history: the bricks themselves, their narrative logic and form, in effect suggested the existence of the larger building and its principles.

A consequence of this analysis is that the naturalistic and historical assumptions which we have learnt to recognize as typically western need to be understood primarily as implicit mechanisms in the use of everyday language for practical purposes, a use which is often unconscious and unsystematic, and to a large extent independent of the various explicit definitions of nature and history which are possible in each period. In their implicit form (although not in their complex literary elaborations) these fundamental narrative assumptions can be found in different cultures – in sixteenth-century India they appear in Muslim, Hindu and Christian sources alike. It was only after a long and original process that a particular kind of language-game about nature and about history developed in the European Christian tradition. This was a critical, systematic and empirical kind of discourse in which nature and history were central to the definition of authoritative, erudite genres, and they were central precisely because theological figurations and moral values could be relativized by reference to them. This kind of discourse was critical insofar as it was prepared to identify and revise assumptions without fear, systematic insofar as it was carried on coherently in the framework of an institutionalized language-game, and empirical insofar as it stressed the importance of particular human experiences as an authoritative source of knowledge.

The process of the emergence of these empirical human and natural sciences, as it developed in the Renaissance, took the form of a dialogue with classical models, and required, against the theological emphasis of medieval culture, the painful separation of *faith* and *reason* as two independent areas of discourse (and here I refer to reason and faith as areas of discourse, not as the abstract definitions of two fundamental human psychological faculties). Within the religious systems of the Reformation and the Counter-Reformation, faith and reason were still, ideally, acting together. However, as I have sought to illustrate, the impulse towards historicization and rationalization influenced and supported the religious discourses of mission and Biblical studies at the same time as it weakened their foundations. While faith essentially relied on the maintenance of a traditional Christian mythology (even as it was renewed through the experience of the ineffable, in ritual and in the methodical discipline of spiritual exercises), reason constituted itself as a guiding principle, almost an alternative myth, which presided over the new critical, systematic and empirical discourses. That this kind of discourse became central (but neither unique, nor exclusive) in Europe owed a great deal to the early colonial experiences and to the contribution of the different genres of travel literature.

The place of humanism and scepticism in this process was essential, and an understanding of the role of travel literature and its transformation helps us re-define their contribution. Humanism did not simply offer a model of rational, secular civilization and artistic achievement based on classical precedents; rather, by the early seventeenth century it also sustained an intellectual perspective concerned with the variety and purpose of human beliefs and customs, one in which the experience overseas even helped relativize the idealizing role of the ancient Greeks and Romans. There was thus a secular universalism behind the idea of the cosmopolitan humanist traveller which was an alternative to exclusive forms of religious universalism. The religious framework did not of course disappear from this perspective, but it was no longer indispensable. Scepticism operated as a force for criticism, rather than destruction, within these universalist concerns. It sustained the inductive method against the limitation of traditional dialectics; it dwelt on the evidence of a plurality of opinions as a resource to question traditional philosophical arguments; it helped test anti-despotic and anti-dogmatic ideas in alternative scenarios, sometimes fictional but more often inspired by travellers' observations of human diversity. The question is not really the existence of pure scepticism – Montaigne, Descartes, Bayle and Voltaire can be seen to have held fideistic or deistic positions – but rather the criticism of traditional religion as morally or philosophically coherent.

Empiricism alone did not create secularism.[9] There were, essentially, two roads towards the rationalism of the seventeenth century. One, stretching from Abelard and Llull to Grotius and Descartes, rationalized Christian faith through an imaginary dialogue with a gentile who would never be convinced of the truth of the Incarnation and the Trinity, or even of the existence of God, simply with arguments based on an external authority, which could eventually be subject to sceptical doubt. The other road was the road of the traveller as empirical observer, created from the times of Gerald of Wales and Marco Polo to those of Pietro

---

[9] As Susan Rosa has recently reminded us, 'the origins of rationalized discourse about religion and its consequent transformation from a way of thinking to an object of thought are to be found squarely within orthodoxy itself', and in particular within the controversy between different churches created by the Reformation, which stimulated rational arguments: S. Rosa, 'Seventeenth-century Catholic polemic and the rise of cultural rationalism: an example from the empire', *Journal of the History of Ideas*, 57 (1996): 87–107. I would argue that the rationalizing impulse, however, did not exclusively emerge within the European Christian controversy of this period.

della Valle and François Bernier. These were not, however, two separate, independent roads, but rather one single road with two dimensions. The dialogue with the Jew, the Muslim and the gentile was not purely rhetorical: it was based on real concerns and experiences, and in the same way that European debates came to inform the attitudes of observers abroad, thus did the observations of travellers, as missionaries, as traders and colonial agents, or as curious humanists, come to inform the theological, scientific and philosophical debates that created the Enlightenment. Therefore, we may conclude that the rationalist transformation of European culture during the sixteenth and seventeenth centuries cannot be explained without the structuring agency of the discourses of travel literature, in all their moral and empirical diversity.

Appendix

Pietro della Valle's sonnets in honour of the *sati* Giaccamà, whom he met at Ikkeri in November 1623 (Biblioteca Apostolica Vaticana, ms. Lat. 10,389).

In Ikkeri, città regia de Venktapa Naieka principe gentile. D'una donna che si brugiò viva per la morte di suo marito.

> In India è una città detta Ikerì
> Dove, morto il marito a Giaccamà
> Ch'era donna di razza Telengà
> Ne la contrada di Malars Kinì,
>
> Non volendo ella dimorar più qui
> Ma col diletto andarsene colà
> Ne l'altro mondo vi pensa'l trovarà
> Spontaneamente sua vita finì.
>
> E, com'è lor costume si bruggiò
> Poco dopo ch'estinto, et arso fù
> Lo sposo; senza lui, viver non vuòl.
>
> O amor degno di fama, e che qua giù
> Sia celebrato almen, poi che non può
> Lo spirito, ch'è infedile, andar là su.

Alla medesima donna.

> O Giaccamà, si quanto a Dio infedele
> Altretanto al tuo sposo fossi stata,
> Non ti saresti mai viva brugiata
> Per serbare altrai fede, a te crudele.

399

O Giaccamà, se a Dio così fedele
Come al tuo sposo ti fossi mostrata,
La vita ti saresti conservata,
Ma con perpetue lagrime e querele.

Io così faccio, et a farlo mi insegna
La santa legge che dal ciel discese,
Che sola al mondo d'osservarsi e degna.

Vorrei seguir chi in paradiso ascesa,
Ma per non far di ciò l'alma mia indegna
Aspetto che mi chiami chi lei presa.

*

Non penso Giaccamà che habbia men pena
Chi vive a lungo in perpetuo dolore,
Che chi per dare al suo mal fine, muore,
E abbrucciando i tormenti, il duòlo affrena.

Vita d'affani e di miseria piena
Senza por mai in oblio'l perduto amore
Peggio e che morte, e ha ben duro il cuore
Ch'in tale statio molti anni la mena.

Ne più gran segno è di fede, o costanza,
Brugiar se stesso che soffrir vivendo
Un'incendio continuo e prolongato.

Ja che l'anima e'l cor si va straggendo,
Et con maggior martiri è consumato
Quanto più lunga è del fin la speranza.

Bibliography

MANUSCRIPT SOURCES

Archivio Segreto Vaticano, Della Valle-Bufalo: 52, 53, 186.
Archivium Romanum Societatis Iesu (ARSI): Goa 14, 15, 16, 24, 33.
Biblioteca Apostolica Vaticana (BAV): Lat. 10,389; Barberini Lat. 5,206; Barberini Lat. 5,181; Ottob. 3,382; Ottob. 3,385.
Biblioteca Nazionale di Firenze: Palatino 1,125; B. R. 233.
Biblioteca Riccardiana di Firenze: 871, 1,910.
Bibliothèque Nationale de Paris: Portugais 65.
British Library (BL): Sloane 1,820; Add. 16,613; Add. 28,461.

PRIMARY SOURCES

'Abd al-Razzāq. *Matla'as-Sa'dain va Majma'al-Bahrain*, partial edition and translation in E. M. Quatremère (ed.) *Notices et extraits*.
El Abencerraje (novela y romancero), ed. by F. López Estrada. Madrid, 1987.
Acosta, José de. *Historia natural y moral de las Indias*, ed. by E. O'Gorman. Mexico City, 1962.
Al-Biruni. *Albiruni's India*, trans. and ed. by E. C. Sachau, London, 1888; repr. 1910.
Albuquerque, Affonso de. *Cartas de Affonso de Albuquerque*, ed. Raimundo António de Bulhão Pato and Henrique Lopes de Mendoça, 7 vols. Lisbon, 1884–1935.
Albuquerque, Braz de. *Comentários de Affonso d'Albuquerque*, by A. d'Albuquerque [*sic*], ed. by A. Bião, 2 vols. Coimbra, 1922–3.
Alvarez, Francisco, *The Prester John of the Indies . . . being the narrative of the Portuguese embassy to Ethiopia in 1520*, ed. by F. Beckingham, and G. W. B. Huntingford. Hakluyt Society, 2 vols. Cambridge, 1961.
André J. and Filliozat, J. (eds.) *L'inde vue du Rome. Textes latins de l'antiquité relatifs à l'Inde*. Paris, 1986.
Aquinas, Thomas. *Selected political writings*, ed. by A. P. d'Entreves. Oxford, 1959.
Arrian. *History of Alexander and Indica*, ed. and trans. by P. A. Brunt. Loeb Classical Library, 2 vols. London, 1983.

[Azevedo, Agostinho d'], 'Estado da India' (BL ms. Add 28,461, no. 36), *Documentação ultramarina portuguesa*, vol. I, pp. 197–263.

Azurara, Gomes Eanes de. *Crónica do descobrimento e conquista da Guiné*, ed. by Reis Brasil. Lisbon, 1989.

Babur. *Babur-Nama (Memoirs of Babur)*, trans. and ed. by A. S. Beveridge, 2 vols. London, 1921.

Balbi, Gasparo. 'Viaggio dell'Indie Orientali di Gasparo Balbi, Gioilliero Venetiano' (Venice, 1590), in O. Pinto (ed.) *Viaggi di C. Federici e G. Balbi*.

Barbaro, Iosafa. 'Viaggi del Magnifico messer Josephat Barbaro' in *Viaggi fatti da Vinetia alla Tana, in Persia, in India, et in Costantinopoli*, ed. by A. Manuzio, 2nd edn. Venice, 1545.

Barbosa, Duarte. *The book of Duarte Barbosa*, ed. by M. L. Dames. Hakluyt Society, 2nd series, 2 vols. London, 1918–21.

Livro em que dá relação do que viu e ouviu no Oriente, ed. by Augusto Reis Machado. Lisbon, 1946.

Livro do que viu e ouviu no Oriente, ed. by M. A. Veiga e Sousa. Lisbon, 1989.

O livro de Duarte Barbosa, ed. by Maria Augusta da Veiga e Sousa, vol. I. Lisbon, 1996.

Barros, João de. *Da Ásia*. Décadas I–IV. Lisbon, 1777–8.

Ásia, 3 vols. (Decades I–III). Lisbon, 1932–92.

Barros, João de and João Baptista Lavanha. *Quarta decada da Asia*. Madrid, 1615.

Beatis, A. de. *The travel journal of Antonio de Beatis*, ed. by J. R. Hale. Hakluyt Society, 2nd series. London, 1979.

Beauvais, Vincent of. *Speculum historiale*. Augsburg, 1474.

Belleforest, François de. *L'histoire universelle du monde*, 2 vols. Paris, 1570.

La cosmographie universelle de tout le monde . . . auteur en partie Munster. Paris, 1575.

Benavente, Fray Toribio de. *Historia de los Indios de la Nueva España*, ed. by Claudio Esteva. Madrid, 1985.

Benjamin of Tudela. *The itinerary of Benjamin of Tudela*, ed. by M. A. Signer and M. N. Adler. Joseph Simon, 1983.

Bernier, François. *Travels in the Moghul Empire, A.D. 1656–1668*, trans. I. Brock, ed. A. Constable. London, 1891.

Voyage dans les etats du Grand Mogol, ed. F. B. Hattacharya. Fayard, 1981.

Betanzos, Juan de. *Suma y narración de los Incas*, ed. by M. del C. Martín Rubio. Madrid, 1987.

Bocarro, António. *Década XIII da História da Índia*, ed. by R. J. de Lima Felner. 2 vols. Lisbon, 1876.

'Livro das plantas de todas as fortalezas, cidades e povoações do Estado da Índia oriental', ed. by A. B. de Bragança Pereira. *Arquivo Português Oriental*, tomo IV, vol. 2, part 2. Goa, 1938.

Bonner, A. (ed.) *Selected works of Ramon Llull*, 2 vols. Princeton, 1985.

Botero, Giovanni. *Relationi universali*, 4 parts. Vicenza, 1595–6; Venice, 1618.

The travellers breviat, or an historicall description of the most famous kingdomes in the world, trans. by Robert Johnson. London, 1601.

Delle cause della grandeza e magnificenza delle città libri III. Rome, 1588.

Boxer, C. R. (ed.) *South China in the sixteenth century.* Hakluyt Society, 2nd series. London, 1953.

Broquière, Bertrandon de la. *Le voyage d'Outremer*, ed. by C. Schefer. Paris, 1892.

The voyage d'Outremer by Bertrandon de la Broquière, ed. by G. R. Kline. New York, 1988.

Bull, G. (ed.) *The pilgrim. The travels of Pietro della Valle*, ed. and trans. by George Bull. London, 1990.

Busbecq, Ogier. *Omnia quae extant. Legationis Turcicae epistolae quatuor.* Leiden, 1633.

Camões, Luís de. *Os Lusíadas.* Lisbon, 1572.

Careri, G. F. G. *Indian travels of Thevenot and Careri*, ed. by Surendranath Sen. New Delhi, 1949.

Carletti, Francesco. *Ragionamento del mio viaggio intorno al mondo*, ed. by G. Silvestro. Turin, l958.

Carpini, John of Piano. 'Ystoria Mongalorum quos nos Tartaros apellamus', in van den Wyngaert (ed.) *Sinica Franciscana.*

Castanheda, Fernão Lopes de. *História do descobrimento & conquista da Índia pelos Portugueses*, ed. by M. Lopes de Almeida, 2 vols. Porto, 1979.

Catalani de Sévérac. Jordanus. *Mirabilia descripta*, ed. H. Yule. London, 1863.

Mirabilia descripta. Les merveilles de l'Asie, ed. by H. Cordier. Paris, 1925.

Cessi, R. (ed.) 'L'itinerario indiano di Francesco dal Bocchier'. *Atti della Accademia nazionale dei Lincei. Rendiconti della classe di scienze morali, storiche e filologiche*, ser. VIII, 6 (1951): 232–49.

Chardin, Jean. *Journal du voyage du Chevalier Chardin en Perse et aux Indes Orientales.* London, 1686.

Cieza de León, Pedro. *Parte primera de la chrónica del Perú.* Seville, 1553.

Descubrimiento y conquista del Perú, ed. by F. Cantù. Rome 1979.

Crónica del Perú. Segunda parte, ed. by F. Cantù, 2nd edn. Lima, 1986.

Clavijo, Ruy González de. *Embajada a Tamorlán*, ed. by F. López Estrada. Madrid, 1943.

Embajada a Tamerlán, ed. by Ramon Alba. Madrid, 1984.

Columbo, Fernando. *Histories del signor don Fernando Colombo . . . relatione della vita e de fatti dell'ammiraglio don Christoforo Colombo suo padre.* Venice, 1571.

Columbus, Christopher. *The four voyages of Columbus*, ed. by Cecil Jane. New York, 1988. (Originally published by the Hakluyt Society. London, 1930 and 1933.)

The journal of the first voyage, ed. by B. W. Ife. London, 1990.

Conti, N. 'The travels of Nicolò Conti in the East', with independent pagination in R. H. Major (ed.) *India in the fifteenth century*, pp. 1–39.

Correa, Gaspar. *Lendas da Índia*, ed. by Rodrigo José de Lima Felner, 5 vols. Lisbon, 1858–66.

Cortés, Hernán. *Cartas de relación*, ed. by A. Delgado Gómez. Madrid, 1993.

Couto, Diogo do. *Décadas*, IV–XII. Lisbon, 1778–88 (as a continuation of Barros, *Da Ásia*. Lisbon, 1777–8).

Década quinta da 'Ásia', ed. by M. de Jong, Coimbra 1937.

Coutre, Jacques de. *Andanzas asiáticas*, ed. by Eddy Stols, B. Teensma and J. Werberckmoes. Madrid, 1991.

Cresques, Abraham. *Atlas Català de Cresques Abraham*, ed. by J. Matas. Barcelona 1975.

Cronica do descobrimento e conquista da India pelos Portugueses [Anonymous Codex, British Museum, Egerton 20901], ed. by Luís de Albuquerque. Lisbon, 1974.

Dahmen, P. (ed.) *Un Jésuite Brahme. Robert de Nobili S. I. 1577–1656.* Louvain, 1924.

Dante [Aligieri], *The Divine Comedy*, trans. and ed. by J. D. Sinclair. New York, 1939.

Della Valle, Pietro. *Nel funerale de Sitti Maani Gioerida sua consorte.* Rome, 1627.
Delle conditioni di Abbas, Re di Persia. Venice, 1628.
Viaggi di Pietro della Valle il Pellegrino. Parte prima della Persia. Parte seconda della Persia, 2 vols. Rome, 1658.
Viaggi di Pietro della Valle il Pellegrino. La Turchia. 2nd edition. Rome, 1662.
Viaggi di Pietro della Valle il pellegrino descritti da lui medesimo in lettere familiari all'erudito suo amico Mario Schipano. Parte terza, cioè l'India, co'l ritorno alla patria. Rome, 1663.
The travels of Pietro della Valle in India from the old English translation of 1664 by G. Havers, ed. by E. Grey, 2 vols. London, 1892.
I viaggi di Pietro della Valle. Lettere dalla Persia, vol. I, ed. by F. Gaeta and L. Lockhart. Rome, 1972.

Díaz del Castillo, Bernal. *Historia verdadera de la conquista de la Nueva España*, ed. by Miguel-León Portilla, 2 vols. Madrid, 1984.

Diodorus Siculus. *The library of history*, trans. by C. H. Oldfather et al. Loeb Classical Library, 12 vols. Cambridge, Mass. and London, 1933–67.

Documentacão ultramarina portuguesa, ed. by A. de Silva Rego (vols. I–V) and E. Sanceau (vols VI–VIII). Lisbon, 1960–83.

Documentos remetidos da Índia, ou livros das Monções, ed. by R. A. de Bulhão Pato (vols. I–IV) and A. da Silva Rego (vols. VI–X). Lisbon, 1880–1982.

Dubois, Abbé J.-A. *Character, manners and customs of the people of India*, ed. by Rev. G. U. Pope. Madras, 1879.

Elliot, H. M. and Dowson, J. (eds.) *The History of India as told by its own historians*, 7 vols. London, 1867–77.

Faria y Sousa, Manuel de. *Asia portuguesa*, 3 vols. Lisbon, 1666–75.

Federici, Cesare. 'Viaggio nell'india Orientale' (Venezia, 1587), in O. Pinto (ed.) *Viaggi di C. Federici e G. Balbi.*
'The voyage and travell of M. Caesar Fredericke, marchant of Venice, into the East India', trans. by T. Hickock, in R. Hakluyt (ed.) *Principal navigations*, vol. III, 198–269.

Fenicio, Jacomé. *Livro da seita dos Indios orientais*, ed. by J. Charpentier. Uppsala, 1933.

Ferishta, M. Q. *History of the rise of the Mahomedan power in India till the year 1612*, trans. by J. Briggs, 4 vols. Calcutta, 1908–10.

Fernandes, Gonçalo. *Tratado do P. Gonçalo Fernandes Trancoso sobre o Hinduísmo*, ed. by J. Wicki. Lisbon, 1973.

Fernandes, Valentim (ed.) *Marco Paulo.* Lisbon, 1502.

O Manuscrito 'Valentim Fernandes', ed. by A. Bião. Lisbon, 1940.

Fernández de Figueroa, Martín. *Conquista de las Indias, de Persia et Arabia* (Salamanca, 1512), in J. B. McKenna (ed.) *A Spaniard in the Portuguese Indies*.

Ferrando, R. (ed.) *Relaciones de la Camboya y el Japón*. Madrid, 1988.

Foster, W. (ed.) *Early travels in India 1583–1619*. London, 1921.

Fróis, Luís. 'Tratado en que se contem . . . algumas contradições e diferenças de custumes antre a gente de Europa e esta provincia de Japaõ', ed. by J. F. Schütte, *Kulturgegensätze Europa-Japan (1585)*. Tokyo, 1955.

Historia de Japam (1549–1593), ed. by J. Wicki, 5 vols. Lisbon 1976–84.

García Mercadal, J. (ed.) *Viajes de extrangeros por España y Portugal*. Madrid, 1952.

Garcilaso de la Vega, el Inca. *Comentarios reales, que tratan del orígen de los Incas*. Lisbon, 1609.

Garin, E. (ed.) *Prosatori latini del quattrocento*, in *La letteratura Italiana. Storia e testi*, vol. XIII. Milan and Naples, 1952.

Geoffrey of Monmouth. *The history of the kings of Britain*, ed. by L. Thorpe. Harmondsworth, 1966.

Gerald of Wales, *Giraldi Cambrensis opera*, vols. V and VI edited by J. F. Dimock. London, 1867–8.

The journey through Wales/The description of Wales, ed. and trans. by L. Thorpe. Harmondsworth, 1978.

The history and topography of Ireland, ed. and trans. by J. J. O'Meara, revised edn. Harmondsworth, 1982.

Gil, J. and Varela, C. (eds.) *Cartas de particulares a Colón y Relaciones coetáneas*. Madrid, 1984.

Giorgetti, A. (ed.) 'Lettere di Giovanni da Empoli e di Raffaelo Galli', *Archivio Storico Italiano*, ser. IV, 6 (1880): 165–74.

Giovio, Paolo. *Historiae sui temporis*, from *Opera*, vols. III–IV, Ed. by D. Visconti. Rome, 1956–64.

Góis, Damião de. *Chronica do felicissimo rei Dom Emanuel*, ed. by D. Lopes, 4 vols. Coimbra, 1949–55.

Goldschmidt, E. P. (ed.) 'Le voyage de Hieronimus Monetarius à travers la France', *Humanisme et Renaissance* 6 (1939).

Gómara, Francisco López de. *Historia de las Indias*. Zaragoza, 1552.

Gonçalves, Diogo. *Historia do Malavar*, ed. by J. Wicki. Münster, 1955.

Gonçalves, Sebastiam, *Primeira parte da História dos religiosos da Companhia de Jesus*, ed. by J. Wicki, 3 vols. Coimbra, 1957–62.

González de Mendoza, Juan. *Historia de las cosas más notables, ritos y costumbres del gran reino de la China*. Rome, 1585.

Historia del gran reino de la China, ed. by Ramon Alba. Madrid, 1990.

[Goulard, Simon] *Histoire de Portugal, contenant les enterprises, navigations et gestes memorables des Portugallois*. Geneva, 1581.

Greenlee, W. B. (ed.) *The voyage of Pedro Alvares Cabral to Brazil and India*. London, 1938.

Guerreiro, Fernão. *Relação anual das coisas que fizeram os padres da Companhia de Jesus nas suas missões . . . nos anos de 1600 a 1609*, ed. by A. Viegas, 3 vols. Coimbra, 1930–42.

Guicciardini, Francesco. 'Diario del viaggio in Spagna', in R. Palmarocchi (ed.) *Scritti autobiografici e rari*. Bari, 1936.

Storia d'Italia, 3 vols. Milan, 1988.

Guzmán, Luis de. *Historia de las missiones que han hecho los religiosos de la Compañía de Jesús para predicar el sancto evangelio en la India Oriental, y en los reynos de la China y Japón*. Alcalá, 1601.

Hakluyt, Richard. (ed.) *Principal navigations, voyages, traffiques and discoveries of the English nation*, ed. by J. Masefield. 7 vols. London, 1907.

Harff, Arnold von. *The pilgrimage of Arnold von Harff, knight from Cologne*, ed. by M. Letts. Hakluyt Society, 2nd series. London, 1946.

Hayton, Prince of Armenia. 'La flor des estoires de la terre d'Orient', in *Recueil des histoires des croisades. Documents Arméniens*, vol. II. Paris, 1906.

Hernández, Francisco. *Antigüedades de la Nueva España*, ed. by A. H. de León-Portilla. Madrid, 1986.

Herodotus. *The histories*, ed. by A. R. Burn, trans. Aubrey de Sélincort. Harmondsworth, 1972.

Hippocratic writings, ed. by G. E. R. Lloyd, trans. J. Chadwick and W. N. Mann. Harmondsworth, 1978.

Ibn Battūta. *The travels of Ibn Battūta, 1325–1354*, ed. and trans. from the Arabic version by C. Defrémery and B. R. Sanguinetti, by H. A. R. Gibb and C. F. Beckingham, 4 vols. to date. Cambridge and London, 1958–94.

A través del Islam, trans. and ed. by S. Fanjul and F. Arbós. Madrid, 1987.

Ibn Khaldūn. *The Muqaddimah*, trans. by F. Rosenthal, abridged and ed. by N. J. Dawood. London, 1967.

Intino, R. d' (ed.) *Enformação das cousas da China. Textos do século XVI*. Lisbon, 1989.

Jahn, K. (ed. and trans.) *Histoire universelle de Rasid al-Din Fadl Allah Abul Kabir*, vol. I: *Histoire des Francs*. Leiden, 1951.

Jarric, Pierre du. *Histoire des choses plus memorables*, 3 parts. Bordeaux 1608–14.

Kalidasa. *Theater of memory*, ed. by B. Stoler Miller. Columbia 1984.

Kircher, Athanasius. *Lingua Aegyptiaca restituta*. Rome, 1644.

China illustrata, trans. by Charles Van Tuyl. Bloomington, Ind., 1987.

Las Casas, Fray Bartolomé de. *Historia de las Indias*, ed. by A. Millares Carlo, 3 vols. Mexico City, 1951.

Laws of Manu, ed. and trans. by W. Doniger with B. K. Smith. Harmondsworth, 1991.

Le Bouvier, Gilles. 'Le livre de la description des pays', ed. by E. T. Hamy, in *Recueil des voyages et de documents pour servir à l'histoire de la géographie*, vol. XXII. Paris, 1908.

Le Roy, Louis. *De la vicissitude ou varieté des choses en l'univers*. Paris, 1575.

Letts, M. (ed.) *The travels of Leo of Rozmital through Germany, Flanders, England, France, Spain and Italy 1465–1467*. Hakluyt Society, 2nd series. London, 1957.

Libro del Conosçimiento de todos los reinos e tierras e señoríos que son por el mundo, ed. by Marcos Jiménez de la Espada. (1877); Repr. Barcelona, 1980.

Lima Cruz, M. A. (ed.) *Diogo do Couto e a década 8a da Ásia*, 2 vols. Lisbon, 1993.

Linschoten, Jan Huyghen van. *The voyage to the East Indies, from the English translation of 1598*, ed. by A. C. Burnell and P. A. Tiele, 2 vols. London, 1885.

'Livro das cidades e fortalezas que a coroa de Portugal tem nas partes da Índia', ed. by F. P. Mendes da Luz. *Studia*, 6 (1960).

Llull, Ramon. *Llibre de meravelles*, ed. by M. Gustà and J. Molas. Barcelona, 1980.

Lopes, D. (ed.) *Chronica dos reis de Bisnaga*. Lisbon, 1897.

(ed.) *Historia dos Portugueses no Malabar por Zinadím. Manuscripto arabe do seculo XVI*. Lisbon, 1898.

Lopes, F. *Crónica de D. João I*, ed. by H. Baquero Moreno. Lisbon, 1983.

Lord, Henry. *Display of two forraigne sects in the East Indies*. London, 1630.

Lucena, João de. *Historia da vida do Padre Francisco de Xavier*. Lisbon, 1600.

Ludolphus of Suchen, *De itinere terrae sancter liber*, ed. by F. Deycks. Stuttgart, 1851.

Ma Huan. *The overall survey of the ocean shores 1433*, ed. by J. V. G. Mills. Cambridge, 1970.

Maffei, Giovan Pietro. *Historiarum indicarum libri XVI*. Florence, 1588.

Mahabharata, trans. by J. A. B van Buitenen, books 1–5, 3 vols. Chicago, 1973–).

Major, R. H. (ed.) *India in the fifteenth century*. Hakluyt Society, 1st series. London, 1857.

Mandeville, John. *Mandeville's travels: texts and translations*, ed. by M. Letts. Hakluyt Society, 2nd series, 2 vols. London, 1953.

Manucci, Niccolao. *Storia do Mogor*, English ed. W. Irvine, 4 vols. London, 1907–8.

Manuzio, Antonio (ed.) *Viaggi fatti da Vinetia alla Tana, in Persia, in India et in Constantinopoli*. Venice, 1543.

Marana, Giovanni Paolo. *L'espion du Grand Seigneur*. Paris, 1684–6.

Marignolli, John of, 'Recollections of eastern travel', in Yule and Cordier (eds.) *Cathay and the way thither*, vol. III.

Matos, L. de (ed.) *Imagens do Oriente no século XVI. Reprodução do códice Portugês da Biblioteca Casanatense*. Lisbon, 1985.

McKenna, J. B. (ed.) *A Spaniard in the Portuguese Indies. The narrative of Martín Fernández de Figueroa*. Cambridge, Mass., 1967.

Le meraviglie dell'India, ed. by G. Tardiola. Rome, 1991.

Methwold, William. 'Relation', in *Relations from Golconda in the seventeenth century*, ed. by W. H. Moreland. London, 1931.

Monga, L. (ed.) *Un mercante di Milano in Europa. Diario di viaggio del primo cinquecento*. Milan, 1985.

Monserrate, Antonio. 'Mongolicae legationis commentarius', ed. by H. Hosten, in *Memoirs of the Asiatic Society of Bengal*, vol. III. Calcutta, 1914.

The commentary . . . on his journey to the court of Akbar, trans. J. S. Hoyland and annotated by S. N. Banerjee. Oxford, 1922.

Montaigne, Michel de. *The complete essays*, trans. and ed. by M. Screech. Harmonsworth, 1993.

Montalboddo, Francanzano da (ed.) *Paesi novamenti retrovati. Et novo mondo da Alberico Vesputio Florentino intitulato*. Vicenza, 1507.

Mundy, Peter. *The travels of Peter Mundy in Europe and Asia, 1608–1667*, ed. by Sir R. Carnac Temple, 6 vols. Hakluyt Society. London, 1907–36.

Muntaner, Ramon, 'Crònica', ed. by F. Soldevila, in *Les quatre grans cròniques*. Barcelona, 1971.

Navarrete, Fray Domingo, *The travels and controversies of friar Domingo Navarrete, 1616–1686*, ed. by J. S. Cummins. Hakluyt Society, 2 vols. London, 1962.

Nikitin, Afanasii. *Travels of Athanasius Nikitin*, with independent pagination in R. H. Major (ed.) *India in the fifteenth century*, pp. 1–32.

Nizamuddin Ahmad, Khwajah. *Tbaqat-i-Akbari. A history of India from the early Musalman invasions to the thirty-sixth year of the reign of Akbar*, trans. by Brajendanath De and ed. by Baini Prashad, 3 vols. Calcutta, 1911–39.

Nobili, Roberto de. *On Indian customs*, ed. by S. Rajamanickam. Palayamkottai, 1972.

Nunes, Leonardo. *Crónica de dom João de Castro*, ed. by J. D. M. Ford. Cambridge, Mass., 1936.

Ordóñez de Ceballos, Pedro, *Viaje del mundo*, ed. by F. Muradás. Madrid, 1993.

Orta, Garcia da. *Coloquios dos simples e drogas da India*. Goa, 1563.

Osorius, Hieronymus. *De rebus Emmanuelis regis lusitaniae libri XII*. Lisbon, 1571.

Oviedo, Gonzalo Fernández de *Historial general y natural de las Indias*. Seville, 1535.

   Historia general y natural de las Indias, ed. by J. Amador de los Ríos, 4 vols. Madrid, 1851–5.

Pacifici, S. J. (ed. and trans.) *Copy of a letter of the king of Portugal sent to the king of Castile concerning the voyage and success of India ('Copia di una lettera del re di Portogallo mandata al re de Castella del viaggio et successo de India', Roma 1505)*. Minneapolis, 1955.

Paez, Pedro. *Historia de Ethiopia*, ed. by E. Sanceau and A. Feio, 2 vols. Oporto, 1945.

Pegolotti, Francesco Balducci. *La practica della mercatura*, ed. by A. Evans. Cambridge, Mass., 1936.

Peragallo, P. (ed.) 'Viaggio di Matteo di Bergamo in India sulla flotta di Vasco da Gama (1502–3)'. *Bollettino della Società Geografica Italiana*, 4th series, 3 (1902): 92–129.

Perellós, Ramon de. 'Viatge al Purgatori nomenat de Sant Patrici', in *Novel·les amoroses i morals*, ed. by A. Pacheco and A. Bover i Font. Barcelona, 1982.

Piccolomini, Aeneas Sylvius [Pius II], *Memoirs of a Renaissance pope*, trans. and ed. by F. A. Gragg and L. C. Gabel, *Smith College Studies in History*, 5 vols. Northampton Mass., 1937–57.

   Descripción de Asia, ed. by F. Socas, in *Biblioteca de Colón*, vol. III. Madrid, 1992.

Pigafetta, Antonio. *Relation du primer voyage autour du monde*, ed. by J. Denucé. Anvers and Paris, 1923.

   La mia longa et pericolosa navigatione, ed. by L. Giovannini. Milan, 1989.

Pignoria, Lorenzo. *Vestustissimae tabulae Aeneae explicatio*. Venice, 1605.

   Le vere e nove imagini de gli dei delli antichi . . . et un discorso intorno le deità dell'Indie orientali et occidentali. Padua, 1615.

Pimenta, Nicolas. *Epistola patris Nicolai Pimentae . . . ad R. P. Claudium Aquavivam*. Rome, 1601.

Pinto, Fernão Mendes. *Peregrinaçam*. Lisbon, 1614.

Cartas de Fernão Mendes Pinto e outros documentos, ed. by R. Catz. Lisbon, 1983.

Pinto, O. (ed.) *Viaggi di C. Federici e G. Balbi alle Indie Orientali*. Rome, 1962.

Pires, Tomé. *The Suma Oriental of Tomé Pires, an account of the East . . . written in 1512–1515. And the book of Francisco Rodrigues, rutter of a voyage*, ed. and trans. by A. Cortesão. Hakluyt Society, 2nd series, 2 vols. London, 1944.

O manuscrito de Lisboa da 'Suma Oriental' de Tomé Pires, ed. by R. M. Loureiro. Macao, 1996.

Pliny. *Natural history*, ed. and trans. by H. Rackham. Loeb Classical Library, 10 vols. Cambridge, Mass. and London, 1938–62.

Poggio Bracciolini. *Opera omnia*, 4 vols. Turin, 1964–9.

De varietate fortunae, ed. by O. Merisalo. Helsinki, 1993.

Facezie, ed. by M. Ciccuto. Milan, 1994.

Polo, Marco. *Il milione*, ed by L. F. Benedetto. Florence, 1928.

The description of the world, ed. by A. C. Moule and Paul Pelliot, 2 vols. London, 1938.

The travels, ed. and trans. by R. Latham. Harmondsworth, 1958.

Popelinière, sieur de la [H. L. Voisin]. *L'idée d'histoire accomplie*. Paris, 1599.

Pordenone, Odoric of. *Viaggio del Beato Odorico da Pordenone*, ed. by G. Pullè. Milan, 1931.

Memoriale toscano. Viaggio in India e Cina (1318–1330) di Odorico da Pordenone, ed. by L. Monaco. Alessandria, 1990.

Purchas, Samuel (ed.) *Hakluytus posthumus; or, Purchas his pilgrimes*. London, 1625.

Pilgrimage, or relations of the world and the religions observed in all ages and places discovered, 4th edn. London, 1626.

Pyrard de Laval, François. *Voyage de François Pyrard de Laval aux Indes orientales (1601–1611)*, ed. by Xavier de Castro, 2 vols. Paris, 1998.

Quatremère, E. M. (ed.) *Notices et extraits des manuscrits de la Biblothèque du Roi*, vol. XIV, part I, pp. 1–473. Paris, 1843.

Queyroz, Fernão de. *Conquista temporal e espiritual de Ceylão*. Colombo, 1916.

Ramusio, Giovanni Battista (ed.) *Navigationi et viaggi*, 3 vols. Venice 1550 (I), 1556 (III), 1559 (II).

Navigazioni e viaggi, ed. by Marica Milanesi, 6 vols. Turin, 1978–88.

Ragvagli d'alcune missioni fatte dalli padri della Compagnia di Giesù . . . nell'Indie orientale. Rome, 1615.

Ravenstein, E. G. (ed.) *A journal of the first voyage of Vasco da Gama, 1497–1499*. Hakluyt Society. London, 1898.

Rego, A. da Silva (ed.) *Documentação para a história das missões do padroado português do Orientê: India*, 12 vols. Lisbon, 1947–58.

Relazioni degli ambascatori veneti al senato, ed. by E. Albèri, 15 vols. Florence, 1839–63.

Ribeiro, L. (ed.) 'Uma geografia quinhentista'. *Studia*, 7 (1961): 151–318.

Roe, Thomas. *The embassy of Sir Thomas Roe to the court of the Great Mogul, 1615–1619*, ed. by W. Foster, 2 vols. London, 1899.

Rogerius, Abraham. *Le théatre de l'idolatrie, ou la porte ouverte pour parvenir à la connoissance du paganisme caché*. Amsterdam, 1670.

De open-deure tot het verborgen heydendom, ed. by W. Caland. The Hague, 1915.

Rubruck, William of. *The mission of friar William of Rubruck*, trans. and ed. by P. Jackson. Hakluyt Society, 2nd series. London, 1990.

Sahagún, Bernardino de. *Historia general de las cosas de nueva España*, ed. by J. C. Temprano. Madrid, 1990.

San Antonio, Gabriel de. 'Breve y verdadera relación de los sucesos del reino de Camboxa' (Valladolid, 1604), in Ferrando (ed.) *Relaciones de la Camboya y el Japón*.

Sandoval, Alonso de. *Un tratado sobre la esclavitud*, ed. by E. Vila Vilar. Madrid, 1987.

Sansovino, Francesco. *Del governo de i regni et delle republiche così antiche come moderne*. Venice, 1561.

Dell'historie universale dell'origine et Imperio de Turchi. Venice 1561; 2nd edn, 1564.

Sanuto, Marino. *I Diarii*, 58 vols. Venice, 1879–1903.

Sassetti, Filippo. *Lettere di vari paesi*, ed. by V. Bramanti. Milan, 1970.

Simon, Richard (ed.) *Antiquitates ecclesiae orientalis*. London, 1682.

Soledade, Fernando da. *História Seráfica cronológica da Ordem de San Francisco na Província de Portugal*, vol. III. Lisbon, 1705.

Stoneman, R. (ed.) *Legends of Alexander the Great*. London, 1994.

Strabo. *The geography of Strabo*, trans. by H. L. Jones. Loeb Classical Library, 8 vols. Cambridge, Mass. and London, 1917–32.

Sylvius, Aeneas [Piccolomini]. *Storia di due amanti*, ed. by M. L. Doglio, introductory essay by L. Firpo. Milan, 1990.

Tafur, Pero. *Andanças e viajes*, ed. by F. López Estrada. Barcelona, 1982 (reprint of the 1874 edition by Marcos Jiménez de la Espada).

Tavernier, Jean-Baptiste. *Travels in India (1640–67)*, trans. by V. Ball and revised by W. Crooke. London, 1925.

Thackston, W. M. (ed.) *A century of princes. Sources on Timurid history and art*. Cambridge, Mass., 1989.

Thévenot, M. *Indian travels of Thévenot and Careri*, ed. by S. Sen. New Delhi, 1949.

Thévet, André. *Cosmographie universelle*. Paris, 1575.

Trigault, Nicolas [Ricci, Matteo]. *Histoire de l'expedition chretienne au Royaume de la Chine, 1582–1610*, ed. by L. Shih and G. Bessière, 1978.

Trindade, Paulo de. *Conquista espiritual do Oriente*, ed. by F. Felix Lopes, 3 vols. Lisbon, 1962–7.

Valignano, Alessandro. *Historia del principio y progreso de la Compañía de Jesús en las Indias Orientales 1542–64*, ed. by Josef Wicki. Rome, 1944.

Sumario de las cosas del Japón, ed. by J. L. Álvarez-Taladriz. Tokyo, 1954.

Varthema, Ludovico de. *The travels of Ludovico di Varthema*, trans. by J. Winter Jones and ed. by G. P. Badger. Hakluyt Society. London, 1863.

Itinerary, trans. by J. Winter Jones (1863), ed. by R. C. Temple. London, 1928.

Itinerario, ed. by Paolo Guidici, 2nd edn. Milan, 1929.

[Velho, Alvaro], *Diário da viagem de Vasco da Gama*, ed. by D. Peres, A. Bião and A. Magalhães Basto. Porto, 1945.

'Relação da primeira viagem de Vasco da Gama', ed. by Luís de Albuquerque, in *Grandes viagens marítimas*. Lisbon, 1989.

Vespucci, Amerigo. *Cartas de viaje*, ed. by L. Formisano. Madrid, 1986.

Il mondo nuovo di Amerigo Vespucci, ed. by M. Pozzi. Turin, 1993.

Vettori, Francesco. *Scritti storici e politici*, ed. by E. Niccolini. Bari, 1972.

Vitoria, Francisco de. *Political writings*, ed. by A. Pagden and J. Lawrence. Cambridge, 1991.

Voyage dans les deltas du Gange et de l'Irraouaddy 1521, ed. by G. Bouchon and L. F. Thomaz, with Portuguese text and French and English translations. Paris, 1988.

Voyages de Vasco de Gama. Relations des expéditions de 1497–1499 & 1502–1503, ed. by P. Teyssier, P. Valentin and J. Aubin. Paris, 1995.

Warren, Edouard de. *L'Inde anglaise en 1843–1844*, 2nd edn, 3 vols. Paris, 1845.

van den Wyngaert, A. OFM (ed.) *Sinica Franciscana. Itinera et relationes fratrum minorum saeculi XIII et XIV*, vol. I. Karachi and Florence, 1929.

Xavier, Francis. *Epistolae S. Francisci Xaverii*, ed. by G. Schurhammer and J. Wicki, 2 vols. Rome, 1944–5.

Yule, H. (ed.) *Cathay and the way thither, being a collection of medieval notices of China*, revised by H. Cordier. Hakluyt Society, 2nd series, 4 vols. London, 1913–16.

SECONDARY SOURCES

Abulafia, A. *Christians and Jews in the twelfth-century Renaissance*. London, 1995.

Actas do II seminario internacional de Historia Indo-Portuguesa. Lisbon, 1985.

Adas, M. *Machines as the measure of men. Science, technology and ideologies of western dominance*. Ithaca and London, 1989.

Al-Ahmed, A. 'Barbarians in Arab eyes'. *Past and Present*, 134 (1992): 3–18.

Alam, M. and Subrahmanyam, S. 'From an ocean of wonders: Mahmud bin Amir Wali Balkh and his Indian travels, 1625–31', in C. Salmon (ed.) *Récits de voyage des Asiatiques: Genres, mentalités, conception de l'espace*. Paris, 1996, pp. 161–89.

Albuquerque, L. de, Ferronha, A. L., Horta, J. da Silva and Loureiro, R. *O confronto do olhar. O encontro dos povos na época das navegações portuguesas*. Lisbon, 1991.

Almagià, R. 'Per una conoscenza più completa della figura e dell'opera di Pietro della Valle'. *Rendiconti dell'Academia Nazionale dei Lincei (scienze morali)*, series 8, 6 (1951): pp. 375–81.

Alves, J. Manuel dos Santos. 'A cruz, os diamantes e os cavalos; Frei Luís do Salvador, primeiro missionário e embaixador português em Vijayanagara (1500–1510)'. *Mare Liberum*. 5 (1993): 9–20.

Andreu, F. 'Carteggio inedito di Pietro della Valle col P. Avitabile e i missionari Teatini della Georgia'. *Regnum Dei*. 23–4 (1950): 57–99; 25 (1951): 19–50; 26–7 (1951): 118–38.

Aparicio López, T. 'La orden de San Agustín en la India 1572–1622'. *Studia*, 38 (1974): 563–707.

Armitage, D. 'The "procession portrait" of Queen Elizabeth I. A note on a tradition'. *Journal of the Warburg and Courtauld Institutes*, 53 (1990): 301–7.

Arokiasamy, S. *Dharma, Hindu and Christian according to Roberto de Nobili*. Rome, 1986.

Atkinson, G. *Les noveaux horizons de la Renaissance française*. Geneva, 1936.

Aubin, J. 'Francisco de Albuquerque, un juif castillan au service de l'Inde Portugaise (1510–1515)'. *Arquivos do Centro Cultural Português*, 7 (1973): 175–88.

'Deux chrétiens au Yémen Tahiride'. *Journal of the Royal Asiatic Society*, 3rd series, 3 (1993): 33–75.

Bartlett, R. *Gerald of Wales 1146–1223*. Oxford, 1982.

Basham, A. L. (ed.) *A cultural history of India*. Delhi, 1975.

Baudot, G. *Utopie et histoire au Mexique*. Toulouse, 1977.

Bayly, S. *Saints, goddesses and kings: Muslims and Christians in South Indian society 1700–1900*. Cambridge, 1989.

Beazley, C. R. *The dawn of modern geography*, 3 vols. London, 1897–1906.

Beckingham, C. F. *Between Islam and Christendom: travellers, facts, legends in the late Middle Ages and the Renaissance*. London, 1983.

Bell, A. F. G. *Diogo do Couto*. Oxford 1924.

Gaspar Correa. Oxford 1924.

Bietenholz, P. G. *Pietro della Valle (1586–1652). Studien zur Geschichte der Orientkenntnis und des Orientbildes im Abendlande*. Stuttgart, 1962.

Bitterli, U. *Cultures in conflict. Encounters between European and non-European cultures, 1492–1800*. Cambridge, 1989.

Blunt, W. *Pietro's pilgrimage: a journey to India and back at the beginning of the seventeenth century*. London, 1953.

Bolgar, R. R. *The classical heritage and its beneficiaries*. Cambridge, 1954.

Bouchon, G. *L'Asie du sud à l'époque des grandes découvertes*, collected studies. London, 1987.

'L'Inde dans l'Europe de la Renaissance', in C. Weinberger-Thomas (ed.) *L'Inde et l'imaginaire*. Paris, 1988.

'Regent of the sea'. *Cannanore's response to Portuguese expansion, 1507–1528*. Oxford, 1988.

Albuquerque. Le lion des mers d'Asie. Paris, 1992.

Bouwsma, W. J. *Concordia Mundi: the career and thought of Guillaume Postel*. Cambridge, 1957.

Boxer, C. R. *João de Barros, Portuguese humanist and historian of Asia*. New Delhi, 1981.

Brading, D. *The first America. The Spanish monarchy, creole patriots and the liberal state, 1492–1867*. Cambridge, 1991.

Brown, L. W. *The Indian Christians of Saint Thomas*. Cambridge, 1956.

Browne, E. G. *A literary history of Persia*, 4 vols. Cambridge, 1902–24.

Bugge, H. and Rubiés, J. P. *Shifting cultures. Interaction and discourse in the expansion of Europe*. Münster, 1995.

Bull, M. *Knightly piety and the lay response to the first crusade. The Limousin and Gascony, c. 970–c. 1130*. Oxford, 1993.

Burke, P. *The Renaissance sense of the past*. London, 1969.

Montaigne. Oxford, 1981.

'European views of world history from Giovio to Voltaire', in *History of European Ideas*, 6, 3 (1985).

Varieties of cultural history. Cambridge, 1997.

'The philosopher as traveller: Bernier's Orient', in J. Elsner and J. P. Rubiés (eds.) *Voyages and visions. Towards a cultural history of travel.* London 1999.

Burns, R. I. *Christians, Muslims and Jews in the crusader kingdom of Valencia.* Cambridge, 1984.

Cambridge History of India, ed. H. Dodwell, 6 vols. Cambridge, 1922–53.

Camille, M. *The gothic idol. Ideology and image-making in medieval art.* Cambridge, 1989.

Campbell, M. B. *The witness and the other world: exotic European travel writing 400–1600.* Ithaca and London, 1988.

Cannadine, D. and Price, S. (eds.) *Rituals of royalty. Power and ceremonial in traditional societies.* Cambridge, 1987.

Carrasco Urgoiti, S. *El moro de Granada en la literatura (del siglo XV al siglo XVII).* Madrid, 1956.

Cary, G. *The medieval Alexander.* Cambridge, Mass., 1956.

Céard, J. and Margolin, J. C. *Voyager à la Renaissance. Actes du colloque de Tours 1983.* Paris, 1987.

Chabod, F. 'Giovanni Botero', in *Scritti sul Rinascimento.* Turin, 1974.

Chandeigne, M. (ed.) *Lisbonne hors les murs 1415–1580. L'invention du monde par les navigateurs portugais.* Paris, 1990.

Chartier, R. 'Intellectual history or sociocultural history? The French trajectories', in D. LaCapra and S. L. Kaplan (eds.) *Modern European intellectual history.* Ithaca, 1982.

Chaudhuri, K. N. *Trade and civilisation in the Indian Ocean.* Cambridge, 1985.

Ciampi, I. *Della vita e delle opere di Pietro della Valle il Pellegrino.* Rome, 1880.

Clendinnen, I. *Ambivalent conquests: Maya and Spaniard in Yucatan 1517–1570.* Cambridge, 1987.

Clifford, J. *The Predicament of culture.* Harvard, 1988.

Cochrane, E. *Historians and historiography in the Italian Renaissance.* Chicago, 1981.

Colas, G. 'Vie Légumineuse et pensée travestie. A propos de l'adaptation des Jésuites en Inde aux XVIIe et XVIIIe siècles'. *Purusartha* 19 (1996): 199–220.

Correia-Affonso, J. *Jesuit letters and Indian history.* Bombay, 1955.

(ed.) *Indo-Portuguese history: sources and problems.* Oxford, 1981.

Critchley, J. *Marco Polo's book.* London, 1993.

Cronin, V. *A pearl to India. The life of Roberto de Nobili.* London, 1959.

Dallapiccola, A. and Zingel-Ave, S. (eds.) *Vijayanagara: city and empire*, 2 vols. Stuttgart, 1985.

Deluz, C. *Le livre de Jehan de Mandeville. Une 'géographie' au XIVe siècle.* Louvain-la-Neuve, 1988.

Derrett, J. D. M. *The Hoysalas.* Oxford, 1957.

Religion, law and the state in India. London, 1968.

'Rajadharma'. *Journal of Asiatic Society*, 35 (1976): 597–609.

Dias, J. S. da Silva. *Os descobrimentos e a problemática cultural do século XVI.* Lisbon, 1973.

Diffie, B. and Winius, G. *Foundations of the Portuguese empire 1415–1580.* Oxford, 1977.

Dirks, N. B. *The hollow crown. Ethnohistory of an Indian kingdom.* Cambridge, 1988.

Disney, A. R. *Twilight of the Pepper Empire: Portuguese trade in southwest India in the early seventeenth century.* Cambridge, Mass., 1978.

Dodds, M. *Les récits de voyages: sources de L'esprit des Loys de Montesquieu.* Paris, 1929.

Eaton, R. *Sufis of Bijapur, 1300–1700.* Princeton, 1978.

Elliott, J. H. *The old world and the new, 1492–1650.* Cambridge, 1970.

'Spain and America before 1700', in L. Bethell (ed.) *Colonial Spanish America.* Cambridge, 1987.

Elsner, J. and Rubiés, J. P. (eds.) *Voyages and visions. Towards a cultural history of travel.* London, 1999.

Embree, A. T. (ed.) *Sources of Indian tradition,* vol. I. New York, 1988.

Encyclopaedia of Islam, new edition. Leiden and London, 1960– .

Fernández-Armesto, F. 'Medieval ethnography'. *Journal of the Anthropological Society of London,* 13 (1982): 272–86.

Before Columbus. Exploration and colonisation from the Mediterranean to the Atlantic, 1229–1492. Basingstoke, 1987.

Feyerabend, P. K. *Farewell to reason.* London, 1987.

Fletcher, R. *The quest for El Cid.* Oxford, 1989.

Flores, M. da C. *Os portugueses e o Sião no século XVI.* Lisbon, 1995.

Frappier, J. *Chrétien de Troyes et le mythe du Graal.* Paris, 1972.

Fritz, J. M. and Michell, G. *City of victory. Vijayanagara, the medieval Hindu capital of Southern India,* with photographs by John Gollings. New York, 1991.

Fritz, J. M., Michell, G. and Nagaraja Rao, M. S. *Where kings and gods meet. The royal centre at Vijayanagara.* Tucson, 1984.

Fubini, R. 'Il "teatro del mondo" nelle prospettive morali e storico-politiche di Poggio Bracciolini', in *Poggio Bracciolini 1380–1980.* Florence, 1982.

Garin, E. 'Ritratto di Enea Silvio Piccolomini', in his *La cultura filosofica del Rinascimento italiano.* Florence, 1961.

Ermetismo del Rinascimento. Rome, 1988.

Gavetas do Torre do Tombo, ed. by A. da Silva Rego, 12 vols. Lisbon, 1960–77.

Geertz, C. *Local knowledge.* New York, 1983.

Gentile, S. *Firenze e la scoperta dell'America. Umanesimo e geografia nel '400 Fiorentino.* Florence, 1992.

'Toscanelli, Traversari, Niccoli e la geografia'. *Rivista Geografica Italiana,* 100 (1993): 113–31.

Gerbi, A. *The dispute of the New World. The history of a polemic 1750–1900.* Pittsburgh, 1973.

Gernet, J. *China and the Christian impact.* Cambridge, 1985.

Gliozzi, G. *Adamo e il nuovo mondo. La nascita dell'antropologia come ideologia coloniale.* Florence, 1977.

Gölner, C. *Turcica: die europäischen Turkendrücke des XVI Jahrhunderts,* 2 vols. Berlin, 1961–68.

Goodman, J. F. *Chivalry and exploration 1298–1630.* London, 1998.

Grafton, A. *Joseph Scaliger. A study in the history of classical scholarship in the age of science 1450–1800,* 2 vols. Oxford, 1983–93.

'Humanism, magic and science', in A. Goodman and A. Mackay (eds.) *The impact of humanism on western Europe*. London and New York, 1990.

Greenblatt, S. *Marvellous possessions*. Oxford, 1991.

(ed.) *New world encounters*. Berkeley, 1994.

Greiff, B. *Tagebuch des Lucas Rem aus den Jahren 1494–1541*. Augsburg, 1861.

Groslier, B. P. *Angkor et la Cambodge au XVIe siècle d'après les sources portugaises et espagnols*. Paris, 1958.

Gubernatis, A. de. *Storia dei viaggiatori italiani nelle Indie Orientali*. Livorno, 1875.

Guerreiro, I. and Rodrigues, V. L. G. 'O grupo de Cochim e a oposição a Afonso de Albuquerque'. *Studia*, 51 (1992): 119–44.

Gurney, J. D. 'Pietro della Valle and the limits of perception'. *Bulletin of the School of Oriental and African Studies*, 49 (1986): 193–216.

Hahn, T. 'Indians East and West'. *Journal of Medieval and Renaissance Studies*, 8 (1978).

'The Indian tradition in western medieval intellectual history'. *Viator*, 9 (1978): 213–34.

Hale, J. R. *Renaissance Europe. Individual and society, 1480–1520*. London, 1971.

Hanke, L. *All mankind is one. A study of the disputation between Bartolomé de Las Casas and Juan Ginés de Sepúlveda on the religious and intellectual capacity of the American Indians*. DeKalb, Ill., 1974.

Hardy, Peter. *Historians of medieval India. Studies in Indo-Muslim historical writing*. London, 1960.

Harle, J. C. *The art and architecture of the Indian subcontinent*. Harmondsworth, 1986.

Harrison, J. B. 'Five Portuguese historians', in C. H. Phillips (ed.) *Historians of India, Pakistan and Ceylon*. London, 1961.

Hartog, F. *The mirror of Herodotus*. California, 1988.

Haynes, J. *The humanist as traveller. George Sandy's 'Relation of a journey begun A. Dom. 1610'*. Rutherford and London, 1986.

Hazard, P. *La crise de la conscience européene*. Paris, 1935.

Heers, J. *Marco Polo*. Paris, 1983.

Heras, H. 'Early relations between Vijayanagara and Portugal'. *Quarterly Journal of the Mythic Society*, (1925): 63–74 (Bangalore).

The Aravidu dynasty of Vijayanagara. Madras, 1927.

Higgins, I. M. *Writing East. The 'travels' of Sir John Mandeville*. Philadelphia, 1997.

Hobson-Jobson. The Anglo-Indian Dictionary, ed. by H. Yule and A. C. Burnell, 2nd edn. London, 1903.

Hocart, A. M. *Kings and councillors*. Cairo, 1936; repr. Chicago, 1970.

Hodgen, M. *Early anthropology in the sixteenth and seventeenth centuries*. Philadelphia, 1964.

Hodgson, M. G. S. *The venture of Islam*, 3 vols. Chicago, 1974.

Hooykaas, R. 'Humanism and the voyages of discovery in 16th century Portuguese science and letters'. *Medeelingen der Koninklijke Nederlandse Akademie van Wetenschappen* (1979): 93–160.

Horta, J. da Silva. 'A representação do Africano na literatura de viagens, do Senegal à Serra Leoa (1453–1508)'. *Mare Liberum* 2 (1991): pp. 209–339.

'Uma leitura de Zurara por João de Barros', *Amar, sentir e viver a História.* *Estudos de homenagem a Joaquim Veríssimo Serrão.* Lisbon, 1995.

Huddleston, L. E. *Origins of the American Indians. European concepts 1492–1729.* Austin, Tex., 1967.

Hyde, J. K. 'Real and imaginary journeys in the later Middle Ages'. *Journal of the John Rylands Library*, 65 (1982).

Iversen, E. *The myth of Egypt and its hieroglyphs in European tradition.* Copenhagen, 1961.

Jackson, P. *The Delhi sultanate. A political and military history.* Cambridge, 1999.

Jackson, P. and Lockhart, L. (eds.) *The Timurid and Safavid periods*, in *The Cambridge History of Iran*, vol. VI. Cambridge, 1986.

Jahn, K. *Rashid al-Din's 'History of India'.* The Hague, 1965.

Kane, P. V. *History of Dharmasastra*, 5 vols. Poona, 1930–62.

Karashima, N. 'Nayaka rule in North and South Arcot districts in South India during the sixteenth century'. *Acta Asiatica*, 48 (1985): 1–26.

Karttunen, K. 'India in early Greek Literature'. *Studia Orientalia*, 65 (1989): 1–293 (Helsinki).

Kedar, B. Z. *Crusade and mission.* Princeton, 1984.

Keen, B. *The Aztec image in Western thought.* New Brunswick, 1971.

Kieckhefer, R. *Magic in the Middle Ages.* Cambridge, 1989.

Kimble, G. H. T. *Geography in the Middle Ages.* London, 1938.

Krantz, F. 'Between Bruni and Machiavelli: history, law and historicism in Poggio Bracciolini', in P. Mack and M. Jacob (eds.) *Politics and culture in early modern Europe.* Cambridge, 1987, pp. 119–51.

Krishnaswami Aiyangar, S. *Sources of Vijayanagar history.* Madras, 1919.

South India and her Muhammadan invaders. Madras, 1921.

Kulke, H. 'Maharajas, mahants and historians. Reflections on the historiography of early Vijayanagara and Sringeri', in A. Dallapiccola and S. Zingel-Ave (eds.) *Vijayanagara: city and empire*, 2 vols. Stuttgart, 1985, vol. I, pp. 120–43.

Kupperman, K. O. *Settling with the Indians. The meeting of English and Indian cultures in America, 1580–1640.* Totowa, N.J., 1980.

(ed.) *America in European consciousness 1493–1750.* Chapel Hill and London, 1995.

Lach, D. F. *Asia in the making of Europe.* Vol. I: *The century of discovery* (two books), Chicago 1965; vol. II: *The century of wonder* (three books), Chicago, 1970–7; vol. III (with E. J. Van Kley): *A century of advance* (four books), Chicago, 1993.

Lapa, Rodrigues. *Historiadores quinhenistas.* Lisbon, 1942.

Le Goff, J. 'L'occident médiéval et l'océan indien: un horizon onirique', in Le Goff, *Pour un autre Moyen Age.* Paris, 1977.

Lewis, B. *Race and slavery in the Middle East.* Oxford, 1990.

Linehan, P. *History and the historians of medieval Spain.* Oxford, 1993.

Lloyd, G. E. R. *Demystifying mentalities*, Cambridge, 1990.

Lockhart, L. 'European contacts with Persia, 1350–1736', in P. Jackson and L. Lockhart (eds.) *Cambridge History of Iran*, vol. VI, pp. 373–409.

Longhena, M. 'I manoscritti del IV libro del *De Varietate Fortunae* di Poggio Bracciolini'. *Bollettino della Società Geografica Italiana* (1925): 191–215.

Longhurst, A. H. *Hampi ruins described and illustrated.* Calcutta, 1917.

Loomis, R. S. (ed.) *Arthurian literature in the Middle Ages.* Oxford, 1959.

Löschhorn, E. 'Vijayanagara as seen by European visitors', in A. Dallapiccola and S. Zingel-Ave (eds.) *Vijayanagara: city and empire*, 2 vols. Stuttgart, 1985, pp. 344–53.

Loureiro, R. 'O descobrimento da civilizacão Indiana nas cartas Jesuítas (século XVI)', in B. Ares Queija and S. Gruzinski (eds.) *Entre dos mundos. Fronteras culturales y agentes mediadores.* Seville, 1997, pp. 299–327.

A China na cultura Portuguesa do século XVI. (forthcoming).

MacCormack, S. *Religion in the Andes. Vision and imagination in early colonial Peru.* Princeton, 1991.

Maclagan, E, *The Jesuits and the Great Mogul.* London, 1932.

Maffei, D. (ed.) *Enea Silvio Piccolomini. Atti del convengo per il quinto centenario della morte.* Siena, 1968.

Magalhães-Godinho, V. *L'économie de l'empire portugais aux XVe et XVIe siècles.* Paris, 1969.

Mahalingam, T. V. *Administration and social life under Vijayanagara.* Madras, 1940.

Marshall, P. J. and Williams, G. *The great map of mankind. British perceptions of the world in the age of Enlightenment.* London, 1982.

Martels, Z. R. W. M. von. 'Augerius Gislenius Busbequius: leven en werk van de keizerlijke gezant aan het hof van Süleyman de Grote. Een biografrische, literaire en historische studie met editie van onuigegeven teksten'. Ph. D. thesis, University of Groningen, 1989.

Mathew, K. S. *Portuguese and the sultanate of Gujarat (1500–1573).* New Delhi, 1985, pp. 344–53.

McPherson, K. 'Paravas and Portuguese. A study of Portuguese strategy and its impact on an Indian seafaring community'. *Mare Liberum*, 13 (1997): 69–82.

Meilink-Roelofsz, M. A. P. *Asian trade and European influence in the Indonesian archipelago between 1500 and about 1630.* The Hague, 1962.

Merisalo, O. 'Le prime edizioni stampate del De Varietate Fortunae di Poggio Bracciolini'. *Arctos. Acta Philologica Fennica*, 19 (1985): 81–102; and 20 (1986): 101–29.

Metzler, I. 'Perceptions of hot climate in medieval cosmography and travel literature'. *Reading Medieval Studies*, 23 (1997): 69–105.

Michell, G. *The Penguin guide to the monuments of India*, vol. I: *Buddhist, Jain, Hindu.* Harmondsworth, 1989.

The Vijayanagara courtly style. New Delhi, 1992.

Miller, P. 'An antiquary between philology and history. Peiresc and the Samaritans', in D. Kelley (ed.) *History and the disciplines. The reclassification of knowledge in early modern Europe.* Rochester and London, 1997.

'A philologist, a traveller and an antiquary rediscover the Samaritans in seventeenth-century Paris, Rome and Aix: Jean Morin, Pietro della Valle and N.-C. Fabri de Peiresc', in H. Zedelmaier and M. Mulsow (eds.) *Gelehrsamkeit als Praxis: Arbeitsweisen, Funktionen, Grenzbereiche* (forthcoming).

Miquel, A. *La géographie humaine du monde musulman*, 4 vols. Paris and The Hague, 1967–88.

Mitter, P. *Much maligned monsters. History of European reactions to Indian art.* Oxford, 1977.

Momigliano, A. *The classical foundations of modern historiography.* Berkeley, 1990.

Moran, J. F. *The Japanese and the Jesuits: Alessandro Valignano in sixteenth-century Japan.* London, 1993.

Morris, C. *The discovery of the individual 1050–1200.* 1972; repr. Toronto, 1987.

Murr, S. 'Les conditions d'émergence du discours sur l'Inde au siècle des Lumières', in *Inde et littératures.* Paris, 1983, pp. 233–84.

L'Inde philosophique entre Bossuet et Voltaire, 2 vols. Paris, 1987.

'Généalogies et analogies entre paganisme ancien et "gentilité des Indes" dans l'apologétique Jésuite au siècle des lumières', in F. Laplanche and Ch. Grell (eds.) *Les religions du paganisme antique dans l'Europe chrétienne XVIe–XVIIIe siècle.* Paris, 1988, pp. 141–61.

'La politique "au Mogol" selon Bernier: appareil conceptuel, rhétorique stratégique, philosophie morale', in J. Pouchepadass and H. Stern, *De la royauté à l'état. Anthropologie et histoire du politique dans le monde indien.* Paris, 1991, pp. 239–311.

Nanda, M. *European travel accounts during the reigns of Shahjahan and Aurangzeb.* Kurukshetra, 1994.

Napoli, G. di. *Lorenzo Valla. Filosofia e religione nell'umanesimo Italiano.* Rome, 1971.

Newitt, M. (ed.) *The first Portuguese colonial empire.* Exeter, 1986.

Newton, A. P. (ed.) *Travel and travellers of the Middle Ages.* London, 1926.

Nilakanta Sastri, K. A. 'Marco Polo on India', *Oriente Poliano.* Rome, 1957.

A history of South India, 3rd, edn. Madras 1966.

Nilakanta Sastri, K. A. and Venkataramanayya N. *Further sources of Vijayanagara history*, 3 vols. Madras, 1946.

O'Flaherty, E. G. 'Relativism and criticism in seventeenth-century French thought'. Ph. D. thesis, University of Cambridge, 1987.

O'Malley, J. W. *The first Jesuits.* Cambridge, Mass., 1993.

Olschki, L. *L'Asia di Marco Polo.* Florence, 1957.

Oxford Companion to Philosophy, ed. by T. Honderich. Oxford and New York, 1996.

Pagden, A. *The fall of natural man. The American Indian and the origins of comparative ethnology*, 2nd edn. Cambridge, 1986.

European encounters with the New World, from Renaissance to Romanticism. New Haven and London, 1993.

Pastor, B. *The armature of conquest. Spanish accounts of the discovery of America, 1492–1589.* Stanford, 1992.

Pastine, D. *La nascita dell'idolatria. L'Oriente religioso di Athanasius Kircher.* Florence, 1978.

Pearson, M. N. *The Portuguese in India.* Cambridge, 1987.

Pelliot, P. *Notes on Marco Polo.* Paris, 1959.

Pennington, L. E. (ed.) *The Purchas handbook. Studies of the life, times and writings of Samuel Purchas 1577–1626.* Hakluyt Society 2nd series, 2 vols. London, 1997.

Penrose, B. *Travel and discovery in the Renaissance, 1420–1620.* Cambridge, Mass., 1952.

Phillips, J. R. S. *The medieval expansion of Europe.* Oxford, 1988.

Pinker, S. *The language instinct.* Harmondsworth, 1994.

Pintard, R. *Le libertinage érudit dans la première moitié du XVIIe siècle,* 2 vols. Paris, 1943.

Popkin, R. H. *The history of scepticism from Erasmus to Spinoza.* Berkeley, 1979.

Isaac La Peyrère (1596–1676), his life, work, and influence. Leiden and New York, 1987.

Radulet, C. *Os descobrimentos Portugueses e a Itália.* Lisbon, 1991.

Rajamanickam, S. *The first oriental scholar.* Tirunelveli, 1972.

Rama Sarma, S. *Saluva dynasty of Vijayanagar.* Hyderabad, 1979.

Ramanujan, A. K., Narayana Rao, V. and Shulman, D. *When God is a customer. Telugu courtesan songs by Ksetrayya and others.* Berkeley and Los Angeles, 1994.

Randles, W. G. L., ' "Peuples sauvages" et "états despotiques": la pertinence, au XVIe siècle, de la grille aristotélicienne pour classer les nouvelles sociétés révélées par les découvertes en Brésil, en Afrique et en Asie', *Mare Liberum,* 3 (1991): 299–307.

Rangasvami Sarasvati, A. 'Political maxims of the emperor-poet Krishnadeva Raya'. *Journal of Indian History,* 4 (1926): 61–88.

Rao, V. Narajana, Shulman, D. and Subrahmanyam, S. *Symbols of substance. Court and state in Nayaka period Tamil Nadu.* Delhi, 1992.

Rebelo, L. de Sousa. 'Providencialismo e profecia nas crónicas portuguesas da expansão'. *Bulletin of Hispanic Studies,* 71 (1994): 67–86.

Rego, A. da Silva. *História das missões do padroado português do Oriente. Índia (1500–42).* Lisbon, 1949.

Richard, J. *Croisés, missionaires et voyageurs: les perspectives orientales du monde latin médiéval.* London, 1983.

Roger, F. M. *The quest for Eastern Christians: travels and rumor in the age of discovery.* Minneapolis, 1962.

Rosa, S. 'Seventeenth-century Catholic polemic and the rise of cultural rationalism: an example from the empire'. *Journal of the History of Ideas,* 57 (1996): 87–107.

Rossi, E. 'Versi Turchi e altri scritti inediti di Pietro della Valle'. *Rivista degli Studi Orientali,* 22 (1947): 92–8.

'Poesie inedite in Persiano di Pietro della Valle'. *Revista degli Studi Orientali,* 28 (1953): 108–17.

Rubiés, J. P. 'Hugo Grotius's dissertation on the origin of the American peoples and the use of comparative methods'. *Journal of the History of Ideas,* 52, 2 (1991): 221–44.

'New worlds and Renaissance ethnology'. *History and Anthropology,* 6 (1993): 157–97.

'The oriental voices of Mendes Pinto, or the traveller as ethnologist in Portuguese India'. *Portuguese Studies* 10 (1994): pp. 24–43.

'Instructions for travellers: teaching the eye to see', in J. Stagl and C. Pinney (eds.) *From travel literature to ethnography.* Special issue of *History and Anthropology,* 9 (1996): 139–90.

'Giovanni di Buonagrazia's letter to his father concerning his participation in the second expedition of Vasco da Gama (1502–3)'. *Mare Liberum*, 16 (1998): 87–112.

'The Jesuit discovery of Hinduism: Antonio Rubino's account of the history and religion of Vijayanagara (1608)'. *Archiv für Religionsgeschichte* (forthcoming).

'Travel writing as a genre: facts, fictions and the invention of a scientific discourse in early modern Europe'. *Journeys*, 1 (2000): 5–33.

'A western rationality? Late medieval travellers and the practice of cross-cultural encounters' (forthcoming).

Runciman, S. *A History of the Crusades*, vol. III: *The kingdom of Acre*. Cambridge, 1954; repr. Harmondsworth, 1978.

Saenger, P. 'Manières de lire médiévales', in H.-J. Martin and R. Chartier (eds.) *Histoire de l'édition française*. Paris, 1983–7, vol. I: *Le livre conquérant, du Moyen Age au milieu du XVIIe siècle*, pp. 131–41.

Said, E. W. *Orientalism*. Harmondsworth, 1978.

Saletore, B. A. *Social and political life in the Vijayanagara Empire*, 2 vols. Madras, 1932.

Sargent-Baur, B. N. (ed.) *Journeys towards God. Pilgrimage and Crusade*. Kalamazoo, 1992.

Sarojini Devi, K. *Religion in Vijayanagara empire*. New Delhi, 1990.

Schütte, J. F. *Valignano's mission principles for Japan*. 2 vols. Institute for Jesuit Sources, St Louis, 1980–5.

Schurhammer, G. *Gesammelte Studien*, 4 vols. Lisbon and Rome, 1965.
    Francis Xavier: his life, his times, 4 vols. Vol. II: *India 1541–45*. Rome, 1977.

Schwartz, S. B. (ed.) *Implicit understandings: observing, reporting and reflecting on the encounters between Europeans and other peoples in the early modern era*. Cambridge, 1994.

Seed, P. *Ceremonies of possession in Europe's conquest of the New World, 1492–1640*. Cambridge, 1995.

Sensburg, W. 'Poggio Bracciolini und Nicolo Conti in ihrer Bedeutung für die Geografie des Renaissancezeitalters'. *Mitteilungen der K. K. Geographischen Gesellschaft in Wien*, 49 (1906): pp. 83–109.

Serrão, J. (ed.) *Dicionário da história de Portugal*, 4 vols. Lisbon, 1963–71.

Sewell, R. *A forgotten empire (Vijayanagar)*. London, 1900.

Shastry, B. S. *Studies in Indo-Portuguese history*. Bangalore, 1981.

Sherwani, H. K. *The Bahmanis of the Deccan*, 2nd edn. New Delhi, 1985.

Shulman, D. D. *The king and the clown in South Indian myth and poetry*. Princeton, 1985.

Silva, D. da. *The Portuguese in Asia. An annotated bibliography of studies in Portuguese colonial history in Asia, 1498–c. 1800*. Zug, Switzerland, 1987.

Simon Díaz, J. *Bibliografía de las literaturas hispánicas*, 3 vols. Madrid, 1963.

Smith, J. M. 'No more language games: words, beliefs and the political culture of early modern France'. *American Historical Review*, 102 (1997): 1413–40.

Southern, R. W. *Western views of Islam in the Middle Ages*. Cambridge, Mass., 1961.

Spallanzani, M. *Giovanni da Empoli, mercante navigatore fiorentino*. Florence, 1984.

Mercanti fiorentini nell'Asia portoghese. Florence, 1997.

Spence, J. D. *The memory palace of Matteo Ricci.* New York, 1984

Sridhara Babu, D. 'Kingship: state and religion in South India'. Inaugural dissertation, Göttingen, 1975.

Stein, B. *Peasant state and society in medieval South India.* New Delhi, 1980.

'Vijayanagara and the transition to patrimonial systems', in A. Dallapiccola and S. Zingel-Ave (eds.) *Vijayangara: city and empire.* Stuttgart, 1985.

Vijayanagara. Cambridge, 1989.

A history of India. Oxford, 1998.

Strayer, J. 'Feudalism in Western Europe', in R. Coulbourn (ed.) *Feudalism in history.* Hamden, Conn., 1965.

Subrahmanyam, S. *Improvising empire. Portuguese trade and settlement in the Bay of Bengal 1500–1700.* Oxford, 1990.

The Portuguese empire in Asia, 1500–1700. A political and economic history. London and New York, 1993.

'Agreeing to disagree: Burton Stein on Vijayanagara'. *South Asia Research* 17 (1997): 127–39.

Tate, R. B. 'López de Ayala, humanist historian?' *Hispanic Review,* 25 (1957): 157–74.

'Mythology in Spanish historiography of the Middle Ages and the Renaissance'. *Hispanic Review,* 25 (1957): 1–18.

Taylor, E. G. R. *Late Tudor and early Stuart geography, 1583–1650.* London, 1934.

Teltscher, K. *India inscribed. European and British writing on India 1600–1800.* New Delhi, 1995.

Thapar, R. *A history of India from the discovery to 1526.* Harmondsworth, 1966; repr. 1987.

'Epic and history: tradition, dissent and politics in India'. *Past and Present,* 125 (1989): 3–26.

Thomaz, L. F. 'Malaka et ses communautés marchandes au tournant du 16e siècle', in D. Lombard and J. Aubin (eds.) *Marchands et hommes d'affaires asiatiques dans l'océan Indien et la mer de Chine 13e–20e siècles.* Paris, 1988.

'L'idée impériale Manueline', in J. Aubin (ed.) *La découverte, le Portugal et l'Europe.* Paris, 1990.

Tiele, P. A. *Mémoire bibliographique sur les journaux des navigateurs néerlandais.* Amsterdam, 1867.

Valensi, L. *The birth of the despot. Venice and the Sublime Porte.* Ithaca and London, 1993.

Veluthat, K. *The political structure of early medieval South India.* London, 1993.

Venkataramanayya, N. *Vijayanagara. Origin of the city and the empire.* Madras, 1933.

Studies in the history of the third dynasty of Vijayanagara. Madras, 1935.

Vives Gatell, J. 'Andanças e viajes de un hidalgo Español'. *Spanische Forschungen der Görresgesellschaft,* 7 (1938); reprinted in Tafur, *Andanças e viajes de Pero Tafur,* ed. by F. López Estrada. Barcelona, 1982.

Vogel, K. A. 'Cultural variety in a Renaissance perspective: Johannes Boemus on "The manners, laws and customs of all peoples" (1520)', in H. Bugge and J. P. Rubiés (eds.) *Shifting cultures.* Münster, 1995.

Wagoner, Ph. B. *Tidings of the king. A translation and ethnohistorical analysis of the 'Rayavacakamu'*. Honolulu, 1993.

'"Sultan among Hindu Kings": dress, titles and islamicization of Hindu culture at Vijayanagara'. *Journal of Asian Studies*, 55 (1996), 851–80.

Weinberger-Thomas, C. (ed.) *L'Inde et l'imaginaire*. Paris, 1988.

Weiss, R. 'Ciriaco d'Ancona in Oriente', in A. Pertusi (ed.) *Venezia e l'Oriente fra tardo medioevo e rinascimento*. Venice, 1966.

Wicki, J. (ed.) *Documenta indica*, 18 vols. Rome, 1964–88.

Wilks, M. *Historical sketches of the South of India in an attempt to trace the history of Mysoor*, vol. I. Madras, 1869.

Winius, G. 'The life of Jacques de Coutre: a prime source emerges from the shades'. *Itinerario*, 9 (1985): 137–44.

Wittkower, R. 'Marvels of the East: a study in the history of monsters', *Journal of the Warburg and Courtauld Institutes*, 5 (1942): 159–97.

'Marco Polo and the pictorial tradition of the marvels of the East', in *Oriente Poliano*. Rome, 1957, pp. 155–72.

Wolfzettel, F. *Le discours du voyageur*. Paris, 1996.

Wood, F. *Did Marco Polo go to China?* London, 1995.

Yapp, M. E. 'Europe in the Turkish mirror'. *Past and Present*, 137 (1992): 134–55.

Zoli, S. *L'Europa libertina tra controriforma e illuminismo. L'oriente dei libertini e le origini dell'illuminismo*. Bologna, 1989.

Zupanov, Ines G. 'Aristocratic analogies and demotic descriptions in the seventeenth century Madurai Mission'. *Representations*, 41 (1993): 123–48.

'Writing and acting culture: the Jesuit experiments in 17th century South India'. Ph.D. University of California at Berkeley, 1991; on microfilm, 1994.

Index

Past and Present Publications

General Editor: JOANNA INNES, *Somerville College, Oxford*

Family and Inheritance: Rural Society in Western Europe 1200–1800, edited by Jack Goody, Joan Thirsk and E. P. Thompson*

French Society and the Revolution, edited by Douglas Johnson

Peasants, Knights and Heretics: Studies in Medieval English Social History, edited by R. H. Hilton*

Town in Societies: Essays in Economic History and Historical Sociology, edited by Philip Abrams and E. A. Wrigley*

Desolation of a City: Coventry and the Urban Crisis of the Late Middle Ages, Charles Phythian-Adams

Puritanism and Theatre: Thomas Middleton and Opposition Drama under the Early Stuarts, Margot Heinemann*

Lords and Peasants in a Changing Society: The Estates of the Bishopric of Worcester 680–1450, Christopher Dyer

Life, Marriage and Death in a Medieval Parish: Economy, Society and Demography in Halesowen 1270–1400, Ziv Razi

Biology, Medicine and Society 1740–1940, edited by Charles Webster

The Invention of Tradition, edited by Eric Hobsbawm and Terence Ranger*

Industrialization before Industrialization: Rural Industry and the Genesis of Capitalism, Peter Kriedte, Hans Medick and Jürgen Schlumbohm*

The Republic in the Village: The People of the Var from the French Revolution to the Second Republic, Maurice Agulhon†

Social Relations and Ideas: Essays in Honour of R. H. Hilton, edited by T. H. Aston, P. R. Coss, Christopher Dyer and Joan Thirsk

A Medieval Society: The West Midlands at the End of the Thirteenth Century, R. H. Hilton

Winstanley: 'The Law of Freedom' and Other Writings, edited by Christopher Hill

Crime in Seventeenth-Century England: A County Study, J. A. Sharpe†

The Crisis of Feudalism: Economy and Society in Eastern Normandy c. 1300–1500, Guy Bois†

The Development of the Family and Marriage in Europe, Jack Goody*

Disputes and Settlements: Law and Human Relations in the West, edited by John Bossy

Rebellion, Popular Protest and the Social Order in Early Modern England, edited by Paul Slack

Studies on Byzantine Literature of the Eleventh and Twelfth Centuries, Alexander Kazhdan in collaboration with Simon Franklin†

The English Rising of 1381, edited by R. H. Hilton and T. H. Aston*

Praise and Paradox: Merchants and Craftsmen in Elizabethan Popular Literature, Laura Caroline Stevenson

The Brenner Debate: Agrarian Class Structure and Economic Development in Pre-Industrial Europe, edited by T. H. Aston and C. H. E. Philpin*

Eternal Victory: Triumphant Rulership in Late Antiquity, Byzantium, and the Early Medieval West, Michael McCormick†*

East-Central Europe in Transition: From the Fourteenth to the Seventeenth Century, edited by Antoni Mączak, Henryk Samsonowicz and Peter Burke*

Small Books and Pleasant Histories: Popular Fiction and its Readership in Seventeenth-Century England, Margaret Spufford*

Society, Politics and Culture: Studies in Early Modern England, Mervyn James*

Horses, Oxen and Technological Innovation: The Use of Draught Animals in English Farming 1066–1500, John Langdon

Nationalism and Popular Protest in Ireland, edited by C. H. E. Philpin

Rituals of Royalty: Power and Cremonial in Traditional Societies, edited by David Cannadine and Simon Price*

The Margins of Society in Late Medieval Paris, Bronisław Geremek†

Landlords, Peasants and Politics in Medieval England, edited by T. H. Aston

Geography, Technology, and War: Studies in the Maritime History of the Mediterranean, 649–1571, John H. Pryor*

Church Courts, Sex and Marriage in England, 1570–1640, Martin Ingram*

Searches for an Imaginary Kingdom: The Legend of the Kingdom of Prester John, L. N. Gumilev

Crowds and History: Mass Phenomena in English Towns, 1790–1835, Mark Harrison

Concepts of Cleanliness: Changing Attitudes in France since the Middle Ages, Georges Vigarello†

The First Modern Society: Essays in English History in Honour of Lawrence Stone, edited by A. L. Beier, David Cannadine and James M. Rosenheim

The Europe of the Devout: The Catholic Reformation and the Formation of a New Society, Louis Châtellier†

English Rural Society, 1500–1800: Essays in Honour of Joan Thirsk, edited by John Chartres and David Hey

From Slavery to Feudalism in South-Western Europe, Pierre Bonnassie†

Lordship, Knighthood and Locality: A Study in English Society c. 1180–c. 1280, P. R. Coss

English and French Towns in Feudal Society: A Comparative Study, R. H. Hilton*

An Island for Itself: Economic Development and Social Change in Late Medieval Sicily, Stephan R. Epstein

Epidemics and Ideas: Essays on the Historical Perception of Pestilence, edited by Terence Ranger and Paul Slack*

The Political Economy of Shopkeeping in Milan, 1886–1922, Jonathan Morris

After Chartism: Class and Nation in English Radical Politics, 1848–1874, Margot C. Finn

Commoners: Common Right, Enclosure and Social Change in England, 1700–1820, J. M. Neeson*

* Also published in paperback
† Co-published with the Maison des Sciences de l'Homme, Paris